THE Billboard BOOK OF TOP 40 ALBUMS

JOEL WHITBURN

BILLBOARD PUBLICATIONS, INC./NEW YORK

Photo captions by Ira Robbins
Picture sleeves selected from Joel Whitburn's personal collection
Photography by Malcolm Hjerstedt of Munroe Studios, Inc.
Chart typesetting by Arcata Graphics/Kingsport
Edited by Marisa Bulzone and Liz Harvey
Graphic Production by Ellen Greene
Book design by Bob Fillie
Cover design by Bob Fillie
Cover illustration © by Carmine Vecchio

First published 1987 by Billboard Publications, Inc., 1515 Broadway, New York, NY 10036.

Library of Congress Cataloging-in-Publication Data

Whitburn, Joel.
  The Billboard book of top 40 albums.

  Includes index.
  1. Popular music—Discography.   I. Billboard.
II. Title.   III. Title: Billboard book of top forty
albums.   IV. Title: Book of top 40 albums.   V. Title:
Book of top forty albums.
ML156.4.P66W43   1987   016.7899'12   87-24982
ISBN 0-8230-7513-3 (pbk.)

Distributed in the United Kingdom by Guinness Books, 33 London Road, Enfield, Middlesex, England EN2 6DJ.

"Guinness" is a registered trademark of Guinness Superlatives, Inc.

ISBN 0-85112-887-4

Manufactured in the United States of America

First printing, 1987

1 2 3 4 5 6 7 8 9/92 91 90 89 88 87

This book is dedicated to
the 12-inch vinyl album configuration.
If its days are numbered as many suggest,
I will sorely miss its art form and
the gentle placement of a stylus
into its shiny black grooves.

The author wishes to give thanks to
the entire staff of RECORD RESEARCH:

> Bill Hathaway
> Brent Olynick
> Fran Whitburn
> Kim Whitburn
> Kim Gaardner
> Joanne Wagner
> John Novak
> Lori Wasedalek
> Jeff Samp
> Phil Summers
> Oscar Vidotto

A special note of thanks to my mother
for her research contributions to this book.

CONTENTS

AUTHOR'S NOTE

Welcome to the first edition of *The Billboard Book of Top 40 Albums*. For the past several years, *The Billboard Book of Top 40 Singles* has been available in bookstores, so the time for the album edition is long overdue.

If you are familiar with the other *Billboard* books I have researched, you will find that the format herein is the same basic one I have used in many of the earlier editions. In a sentence, this book gives a concise look at the hottest albums of the rock era and the artists who made them the "cream of the crop."

When you realize that the 4,700 titles listed in this volume represent only 25 percent of the total number of albums that have made the *Billboard* Top 200 weekly "Pop Albums" charts, you know that these are exclusive achievers. Of the forty or so albums that are released each week, only two or three of these crack the Top 40 hierarchy. Competition in the weekly Top 40 race is ferocious; it is, perhaps, a more highly competitive race than those fought in sports arenas. It is the one race that continues year round, it never starts over, and yet it provides new standings every week of the year. With a plethora of Top 40 countdown programs on America's airwaves, it is clear that this country is hooked on this unending dash to the top.

Most involved in the ongoing pursuit of the top position are the dynamic contenders—the artists. Not only do they influence American popular culture, they affect Western cultural heritage. Think back to the days of a wonderful new Frank Sinatra release, another in a string of hit Kingston Trio albums, a heralded new Bob Dylan album, the Beatles' innovative *Sgt. Pepper's Lonely Hearts Club Band*, and Michael Jackson's masterpiece, *Thriller*, which captured most of America's youth. Rising into the Top 40 stratosphere places an artist in elite company. Holding down a slot in this golden territory may be tougher than making the NBA playoffs.

Whether you are a rabid or a casual fan of American popular music, you will undoubtedly find most of your favorite albums and artists among the prestigious ones listed in this volume. And whether you use this edition as a serious reference guide to the rock era, as a tool to catalog your private album collection, or as a casual reference and trivia guide, I hope you will be enthralled and entertained as you delve into an era of America's greatest hits.

JOEL WHITBURN
July 1987

JOEL WHITBURN:
ON TOP OF THE POP ALBUM CHARTS FOR OVER THIRTY YEARS

Only one person has covered every position on *Billboard*'s "Top Pop Albums" charts from 1955 to the present: chart authority Joel Whitburn.

But for Joel, merely tracking the rise and fall of every album that ever appeared on the industry's most authoritative pop albums chart isn't enough. So he's gone a step further: he has actually *collected* a copy of each charted album to make sure that every piece of information published in his books is accurate and indisputable.

Joel's mammoth collection of 30,000 albums and 40,000 singles—which also includes every record to ever hit *Billboard*'s "Hot 100" pop singles chart—is housed in a specially built, environmentally controlled underground vault adjacent to his Record Research offices in Joel's home in Menomonee Falls, Wisconsin.

The largest privately owned record collection in the world grew from the modest origins of the 45 RPM singles Joel began collecting as a hobby in the early 1950s. The burgeoning size and scope of the collection soon prompted Joel to begin keeping track of each record by filing it according to its highest position on *Billboard*'s "Hot 100." He later published this information in a slender volume titled simply *Record Research*.

Today, the Record Research books and supplements can be found on record collectors' bookshelves, on radio station reference racks, and in artists' private libraries all over the world. They provide essential statistics and data on *Billboard*'s pop singles, pop albums, country, black, adult contemporary, and other major charts.

Widely recognized as the foremost authority on charted music, Joel regularly supplies chart information to Casey Kasem, Dick Clark, and other prominent disc jockeys and music show hosts across America. In addition, he also makes frequent guest appearances on radio talk shows throughout the country.

An avid sports fan and outdoor enthusiast, 6'6" Joel enjoys relaxing with wife Fran and daughter Kim at his vacation home and second office in northern Wisconsin. Here he spends his time swimming, boating, water skiing, cycling, and hunting—and staying forever on top of *Billboard*'s "Top Pop Albums" charts.

A SYNOPSIS OF THE BILLBOARD ALBUM CHARTS

DATE	POSITIONS	CHART TITLE
1/1/55	15	BEST-SELLING POPULAR ALBUMS (mostly biweekly charts with the exception of a 7-week gap and several 3-week gaps)
3/24/56	10-15-20-30	BEST-SELLING POPULAR ALBUMS (charts published weekly with size varying from a top 10 to a top 30)
6/2/56	15	BEST-SELLING POP ALBUMS
9/2/57	25	BEST-SELLING POP LP's
5/25/59	50	BEST-SELLING MONOPHONIC LP's
5/25/59	30	BEST-SELLING STEREOPHONIC LP's (separate Stereo and Mono charts published through 8/10/63)
1/4/60	40	MONO ACTION CHARTS (mono albums charted 39 weeks or less)
1/4/60	30	STEREO ACTION CHARTS (stereo albums charted 19 weeks or less—changed to 29 weeks or less on 5/30/60)
1/4/60	25	ESSENTIAL INVENTORY—MONO (mono albums charted 40 weeks or more)
1/4/60	20	ESSENTIAL INVENTORY—STEREO (stereo albums charted 20 weeks or more—changed to 30 weeks or more on 5/30/60)
1/9/61	25	ACTION ALBUMS—MONOPHONIC (mono albums charted 9 weeks or less)
1/9/61	15	ACTION ALBUMS—STEREOPHONIC (stereo albums charted 9 weeks or less)
1/9/61	—	Approximately 200 albums listed by category (no positions) and shown as essential inventory
4/3/61	150	TOP LP's—MONAURAL
4/3/61	50	TOP LP's—STEREO
8/17/63	150	TOP LP's (1 chart)
4/1/67	175	TOP LP's
5/13/67	200	TOP LP's
11/25/67	200	TOP LP's (3 pages)
2/15/69	200	TOP LP's (2 pages with A-Z artist listing)
2/19/72	200	TOP LP's & TAPES
10/20/84	200	TOP 200 ALBUMS
1/5/85	200	TOP POP ALBUMS

An album appearing on both the Mono and Stereo charts in the same week is tabulated as one weekly appearance.

The album's highest position is determined by the chart (Mono or Stereo) on which the album reached its highest position.

The Essential Inventory charts list albums that have already been charted for months on the Mono & Stereo charts and, therefore, the album was researched for weeks charted only—its chart positions were not used.

THE
TOP 40
ALBUMS

ALBUMS BY ARTIST

This section lists, alphabetically by artist name, every album release to hit the Top 40 on *Billboard*'s pop album charts from 1955 through 1986.

Each artist's charted hits are listed in chronological order. A sequential number is shown in front of each song title to indicate the artist's number of charted albums. All top ten albums are highlighted in dark type.

All top ten singles from *Billboard*'s "Hot 100" are listed below the album they came from. The highest position each single reached is indicated in parentheses after the title. Singles listed without a highest position are noteworthy non-top ten hits.

Explanation of Headings and Symbols

DATE: Date album debuted on the charts

POS: Album's highest charted position (highlighted in bold type)

WKS: Total weeks charted in Top 40

LABEL & NO.: Original album label and number

( ) The number in parentheses after No. 1 and No. 2 albums indicates the total weeks the album held that position.

† Indicates the weeks the charted data is subject to change since the album was still charted in the Top 40 as of the June 20, 1987 cutoff date.

[ ] The number in the brackets following the label number indicates amount of records in the album.

• RIAA certified gold album (500,000 units sold)

▲ RIAA certified platinum album (1,000,000 units sold)

The Record Industry Association of America began certifying gold albums in 1958 and platinum albums in 1976. Before these dates, there are most certainly some hits that would have qualified for these certifications. Also, some record labels have never requested RIAA certification for their hits.

Letter(s) in brackets after titles indicate the following:

[C] Comedy Recording
[E] Early Recording
[EP] 7″ Extended Play (E.P.)
[F] Foreign Language Recording
[G] Greatest Hits
[I] Instrumental Recording
[K] Compilation
[L] Live Recording

[M] Mini-album Recording
        (10″ or 12″ E.P.)
[N] Novelty Recording
[OC] Original Cast Recording
[R] Reissue of Previously Charted
        Album
[S] Soundtrack
[T] Talk/Spoken Word Recording
[TV] Television Soundtrack
[X] Christmas Recording

DATE	POS	WKS	ARTIST—RECORD TITLE	LABEL & NO.

A

DATE	POS	WKS	ARTIST—RECORD TITLE	LABEL & NO.
			ABBA	
			Pop quartet formed in Stockholm, Sweden in 1970. Consisted of Frida Lyngstad and Agnetha Faltskog (vocals), Bjorn Ulvaeus (guitar) and Benny Anderson (keyboards). Benny and Bjorn recorded together in 1966. Bjorn and Agnetha married in 1971, divorced in 1978. Benny and Frida married in 1978, divorced in 1981.	
2/26/77	20	9	● 1. Arrival	Atlantic 18207
			"Dancing Queen"(1)	
3/25/78	14	17	▲ 2. The Album	Atlantic 19164
			"Take A Chance On Me"(3)	
7/28/79	19	12	● 3. Voulez-Vous	Atlantic 16000
12/27/80	17	16	● 4. Super Trouper	Atlantic 16023
			"The Winner Takes It All"(8)	
1/23/82	29	6	5. The Visitors	Atlantic 19332
			GREGORY ABBOTT	
			Soul singer, songwriter from New York City.	
12/27/86	22	16	● 1. Shake You Down	Columbia 40437
			"Shake You Down"(1)	
			ABC	
			New wave rock group from Sheffield, England. Martin Fry, lead singer.	
11/20/82	24	20	1. the Lexicon of Love	Mercury 4059
			"The Look Of Love"	
10/26/85	30	15	2. how to be a...Zillionaire!	Mercury 824904
			"Be Near Me"(9)	
			AC/DC	
			Hard rock band formed in Sydney, Australia in 1974. Consisted of brothers Angus and Malcolm Young (guitars), Bon Scott (lead singer), Phil Rudd (drums) and Mark Evans (bass). Cliff Williams replaced Evans in 1977. Bon Scott died on 2/19/80 from alcohol abuse and was replaced by Brian Johnson. Simon Wright replaced Rudd in 1985.	
9/15/79	17	10	▲ 1. Highway To Hell	Atlantic 19244
8/23/80	4	45	▲ 2. **Back In Black**	Atlantic 16018
			Brian Johnson replaces Bon Scott as lead singer	
4/18/81	3	19	▲ 3. **Dirty Deeds Done Dirt Cheap** [R]	Atlantic 16033
			recorded in 1976	
12/12/81	1(3)	16	▲ 4. **For Those About To Rock We Salute You**	Atlantic 11111
9/10/83	15	11	● 5. Flick Of The Switch	Atlantic 80100
8/17/85	32	5	● 6. Fly On The Wall	Atlantic 81263
8/09/86	33	6	▲ 7. Who Made Who [S K]	Atlantic 81650
			soundtrack from the film "Maximum Overdrive" - includes 3 new songs	
			ACE	
			British pub-rock quintet. Paul Carrack, lead singer.	
4/05/75	11	11	1. Five-A-Side (an Ace album)	Anchor 2001
			"How Long"(3)	

DATE	POS	WKS	ARTIST—RECORD TITLE	LABEL & NO.
			BRYAN ADAMS	
			Born on 11/5/59 in Vancouver, Canada. Rock singer, songwriter, guitarist.	
4/02/83	8	24	▲ 1. Cuts Like A Knife	A&M 4919
			"Straight From The Heart"(10)	
12/01/84	1(2)	66	▲ 2. Reckless	A&M 5013
			"Run To You"(6)	
			"Heaven"(1)	
			"Summer Of '69"(5)	
			CANNONBALL ADDERLEY	
			Born Julian Edwin Adderley on 9/15/28 in Tampa. Alto saxophonist, leader of jazz combo featuring brother Nat Adderley (cornet) and Joe Zawinul (piano). Cannonball died of a stroke on 8/8/75 in Gary, Indiana.	
7/07/62	30	5	1. Nancy Wilson/Cannonball Adderley	Capitol 1657
4/13/63	11	11	2. Jazz Workshop Revisited [I-L]	Riverside 444
3/25/67	13	9	3. Mercy, Mercy, Mercy! [I-L]	Capitol 2663
			AEROSMITH	
			Hard-rock band formed in Sunapee, NH in 1970. Consisted of Steve Tyler (lead singer), Joe Perry and Brad Whitford (guitars), Tom Hamilton (bass) and Joey Kramer (drums). Perry left for own Joe Perry Project in 1979. Whitford left in 1980. Original band reunited in April of 1984.	
5/24/75	11	31	▲ 1. Toys In The Attic	Columbia 33479
			"Walk This Way"(10)	
3/20/76	21	8	▲ 2. Aerosmith	Columbia 32005
			"Dream On"(6)	
5/29/76	3	21	▲ 3. Rocks	Columbia 34165
1/07/78	11	8	▲ 4. Draw The Line	Columbia 34856
11/18/78	13	13	▲ 5. Live! Bootleg [L]	Columbia 35564 [2]
12/15/79	14	12	● 6. Night In The Ruts	Columbia 36050
10/02/82	32	6	7. Rock In A Hard Place	Columbia 38061
12/14/85	36	5	8. Done With Mirrors	Geffen 24091
			AFTER THE FIRE	
			English band led by Andy Piercy.	
4/16/83	25	8	1. ATF	Epic 38282
			"Der Kommisar"(5)	
			A-HA	
			Trio formed in Oslo, Norway: Morten Harket (vocals), Pal Waaktaar (guitar, keyboards) and Mags Furuholem (keyboards).	
9/07/85	15	26	● 1. Hunting High And Low	Warner 25300
			"Take On Me"(1)	
			AIR FORCE - see GINGER BAKER	
			AIR SUPPLY	
			Melbourne, Australia duo: Russ Hitchcock (b: 6/15/49) & Graham Russell (b: 6/1/50).	
9/06/80	22	19	▲ 1. Lost In Love	Arista 4268
			"Lost In Love"(3)	
			"All Out Of Love"(2)	
			"Every Woman In The World"(5)	

DATE	POS	WKS	ARTIST—RECORD TITLE	LABEL & NO.
6/27/81	10	25	▲ 2. **The One That You Love**	Arista 9551
			"The One That You Love"(1)	
			"Here I Am"(5)	
			"Sweet Dreams"(5)	
7/17/82	25	8	▲ 3. Now And Forever	Arista 9587
			"Even The Nights Are Better"(5)	
9/03/83	7	26	▲ 4. **Greatest Hits** [G]	Arista 8024
			"Making Love Out Of Nothing At All"(2)	
7/06/85	26	8	● 5. Air Supply	Arista 8283

ALABAMA

Quartet from Fort Payne, Alabama: Randy Owen (vocals, guitar), Jeff Cook (guitar, fiddle, keyboards), Teddy Gentry (bass, vocals) and Mark Herndon (drums, vocals). Randy, Jeff and Teddy are cousins. Country music's current #1 act.

DATE	POS	WKS	ARTIST—RECORD TITLE	LABEL & NO.
5/02/81	16	41	▲ 1. Feels So Right	RCA 3930
3/20/82	14	20	▲ 2. Mountain Music	RCA 4229
3/26/83	10	15	▲ 3. **The Closer You Get...**	RCA 4663
2/18/84	21	17	▲ 4. Roll On	RCA 4939
3/16/85	28	5	▲ 5. 40 Hour Week	RCA 5339
3/08/86	24	15	6. Greatest Hits [G]	RCA 7170

THE ALARM

British rock quartet - Mike Peters, lead singer.

DATE	POS	WKS	ARTIST—RECORD TITLE	LABEL & NO.
2/15/86	39	3	1. Strength	I.R.S. 5666

MORRIS ALBERT

Brazilian singer/songwriter.

DATE	POS	WKS	ARTIST—RECORD TITLE	LABEL & NO.
11/29/75	37	2	1. Feelings	RCA 1018
			"Feelings"(6)	

RONNIE ALDRICH & His Two Pianos

DATE	POS	WKS	ARTIST—RECORD TITLE	LABEL & NO.
11/06/61	20	13	1. Melody And Percussion For Two Pianos [I]	London P. 4 44007
10/20/62	36	2	2. Ronnie Aldrich & His Two Pianos [I]	London P. 4 44018

DAVIE ALLAN & THE ARROWS

Davie began as a session guitarist for Mike Curb in Los Angeles.

DATE	POS	WKS	ARTIST—RECORD TITLE	LABEL & NO.
12/03/66	17	13	1. The Wild Angels [S]	Tower 5043

DAYTON ALLEN

Comedian on the Steve Allen TV show.

DATE	POS	WKS	ARTIST—RECORD TITLE	LABEL & NO.
12/19/60	35	1	1. Why Not! [C]	Grand Award 424

STEVE ALLEN

Born on 12/26/21 in New York City. Well-known television personality. Founded "Tonight Show" in 1954. Played title role in 1956 movie "The Benny Goodman Story".

DATE	POS	WKS	ARTIST—RECORD TITLE	LABEL & NO.
5/14/55	7	10	1. **Music For Tonight** [I]	Coral 57004

THE ALLMAN BROTHERS BAND

Southern rock band formed in Macon, Georgia in 1968. Consisted of brothers Duane (lead guitar) and Gregg Allman (keyboards), Dickey Betts (guitar), Berry Oakley (bass), and the drum duo of Jai Johnny Johanson and Butch Trucks. Duane and Gregg known earlier as Allman Joys and Hour Glass. Duane was the top session guitarist at Muscle Shoals studio. He was killed in a motorcycle crash on

DATE	POS	WKS	ARTIST—RECORD TITLE	LABEL & NO.
			10/29/71 at the age of 24. On 11/11/72, Oakley was killed in another cycle accident. He was replaced by Lamar Williams. Chuck Leavill (keyboards) added in 1972. After much turmoil, band regrouped in 1978 with a new lineup led by Gregg Allman and Dickey Betts.	
12/05/70	**38**	2	1. Idlewild South	Atco 342
7/31/71	**13**	11	● 2. At Fillmore East [L]	Capricorn 802 [2]
3/18/72	**4**	29	● 3. **Eat A Peach** [L]	Capricorn 0102 [2]
			includes Duane's last 3 studio recordings	
4/07/73	**25**	6	● 4. Beginnings [R]	Atco 805 [2]
			reissue of album #1 above and LP "The Allman Brothers Band" (1970)	
8/25/73	**1**(5)	24	● 5. **Brothers And Sisters**	Capricorn 0111
			"Ramblin Man"(2)	
9/27/75	**5**	8	● 6. **Win, Lose Or Draw**	Capricorn 0156
3/24/79	**9**	13	● 7. **Enlightened Rouges**	Capricorn 0218
9/06/80	**27**	6	● 8. Reach For The Sky	Arista 9535
			DUANE ALLMAN	
			Born on 11/20/46. The Allman Brothers Band guitarist. Died on 10/29/71 in a motorcycle mishap.	
1/20/73	**28**	6	● 1. An Anthology [K]	Capricorn 0108 [2]
			features Duane's session work	
			GREGG ALLMAN	
			Born on 12/8/47 in Nashville. Keyboardist for The Allman Brothers Band. Married briefly to Cher in 1975.	
12/08/73	**13**	17	● 1. Laid Back	Capricorn 0116
			LAURINDO ALMEIDA & The Bossa Nova All Stars	
12/08/62	**9**	22	1. **Viva Bossa Nova!** [I]	Capitol 1759
			HERB ALPERT & THE TIJUANA BRASS	
			Herb was born on 3/31/35 in Los Angeles. Producer, composer, trumpeter, bandleader. Played trumpet since age eight. A&R for Keen Records, produced first Jan & Dean session, wrote "Wonderful World" hit for Sam Cooke. Formed A&M Records with Jerry Moss in 1962. Used studio musicians until early 1965, then own band.	
1/26/63	**24**	49	● 1. The Lonely Bull [I]	A&M 101
			"The Lonely Bull"(6)	
6/12/65	**1**(8)	41	● 2. **Whipped Cream & Other Delights** [I]	A&M 110
			"Taste Of Honey"(7)	
11/06/65	**1**(6)	07	● 3. **Going Places** [I]	A&M 112
12/18/65	**6**	52	● 4. **South Of The Border** [I]	A&M 108
3/05/66	**17**	13	● 5. Herb Alpert's Tijuana Brass, Volume 2 [I]	A&M 103
			Herb's 2nd album, recorded in 1963	
5/21/66	**1**(9)	59	● 6. **What Now My Love** [I]	A&M 4114
5/21/66	**30**	59	7. The Brass Are Comin' [I]	A&M 4228
12/17/66	**2**(6)	38	● 8. **S.R.O.** [I]	A&M 4119
6/10/67	**1**(1)	36	● 9. **Sounds Like** [I]	A&M 4124
12/30/67	**4**	18	● 10. **Herb Alpert's Ninth** [I]	A&M 4134
5/18/68	**1**(2)	28	● 11. **The Beat Of The Brass** [I]	A&M 4146
			"This Guy's In Love With You"(1)	
7/19/69	**28**	7	● 12. Warm [I]	A&M 4190

DATE	POS	WKS	ARTIST—RECORD TITLE	LABEL & NO.
10/20/79	6	19	▲ 13. **Rise** [I]	A&M 4790
			"Rise"(1)	
8/09/80	28	4	14. Beyond [I]	A&M 3717
			AMBROSIA	
			Los Angeles-based trio: David Pack, Joe Puerta & Burleigh Drummond.	
7/26/75	22	8	1. Ambrosia	20th Century 434
11/04/78	19	9	2. Life Beyond L.A.	Warner 3135
			"How Much I Feel"(3)	
5/31/80	25	7	3. One Eighty	Warner 3368
			"Biggest Part Of Me"(3)	
			AMERICA	
			Trio formed in London, England, 1969. Consisted of Dan Peek, Gerry Beckley and Dewey Bunnell. All played guitars. Met at US Air Force base. With group Daze in 1970. Moved to U.S. in February, 1972. Peek left in 1976.	
3/04/72	1(5)	22	▲ 1. **America**	Warner 2576
			"A Horse With No Name"(1)	
			"I Need You"(9)	
12/16/72	9	16	● 2. **Homecoming**	Warner 2655
			"Ventura Highway"(8)	
12/01/73	28	5	3. Hat Trick	Warner 2728
8/24/74	3	17	● 4. **Holiday**	Warner 2808
			"Tin Man"(4)	
			"Lonely People"(5)	
4/19/75	4	17	● 5. **Hearts**	Warner 2852
			"Sister Golden Hair"(1)	
11/29/75	3	22	▲ 6. **History/America's Greatest Hits** [G]	Warner 2894
5/08/76	11	8	● 7. Hideaway	Warner 2932
3/26/77	21	4	8. Harbor	Warner 3017
			THE AMES BROTHERS	
			Vocal group from Malden, MA, formed in the late 40s. Family name Urick. Consisted of Ed (b: 7/9/27), Gene (b: 2/13/25), Joe (b: 5/3/24) and Vic (b: 5/20/26, d: 1/23/78). After local work in Boston, did extensive touring. Own TV series in 1955.	
12/02/57	16	4	1. There'll Always Be A Christmas [X]	RCA 1541
			ED AMES	
			One of the Ames Brothers. Played an Indian on the "Daniel Boone" TV series.	
3/18/67	4	19	● 1. **My Cup Runneth Over**	RCA 3774
			"My Cup Runneth Over"(8)	
1/20/68	24	8	2. When The Snow Is On The Roses	RCA 3913
3/23/68	13	18	● 3. Who Will Answer?	RCA 3961
			Our Time	
			BILL ANDERSON	
			Born 11/1/37 in Columbia, SC. Host of Nashville Network's TV quiz show "Fandango".	
7/27/63	36	5	1. Still	Decca 74427
			"Still"(8)	

DATE	POS	WKS	ARTIST—RECORD TITLE	LABEL & NO.
			ERNESTINE ANDERSON	
			Jazz singer formerly with Eddie Heywood and Lionel Hampton.	
10/20/58	15	6	1. Hot Cargo!	Mercury 20354
			LYNN ANDERSON	
			Born on 9/26/47 in Grand Forks, ND. Daughter of country singer Liz Anderson.	
2/13/71	19	12	▲ 1. Rose Garden	Columbia 30411
			"Rose Garden"(3)	
			THE ANGELS	
			Female pop trio from Orange, NJ, formed as the Starlets with sisters Phyllis "Jiggs" (b: 9/24/42) & Barbara Allbut (b: 9/24/40), and Linda Jansen (lead singer). First recorded for Astro in 1960. Jansen was replaced by Peggy Santiglia in 1962.	
11/16/63	33	3	1. My Boyfriend's Back	Smash 67039
			"My Boyfriend's Back"(1)	
			THE ANIMALS	
			Formed in Newcastle, England in 1958 as the Alan Price Combo. Consisted of Eric Burdon (vocals), Alan Price (keyboards), Bryan "Chas" Chandler (bass), Hilton Valentine (guitar) and John Steel (drums). Price left in May of 1965, replaced by Dave Rowberry. Steel left in 1966, replaced by Barry Jenkins. Group disbanded in July, 1968. After a period with War, Burdon and the other originals reunited, 1983.	
10/03/64	7	15	1. **The Animals**	MGM 4264
			"The House Of The Rising Sun"(1)	
3/12/66	6	51	● 2. **The Best Of The Animals** [G]	MGM 4324
9/24/66	20	12	3. Animalization	MGM 4384
			"See See Rider"(10)	
1/14/67	33	3	4. Animalism	MGM 4414
			ANIMOTION	
			Techno-pop quintet led by Astrid Plane and Bill Wadhams.	
4/20/85	28	7	1. Animotion	Mercury 822580
			"Obsession"(6)	
			PAUL ANKA	
			Born on 7/30/41 in Ottawa, Canada. Performer since age 12. Father financed first recording in 1956 "I Confess" (RPM 472). Wrote "My Way" for Frank Sinatra, "She's A Lady" for Tom Jones. Also wrote Theme for the "Tonight Show". Own variety show in 1973. Long-time entertainer in Las Vegas.	
7/04/60	4	54	1. **Paul Anka Sings His Big 15** [G]	ABC-Para. 323
12/05/60	23	3	2. Anka At The Copa [L]	ABC-Para. 353
9/28/74	9	14	● 3. **Anka**	United Art. 314
			"(You're) Having My Baby"(1)	
			"One Man Woman/One Woman Man"(7)	
5/24/75	36	3	4. Feelings	United Art. 367
			"I Don't Like To Sleep Alone"(8)	
1/17/76	22	9	● 5. Times Of Your Life [K]	United Art. 569
			9 of 10 cuts from previous 2 United Artists albums	
			"Times Of Your Life"(7)	

DATE	POS	WKS	ARTIST—RECORD TITLE	LABEL & NO.
			ANNETTE	
			Born Annette Funicello on 10/22/42 in Utica, NY. Became a Mousketeer in 1955. In several teen films in the early 60s. Backing group: The Afterbeats.	
3/21/60	21	21	1. Annette Sings Anka	Buena Vista 3302
9/26/60	38	3	2. Hawaiiannette	Buena Vista 3303
12/14/63	39	1	3. Annette's Beach Party [S]	Buena Vista 3316
			half of the songs are from the film "Beach Party"	
			RAY ANTHONY	
			Born Raymond Antonini on 1/20/22 in Bentleyville, PA. Trumpeter bandleader. Raised in Cleveland. Joined Al Donahue in 1939, then with Glenn Miller and Jimmy Dorsey from 1940-42. Led US Army band. Formed own band in 1946. Very popular with college audiences. Appeared in film "Daddy Long Legs" with Fred Astaire in 1955.	
3/19/55	10	6	1. **Golden Horn** [I]	Capitol 563
6/23/56	15	1	2. Dream Dancing [I]	Capitol 723
10/28/57	11	21	3. Young Ideas [I]	Capitol 866
5/19/58	12	10	4. The Dream Girl [I]	Capitol 969
8/11/62	14	13	5. Worried Mind [I]	Capitol 1752
			ADAM ANT	
			Born Stuart Goddard on 11/3/54 in London, England. Formed Adam & The Ants in 1976.	
12/11/82	16	16	● 1. Friend Or Foe	Epic 38370
			"Goody Two Shoes"	
			CARMINE APPICE - see BECK, BOGERT, APPICE	
			APRIL WINE	
			Rock quintet from Montreal, Canada led by Myles Goodwyn.	
2/28/81	26	12	▲ 1. The Nature Of The Beast	Capitol 12125
8/07/82	37	3	2. Power Play	Capitol 12218
			ARCADIA	
			English group features Duran Duran's Simon Lebon, Nick Rhodes & Roger Taylor	
12/21/85	23	9	▲ 1. So Red The Rose	Capitol 12428
			"Election Day"(6)	
			ARGENT	
			British rock quartet, consisted of ex-Zombies member Rod Argent (vocals, keyboards), John Verity (guitar), Jim Rodford (bass) and Robert Henrit (drums).	
9/02/72	23	7	1. All Together Now	Epic 31556
			"Hold Your Head Up"(5)	
			JOAN ARMATRADING	
			Born on 12/9/50 in St. Kitts, West Indies. Vocalist, pianist, guitarist, composer. To Birmingham, England in 1958. First recorded for Cube in 1971.	
7/26/80	28	5	1. Me Myself I	A&M 4809
5/28/83	32	3	2. The Key	A&M 4912

DATE	POS	WKS	ARTIST—RECORD TITLE	LABEL & NO.
			LOUIS ARMSTRONG	
			Born Daniel Louis Armstrong on 7/4/1900 in New Orleans; died on 7/6/71 in New York. Nickname: Satchmo. Trumpeter, vocalist. Resident of Colored Waif's Home in New Orleans and played cornet in the Home's band. Joined Joe "King" Oliver in Chicago in 1922. By 1929, had become the most widely known black musician. Influenced dozens of singers and trumpet players, both black and white. Made numerous appearances on radio, TV and in films.	
10/01/55	10	2	1. **Satch Plays Fats**	Columbia 708
			a tribute to Fats Waller	
12/15/56	12	2	2. Ella And Louis	Verve 4003
			ELLA FITZGERALD & LOUIS ARMSTRONG	
			backing by the Oscar Peterson Trio, plus Buddy Rich	
5/23/64	1(6)	48	● 3. **Hello, Dolly!**	Kapp 3364
			"Hello, Dolly"(1)	
			EDDY ARNOLD	
			Born on 5/15/18 near Henderson, TN. Became popular on Nashville's Grand Ole Opry as a singer with Pee Wee King (1940-43). Country music's all-time #1 artist.	
11/27/65	7	28	● 1. **My World**	RCA 3466
			"Make The World Go Away"(6)	
5/21/66	26	5	2. I Want To Go With You	RCA 3507
3/11/67	36	2	3. Somebody Like Me	RCA 3715
6/24/67	34	2	● 4. The Best Of Eddy Arnold [G]	RCA 3565
11/25/67	34	5	5. Turn The World Around	RCA 3869
			ARROWS - see DAVIE ALLAN	
			ARTISTS UNITED AGAINST APARTHEID	
			Benefit group of 49 superstar artists formed in protest of the South African government - proceeds to benefit political prisoners in South Africa.	
12/07/85	31	4	1. Sun City	Manhattan 53019
			ASHFORD & SIMPSON	
			R&B vocal/songwriting husband and wife duo: Nickolas Ashford (b: 5/4/42, Fairfield, SC) and Valerie Simpson (b: 8/26/46, New York, NY). Team wrote for Chuck Jackson and Maxine Brown. Joined staff at Motown and wrote and produced for many of the label's top stars.	
9/23/78	20	12	● 1. Is It Still Good To Ya	Warner 3219
9/08/79	23	9	● 2. Stay Free	Warner 3357
9/13/80	38	2	3. A Musical Affair	Warner 3458
2/09/85	29	10	4. Solid	Capitol 12366
			ASIA	
			English rock supergroup composed of Steve Howe (Yes), Carl Palmer (Emerson, Lake & Palmer), Geoff Downes (Buggles, Yes) and John Wetton (King Crimson, Uriah Heep, Roxy Music). Howe replaced by Mandy Meyer (Krokus) in 1985.	
4/03/82	1(9)	35	▲ 1. **Asia**	Geffen 2008
			"Heat Of The Moment"(4)	
8/27/83	6	11	▲ 2. **Alpha**	Geffen 4008
			"Don't Cry"(10)	

DATE	POS	WKS	ARTIST—RECORD TITLE	LABEL & NO.
			THE ASSOCIATION	
			Group formed in Los Angeles in 1965. Consisted of Terry Kirkman (plays 23 wind, reed and percussion instruments), Jules Alexander (guitar), Brian Cole (bass), Jim Yester (guitar), Ted Buechel Jr. (drums) and Russ Giguere (percussion). Larry Ramos joined in early 1968. Richard Thompson (keyboards) replaced Giguere in 1970. Cole died on 8/2/73 of a drug overdose. Thompson replaced by Rick Ulsky in 1974. Regrouped with original surviving members on 9/26/80.	
10/01/66	5	15	● 1. **And Then...Along Comes The Association**	Valiant 5002
			"Along Comes Mary"(7)	
			"Cherish"(1)	
3/04/67	34	3	2. Renaissance	Valiant 5004
8/05/67	8	25	● 3. **Insight Out**	Warner 1696
			"Windy"(1)	
			"Never My Love"(2)	
5/25/68	23	6	4. Birthday	Warner 1733
			"Everything That Touches You"(10)	
1/25/69	4	23	▲ 5. **Greatest Hits** [G]	Warner 1767
10/18/69	32	4	6. The Association	Warner 1800
			CHET ATKINS	
			Born on 6/20/24 in Luttrell, Tennessee. Elected to the Country Music Hall of Fame in 1973. Nashville's top guitarist.	
6/16/58	21	4	1. Chet Atkins At Home [I]	RCA 1544
2/22/60	16	12	2. Teensville [I]	RCA 2161
2/13/61	7	9	3. **Chet Atkins' Workshop** [I]	RCA 2232
4/28/62	31	4	4. Down Home [I]	RCA 2450
10/13/62	33	6	5. Caribbean Guitar [I]	RCA 2549
			ATLANTA RHYTHM SECTION	
			Group formed of musicians from Studio One, Doraville, GA in 1971. Consisted of Rodney Justo (vocals), Barry Bailey, Paul Goddard, J.R. Cobb (guitars), Dean Daughtry (keyboards) and Robert Nix (drums). Cobb, Daughtry and band manager Buddy Buie had been with the Classics IV; others had been with Roy Orbison. Justo left after first album, replaced by Ronnie Hammond.	
3/12/77	11	14	● 1. A Rock And Roll Alternative	Polydor 6080
			"So In To You"(7)	
4/08/78	7	15	▲ 2. **Champagne Jam**	Polydor 6134
			"Imaginary Lover"(7)	
7/07/79	26	7	● 3. Underdog	Polydor 6200
			ATLANTIC STARR	
			Originally an eight-man, one-woman band, formed in New York City in 1976. Lead singers: brothers Wayne & David Lewis and Sharon Bryant (replaced by Barbara Weathers in 1985).	
4/17/82	18	7	1. Brillance	A&M 4883
2/22/86	17	14	● 2. **As The Band Turns**	A&M 5019
			"Secret Lovers"(3)	
			AURRA	
			Consisted of ex-Slave members Steve Washington and Tom Lockett, Jr., saxophones; with vocalists Starleana Young and Curt Jones.	
4/17/82	38	3	1. A Little Love	Salsoul 8551

DATE	POS	WKS	ARTIST—RECORD TITLE	LABEL & NO.
			PATTI AUSTIN	
			Born on 8/10/48 in New York City. Backup work in New York. Goddaughter of Quincy Jones. Also see Yutaka.	
1/29/83	36	11	1. Every Home Should Have One	Qwest 3591
			"Baby, Come To Me"(1-with James Ingram)	
			AUTOGRAPH	
			Los Angeles-based rock quintet - Steve Plunkett, lead singer.	
2/23/85	29	12	● 1. Sign in Please	RCA 8040
			"Turn Up The Radio"	
			FRANKIE AVALON	
			Born Francis Avallone on 9/18/39 in Philadelphia. Worked in bands in Atlantic City, NJ in 1953. Radio and TV with Paul Whiteman, mid-50s. Singer, trumpet player with Rocco & His Saints in 1957. Film "Disc Jockey Jamboree" in 1957. Teen idol managed by Bob Marucci. Frequent appearances in films with Annette. Also films "Guns Of The Timberland" in 1960, "The Carpetbaggers" in 1962.	
1/04/60	9	13	1. Swingin' On A Rainbow	Chancellor 5004
			AVERAGE WHITE BAND	
			Vocal/instrumental group formed in Scotland in 1972. Consisted of Alan Gorrie (vocal, bass), Hamish Stuart (vocal, guitar), Onnie McIntyre (vocal, guitar), Malcolm Duncan (saxophone), Roger Ball (keyboards, saxophone) and Robbie McIntosh (drums). McIntosh died of drug poisoning in 1974, replaced by Steve Ferrone.	
12/21/74	1(1)	17	● 1. **AWB**	Atlantic 7308
			"Pick Up The Pieces"(1)	
5/17/75	39	2	2. Put It Where You Want It [R]	MCA 475
			reissue of 1973 album "Show Your Hand"	
7/05/75	4	11	● 3. **Cut The Cake**	Atlantic 18140
			"Cut The Cake"(10)	
7/31/76	9	10	▲ 4. **Soul Searching**	Atlantic 18179
2/05/77	28	5	● 5. Person To Person [L]	Atlantic 1002 [2]
8/20/77	33	5	6. Benny And Us	Atlantic 19105
			AVERAGE WHITE BAND & BEN E. KING	
4/22/78	28	5	● 7. Warmer Communications	Atlantic 19162
5/05/79	32	3	8. Feel No Fret	Atlantic 19207
			ROY AYERS	
			R&B/jazz vibraphonist.	
4/15/78	33	3	1. Let's Do It	Polydor 6126
			B	
			THE BABYS	
			John Waite, lead singer of British foursome.	
12/17/77	34	3	1. Broken Heart	Chrysalis 1150
3/10/79	22	10	2. Head First	Chrysalis 1195

DATE	POS	WKS	ARTIST—RECORD TITLE	LABEL & NO.
			BURT BACHARACH	
			Born on 5/12/28 in Kansas City. Conductor, arranger and top composer who often worked with lyricist Hal David. Formerly married to Angie Dickinson, currently married to songwriter Carole Bayer Sager.	
6/26/71	**18**	12	● 1. Burt Bacharach	A&M 3501
			BACHMAN-TURNER OVERDRIVE	
			Hard-rock group formed in Vancouver, Canada in 1972. Randy Bachman (vocals, guitar), Tim Bachman (guitar), C. Fred Turner (vocals, bass) and Robbie Bachman (drums). Originally known as Brave Belt. Randy had been in the Guess Who and recorded solo. Tim Bachman left in 1973, replaced by Blair Thornton. Randy Bachman left in 1977. Randy and Tim regrouped with C.F. Turner in 1984.	
3/09/74	**4**	35	● 1. **Bachman-Turner Overdrive II**	Mercury 696
			"Let It Ride"/"Takin' Care Of Business"	
9/14/74	**1**(1)	25	● 2. **Not Fragile**	Mercury 1004
			"You Ain't Seen Nothing Yet"(1)	
6/07/75	**5**	9	● 3. **Four Wheel Drive**	Mercury 1027
1/31/76	**23**	7	● 4. Head On	Mercury 1067
9/11/76	**19**	6	● 5. Best Of B.T.O (So Far) [G]	Mercury 1101
			BAD COMPANY	
			British: Paul Rodgers (vocals), Mick Ralphs (guitar), Simon Kirke (drums) & Boz Burrell (bass). Paul and Simon from Free; Mick from Mott The Hoople; and Boz from King Crimson.	
8/03/74	**1**(1)	15	● 1. **Bad Company**	Swan Song 8410
			"Can't Get Enough"(5)	
4/26/75	**3**	11	● 2. **Straight Shooter**	Swan Song 8413
			"Feel Like Makin' Love"(10)	
2/21/76	**5**	15	▲ 3. **Run With The Pack**	Swan Song 8415
4/02/77	**15**	8	● 4. **Burnin' Sky**	Swan Song 8500
3/31/79	**3**	24	▲ 5. **Desolation Angels**	Swan Song 8506
9/18/82	**26**	6	6. Rough Diamonds	Swan Song 90001
			BADFINGER	
			British quartet originally known as The Iveys - leader Pete Ham commited suicide on 4/23/75 (27).	
12/05/70	**28**	5	1. No Dice	Apple 3367
			"No Matter What"(8)	
2/19/72	**31**	3	2. Straight Up	Apple 3387
			produced by Todd Rundgren & George Harrison	
			"Day After Day"(4)	
			JOAN BAEZ	
			Folk song stylist born in New York City on 1/9/41. Became a political activist while attending Boston University in the late 50s.	
12/18/61	**13**	70	● 1. Joan Baez, Vol. 2	Vanguard 2097
4/14/62	**15**	45	● 2. Joan Baez	Vanguard 2077
			Joan's first album, recorded in 1960	
11/03/62	**10**	70	● 3. **Joan Baez In Concert** [L]	Vanguard 2122
12/14/63	**7**	23	4. **Joan Baez In Concert, Part 2** [L]	Vanguard 2123
12/05/64	**12**	28	5. Joan Baez/5	Vanguard 79160
11/13/65	**10**	9	6. **Farewell, Angelina**	Vanguard 79200

DATE	POS	WKS	ARTIST—RECORD TITLE	LABEL & NO.
10/14/67	38	2	7. Joan	Vanguard 79240
2/15/69	30	5	● 8. Any Day Now	Vanguard 79306 [2]
			Songs of Bob Dylan	
7/26/69	36	2	9. David's Album	Vanguard 79308
			dedicated to her imprisoned husband, David Harris	
10/02/71	11	10	● 10. Blessed Are	Vanguard 6570 [2]
			"The Night They Drove Old Dixie Down"(3)	
6/14/75	11	17	● 11. Diamonds & Rust	A&M 4527
3/06/76	34	3	12. From Every Stage [L]	A&M 3704 [2]

PHILIP BAILEY

Born on 5/8/51 in Denver. Former co-lead vocalist for Earth, Wind & Fire.

DATE	POS	WKS	ARTIST—RECORD TITLE	LABEL & NO.
1/19/85	22	11	1. Chinese Wall	Columbia 39542
			"Easy Lover"(2-with Phil Collins)	

ANITA BAKER

Soul singer from Detroit. Former lead singer of Chapter 8.

DATE	POS	WKS	ARTIST—RECORD TITLE	LABEL & NO.
9/13/86	11	41+	▲ 1. Rapture	Elektra 60444
			"Sweet Love"(8)	

GINGER BAKER'S AIR FORCE

Ginger was drummer for Cream and Blind Faith. Group features Steve Winwood and Denny Laine.

DATE	POS	WKS	ARTIST—RECORD TITLE	LABEL & NO.
6/06/70	33	3	1. Ginger Baker's Air Force [L]	Atco 703 [2]
			recorded live at London's Royal Albert Hall	

MARTY BALIN

Born on 1/30/43 in Cincinnati. Co-founder of Jefferson Airplane/Jefferson Starship/KBC.

DATE	POS	WKS	ARTIST—RECORD TITLE	LABEL & NO.
8/15/81	35	3	1. Balin	EMI America 17054
			"Hearts"(8)	

KENNY BALL & His Jazzmen

English dixieland jazz band.

DATE	POS	WKS	ARTIST—RECORD TITLE	LABEL & NO.
4/14/62	13	15	1. Midnight In Moscow [I]	Kapp 1276
			"Midnight In Moscow"(2)	

BANANARAMA

Female trio from London, England: Sarah Dallin, Keren Woodward and Siobhan Fahey.

DATE	POS	WKS	ARTIST—RECORD TITLE	LABEL & NO.
9/15/84	30	7	1. Bananarama	London 820036
			reissued (#820165) October, 1984 with new song "Wild Life"	
			"Cruel Summer"(9)	
8/23/86	15	11	● 2. True Confessions	London 828013
			"Venus"(1)	

THE BAND

Formed in Woodstock, New York in 1967: Robbie Robertson (guitar), Levon Helm (drums), Rick Danko (bass), Richard Manuel and Garth Hudson (keyboards). All from Canada (except Helm from Arkansas) and all were with Ronnie Hawkins' Hawks. Recorded extensively with Bob Dylan. Disbanded on Thanksgiving Day in 1976. Manuel committed suicide on 3/4/86 (42). Also see Bob Dylan.

DATE	POS	WKS	ARTIST—RECORD TITLE	LABEL & NO.
10/19/68	30	7	1. Music From Big Pink	Capitol 2955
			Big Pink: The Band's communal home in Woodstock	
10/18/69	9	24	● 2. **The Band**	Capitol 132
9/05/70	5	14	● 3. **Stage Fright**	Capitol 425

Chet Atkins is not only recognized as one of America's finest guitarists, he is highly regarded as a Nashville record producer and executive. He played on and produced many of Elvis Presley's early sessions, including "Heartbreak Hotel" and "Love Me Tender."

Bad Company, formed in 1973 by former members of Free, King Crimson, and Mott the Hoople, immediately found far greater commercial success than any of those estimable groups. The first Bad Company album went to No. 1; *Straight Shooter,* the follow-up, reached No. 3.

Joan Baez has long been associated with Bob Dylan and has performed on-stage with him numerous times. Over the years, Baez has recorded many Dylan compositions. *Any Day Now* is an entire album of his songs; *5* includes "It Ain't Me Babe."

The Beach Boys released seven albums and twelve singles in its first three years (1962–64) as national recording artists. *Shut Down Volume 2,* the group's fifth chart album, features such classic tunes as "Don't Worry Baby," "Fun, Fun, Fun," and "The Warmth of the Sun."

The Beatles began recording *Sgt. Pepper* on Nov. 28, 1966, in the same week the Jimi Hendrix Experience played its first gig and the Monkees received a gold record for "I'm a Believer." The album was released on June 1, 1967, two days before "Light My Fire" entered the charts. The first song the Beatles recorded for *Sgt. Pepper* was "When I'm 64"; the last was "With a Little Help from My Friends."

The Beatles had a very busy 1964. In the months of June and July alone the group began a world tour; premiered *A Hard Day's Night,* its first movie; and released the *Something New* album, as well as the film soundtrack, a single of the movie's title song, and two other singles, including "And I Love Her."

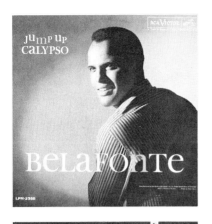

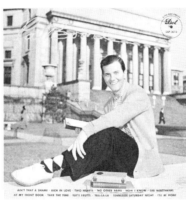

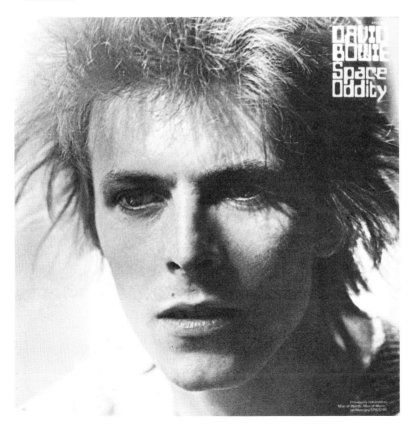

Harry Belafonte has not had a hit single since 1957, but can claim two dozen albums that have made the charts, six of which went gold. The New York native has recorded with such diverse singing partners as Miriam Makeba, Lena Horne, Odetta, and Nana Mouskori and remains America's best-known calypso advocate.

Chuck Berry has been an American rock'n'roll institution since recording "Maybellene" in 1955. The following year, he played 101 concerts in 101 days, a monumental tour that began and ended in New York.

Bobby Bland, the great blues singer, had a two-sided hit in 1963: "Call on Me" went to No. 22, while its flip, "That's the Way Love Is," reached No. 33 on its own: The album (also 1963) that contains both songs, however, did better than either of them, peaking at No. 11.

The Blues Magoos was from the Bronx. Originally known as the Bloos Magoos, the group built its reputation on the New York club scene, wearing custom-made clothing that lit up onstage. Despite a lengthy career, the group's biggest single was its first: "(We Ain't Got) Nothin' Yet," a classic slice of psychedelic punk, which was included on its debut album, *Psychedelic Lollipop* (1966).

Pat Boone first gained fame by winning Ted Mack's "Original Amateur Hour" three times in the early 1950s. By 1957 he was a huge star, thanks to his records, movies, and a regular part on the "Arthur Godfrey and His Friends" television show (in which he succeeded Julius LaRosa).

David Bowie originally released this album in England under the title *David Bowie*. The American version was retitled *Man of Words, Man of Music* and, three years later, reissued as *Space Oddity*. The title track, Bowie's first British hit in 1969, actually became his first American Top 40 hit as well, in 1973.

DATE	POS	WKS	ARTIST—RECORD TITLE	LABEL & NO.
10/16/71	21	5	4. Cahoots	Capitol 651
9/23/72	6	14	● 5. **Rock Of Ages** **[L]**	Capitol 11045 [2]
12/15/73	28	6	6. Moondog Matinee	Capitol 11214
1/03/76	26	5	7. Northern Lights-Southern Cross	Capitol 11440
5/20/78	16	8	8. The Last Waltz **[S-L]**	Warner 3146 [3]
			<div align="center">farewell concert at the San Francisco Winterland with guests Bob Dylan, Eric Clapton, Neil Diamond, Ringo Starr & others</div>	
			BANGLES	
			Female rock quartet formed in Los Angeles in January, 1981: sisters Vicki (lead guitar) and Debbi Peterson (drums), Michael Steele (bass) and Susanna Hoffs (guitar). Originally named The Bangs.	
3/08/86	2(2)	46	▲ 1. **Different Light**	Columbia 40039
			"Manic Monday"(2)	
			"Walk Like An Egyptian"(1)	
			BAR-KAYS	
			R&B instrumental combo consisting of Jimmy King (guitar), Ronnie Caldwell (organ), James Alexander (bass), Carl Cunningham (drums), Phalon Jones (saxophone) and Ben Cauley (trumpet). Formed by Al Jackson, drummer with Booker T & The MG's. The plane crash that killed Otis Redding (10/10/67) also claimed the lives of all the Bar-Kays except Cauley and Alexander (who were not on the plane). Alexander re-formed the band. Appeared in the film "Wattstax"; much session work at Stax.	
12/15/79	35	3	● 1. Injoy	Mercury 3781
			COUNT BASIE	
			Born William Basie on 8/21/04 in Red Bank, New Jersey. Died on 4/26/84. Pianist, organist, bandleader. Learned music and piano from mother, organ from Fats Waller. First recorded with own band in 1937 for Decca. Many films and continued touring into the 70s.	
2/09/63	5	22	1. **Sinatra-Basie**	Reprise 1008
			FRANK SINATRA/COUNT BASIE	
7/20/63	19	4	2. This Time By Basie! Hits of the 50's	
			And 60's **[I]**	Reprise 6070
9/12/64	13	15	3. It Might As Well Be Swing	Reprise 1012
			FRANK SINATRA/COUNT BASIE	
			TONI BASIL	
			Los Angeles vocalist, actress, choreographer, and video director.	
11/27/82	22	9	● 1. Word Of Mouth	Chrysalis 1410
			"Mickey"(1)	
			LES BAXTER	
			Born 3/14/22 in Mexia, Texas. Began as a conductor on radio shows in the 30s. Musical arranger for Capitol Records in the 50s.	
1/28/56	6	2	1. **Tamboo!** **[I]**	Capitol 655
3/16/57	21	2	2. Skins! **[I]**	Capitol 774
			BAY CITY ROLLERS	
			Formed in 1967 in Edinburgh, Scotland as the Saxons. Original members: brothers Alan & Derek Longmuir, Les McKeoun (lead singer), Eric Faulkner and Stuart "Woody" Wood.	
12/13/75	20	9	● 1. Bay City Rollers	Arista 4049
			"Saturday Night"(1)	
7/24/76	31	4	● 2. Rock N' Roll Love Letter	Arista 4071
			"Money Honey"(9)	

DATE	POS	WKS	ARTIST—RECORD TITLE		LABEL & NO.
10/09/76	26	7	● 3. Dedication		Arista 4093
7/30/77	23	7	● 4. It's A Game		Arista 7004
			"You Made Me Believe In Magic"(10)		

THE BEACH BOYS

Group formed in Hawthorne, California in 1961. Consisted of brothers Brian (keyboards, bass), Carl (guitar), and Dennis Wilson (drums); their cousin Mike Love (lead vocals, saxophone), and Al Jardine (guitar). Known in high school as Kenny & The Cadets, Carl & The Passsions, then The Pendletones. First recorded for X/Candix in 1961. Jardine was replaced by David Marks from March, 1962 to March, 1963. Brian replaced by Bruce Johnston for personal appearances since April, 1965. Dennis Wilson drowned on 12/28/83 (39).

DATE	POS	WKS	ARTIST—RECORD TITLE		LABEL & NO.
12/08/62	32	7	1. Surfin' Safari		Capitol 1808
5/18/63	2(2)	30	● 2. **Surfin' U.S.A.**		Capitol 1890
			"Surfin' U.S.A."(3)		
10/26/63	7	18	● 3. **Surfer Girl**		Capitol 1981
			"Surfer Girl"(7)		
12/07/63	4	20	● 4. **Little Deuce Coupe**		Capitol 1998
			"Be True To Your School"(6)		
5/02/64	13	22	● 5. Shut Down, Volume 2		Capitol 2027
			"Fun, Fun, Fun"(5)		
			Volume 1 - see Miscellaneous section: Cars		
8/08/64	4	38	● 6. **All Summer Long**		Capitol 2110
			"I Get Around"(1)		
11/21/64	1(4)	40	● 7. **Beach Boys Concert**	[L]	Capitol 2198
4/17/65	4	29	● 8. **The Beach Boys Today!**		Capitol 2269
			"When I Grow Up"(9)		
			"Dance, Dance, Dance"(8)		
8/07/65	2(1)	17	● 9. **Summer Days (And Summer Nights!!)**		Capitol 2354
			"Help Me Rhonda"(1)		
			"California Girls"(3)		
12/04/65	6	14	10. **Beach Boys' Party!**		Capitol 2398
			"Barbara Ann"(2)		
6/11/66	10	21	11. **Pet Sounds**		Capitol 2458
			"Sloop John B"(3)		
			"Wouldn't It Be Nice"(8)		
8/13/66	8	18	● 12. **Best Of The Beach Boys**	[G]	Capitol 2545
1/27/68	24	9	13. Wild Honey		Capitol 2859
10/02/71	29	7	14. Surf's Up		Brother 6453
3/10/73	36	3	15. Holland		Brother 2118
1/05/74	25	5	● 16. The Beach Boys In Concert	[L]	Brother 6484 [2]
8/03/74	1(1)	19	● 17. **Endless Summer**	[K]	Capitol 11307 [2]
5/17/75	8	13	● 18. **Spirit Of America**	[K]	Capitol 11384 [2]
8/09/75	25	5	19. Good Vibrations-Best Of The Beach Boys	[G]	Brother 2223
7/24/76	8	12	● 20. **15 Big Ones**		Brother 2251
			15: age of band and number of tracks		
			"Rock And Roll Music"(5)		

DATE	POS	WKS	ARTIST—RECORD TITLE		LABEL & NO.
			BEASTIE BOYS		
			New York white rap trio formed in 1981, consisting of King Ad-Rock (Adam Horovitz - son of playwright Israel Horovitz), MCA (Adam Yauch) and Mike D (Michael Diamond).		
12/20/86	**1**(7)	27+	▲ 1. **Licensed To Ill**		Def Jam 40238
			"(You Gotta) Fight For Your Right (To Party!)"(7)		
			THE BEATLES		
			The world's #1 rock group was formed in Liverpool, England in the late 1950s. Known in early forms as the Quarrymen, Johnny & the Moondogs, The Rainbows, and the Silver Beatles. Named The Beatles in 1960. Originally consisted of John Lennon, Paul McCartney, George Harrison (guitars), Stu Sutcliffe (bass) and Pete Best (drums). Sutcliffe left in April, 1961 (died on 4/10/62); McCartney moved to bass. Best replaced by Ringo Starr in August, 1962. Group managed by Brian Epstein (died on 8/27/67) and produced by George Martin. First US tour in February, 1964. Own Apple label in 1968. Disbanded on 4/17/70.		
2/08/64	**1**(11)	27	● 1. **Meet The Beatles!**		Capitol 2047
			"I Want To Hold Your Hand"(1)		
2/15/64	**2**(9)	26	2. **Introducing...The Beatles**		Vee-Jay 1062
			1st U.S. album - released July, 1963		
			"Please Please Me"(3)		
			"Twist And Shout"(2)		
			"Do You Want To Know A Secret"(2)		
			"Love Me Do"*(1)		
			"P.S. I Love You"*(10) * - only on first pressing		
4/25/64	**1**(5)	26	● 3. **The Beatles' Second Album**		Capitol 2080
			"She Loves You"(1)		
6/20/64	**20**	9	4. **The American Tour With Ed Rudy**	[T]	RadioPulsebeat 2
			interviews with The Beatles		
7/18/64	**1**(14)	14	5. **A Hard Day's Night**	[S]	United Art. 6366
			8 vocals - 4 instrumentals		
			"Can't Buy Me Love"(1)		
			"A Hard Day's Night"(1)		
8/15/64	**2**(9)	28	● 6. **Something New**		Capitol 2108
			includes 5 tunes from "A Hard Day's Night" album		
12/19/64	**7**	9	● 7. **The Beatles' Story**	[T]	Capitol 2222 [2]
			narrative featuring bits of their hits		
1/09/65	**1**(9)	38	● 8. **Beatles '65**		Capitol 2228
			"I Feel Fine"(1)		
			"She's A Woman"(4)		
7/10/65	**1**(6)	21	● 9. **Beatles VI**		Capitol 2358
			"Eight Days A Week"(1)		
9/11/65	**1**(9)	33	● 10. **Help!**	[S]	Capitol 2386
			7 vocals - 5 instrumentals		
			"Ticket To Ride"(1)		
			"Help!"(1)		
1/08/66	**1**(6)	39	● 11. **Rubber Soul**		Capitol 2442
7/16/66	**1**(5)	15	● 12. **"Yesterday"...And Today**	[G]	Capitol 2553
			originally featured the "butcher cover"		
			"Yesterday"(1)		
			"We Can Work It Out"(1)		
			"Day Tripper"(5)		
			"Nowhere Man"(3)		

DATE	POS	WKS	ARTIST—RECORD TITLE	LABEL & NO.
9/10/66	1(6)	24	● 13. **Revolver**	Capitol 2576
			"Yellow Submarine"(2)	
6/24/67	1(15)	63	● 14. **Sgt. Pepper's Lonely Hearts Club Band**	Capitol 2653
			also see Soundtrack of the same name	
12/30/67	1(8)	30	● 15. **Magical Mystery Tour** [S-G]	Capitol 2835
			6 tunes from the film + 5 singles hits	
			"Penny Lane"(1)	
			"Strawberry Fields Forever"(8)	
			"All You Need Is Love"(1)	
			"Hello Goodbye"(1)	
12/14/68	1(9)	25	● 16. **The Beatles**	Apple 101 [2]
2/15/69	2(2)	12	● 17. **Yellow Submarine** [S]	Apple 153
			side 1: Beatles; side 2: instrumentals by George Martin	
10/25/69	1(11)	32	● 18. **Abbey Road**	Apple 383
			"Come Together"(1)	
			"Something"(1)	
3/21/70	2(4)	17	● 19. **Hey Jude** [G]	Apple 385
			"Paperback Writer"(1)	
			"Lady Madonna"(4)	
			"Hey Jude"(1)	
			"The Ballad Of John And Yoko"(8)	
6/06/70	1(4)	20	● 20. **Let It Be** [S]	Apple 34001
			film features the Beatles during recording sessions	
			"Get Back"(1)	
			"Let It Be"(1)	
			"The Long And Winding Road"(1)	
4/21/73	3	18	● 21. **The Beatles/1962-1966** [G]	Apple 3403 [2]
4/21/73	1(1)	21	● 22. **The Beatles/1967-1970** [G]	Apple 3404 [2]
6/26/76	2(2)	13	▲ 23. **Rock 'N' Roll Music** [K]	Capitol 11537 [2]
			"Got To Get You Into My Life"(7)	
5/21/77	2(2)	8	▲ 24. **The Beatles At The Hollywood Bowl** [E-L]	Capitol 11638
			concert recordings of 8/23/64 & 8/30/65	
11/19/77	24	6	● 25. Love Songs [K]	Capitol 11711 [2]
4/19/80	21	9	26. Rarities [K]	Capitol 12060
4/10/82	19	8	● 27. Reel Music [K]	Capitol 12199
			tunes from the Beatles' five films	
			THE BEAU BRUMMELS	
			Formed in 1964 in San Francisco. Led by Sal Valentino (vocals) and Ron Elliott (guitar).	
6/26/65	24	7	1. Introducing The Beau Brummels	Autumn 103
			"Just A Little"(8)	
			BECK, BOGERT, APPICE	
4/28/73	12	11	1. Jeff Beck, Tim Bogert, Carmine Appice	Epic 32140
			Bogert & Appice formerly with Cactus and Vanilla Fudge	
			JEFF BECK	
			English rock guitarist - formerly with the Yardbirds ('64-'66).	
9/14/68	15	14	1. Truth	Epic 26413
8/02/69	15	8	2. Beck-Ola	Epic 26478
			above 2 with Rod Stewart (vocals)	
6/03/72	19	9	3. Jeff Beck Group	Epic 31331
4/26/75	4	11	▲ 4. **Blow By Blow** [I]	Epic 33409

DATE	POS	WKS	ARTIST—RECORD TITLE		LABEL & NO.
7/17/76	**16**	9	▲ 5. Wired	[I]	Epic 33849
4/09/77	**23**	6	6. Jeff Beck with The Jan Hammer Group		
			Live	[I-L]	Epic 34433
7/19/80	**21**	8	7. There And Back	[I]	Epic 35684
8/17/85	**39**	2	8. Flash		Epic 39483
			"People Get Ready" sung by Rod Stewart		

THE BEE GEES

Trio of brothers from Manchester, England: Barry (b: 9/1/47) and twins Robin and Maurice Gibb (b: 12/22/49). First performed December, 1955. To Australia in 1958, performed as the Gibbs, later as BG's, finally the Bee Gees. First recorded for Leedon/Festival in 1963. Returned to England in February, 1967, with guitarist Vince Melouney and drummer Colin Peterson. Toured Europe and USA in 1968. Melouney left in December, 1968; Robin left for solo career in 1969. When Peterson left in August of 1969, Barry and Maurice went solo. After eight months, brothers reunited. Composed soundtracks of "Saturday Night Fever" and "Staying Alive"; in film "Sgt. Pepper's Lonely Hearts Club Band". Group was named for Barry Gibb, Bill Goode (a friend), and Bill Gates (a DJ).

DATE	POS	WKS	ARTIST—RECORD TITLE		LABEL & NO.
9/16/67	**7**	18	1. **Bee Gees' 1st**		Atco 223
2/24/68	**12**	7	2. Horizontal		Atco 233
9/28/68	**17**	7	3. Idea		Atco 253
			"I've Gotta Get A Message To You"(8)		
			"I Started A Joke"(6)		
3/08/69	**20**	10	4. Odessa		Atco 702 [2]
8/02/69	**9**	16	• 5. **Best Of Bee Gees**	[G]	Atco 292
2/06/71	**32**	5	6. 2 Years On		Atco 353
			"Lonely Days"(3)		
10/02/71	**34**	6	7. Trafalgar		Atco 7003
			"How Can You Mend A Broken Heart"(1)		
12/16/72	**35**	3	8. To Whom It May Concern		Atco 7012
8/16/75	**14**	22	• 9. Main Course		RSO 4807
			"Jive Talkin'"(1)		
			"Nights On Broadway"(7)		
10/02/76	**8**	28	▲ 10. **Children Of The World**		RSO 3003
			"You Should Be Dancing"(1)		
			"Love So Right"(3)		
6/04/77	**8**	31	▲ 11. **Here At Last...Bee Gees...Live**	[L]	RSO 3901 [2]
12/10/77	**1(24)**	54	▲ 12. **Saturday Night Fever**	[S]	RSO 4001 [2]
			6 cuts by the Bee Gees/others by various artists -		
			the #1 selling soundtrack album of all-time (25 million)		
			"How Deep Is Your Love"(1)		
			"Stayin' Alive"(1)		
			"Night Fever"(1)		
2/17/79	**1(6)**	26	▲ 13. **Spirits Having Flown**		RSO 3041
			"Too Much Heaven"(1)		
			"Tragedy"(1)		
			"Love You Inside Out"(1)		
11/17/79	**1(1)**	17	▲ 14. **Bee Gees Greatest**	[G]	RSO 4200 [2]
			RSO hits only		
7/30/83	**6**	14	▲ 15. **Staying Alive**	[S]	RSO 813269
			side 1: Bee Gees; side 2: various artists		

DATE	POS	WKS	ARTIST—RECORD TITLE		LABEL & NO.

HARRY BELAFONTE

Born Harold George Belafonte, Jr. on 3/1/27 in Harlem. Actor in American Negro Theater, Drama Workshop, mid-40s. Started career as a "straight pop" singer. Recorded for Jubilee Records in 1949, shortly afterward began specializing in folk music. Rode the crest of the calypso craze to worldwide stardom. Starred in eight films from 1953-74. Replaced Danny Kaye in 1987 as the goodwill ambassador for UNICEF.

DATE	POS	WKS	ARTIST—RECORD TITLE		LABEL & NO.
1/28/56	3	6	1. **"Mark Twain" And Other Folk Favorites**		RCA 1022
2/25/56	1(6)	62	● 2. **Belafonte**		RCA 1150
6/16/56	1(31)	84	● 3. **Calypso**		RCA 1248
			"Banana Boat"(5)		
3/30/57	2(2)	20	● 4. **An Evening With Belafonte**		RCA 1402
9/16/57	3	16	5. **Belafonte Sings Of The Caribbean**		RCA 1505
10/20/58	16	15	6. Belafonte Sings The Blues		RCA 1972
5/25/59	18	10	7. Love Is A Gentle Thing		RCA 1927
6/22/59	13	19	8. Porgy & Bess		RCA 1507

LENA HORNE/HARRY BELAFONTE

DATE	POS	WKS	ARTIST—RECORD TITLE		LABEL & NO.
11/16/59	3	07	● 9. **Belafonte At Carnegie Hall**	[L]	RCA 6006 [2]
3/21/60	34	1	10. My Lord What A Mornin'		RCA 2022
			spirituals		
12/26/60	3	10	● 11. **Belafonte Returns To Carnegie Hall**	[L]	RCA 6007 [2]
			with Odetta-Miriam Makeba-Chad Mitchell Trio		
9/11/61	3	40	● 12. **Jump Up Calypso**		RCA 2388
6/02/62	8	18	13. **The Midnight Special**		RCA 2449
10/27/62	25	13	14. The Many Moods Of Belafonte		RCA 2574
7/13/63	30	5	15. Streets I Have Walked		RCA 2695
4/25/64	17	10	16. Belafonte At The Greek Theatre	[L]	RCA 6009 [2]

BELL & JAMES

R&B duo: Leroy Bell and Casey James. Began as songwriting team for Bell's uncle, producer Thom Bell.

DATE	POS	WKS	ARTIST—RECORD TITLE		LABEL & NO.
4/07/79	31	4	1. Bell & James		A&M 4728

PAT BENATAR

Real name: Patricia Andrzejewski. Born in 1952 in Brooklyn. Married her record producer, Neil Geraldo in 1982.

DATE	POS	WKS	ARTIST—RECORD TITLE		LABEL & NO.
1/26/80	12	15	▲ 1. **In The Heat Of The Night**		Chrysalis 1236
8/30/80	2(5)	38	▲ 2. **Crimes Of Passion**		Chrysalis 1275
			"Hit Me With Your Best Shot"(9)		
7/25/81	1(1)	30	▲ 3. **Precious Time**		Chrysalis 1346
11/27/82	4	27	▲ 4. **Get Nervous**		Chrysalis 1396
10/22/83	13	16	▲ 5. **Live From Earth**	[L]	Chrysalis 41444
			2 of the 10 songs are new studio tracks		
			"Love Is A Battlefield"(5)		
12/01/84	14	15	▲ 6. **Tropico**		Chrysalis 41471
			"We Belong"(5)		
12/21/85	26	9	7. Seven The Hard Way		Chrysalis 41507
			"Invincible (Theme From "Legend Of Billie Jean")"(10)		

DATE	POS	WKS	ARTIST—RECORD TITLE	LABEL & NO.

TONY BENNETT

Born Anthony Benedetto on 8/13/26 in Queens, NY. Worked local clubs while in high school, sang in US Army bands. Audition record of "Boulevard Of Broken Dreams" earned a Columbia contract in 1950.

DATE	POS	WKS	ARTIST—RECORD TITLE	LABEL & NO.
2/23/57	14	9	1. Tony	Columbia 938
8/25/62	5	83	● 2. **I Left My Heart In San Francisco**	Columbia 8669
12/08/62	37	2	3. Tony Bennett At Carnegie Hall [L]	Columbia 23 [2]
4/06/63	5	23	4. **I Wanna Be Around**	Columbia 8800
9/21/63	24	8	5. This Is All I Ask	Columbia 8856
3/21/64	20	8	6. The Many Moods Of Tony	Columbia 8941
10/02/65	20	18	● 7. Tony's Greatest Hits, Volume III [G]	Columbia 9173
5/14/66	18	12	8. The Movie Song Album	Columbia 9272

GEORGE BENSON

Born on 3/2/43 in Pittsburgh. Played guitar from age eight. Played in Brother Jack McDuff's trio, 1964. House musician at CTI Records to early 1970's. Influenced heavily by Wes Montgomery.

DATE	POS	WKS	ARTIST—RECORD TITLE	LABEL & NO.
5/22/76	1(2)	22	▲ 1. **Breezin'**	Warner 2919
			"This Masquerade"(10)	
2/19/77	9	17	▲ 2. **In Flight**	Warner 2983
2/18/78	5	19	▲ 3. **Weekend In L.A.** [L]	Warner 3139 [2]
			"On Broadway"(7)	
3/24/79	7	13	● 4. **Livin' Inside Your Love**	Warner 3277 [2]
8/09/80	3	20	▲ 5. **Give Me The Night**	Warner 3453
			"Give Me The Night"(4)	
12/12/81	14	14	● 6. The George Benson Collection [G]	Warner 3577 [2]
			"Turn Your Love Around"(5)	
7/02/83	27	11	● 7. In Your Eyes	Warner 23744

BROOK BENTON

Born Benjamin Franklin Peay on 9/19/31 in Camden, SC. Sang with the Camden Jubilee Singers. To New York in 1948, joined Bill Langford's Langfordaires. With Jerusalem Stars in 1951. First recorded under own name for Okeh in 1953.

DATE	POS	WKS	ARTIST—RECORD TITLE	LABEL & NO.
12/29/62	40	1	1. Singing The Blues - Lie To Me	Mercury 60740
3/28/70	27	4	2. Brook Benton Today	Cotillion 9018
			"Rainy Night In Georgia"(4)	

POLLY BERGEN

Born on 7/14/31. Real name: Nellie Burgin. Singer/actress in movies and TV.

DATE	POS	WKS	ARTIST—RECORD TITLE	LABEL & NO.
6/10/57	10	5	1. **Bergen Sings Morgan**	Columbia 994
			Polly portrayed Helen Morgan in a TV film	
11/04/57	20	1	2. The Party's Over	Columbia 1031

BERLIN

Los Angeles electro-pop trio: Terri Nunn (vocals), John Crawford (bass) and Rob Brill (drums). Group went from a 6-piece band to a trio in 1985.

DATE	POS	WKS	ARTIST—RECORD TITLE	LABEL & NO.
3/19/83	30	11	● 1. Pleasure Victim	Geffen 2036
5/26/84	28	4	2. Love Life	Geffen 4025

DATE	POS	WKS	ARTIST—RECORD TITLE	LABEL & NO.
			SHELLEY BERMAN	
			Popular nightclub comedian. Made TV debut on the "Jack Paar Show".	
4/27/59	2(5)	96	1. **Inside Shelley Berman** [C]	Verve 15003
11/30/59	6	39	2. **Outside Shelley Berman** [C]	Verve 15007
7/25/60	4	25	3. **The Edge Of Shelley Berman** [C]	Verve 15013
12/25/61	25	3	4. A Personal Appearance [C]	Verve 15027
			LEONARD BERNSTEIN	
			Born on 8/25/18 in Lawrence, Massachusetts. Conductor, composer, pianist. Premier conductor, has directed numerous major orchestras, worldwide. Composed music for Broadway's "West Side Story" and the film "On The Waterfront".	
12/12/60	13	11	1. Bernstein Plays Brubeck Plays Bernstein [I] side 1: New York Philharmonic with Dave Brubeck Quartet conducted by Leonard Bernstein; side 2: Dave Brubeck Quartet	Columbia 8257
			CHUCK BERRY	
			Born Charles Edward Anderson Berry on 10/18/26 in San Jose, California. Grew up in St. Louis. Muddy Waters introduced Chuck to Leonard Chess (Chess Records) in Chicago. First recording, "Maybellene", was an instant success. Appeared in the film "Rock, Rock, Rock" in 1956, and several others. Regarded by many as rock 'n roll's most influential artist.	
10/05/63	29	2	1. Chuck Berry On Stage [L] live audience dubbed in	Chess 1480
8/22/64	34	3	2. Chuck Berry's Greatest Hits [G] *"Maybellene"(5)* *"School Day"(3)* *"Rock & Roll Music"(8)* *"Sweet Little Sixteen"(2)* *"Johnny B. Goode"(8)*	Chess 1485
8/05/72	8	20	● 3. **The London Chuck Berry Sessions** [L] side 1: studio; side 2: live *"My Ding-A-Ling"(1)*	Chess 60020
			DICKEY BETTS	
			Lead guitarist of The Allman Brothers Band.	
9/28/74	19	7	1. Highway Call side 1: vocals; side 2: instrumentals	Capricorn 0123
5/21/77	31	2	2. Dickey Betts & Great Southern	Arista 4123
			THE B-52'S	
			Quintet from Athens, Georgia.	
9/27/80	18	9	● 1. Wild Planet	Warner 3471
3/06/82	35	4	2. Mesopotamia [M]	Warner 3641
6/04/83	29	6	3. Whammy!	Warner 23819
			BIG BROTHER & THE HOLDING COMPANY	
			Formed in San Francisco in 1965. Janis Joplin joined as lead singer in 1966. Sensation at the Monterey Pop Festival in 1967. Disbanded in 1972.	
9/14/68	1(8)	29	● 1. **Cheap Thrills**	Columbia 9700
			BIG COUNTRY	
			Scottish four-man rock band.	
10/08/83	18	18	● 1. The Crossing	Mercury 812870

DATE	POS	WKS	ARTIST—RECORD TITLE	LABEL & NO.
			MR. ACKER BILK	
			Born Bernard Stanley Bilk on 1/28/29 in Somerset, England. Clarinetist, composer.	
5/19/62	3	24	● 1. **Stranger On The Shore** [I]	Atco 129
			"Stranger On The Shore"(1)	
			ELVIN BISHOP	
			Born on 10/21/42 in Tulsa, Oklahoma. Lead guitarist with Paul Butterfield's Blues Band (1965-68).	
4/24/76	18	8	1. Struttin' My Stuff	Capricorn 0165
			"Fooled Around And Fell In Love"(3)	
10/08/77	38	2	2. Live! Raisin' Hell [L]	Capricorn 0185 [2]
			STEPHEN BISHOP	
			Pop-rock singer, songwriter from San Diego.	
10/08/77	34	3	1. Careless	ABC 954
			"On And On"	
11/04/78	35	4	● 2. Bish	ABC 1082
			THE BLACKBYRDS	
			Founded in 1973 by Donald Byrd while teaching at Howard University, Washington, D.C.	
3/08/75	30	7	1. Flying Start	Fantasy 9472
			"Walking In Rhythm"(6)	
4/03/76	16	9	● 2. City Life	Fantasy 9490
1/29/77	34	4	● 3. Unfinished Business	Fantasy 9518
			BLACK SABBATH	
			British heavy-metal group. Ozzy Osbourne, lead vocals on LP's #1-6. Replaced by Ronnie James Dio on LP's #7-9. Ian Gillan, lead vocalist on LP #10.	
11/28/70	23	10	▲ 1. Black Sabbath	Warner 1871
2/20/71	12	34	▲ 2. Paranoid	Warner 1887
9/11/71	8	17	▲ 3. **Master Of Reality**	Warner 2562
11/04/72	13	13	▲ 4. Black Sabbath, Vol. 4	Warner 2602
2/09/74	11	11	▲ 5. Sabbath Bloody Sabbath	Warner 2695
9/13/75	28	4	6. Sabotage	Warner 2822
6/21/80	28	9	▲ 7. Heaven And Hell	Warner 3372
12/05/81	29	8	● 8. Mob Rules	Warner 3605
2/19/83	37	4	9. Live Evil [L]	Warner 23742 [2]
11/05/83	39	2	10. Born Again	Warner 23978
			BILL BLACK'S COMBO	
			Bill was born on 9/17/26 in Memphis; died of a brain tumor on 10/21/65. Bass guitarist. Session work in Memphis, backed Elvis Presley (with Scotty Moore, guitar; D.J. Fontana, drums) on most of his early records. Formed own band in 1959.	
11/14/60	23	5	1. Solid And Raunchy [I]	Hi 12003
3/17/62	35	3	2. Let's Twist Her [I]	Hi 12006
			STANLEY BLACK	
3/10/62	30	2	1. Exotic Precussion [I]	London P. 4 44004
10/06/62	33	2	2. Spain [I]	London P. 4 44016
			RITCHIE BLACKMORE - see RAINBOW	

DATE	POS	WKS	ARTIST—RECORD TITLE	LABEL & NO.
			BOBBY BLAND	
			Born Robert Calvin Bland on 1/27/30 in Rosemark, TN. Nicknamed "Blue". Sang in gospel group "The Miniatures" in Memphis, late 40s. Member of the Beale Streeters which included Johnny Ace, B.B. King, Rosco Gordon, Earl Forest and Willie Nix in 1949. Driver and valet for B.B. King; appeared in the Johnny Ace Revue, early 50s. First recorded in 1952, for the Modern label. Frequent tours with B.B. King into the 80s.	
8/03/63	**11**	7	1. Call On Me/Thats The Way Love Is	Duke 77
			BLASTERS	
			Los Angeles rockabilly group.	
5/01/82	**36**	4	1. The Blasters	Slash 3680
			BLIND FAITH	
			Eric Clapton, Steve Winwood, Ginger Baker & Rick Grech.	
8/23/69	**1(2)**	20	● 1. **Blind Faith**	Atco 304
			BLONDIE	
			Formed in New York City in 1975. Consisted of Chris Stein & Frank Infante (guitars), Jimmy Destri (keyboards), Gary Valentine (bass), Clem Burke (drums) and Deborah Harry (vocals). Stein and Harry were married. Harry had been in folk/rock group, Wind In The Willows; did solo work from 1980; in films "Union City Blues" and "Roadie". Disbanded in 1983; Burke went with Eurythmics.	
3/17/79	**6**	16	▲ 1. **Parallel Lines**	Chrysalis 1192
			"Heart Of Glass"(1)	
10/27/79	**17**	19	▲ 2. Eat To The Beat	Chrysalis 1225
12/13/80	**7**	23	▲ 3. Autoamerican	Chrysalis 1290
			"The Tide Is High"(1)	
			"Rapture"(1)	
11/21/81	**30**	11	● 4. The Best Of Blondie　　　　　　　[G]	Chrysalis 1337
			"Call Me"(1)	
6/26/82	**33**	4	5. The Hunter	Chrysalis 1384
			BLOODROCK	
			Rock group from Fort Worth, Texas; Jim Rutledge, lead vocals.	
1/23/71	**21**	8	1. Bloodrock 2	Capitol 491
4/17/71	**27**	8	2. Bloodrock 3	Capitol 765
			BLOODSTONE	
			From Kansas City, Missouri. Formed as the Sinceres, consisted of Charles McCormick, Willis Draffen, Charles Love, Henry Williams, and Roger Durham (d: 1973). First recorded for British Decca.	
6/30/73	**30**	7	1. Natural High	London 620
			"Natural High"(10)	
			BLOOD, SWEAT & TEARS	
			Group formed by Al Kooper in 1968. Nucleus consisted of Kooper (keyboards), Steve Katz (guitar), Bobby Colomby (drums) and Jim Fielder (bass). Kooper replaced by lead singer David Clayton-Thomas in 1969. Clayton-Thomas replaced by Jerry Fisher in 1972. Katz left in 1973. Clayton-Thomas rejoined in 1974.	
2/01/69	**1(7)**	66	▲ 1. **Blood, Sweat & Tears**	Columbia 9720
			"You've Made Me So Very Happy"(2)	
			"Spinning Wheel"(2)	
			"And When I Die"(2)	

DATE	POS	WKS	ARTIST—RECORD TITLE	LABEL & NO.
7/18/70	1(2)	19	● 2. **Blood, Sweat & Tears 3**	Columbia 30090
7/17/71	10	11	● 3. **B, S & T; 4**	Columbia 30590
3/25/72	19	6	▲ 4. Blood, Sweat & Tears Greatest Hits [G]	Columbia 31170
11/25/72	32	7	5. New Blood	Columbia 31780
			MIKE BLOOMFIELD	
			Chicago-born blues guitarist - with Paul Butterfield Blues Band, & Electric Flag - died on 2/15/81 (37).	
10/05/68	12	10	● 1. Super Session	Columbia 9701
			MIKE BLOOMFIELD/AL KOOPER/STEVE STILLS	
2/15/69	18	10	2. The Live Adventures Of Mike Bloomfield And Al Kooper [L]	Columbia 6 [2]
			THE BLOW MONKEYS	
			British quartet fronted by Dr. Robert (Robert Howard).	
7/19/86	35	5	1. Animal Magic	RCA 8065
			BLUE CHEER	
			San Francisco hard-rock trio.	
3/30/68	11	11	1. Vincebus Eruptum	Philips 264
			BLUE OYSTER CULT	
			New York hard-rock quintet led by Donald "Buck Dharma" Roeser (lead guitar) and Eric Bloom (lead vocal).	
4/05/75	22	4	● 1. On Your Feet Or On Your Knees [L]	Columbia 33371 [2]
9/25/76	29	9	▲ 2. Agents Of Fortune	Columbia 34164
			"(Don't Fear) The Reaper"	
8/16/80	34	3	3. Cultosaurus Erectus	Columbia 36550
8/01/81	24	11	● 4. Fire Of Unknown Origin	Columbia 37389
6/12/82	29	5	5. Extraterrestrial Live [L]	Columbia 37946 [2]
			BLUES BROTHERS	
			Jake Blues (John Belushi) & Elwood Blues (Dan Aykroyd) - originally created for TV's "Saturday Night Live". Belushi died of a drug overdose on 3/5/82 (33).	
1/06/79	1(1)	16	▲ 1. **Briefcase Full Of Blues**	Atlantic 19217
7/05/80	13	12	● 2. The Blues Brothers [S]	Atlantic 16017
			with Aretha Franklin, James Brown & Ray Charles	
			BLUES MAGOOS	
			Bronx, New York psychedelic rock quintet led by Peppy Castro.	
2/18/67	21	5	1. Psychedelic Lollipop	Mercury 61096
			"(We Ain't Got) Nothin' Yet"(5)	
			ANGELA BOFILL	
			Performed with Dizzy Gillespie and Cannonball Adderley.	
12/22/79	34	8	1. Angel of the Night	GRP 5501
4/02/83	40	3	2. Too Tough	Arista 9616
			TIM BOGERT - see BECK, BOGERT, APPICE	
			RUDI BOHN & his Band	
			German conductor of polkas.	
10/16/61	38	2	1. Percussive Oompah [I]	London P. 4 44009

DATE	POS	WKS	ARTIST—RECORD TITLE	LABEL & NO.
			BON JOVI	
			New Jersey hard rock quintet consisting of Jon Bon Jovi (Bongiovi), lead vocals; Richie Sambora, guitars; Dave Bryan, keyboards; Alec John Such, bass; Tico Torres, drums. America's hottest rock band, 1986-87.	
6/08/85	37	5	▲ 1. 7800 Fahrenheit	Mercury 824509
9/20/86	**1(8)**	40+	▲ 2. **Slippery When Wet**	Mercury 830264
			"You Give Love A Bad Name"(1)	
			"Livin' On A Prayer"(1)	
			GARY U.S. BONDS	
			Born Gary Anderson on 6/6/39 in Jacksonville, Florida. Signed to Legrand Records by Frank Guida in Norfolk, Virginia.	
8/21/61	6	11	1. **Dance 'til Quarter To Three**	Legrand 3001
			"New Orleans"(6)	
			"Quarter To Three"(1)	
			"School Is Out"(5)	
5/16/81	27	7	2. Dedication	EMI America 17051
			KARLA BONOFF	
			Songwriter/singer from Los Angeles.	
10/13/79	31	8	1. Restless Nights	Columbia 35799
			BOOKER T. & THE MG's	
			Band formed by session men from Stax Records in Memphis, 1962. Consisted of Booker T. Jones (b: 11/12/44, Memphis), keyboards; Steve Cropper (b: 10/21/42, Ozark Mountains, MO.), guitar; Donald "Duck" Dunn (b: 11/24/41, Memphis), bass; and Al Jackson, Jr. (b: 11/27/34, Memphis, d: 1975), drums. MG stands for Memphis Group. Cropper and Dunn had been in the Mar-Keys. Much session work. Jones received music degree from Indiana University, and married Priscilla Coolidge, sister of Rita. Produced for Rita Coolidge, Earl Klugh, Bill Withers, and for Willie Nelson's "Stardust" album. Cropper and Dunn joined the Blues Brothers. Group disbanded in 1968, reorganized in 1973 for a short time.	
1/12/63	33	2	1. Green Onions [I]	Stax 701
			"Green Onions"(3)	
9/16/67	35	4	2. Hip Hug-Her [I]	Stax 717
			DEBBY BOONE	
			Pat Boone's daughter. Born on 9/22/56 in Hackensack, New Jersey.	
11/12/77	6	9	▲ 1. **You Light Up My Life**	Warner 3118
			"You Light Up My Life"(1)	
			PAT BOONE	
			Born Charles Eugene Boone on 6/1/34 in Jacksonville, Florida. To Nashville, early 50s, attended Lipscomb College. First recorded for Republic in 1953. Appeared on Ted Mack and Arthur Godfrey amateur shows in 1954. Married Red Foley's daughter Shirley in 1954. Appeared in 15 films. Toured with wife and daughters Cherry, Linda Lee, Deborah Ann and Laura Gene in the mid-60s.	
10/27/56	14	4	1. Howdy!	Dot 3030
6/24/57	13	7	2. A Closer Walk with Thee [EP]	Dot 1056
			7" E.P. (4 sacred songs)	
7/08/57	19	3	3. "Pat"	Dot 3050
9/02/57	5	5	4. **Four By Pat** [EP]	Dot 1057
			7" E.P. (4 songs)	

DATE	POS	WKS	ARTIST—RECORD TITLE	LABEL & NO.
10/07/57	20	2	5. Pat Boone	Dot 3012
			Pat's 1st album	
			"Ain't That A Shame"(1)	
			"At My Front Door"(7)	
			"I'll Be Home"(4)	
10/21/57	3	36	● 6. **Pat's Great Hits** [G]	Dot 3071
			"I Almost Lost My Mind"(1)	
			"Friendly Persuasion"(5)	
			"Don't Forbid Me"(1)	
			"Why Baby Why"(5)	
			"Love Letters In The Sand"(1)	
			"Remember You're Mine"(6)	
12/23/57	12	13	7. April Love [S]	Dot 9000
			"April Love"(1)	
12/23/57	21	4	8. Hymns We Love	Dot 3068
7/28/58	2(1)	32	9. **Star Dust**	Dot 3118
11/24/58	13	2	10. Yes Indeed!	Dot 3121
7/20/59	17	9	11. Tenderly	Dot 3180
5/23/60	26	3	12. Moonglow	Dot 3270
8/07/61	29	6	13. Moody River	Dot 3384
			"Moody River"(1)	
1/13/62	39	1	14. White Christmas [X]	Dot 3222

BOOTSY

William "Bootsy" Collins with his band "Bootsy's Rubber Band"

DATE	POS	WKS	ARTIST—RECORD TITLE	LABEL & NO.
3/05/77	16	12	● 1. Ahh...The Name Is Bootsy, Baby!	Warner 2972
3/11/78	16	10	● 2. Bootsy? Player Of The Year	Warner 3093

BOSTON

Rock group from Boston, spearheaded by Tom Scholz (guitars and keyboards) and Brad Delp (lead vocals). Originally a quintet, group also included Barry Goudreau (guitar), Fran Sheehan (bass) and Sib Hashian (drums). After an absence from the charts for 7 years ('79-'86), Boston returned as basically a duo: Scholz & Delp.

DATE	POS	WKS	ARTIST—RECORD TITLE	LABEL & NO.
10/16/76	3	49	▲ 1. **Boston**	Epic 34188
			"More Than A Feeling"(5)	
9/02/78	1(2)	13	▲ 2. **Don't Look Back**	Epic 35050
			"Don't Look Back"(4)	
10/18/86	1(4)	29	▲ 3. **Third Stage**	MCA 6188
			"Amanda"(1)	
			"We're Ready"(9)	

BOSTON POPS ORCHESTRA/ ARTHUR FIEDLER

Fiedler was born in Boston on 12/17/1894; died on 7/10/79 (84). He first conducted the Boston Pops in 1930.

DATE	POS	WKS	ARTIST—RECORD TITLE	LABEL & NO.
2/02/59	9	16	1. **Offenbach: Gaite Parisienne; Khachaturian: Gayne Ballet Suite [I]** [I]	RCA 2267
9/15/62	29	4	2. Pops Roundup [I]	RCA 2595
3/23/63	36	2	3. Our Man In Boston [I]	RCA 2599
4/13/63	5	18	4. **"Jalousie" And Other Favorites In The Latin Flavor** [I]	RCA 2661

DATE	POS	WKS	ARTIST—RECORD TITLE	LABEL & NO.
6/22/63	29	7	5. Star Dust [I]	RCA 2670
11/07/64	18	12	6. "Pops" Goes The Trumpet [I]	RCA 2729
			AL HIRT/BOSTON POPS/ARTHUR FIEDLER	
			## BOSTON SYMPHONY Orchestra	
5/18/63	17	7	1. Ravel: Bolero/Pavan For A Dead Princess/La Valse [I] Charles Munch, conductor	RCA 2664
			## DAVID BOWIE	
			Born David Robert Jones on 1/8/47 in London, England. First recorded as David Jones And the King Bees, Lower Third, Manish Boys, 1963. Brought highly theatrical values to rock through work with Lindsay Kemp Mime Troupe. Periods of reclusiveness heightened his appeal. Films "The Man Who Fell To Earth", 1976; "Just A Gigolo", 1978; "The Hunger", "Merry Christmas Mr. Lawrence", 1983; "Labyrinth", 1986. In Broadway play "The Elephant Man", 1980.	
3/03/73	16	10	1. Space Oddity [R] 1st rock album, recorded in 1968	RCA 4813
5/26/73	17	8	● 2. Aladdin Sane	RCA 4852
11/24/73	23	9	3. Bowie Pin Ups David's versions of his favorite pop hits from '64-'67	RCA 0291
6/22/74	5	10	● 4. **Diamond Dogs**	RCA 0576
11/09/74	8	8	● 5. **David Live** [L] recorded at the Tower Theatre, Philadelphia	RCA 0771 [2]
3/29/75	9	17	● 6. **Young Americans** "Fame"(1)	RCA 0998
2/14/76	3	13	● 7. **Station To Station** "Golden Years"(10)	RCA 1327
6/26/76	10	8	▲ 8. **Changesonebowie** [G]	RCA 1732
2/05/77	11	7	9. Low	RCA 2030
11/26/77	35	3	10. "Heroes"	RCA 2522
6/23/79	20	8	11. Lodger	RCA 3254
10/18/80	12	11	12. Scary Monsters	RCA 3647
5/07/83	4	34	▲ 13. **Let's Dance**	EMI America 17093
10/20/84	11	11	▲ 14. **Tonight** "Blue Jean"(8)	EMI America 17138
			## BRAM TCHAIKOVSKY	
			Rock quartet led by Bram (real name Peter Bramall).	
8/11/79	36	4	1. Strange Man, Changed Man	Polydor 6211
			## LAURA BRANIGAN	
			Born on 7/3/57 in New York. Pop singer. Has done some acting work.	
11/27/82	34	9	● 1. Branigan "Gloria"(2)	Atlantic 19289
5/14/83	29	5	● 2. Branigan 2 "Solitaire"(7)	Atlantic 80052
6/09/84	23	19	● 3. Self Control "Self Control"(4)	Atlantic 80147

DATE	POS	WKS	ARTIST—RECORD TITLE	LABEL & NO.
			BRASS CONSTRUCTION	
			Formed as Dynamic Soul by Randy Muller in Brooklyn, 1968. Randy produces the band, Skyy.	
3/20/76	**10**	13	▲ 1. **Brass Construction**	United Art. 545
12/04/76	**26**	9	● 2. Brass Construction II	United Art. 677
			BREAD	
			Formed in Los Angeles in 1969. Consisted of leader David Gates (vocals, guitar, keyboards), James Griffin (guitar), Robb Royer (guitar) and Jim Gordon (drums). Originally called Pleasure Faire. Griffin wrote award-winning "For All We Know" as Arthur James in 1969. Gordon was replaced by Mike Botts after first album. Royer replaced by Larry Knechtel in 1971. Disbanded in 1973, reunited briefly in 1976. All songs written, produced and arranged by David Gates.	
8/22/70	**12**	8	● 1. On The Waters	Elektra 74076
			"Make It With You"(1)	
4/10/71	**21**	10	● 2. Manna	Elektra 74086
			"If"(4)	
2/12/72	**3**	20	● 3. **Baby I'm-A Want You**	Elektra 75015
			"Baby I'm-A Want You"(3)	
			"Everything I Own"(5)	
12/02/72	**18**	16	● 4. Guitar Man	Elektra 75047
4/07/73	**2(1)**	23	● 5. **The Best Of Bread** [G]	Elektra 75056
7/06/74	**32**	3	● 6. The Best Of Bread, Volume Two [G]	Elektra 1005
2/05/77	**26**	6	● 7. Lost Without Your Love	Elektra 1094
			"Lost Without Your Love"(9)	
			BREWER & SHIPLEY	
			Folk-rock duo formed in Los Angeles: Mike Brewer & Tom Shipley.	
4/24/71	**34**	3	1. Tarkio	Kama Sutra 2024
			"One Toke Over The Line"(10)	
			BRICK	
			R&B group from Atlanta. Consisted of Jimmy Brown, Ray Ransom, Donald Nevins, Reggie Harris and Eddie Irons.	
12/25/76	**19**	8	1. Good High	Bang 408
			"Dazz"(3)	
10/15/77	**15**	8	2. Brick	Bang 409
			ALICIA BRIDGES	
			Atlanta-based disco singer, songwriter.	
12/16/78	**33**	7	1. Alicia Bridges	Polydor 6158
			"I Love The Nightlife"(5)	
			BRONSKI BEAT	
			British techno-pop trio: Jimmy Somerville (vocals), Steve Bronski & Larry Steinbachek (synthesizers).	
3/02/85	**36**	3	1. The Age Of Consent	MCA 5538
			THE BROTHERS FOUR	
			Dick Foley, Bob Flick, John Paine and Mike Kirkland. Formed while fraternity brothers at the University of Washington.	
4/18/60	**11**	19	1. The Brothers Four	Columbia 1402
			"Greenfields"(2)	
2/13/61	**4**	7	2. **B.M.O.C. (Best Music On/Off Campus)**	Columbia 1578

DATE	POS	WKS	ARTIST—RECORD TITLE		LABEL & NO.
			THE BROTHERS JOHNSON		
			Duo from Los Angeles. Consisted of brothers George (b: 5/17/53) and Louis (b: 4/13/55). Played since age 7, had own band, the Johnson Three + 1, with brother Tommy and cousin Alex Weir. With Billy Preston band to 1975. Also see Quincy Jones.		
4/17/76	9	24	▲ 1. **Look Out For #1**		A&M 4567
			"I'll Be Good To You"(3)		
5/28/77	13	26	▲ 2. **Right On Time**		A&M 4644
			"Strawberry Letter 23"(5)		
8/19/78	7	10	▲ 3. **Blam!!**		A&M 4714
3/15/80	5	16	▲ 4. **Light Up The Night**		A&M 3716
			"Stomp!"(7)		
			THE CRAZY WORLD OF ARTHUR BROWN		
			Arthur was born on 6/24/44 in Whitby, England.		
10/12/68	7	10	1. **The Crazy World Of Arthur Brown**		Track 8198
			"Fire"(2)		
			CHUCK BROWN & THE SOUL SEARCHERS		
			Washington, DC-based 9-member group.		
3/10/79	31	5	● 1. **Bustin' Loose**		Source 3076
			JAMES BROWN		
			Born on 5/3/28 in Macon, Georgia. Raised in Augusta, Georgia. Sang in a gospel group, formed own vocal group, the Famous Flames. Cut a demo record of own composition "Please Please Please", November, 1955, at radio station WIBB in Macon. Signed to King/Federal Records in January, 1956 and re-recorded the song. Cameo appearances in films "The Blues Brothers" and "Rocky IV". One of the originators of "Soul" music, billed as "The Godfather Of Soul".		
7/06/63	2(2)	33	1. **Live At The Apollo** [L]		King 826
			recorded at the Apollo Theater, New York City, 10/24/62		
3/28/64	10	13	2. **Pure Dynamite! Live At The Royal** [L]		King 883
			recorded at the Royal Theater, Baltimore, Maryland		
12/04/65	26	8	3. **Papa's Got A Brand New Bag**		King 938
			"Papa's Got A Brand New Bag"(8)		
2/26/66	36	4	4. **I Got You (I Feel Good)**		King 946
			"I Got You (I Feel Good)"(3)		
10/28/67	35	2	5. **Cold Sweat**		King 1020
			"Cold Sweat"(7)		
4/13/68	17	6	6. **I Can't Stand Myself (When You Touch Me)**		King 1030
12/14/68	32	7	7. **Live At The Apollo, Volume II** [L]		King 1022 [2]
9/13/69	26	7	8. **It's A Mother**		King 1063
9/27/69	40	1	9. **James Brown plays & directs The Popcorn** [I]		King 1055
10/24/70	29	6	10. **Sex Machine** [L]		King 1115 [2]
9/18/71	22	7	11. **Hot Pants**		Polydor 4054
1/29/72	39	2	12. **Revolution Of The Mind - Live At The Apollo, Volume III** [L]		Polydor 3003 [2]
4/07/73	31	5	13. **Black Caesar** [S]		Polydor 6014
3/30/74	34	8	● 14. **The Payback**		Polydor 3007 [2]
9/07/74	35	2	15. **Hell**		Polydor 9001 [2]

DATE	POS	WKS	ARTIST—RECORD TITLE	LABEL & NO.
			LES BROWN & His Band of Renown	
			Worked with Bob Hope for over two decades.	
2/19/55	**15**	2	1. Concert At The Palladium [I-L]	Coral CX-1 [2]
			recorded at the Hollywood Palladium, September 1953	
			PETER BROWN	
			Born on 12/25/40 in Chicago. Vocalist, keyboards, producer.	
4/01/78	**11**	19	1. A Fantasy Love Affair	Drive 104
			"Dance With Me"(8)	
			JACKSON BROWNE	
			Born on 10/9/48 in Heidelberg, Germany. Vocalist, guitar, piano, composer. To Los Angeles in 1951. With Tim Buckley and Nico in 1967 in New York City. Returned to Los Angeles, concentrated on songwriting. His songs were recorded by Linda Ronstadt, Tom Rush, Joe Cocker, The Byrds, Johnny Rivers, Bonnie Raitt, and many others. Worked with the Eagles, produced Warren Zevon's first album. Wife Phyllis committed suicide on 3/25/76. Activist against nuclear power.	
11/02/74	**14**	12	● 1. Late For The Sky	Asylum 1017
11/27/76	**5**	18	▲ 2. **The Pretender**	Asylum 1079
1/07/78	**3**	25	▲ 3. **Running On Empty**	Asylum 113
7/19/80	**1(1)**	21	▲ 4. **Hold Out**	Asylum 511
8/27/83	**8**	12	● 5. **Lawyers In Love**	Asylum 60268
3/22/86	**23**	9	● 6. Lives In The Balance	Asylum 60457
			TOM BROWNE	
			Jazz/funk trumpet player.	
9/20/80	**18**	9	● 1. Love Approach [I]	GRP 5008
3/21/81	**37**	2	2. Magic	GRP 5503
			DAVE BRUBECK QUARTET	
			David was born David Warren on 12/6/20 in Concord, California. Besides Brubeck (piano), quartet consists of Paul Desmond (alto sax), Joe Morello (drums), and Eugene Wright (bass). One of America's all-time most popular jazz groups on college campuses.	
2/05/55	**8**	6	1. **Dave Brubeck At Storyville: 1954** [I-L]	Columbia 590
3/19/55	**5**	22	2. **Brubeck Time** [I]	Columbia 622
11/12/55	**7**	3	3. **Jazz: Red Hot And Cool** [I-L]	Columbia 699
7/08/57	**18**	1	4. Jazz Impressions of the U.S.A. [I]	Columbia 984
9/30/57	**24**	1	5. Jazz Goes To Junior College [I-L]	Columbia 1034
11/28/60	**2(1)**	86	● 6. **Time Out Featuring "Take Five"** [I]	Columbia 8192
12/12/60	**13**	11	7. Berstein Plays Brubeck Plays Bernstein [I]	Columbia 8257
			side 1: New York Philharmonic with Dave Brubeck Quartet conducted by Leonard Bernstein; side 2: Dave Brubeck Quartet	
1/27/62	**8**	31	8. **Time Further Out** [I]	Columbia 8490
7/07/62	**24**	9	9. Countdown - Time In Outer Space [I]	Columbia 8575
3/23/63	**14**	10	10. Bossa Nova U.S.A. [I]	Columbia 8798
8/03/63	**37**	2	11. The Dave Brubeck Quartet At Carnegie Hall [I-L]	Columbia 826 [2]

DATE	POS	WKS	ARTIST—RECORD TITLE	LABEL & NO.
			PEABO BRYSON	
			Born Robert Peabo Bryson on 4/13/51 in Greenville, SC. Also see Michael Zager.	
2/10/79	35	4	● 1. Crosswinds	Capitol 11875
2/27/82	40	2	2. I Am Love	Capitol 12179
9/10/83	25	14	● 3. Born To Love	Capitol 12284
			PEABO BRYSON/ROBERTA FLACK	
			B.T. EXPRESS	
			Brooklyn, New York disco septet. B.T. stands for Brothers Trucking.	
12/14/74	5	18	● 1. **Do It ('Til You're Satisfied)**	Roadshow 5117
			"Do It ('Til You're Satisfied)"(2)	
			"Express"(4)	
8/23/75	19	8	2. Non-Stop	Roadshow 41001
			LINDSEY BUCKINGHAM	
			Born on 10/3/47 in California. Lindsey, along with Stevie Nicks, joined Fleetwood Mac in 1975.	
11/28/81	32	5	1. Law And Order	Asylum 561
			"Trouble"(9)	
			BUCKNER & GARCIA	
			Atlanta-based duo: Jerry Buckner and Gary Garcia.	
5/08/82	24	5	● 1. Pac-Man Fever [N]	Columbia 37941
			album inspired by popular video games	
			"Pac-Man Fever"(9)	
			JIMMY BUFFETT	
			Born on 12/25/46 in Mobile, Alabama. Backed by the Coral Reefer Band since 1975.	
3/29/75	25	4	1. A1A	Dunhill 50183
			A1A: beach access road off U.S. 1 in Florida	
3/26/77	12	19	▲ 2. Changes In Latitudes, Changes In Attitudes	ABC 990
			"Margaritaville"(8)	
4/15/78	10	9	▲ 3. **Son Of A Son Of A Sailor**	ABC 1046
9/22/79	14	11	● 4. Volcano	MCA 5102
3/14/81	30	4	5. Coconut Telegraph	MCA 5169
1/30/82	31	6	6. Somewhere Over China	MCA 5285
			ERIC BURDON & WAR	
			Eric was born on 5/11/41 in Newcastle-On-Tyne, England. Lead singer of The Animals.	
7/11/70	18	13	1. Eric Burdon Declares "War"	MGM 4663
			"Spill The Wine"(3)	
			KATE BUSH	
			Born on 7/30/58 in Plumstead, England.	
11/09/85	30	6	1. Hounds Of Love	EMI America 17171
			"Running Up That Hill"	
			JOE BUSHKIN	
			Pianist.	
5/26/56	14	1	1. Midnight Rhapsody [I]	Capitol

DATE	POS	WKS	ARTIST—RECORD TITLE	LABEL & NO.
			JERRY BUTLER	
			Born on 12/8/39 in Sunflower, Mississippi. To Chicago, 1944. Sang with church groups, and the Northern Jubilee Gospel Singers, with Curtis Mayfield. Later with R&B group, the Quails. In 1957, he and Mayfield joined a vocal group, the Roosters, with Sam Gooden, Arthur Brooks and Richard Brooks. Changed name to the Impressions in 1957. Left for solo career in autumn of 1958. Teamed again with Curtis Mayfield for a string of hits with Vee-Jay from 1960-64.	
5/10/69	29	6	1. The Ice Man Cometh	Mercury 61198
			"Only The Strong Survive"(4)	
			BILLY BUTTERFIELD - see RAY CONNIFF	
			CHARLIE BYRD	
			Born on 9/16/25 in Chuckatuch, Virginia. Jazz and classical guitar virtuoso.	
10/13/62	1(1)	44	1. **Jazz Samba** [I]	Verve 8432
			STAN GETZ/CHARLIE BYRD	
			DONALD BYRD	
			Born on 12/9/32 in Detroit. Trumpet, flugelhorn. Founded the Blackbyrds in 1973..	
7/14/73	36	2	1. Black Byrd	Blue Note 047
5/11/74	33	3	2. Street Lady [I]	Blue Note 140
			THE BYRDS	
			Folk-rock group formed in Los Angeles, 1964. Consisted of James (Roger) McGuinn, 12-string guitar; David Crosby, guitar; Gene Clark, percussion; Chris Hillman, bass; and Mike Clarke, drums. McGuinn, who changed his name to Roger in 1968, had been with Bobby Darin and the Chad Mitchell Trio. Clark had been with the New Christy Minstrels. All except Clarke had folk music background. Professional debut March, 1965. First recorded as the Beefeaters for Elektra, 1965. Also recorded as the Jet Set. Clark left after "Eight Miles High". Crosby left in 1968 to form Crosby, Stills, And Nash. Reformed in 1968 with McGuinn, Hillman, Kevin Kelly, drums; and Gram Parsons, guitar. Hillman and Parsons left to form the Flying Burrito Brothers. McGuinn again reformed with Clarence White, guitar; John York, bass; and Gene Parsons, drums. Reunions with original members in 1973 and 1979.	
7/17/65	6	4	1. **Mr. Tambourine Man**	Columbia 9172
			"Mr. Tambourine Man"(1)	
2/12/66	17	10	2. Turn! Turn! Turn!	Columbia 9254
			"Turn! Turn! Turn!"(1)	
9/17/66	24	8	3. Fifth Dimension	Columbia 9349
4/22/67	24	5	4. Younger Than Yesterday	Columbia 9442
9/16/67	6	15	▲ 5. **The Byrds' Greatest Hits** [G]	Columbia 9516
1/10/70	36	3	6. Ballad Of Easy Rider	Columbia 9942
11/28/70	40	2	7. The Byrds (Untitled)	Columbia 30127 [2]
4/14/73	20	7	8. Byrds	Asylum 5058
			reunion of original 5 Byrds	

DATE	POS	WKS	ARTIST—RECORD TITLE	LABEL & NO.

C

JOHN CAFFERTY & THE BEAVER BROWN BAND

Rock sextet from Rhode Island. Wrote and recorded the music for the soundtrack "Eddie & The Cruisers".

DATE	POS	WKS	ARTIST—RECORD TITLE	LABEL & NO.
8/25/84	9	24	▲ 1. **Eddie And The Cruisers** [S]	Scotti Br. 38929
			"On The Dark Side"(7)	
			"Tender Years"	
7/06/85	40	3	2. Tough All Over	Scotti Br. 39405

BOBBY CALDWELL

Born on 8/15/51 in New York City. Vocalist, pianist, percussionist, composer. Plays many instruments. Wrote tracks for "New Mickey Mouse Club" TV show, and commercials. With Johnny Winter in early 70s.

DATE	POS	WKS	ARTIST—RECORD TITLE	LABEL & NO.
2/17/79	21	10	1. Bobby Caldwell	Clouds 8804
			"What You Won't Do For Love"(9)	

CAMEO

Soul/funk group from New York City, led by Larry Blackmon.

DATE	POS	WKS	ARTIST—RECORD TITLE	LABEL & NO.
7/12/80	25	10	● 1. Cameosis	Choc. City 2011
4/24/82	23	6	● 2. Alligator Woman	Choc. City 2021
4/07/84	27	9	● 3. She's Strange	Atlanta A. 814984
10/11/86	8	31	● 4. **Word Up!**	Atlanta A. 830265
			"Word Up"(6)	

GLEN CAMPBELL

Born on 4/22/36 near Delight, Arkansas. Vocalist, guitar, composer. With his uncle Dick Bills' band, 1954-58. To Los Angeles; recorded with The Champs in 1960; became prolific studio musician; with The Beach Boys, 1965. Own TV show, "The Glen Campbell Goodtime Hour", 1968-72. In films "True Grit", "Norwood" and "Strange Homecoming".

DATE	POS	WKS	ARTIST—RECORD TITLE	LABEL & NO.
4/27/68	15	35	● 1. By The Time I Get To Phoenix	Capitol 2851
6/08/68	26	4	● 2. Hey, Little One	Capitol 2878
8/10/68	5	40	● 3. **Gentle On My Mind**	Capitol 2809
9/14/68	24	5	4. A New Place In The Sun	Capitol 2907
11/09/68	11	13	● 5. Bobbie Gentry & Glen Campbell	Capitol 2928
11/30/68	1(5)	29	● 6. **Wichita Lineman**	Capitol 103
			"Wichita Lineman"(3)	
4/12/69	2(1)	18	● 7. **Galveston**	Capitol 210
			"Galveston"(4)	
9/27/69	13	14	● 8. Glen Campbell - "Live" [L]	Capitol 0268 [2]
2/14/70	12	11	● 9. Try A Little Kindness	Capitol 389
6/20/70	38	3	10. Oh Happy Day	Capitol 443
10/31/70	27	5	11. The Glen Campbell Goodtime Album	Capitol 493
			"It's Only Make Believe"(10)	
5/29/71	39	1	● 12. Glen Campbell's Greatest Hits [G]	Capitol 752
9/06/75	17	13	● 13. Rhinestone Cowboy	Capitol 11430
			"Rhinestone Cowboy"(1)	

DATE	POS	WKS	ARTIST—RECORD TITLE	LABEL & NO.
4/16/77	**22**	7	● 14. Southern Nights	Capitol 11601
			"Southern Nights"(1)	
			CANNED HEAT	
			Blues-rock band formed in Los Angeles in 1966. Consisted of Bob 'The Bear' Hite (vocals, harmonica), Alan 'Blind Owl' Wilson (guitar, harmonica, vocals), Henry Vestine (guitar), Larry Taylor (bass) and Frank Cook (drums). Cook replaced by Fito de la Parra in 1968. Vestine replaced by Harvey Mandel in 1969. Wilson died of a drug overdose on 9/3/70 (27). Hite died of a drug-related heart attack on 4/6/81 (36).	
9/07/68	**16**	14	1. Boogie With Canned Heat	Liberty 7541
			"On The Road Again"	
12/28/68	**18**	9	2. Living The Blues [L]	Liberty 27200 [2]
			record 2 recorded live	
			"Going Up The Country"	
8/30/69	**37**	2	3. Hallelujah	Liberty 7618
			EDDIE CANO	
			Jazz/latin quartet led by Eddie on piano.	
9/01/62	**31**	3	1. Eddie Cano At P.J.'s [I]	Reprise 6030
			CAPTAIN & TENNILLE	
			The Captain: Daryl Dragon (b: 8/27/42, Los Angeles); and Toni Tennille (b: 5/8/43, Montgomery, AL). Husband and wife, both play piano. Dragon is son of notable conductor Carmen Dragon. Keyboardist with The Beach Boys, nicknamed the "Captain" by Mike Love. Duo had own TV show on ABC, 1976-77.	
6/21/75	**2(1)**	14	● 1. **Love Will Keep Us Together**	A&M 3405
			"Love Will Keep Us Together"(1)	
			"The Way I Want To Touch You"(4)	
3/27/76	**9**	16	▲ 2. **Song Of Joy**	A&M 4570
			"Lonely Night"(3)	
			"Shop Around"(4)	
			"Muskrat Love"(4)	
4/23/77	**18**	7	● 3. Come In From The Rain	A&M 4700
1/05/80	**23**	9	● 4. Make Your Move	Casablanca 7188
			"Do That To Me One More Time"(1)	
			GEORGE CARLIN	
			Born on 5/12/37 in New York City. Comedian, actor. In films "Outrageous Fortune", "Car Wash" and "Americathon".	
3/18/72	**13**	16	● 1. FM & AM [C]	Little David 7214
10/28/72	**22**	10	● 2. Class Clown [C]	Little David 1004
12/01/73	**35**	5	● 3. Occupation: Foole [C]	Little David 1005
1/04/75	**19**	7	● 4. Toledo Window Box [C]	Little David 3003
12/27/75	**34**	3	5. An Evening With Wally Londo Featuring Bill Slaszo [C]	Little David 1008
			BELINDA CARLISLE	
			Born on 8/16/58 in Hollywood. Lead singer of the Go-Go's, 1978-84.	
7/05/86	**13**	16	● 1. Belinda	I.R.S. 5741
			"Mad About You"(3)	
			WALTER CARLOS	
			Classical music performed on the Moog Synthesizer.	
3/01/69	**10**	17	● 1. **Switched-On Bach** [I]	Columbia 7194

DATE	POS	WKS	ARTIST—RECORD TITLE	LABEL & NO.
			CARL CARLTON	
			Born in 1952 in Detroit. Singing since age nine. First recorded for Lando in 1964.	
10/03/81	34	3	1. Carl Carlton	20th Century 628
			ERIC CARMEN	
			Born on 8/11/49 in Cleveland. Lead singer of the Raspberries, 1970-74.	
2/21/76	21	8	● 1. Eric Carmen	Arista 4057
			"All By Myself"(2)	
			KIM CARNES	
			Born on 7/20/45 in Los Angeles. Vocalist, pianist, composer. Member of New Christy Minstrels with husband/co-writer Dave Ellingson and Kenny Rogers, late 1960s. Wrote and performed commercials.	
5/09/81	1(4)	23	▲ 1. **Mistaken Identity**	EMI America 17052
			"Bette Davis Eyes"(1)	
			CARPENTERS	
			Richard Carpenter (b: 10/15/46) and sister Karen (b: 3/2/50; d: 2/4/83 of anorexia [32]). From New Haven, CT. Richard played piano from age nine. To Downey, CA, 1963. Karen played drums in group with Richard and bass player Wes Jacobs in 1965. The trio recorded for RCA in 1966. After a period with the band Spectrum, the Carpenters recorded as a duo for A&M in 1969. Hosts of TV variety show "Make Your Own Kind Of Music" in 1971.	
9/26/70	2(1)	53	● 1. **Close To You**	A&M 4271
			"Close To You"(1)	
			"We've Only Just Begun"(2)	
6/05/71	2(2)	39	● 2. **Carpenters**	A&M 3502
			"For All We Know"(3)	
			"Rainy Days And Mondays"(2)	
			"Superstar"(2)	
7/08/72	4	19	● 3. **A Song For You**	A&M 3511
			"Hurting Each Other"(2)	
			"Goodbye To Love"(7)	
6/09/73	2(1)	19	● 4. **Now & Then**	A&M 3519
			side 2: medley of '60's hits with D.J. Tony Peluso	
			"Sing"(3)	
			"Yesterday Once More"(2)	
12/08/73	1(1)	17	● 5. **The Singles 1969-1973** [G]	A&M 3601
			"Top Of The World"(1)	
6/28/75	13	11	● 6. **Horizon**	A&M 4530
			"Please Mr. Postman"(1)	
			"Only Yesterday"(4)	
7/31/76	33	5	● 7. A Kind Of Hush	A&M 4581
			VIKKI CARR	
			Born Florencia Martinez Cardona on 7/19/41 in El Paso, Texas. A regular on the Ray Anthony musical variety TV show in 1962.	
12/02/67	12	16	1. It Must Be Him	Liberty 7533
			"It Must Be Him"(3)	
6/07/69	29	7	2. For Once In My Life [L]	Liberty 7604

The Breakfast Club, John Hughes' 1984 film about five disaffected high school students, had quite an impact on one Scottish band. After making seven fine albums of challenging, artistic music that went nowhere in the U.S., Simple Minds recorded producer Keith Forsey's film theme, "Don't You (Forget About Me)," and landed at the top of the American charts.

The Brothers Four members weren't actually related; they met at a University of Washington fraternity in the late 1950s. The folk quartet's one huge hit single, "Greenfields," appears on its 1960 debut album, *The Brothers Four.*

James Brown signed his first recording contract in a Macon, GA barbershop in 1956; the classic single "Please, Please, Please" was in stores less than six weeks later, launching an electrifying career that shows no sign of ending.

Jimmy Buffett, a onetime journalism student, did a stint writing for *Billboard* before turning to a life of singing and occasional film acting. *Son of a Son of a Sailor* (1978) is Buffett's biggest selling album, although his best-known song, "Margaritaville," is on an earlier album.

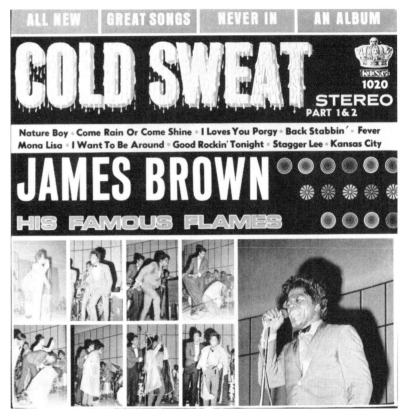

The Cars' time has been filled with a great deal of extracurricular work since the group's debut in 1978 with a platinum album. Besides building and operating Syncro Sound, a Boston recording studio, Ric Ocasek has cut two solo albums and produced everyone from Bebe Buell to the Bad Brains, while Benjamin Orr, Elliot Easton, and Greg Hawkes have also done solo records.

Ray Charles is not only a giant of R&B, but also of country, blues, and jazz. The pianist and singer, whose career began in the 1940s, once said of soul music, "We don't know what it is, but it's a force that can light a room. The force radiates from a sense of selfhood, a sense of knowing where you've been and what it means. Soul is a way of life, but it's always the hard way."

Eric Clapton was the second guitarist (chronologically speaking) in the fabled Yardbirds, preceding both Jeff Beck and Jimmy Page in the lineup. After recording "For Your Love," Clapton left to join John Mayall's Bluesbreakers, and then moved on to Cream, Blind Faith, Derek and the Dominos, and finally a solo career in 1974.

The Dave Clark Five formed in London in 1960 to raise money for Clark's soccer team, which wanted to travel to Holland for a game. In January 1964, the band's "Glad All Over" pushed the Beatles' "I Want to Hold Your Hand" out of the No. 1 spot on the British charts. Later, it became the second British Invasion group (after the Beatles) to appear on "The Ed Sullivan Show."

Nat King Cole, born Nathaniel Adams Coles, didn't begin to sing until 1940 although his recording career, as a pianist in various small combos, dates back to the 1930s. Early sides by the man responsible for "Ramblin' Rose" had such titles as "Anesthetic for Lovers," "Hit That Jive, Jack," and "Vom Vim Veedle."

Judy Collins' first public performance was as a 13-year-old playing Mozart with the Denver Symphony. She has since recorded songs by Joni Mitchell, Stephen Sondheim, and Leonard Cohen. The only hit single know to be written specifically about Collins is Crosby, Stills and Nash's "Suite: Judy Blue Eyes."

Sam Cooke released his first pop single under the name Dale Cook because he was concerned about alienating his fans, who knew him as the gospel-singing leader of the Soul Stirrers.

Bill Cosby may be enjoying an extraordinary level of fame and fortune in the mid-1980s, but he wasn't exactly unknown in 1966, a year in which he co-starred on "I Spy"; released his fourth gold album, *Wonderfulness;* and won a Grammy for "Best Comedy Artist."

DATE	POS	WKS	ARTIST—RECORD TITLE	LABEL & NO.
			DAVID CARROLL	
			Born Nook Schrier on 10/15/13 in Chicago. Arranger, conductor since 1951 for many top Mercury artists.	
6/01/59	21	6	1. Let's Dance	Mercury 60001
1/11/60	6	30	2. **Let's Dance Again**	Mercury 60152
			THE CARS	
			Rock group formed in Boston in 1976. Consisted of Ric Ocasek (lead vocals, guitar), Elliot Easton (guitar), Greg Hawkes (keyboards), Benjamin Orr (bass) and David Robinson (drums). Ocasek, Orr and Hawkes had been in trio, early 70s. Group named by Robinson, got start at the Rat Club in Boston. All songs written by Ocasek.	
9/23/78	18	38	▲ 1. The Cars	Elektra 135
7/07/79	3	21	▲ 2. **Candy-O**	Elektra 507
9/06/80	5	11	▲ 3. **Panorama**	Elektra 514
11/28/81	9	24	▲ 4. **Shake It Up**	Elektra 567
			"Shake It Up"(4)	
4/07/84	3	48	▲ 5. **Heartbeat City**	Elektra 60296
			"You Might Think"(7)	
			"Drive"(3)	
11/23/85	12	16	▲ 6. The Cars Greatest Hits [G]	Elektra 60464
			"Tonight She Comes"(7)	
			JOHNNY CASH	
			Born on 2/26/32 in Kingsland, Arkansas. To Dyess, AR at age 3. Brother Roy had Dixie Rhythm Ramblers band, late 40s. In US Air Force, 1950-54. Formed trio with Luther Perkins (guitar) and Marshall Grant (bass) in 1955. First recorded for Sun in 1955. On "Louisiana Hayride" and "Grand Ole Opry" shows, 1957. Own TV show for ABC, 1969-71. Worked with June Carter from 1961, married her in March, 1968. Daughter Rosanne Cash and stepdaughter Carlene Carter currently enjoying successful singing careers.	
12/08/58	19	9	1. The Fabulous Johnny Cash	Columbia 1253
9/14/63	26	9	● 2. Ring Of Fire (The Best Of Johnny Cash) [K]	Columbia 8853
7/20/68	13	39	▲ 3. Johnny Cash At Folsom Prison [L]	Columbia 9639
7/12/69	1(4)	35	▲ 4. **Johnny Cash At San Quentin** [L]	Columbia 9827
			"A Boy Named Sue"(2)	
2/21/70	6	17	● 5. **Hello, I'm Johnny Cash**	Columbia 9943
			ROSANNE CASH	
			Johnny Cash's daughter. Married to Rodney Crowell since 1979.	
6/06/81	26	9	● 1. Seven Year Ache	Columbia 36965
			DAVID CASSIDY	
			Born on 4/12/50 in New York City. Son of actor Jack Cassidy and actress Evelyn Ward. Played Keith and was lead singer for TV's "The Partridge Family".	
2/19/72	15	8	● 1. Cherish	Bell 6070
			"Cherish"(9)	

DATE	POS	WKS	ARTIST—RECORD TITLE	LABEL & NO.
			SHAUN CASSIDY	
			Born on 9/27/59 in Los Angeles. Son of actor Jack Cassidy and actress Shirley Jones. Played Joe Hardy on TV's "The Hardy Boys". Shaun & David Cassidy are half-brothers. Joined the cast of TV's soap series "General Hospital" in 1987.	
7/09/77	3	26	▲ 1. **Shaun Cassidy**	Warner 3067
			"Da Doo Ron Ron"(1)	
			"That's Rock 'N' Roll"(3)	
12/03/77	6	11	▲ 2. **Born Late**	Warner 3126
			"Hey Deanie"(7)	
9/02/78	33	4	▲ 3. Under Wraps	Warner 3222
			THE JIMMY CASTOR BUNCH	
			Jimmy was born on 6/2/43 in New York City. Vocalist, saxophone, composer, arranger. Formed the Jimmy Castor Bunch in 1972, with Gerry Thomas (keyboards), Doug Gibson (bass), Harry Jensen (guitar), Lenny Fridie, Jr. (congas) & Bobby Manigault (drums).	
6/24/72	27	6	1. It's Just Begun	RCA 4640
			"Troglodyte"(6)	
			CARMEN CAVALLARO	
			Pianist imitating Eddy Duchin's style.	
5/26/56	1(1)	99	1. **The Eddy Duchin Story** [S-I]	Decca 8289
			biographical film about the popular pianist/orchestra leader	
			PETER CETERA	
			Born on 9/13/44 in Chicago. Lead singer and bass guitarist of Chicago for their first 17 albums.	
7/26/86	23	25	● 1. Solitude/Solitaire	Warner 25474
			"Glory Of Love"(1)	
			"The Next Time I Fall"(1-with Amy Grant)	
			FRANK CHACKSFIELD	
			Born on 5/9/14 in Sussex, England. Orchestra leader.	
1/09/61	36	1	1. Ebb Tide	Richmond 30078
			CHAD & JEREMY	
			Chad Stuart (b: 12/10/43, England) & Jeremy Clyde (b: 3/22/44, England). Folk-rock duo formed in early 60s, broke up in 1967.	
1/23/65	22	11	1. Yesterday's Gone	World Art. 2002
			"A Summer Song"(7)	
8/21/65	37	3	2. Before And After	Columbia 9174
			GEORGE CHAKIRIS	
			Portrayed Bernardo in the film "West Side Story".	
9/15/62	28	4	1. George Chakiris	Capitol 1750
			RICHARD CHAMBERLAIN	
			Born on 3/31/35. Leading actor in films, theatre and television. Played lead role in TV's "Dr. Kildare", 1961-66.	
2/16/63	5	24	1. **Richard Chamberlain Sings**	MGM 4088
			"Theme From Dr. Kildare"(10)	
			THE CHAMBERS BROTHERS	
			Four Mississippi-born brothers: George (b: 9/26/31), bass; Willie (b: 3/3/38), guitar; Lester (b: 4/13/40), harmonica; and Joe (b: 8/22/42), guitar. Started as a gospel group in the fifties. Drummer Brian Keenan (b: 1/28/44) added in 1965.	
9/14/68	4	17	● 1. **The Time Has Come**	Columbia 9522
11/23/68	16	6	2. A New Time-A New Day	Columbia 9671

DATE	POS	WKS	ARTIST—RECORD TITLE	LABEL & NO.
			CHANGE	
			European/American studio group formed by Italian producer Jacques Fred Petrus. Luther Vandross sang on several songs from group's first two albums. Later group, based in New York, included lead vocals by James Robinson and Deborah Cooper.	
6/21/80	29	7	● 1. The Glow Of Love	RFC 3438
			CHANTAY'S	
			Teenage surf/rock quintet from Santa Ana, CA: Bob Spickard (lead guitar), Brian Carman (rhythm guitar), Bob Marshall (piano), Warren Waters (bass) and Bob Welch (drums).	
6/22/63	26	4	1. Pipeline [I]	Dot 25516
			"Pipeline"(4)	
			HARRY CHAPIN	
			Folk-rock storyteller. Born on 12/7/42 in New York City. Died in an auto accident on 7/16/81.	
10/26/74	4	17	● 1. **Verities & Balderdash**	Elektra 1012
			"Cat's In The Cradle"(1)	
			CHARLENE	
			Full name: Charlene Duncan. From Los Angeles.	
6/05/82	36	3	1. I've Never Been To Me	Motown 6009
			"I've Never Been To Me"(3)	
			RAY CHARLES	
			Born Ray Charles Robinson on 9/23/30 in Albany, Georgia. To Greenville, Florida while still an infant. Partially blind at age 5, completely blind at 7 (glaucoma). Studied classical piano and clarinet at State School for Deaf and Blind Children, St. Augustine, Florida, 1937-45. With local Florida bands, moved to Seattle in 1948. Formed the McSon Trio (also known as the Maxim Trio and the Maxine Trio) with G.D. McGhee (guitar) and Milton Garred (bass). First recordings were very much in the King Cole Trio style. Formed own band in 1954. Extremely popular performer with many TV and film appearances.	
2/15/60	17	37	1. The Genius Of Ray Charles	Atlantic 1312
7/18/60	13	18	2. Ray Charles In Person [L]	Atlantic 8039
			recorded on 5/28/59 at Herndon Stadium, Atlanta, Georgia	
10/10/60	9	13	3. **The Genius Hits The Road**	ABC-Para. 335
			"Georgia On My Mind"(1)	
3/06/61	11	16	4. Dedicated To You	ABC-Para. 355
3/27/61	4	29	5. **Genius + Soul Jazz**	Impulse! 2
			featuring top jazz artists including Count Basie's band	
			"One Mint Julep"(8)	
1/20/62	11	52	6. Do The Twist! [K]	Atlantic 8054
5/12/62	1(14)	59	● 7. **Modern Sounds In Country And Western Music**	ABC-Para. 410
			"I Can Stop Loving You"(1)	
			"You Don't Know Me"(2)	
6/23/62	20	4	8. What'd I Say [K]	Atlantic 8029
			"What'd I Say"(6)	
9/01/62	5	23	● 9. **Ray Charles' Greatest Hits** [G]	ABC-Para. 415
			"Hit The Road Jack"(1)	
			"Unchain My Heart"(9)	
9/01/62	14	9	10. The Ray Charles Story [K]	Atlantic 900 [2]
			all of above Atlantic albums recorded 1952-1959	

DATE	POS	WKS	ARTIST—RECORD TITLE	LABEL & NO.
11/10/62	2(2)	38	● 11. **Modern Sounds In Country And Western Music (Volume Two)**	ABC-Para. 435
			"You Are My Sunshine"(7)	
			"Take These Chains From My Heart"(8)	
9/14/63	2(2)	21	12. **Ingredients In A Recipe For Soul**	ABC-Para. 465
			"Busted"(4)	
4/04/64	9	11	13. **Sweet & Sour Tears**	ABC-Para. 480
9/26/64	36	5	14. **Have A Smile With Me**	ABC-Para. 495
4/30/66	15	20	15. **Crying Time**	ABC-Para. 544
			"Crying Time"(6)	
			THE RAY CHARLES SINGERS	
			Ray was born on 9/13/18 in Chicago. Arranger and conductor for many TV shows including "Perry Como Show", "Glen Campbell Show" and "Sha-Na-Na".	
5/30/64	11	15	1. **Something Special For Young Lovers**	Command 866
			"Love Me With All Your Heart"(3)	
			CHARLESTON CITY ALL-STARS	
			Conducted by Enoch Light.	
9/02/57	16	14	1. The Roaring 20's, Volume 2 [I]	Grand Award 340
9/02/57	17	2	2. The Roaring 20's, Volume 3 [I]	Grand Award 353
			CHASE	
			Jazz-rock band organized by trumpeter Bill Chase (formerly with Woody Herman, and Stan Kenton). Bill Chase and 3 other members were killed in a plane crash on 8/9/74.	
7/03/71	22	10	1. Chase	Epic 30472
			CHEAP TRICK	
			Rock quartet from Rockford, Illinois consisting of Rick Nielsen, guitar; Bun E. Carlos, drums; Robin Zander, vocals; and Tom Petersson, bass (replaced by Jon Brant in 1980).	
3/03/79	4	30	▲ 1. **Cheap Trick At Budokan** [L]	Epic 35795
			"I Want You To Want Me"(7)	
10/06/79	6	10	▲ 2. **Dream Police**	Epic 35773
7/19/80	39	2	3. Found All The Parts [M]	Epic 36453
			10" mini LP - recorded 1976-1979	
11/22/80	24	6	● 4. **All Shook Up**	Epic 36498
6/19/82	39	10	5. **One On One**	Epic 38021
10/05/85	35	4	6. **Standing On The Edge**	Epic 39592
			CHUBBY CHECKER	
			Born Ernest Evans on 10/3/41 in Philadelphia. His cover version of Hank Ballard's "The Twist" started a worldwide dance craze.	
10/31/60	3	42	1. **Twist With Chubby Checker**	Parkway 7001
			"The Twist"(1)	
12/04/61	11	16	2. Let's Twist Again	Parkway 7004
			"Let's Twist Again"(8)	
12/18/61	2(6)	37	3. **Your Twist Party** [K]	Parkway 7007
			features songs from above 3 albums and "It's Pony Time" LP	
12/25/61	7	11	4. **Bobby Rydell/Chubby Checker**	Cameo 1013
1/20/62	8	22	5. **For Twisters Only**	Parkway 7002

DATE	POS	WKS	ARTIST—RECORD TITLE	LABEL & NO.
4/14/62	**17**	17	6. For Teen Twisters Only	Parkway 7009
			"The Fly"(7)	
			"Slow Twistin'"(3)	
7/21/62	**29**	3	7. Don't Knock The Twist [S]	Parkway 7011
			6 cuts by Chubby, who also stars in the film	
11/10/62	**23**	8	8. All The Hits (For Your Dancin' Party)	Parkway 7014
			"Limbo Rock"(2)	
12/29/62	**11**	19	9. Limbo Party	Parkway 7020
2/09/63	**27**	8	10. Chubby Checker's Biggest Hits [G]	Parkway 7022
			"Popeye The Hitchhiker"(10)	

CHEECH & CHONG

Comedians Richard 'Cheech' Marin & Thomas Chong. Cheech was born in Watts, CA; Chong in Edmonton, Alberta, Canada. Starred in movies since 1980.

DATE	POS	WKS	ARTIST—RECORD TITLE	LABEL & NO.
1/29/72	**28**	10	● 1. Cheech And Chong [C]	Ode 77010
7/15/72	**2(1)**	20	● 2. **Big Bambu** [C]	Ode 77014
9/08/73	**2(1)**	29	● 3. **Los Cochinos** [C]	Ode 77019
10/26/74	**5**	9	● 4. **Cheech & Chong's Wedding Album** [C]	Ode 77025
			"Earache My Eye Featuring Alice Bowie"(9)	
7/10/76	**25**	6	5. Sleeping Beauty [C]	Ode 77040

CHER

Born Cherilyn LaPierre on 5/20/46 in El Centro, California. Worked as back-up singer for Phil Spector. Recorded with Sonny Bono as "Caesar & Cleo" in 1963. Recorded as "Bonnie Jo Mason" and "Cherilyn" in 1964. Married Bono in 1963, divorced in 1974. Married for a short time to Gregg Allman. Own TV series with Bono from 1971-77. Acclaimed as actress in films "Silkwood" and "Mask".

DATE	POS	WKS	ARTIST—RECORD TITLE	LABEL & NO.
10/16/65	**16**	10	1. All I Really Want To Do	Imperial 12292
6/18/66	**26**	7	2. The Sonny Side Of Cher	Imperial 12301
			"Bang Bang"(9)	
10/30/71	**16**	11	3. Gypsys, Tramps & Thieves	Kapp 3649
			"Gypsys, Tramps & Thieves"(1)	
			"The Way of Love"(7)	
10/27/73	**28**	4	● 4. Half-Breed	MCA 2104
			"Half-Breed"(1)	
4/14/79	**25**	6	● 5. Take Me Home	Casablanca 7133
			"Take Me Home"(8)	

CHERRELLE

Real name: Cheryl Norton. From Los Angeles.

DATE	POS	WKS	ARTIST—RECORD TITLE	LABEL & NO.
4/12/86	**36**	1	1. High Priority	Tabu 40094

DON CHERRY

Born in Wichita, Texas on 1/11/24. Sang briefly with postwar Tommy Dorsey and Victor Young orchestras; left music to become a pro golfer in the late 50s.

DATE	POS	WKS	ARTIST—RECORD TITLE	LABEL & NO.
9/22/56	**15**	7	1. Swingin' For Two	Columbia 893
			with Ray Conniff & His Orchestra	

DATE	POS	WKS	ARTIST—RECORD TITLE	LABEL & NO.
			THE CHI-LITES	
			R&B vocal group from Chicago. Consisted of Eugene Record (lead vocals), Robert Lester (tenor), Marshall Thompson (baritone) and Creadel Jones (bass). First recorded as the Hi-Lites on Daran in 1963.	
9/25/71	12	14	1. (For God's Sake) Give More Power To The People	Brunswick 754170
			"Have You Seen Her"(3)	
5/13/72	5	16	2. **A Lonely Man**	Brunswick 754179
			"Oh Girl"(1)	
			CHIC	
			Disco group formed in New York City by producers Bernard Edwards, bass; and Nile Rodgers, guitar. Vocalists were Norma Jean Wright (replaced by Alfa Anderson) and Luci Martin; and Tony Thompson on drums. Rodgers joined the Honeydrippers in 1984. Thompson joined the Power Station in 1985 and Edwards became their producer.	
2/04/78	27	9	● 1. Chic	Atlantic 19153
			"Dance, Dance, Dance"(6)	
12/09/78	4	22	▲ 2. **C'est Chic**	Atlantic 19209
			"Le Freak"(1)	
			"I Want Your Love"(7)	
8/25/79	5	11	▲ 3. **Risque**	Atlantic 16003
			"Good Times"(1)	
8/23/80	30	3	4. Real People	Atlantic 16016
			CHICAGO	
			Jazz-oriented rock group formed in Chicago in 1967. Consisted of Robert Lamm, keyboards; James Pankow, trombone; Lee Loughnane, trumpet; Terry Kath, guitar (d: 1/23/78 [31] playing Russian roulette); Walt Parazaider, reeds; Peter Cetera, bass; and Danny Seraphine, drums. Originally called The Big Thing, later Chicago Transit Authority. To Los Angeles in late 60s. Kath replaced by Donnie Dacus. Bill Champlin, keyboards, joined in 1982. Cetera left in 1985, replaced by Jason Scheff.	
5/31/69	17	41	▲ 1. Chicago Transit Authority	Columbia 8 [2]
			"Does Anybody Really Know What Time It Is?"(7)	
			"Beginnings"(7)	
2/21/70	4	53	● 2. **Chicago II**	Columbia 24 [2]
			"Make Me Smile"(9)	
			"25 Or 6 To 4"(4)	
1/30/71	2(2)	22	▲ 3. **Chicago III**	Columbia 30110 [2]
11/20/71	3	19	▲ 4. **Chicago At Carnegie Hall** [L]	Columbia 30865 [4]
			4 album boxed set	
7/29/72	1(9)	20	▲ 5. **Chicago V**	Columbia 31102
			"Saturday In The Park"(3)	
7/21/73	1(5)	27	▲ 6. **Chicago VI**	Columbia 32400
			"Feelin' Stronger Every Day"(10)	
			"Just You 'N' Me"(4)	
4/06/74	1(1)	35	▲ 7. **Chicago VII**	Columbia 32810 [2]
			"(I've Been) Searchin' So Long"(9)	
			"Call On Me"(6)	
4/12/75	1(2)	15	▲ 8. **Chicago VIII**	Columbia 33100
			"Old Days"(5)	
11/29/75	1(5)	22	▲ 9. **Chicago IX - Chicago's Greatest Hits** [G]	Columbia 33900

DATE	POS	WKS	ARTIST—RECORD TITLE	LABEL & NO.
7/04/76	3	30	▲ 10. **Chicago X**	Columbia 34200
			"If You Leave Me Now"(1)	
10/01/77	6	10	▲ 11. **Chicago XI**	Columbia 34860
			"Baby, What A Big Surprise"(4)	
10/21/78	12	10	▲ 12. Hot Streets	Columbia 35512
9/08/79	21	5	● 13. Chicago 13	Columbia 36105
7/17/82	9	18	▲ 14. **Chicago 16**	Full Moon 23689
			"Hard To Say I'm Sorry"(1)	
6/16/84	4	44	▲ 15. **Chicago 17**	Full Moon 25060
			"Hard Habit To Break"(3)	
			"You're The Inspiration"(3)	

THE CHIPMUNKS

Characters created by Ross Bagdasarian ("David Seville"). Named Alvin, Simon and Theodore after Liberty executives Alvin Bennett, Simon Waronker & Theodore Keep. Bagdasarian died on 1/16/72 (52); his son resurrected the act in 1980.

DATE	POS	WKS	ARTIST—RECORD TITLE		LABEL & NO.
12/07/59	4	28	1. **Let's All Sing With The Chipmunks**	[N]	Liberty 3132
			"The Chipmunk Song"(1)		
			"Alvin's Harmonica"(3)		
6/20/60	31	5	2. Sing Again With The Chipmunks	[N]	Liberty 3159
9/19/64	14	11	3. The Chipmunks Sing The Beatles Hits	[N]	Liberty 7388
8/23/80	34	6	● 4. Chipmunk Punk	[N]	Excelsior 6008
			'group' resurrected by Seville's son		

JUNE CHRISTY

9/29/56	14	4	1. The Misty Miss Christy	Capitol 725
7/22/57	16	4	2. June - Fair and Warmer!	Capitol 833

CINDERELLA

Pennsylvania-based heavy-metal band, consisting of Tom Keifer (lead singer, guitar, piano), Jeff LaBar (guitar), Eric Brittingham (bass) & Fred Coury (drums).

8/23/86	3	44+	▲ 1. **Night Songs**	Mercury 830076

ERIC CLAPTON

Born on 3/30/45 in Ripley, England. Vocalist, guitarist. With The Roosters in 1963, The Yardbirds, 1963-65, and John Mayall's Bluesbreakers, 1965-66. Formed Cream with Jack Bruce and Ginger Baker, 1966. Formed Blind Faith in 1968; worked with John Lennon's Plastic Ono Band, and Delaney & Bonnie. Formed Derek & The Dominos, 1970. After 2 years of reclusion (1971 & 72), Clapton performed his comeback concert at London's Rainbow Theatre in January, 1973. Began actively recording and touring again in 1974. Also see Derek & The Dominos, and Delaney & Bonnie.

DATE	POS	WKS	ARTIST—RECORD TITLE		LABEL & NO.
8/08/70	13	10	1. Eric Clapton		Atco 329
4/22/72	6	22	● 2. **History Of Eric Clapton**	[K]	Atco 803 [2]
			recordings with groups listed in above artist notes		
10/06/73	18	6	3. Eric Clapton's Rainbow Concert	[L]	RSO 877
			Clapton's comeback concert at London's Rainbow Theatre with Pete Townshend, Steve Winwood, Ron Wood & Jim Capaldi		
7/27/74	1(4)	14	● 4. **461 Ocean Boulevard**		RSO 4801
			address where recorded in Miami, Florida		
			"I Shot The Sheriff"(1)		
4/26/75	21	5	5. There's One In Every Crowd		RSO 4806
9/13/75	20	7	6. E.C. Was Here	[L]	RSO 4809

DATE	POS	WKS	ARTIST—RECORD TITLE	LABEL & NO.
10/16/76	**15**	11	7. No Reason To Cry	RSO 3004
12/24/77	**2(5)**	30	▲ 8. **Slowhand**	RSO 3030
			"Lay Down Sally"(3)	
12/02/78	**8**	17	▲ 9. **Backless**	RSO 3039
			"Promises"(9)	
5/10/80	**2(6)**	19	● 10. **Just One Night** [L]	RSO 4202 [2]
			recorded live at the Budokan Theatre, Japan	
3/21/81	**7**	13	● 11. **Another Ticket**	RSO 3095
			"I Can't Stand It"(10)	
2/26/83	**16**	10	12. Money And Cigarettes	Duck 23773
4/13/85	**34**	7	● 13. Behind the Sun	Duck 25166

THE DAVE CLARK FIVE

Rock group formed in Tottenham, England in 1962. Consisted of Dave Clark (drums), Mike Smith (lead vocals, keyboards), Lenny Davidson (guitar), Dennis Payton (sax) and Rick Huxley (bass). First recorded for Ember/Pye in 1962. On Ed Sullivan show in March, 1964. Film "Having A Wild Weekend", 1965. Disbanded in 1973. Clark had been a stuntman in films, formed group to raise money for his soccer team, the Tottenham Hotspurs. Clark wrote the new London stage musical "Time".

DATE	POS	WKS	ARTIST—RECORD TITLE	LABEL & NO.
4/25/64	**3**	25	● 1. **Glad All Over**	Epic 26093
			"Glad All Over"(6)	
			"Bits And Pieces"(4)	
7/04/64	**5**	13	2. **The Dave Clark Five Return!**	Epic 26104
			"Can't You See That She's Mine"(4)	
9/05/64	**11**	9	3. American Tour	Epic 26117
			"Because"(3)	
1/16/65	**6**	13	4. **Coast To Coast**	Epic 26128
5/15/65	**24**	6	5. Weekend In London	Epic 26139
9/18/65	**15**	11	6. Having A Wild Weekend [S]	Epic 26162
			the Dave Clark Five star in the film	
			"Catch Us If You Can"(4)	
1/22/66	**32**	6	7. I Like It Like That	Epic 26178
			"I Like It Like That"(7)	
4/02/66	**9**	20	● 8. **The Dave Clark Five's Greatest Hits** [G]	Epic 26185
			"Over And Over"(1)	

DICK CLARK - see RADIO/TV CELEBRITY COMPILATIONS

PETULA CLARK

Born on 11/15/32 in Epsom, England. On radio at age nine; own show "Pet's Parlour" at age eleven. TV series in England in 1950. First US record release for Coral in 1951. Appeared in over 20 British films, 1944-57; revived her film career in late 60s, starring in "Finian's Rainbow" and "Goodbye Mr. Chips". Also see Soundtracks "Finian's Rainbow"/"Goodbye, Mr. Chips".

DATE	POS	WKS	ARTIST—RECORD TITLE	LABEL & NO.
3/20/65	**21**	16	1. Downtown	Warner 1590
			"Downtown"(1)	
9/23/67	**27**	10	2. These Are My Songs	Warner 1698
			"This Is My Song"(3)	
			"Don't Sleep In The Subway"(5)	
5/24/69	**37**	3	3. Portrait Of Petula	Warner 1789

DATE	POS	WKS	ARTIST—RECORD TITLE	LABEL & NO.
			STANLEY CLARKE	
			Born on 6/30/51 in Philadelphia. Bass, violin, cello. With Chick Corea in Return To Forever.	
11/29/75	34	3	1. Journey To Love [I]	Nemperor 433
10/23/76	34	4	2. School Days [I]	Nemperor 439
6/06/81	33	8	3. The Clarke/Duke Project	Epic 36918
			STANLEY CLARKE/GEORGE DUKE	
			THE CLASH	
			Eclectic new wave rock group formed in London in 1976. Consisted of Joe Strummer (vocals, lyricist), Mick Jones (guitar), Paul Simonon (bass) and Topper Headon (drums). Headon left in May, 1983; replaced by Peter Howard. Jones left band in 1984 to form Big Audio Dynamite. Political activists, they wrote songs protesting racism and oppression. Strummer disbanded The Clash in early 1986.	
3/08/80	27	9	1. London Calling	Epic 36328 [2]
2/28/81	24	4	2. Sandinista!	Epic 37037 [3]
6/26/82	7	39	▲ 3. **Combat Rock**	Epic 37689
			"Rock The Casbah"(8)	
			VAN CLIBURN	
			Classical pianist from Kilgore, Texas.	
8/04/58	1(7)	25	● 1. **Tchaikovsky: Piano Concerto No. 1** [I]	RCA 2252
			Kiril Kondrashin, conductor	
7/13/59	10	37	2. **Rachmaninoff: Piano Concerto No. 3** [I-L]	RCA 2355
			Carnegie Hall performance of 5/19/58	
3/24/62	25	7	3. Brahms: Piano Concerto No. 2 [I]	RCA 2581
			Fritz Reiner conducts the Chicago Symphony Orchestra	
			LINDA CLIFFORD	
			Vocalist from Brooklyn. Former Miss New York State. With Jericho Jazz Singers, then own trio, 1967. Worked Chicago clubs, 1973-77. First recorded for ABC, 1974.	
7/01/78	22	5	1. If My Friends Could See Me Now	Curtom 5021
4/21/79	26	8	2. Let Me Be Your Woman	RSO 3902 [2]
			CLIMAX BLUES BAND	
			Blues/rock quintet formed in Stafford, England; led by Colin Cooper & Peter Haycock.	
10/05/74	37	2	1. Sense Of Direction	Sire 7501
6/11/77	27	6	2. Gold Plated	Sire 7523
			"Couldn't Get It Right"(3)	
			GEORGE CLINTON	
			'P-Funk' innovator. Also see Funkadelic and Parliament.	
4/30/83	40	1	1. Computer Games	Capitol 12246
			ROSEMARY CLOONEY - see HI-LO's	
			BILLY COBHAM	
			Jazz/rock drummer. Formerly with John McLaughlin.	
1/12/74	26	9	1. Spectrum [I]	Atlantic 7268
5/25/74	23	6	2. Crosswinds [I]	Atlantic 7300
1/25/75	36	1	3. Total Eclipse [I]	Atlantic 18121

DATE	POS	WKS	ARTIST—RECORD TITLE	LABEL & NO.
			JOE COCKER	
			Born John Robert Cocker on 5/20/44 in Sheffield, England. Own skiffle band, the Cavaliers, late 50s, later reorganized as Vance Arnold & The Avengers. Assembled the Grease Band, mid-60s. First US tour, Woodstock Festival, in August, 1969. Successful tour with 43-piece revue, Mad Dogs And Englishmen, 1970. Notable spastic stage antics were based on Ray Charles' movements at the piano.	
7/19/69	**35**	3	● 1. With A Little Help From My Friends	A&M 4182
			with Jimmy Page & Stevie Winwood	
11/29/69	**11**	26	● 2. Joe Cocker!	A&M 4224
			with Leon Russell and The Grease Band	
9/05/70	2(1)	16	● 3. **Mad Dogs & Englishmen** [S-L]	A&M 6002 [2]
			title refers to Cocker's 1970 concert tour with an entourage of 43 including Leon Russell & Chris Stainton	
			"The Letter"(7)	
12/30/72	**30**	7	4. Joe Cocker	A&M 4368
9/21/74	**11**	10	5. I Can Stand A Little Rain	A&M 3633
			"You Are So Beautiful"(5)	
			DENNIS COFFEY & The Detroit Guitar Band	
			Session guitarist for The Temptations, Jackson 5 and others.	
1/08/72	**36**	4	1. Evolution [I]	Sussex 7004
			"Scorpio"(6)	
			COLD BLOOD	
			Bay-area rock group led by Lydia Pense.	
3/07/70	**23**	6	1. Cold Blood	San Francisco 200
			NAT KING COLE	
			Born Nathaniel Adams Coles on 3/17/17 in Montgomery, Alabama. Died of lung cancer on 2/15/65 in Santa Monica, CA (48). Raised in Chicago. Own band, the Royal Dukes, at age 17. First recorded in 1936 in band led by brother Eddie. Toured with "Shuffle Along" musical revue, stayed in Los Angeles. Formed trio in 1939, consisting of Nat, piano; Oscar Moore, guitar; and Wesley Prince, bass (replaced several years later by Johnny Miller). Long series of top-selling records led to his going solo in 1950. In films "St. Louis Blues", "Cat Ballou" and many other film and TV appearances. Last performed in 1964, due to ill health. Daughter Natalie is also a recording star.	
4/28/56	**16**	2	1. Ballads Of The Day	Capitol 680
			"Darling Je Vous Aime Beaucoup"(7)	
			"A Blossom Fell"(2)	
3/09/57	**13**	2	2. After Midnight	Capitol 782
			with the King Cole Trio	
4/06/57	1(8)	66	● 3. **Love Is The Thing**	Capitol 824
9/23/57	**18**	3	4. This Is Nat "King" Cole	Capitol 870
12/16/57	**18**	6	5. Just One Of Those Things	Capitol 903
5/05/58	**18**	3	6. St. Louis Blues [S]	Capitol 993
			Nat portrayed W.C. Handy in the film about Handy's life	
9/22/58	**12**	5	7. Cole Espanol [F]	Capitol 1031
12/01/58	**17**	2	8. The Very Thought Of You	Capitol 1084
4/18/60	**33**	2	9. Tell Me All About Yourself	Capitol 1331
10/24/60	**4**	23	10. **Wild Is Love**	Capitol 1392
5/12/62	**27**	9	11. Nat King Cole sings/George Shearing plays	Capitol 1675

DATE	POS	WKS	ARTIST—RECORD TITLE	LABEL & NO.
9/29/62	3	53	● 12. **Ramblin' Rose**	Capitol 1793
			"Ramblin' Rose"(2)	
1/05/63	24	10	13. Dear Lonely Hearts	Capitol 1838
7/20/63	14	9	14. Those Lazy-Hazy-Crazy Days Of Summer	Capitol 1932
			"Those Lazy-Hazy-Crazy Days Of Summer"(6)	
8/22/64	18	4	15. I Don't Want To Be Hurt Anymore	Capitol 2118
3/06/65	4	25	16. **L-O-V-E**	Capitol 2195
5/08/65	30	11	● 17. Unforgettable [R]	Capitol 357
			reissue of 1953 10" album	

NATALIE COLE

Born on 2/6/50 in Los Angeles. Daughter of Nat "King" Cole. Professional debut at age 11. Married her producer, Marvin Yancy, in 1976.

DATE	POS	WKS	ARTIST—RECORD TITLE	LABEL & NO.
11/01/75	18	8	● 1. Inseparable	Capitol 11429
			"This Will Be"(6)	
6/05/76	13	11	● 2. Natalie	Capitol 11517
3/12/77	8	13	▲ 3. **Unpredictable**	Capitol 11600
			"I've Got Love On My Mind"(5)	
1/28/78	16	17	▲ 4. Thankful	Capitol 11708
			"Our Love"(10)	
8/05/78	31	7	● 5. Natalie...Live! [L]	Capitol 11709 [2]

JUDY COLLINS

Contemporary folksinger born on 5/1/39 in Denver, Colorado.

DATE	POS	WKS	ARTIST—RECORD TITLE	LABEL & NO.
7/13/68	5	19	● 1. **Wildflowers**	Elektra 74012
			"Both Sides Now"(8)	
2/01/69	29	11	● 2. Who Knows Where The Time Goes	Elektra 74033
10/11/69	29	3	3. Recollections [K]	Elektra 74055
			recorded 1963-1965	
12/12/70	17	16	● 4. Whales & Nightingales	Elektra 75010
7/01/72	37	3	● 5. Colors Of The Day/The Best Of Judy Collins [G]	Elektra 75030
3/24/73	27	4	6. True Stories And Other Dreams	Elektra 75053
5/03/75	17	17	● 7. Judith	Elektra 1032
			"Send In The Clowns"	
9/25/76	25	4	8. Bread & Roses	Elektra 1076

PHIL COLLINS

Born on 1/31/51 in London, England. Vocalist, drummer, composer. Stage actor as a young child. With group Flaming Youth. Joined Genesis in 1970, became lead singer in 1975. Also with jazz/rock group Brand X. First solo album in 1981.

DATE	POS	WKS	ARTIST—RECORD TITLE	LABEL & NO.
4/04/81	7	26	▲ 1. **Face Value**	Atlantic 16029
12/04/82	8	21	● 2. **Hello, I Must Be Going!**	Atlantic 80035
			"You Can't Hurry Love"(10)	
3/09/85	1(7)	70	▲ 3. **No Jacket Required**	Atlantic 81240
			"One More Night"(1)	
			"Sussudio"(1)	
			"Don't Lose My Number"(4)	
			"Take Me Home"(7)	
			1985 Grammy winner: Album of the Year	

DATE	POS	WKS	ARTIST—RECORD TITLE	LABEL & NO.
			WILLIAM COLLINS - see BOOTSY	
			COMMAND ALL-STARS - see ENOCH LIGHT	
			COMMODORES	
			Formed in Tuskegee, Alabama in 1970. Consisted of Lionel Richie (vocals, saxophone), William King (trumpet), Thomas McClary (guitar), Milan Williams (keyboards), Ronald LaPread (bass) and Walter "Clyde" Orange (drums). First recorded for Motown in 1972. In film "Thank God It's Friday". Richie began solo work in 1981.	
7/05/75	26	5	1. Caught In The Act	Motown 820
11/29/75	29	6	2. Movin' On	Motown 848
			"Sweet Love"(5)	
8/07/76	12	25	3. Hot On The Tracks	Motown 867
			"Just To Be Close To You"(7)	
4/16/77	3	31	4. **Commodores**	Motown 884
			"Easy"(4)	
			"Brick House"(5)	
11/12/77	3	16	5. **Commodores Live!** [L]	Motown 894 [2]
6/03/78	3	23	▲ 6. **Natural High**	Motown 902
			"Three Times A Lady"(1)	
12/23/78	23	6	7. Commodores' Greatest Hits [G]	Motown 912
8/18/79	3	30	8. **Midnight Magic**	Motown 926
			"Sail On"(4)	
			"Still"(1)	
6/28/80	7	15	▲ 9. **Heroes**	Motown 939
7/11/81	13	19	▲ 10. In The Pocket	Motown 955
			"Lady (You Bring Me Up)"(8)	
			"Oh No"(4)	
1/15/83	37	4	11. All The Great Hits [G]	Motown 6028
3/23/85	12	15	● 12. Nightshift	Motown 6124
			"Nightshift"(3)	
			PERRY COMO	
			Born on 5/18/12 in Canonsburg, Pennsylvania. Owned barbershop in hometown. With Freddy Carlone band, 1933; with Ted Weems, 1936-1942. Films "Something For The Boys", 1944; "Doll Face", "If I'm Lucky", 1946; "Words And Music", 1948. Own "Supper Club" radio series to late 1940s. Television shows (15 minutes) from 1948-1955. Host of hourly TV shows from 1955-1963.	
10/15/55	7	15	1. **So Smooth**	RCA 1085
9/02/57	8	10	2. **We Get Letters**	RCA 1463
12/16/57	8	5	● 3. **Merry Christmas Music** [X]	RCA 1243
12/16/57	11	9	4. Dream Along With Me	RCA Camden 403
6/23/58	18	2	5. Saturday Night With Mr. C.	RCA 1004
9/01/58	24	2	6. Como's Golden Records [G]	RCA 1007
			"Hot Diggity"(1)	
			"Round And Round"(1)	
			"Catch A Falling Star"(1)	
			"Magic Moments"(4)	
12/15/58	9	4	7. **Merry Christmas Music** [X-R]	RCA 1243
1/05/59	16	7	8. When You Come To The End Of The Day	RCA 1885
11/02/59	17	3	9. Como Swings	RCA 2010

DATE	POS	WKS	ARTIST—RECORD TITLE	LABEL & NO.
1/04/60	22	1	● 10. Season's Greetings [X]	RCA 2066
12/31/60	27	1	11. Season's Greetings [X-R]	RCA 2066
1/13/62	33	1	12. Season's Greetings [X-R]	RCA 2066
12/08/62	32	3	13. By Request	RCA 2567
2/06/71	22	12	14. It's Impossible	RCA 4473
			"It's Impossible"(10)	
7/07/73	34	4	● 15. And I Love You So	RCA 0100

CON FUNK SHUN

Soul band formed as Project Soul in Vallejo, California in 1968 by high school classmates Mike Cooper (lead vocals, guitar) and Louis McCall (drums). To Memphis in 1972, changed name to Con Funk Shun.

DATE	POS	WKS	ARTIST—RECORD TITLE	LABEL & NO.
8/05/78	32	7	● 1. Loveshine	Mercury 3725
5/10/80	30	5	● 2. Spirit Of Love	Mercury 3806

RAY CONNIFF

Born on 11/6/16 in Attleboro, Massachusetts. Trombonist-arranger with Bunny Berigan, Bob Crosby, Harry James, Vaughn Monroe, and Artie Shaw bands; later conductor- arranger on many hit albums in the 50s and 60s.

DATE	POS	WKS	ARTIST—RECORD TITLE	LABEL & NO.
3/23/57	11	16	1. 'S Wonderful! [I]	Columbia 925
12/23/57	10	37	● 2. 'S Marvelous [I]	Columbia 1074
6/23/58	9	52	3. 'S Awful Nice [I]	Columbia 1137
9/29/58	9	40	● 4. Concert In Rhythm [I]	Columbia 1163
7/06/59	29	5	5. Hollywood In Rhythm [I]	Columbia 1310
12/14/59	8	33	6. Conniff Meets Butterfield [I]	Columbia 1346
			RAY CONNIFF & BILLY BUTTERFIELD (trumpeter)	
1/04/60	14	1	● 7. Christmas With Conniff [X]	Columbia 1390
2/15/60	8	47	8. It's The Talk Of The Town	Columbia 1334
3/07/60	13	29	9. Concert In Rhythm - Volume II [I]	Columbia 1415
8/15/60	6	22	10. Young At Heart	Columbia 1489
10/10/60	4	37	11. Say It With Music (A Touch Of Latin) [I] [I]	Columbia 1490
12/31/60	15	1	12. Christmas With Conniff [X-R]	Columbia 1390
2/13/61	4	46	● 13. Memories Are Made Of This [I]	Columbia 1574
3/27/61	10	3	14. Broadway In Rhythm [I]	Columbia 1252
9/18/61	14	21	15. Somebody Loves Me	Columbia 1642
1/06/62	16	3	16. Christmas With Conniff [X-R]	Columbia 1390
			made top 10 on Billboard's special Christmas charts (1969)	
2/17/62	5	23	● 17. So Much In Love	Columbia 1720
5/12/62	6	18	18. 'S Continental [I]	Columbia 1776
10/27/62	28	5	19. Rhapsody In Rhythm [I]	Columbia 1878
12/22/62	32	2	● 20. We Wish You A Merry Christmas [X]	Columbia 1892
			made top 10 on Billboard's special Christmas charts (1963/64/72)	
3/09/63	20	8	21. The Happy Beat [I]	Columbia 8749
11/14/64	23	11	22. Invisible Tears	Columbia 9064
7/10/65	34	6	23. Music From Mary Poppins, The Sound Of Music, My Fair Lady, & Other Great Movie Themes	Columbia 9166
7/30/66	3	41	▲ 24. Somewhere My Love	Columbia 9319
			"Somewhere My Love"(9)	
7/08/67	30	6	25. This Is My Song	Columbia 9476

DATE	POS	WKS	ARTIST—RECORD TITLE	LABEL & NO.
1/06/68	39	2	26. Hawaiian Album	Columbia 9547
3/30/68	25	13	● 27. It Must Be Him	Columbia 9595
7/27/68	22	9	● 28. Honey	Columbia 9661
			NORMAN CONNORS	
			Born on 3/1/48 in Philadelphia. Jazz drummer with Archie Shepp, John Coltrane, Pharoah Sanders, and others. Own group on Buddah in 1972.	
10/09/76	39	1	● 1. You Are My Starship	Buddah 5655
			SAM COOKE	
			Born on 1/22/35 in Chicago. Died from a gunshot wound on 12/11/64 (29) in Los Angeles. Son of a Baptist minister, sang in choir from age six. Joined gospel group, the Highway Q.C.'s. Joined the Soul Stirrers in 1950, lead singer until 1956. First recorded secular songs in 1956 as "Dale Cook" on Specialty. String of hits on Keen label led to contract with RCA. Shot by female motel manager under mysterious circumstances. Considered by many as the definitive soul singer.	
3/10/58	16	2	1. Sam Cooke	Keen 2001
			"You Send Me"(1)	
11/03/62	22	7	2. The Best Of Sam Cooke [G]	RCA 2625
			"Chain Gang"(2)	
7/04/64	34	3	3. Ain't That Good News	RCA 2899
			"Another Saturday Night"(10)	
2/20/65	29	5	4. Sam Cooke At The Copa [L]	RCA 2970
			RITA COOLIDGE	
			Born on 5/1/45 in Nashville. Began career as one of the Friends of Delaney & Bonnie; toured with Joe Cocker's "Mad Dogs & Englishmen" troupe. Prolific backing singer, early 70s. Married to Kris Kristofferson, 1973-79. Sister Priscilla married to Booker T. Jones (Booker T. & The MG's).	
10/13/73	26	6	● 1. Full Moon	A&M 4403
			KRIS KRISTOFFERSON & RITA COOLIDGE	
7/09/77	6	21	▲ 2. Anytime...Anywhere	A&M 4616
			"(Your Love Has Lifted Me) Higher And Higher"(2)	
			"We're All Alone"(7)	
7/15/78	32	5	● 3. Love Me Again	A&M 4699
			ALICE COOPER	
			Born Vincent Furnier on 2/4/48 in Detroit. Formed rock group in Phoenix in 1965; changed name to Alice Cooper in 1966. To Los Angeles in 1968, then to Detroit in 1969. Alice is known primarily for his bizarre stage antics.	
4/03/71	35	6	● 1. Love It To Death	Warner 1883
12/18/71	21	16	▲ 2. Killer	Warner 2567
7/15/72	2(3)	15	● 3. School's Out	Warner 2623
			"School's Out"(7)	
3/24/73	1(1)	23	▲ 4. Billion Dollar Babies	Warner 2685
12/15/73	10	10	● 5. Muscle Of Love	Warner 2748
9/28/74	8	10	▲ 6. Alice Cooper's Greatest Hits [G]	Warner 2803
3/29/75	5	17	● 7. Welcome To My Nightmare	Atlantic 18130
8/21/76	27	7	● 8. Alice Cooper Goes To Hell	Warner 2896

DATE	POS	WKS	ARTIST—RECORD TITLE	LABEL & NO.
			CORNELIUS BROTHERS & SISTER ROSE	
9/30/72	29	6	Miami-based trio consisting of Eddie, Carter and Rose Cornelius. 1. Cornelius Brothers & Sister Rose *"Treat Her Like A Lady"*(3) *"Too Late To Turn Back Now"*(2)	United Art. 5568
			BILL COSBY	
			Born on 7/12/38 in Philadelphia. Top comedian of records, nightclubs, film and TV. His first 7 comedy albums were all million sellers. Played Alexander Scott on TV series "I Spy". Star of the current #1 NBC-TV series "The Cosby Show".	
2/06/65	32	5	▲ 1. I Started Out As A Child [C]	Warner 1567
10/23/65	19	55	● 2. Why Is There Air? [C]	Warner 1606
6/18/66	7	54	▲ 3. **Wonderfulness** [C]	Warner 1634
7/09/66	21	34	▲ 4. Bill Cosby Is A Very Funny Fellow, Right! [C]	Warner 1518
5/20/67	2(1)	28	● 5. **Revenge** [C]	Warner 1691
9/09/67	18	12	6. Bill Cosby Sings/Silver Throat *"Little Ole Man"*(4)	Warner 1709
4/13/68	7	23	● 7. **To Russell, My Brother, Whom I Slept With** [C]	Warner 1734
11/16/68	16	11	● 8. 200 M.P.H. [C]	Warner 1757
3/08/69	37	3	9. It's True! It's True! [C]	Warner 1770
7/05/86	26	4	● 10. Those Of You With Or Without Children, You'll Understand [C]	Geffen 24104
			ELVIS COSTELLO	
			Born Declan McManus in Liverpool, England on 8/25/55. Changed name to Elvis Costello in 1976. Formed backing band, The Attractions in 1977. Leading eclectic rock singer for a decade.	
3/04/78	32	5	● 1. My Aim Is True	Columbia 35037
5/06/78	30	4	2. This Year's Model	Columbia 35331
2/03/79	10	11	● 3. **Armed Forces**	Columbia 35709
3/22/80	11	8	4. Get Happy!!	Columbia 36347
10/25/80	28	3	5. Taking Liberties [K] previously released and unreleased tracks	Columbia 36839
2/21/81	28	4	6. Trust	Columbia 37051
8/28/82	30	7	7. Imperial Bedroom	Columbia 38157
8/20/83	24	12	8. Punch The Clock	Columbia 38897
7/21/84	35	3	9. Goodbye Cruel World	Columbia 39429
4/05/86	39	3	10. The Costello Show (Featuring Elvis Costello) - King Of America	Columbia 40173
			JOHN COUGAR - see MELLENCAMP	
			COUNTRY JOE & THE FISH	
			Country Joe (Joseph McDonald, b: 1/1/42) & The Fish were San Francisco's leading political rock band of the 60s.	
9/23/67	39	3	1. Electric Music For The Mind And Body	Vanguard 79244
7/27/68	23	7	2. Together	Vanguard 79277

DATE	POS	WKS	ARTIST—RECORD TITLE	LABEL & NO.
			NOEL COWARD	
			British actor/writer. Died in 1973 (73).	
1/28/56	**14**	2	1. Noel Coward At Las Vegas [L]	Columbia 5063
			THE COWSILLS	
			Family group from Rhode Island. Consisted of five brothers, their little sister and mother, who died on 1/31/85 (56).	
12/09/67	**31**	7	1. The Cowsills	MGM 4498
			"The Rain, The Park & Other Things"(2)	
5/17/69	**16**	10	2. The Cowsills In Concert [L]	MGM 4619
			"Hair"(2)	
			LES CRANE	
			TV talk-show host from San Francisco.	
12/25/71	**32**	4	1. Desiderata	Warner 2570
			Les talks, accompanied by a musical background	
			"Desiderata"(8)	
			JOHNNY CRAWFORD	
			Born on 3/26/46 in Los Angeles. One of the original Mouseketeers. Played Chuck Connor's son (Mark McCain) in the TV series, "The Rifleman", 1958-63.	
9/22/62	**40**	1	1. A Young Man's Fancy	Del-Fi 1223
			"Cindy's Birthday"(8)	
			CRAZY OTTO	
			German pianist Fritz Schulz-Reichel. Also see Johnny Maddox.	
4/16/55	**1(2)**	20	1. **Crazy Otto** [I]	Decca 8113
			CREAM	
			British supergroup: Eric Clapton (guitar), Ginger Baker (drums) & Jack Bruce (bass).	
12/23/67	**4**	50	● 1. **Disraeli Gears**	Atco 232
			"Sunshine Of Your Love"(5)	
7/20/68	**1(4)**	30	● 2. **Wheels Of Fire** [L]	Atco 700 [2]
			record 1: studio; record 2: Live At The Fillmore	
			"White Room"(6)	
8/31/68	**39**	1	● 3. Fresh Cream	Atco 206
3/15/69	**2(2)**	20	● 4. Goodbye	Atco 7001
7/26/69	**3**	20	● 5. **Best Of Cream** [G]	Atco 291
5/09/70	**15**	9	6. Live Cream [L]	Atco 328
4/15/72	**27**	5	7. Live Cream - Volume II [L]	Atco 7005
			CREEDENCE CLEARWATER REVIVAL	
			Rock group formed while members attended high school at El Cerrito, California. Consisted of John Fogerty (vocals, guitar), Tom Fogerty (guitar), Stu Cook (keyboards, bass) and Doug Clifford (drums). First recorded as the Blue Velvets for the Orchestra label in 1959. Recorded as the Golliwogs for Fantasy in 1964. Tom Fogerty left for a solo career in 1971 and group disbanded in October, 1972.	
3/01/69	**7**	37	● 1. **Bayou Country**	Fantasy 8387
			"Proud Mary"(2)	
9/20/69	**1(4)**	23	● 2. **Green River**	Fantasy 8393
			"Bad Moon Rising"(2)	
			"Green River"(2)	

DATE	POS	WKS	ARTIST—RECORD TITLE		LABEL & NO.
12/20/69	3	24	● 3. **Willy and the Poorboys**		Fantasy 8397
			"Down On The Corner"(3)		
7/25/70	**1(9)**	27	● 4. **Cosmo's Factory**		Fantasy 8402
			"Travelin' Band"(2)		
			"Up Around The Bend"(4)		
			"Lookin' Out My Back Door"(2)		
12/26/70	5	22	● 5. **Pendulum**		Fantasy 8410
			"Have You Ever Seen The Rain"(8)		
5/06/72	12	12	● 6. Mardi Gras		Fantasy 9404
			"Sweet Hitch-Hiker"(6)		
1/06/73	15	6	● 7. Creedence Gold	[G]	Fantasy 9418
			THE CRICKETS - see BUDDY HOLLY/ BOBBY VEE		
			JIM CROCE		
			Born on 1/10/43 in Philadelphia. Killed in a plane crash on 9/20/73 (30) in Natchitoches, LA. Vocalist, guitarist, composer. Recorded with wife Ingrid for Capitol in 1968. Lead guitarist on his hits, Maury Muehleisen, was killed in the same plane crash.		
9/09/72	**1(5)**	42	● 1. **You Don't Mess Around With Jim**		ABC 756
			"You Don't Mess Around With Jim"(8)		
			"Time In A Bottle"(1)		
7/21/73	7	26	● 2. **Life And Times**		ABC 769
			"Bad, Bad Leroy Brown"(1)		
12/22/73	**2(2)**	26	● 3. **I Got A Name**		ABC 797
			"I Got A Name"(10)		
			"I'll Have To Say I Love You In A Song"(9)		
10/12/74	**2(2)**	15	● 4. **Photographs & Memories/His Greatest Hits**	[G]	ABC 835
			BING CROSBY		
			The most popular entertainer of the 20th century's first 50 years. Harry Lillis Crosby was born on 5/2/01 (or 04) in Tacoma, Washington. He and singing partner Al Rinker were hired in 1926 by Paul Whiteman; with Harry Barris they became the Rhythm Boys and gained an increasing following. The trio split from Whiteman in 1930, and Bing sang briefly with Gus Arnheim's band. It was his early-1931 smash with Arnheim, "I Surrender, Dear", which earned Bing a CBS radio contract, and launched an unsurpassed solo career. Over the next three decades the resonant Crosby baritone and breezy persona sold more than 300 million records and was featured in over 50 movies (won Academy Award for "Going My Way", 1944). Bing died of a heart attack on a golf course on 10/14/77.		
12/22/56	21	1	1. A Christmas Sing With Bing Around The World	[X]	Decca 8419
			from the CBS Radio Program - featuring various choirs		
12/02/57	**1(1)**	7	● 2. **Merry Christmas**	[X]	Decca 8128
			first charted in 1945 - the #1 Christmas album of all-time		
			"White Christmas"		
3/31/58	13	2	3. Shillelaghs and Shamrocks		Decca 8207
12/15/58	**2(1)**	4	4. **Merry Christmas**	[X-R]	Decca 8128
12/28/59	17	2	5. Merry Christmas	[X-R]	Decca 8128
12/19/60	9	3	6. **Merry Christmas**	[X-R]	Decca 8128
1/06/62	22	3	7. Merry Christmas	[X-R]	Decca 8128

DATE	POS	WKS	ARTIST—RECORD TITLE	LABEL & NO.
			DAVID CROSBY	
			Born on 8/14/41 in Los Angeles. Vocals, guitar with The Byrds, 1964-68. Frequent troubles with the law due to drug charges.	
3/20/71	**12**	10	● 1. If I Could Only Remember My Name	Atlantic 7203
			with West Coast guests Jerry Garcia, Grace Slick, & Joni Mitchell	
			DAVID CROSBY/GRAHAM NASH	
4/29/72	**4**	14	● 1. Graham Nash/David Crosby	Atlantic 7220
10/25/75	**6**	12	● 2. Wind On The Water	ABC 902
8/21/76	**26**	6	● 3. Whistling Down The Wire	ABC 956
			CROSBY, STILLS & NASH	
			David Crosby, guitar (from The Byrds); Stephen Stills, guitar, bass (from Buffalo Springfield); and Graham Nash, guitar (from The Hollies). Neil Young, guitar (from Buffalo Springfield) joined the trio in summer, 1969.	
7/05/69	**6**	40	● 1. Crosby, Stills & Nash	Atlantic 8229
			CROSBY, STILLS, NASH & YOUNG:	
4/04/70	**1(1)**	38	● 2. Deja Vu	Atlantic 7200
4/24/71	**1(1)**	26	● 3. 4 Way Street [L]	Atlantic 902 [2]
9/14/74	**1(1)**	12	● 4. So Far [G]	Atlantic 18100
			CROSBY, STILLS & NASH:	
7/16/77	**2(4)**	20	▲ 5. CSN	Atlantic 19104
			"Just A Song Before I Go"(7)	
7/31/82	**8**	30	▲ 6. Daylight Again	Atlantic 19360
			"Wasted On The Way"(9)	
			CHRISTOPHER CROSS	
			Born Christopher Geppert on 5/3/51 in San Antonio, Texas. Formed own group with Rob Meurer (keyboards), Andy Salmon (bass) and Tommy Taylor (drums) in 1973.	
3/29/80	**6**	81	▲ 1. Christopher Cross	Warner 3383
			"Ride Like The Wind"(2)	
			"Sailing"(1)	
2/26/83	**11**	11	● 2. Another Page	Warner 23757
			"Think Of Laura"(9)	
			THE CRUSADERS	
			Instrumental jazz-oriented group formed in Houston, as the Swingsters, early 1950's. To California, early 1960's, name changed to Jazz Crusaders. Became The Crusaders in 1971. Included Joe Sample (keyboards), Wilton Felder (reeds) and Stix Hooper (drums).	
12/21/74	**31**	3	● 1. Southern Comfort [I]	Blue Thumb 9002 [2]
9/13/75	**26**	5	2. Chain Reaction [I]	Blue Thumb 6022
7/10/76	**38**	3	3. Those Southern Knights [I]	Blue Thumb 6024
8/12/78	**34**	8	● 4. Images [I]	Blue Thumb 6030
6/23/79	**18**	17	● 5. Street Life [I]	MCA 3094
			with guest vocalist Randy Crawford on "Street Life"	
8/02/80	**29**	4	6. Rhapsody And Blues [I]	MCA 5124
			with guest vocalist Bill Withers on "Soul Shadows"	

DATE	POS	WKS	ARTIST—RECORD TITLE	LABEL & NO.
			CULTURE CLUB	
			Formed in London, England in 1981. Consisted of George "Boy George" O'Dowd (b: 6/14/61), vocals; Roy Hay, guitar, keyboards; Mikey Craig, bass; and Jon Moss, drums. Designer Sue Clowes originated distinctive costuming for the group.	
2/12/83	14	38	▲ 1. Kissing To Be Clever	Epic 38398
			"Do You Really Want To Hurt Me"(2)	
			"Time (Clock Of My Heart)"(2)	
			"I'll Tumble 4 Ya"(9)	
11/12/83	2(6)	38	▲ 2. **Colour By Numbers**	Epic 39107
			"Church Of The Poison Mind"(10)	
			"Karma Chameleon"(1)	
			"Miss Me Blind"(5)	
11/24/84	26	11	▲ 3. Waking Up With The House On Fire	Virgin 39881
5/10/86	32	6	4. From Luxury To Heartache	Virgin 40345
			BURTON CUMMINGS	
			Born on 12/31/47 in Winnipeg, Canada. Lead singer of the Guess Who.	
12/18/76	30	7	1. Burton Cummings	Portrait 34261
			"Stand Tall"(10)	
			# D	
			ROGER DALTREY	
			Born on 3/1/44 in London, England. Formed band, the Detours, who later became the Who. Roger was the Who's lead singer, and starred in the films "Tommy", "Lisztomania", and "McVicar".	
8/30/75	28	5	1. Ride A Rock Horse	MCA 2147
8/30/80	22	6	2. McVicar [S]	Polydor 6284
			Daltrey stars in the film - soundtrack features all members of The Who	
			VIC DAMONE	
			Born Vito Farinola on 6/12/28 in Brooklyn. Vic is among the most popular of postwar ballad singers; he also appeared in several movies and hosted a TV series (1956-57).	
10/13/56	14	8	1. That Towering Feeling!	Columbia 900
			BILL DANA	
			Comedian a/k/a Jose Jimenez.	
8/01/60	15	27	1. My Name...Jose Jimenez [C]	Signature 1013
8/21/61	5	19	2. **Jose Jimenez - The Astronaut (The First Man In Space)** [C]	Kapp 1238
4/07/62	32	2	3. Jose Jimenez In Orbit/Bill Dana On Earth [C]	Kapp 1257
11/17/62	16	5	4. Jose Jimenez Talks To Teenagers Of All Ages [C]	Kapp 1304
3/16/63	30	3	5. Jose Jimenez - Our Secret Weapon [C]	Kapp 1320

DATE	POS	WKS	ARTIST—RECORD TITLE	LABEL & NO.
			VIC DANA	
			Born on 8/26/42 in Buffalo, New York.	Dolton 8034
5/01/65	13	11	1. Red Roses For A Blue Lady	
			"Red Roses For A Blue Lady"(10)	
			RODNEY DANGERFIELD	
			Born Jack Roy in 1921 in New York. Owner of Dangerfield's club in New York City. Comedian and star of the films "Caddyshack", "Easy Money", and "Back To School".	
12/24/83	36	3	1. Rappin' Rodney [C]	RCA 4869
			THE CHARLIE DANIELS BAND	
			Charlie was born on 10/28/37 in Wilmington, North Carolina. Sessionman (guitar, fiddle and banjo) in Nashville for Bob Dylan, Ringo Starr, Pete Seeger, and others. Formed own band in 1971. Began hosting annual jam of Southern bands ("Volunteer Jam") in 1975.	
3/15/75	38	2	● 1. Fire On The Mountain	Kama Sutra 2603
6/19/76	35	3	● 2. Saddle Tramp	Epic 34150
6/30/79	5	27	▲ 3. **Million Mile Reflections**	Epic 35751
			"The Devil Went Down To Georgia"(3)	
8/16/80	11	9	▲ 4. Full Moon	Epic 36571
4/24/82	26	6	● 5. Windows	Epic 37694
			BOBBY DARIN	
			Born Walden Robert Cassotto on 5/14/36 in the Bronx, NY. Died of heart failure on 12/20/73 (37) in Los Angeles. Vocalist, piano, guitar, drums. First recorded in 1956 with "The Jaybirds" (Decca). First appeared on TV, in March, 1956, on the Tommy Dorsey Show. Married to actress Sandra Dee, 1960-67. Nominated for an Oscar for his performance in the film "Captain Newman, MD". Formed own record company, Direction, in 1968.	
10/05/59	7	39	1. **That's All**	Atco 104
			"Mack The Knife"(1)	
			"Beyond The Sea"(6)	
3/07/60	6	50	2. **This Is Darin**	Atco 115
10/17/60	9	22	3. **Darin At The Copa** [L]	Atco 122
6/26/61	18	20	4. The Bobby Darin Story [G]	Atco 131
			"Splish Splash"(3)	
			"Queen Of The Hop"(9)	
			"Dream Lover"(2)	
			DAVID & DAVID	
			Los Angeles duo: David Baerwald & David Ricketts.	A&M 5134
12/06/86	39	2	1. Boomtown	
			JOHN DAVIDSON	
			Born on 12/13/41 in Pittsburgh. Singer, actor. Co-hosted TV's "That's Incredible" and currently hosting the new "Hollywood Squares".	
11/19/66	19	10	1. The Time Of My Life!	Columbia 9380

DATE	POS	WKS	ARTIST—RECORD TITLE	LABEL & NO.
			MAC DAVIS	
			Born on 1/21/42 in Lubbock, Texas. Vocalist, guitar, composer. Worked as regional rep for Vee-Jay, and Liberty Records. Wrote "In The Ghetto", "Don't Cry Daddy", hits for Elvis Presley. Host of his own musical variety TV series, 1974-76. Appearances in several films, including "North Dallas Forty" in 1979.	
9/30/72	11	13	▲ 1. Baby Don't Get Hooked On Me	Columbia 31770
			"Baby Don't Get Hooked On Me"(1)	
8/10/74	13	15	● 2. Stop And Smell The Roses	Columbia 32582
			"Stop And Smell The Roses"(9)	
3/08/75	21	5	● 3. All The Love In The World	Columbia 32927
			MILES DAVIS	
			Born on 5/25/26 in Alton, Illinois. Jazz trumpeter. Began career in 1944 with Billy Eckstine's orchestra. Formed own quintet in 1955. Influenced jazz fusion movement.	
6/27/70	35	4	● 1. Bitches Brew [I]	Columbia 26 [2]
			SAMMY DAVIS, JR.	
			Born on 12/8/25 in New York City. Vocalist, dancer, actor. With father and uncle in dance act, Will Mastin Trio, from early 1940's. First recorded for Decca in 1954. Lost his left eye and had his nose smashed in an auto accident in Las Vegas on 11/19/54; returned to performing January, 1955. Frequent appearances on TV, Broadway, and in films.	
5/14/55	1(6)	27	1. **Starring Sammy Davis, Jr.**	Decca 8118
10/15/55	5	9	2. **Just For Lovers**	Decca 8170
11/17/62	14	9	3. What Kind Of Fool Am I and Other Show-Stoppers	Reprise 6051
5/23/64	26	6	4. The Shelter Of Your Arms	Reprise 6114
3/15/69	24	8	5. I've Gotta Be Me	Reprise 6324
6/17/72	11	8	6. Sammy Davis Jr. Now	MGM 4832
			"The Candy Man"(1)	
			DAWN	
			Vocal trio formed in New York City. Consisted of Tony Orlando, Telma Hopkins and Joyce Vincent. Orlando had recorded solo, 1961-63; Hopkins and Vincent had been backup singers. Orlando was manager for April-Blackwood Music at the time of their first hit. All of their hits produced by Hank Medress (The Tokens) and Dave Appell.	
1/30/71	35	3	1. Candida	Bell 6052
			"Candida"(3)	
			"Knock Three Times"(1)	
5/26/73	30	5	● 2. Tuneweaving	Bell 1112
			"Tie A Yellow Ribbon Round The Ole Oak Tree"(1)	
1/11/75	16	8	3. Prime Time	Bell 1317
5/31/75	20	4	4. He Don't Love You (Like I Love You)	Elektra 1034
			"He Don't Love You (Like I Love You)"(1)	
8/02/75	16	6	● 5. Tony Orlando & Dawn/Greatest Hits [G]	Arista 4045

DATE	POS	WKS	ARTIST—RECORD TITLE	LABEL & NO.
			DORIS DAY	
			Born Doris Kappelhoff on 4/3/22 in Cincinnati. Doris sang briefly with Bob Crosby in 1940 and shortly thereafter became a major star with the Les Brown band ("Sentimental Journey"). Her great solo recording success was soon transcended by Hollywood as Doris became the #1 box office star of the late 50s and early 60s; her 1968-73 TV series was also popular.	
2/05/55	15	2	1. Young At Heart [S]	Columbia 6339
			10" LP - 6 songs by Doris; 2 by Frank Sinatra	
6/25/55	1(17)	28	2. **Love Me Or Leave Me** [S]	Columbia 710
			Doris portrayed singer Ruth Etting in the film	
2/09/57	11	6	3. Day By Day	Columbia 942
5/30/60	26	7	4. Listen To Day	Columbia DD1
			MORRIS DAY	
			Leader of Minneapolis funk group, The Time (formerly Prince's backing band).	
11/16/85	37	3	1. Color Of Success	Warner 25320
			DAZZ BAND	
			Cleveland ultrafunk band, formerly Kinsman Dazz. "Dazz" means "danceable jazz".	
5/29/82	14	10	● 1. Keep It Live	Motown 6004
			"Let It Whip"(5)	
			DEAD OR ALIVE	
			British pop-rock quartet. Pete Burns, lead singer.	
8/17/85	31	6	1. Youthquake	Epic 40119
			"You Spin Me Round (Like A Record)"	
			JIMMY DEAN	
			Born Seth Ward on 8/10/28 in Plainview, Texas. Vocalist, piano, guitar, composer. With Tennessee Haymakers in Washington, DC, 1948. Own Texas Wildcats in 1952. Recorded for Four Star in 1952. Own CBS-TV series, 1957-58; ABC-TV series, 1963-66.	
12/11/61	23	28	1. Big Bad John And Other Fabulous Songs And Tales	Columbia 8535
			"Big Bad John"(1)	
			RONNIE DEAUVILLE	
12/09/57	13	2	1. Smoke Dreams	Era 20002
			DeBARGE	
			Family group from Grand Rapids, MI. Consisted of lead vocalist Eldra (keyboards), Mark (trumpet, saxophone), James (keyboards), Randy (bass) and Bunny DeBarge (vocals). Brothers Bobby and Tommy were in Switch.	
5/28/83	24	7	● 1. All This Love	Gordy 6012
2/04/84	36	5	● 2. In A Special Way	Gordy 6061
4/20/85	19	24	● 3. Rhythm Of The Night	Gordy 6123
			"Rhythm Of The Night"(3)	
			"Who's Holding Donna Now"(6)	
			EL DeBARGE	
			Eldra DeBarge (b: 6/4/61). Lead singer of family group DeBarge.	
6/21/86	24	11	● 1. El DeBarge	Gordy 6181
			"Who's Johnny"(3)	

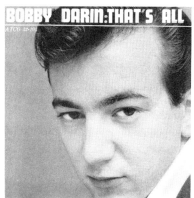

David Crosby and Graham Nash have been musical cohorts for nearly two decades, but they tried a different sort of collaboration on May 16, 1987 when they had a double wedding ceremony at Nash's home in California.

Bobby Darin may have scored over twenty Top 40 singles, but the record for which the late singer will always be remembered is "Mack the Knife," included on his 1959 album, *That's All.*

Doris Day was the singer with Les Brown's band before she passed a screen test and became an actress. In 1948 her first movie, *Romance on the High Seas,* gave her a hit record, "It's Magic." *Calamity Jane* did the same in 1954 with "Secret Love," and Alfred Hitchcock's *The Man Who Knew Too Much* gave Day "Que Sera, Sera" in 1956.

Deep Purple has done extremely well as a band, with six gold albums between 1972 and 1984, but former members have also gone on to great success with such hard-rocking outfits as Rainbow and Whitesnake. Deep Purple's first two American hits were cover versions of songs by Joe South, "Hush," and Neil Diamond, "Kentucky Woman."

Neil Diamond has earned millions of fans and dollars singing his own compositions, but he was originally a songwriter for other artists. The Brooklyn native is responsible for two of the Monkees' most familiar tunes, "I'm a Believer" and "A Little Bit Me, A Little Bit You," and penned material for Jay and the Americans, Sonny and Cher, and the Ronettes as well.

Dion's two 1961 classics, "The Wanderer" and "Runaround Sue," can be heard on the soundtrack of *The Wanderers.* This 1979 film is about a gang of Italian teenagers growing up in the Bronx, a subject that should be quite familiar to Dion DiMucci, formerly of Belmont Avenue.

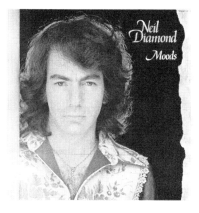

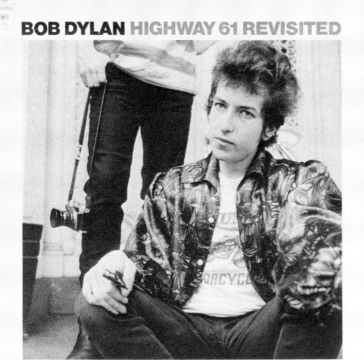

The Doors' *13* (named for the number of cuts on the career compilation) was released just a month after the group's final concert appearance as a quartet in New Orleans, on Nov. 12, 1970. The Doors recorded one final studio album, *L.A. Woman,* before Jim Morrison's departure and death the following year.

Bob Dylan's instrumental credit for "police car" (in addition to guitar, harmonica, and piano) on the back cover of *Highway 61 Revisited* is for a sirenlike whistle he blows on the title track. Joining Dylan in the studio for this 1965 album were Mike Bloomfield (guitar) and Al Kooper (keyboards).

Earth Wind & Fire, led by Maurice White (ex-drummer for the Ramsey Lewis Trio), began its recording career as the Salty Peppers, but achieved success in 1973 when its second Columbia album, *Head to the Sky,* went gold. *Spirit,* Earth Wind & Fire's 1976 album, reached No. 2 and contained "Getaway," the band's third gold single.

Duane Eddy was given his first guitar at the age of 5, but wasn't interested in playing until he was 17. His characteristic twang sound led to over two dozen hit singles, beginning with his first top ten hit in 1958, "Rebel Rouser." He first recorded Henry Mancini's "Peter Gunn" theme in 1960; in 1986, he joined with England's Art of Noise for an entirely different remake of it.

Electric Light Orchestra once appeared on a British television show with masked roadies standing in for three musicians who had left the band. Of the group's original core trio, Roy Wood stayed for only one album before forming Wizzard, and Bev Bevan lasted over a decade before temporarily joining Black Sabbath.

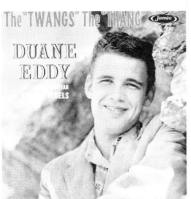

DATE	POS	WKS	ARTIST—RECORD TITLE	LABEL & NO.
			JOEY DEE & THE STARLITERS	
			Born Joseph DiNicola on 6/11/40 in Passaic, NJ. Joey first recorded for the Bonus and Scepter labels in 1960. Joey & The Starliters became the house band at the Peppermint Lounge, New York City in September, 1960. Own club, The Starliter, New York City, 1964. Band then included, for a time, 3 members who later formed the Young Rascals, and Jimi Hendrix, guitar, 1965-66. In films "Hey, Let's Twist" and "Two Tickets To Paris".	
12/25/61	2(6)	36	1. **Doin' The Twist At The Peppermint Lounge** [L]	Roulette 25166
			"Peppermint Twist-Part 1"(1)	
			"Shout"(6)	
3/10/62	18	13	2. Hey, Let's Twist! [S]	Roulette 25168
			with Jo-Ann Campbell, Teddy Randazzo & Kay Armen - filmed at New York's Peppermint Lounge	
			KIKI DEE	
			Born Pauline Matthews on 3/6/47 in Yorkshire, England.	
12/07/74	28	4	1. I've Got The Music In Me	Rocket 458
			LENNY DEE	
			Organist.	
7/09/55	11	6	1. Dee-lightful! [I]	Decca 8114
			DEEP PURPLE	
			British hard-rock band - original lineup: Ritchie Blackmore (guitar), Rod Evans (vocals), Jon Lord (keyboards), Ian Paice (drums) and Nicky Simper (bass). Evans and Simper left in 1969, replaced by Ian Gillan and Roger Glover. Numerous personnel changes from late 1973 on.	
10/12/68	24	10	1. Shades Of Deep Purple	Tetragramm. 102
			"Hush"(4)	
9/04/71	32	3	2. Fireball	Warner 2564
5/06/72	7	30	▲ 3. **Machine Head**	Warner 2607
			"Smoke On The Water"(4)	
2/10/73	15	14	● 4. Who Do We Think We Are!	Warner 2678
5/12/73	6	23	▲ 5. **Made In Japan** [L]	Warner 2701 [2]
3/23/74	9	12	● 6. **Burn**	Warner 2766
			new members: David Coverdale (replaces Gillan), Glenn Hughes (replaces Glover)	
12/14/74	20	6	● 7. Stormbringer	Warner 2832
12/08/84	17	18	▲ 8. Perfect Strangers	Mercury 824003
			reunion of Blackmore/Gillan/Glover/Lord/Paice	
			DEF LEPPARD	
			Heavy-metal quintet formed in Sheffield, England in 1977: Joe Elliott, lead singer; Pete Willis and Steve Clark, lead guitars; Rick Savage, bass; and Rick Allen, drums (lost his left arm in an auto accident on New Year's Eve in 1984). Phil Collen replaced Pete Willis in late 1982.	
10/03/81	38	3	▲ 1. High 'n' Dry	Mercury 4021
2/12/83	2(2)	58	▲ 2. **Pyromania**	Mercury 810308

DATE	POS	WKS	ARTIST—RECORD TITLE	LABEL & NO.
			DELANEY & BONNIE & FRIENDS	
			Delaney Bramlett (b: 7/1/39) & wife Bonnie Lynn Bramlett (b: 11/8/44) & Friends - backing artists who included at various times Leon Russell, Rita Coolidge, Dave Mason, Eric Clapton, Duane Allman, and many others. Friends Bobby Whitlock, Carl Radle and Jim Gordon later became Eric Clapton's Dominos. Delaney & Bonnie dissolved their marriage and group in 1972. Also see The Shindogs.	
4/25/70	29	6	1. Delaney & Bonnie & Friends On Tour with Eric Clapton [L]	Atco 326
			THE DELLS	
			R&B vocal group formed at Thornton Township High School, Harvey, IL. Consisted of Johnny Funches, lead; Marvin Junior, tenor; Verne Allison, tenor; Mickey McGill, baritone; and Chuck Barksdale, bass. First recorded as the El-Rays for Chess, 1953. Recorded for Vee-Jay Records, 1955-65. Group remained intact into the 80s, with exception of Funches, who was replaced by Johnny Carter (ex-Flamingos) in 1960.	
8/10/68	29	5	1. There Is	Cadet 804
			"Stay In My Corner"(10)	
			MARTIN DENNY	
			Born on 4/10/21 in New York City. Composer, arranger, pianist. Originated the "Exotic Sounds of Martin Denny" in Hawaii, featuring Julius Wechter (Baja Marimba Band) on vibes and marimba.	
			THE EXOTIC SOUNDS OF MARTIN DENNY:	
5/04/59	1(5)	61	1. **Exotica** [I]	Liberty 7034
			"Quiet Village"(4)	
9/14/59	8	48	2. **Quiet Village** [I]	Liberty 7122
10/06/62	6	21	3. **A Taste Of Honey** [I]	Liberty 7237
			JOHN DENVER	
			Born John Henry Deutschendorf on 12/31/43 in Roswell, New Mexico. To Los Angeles in 1964. With Chad Mitchell Trio, 1965-68. Wrote "Leaving On A Jet Plane". Starred in the film "Oh, God" in 1978.	
6/19/71	15	31	● 1. Poems, Prayers & Promises	RCA 4499
			"Take Me Home, Country Roads"(2)	
11/11/72	4	27	● 2. **Rocky Mountain High**	RCA 4731
			"Rocky Mountain High"(9)	
6/30/73	16	13	● 3. Farewell Andromeda	RCA 0101
7/06/74	1(1)	37	● 4. **Back Home Again**	RCA 0548
			"Annie's Song"(1)	
			"Back Home Again"(5)	
3/08/75	2(2)	19	● 5. **An Evening With John Denver** [L]	RCA 0764 [2]
			"Thank God I'm A Country Boy"(1)	
10/04/75	1(2)	22	● 6. **Windsong**	RCA 1183
			"I'm Sorry"(1)	
12/06/75	14	6	● 7. Rocky Mountain Christmas [X]	RCA 1201
9/04/76	7	14	▲ 8. **Spirit**	RCA 1694
3/05/77	1(3)	7	● 9. **John Denver's Greatest Hits** [G]	RCA 0374
			"Sunshine On My Shoulders"(1)	
3/05/77	6	7	▲ 10. **John Denver's Greatest Hits, Volume 2** [G]	RCA 2195
2/10/79	25	6	● 11. John Denver	RCA 3075
12/22/79	26	4	▲ 12. A Christmas Together [X]	RCA 3451

DATE	POS	WKS	ARTIST—RECORD TITLE	LABEL & NO.
			JOHN DENVER & THE MUPPETS	
			made top 10 on Billboard's special Christmas charts (1983)	
4/19/80	39	2	13. Autograph	RCA 3449
9/05/81	32	4	● 14. Some Days Are Diamonds	RCA 4055
5/22/82	39	2	● ·15. Seasons Of The Heart	RCA 4256
			DEODATO	
			Born Eumire Deodato Almeida on 6/21/42 in Rio de Janeiro, Brazil. Keyboardist, composer, arranger, producer. Kool & The Gang's producer from 1979-82.	
2/24/73	3	13	1. **Prelude** [I]	CTI 6021
			"Also Sprach Zarathustra (2001)"(2)	
9/08/73	19	10	2. Deodato 2 [I]	CTI 6029
			DEREK & THE DOMINOS	
			A gathering of alumni from Delaney & Bonnie & Friends. Featuring Eric Clapton (Derek), Bobby Whitlock, Jim Gordon and Carl Radle (died on 5/30/80).	
11/28/70	16	19	● 1. Layla	Atco 704 [2]
			with Duane Allman	
			"Layla"(10)	
2/17/73	20	9	● 2. Derek & The Dominos In Concert [L]	RSO 8800 [2]
			RICK DERRINGER	
			Born Richard Zehringer on 8/5/47 in Celina, Ohio. Lead singer and guitarist of The McCoys. Performed on and produced sessions for both Edgar & Johnny Winter's bands.	
1/05/74	25	8	1. All American Boy	Blue Sky 32481
			JOHNNY DESMOND - see GLENN MILLER	
			DEVO	
			Robotic rock group formed in Akron, Ohio, consisting of brothers Mark and Bob Mothersbaugh, brothers Jerry and Bob Casale, and Alan Myers.	
10/11/80	22	16	▲ 1. Freedom Of Choice	Warner 3435
10/17/81	23	6	2. New Traditionalists	Warner 3595
			DEXYS MIDNIGHT RUNNERS	
			Kevin Rowland, leader of 8-piece Birmingham, England band.	
3/19/83	14	12	1. Too-Rye-Ay	Mercury 4069
			"Come On Eileen"(1)	
			DENNIS DeYOUNG	
			Born on 2/18/47 in Chicago. Lead singer and keyboardist for Styx.	
11/10/84	29	4	1. Desert Moon	A&M 5006
			"Desert Moon"(10)	
			NEIL DIAMOND	
			Born on 1/24/41 in Brooklyn. Vocalist, guitar, prolific composer. With Roadrunners folk group, 1954-56. Worked as song-plugger, staff writer in New York City. Wrote for The Monkees' TV show. First recorded for Duel in 1961. Wrote score for "Jonathan Livingston Seagull" film; starred in and composed the music for "The Jazz Singer".	
1/17/70	30	6	● 1. Touching You Touching Me	Uni 73071
			"Holly Holy"(6)	
8/29/70	10	19	● 2. **Neil Diamond/Gold** [L]	Uni 73084
			recorded at the Troubadour in Hollywood	

DATE	POS	WKS	ARTIST—RECORD TITLE		LABEL & NO.
11/21/70	13	14	● 3. Tap Root Manuscript "Cracklin' Rosie"(1)		Uni 73092
11/20/71	11	13	● 4. Stones "I Am...I Said"(4)		Uni 93106
7/22/72	5	24	● 5. **Moods** "Song Sung Blue"(1)		Uni 93136
12/23/72	5	19	● 6. **Hot August Night** recorded 8/24/72 at the Greek Theatre, Los Angeles	[L]	MCA 8000 [2]
3/10/73	36	4	7. Double Gold	[K]	Bang 227 [2]
9/29/73	35	4	● 8. Rainbow reissue of cuts from Uni albums	[K]	MCA 2103
11/17/73	2(1)	16	▲ 9. **Jonathan Livingston Seagull**	[S]	Columbia 32550
6/29/74	29	7	● 10. Neil Diamond/His 12 Greatest Hits	[G]	MCA 2106
11/09/74	3	19	▲ 11. **Serenade** "Longfellow Serenade"(5)		Columbia 32919
7/04/76	4	16	▲ 12. **Beautiful Noise**		Columbia 33965
3/05/77	8	9	▲ 13. **Love At The Greek** recorded August, 1976 at the Greek Theatre	[L]	Columbia 34404 [2]
12/10/77	6	14	▲ 14. **I'm Glad You're Here With Me Tonight**		Columbia 34990
12/16/78	4	12	▲ 15. **You Don't Bring Me Flowers** "You Don't Bring Me Flowers"(1-with Barbra Streisand)		Columbia 35625
1/19/80	10	10	▲ 16. **September Morn**		Columbia 36121
11/29/80	3	32	▲ 17. **The Jazz Singer** "Love On The Rocks"(2) "Hello Again"(6) "America"(8) film is a remake of Al Jolson's 1927 classic	[S]	Capitol 12120
12/05/81	17	11	▲ 18. On The Way To The Sky		Columbia 37628
10/23/82	9	19	▲ 19. **Heartlight** "Heartlight"(5)		Columbia 38359
9/01/84	35	5	● 20. Primitive		Columbia 39199
5/31/86	20	11	● 21. Headed For The Future		Columbia 40368
			DIO Ronnie James Dio, former lead singer of Black Sabbath & Rainbow.		
7/28/84	23	10	▲ 1. The Last In Line		Warner 25100
9/14/85	29	10	● 2. Sacred Heart		Warner 25292
			DION Born Dion DiMucci on 7/18/39 in the Bronx, New York. Formed Dion & The Timberlanes in 1957, then Dion & The Belmonts in 1958. Went solo in 1960. Moved to Miami in 1968. Brief reunion with the Belmonts, 1967 and 1972, periodically since then. Currently records contemporary Christian songs.		
12/04/61	11	21	1. Runaround Sue "Runaround Sue"(1) "The Wanderer"(2)		Laurie 2009
7/28/62	12	12	2. Lovers Who Wander "Lovers Who Wander"(3) "Little Diane"(8)		Laurie 2012

DATE	POS	WKS	ARTIST—RECORD TITLE	LABEL & NO.
2/23/63	29	3	3. Dion Sings His Greatest Hits　　　　　　[G] 2 cuts: Dion; 10 cuts: Dion & The Belmonts "A Teenager In Love"(5) "Where Or When"(3)	Laurie 2013
4/06/63	20	6	4. Ruby Baby "Ruby Baby"(2)	Columbia 8810

DIRE STRAITS

Rock group formed in London by Mark Knopfler (lead vocals, lead guitar, songwriter, producer) and his brother David Knopfler (guitar), with John Illsley (bass) and Pick Withers (drums). David left in late 1979, replaced by Hal Lindes (who left in 1985). Added keyboardist Alan Clark in 1982. Terry Williams replaced drummer Pick Withers in 1983.

DATE	POS	WKS	ARTIST—RECORD TITLE	LABEL & NO.
2/03/79	2(1)	21	▲ 1. **Dire Straits** "Sultans Of Swing"(4)	Warner 3266
7/07/79	11	8	● 2. Communique	Warner 3330
11/22/80	19	17	● 3. Making Movies	Warner 3480
10/16/82	19	8	● 4. Love Over Gold	Warner 23728
6/15/85	1(9)	55	▲ 5. **Brothers In Arms** "Money For Nothing"(1) "Walk Of Life"(7) "So Far Away"	Warner 25264

SENATOR EVERETT McKINLEY DIRKSEN

U.S. senator from Illinois, 1950-69 - died on 9/7/69 (73).

DATE	POS	WKS	ARTIST—RECORD TITLE	LABEL & NO.
1/28/67	16	8	1. Gallant Men　　　　　　　　　　　[T]	Capitol 2643

DISCO TEX & THE SEX-O-LETTES

Disco studio group assembled by producer Bob Crewe. Featuring lead voice Sir Monti Rock III (real name: Joseph Montanez, Jr.), owner of a chain of hairdressing salons.

DATE	POS	WKS	ARTIST—RECORD TITLE	LABEL & NO.
8/23/75	36	3	1. Disco Tex & His Sex-O-Lettes "Get Dancin'"(10)	Chelsea 505

DR. BUZZARD'S ORIGINAL "SAVANNAH" BAND

New York City Thirties-styled disco group formed by brothers Stony Browder and August Darnell (born: Thomas Browder), with Cory Daye, lead singer. Darnell left in 1980 to form Kid Creole & The Coconuts.

DATE	POS	WKS	ARTIST—RECORD TITLE	LABEL & NO.
10/09/76	22	18	● 1. Dr. Buzzard's Original Savannah Band	RCA 1504
3/11/78	36	3	2. Dr. Buzzard's Original Savannah Band Meets King Penett	RCA 2402

DR. JOHN

Born Malcolm "Mac" Rebennack on 11/21/40 in New Orleans. Pioneer 'swamp rock' styled instrumentalist.

DATE	POS	WKS	ARTIST—RECORD TITLE	LABEL & NO.
6/09/73	24	9	1. In The Right Place "Right Place Wrong Time"(9)	Atco 7018

DOKKEN

Los Angeles-based hard rock quartet led by Don Dokken.

DATE	POS	WKS	ARTIST—RECORD TITLE	LABEL & NO.
2/01/86	32	5	1. Under Lock And Key	Elektra 60458

DATE	POS	WKS	ARTIST—RECORD TITLE	LABEL & NO.
			THOMAS DOLBY	
			Born Thomas Morgan Dolby Robertson of British parentage on 10/14/58 in Cairo, Egypt. Master of computer-generated music and self-directed videos. Played keyboards as a member of Bruce Woolley & The Camera Club, and the Lene Lovich band, 1979-80. Began solo career in 1981.	
3/12/83	20	11	1. Blinded By Science [M]	Harvest 15007
			"She Blinded Me With Science"(5)	
4/23/83	13	13	2. The Golden Age Of Wireless	Capitol 12271
4/14/84	35	3	3. The Flat Earth	Capitol 12309
			PLACIDO DOMINGO	
			Spanish operatic tenor.	
12/26/81	18	8	● 1. Perhaps Love	CBS 37243
			with John Denver on the title cut	
			FATS DOMINO	
			Born Antoine Domino on 2/26/28 in New Orleans. Classic New Orleans R&B piano-playing vocalist - heavily influenced by Fats Waller and Albert Ammons. Joined Dave Bartholomew Band, mid-40s. Signed to Imperial record label in 1949. His first recording "The Fat Man" reportedly was a million-seller. Heard on many sessions cut by other R&B artists, including Lloyd Price and Joe Turner. Films "Shake Rattle And Roll", "Jamboree", "The Big Beat", "The Girl Can't Help It". Teamed with co-writer Dave Bartholomew on the majority of his hits. Lives in New Orleans with wife Rosemary and eight children. Frequently appears in Las Vegas. One of the most influential and popular R&B stars.	
11/10/56	18	6	1. Fats Domino - Rock And Rollin'	Imperial 9009
			"I'm In Love Again"(3)	
2/23/57	19	2	2. This Is Fats Domino!	Imperial 9028
			"Blueberry Hill"(2)	
			"Blue Monday"(5)	
3/23/57	17	4	3. Rock And Rollin' With Fats Domino	Imperial 9004
			Fats' first album	
			"Ain't That A Shame"(10)	
			DONOVAN	
			Born Donovan Phillip Leitch on 2/10/46 near Glasgow, Scotland. Singer-songwriter- guitarist. To London at age ten. Worked Newport Folk Festival in 1965. Wrote score for film "If It's Tuesday This Must Be Belgium". Films, "The Pied Piper Of Hamlin", 1972, "Brother Sun, Sister Moon", 1973. In retirement from 1974-81.	
10/30/65	30	4	1. Catch The Wind	Hickory 123
10/15/66	11	12	2. Sunshine Superman	Epic 26217
			"Sunshine Superman"(1)	
3/11/67	14	8	3. Mellow Yellow	Epic 26239
			"Mellow Yellow"(2)	
1/27/68	19	7	● 4. A Gift From A Flower To A Garden	Epic 171 [2]
			deluxe box set of previous 2 albums	
8/10/68	18	14	5. Donovan In Concert [L]	Epic 26386
11/16/68	20	9	6. The Hurdy Gurdy Man	Epic 26420
			"Hurdy Gurdy Man"(5)	

DATE	POS	WKS	ARTIST—RECORD TITLE	LABEL & NO.
3/01/69	4	33	● 7. **Donovan's Greatest Hits** [G]	Epic 26439
10/11/69	23	6	8. Barabajagal	Epic 26481
			with The Jeff Beck Group on 2 cuts	
			"Atlantis"(7)	
7/25/70	16	6	9. Open Road	Epic 30125
5/05/73	25	8	10. Cosmic Wheels	Epic 32156

THE DOOBIE BROTHERS

Group formed in San Jose, CA in 1970. Consisted of Pat Simmons (vocals, guitar), Tom Johnston (lead vocals, guitar, keyboards), John Hartman (percussion) and Dave Shogren (bass). First recorded for Warner in 1971. Shogren replaced by Tiran Porter (bass). Mike Hossack (percussion), added in 1972 (later replaced by Keith Knudsen). Toured England in 1974. Jeff "Skunk" Baxter (slide guitar), formerly with Steely Dan, added in 1974. Michael McDonald (lead vocals, keyboards), added, 1975. Johnston left in 1978. Baxter, Hartman replaced by Cornelius Bumpus (keyboards, saxophone), John McFee (guitar) and Chet McCracken (drums) in 1979. Tom Johnston wrote majority of hits from 1972-75; Michael McDonald from 1976-83. Disbanded in 1983.

DATE	POS	WKS	ARTIST—RECORD TITLE	LABEL & NO.
10/28/72	21	9	▲ 1. **Toulouse Street**	Warner 2634
4/28/73	7	33	▲ 2. **The Captain And Me**	Warner 2694
			"Long Train Runnin'"(8)	
3/23/74	4	30	▲ 3. **What Were Once Vices Are Now Habits**	Warner 2750
			"Black Water"(1)	
5/24/75	4	13	● 4. **Stampede**	Warner 2835
4/24/76	8	10	▲ 5. **Takin' It To The Streets**	Warner 2899
11/27/76	5	14	▲ 6. **Best Of The Doobies** [G]	Warner 2978
9/24/77	10	8	● 7. **Livin' On The Fault Line**	Warner 3045
1/06/79	1(5)	30	▲ 8. **Minute By Minute**	Warner 3193
			"What A Fool Believes"(1)	
10/11/80	3	18	▲ 9. **One Step Closer**	Warner 3452
12/05/81	39	3	● 10. Best Of The Doobies, Volume II [G]	Warner 3612

THE DOORS

Rock group formed in Los Angeles in 1965. Consisted of Jim Morrison (b: 12/8/43, Melbourne, FL; d: 7/3/71, Paris, France), lead singer; Ray Manzarek, keyboards; Robby Krieger, guitar; and John Densmore, drums. Controversial onstage performances by Morrison caused several arrests and cancellations. Morrison left group, 12/12/70. Film "A Feast Of Friends". Group disbanded in 1973.

DATE	POS	WKS	ARTIST—RECORD TITLE	LABEL & NO.
6/24/67	2(2)	53	● 1. **The Doors**	Elektra 74007
			"Light My Fire"(1)	
11/11/67	3	23	● 2. **Strange Days**	Elektra 74014
8/17/68	1(4)	14	● 3. **Waiting For The Sun**	Elektra 74024
			"Hello, I Love You"(1)	
8/09/69	6	2	● 4. **The Soft Parade**	Elektra 75005
			"Touch Me"(3)	
3/14/70	4	12	● 5. **Morrison Hotel/Hard Rock Cafe**	Elektra 75007
8/15/70	8	12	● 6. **Absolutely Live** [L]	Elektra 9002 [2]
12/26/70	25	7	● 7. 13 [G]	Elektra 74079
5/15/71	9	22	● 8. **L.A. Woman**	Elektra 75011
11/27/71	31	5	9. Other Voices	Elektra 75017

DATE	POS	WKS	ARTIST—RECORD TITLE	LABEL & NO.
11/15/80	17	17	▲ 10. The Doors Greatest Hits　　　　　　[G]	Elektra 515
11/26/83	23	7	11. Alive, She Cried　　　　　　　　　[E-L] 　　　　recorded 1968-1970	Elektra 60269
			ANTAL DORATI	
			Conductor.	
3/16/59	3	46	● 1. **Tchaikovsky: 1812 Festival** 　　**Overture/Capriccio Italien**　　[I] 　　with the Minneapolis Symphony Orchestra	Mercury 50054
7/03/61	20	8	2. Beethoven: Wellington's Victory/Leonore 　　Overture No. 3/Prometheus 　　Overture　　　　　　　　　　　[I] 　　with the London Symphony Orchestra	Mercury 9000
			JIMMY DORSEY	
			Jimmy was born on 2/29/04 in Shenandoah, PA; died of cancer on 6/12/57. Great alto sax & clarinet soloist and bandleader beginning in 1935.	
10/07/57	19	4	1. The Fabulous Jimmy Dorsey 　　8 of 12 cuts were recorded after Jimmy's death 　　*"So Rare"*(2)	Fraternity 1008
			THE TOMMY DORSEY ORCHESTRA	
			Tommy was born on 11/19/05 in Mahanoy City, PA; choked to death on 11/26/56. Great trombonist and bandleader beginning in 1935. Tommy and brother Jimmy recorded together as the Dorsey Brothers Orchestra from 1928-35, reunited 1953-56. Hosted musical variety TV show, 1954-56. Warren Covington fronted band after Tommy's death.	
6/01/59	38	2	1. Tea For Two Cha Chas　　　　　　　[I] 　　band led by Warren Covington	Decca 8842
			TOMMY & JIMMY DORSEY	
5/19/58	15	6	1. The Fabulous Dorseys In Hi-Fi　　　[I] 　　Tommy Dorsey & his orchestra featuring Jimmy Dorsey	Columbia 1190
			DOUBLE	
			Euro-pop quartet from Germany. Led by Kurt Maloo & Felix Haug.	
9/13/86	30	6	1. Blue	A&M 5133
			CARL DOUGLAS	
			Born in Jamaica, West Indies.	
1/25/75	37	2	1. Kung Fu Fighting And Other Great Love 　　Songs 　　*"Kung Fu Fighting"*(1)	20th Century 464
			RONNIE DOVE	
			Born on 9/7/40 in Herndon, Virginia; discovered while singing in Baltimore. Nearly all of Ronnie's hits were produced by Phil Kahl (V.P. of Diamond Records).	
6/04/66	35	6	1. The Best Of Ronnie Dove　　　　　[G]	Diamond 5005
			CARMEN DRAGON	
			Carmen conducted the Capitol Symphony Orchestra. Died on 3/28/84 (69). Father of Daryl Dragon (of Captain & Tennille). Also see Leonard Pennario.	
4/28/62	36	3	1. Nightfall　　　　　　　　　　　[I] 　　classical melodies	Capitol 8575

DATE	POS	WKS	ARTIST—RECORD TITLE	LABEL & NO.
			THE DRAMATICS	
			Soul group from Detroit. First recorded for Wingate as the Dynamics, 1966. Members in 1971: Ron Banks (lead singer), William Howard, Larry Demps, Willie Ford and Elbert Wilkins. Howard and Wilkins replaced by L.J. Reynolds and Lenny Mayes, 1973.	
3/04/72	20	11	1. Whatcha See Is Whatcha Get	Volt 6018
			"Whatcha See Is Whatcha Get"(9)	
			"In The Rain"(5)	
5/17/75	31	3	2. The Dramatic Jackpot	ABC 867
			THE DREAM ACADEMY	
			English trio: Nick Laird-Clowes (guitar/vocals), Gilbert Gabriel (keyboards), Kate St. John (vocals/oboe/saxophone).	
2/08/86	20	9	1. The Dream Academy	Warner 25265
			"Life In A Northern Town"(7)	
			THE DRIFTERS	
			Vocal group formed to showcase lead singer Clyde McPhatter on Atlantic in 1953. Included Gerhart and Andrew Thrasher, Bill Pinkney and McPhatter who went solo in 1955. Group continued with various lead singers until 1958. In 1958, manager George Treadwell disbanded the group and brought in The Five Crowns and renamed them The Drifters. The majority of The Drifters' pop hits were sung by 3 different lead singers: Ben E. King, 1959-60; Rudy Lewis, 1961-63; and Johnny Moore, 1957, and 1963-66. Rudy died of a heart attack in summer of 1964. Many personnel changes throughout career and several groups have used the name in later years.	
11/07/64	40	2	1. Under The Boardwalk	Atlantic 8099
			"On Broadway"(9)	
			"Under The Boardwalk"(4)	
			EDDY DUCHIN - see CARMEN CAVALLARO	
			GEORGE DUKE	
			Born on 1/12/46 in San Rafael, CA. Top jazz/rock keyboardist. Played with Jean-Luc Ponty, the Mothers of Invention, and Cannonball Adderley's band.	
12/03/77	25	8	● 1. Reach For It	Epic 34883
7/08/78	39	1	2. Don't Let Go	Epic 35366
6/06/81	33	8	3. The Clarke/Duke Project	Epic 36918
			STANLEY CLARKE/GEORGE DUKE	
			DUKES OF DIXIELAND	
			Dixieland jazz combo.	
9/09/57	6	26	1. Marching Along With The Dukes Of Dixieland, Vol. 3 [I]	Audio Fidel. 1851
12/11/61	10	21	2. The Best Of The Dukes Of Dixieland [G-I]	Audio Fidel. 1956
			DURAN DURAN	
			Romantic-styled band formed in Birmingham, England in 1980. Consisted of Simon LeBon (b: 10/27/58), vocals; Andy Taylor (b: 2/16/61), guitar; Nick Rhodes (b: 6/8/62), keyboards; John Taylor (b:	

DATE	POS	WKS	ARTIST—RECORD TITLE	LABEL & NO.
			6/20/60), bass; and Roger Taylor (b: 4/26/60), drums. Named after villain in the Jane Fonda film "Barbarella". None of the Taylors are related. MTV appearances helped spread group's popularity. Andy Taylor and John Taylor recorded with The Power Station, 1985; LeBon, Rhodes & Roger Taylor recorded as Arcadia in 1985. As of 1986, group now a trio: LeBon, Rhodes and John Taylor.	
1/29/83	6	21	▲ 1. **Rio**	Harvest 12211
			"Hungry Like The Wolf"(3)	
7/02/83	10	14	▲ 2. **Duran Duran** [R]	Capitol 12158
			their first album, released in 1981	
			"Is There Something I Should Know"(4)	
12/10/83	8	41	▲ 3. **Seven And The Ragged Tiger**	Capitol 12310
			"Union Of The Snake"(3)	
			"New Moon On Monday"(10)	
			"The Reflex"(1)	
12/08/84	4	17	▲ 4. **Arena** [L]	Capitol 12374
			"The Wild Boys"(2)	
12/20/86	12	14	▲ 5. **Notorious**	Capitol 12540
			"Notorious"(2)	
			JIMMY DURANTE	
			Much-beloved comedian who started on vaudeville and became star of many Broadway shows and movies as well as his own TV show (1954-56); the great "Schnozzola" died on 1/29/80 (86).	
10/26/63	30	4	1. **September Song**	Warner 1506
			serious singing by the great comedian	
			BOB DYLAN	
			Born Robert Allen Zimmerman on 5/24/41 in Duluth, Minnesota. Singer-songwriter- guitarist-harmonica player. Took stage name from poet, Dylan Thomas. To New York City in December, 1960. Worked Greenwich Village folk clubs. Signed to Columbia Records in October, 1961. Innovator of folk-rock style, 1965. Motorcycle crash on 7/29/66 led to short retirement. Films "Don't Look Back", 1965, "Eat The Document", 1969, "Pat Garrett And Billy The Kid", 1973. Toured with Rolling Thunder Revue, 1976. Made film "Renaldo And Clara", 1978. Became a born-again Christian in 1979, songs reflecting his new faith. One of rock music's most influential artists.	
9/28/63	22	14	● 1. The Freewheelin' Bob Dylan	Columbia 8786
3/28/64	20	5	2. The Times They Are A-Changin'	Columbia 8905
5/15/65	6	32	● 3. **Bringing It All Back Home**	Columbia 9128
10/09/65	3	24	● 4. **Highway 61 Revisited**	Columbia 9189
			"Like A Rolling Stone"(2)	
8/06/66	9	15	● 5. **Blonde On Blonde**	Columbia 841 [2]
			"Rainy Day Women #12 & 35"(2)	
5/20/67	10	21	▲ 6. **Bob Dylan's Greatest Hits** [G]	Columbia 9463
			"Positively 4th Street"(7)	
2/10/68	2(4)	21	● 7. **John Wesley Harding**	Columbia 9604
5/03/69	3	31	▲ 8. **Nashville Skyline**	Columbia 9825
			"Lay Lady Lay"(7)	
7/11/70	4	12	● 9. **Self Portrait**	Columbia 30050 [2]
11/14/70	7	12	● 10. **New Morning**	Columbia 30290

DATE	POS	WKS	ARTIST—RECORD TITLE	LABEL & NO.
12/11/71	**14**	17	▲ 11. Bob Dylan's Greatest Hits, Vol. II [G]	Columbia 31120 [2]
9/01/73	**16**	14	12. Pat Garrett & Billy The Kid [S]	Columbia 32460
			Dylan appeared as Alias in the film - (3 vocals by Dylan)	
1/05/74	**17**	7	● 13. Dylan [K]	Columbia 32747
			outtake recordings from 1969-70	
2/09/74	**1**(4)	12	● 14. **Planet Waves**	Asylum 1003
			with The Band	
7/20/74	**3**	10	● 15. **Before The Flood** [L]	Asylum 201 [2]
			the Bob Dylan/Band concert tour	
2/08/75	**1**(2)	14	● 16. **Blood On The Tracks**	Columbia 33235
8/02/75	**7**	9	17. **The Basement Tapes** [E]	Columbia 33682 [2]
			recorded at Big Pink in Woodstock with The Band in 1967	
1/24/76	**1**(5)	17	▲ 18. **Desire**	Columbia 33893
10/09/76	**17**	5	● 19. Hard Rain [L]	Columbia 34349
			recorded during his tour, the "Rolling Thunder Revue"	
7/15/78	**11**	8	● 20. Street-Legal	Columbia 35453
5/19/79	**13**	7	21. Bob Dylan At Budokan [L]	Columbia 36067 [2]
			recorded in Japan on 3/1/78	
9/15/79	**3**	13	▲ 22. **Slow Train Coming**	Columbia 36120
7/19/80	**24**	5	23. Saved	Columbia 36553
9/19/81	**33**	3	24. Shot Of Love	Columbia 37496
11/26/83	**20**	10	● 25. Infidels	Columbia 38819
6/29/85	**33**	6	26. Empire Burlesque	Columbia 40110
1/11/86	**33**	2	27. Biograph [K]	Columbia 38830 [5]
			53-song collection from 1962-81 (18 songs previously unreleased)	

E

EAGLES

Formed in Los Angeles in 1971. Consisted of Glenn Frey (vocals, guitar), Bernie Leadon (guitar), Randy Meisner (bass) and Don Henley (drums). Meisner had founded Poco; Leadon had been in the Flying Burrito Brothers; and Frey and Henley were with Linda Ronstadt. Debut album recorded in England in 1972. Don Felder (guitar) added in 1975. Leadon replaced by Joe Walsh in 1975; and Meisner replaced by Timothy B. Schmit in 1977. Disbanded in 1982.

DATE	POS	WKS	ARTIST—RECORD TITLE	LABEL & NO.
7/22/72	**22**	7	● 1. Eagles	Asylum 5054
			"Witchy Woman"(9)	
4/27/74	**17**	24	● 2. On The Border	Asylum 1004
			"Best Of My Love"(1)	
6/28/75	**1**(5)	43	● 3. **One Of These Nights**	Asylum 1039
			"One Of These Nights"(1)	
			"Lyin' Eyes"(2)	
			"Take It To The Limit"(4)	
3/06/76	**1**(5)	57	▲ 4. **Eagles/Their Greatest Hits 1971-1975** [G]	Asylum 1052
12/25/76	**1**(8)	32	▲ 5. **Hotel California**	Asylum 1084
			"New Kid In Town"(1)	
			"Hotel California"(1)	

DATE	POS	WKS	ARTIST—RECORD TITLE	LABEL & NO.
10/20/79	1(9)	36	▲ 6. **The Long Run**	Asylum 508
			"Heartache Tonight"(1)	
			"The Long Run"(8)	
			"I Can't Tell You Why"(8)	
11/29/80	6	16	▲ 7. **Eagles Live** [L]	Asylum 705 [2]

EARTH, WIND & FIRE

R&B group formed in Los Angeles in 1969, by Chicago-bred Maurice White (b: 12/19/41, Memphis), lead vocals, percussion, kalimba, songwriter, producer. Co-lead singer Philip Bailey joined in 1972. White had been a session drummer for Chess Records and with the Ramsey Lewis Trio, 1966-1969. Group generally contained 8-10 members, with frequent personnel shuffling. In films "Sgt. Pepper's Lonely Hearts Club Band", and "That's The Way Of The World".

DATE	POS	WKS	ARTIST—RECORD TITLE	LABEL & NO.
7/14/73	27	10	● 1. Head To The Sky	Columbia 32194
4/13/74	15	18	▲ 2. Open Our Eyes	Columbia 32712
3/22/75	1(3)	29	▲ 3. **That's The Way Of The World** [S]	Columbia 33280
			group portrayed a rock band in the film	
			"Shining Star"(1)	
12/13/75	1(3)	21	▲ 4. **Gratitude** [L]	Columbia 33694 [2]
			contains some studio cuts	
			"Sing A Song"(5)	
10/16/76	2(2)	18	▲ 5. **Spirit**	Columbia 34241
12/10/77	3	18	▲ 6. **All 'N All**	Columbia 34905
12/02/78	6	18	▲ 7. **The Best Of Earth, Wind & Fire, Vol. I** [G]	ARC 35647
			"Got To Get You Into My Life"(9)	
			"September"(8)	
6/23/79	3	20	▲ 8. **I Am**	ARC 35730
			"Boogie Wonderland"(6)	
			"After The Love Has Gone"(2)	
11/22/80	10	12	● 9. **Faces**	ARC 36795 [2]
11/14/81	5	18	▲ 10. **Raise!**	ARC 37548
			"Let's Groove"(3)	
3/12/83	12	12	● 11. **Powerlight**	Columbia 38367
1/07/84	40	2	12. Electric Universe	Columbia 38980

SHEENA EASTON

Born on 4/27/59 in Glasgow, Scotland. Vocalist, actress. Starred in BBC-TV documentary "The Big Time", playing a singer, 1980. Sang on the opening credits for the James Bond film "For Your Eyes Only".

DATE	POS	WKS	ARTIST—RECORD TITLE	LABEL & NO.
5/02/81	24	8	● 1. Sheena Easton	EMI America 17049
			"Morning Train (Nine To Five)"(1)	
10/01/83	33	9	2. Best Kept Secret	EMI America 17101
			"Telefone (Long Distance Love Affair)"(9)	
11/24/84	15	21	● 3. A Private Heaven	EMI America 17132
			"Strut"(7)	
			"Sugar Walls"(9)	
12/14/85	40	2	4. Do You	EMI America 17173

DATE	POS	WKS	ARTIST—RECORD TITLE		LABEL & NO.
			DUANE EDDY		
			Born on 4/26/38 in Corning, New York. Began playing guitar at age 5. At age 13, moved to Tucson, then to Coolidge, Arizona. To Phoenix in 1955, and then began long association with producer, songwriter Lee Hazlewood. Eddy's backing band, The Rebels, included 3 top session men, Larry Knechtel on piano and Jim Horn and Steve Douglas on sax. Films "Because They're Young", "A Thunder Of Drums", "The Wild Westerners", "The Savage Seven" and "Kona Coast". Married to Jesse Colter, 1962-68. Duane originated the "twangy" guitar sound and is the all-time #1 rock and roll instrumentalist.		
1/19/59	5	72	1. **Have 'Twangy' Guitar-Will Travel** [I]		Jamie 3000
			"Rebel-'Rouser"(6)		
8/17/59	24	13	2. Especially For You... . [I]		Jamie 3006
1/25/60	18	24	3. The "Twangs" The "Thang" [I]		Jamie 3009
12/26/60	11	14	4. 000,000.00 Worth Of Twang [I-G]		Jamie 3014
			"Forty Miles Of Bad Road"(9)		
			"Because They're Young"(4)		
			VINCENT EDWARDS		
			Born Vincento Eduardo Zoine on 7/9/28 in New York City. Stage, film and TV actor. Best known as the star of the TV series "Ben Casey".		
7/21/62	5	11	1. **Vincent Edwards Sings**		Decca 4311
			ELECTRIC FLAG		
			Chicago blues band formed by Mike Bloomfield and Buddy Miles.		
5/11/68	31	5	1. A Long Time Comin'		Columbia 9597
			ELECTRIC LIGHT ORCHESTRA		
			Group formed in Birmingham, England in 1971, by Roy Wood, Bev Bevans and Jeff Lynne of The Move. Wood left after their first album, leaving Lynne as the group's leader. Much personnel shuffling from then on. From a group size of 8 in 1971, the 1986 ELO consisted of 3 members: Lynne (vocals, guitar, keyboards), Bevan (drums) and Richard Tandy (keyboards).		
11/09/74	16	17	● 1. Eldorado		United Art. 339
			"Can't Get It Out Of My Head"(9)		
11/08/75	8	14	● 2. **Face The Music**		United Art. 546
			"Evil Woman"(10)		
7/17/76	32	5	● 3. Ole ELO [K]		United Art. 630
11/13/76	5	44	▲ 4. **A New World Record**		United Art. 679
			"Telephone Line"(7)		
11/26/77	4	21	▲ 5. **Out Of The Blue**		Jet 823 [2]
6/23/79	5	17	▲ 6. **Discovery**		Jet 35769
			"Shine A Little Love"(8)		
			"Don't Bring Me Down"(4)		
12/15/79	30	8	▲ 7. ELO's Greatest Hits [G]		Jet 36310
8/09/80	4	15	▲ 8. **Xanadu** [S]		MCA 6100
			side 1: Olivia Newton-John; side 2: ELO		
			"Xanadu"(8 - with Olivia Newton John)		
8/22/81	16	12	● 9. Time		Jet 37371
			"Hold On Tight"(10)		
8/20/83	36	1	10. Secret Messages		Jet 38490

DATE	POS	WKS	ARTIST—RECORD TITLE	LABEL & NO.
			LARRY ELGART & His Manhattan Swing Orchestra	
			Larry was born on 3/20/22 in New London, Connecticut. Alto saxman in brother Les' band and his own band.	
7/03/82	24	15	▲ 1. Hooked On Swing [I]	RCA 4343
			LES ELGART	
			Les was born on 8/3/18 in New Haven, CT. Trumpeter and bandleader since 1945.	
11/03/56	13	7	1. The Elgart Touch [I]	Columbia 875
8/19/57	14	7	2. For Dancers Also [I]	Columbia 1008
			YVONNE ELLIMAN	
			Born on 12/29/51 in Honolulu, Hawaii. Portrayed Mary Magdalene in the rock opera "Jesus Christ, Superstar". Joined with Eric Clapton during his 1974 comeback tour.	
4/29/78	40	2	1. Night Flight	RSO 3031
			"If I Can't Have You"(1)	
			DUKE ELLINGTON	
			Born Edward Kennedy Ellington on 4/29/1899 in Washington, D.C. Jazz music's leading bandleader, composer and arranger. Died on 5/24/74.	
6/24/57	14	1	1. Ellington At Newport [I-L]	Columbia 934
			recorded at the Newport Jazz Festival on 7/7/56	
			EMERSON, LAKE & PALMER	
			English classical oriented rock trio formed in 1969. Consisted of Keith Emerson (with The Nice), keyboards; Greg Lake (King Crimson), vocals, bass, guitars; and Carl Palmer (Atomic Rooster), drums. Group split up in 1979, with Palmer joining supergroup Asia. Emerson & Lake regrouped in 1986 with new drummer Cozy Powell. Palmer returned in 1987, replacing Powell.	
2/27/71	18	18	● 1. Emerson, Lake & Palmer	Cotillion 9040
7/10/71	9	11	● 2. **Tarkus**	Cotillion 9900
1/29/72	10	12	● 3. **Pictures At An Exhibition** [L]	Cotillion 66666
			based on Mussorgsky's classical composition	
8/05/72	5	20	● 4. **Trilogy**	Cotillion 9903
12/29/73	11	16	● 5. **Brain Salad Surgery**	Manticore 66669
9/14/74	4	11	● 6. **Welcome back, my friends, to the show that never ends, Ladies and Gentlemen-** [L]	Manticore 200 [3]
4/16/77	12	10	● 7. Works, Volume 1	Atlantic 7000 [2]
1/07/78	37	3	● 8. Works, Volume 2	Atlantic 19147
			above 2 albums feature mostly solo material	
			EMERSON, LAKE & POWELL	
6/28/86	23	12	1. Emerson, Lake & Powell	Polydor 829297
			THE EMOTIONS	
			Black female trio from Chicago, consisting of sisters Wanda (lead), Sheila and Jeanette Hutchinson. First worked as child gospel group called the Heavenly Sunbeams. Left gospel, became The Emotions in 1968. Jeanette replaced by cousin Theresa Davis in 1970, and later by sister Pamela.	
7/02/77	7	21	▲ 1. **Rejoice**	Columbia 34762
			"Best Of My Love"(1)	
9/09/78	40	3	● 2. Sunbeam	Columbia 35385

DATE	POS	WKS	ARTIST—RECORD TITLE	LABEL & NO.
			ENGLAND DAN & JOHN FORD COLEY	
			Pop duo from Austin Texas: Dan Seals (b: 2/8/50) and Coley (b: 10/13/51). Dan (brother of Jim Seals of Seals & Crofts) is currently a hot Country artist. Also see Dan Seals.	
9/25/76	**17**	12	● 1. Nights Are Forever	Big Tree 89517
			"I'd Really Love To See You Tonight"(2)	
			"Nights Are Forever Without You"(10)	
			ENGLISH BEAT	
			English sextet led by Ranking Roger & Dave Wakeling of General Public.	
4/09/83	**39**	3	1. Special Beat Service	I.R.S. 70032
			PRESTON EPPS	
			Bongo player from Oakland. Discovered by Original Sound owner, Art Laboe.	
8/15/60	**35**	3	1. Bongo Bongo Bongo [I]	Original Snd. 5002
			DAVID ESSEX	
			Born David Cook on 7/23/47 in London, England. Portrayed Christ in the London production of "Godspell". Star of British films since 1970.	
3/09/74	**32**	3	1. Rock On	Columbia 32560
			"Rock On"(5)	
			EURYTHMICS	
			Synth/pop duo: David Stewart (b: 9/9/52, England), keyboards, guitar, synthesizer, composer; and Annie Lennox (b: 12/25/54, Scotland), vocals, keyboards, flute, composer. Both had been in the Tourists, 1977-1980. First album recorded in Cologne, Germany, with drummer Clem Burke, formerly of Blondie.	
7/16/83	**15**	17	● 1. Sweet Dreams (Are Made Of This)	RCA 4681
			"Sweet Dreams (Are Made Of This)"(1)	
2/11/84	**7**	23	▲ 2. **Touch**	RCA 4917
			"Here Comes The Rain Again"(4)	
6/01/85	**9**	24	▲ 3. **Be Yourself Tonight**	RCA 5429
			"Would I Lie To You?"(5)	
8/16/86	**12**	15	● 4. Revenge	RCA 5847
			THE EVERLY BROTHERS	
			Donald was born on 2/1/37 in Brownie, Kentucky; Philip on 1/19/39 in Chicago. Vocal duo, guitarists, songwriters. Parents were folk and country singers. Don (beginning at age 8) and Phil (age 6) sang with parents through high school. Invited to Nashville by Chet Atkins and first recorded there for Columbia in 1955. Signed to Archie Bleyer's Cadence Records in 1957. Duo split up in July, 1973, and reunited in September, 1983. The #1 duo of the rock era.	
2/10/58	**16**	3	1. The Everly Brothers	Cadence 3003
			"Bye Bye Love"(2)	
			"Wake Up Little Susie"(1)	
5/23/60	**9**	10	2. It's Everly Time!	Warner 1381
			"So Sad (To Watch Good Love Go Bad)"(7)	
8/22/60	**23**	19	3. The Fabulous Style Of The Everly	
			Brothers [K]	Cadence 3040
			"('Til) I Kissed You"(4)	
			"Let It Be Me"(7)	
			"When Will I Be Loved"(8)	

DATE	POS	WKS	ARTIST—RECORD TITLE	LABEL & NO.
12/05/60	9	15	4. **A Date With The Everly Brothers**	Warner 1395
			"Cathy's Clown"(1)	
9/15/62	35	3	5. The Golden Hits Of The Everly Brothers [G]	Warner 1471
			"Ebony Eyes"(8)	
			"Walk Right Back"(7)	
			"Crying In The Rain"(6)	
			"That's Old Fashioned"(9)	
10/27/84	38	3	6. EB 84	Mercury 822431
			EXILE	
			Quintet formed in Kentucky in 1965. J.P. Pennington, lead singer. Currently a hot Country act.	
9/23/78	14	8	● 1. Mixed Emotions	Warner 3205
			"Kiss You All Over"(1)	
			F	
			FABIAN	
			Born Fabian Forte on 2/6/43 in Philadelphia. Discovered at age 14 (because of his good looks and intriguing name) by a chance meeting with Bob Marcucci, owner of Chancellor Records. Began acting career in 1959 with "Hound Dog Man".	
5/18/59	5	18	1. **Hold That Tiger!**	Chancellor 5003
			"Turn Me Loose"(9)	
12/28/59	3	19	2. **Fabulous Fabian**	Chancellor 5005
			BENT FABRIC & His Piano	
			Born Bent Fabricius-Bjerre on 12/7/42 in Copenhagen. Head of Metronome Records in Denmark. Composer, pianist, TV personality and A&R man.	
11/24/62	13	22	1. Alley Cat [I]	Atco 148
			"Alley Cat"(7)	
			THE FABULOUS THUNDERBIRDS	
			Austin, Texas rock and roll quartet. Kim Wilson, lead singer.	
4/26/86	13	25	● 1. Tuff Enuff	CBS Assoc. 40304
			"Tuff Enuff"(10)	
			FACES	
			Rod Stewart (joined by Ron Wood of the Jeff Beck Group) replaced Steve Marriott as leader of the revamped British group, Small Faces, in 1969.	
4/03/71	29	5	1. Long Player	Warner 1892
1/01/72	6	14	● 2. **A Nod Is As Good As A Wink...To A Blind Horse**	Warner 2574
5/12/73	21	7	3. Ooh La La	Warner 2665
			DONALD FAGEN	
			Born on 1/10/48 in Passaic, NJ. Fagen and Walter Becker founded Steely Dan.	
11/06/82	11	10	● 1. The Nightfly	Warner 23696

DATE	POS	WKS	ARTIST—RECORD TITLE	LABEL & NO.
			PERCY FAITH	
			Born on 4/7/08 in Toronto, Canada. Moved to the United States in 1940. Joined Columbia Records in 1950 as conductor-arranger for their leading singers (Tony Bennett, Doris Day, Rosemary Clooney, Johnny Mathis, and others). Died on 2/9/76 (67).	
7/28/56	18	2	1. Passport To Romance [I]	Columbia 880
4/29/57	8	2	2. **My Fair Lady** [I]	Columbia 895
5/25/59	17	14	3. Porgy And Bess [I]	Columbia 8105
1/11/60	7	17	● 4. **Bouquet** [I]	Columbia 8124
11/28/60	7	15	5. **Jealousy** [I]	Columbia 8292
1/09/61	6	16	6. **Camelot** [I]	Columbia 8370
11/06/61	38	7	7. Mucho Gusto! More Music Of Mexico [I]	Columbia 8439
4/14/62	26	5	8. Bouquet Of Love [I]	Columbia 8481
6/29/63	12	13	● 9. Themes for Young Lovers [I]	Columbia 8823
			MARIANNE FAITHFULL	
			English songstress. Discovered by Rolling Stones' manager, Andrew Loog Oldham. Involved in a long, tumultuous relationship with Mick Jagger. Acted in several stage and screen productions.	
8/14/65	12	15	1. Marianne Faithfull	London 423
			FALCO	
			Falco (Johann Holzel) was born in Vienna, Austria.	
3/15/86	3	18	● 1. **Falco 3**	A&M 5105
			"Rock Me Amadeus"(1)	
			EILEEN FARRELL	
			Operatic soprano.	
1/09/61	15	7	1. I've Got A Right To Sing The Blues	Columbia 1465
			FASTWAY	
			British rock trio led by Fast Eddie Clarke (Motorhead).	
8/13/83	31	6	1. Fastway	Columbia 38662
			JOSE FELICIANO	
			Born on 9/10/45 in Puerto Rico. Blind since birth, Jose moved with his family to New York City at the age of 5. Virtuoso acoustic guitarist.	
8/17/68	2(3)	26	● 1. **Feliciano!**	RCA 3957
			"Light My Fire"(3)	
1/11/69	24	4	2. Souled	RCA 4045
8/02/69	16	13	● 3. Feliciano/10 To 23	RCA 4185
			featuring a recording by Jose at age 10	
1/03/70	29	4	● 4. Alive Alive-O! [L]	RCA 6021 [2]
			in concert at the London Palladium	
			FREDDY FENDER	
			Born Baldermar Huerta on 6/4/37 in San Benito, Texas. Mexican-American singer, guitarist.	
6/07/75	20	11	● 1. Before The Next Teardrop Falls	ABC/Dot 2020
			"Before The Next Teardrop Falls"(1)	
			"Wasted Days And Wasted Nights"(8)	
			MAYNARD FERGUSON	
			Born on 5/4/28 in Quebec, Canada. Moved to the United States in 1949. Played trumpet for Charlie Barnet and then Stan Kenton's Band (1950-53).	
5/21/77	22	7	● 1. Conquistador [I]	Columbia 34457

DATE	POS	WKS	ARTIST—RECORD TITLE	LABEL & NO.
			FERRANTE & TEICHER	
			Piano duo: Arthur Ferrante (b: 9/7/21, New York City) and Louis Teicher (b: 8/24/24, Wilkes-Barre, PA). Met as children while attending the Juilliard School.	
12/11/61	**10**	27	1. **West Side Story & Other Motion Picture & Broadway Hits** [I]	United Art. 6166
			"Tonight"(8)	
12/25/61	**23**	7	2. Love Themes [I]	United Art. 8514
3/24/62	**30**	2	3. Golden Piano Hits [I]	United Art. 8505
			"Exodus"(2)	
3/31/62	**11**	25	4. Tonight [I]	United Art. 6171
7/13/63	**23**	8	5. Love Themes From Cleopatra [I]	United Art. 6290
1/02/65	**35**	6	6. The People's Choice [I]	United Art. 6385
			RICHARD "DIMPLES" FIELDS	
			R&B vocalist; owner of the Cold Duck Music Lounge in San Francisco.	
8/29/81	**33**	4	1. Dimples	Boardwalk 33232
			W.C. FIELDS	
			Classic comedian of American film. Died on 12/25/46 (67).	
2/08/69	**30**	11	1. The Original Voice Tracks From His Greatest Movies [C]	Decca 79164
			THE 5TH DIMENSION	
			Los Angeles-based group formed in 1966. Consisted of Marilyn McCoo, Florence LaRue, Billy Davis, Jr., Lamont McLemore and Ron Townson. McLemore and McCoo had been in the Hi-Fi's; Townson and Davis had been with groups in St. Louis. First called the Versatiles. Davis and McCoo were married, 1969, and recorded as a duo from 1976.	
7/08/67	**8**	11	● 1. **Up, Up And Away**	Soul City 92000
			"Up-Up And Away"(7)	
9/28/68	**21**	8	2. Stoned Soul Picnic	Soul City 92002
			"Stoned Soul Picnic"(3)	
5/31/69	**2**(2)	30	● 3. **The Age Of Aquarius**	Soul City 92005
			"Aquarius/Let The Sunshine In"(1)	
			"Wedding Bell Blues"(1)	
5/23/70	**5**	18	● 4. **The 5th Dimension/Greatest Hits** [G]	Soul City 33900
5/23/70	**20**	16	● 5. Portrait	Bell 6045
			"One Less Bell To Answer"(2)	
3/27/71	**17**	8	● 6. Love's Lines, Angles And Rhymes	Bell 6060
11/13/71	**32**	4	● 7. The 5th Dimension/Live!! [L]	Bell 9000 [2]
10/14/72	**14**	10	● 8. Greatest Hits On Earth [G]	Bell 1106
			greatest hits from both Soul City and Bell labels	
			50 GUITARS OF TOMMY GARRETT	
			A Tommy "Snuff" Garrett production. Guitar solos by Tommy Tedesco.	
1/20/62	**36**	6	1. 50 Guitars Go South Of The Border [I]	Liberty 14005

DATE	POS	WKS	ARTIST—RECORD TITLE	LABEL & NO.
			THE FIREBALLS Rock and roll band formed while high schoolers in Raton, New Mexico: George Tomsco (lead guitar), Dan Trammell (rhythm guitar), Eric Budd (drums), Stan Lark (bass) and Chuck Tharp (vocalist). Tharp quit group in 1960 and was replaced by Jimmy Gilmer (lead vocals, piano). Gilmer was introduced to The Fireballs by their record producer Norman Petty at his famed Clovis, New Mexico studio.	
11/30/63	26	5	1. Sugar Shack *"Sugar Shack"(1)*	Dot 25545
			FIREFALL Mellow rock group formed in Boulder, Colorado by lead singer Rick Roberts.	
7/04/76	28	13	● 1. Firefall *"You Are The Woman"(9)*	Atlantic 18174
9/03/77	27	5	● 2. Luna Sea	Atlantic 19101
12/02/78	27	6	▲ 3. Elan	Atlantic 19183
			THE FIRM British: Jimmy Page (Led Zeppelin/guitar), Paul Rodgers (Bad Company/vocals), Chris Slade (Manfred Mann/drums) and Tony Franklin (keyboards).	
3/09/85	17	16	● 1. The Firm *"Radioactive"*	Atlantic 81239
3/01/86	22	7	2. Mean Business	Atlantic 81628
			FIRST EDITION - see KENNY ROGERS	
			EDDIE FISHER Born Edwin Jack Fisher on 8/10/28 in Philadelphia. Radio work while still in high school; at Copacabana night club, New York, at age 17. With Buddy Morrow, Charlie Ventura, 1946. On Eddie Cantor radio show in 1949. Armed Forces Special Services, 1952-53. Married Debbie Reynolds in 1955. Other marriages to Elizabeth Taylor, and Connie Stevens. Own "Coke Time" 15-minute TV series, 1953-57. Films "All About Eve", 1950; "Bundle Of Joy", 1956; and "Butterfield 8", 1960. Eddie was the #1 idol of bobbysoxers during the early 1950's.	
4/30/55	8	10	1. **I Love You**	RCA 1097
			ELLA FITZGERALD The most honored jazz singer of all time. Ella Fitzgerald was born on 4/25/18 in Newport News, VA. Discovered after winning the Harlem Amateur Hour in 1934, she was hired by Chick Webb and in 1938 created a popular sensation with "A-Tisket, A-Tasket". Following Chick's death in 1939 Ella took over the band for three years. Winner of the Down Beat poll as top female vocalist more than 20 times, she remains among the undisputed royalty of 20th century popular music.	
9/17/55	7	10	1. **Songs from Pete Kelly's Blues**	Decca 8166
			PEGGY LEE & ELLA FITZGERALD	
7/28/56	15	1	2. Ella Fitzgerald sings the Cole Porter Song Book	Verve 4001 [2]
12/15/56	12	2	3. Ella And Louis	Verve 4003

DATE	POS	WKS	ARTIST—RECORD TITLE	LABEL & NO.
			ELLA FITZGERALD & LOUIS ARMSTRONG	
			backing by the Oscar Peterson Trio, plus Buddy Rich	
3/16/57	11	4	4. Ella Fitzgerald sings the Rodgers and Hart Song Book	Verve 4002 [2]
			albums 2 & 4 above arranged and conducted by Buddy Bregman	
9/12/60	11	25	5. Mack The Knife - Ella In Berlin [L]	Verve 4041
1/06/62	35	1	6. Ella In Hollywood [L]	Verve 4052
			THE FIXX	
			London-based techno-pop group: Cy Curnin (lead singer, piano), Jamie West-Oram (guitars), Rupert Greenall (keyboards), Adam Woods (drums) and Dan K. Brown (bass).	
11/26/83	8	28	▲ 1. **Reach The Beach**	MCA 39001
			"One Thing Leads To Another"(4)	
9/15/84	19	10	● 2. Phantoms	MCA 5507
7/05/86	30	8	3. Walkabout	MCA 5705
			ROBERTA FLACK	
			Born on 2/10/39 in Asheville, NC. Grew up in Arlington, VA. Discovered by Les McCann. Signed to Atlantic Records in 1969.	
10/17/70	33	13	● 1. Chapter Two	Atlantic 1569
12/11/71	18	21	● 2. Quiet Fire	Atlantic 1594
3/25/72	1(5)	26	● 3. **First Take**	Atlantic 8230
			"The First Time Ever I Saw Your Face"(1)	
9/01/73	3	14	● 4. **Killing Me Softly**	Atlantic 7271
			"Killing Me Softly With His Song"(1)	
4/19/75	24	5	5. Feel Like Makin' Love	Atlantic 18131
			"Feel Like Makin' Love"(1)	
2/18/78	8	17	● 6. **Blue Lights In The Basement**	Atlantic 19149
			"The Closer I Get To You"(2)	
4/26/80	3	10	● 7. **Roberta Flack & Donny Hathaway**	Atlantic 7216
			"Where Is The Love"(5)	
4/26/80	25	10	● 8. Roberta Flack Featuring Donny Hathaway	Atlantic 16013
9/10/83	25	14	● 9. Born To Love	Capitol 12284
			PEABO BRYSON/ROBERTA FLACK	
			FLASH	
			English rock quartet led by Peter Banks (guitar) & Colin Carter (vocals).	
8/26/72	33	5	1. Flash	Capitol 11040
			FLEETWOOD MAC	
			Formed as a British blues band in 1967 by ex-John Mayall's Bluesbreakers Peter Green (guitar), Mick Fleetwood (drums) and John McVie (bass), along with guitarist Jeremy Spencer. Many lineup changes followed as group headed toward rock super- stardom. Green and Spencer left in 1970. Christine McVie (keyboards) joined in August, 1970. Bob Welch (guitar) joined in April, 1971, stayed thru 1974. Group relocated to California in 1974, whereupon Lindsey Buckingham (guitar) and Stevie Nicks (vocals) joined in January, 1975.	
11/16/74	34	2	1. Heroes Are Hard To Find	Reprise 2196
8/23/75	1(1)	68	▲ 2. **Fleetwood Mac**	Reprise 2225
			Americans Stevie Nicks & Lindsey Buckingham join group	
2/26/77	1(31)	59	▲ 3. **Rumours**	Warner 3010
			"Go Your Own Way"(10)	
			"Dreams"(1)	

DATE	POS	WKS	ARTIST—RECORD TITLE	LABEL & NO.
			"Don't Stop"(3)	
			"You Make Loving Fun"(9)	
11/03/79	4	22	▲ 4. **Tusk**	Warner 3350 [2]
			"Tusk"(8)	
			"Sara"(7)	
1/10/81	14	8	● 5. Fleetwood Mac Live [L]	Warner 3500 [2]
7/24/82	1(5)	21	▲ 6. **Mirage**	Warner 23607
			"Hold Me"(4)	
			THE FLOATERS	
			Detroit soul group.	
7/23/77	10	13	▲ 1. **Floaters**	ABC 1030
			"Float On"(2)	
			A FLOCK OF SEAGULLS	
			British techno-rock quartet - Mike Score, lead singer.	
7/03/82	10	25	● 1. **A Flock Of Seagulls**	Jive 66000
			"I Ran (So Far Away)"(9)	
6/04/83	16	11	2. Listen	Jive 8013
			FOCUS	
			Dutch progressive rock quartet led by guitar virtuoso Jan Akkerman and flutist Thijs Van Leer.	
3/03/73	8	21	● 1. **Moving Waves** [I]	Sire 7401
			"Hocus Pocus"(9)	
6/09/73	35	4	● 2. Focus 3 [I]	Sire 3901 [2]
			DAN FOGELBERG	
			Born on 8/13/51 in Peoria, IL. Vocalist, composer. Worked as folk singer in Los Angeles. With Van Morrison, early 1970's. Session work in Nashville. Toured with the Eagles in 1975.	
1/18/75	17	11	▲ 1. Souvenirs	Full Moon 33137
			Joe Walsh, producer and guitarist	
10/18/75	23	6	● 2. Captured Angel	Full Moon 33499
6/18/77	13	12	▲ 3. Nether Lands	Full Moon 34185
9/23/78	8	13	▲ 4. **Twin Sons Of Different Mothers**	Full Moon 35339
			DAN FOGELBERG & TIM WEISBERG	
12/15/79	3	27	▲ 5. **Phoenix**	Full Moon 35634
			"Longer"(2)	
9/19/81	6	31	▲ 6. **The Innocent Age**	Full Moon 37393 [2]
			"Same Old Lang Syne"(9)	
			"Hard To Say"(7)	
			"Leader Of The Band"(9)	
11/20/82	15	12	▲ 7. Dan Fogelberg/Greatest Hits [G]	Full Moon 38308
2/25/84	15	10	● 8. Windows and Walls	Full Moon 39004
5/25/85	30	5	9. High Country Snows	Full Moon 39616
			JOHN FOGERTY	
			Born on 5/28/45 in Berkeley, CA. Leader of Creedence Clearwater Revival. Although listed as a group, John recorded entirely solo as The Blue Ridge Rangers.	
2/02/85	1(1)	28	▲ 1. **Centerfield**	Warner 25203
			"The Old Man Down The Road"(10)	
10/18/86	26	6	● 2. Eye Of The Zombie	Warner 25449

DATE	POS	WKS	ARTIST—RECORD TITLE	LABEL & NO.
			FOGHAT	
			British rock quartet led by Lonesome Dave Peverett - formerly with Savoy Brown. Settled in New York City in 1975.	
3/16/74	34	3	● 1. Energized	Bearsville 6950
11/30/74	40	2	● 2. Rock And Roll Outlaws	Bearsville 6956
3/06/76	23	7	▲ 3. Fool For The City	Bearsville 6959
12/11/76	36	2	● 4. Night Shift	Bearsville 6962
9/24/77	11	9	▲ 5. Foghat Live [L]	Bearsville 6971
6/10/78	25	7	● 6. Stone Blue	Bearsville 6977
10/20/79	35	3	7. Boogie Motel	Bearsville 6990
			JANE FONDA - see AEROBICS section	
			FRANK FONTAINE	
			"Crazy Guggenheim" on the Jackie Gleason TV show.	
2/23/63	1(5)	28	● 1. **Songs I Sing On The Jackie Gleason Show**	ABC-Para. 442
			STEVE FORBERT	
			Born in 1955 in Meridian, Mississippi. To New York City in 1976.	
2/02/80	20	6	1. Jackrabbit Slim	Nemperor 36191
			TENNESSEE ERNIE FORD	
			Born Ernest Jennings Ford on 2/13/19 in Bristol, TN. Began career as a disc jockey. Host of musical variety TV shows from 1955-65. America's favorite hymn singer.	
4/28/56	12	3	1. This Lusty Land!	Capitol 700
1/05/57	2(3)	85	● 2. **Hymns**	Capitol 756
5/06/57	5	56	● 3. **Spirituals**	Capitol 818
6/09/58	5	61	● 4. **Nearer The Cross**	Capitol 1005
12/22/58	4	3	● 5. **The Star Carol** [X]	Capitol 1071
12/28/59	7	2	6. **The Star Carol** [X-R]	Capitol 1071
5/02/60	23	26	7. Sing A Hymn With Me	Capitol 1332
			includes a hymn book	
12/31/60	28	1	8. The Star Carol [X-R]	Capitol 1071
			FOREIGNER	
			British/American rock group formed in New York City, 1976. Consisted of Mick Jones, guitar; Lou Gramm, vocals; Ian McDonald, guitar, keyboards; Al Greenwood, keyboards; Ed Gagliardi, bass; and Dennis Elliott, drums. Most of their material was written by Jones (formerly with Spooky Tooth) and Gramm. Reformed in 1980 with Jones, Gramm, Elliott and Rick Wills, bass. Gramm, Gagliardi and Greenwood are from New York.	
5/07/77	4	43	▲ 1. **Foreigner**	Atlantic 18215
			"Feels Like The First Time"(4)	
			"Cold As Ice"(6)	
7/08/78	3	37	▲ 2. **Double Vision**	Atlantic 19999
			"Hot Blooded"(3)	
			"Double Vision"(2)	
9/29/79	5	22	▲ 3. **Head Games**	Atlantic 29999
7/25/81	1(10)	52	▲ 4. **4**	Atlantic 16999
			"Urgent"(4)	
			"Waiting For A Girl Like You"(2)	

Ella Fitzgerald, unanimously acclaimed as America's greatest female jazz singer, has recorded with the Ink Spots (1944), Louis Armstrong (1956), Count Basie (1963), and many others. She recorded hit albums of songs by Rodgers and Hart in 1957 and George and Ira Gershwin in 1964.

Focus was a Dutch jazz-classical-rock quartet led by flautist Thijs Van Leer. Included on the *Moving Waves* album (1973), the group's lone American hit, "Hocus Pocus" (by Focus) presented no small verbal challenge for disc jockeys and record buyers alike.

Jane Fonda's Workout Record (a platinum release featuring music by the Jacksons, REO Speedwagon, and others) is just one of the exercise products that has made Fonda the nation's leading physical fitness guru.

Frank Fontaine played Crazy Guggenheim on Jackie Gleason's variety show between 1962 and 1966, mugging wildly in the Great One's "Joe the Bartender" sketches. Fontaine made several albums during that time; *Songs I Sing on the Jackie Gleason Show* spent fifty-three weeks on the charts and hit No. 1 in March 1963.

The Four Seasons' first record, "Sherry," reached No. 1 in September 1962 and remained there five weeks. The group's next hit, "Big Girls Don't Cry," became No. 1 one month later. The New Jersey quartet had six more Top 40 records before the end of the following year.

Freddie & the Dreamers was part of the original British Invasion, scoring four Top 40 hits in America in 1965 and starting a dance craze called the Freddie. Although the group formed in Manchester in 1959, singer Freddie Garrity worked as a milkman until it was signed four years later. *Freddie & the Dreamers* was the only one of the group's six American albums to make the Top 40.

Gerry and the Pacemakers offered, in 1962 and 1963, serious competition for another (better-remembered) Liverpool band. The group was managed by Brian Epstein, produced by George Martin, and had No. 1 British hits with its first three singles, a unique feat.

Eydie Gorme, a Bronx native, met her future husband when she and Steve Lawrence were both regular performers on "The Tonight Show," during the period Steve Allen hosted it in the mid-1950s. Although the two vocalists, who married in 1957, have generally recorded together, Gorme had a big solo hit in 1963, "Blame It on the Bossa Nova."

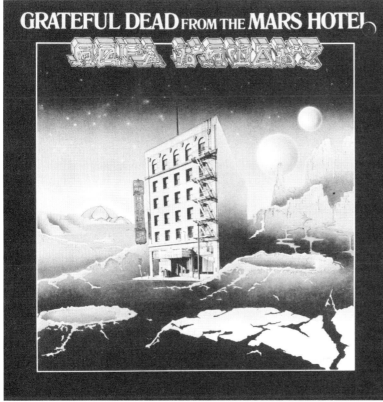

The Grateful Dead grew out of a legendary San Francisco band called the Warlocks. The group became the Grateful Dead in 1965, taking its name from an Egyptian prayer. *From the Mars Hotel* (1974) was the second album released by the band on its own Grateful Dead record label.

Hair, billed as a "tribal love-rock musical," premiered in New York on Oct. 29, 1967 and opened on Broadway in April 1968. The cast album spent three years on the charts, and it is estimated that by the end of 1970, over 800 recordings of material from the show's score had been issued around the world.

Isaac Hayes' first band, in the 1950s, was called Sir Isaac and the DooDads; since then the Tennessee native has done everything from session work on Otis Redding records to co-writing such classics as "Soul Man." He also won an Academy Award and two Grammys for "The Theme from *Shaft*" and played a recurring role on "The Rockford Files" in the 1970s.

DATE	POS	WKS	ARTIST—RECORD TITLE	LABEL & NO.
12/25/82	**10**	12	● 5. **Foreigner Records** [G]	Atlantic 80999
1/05/85	**4**	24	▲ 6. **Agent Provocateur**	Atlantic 81999
			"I Want To Know What Love Is"(1)	
			"That Was Yesterday"	

PETE FOUNTAIN

Born on 7/3/30 in New Orleans. Clarinetist. With Al Hirt, 1956-57. Performed on Lawrence Welk's weekly TV show, 1957-59. Own club in New Orleans, The French Quarter Inn.

DATE	POS	WKS	ARTIST—RECORD TITLE	LABEL & NO.
2/22/60	**8**	43	1. **Pete Fountain's New Orleans** [I]	Coral 57282
5/09/60	**31**	4	2. Pete Fountain Day [I-L]	Coral 57313
8/04/62	**30**	4	3. Music From Dixie [I]	Coral 57401

THE FOUR FRESHMEN

Jazz-styled vocal and instrumental group formed in 1948 while at Arthur Jordan Conservatory of Music in Indianapolis: brothers Ross & Don Barbour, their cousin Bob Flanigan and Ken Errair.

DATE	POS	WKS	ARTIST—RECORD TITLE	LABEL & NO.
2/25/56	**6**	33	1. **Four Freshmen and 5 Trombones**	Capitol 683
10/13/56	**11**	8	2. **Freshmen Favorites** [G]	Capitol 743
3/02/57	**9**	7	3. **4 Freshmen and 5 Trumpets**	Capitol 763
11/18/57	**25**	1	4. Four Freshmen and Five Saxes	Capitol 844
9/29/58	**17**	1	5. The Four Freshmen In Person [L]	Capitol 1008
11/03/58	**11**	6	6. Voices In Love	Capitol 1074
1/11/60	**40**	1	7. The Four Freshmen and Five Guitars	Capitol 1255

THE FOUR LADS

Vocal group from Toronto, Canada: Bernie Toorish (lead tenor), Jimmie Arnold (second tenor), Frankie Busseri (baritone) and Connie Codarini (bass). Sang in choir at St. Michael's Cathedral in Toronto. Worked local hotels and clubs. Worked Le Ruban Bleu in New York City. Signed as backup singers by Columbia in 1950. Backed Johnnie Ray on his #1 hit "Cry".

DATE	POS	WKS	ARTIST—RECORD TITLE	LABEL & NO.
10/06/56	**14**	2	1. On The Sunny Side	Columbia 912

THE FOUR PREPS

Vocal group formed while at Hollywood High School: Bruce Belland, Glen Larson, Ed Cobb and Marvin Ingraham. Belland was later in duo with Dave Somerville of the Diamonds.

DATE	POS	WKS	ARTIST—RECORD TITLE	LABEL & NO.
9/04/61	**8**	13	1. **The Four Preps On Campus** [L]	Capitol 1566
5/12/62	**40**	1	2. Campus Encore [L]	Capitol 1647

THE 4 SEASONS

Vocal group formed in Newark, New Jersey. In 1955, lead singer Frankie Valli (Francis Castelluccio) formed the Variatones with brothers Nick and Tommy DeVito, and Hank Majewski. Changed name to The Four Lovers in 1956. Bob Gaudio (of The Royal Teens) joined as keyboardist and songwriter in 1959, replacing Nick DeVito. Nick Massi replaced Majewski, and their 1961 line-up was set: Valli, Gaudio, Massi and Tommy DeVito. Group had been doing session work for their producer Bob Crewe and took their new name from a New Jersey bowling alley, The Four Seasons. In 1965, Nick Massi was replaced by the group's arranger Charlie Callelo and then by Joe Long. In 1971, Tommy DeVito retired, and Gaudio left (as a performer) the following year. Numerous personnel changes from then on.

DATE	POS	WKS	ARTIST—RECORD TITLE	LABEL & NO.
11/03/62	**6**	20	1. **Sherry & 11 others**	Vee-Jay 1053
			"Sherry"(1)	
			"Big Girls Don't Cry"(1)	
10/05/63	**15**	11	2. Golden Hits of the 4 Seasons [G]	Vee-Jay 1065

DATE	POS	WKS	ARTIST—RECORD TITLE		LABEL & NO.
4/04/64	6	10	3. **Dawn (Go Away) and 11 other great songs**		Philips 124
			"Dawn (Go Away)"(3)		
8/15/64	7	13	4. **Rag Doll**		Philips 146
			"Ronnie"(6)		
			"Rag Doll"(1)		
			"Save It For Me"(10)		
1/15/66	10	22	● 5. **The 4 Seasons' Gold Vault of Hits**	[G]	Philips 196
			"Let's Hang On!"(3)		
1/07/67	22	10	● 6. 2nd Vault Of Golden Hits	[G]	Philips 221
			9 of 12 cuts are Vee-Jay hits		
			"I've Got You Under My Skin"(9)		
7/22/67	8	2	7. **Big Girls Don't Cry and Twelve others**		Vee-Jay 1056
			"Walk Like A Man"(1)		
7/22/67	37	2	8. New Gold Hits		Philips 243
			"Tell It To The Rain"(10)		
			"C'mon Marianne"(9)		
3/01/69	37	2	● 9. Edizione D'Oro (The 4 Seasons Gold Edition-29 Gold Hits)	[G]	Philips 6501 [2]
1/24/76	38	2	10. Who Loves You		Warner 2900
			"Who Loves You"(3)		
			"December, 1963 (Oh, What A Night)"(1)		

FOUR TOPS

R&B group formed in their native Detroit in 1954 as the Four Aims. Consisted of Levi Stubbs (lead singer), Renaldo "Obie" Benson, Lawrence Payton and Abdul "Duke" Fakir. First recorded for Chess in 1956, then Red Top and Columbia, before signing with Motown in 1963. Group has had no personnel changes since its formation. Stubbs is the voice of Audrey II (the voracious vegetation) in the film "Little Shop of Horrors".

DATE	POS	WKS	ARTIST—RECORD TITLE		LABEL & NO.
1/08/66	20	8	1. Four Tops Second Album		Motown 634
			"I Can't Help Myself"(1)		
			"It's The Same Old Song"(5)		
10/29/66	32	5	2. 4 Tops On Top		Motown 647
1/28/67	17	18	3. Four Tops Live!	[L]	Motown 654
8/19/67	11	14	4. Four Tops Reach Out		Motown 660
			"Reach Out I'll Be There"(1)		
			"Standing In The Shadows Of Love"(6)		
			"Bernadette"(4)		
10/07/67	4	37	5. **The Four Tops Greatest Hits**	[G]	Motown 662
6/27/70	21	14	6. Still Waters Run Deep		Motown 704
12/30/72	33	3	7. Keeper Of The Castle		Dunhill 50129
			"Keeper Of The Castle"(10)		
			"Ain't No Woman (Like The One I've Got)"(4)		
10/31/81	37	4	8. Tonight!		Casablanca 7258

FOXY

Miami-based Latino dance band. Four of 5 members came to Florida with the Cuban emigrees of 1959.

DATE	POS	WKS	ARTIST—RECORD TITLE		LABEL & NO.
8/26/78	12	12	1. Get Off		Dash 30005
			"Get Off"(9)		
4/28/79	29	6	2. Hot Numbers		Dash 30010

DATE	POS	WKS	ARTIST—RECORD TITLE	LABEL & NO.
			PETER FRAMPTON	
			Born on 4/22/50 in Beckenham, England. Vocalist, guitarist, composer. Joined British band The Herd at age 16, before forming Humble Pie in 1969, which he left in 1971 to form Frampton's Camel.	
5/10/75	32	3	● 1. Frampton	A&M 4512
2/14/76	1(10)	56	▲ 2. **Frampton Comes Alive!** [L]	A&M 3703 [2]
			"Show Me The Way"(6)	
			"Do You Feel Like We Do"(10)	
6/25/77	2(4)	15	▲ 3. **I'm In You**	A&M 4704
			"I'm In You"(2)	
6/30/79	19	7	● 4. Where I Should Be	A&M 3710
			SERGIO FRANCHI	
			Italian tenor.	
12/08/62	17	9	1. Sergio Franchi	RCA 2640
			CONNIE FRANCIS	
			Born Concetta Rosa Maria Franconero on 12/12/38 in Newark, New Jersey. First recorded for MGM in 1955. Films: "Where The Boys Are", "Follow The Boys", "Looking For Love" and "When The Boys Meet The Girls", 1961-65. Connie stopped performing after she was raped on 11/8/74, for which she was awarded $3,000,000 in damages. Began comeback with a performance on "Dick Clark's Live Wednesday" TV show in 1978.	
2/08/60	4	81	1. **Italian Favorites** [F]	MGM 3791
			"Mama"(8)	
2/22/60	17	00	2. Connie's Greatest Hits [G]	MGM 3793
			"Who's Sorry Now"(4)	
			"My Happiness"(2)	
			"Lipstick On Your Collar"(5)	
			"Frankie"(9)	
12/12/60	9	14	3. **More Italian Favorites** [F]	MGM 3871
9/25/61	39	17	4. More Greatest Hits [G]	MGM 3942
			"Among My Souvenirs"(7)	
			"Everybody's Somebody's Fool"(1)	
			"My Heart Has A Mind Of Its Own"(1)	
			"Many Tears Ago"(7)	
			"Where The Boys Are"(4)	
11/06/61	11	23	5. Never On Sunday and other title songs from motion pictures	MGM 3965
10/27/62	22	2	6. Country Music Connie Style	MGM 4079
			FRANKE & THE KNOCKOUTS	
			Soft rock quintet led by Franke Previte of New Brunswick, New Jersey.	
5/23/81	31	5	1. Franke & The Knockouts	Millennium 7755
			"Sweetheart"(10)	
			FRANKIE GOES TO HOLLYWOOD	
			Rock quintet from Liverpool, England of gay persona; vocals by Holly Johnson and Paul Rutherford.	
12/08/84	33	14	1. Welcome To The Pleasuredome	Island 90232 [2]
			"Relax"(10)	
			"Two Tribes"	

DATE	POS	WKS	ARTIST—RECORD TITLE	LABEL & NO.
			ARETHA FRANKLIN	
			Born on 3/25/42 in Memphis. Daughter of gospel recording artist, Rev. C.L. Franklin, pastor of New Bethel Church in Detroit. Signed to Columbia Records in 1960 by John Hammond, then dramatic turn in style and success after signing with Atlantic and working with producer Jerry Wexler. Appeared in the 1980 film "The Blues Brothers". The all-time Queen of Soul Music.	
4/29/67	2(3)	28	● 1. **I Never Loved A Man The Way I Love You**	Atlantic 8139
			"I Never Loved A Man (The Way I Love You)"(9)	
			"Respect"(1)	
9/02/67	5	19	2. **Aretha Arrives**	Atlantic 8150
			"Baby I Love You"(4)	
2/24/68	2(2)	33	● 3. **Aretha: Lady Soul**	Atlantic 8176
			"A Natural Woman"(8)	
			"Chain of Fools"(2)	
			"(Sweet Sweet Baby) Since You've Been Gone"(5)	
7/20/68	3	20	● 4. **Aretha Now**	Atlantic 8186
			"Think"(7)	
			"I Say A Little Prayer"(10)	
12/07/68	13	9	5. Aretha In Paris [L]	Atlantic 8207
			record at the Olympia Theatre in Paris, France, on 5/7/68	
2/22/69	15	12	6. Aretha Franklin: Soul '69	Atlantic 8212
7/26/69	18	11	7. Aretha's Gold [G]	Atlantic 8227
			"The House That Jack Built"(6)	
2/21/70	17	13	8. This Girl's In Love With You	Atlantic 8248
9/26/70	25	8	9. Spirit In The Dark	Atlantic 8265
6/12/71	7	18	● 10. **Aretha Live At Fillmore West** [L]	Atlantic 7205
10/09/71	19	10	11. Aretha's Greatest Hits [G]	Atlantic 8295
			"Bridge Over Troubled Water"(6)	
			"Spanish Harlem"(2)	
2/26/72	11	17	● 12. Young, Gifted & Black	Atlantic 7213
			"Rock Steady"(9)	
			"Day Dreaming"(5)	
7/01/72	7	11	● 13. **Amazing Grace** [L]	Atlantic 906 [2]
			with James Cleveland & The Southern California Comm. Choir	
8/11/73	30	7	14. Hey Now Hey (The Other Side Of The Sky)	Atlantic 7265
3/30/74	14	11	15. Let Me In Your Life	Atlantic 7292
			"Until You Come Back To Me (That's What I'm Gonna Do)"(3)	
7/04/76	18	11	● 16. Sparkle [S]	Atlantic 18176
9/26/81	36	3	17. Love All The Hurt Away	Arista 9552
9/04/82	23	9	● 18. Jump To It	Arista 9602
8/20/83	36	3	19. Get It Right	Arista 8019
8/10/85	13	35	● 20. Who's Zoomin' Who?	Arista 8286
			"Freeway Of Love"(3)	
			"Who's Zoomin' Who"(7)	
12/13/86	32	8	21. Aretha	Arista 8442
			"I Knew You Were Waiting (For Me)"(1-with George Michael)	

DATE	POS	WKS	ARTIST—RECORD TITLE	LABEL & NO.
			STAN FREBERG	
			Born on 8/7/26 in Los Angeles. Began career doing impersonations on Cliffie Stone's radio show in 1943. Did cartoon voices for the major film studios. His first in a long string of brilliant satirical recordings was "John And Marsha" in 1951.	
7/24/61	34	3	1. Stan Freberg Presents The United States Of America [C]	Capitol 1573
			with Jesse White and Paul Frees - musical score by Billy May	
			FREDDIE & THE DREAMERS	
			Freddie Garrity was born on 11/14/40 in Manchester, England. Formed The Dreamers in 1961, consisting of Garrity (lead singer), Derek Quinn (lead guitar), Roy Crewsdon (guitar), Peter Birrell (bass) and Bernie Dwyer (drums).	
5/22/65	19	7	1. Freddie & The Dreamers	Mercury 61017
			FREE	
			British band formed in 1968: Paul Rodgers (vocals), Paul Kossoff (guitar), Simon Kirke (drums) and Andy Fraser (bass). Kossoff left to form Back Street Crawler, but died of drug-induced heart failure in 1976. Rodgers and Kirke formed Bad Company in 1974.	
9/26/70	17	11	1. Fire And Water	A&M 4268
			"All Right Now"(4)	
			ACE FREHLEY	
			Born on 4/27/51 in the Bronx, New York. Kiss' lead guitarist until 1983.	
11/25/78	26	10	▲ 1. Ace Frehley	Casablanca 7121
			GLENN FREY	
			Born on 11/6/48 in Detroit. Singer, songwriter, guitarist. Founding member of the Eagles.	
7/24/82	32	11	● 1. No Fun Aloud	Asylum 60129
8/25/84	22	14	● 2. The Allnighter	MCA 5501
			THE FRIENDS OF DISTINCTION	
			Los Angeles-based soul/MOR group: Floyd Butler (b: 6/5/41, San Diego); Harry Elston (b: 11/4/38, Dallas); Jessica Cleaves (b: 12/10/48, Los Angeles); and Barbara Jean Love (b: 7/24/41, Los Angeles). Butler and Elston were in the Hi Fi's with LaMonte McLemore and Marilyn McCoo (later with The Fifth Dimension).	
7/05/69	35	3	1. Grazin'	RCA 4149
			"Grazing In The Grass"(3)	
			FRIJID PINK	
			Rock group formed in Detroit. Kelly Green, lead singer.	
3/07/70	11	12	1. Frijid Pink	Parrot 71033
			"House Of The Rising Sun"(7)	
			DAVID FRYE	
			Comedian/impressionist.	
1/10/70	19	8	1. I Am The President [C]	Elektra 75006
			FUNKADELIC	
			Part of producer George Clinton's "P.Funk" battalion. Also see Parliament.	
10/07/78	16	9	▲ 1. One Nation Under A Groove	Warner 3209
10/20/79	18	6	● 2. Uncle Jam Wants You	Warner 3371

DATE	POS	WKS	ARTIST—RECORD TITLE	LABEL & NO.

G

DATE	POS	WKS	ARTIST—RECORD TITLE	LABEL & NO.
			PETER GABRIEL	
			Born on 5/13/50 in London, England. Lead singer of Genesis from 1966-1975.	
4/30/77	38	2	1. Peter Gabriel	Atco 147
7/05/80	22	14	2. Peter Gabriel	Mercury 3848
10/16/82	28	11	● 3. Peter Gabriel (Security)	Geffen 2011
6/14/86	2(3)	30	▲ 4. **So**	Geffen 24088
			"Sledgehammer"(1)	
			"Big Time"(8)	
			THE GAP BAND	
			Brother trio from Tulsa, Oklahoma: Charles, Ronnie and Robert Wilson. Named for three streets in Tulsa: Greenwood, Archer and Pine.	
2/14/81	16	17	▲ 1. The Gap Band III	Mercury 4003
6/26/82	14	17	▲ 2. Gap Band IV	Total Exp. 3001
9/24/83	28	7	● 3. Gap Band V - Jammin'	Total Exp. 3004
			JERRY GARCIA	
			Founder and lead guitarist of the Grateful Dead.	
2/12/72	35	3	1. Garcia	Warner 2582
			DAVE GARDNER	
			Born on 6/11/26 in Jackson, Tennessee. "Brother Dave" had 6 comedy albums chart in the early 60s.	
6/20/60	5	40	1. **Rejoice, Dear Hearts!** [C]	RCA 2083
8/29/60	5	31	2. **Kick Thy Own Self** [C]	RCA 2239
9/18/61	15	10	3. Ain't That Weird? [C]	RCA 2335
5/18/63	28	5	4. It Don't Make No Difference [C]	Capitol 1867
			ART GARFUNKEL	
			Born on 10/13/42 in Queens, New York. Appeared in films "Catch 22", "Carnal Knowledge" and "Bad Timing". Also see Simon & Garfunkel.	
10/06/73	5	13	● 1. **Angel Clare**	Columbia 31474
			"All I Know"(9)	
11/01/75	7	15	▲ 2. **Breakaway**	Columbia 33700
			"My Little Town"(9-Simon & Garfunkel)	
2/11/78	19	9	● 3. Watermark	Columbia 34975
			JUDY GARLAND	
			Born Frances Gumm on 6/10/22 in Grand Rapids, Michigan. Star of MGM film musicals from 1935-54. Hosted own TV variety series, 1963-64. Died on 1/22/69.	
10/29/55	5	7	1. **Miss Show Business**	Capitol 676
11/10/56	17	5	2. Judy	Capitol 734
6/17/57	17	3	3. Alone	Capitol 835
8/07/61	1(13)	73	● 4. **Judy At Carnegie Hall** [L]	Capitol 1569 [2]
9/08/62	33	5	5. The Garland Touch	Capitol 1710

DATE	POS	WKS	ARTIST—RECORD TITLE	LABEL & NO.
			ERROLL GARNER	
			Jazz pianist. Died on 1/2/77 (53).	
11/25/57	**16**	2	1. Other Voices [I]	Columbia 1014
			featuring the juke-box hit "Misty"	
3/10/58	**12**	7	2. Concert By The Sea [I-L]	Columbia 883
			recorded in 1956 in Carmel, California	
6/26/61	**35**	31	3. Dreamstreet [I]	ABC-Para. 365
			LEIF GARRETT	
			Born on 11/8/61 in Hollywood, California. Began film career in 1969; appeared in all 3 "Walking Tall" films.	
2/04/78	**37**	3	● 1. Leif Garrett	Atlantic 19152
1/20/79	**34**	5	● 2. Feel The Need	Scotti Br. 7100
			"I Was Made For Dancin'"(10)	
			TOMMY GARRETT - see 50 GUITARS	
			JOHN GARY	
			Born in Watertown, New York on 11/29/32. Singer on Don McNeill's radio program, "Breakfast Club", for 2 years.	
11/30/63	**19**	27	1. Catch A Rising Star	RCA 2745
3/07/64	**16**	10	2. Encore	RCA 2804
3/20/65	**17**	8	3. A Little Bit Of Heaven	RCA 2994
8/14/65	**11**	13	4. The Nearness Of You	RCA 3349
12/04/65	**21**	7	5. Your All-Time Favorite Songs	RCA 3411
			MARVIN GAYE	
			Born Marvin Pentz Gay, Jr. on 4/2/39 in Washington, DC. Sang in his father's Apostolic church. In vocal groups the Rainbows and Marquees. Joined Harvey Fuqua in the reformed Moonglows. To Detroit in 1960. Session work as drummer at Motown; married to Berry Gordy's sister Anna, 1961-75. First recorded under own name for Tamla in 1961. In seclusion for several months following the death of Tammi Terrell, 1970. Problems with drugs and the IRS led to his moving to Europe for three years. Fatally shot by his father after a quarrel on 4/1/84 in Los Angeles.	
6/28/69	**33**	4	1. M.P.G.	Tamla 292
			"Too Busy Thinking About My Baby"(4)	
			"That's The Way Love Is"(7)	
6/26/71	**6**	27	2. **What's Going On**	Tamla 310
			"What's Going On"(2)	
			"Mercy Mercy Me"(4)	
			"Inner City Blues"(9)	
1/13/73	**14**	11	3. Trouble Man [S]	Tamla 322
			Marvin sings on 3 of the 13 cuts (others are instrumentals)	
			"Trouble Man"(7)	
9/15/73	**2(1)**	18	4. **Let's Get It On**	Tamla 329
			"Let's Get It On"(1)	
12/08/73	**26**	5	5. Diana & Marvin	Motown 803
			DIANA ROSS & MARVIN GAYE	
7/27/74	**8**	13	6. **Marvin Gaye Live!** [L]	Tamla 333
4/10/76	**4**	15	7. **I Want You**	Tamla 342

DATE	POS	WKS	ARTIST—RECORD TITLE	LABEL & NO.
4/16/77	**3**	19	8. **Marvin Gaye Live At The London Palladium** [L]	Tamla 352 [2]
			"Got To Give It Up"(1)	
1/20/79	**26**	7	9. Here, My Dear	Tamla 364 [2]
2/28/81	**32**	4	10. In Our Lifetime	Tamla 374
11/20/82	**7**	13	▲ 11. **Midnight Love**	Columbia 38197
			"Sexual Healing"(3)	
			CRYSTAL GAYLE	
			Born Brenda Gail Webb on 1/9/51 in Paintsville, Kentucky. Loretta Lynn's younger sister.	
10/22/77	**12**	10	▲ 1. **We Must Believe In Magic**	United Art. 771
			"Don't It Make My Brown Eyes Blue"(2)	
11/24/79	**36**	4	● 2. Miss The Mississippi	Columbia 36203
			GLORIA GAYNOR	
			Born on 9/7/49 in Newark, NJ. With the Soul Satisfiers group in 1971.	
2/22/75	**25**	5	1. Never Can Say Goodbye	MGM 4982
			"Never Can Say Goodbye"(9)	
2/03/79	**4**	15	▲ 2. **Love Tracks**	Polydor 6184
			"I Will Survive"(1)	
			THE J. GEILS BAND	
			Rock group formed in Boston, 1967. Consisted of Jerome Geils (guitar), Peter Wolf (vocals), "Magic" Dick Salwitz (harmonica), Seth Justman (keyboards), Danny Klein (bass) and Stephen Jo Bladd (drums). First recorded for Atlantic in 1970. Wolf left for a solo career in the fall of 1983.	
5/19/73	**10**	14	● 1. **Bloodshot**	Atlantic 7260
11/23/74	**26**	4	2. Nightmares...and other tales from the vinyl jungle	Atlantic 18107
10/25/75	**36**	2	3. Hotline	Atlantic 18147
6/26/76	**40**	1	4. Live - Blow Your Face Out [L]	Atlantic 507 [2]
3/08/80	**18**	17	● 5. Love Stinks	EMI America 17016
11/21/81	**1(4)**	29	▲ 6. **Freeze-Frame**	EMI America 17062
			"Centerfold"(1)	
			"Freeze-Frame"(4)	
12/18/82	**23**	10	● 7. Showtime! [L]	EMI America 17087
			Peter Wolf's last album with group	
			GENERAL PUBLIC	
			Fronted by English Beat vocalists Dave Wakeling & Ranking Roger.	
1/19/85	**26**	11	1. ...All The Rage	I.R.S. 70046
			GENESIS	
			Rock group formed in England, 1967. Consisted of Peter Gabriel (lead vocals), Anthony Phillips (guitar), Tony Banks, (keyboards), Michael Rutherford (guitar, bass) and John Mayhew (drums). Phillips and Mayhew left after second album, replaced by Steve Hackett (guitar) and Phil Collins (drums). Gabriel left in June, 1975, with Collins replacing him as new lead singer. Hackett left in 1977, leaving group as a trio: Collins, Rutherford and Banks.	
5/01/76	**31**	6	1. A Trick Of The Tail	Atco 129
2/19/77	**26**	8	2. Wind & Wuthering	Atco 144

DATE	POS	WKS	ARTIST—RECORD TITLE	LABEL & NO.
4/29/78	**14**	8	● 3. And Then There Were Three...	Atlantic 19173
			from here on, group consists of Banks, Collins & Rutherford	
5/03/80	**11**	21	● 4. Duke	Atlantic 16014
10/24/81	**7**	29	▲ 5. **Abacab**	Atlantic 19313
7/10/82	**10**	11	● 6. **Three Sides Live** [L]	Atlantic 2000 [2]
			side four: studio cuts from '79-'81	
11/05/83	**9**	27	▲ 7. **Genesis**	Atlantic 80116
			"That's All"(6)	
6/28/86	**3**	52+	▲ 8. **Invisible Touch**	Atlantic 81641
			"Invisible Touch"(1)	
			"Throwing It All Away"(4)	
			"Land Of Confusion"(4)	
			"Tonight, Tonight, Tonight"(3)	
			BOBBIE GENTRY	
			Born Roberta Lee Streeter on 7/27/44 in Chickasaw County, Mississippi. Singer, songwriter. Married singer Jim Stafford in 1978.	
9/23/67	**1(2)**	18	● 1. **Ode To Billie Joe**	Capitol 2830
			"Ode To Billie Joe"(1)	
11/09/68	**11**	13	● 2. Bobbie Gentry & Glen Campbell	Capitol 2928
			GEORGIA SATELLITES	
			Rock quartet formed in Atlanta, 1980. Led by Dan Baird (lead vocals) and Rick Richards (lead guitar).	
12/20/86	**5**	20	● 1. **Georgia Satellites**	Elektra 60496
			"Keep Your Hands To Yourself"(2)	
			GERRY & THE PACEMAKERS	
			Group formed in Liverpool, England, 1959. Consisted of Gerry Marsden (b: 9/24/42), vocals, guitar; Leslie Maguire, piano; Les Chadwick, bass; and Freddie Marsden, drums. The Marsdens had been in skiffle bands; Gerry had own rock band, Mars-Bars, in 1958. Signed in 1962 by the Beatles' manager, Brian Epstein.	
8/15/64	**29**	5	1. Don't Let The Sun Catch You Crying	Laurie 2024
			"Don't Let The Sun Catch You Crying"(4)	
			"How Do You Do It?"(9)	
4/03/65	**13**	12	2. Ferry Cross The Mersey [S]	United Art. 6387
			9 of 12 songs by Gerry & The Pacemakers (they star in the film which was set in Liverpool)	
			"Ferry Cross The Mersey"(6)	
			STAN GETZ	
			Jazz tenor saxophonist.	
10/13/62	**1(1)**	44	1. **Jazz Samba** [I]	Verve 8432
			STAN GETZ/CHARLIE BYRD (guitar)	
1/05/63	**13**	20	2. Big Band Bossa Nova [I]	Verve 8494
			with the Gary McFarland Orchestra	
6/20/64	**2(2)**	50	● 3. **Getz/Gilberto**	Verve 8545
			STAN GETZ/JOAO GILBERTO (Brazilian singer/ guitarist)	
			"The Girl From Ipanema"(5-vocal by Joao's wife Astrud)	
2/13/65	**24**	17	4. Getz Au Go Go [L]	Verve 8600
			The New Stan Getz Quartet featuring Astrud Gilberto (vocals)	

DATE	POS	WKS	ARTIST—RECORD TITLE	LABEL & NO.
			ANDY GIBB	
			Born Andrew Roy Gibb on 3/5/58 in Manchester, England. Moved to Australia when 6 months old, then back to England at age 9. Youngest brother of Barry, Robin and Maurice Gibb - The Bee Gees.	
8/27/77	**19**	18	▲ 1. Flowing Rivers	RSO 3019
			"I Just Want To Be Your Everything"(1)	
			"(Love Is) Thicker Than Water"(1)	
6/24/78	**7**	15	▲ 2. **Shadow Dancing**	RSO 3034
			"Shadow Dancing"(1)	
			"An Everlasting Love"(5)	
			"(Our Love) Don't Throw It All Away"(9)	
3/08/80	**21**	7	● 3. After Dark	RSO 3069
			"Desire"(4)	
			JOAO GILBERTO - see STAN GETZ	
			NICK GILDER	
			Born on 11/7/51 in London, England. Moved to Vancouver, Canada at age 10. Founding member of the rock band Sweeney Todd.	
11/11/78	**33**	5	1. City Nights	Chrysalis 1202
			"Hot Child In The City"(1)	
			JIMMY GILMER - see THE FIREBALLS	
			DAVID GILMOUR	
			Born on 3/6/47 in Cambridge, England. Guitarist/vocalist with Pink Floyd.	
8/05/78	**29**	6	1. David Gilmour	Columbia 35388
4/21/84	**32**	10	2. About Face	Columbia 39296
			GIUFFRIA	
			California-based rock quintet led by Gregg Giuffria (keyboardist with Angel) and David Glen Eisley (vocals).	
1/26/85	**26**	11	1. Giuffria	MCA 5524
			GLASS TIGER	
			Canadian rock quintet: Alan Frew, Sam Reid, Al Connelly, Wayne Parker and Michael Hanson.	
10/04/86	**27**	28	● 1. The Thin Red Line	Manhattan 53032
			"Don't Forget Me (When I'm Gone)"(2)	
			"Someday"(7)	
			JACKIE GLEASON	
			Born on 2/26/16 in Brooklyn. Star of stage and screen before enormous popularity on TV's "The Honeymooners" and his own CBS-TV variety series. Although famous as a TV comedian, Jackie's albums feature dreamy mood music by studio orchestras featuring the trumpets of Bobby Hackett & Pee Wee Erwin.	
3/05/55	**5**	16	1. **Music To Remember Her** [I]	Capitol 570
6/25/55	**1(2)**	23	2. **Lonesome Echo** [I]	Capitol 627
11/12/55	**2(2)**	11	3. **Romantic Jazz** [I]	Capitol 568
1/28/56	**7**	7	4. **Music For Lovers Only/Music To Make You Misty** [R-I]	Capitol 475 [2]
			reissue of albums from 1953 & 1954	
2/25/56	**8**	5	5. **Music To Change Her Mind** [I]	Capitol 632

DATE	POS	WKS	ARTIST—RECORD TITLE	LABEL & NO.
6/09/56	10	10	6. **Night Winds** [I]	Capitol 717
12/08/56	16	3	7. Merry Christmas [X-I]	Capitol 758
8/26/57	13	2	● 8. Music For The Love Hours [I]	Capitol 816
9/09/57	16	10	9. Velvet Brass [I]	Capitol 859
12/09/57	14	4	10. Jackie Gleason presents "Oooo!" [I]	Capitol 905
			GO-GO'S	
			Female rock group formed in 1978 in Los Angeles, consisting of Belinda Carlisle, Jane Wiedlin, Charlotte Caffey, Kathy Valentine and Gina Schock. Disbanded in 1984.	
9/26/81	1(6)	38	▲ 1. **Beauty And The Beat**	I.R.S. 70021
			"We Got The Beat"(2)	
8/21/82	8	10	● 2. **Vacation**	I.R.S. 70031
			"Vacation"(8)	
4/21/84	18	18	3. Talk Show	I.R.S. 70041
			GODLEY & CREME	
			Kevin Godley & Lol Creme formed duo after leaving British group, 10cc.	
9/28/85	37	3	1. The History Mix Volume 1	Polydor 825981
			MARTY GOLD & His Orchestra	
4/27/63	10	11	1. **Soundpower!** [I]	RCA 2620
			GOLDEN EARRING	
			Rock band from The Netherlands: Barry Hay (vocals), George Kooymans (guitars, vocals), Cesar Zuiderwijk (drums) and Rinus Gerritsen (bass, keyboards).	
6/15/74	12	13	● 1. Moontan	Track 396
2/26/83	24	12	2. Cut	21 Records 9004
			"Twilight Zone"(10)	
			BOBBY GOLDSBORO	
			Born on 1/18/41 in Marianna, Florida. Singer, songwriter, guitarist. To Dothan, Alabama in 1956. Toured with Roy Orbison, 1962-64.	
5/04/68	5	22	● 1. Honey	United Art. 6642
			"Honey"(1)	
			BENNY GOODMAN	
			"King of Swing" - clarinetist/big band leader since the 1930's.	
3/19/55	7	16	1. **B.G. In Hi-Fi** [I]	Capitol 565
3/24/56	4	10	2. **The Benny Goodman Story** [S-I]	Decca 8252/3 [2]
			Benny is portrayed by Steve Allen in the film, although Benny and his musicians play the music	
			LESLEY GORE	
			Born on 5/2/46 in New York City. Raised in Tenafly, New Jersey. Discovered by Quincy Jones while singing at a hotel in Manhattan. In films "Girls On The Beach", "Ski Party" and "The T.A.M.I. Show".	
7/27/63	24	7	1. I'll Cry If I Want To	Mercury 60805
			"It's My Party"(1)	
			"Judy's Turn To Cry"(5)	

DATE	POS	WKS	ARTIST—RECORD TITLE	LABEL & NO.
			EYDIE GORME	
			Born on 8/16/31 in New York City. Regular on Steve Allen's "Tonight Show" in 1954. Broadway debut with husband Steve Lawrence in "Golden Rainbow", 1967. Married Steve in Las Vegas in December, 1957.	
5/06/57	**14**	10	1. Eydie Gorme	ABC-Para. 150
10/28/57	**19**	4	2. Eydie Swings The Blues	ABC-Para. 192
3/31/58	**19**	4	3. Eydie Gorme Vamps The Roaring 20's	ABC-Para. 218
11/03/58	**20**	1	4. Eydie In Love…	ABC-Para. 246
4/27/63	**22**	9	5. Blame It On The Bossa Nova	Columbia 8812
			"Blame It On The Bossa Nova"(7)	
6/04/66	**22**	9	6. Don't Go To Strangers	Columbia 9276
			MORTON GOULD	
11/09/59	**5**	12	1. **Tchaikovsky: 1812 Overture/**	
			Ravel: Bolero [I]	RCA 2345
7/18/60	**3**	35	2. **Grofe: Grand Canyon Suite/**	
			Beethoven: Wellington's Victory [I]	RCA 2433
			ROBERT GOULET	
			Born on 11/26/33 in Lawrence, Massachusetts. Began concert career in Edmonton, Canada. Launched career in hit musical "Camelot", played part of Sir Lancelot.	
11/10/62	**27**	14	1. Two Of Us	Columbia 8626
1/12/63	**9**	27	2. **Sincerely Yours…**	Columbia 8731
5/04/63	**11**	14	3. The Wonderful World Of Love	Columbia 8793
11/09/63	**16**	10	4. Robert Goulet In Person [L]	Columbia 8888
			recorded live at the Chicago Opera House	
6/27/64	**31**	7	5. Manhattan Tower/The Man Who Loves Manhattan	Columbia 2450
			composed & conducted by Gordon Jenkins	
1/23/65	**5**	18	● 6. **My Love Forgive Me**	Columbia 9096
10/09/65	**31**	5	7. Summer Sounds	Columbia 9180
1/29/66	**33**	4	8. Robert Goulet On Broadway	Columbia 9218
			GQ	
			Bronx, New York soul group: Emmanuel Rahiem LeBlanc (lead singer), Keith Crier, Herb Lane and Paul Service. Group became a trio with the departure of Service, 1980.	
4/21/79	**13**	19	▲ 1. Disco Nights	Arista 4225
			GRAHAM CENTRAL STATION	
			Soul/dance group from Oakland. Formed and led by Larry Graham after his departure from Sly & The Family Stone.	
8/30/75	**22**	6	● 1. Ain't No 'Bout-A-Doubt It	Warner 2876
			LARRY GRAHAM	
			Born on 8/14/46 in Beaumont, Texas. To Oakland at the age of two. Bass player with Sly & The Family Stone, 1966-72. Formed Graham Central Station in 1973.	
8/02/80	**26**	9	● 1. One In A Million You	Warner 3447
			"One In A Million You"(9)	

DATE	POS	WKS	ARTIST—RECORD TITLE	LABEL & NO.
			GRAND FUNK RAILROAD	
			Heavy-metal rock group formed in Flint, Michigan in 1968. Consisted of Mark Farner (guitar), Mel Schacher (bass) and Don Brewer (drums). Brewer and Farner had been in Terry Knight & The Pack; Schacher was former bassist with "? & The Mysterians". Knight became producer and manager for Grand Funk, until he was fired in March, 1972. Craig Frost (keyboards), added in 1973. Disbanded in 1976. Re-formed in 1981, with Farner, Brewer and Dennis Bellinger (bass). Disbanded again shortly thereafter. Also see Terry Knight & The Pack.	
11/08/69	27	8	● 1. On Time	Capitol 307
2/07/70	11	15	● 2. Grand Funk	Capitol 406
7/11/70	6	24	● 3. **Closer To Home**	Capitol 471
12/05/70	5	25	● 4. **Live Album** [L]	Capitol 633 [2]
5/01/71	6	21	● 5. **Survival**	Capitol 764
12/04/71	5	15	● 6. **E Pluribus Funk**	Capitol 853
5/20/72	17	9	● 7. **Mark, Don & Mel 1969-71** [K]	Capitol 11042 [2]
10/21/72	7	13	● 8. **Phoenix**	Capitol 11099
			GRAND FUNK:	
8/18/73	2(2)	17	● 9. **We're An American Band**	Capitol 11207
			"We're An American Band"(1)	
4/06/74	5	21	● 10. **Shinin' On**	Capitol 11278
			"The Loco-Motion"(1)	
1/04/75	10	10	● 11. **All The Girls In The World Beware!!!**	Capitol 11356
			"Some Kind Of Wonderful"(3)	
			"Bad Time"(4)	
			GRAND FUNK RAILROAD:	
9/27/75	21	5	12. Caught In The Act [L]	Capitol 11445 [2]
			AMY GRANT	
			Born on 11/25/60 in Augusta, GA. The first lady of contemporary Christian music.	
8/24/85	35	4	▲ 1. Unguarded	A&M 5060
			"Find A Way"	
			EARL GRANT	
			Organist/pianist/vocalist born in Oklahoma City in 1931. Died in an auto accident on 6/10/70 (39).	
8/28/61	7	32	● 1. **Ebb Tide** [I]	Decca 74165
7/14/62	17	13	2. Beyond The Reef [I]	Decca 74231
			EDDY GRANT	
			Born Edmond Montague Grant on 3/5/48 in Plaisance, Guyana. Moved to London in 1960. Formed group the Equals in London, 1967.	
5/21/83	10	15	● 1. **Killer On The Rampage**	Portrait 38554
			"Electric Avenue"(2)	
			GOGI GRANT - see SOUNDTRACK "Helen Morgan Story"	

DATE	POS	WKS	ARTIST—RECORD TITLE	LABEL & NO.
			THE GRASS ROOTS	
			Rock group formed in Los Angeles by pop producers/songwriters Steve Barri and P.F. Sloan. Recruited the Los Angeles bar band, The Thirteenth Floor, to record as The Grass Roots. Consisted of Warren Entner, Creed Bratton, guitars; Rob Grill, bass; and Rick Coonce, drums. Bratton left, replaced by Dennis Provisor in 1969. New lineup, 1972, included Entner, Grill, Reed Kailing, Joel Larson & Virgil Webber.	
1/25/69	25	6	● 1. Golden Grass [G]	Dunhill 50047
			"Midnight Confessions"(5)	
12/20/69	36	6	2. Leaving It All Behind	Dunhill 50067
			GRATEFUL DEAD	
			Psychedelic rock band formed in San Francisco in 1966. Consisted of Jerry Garcia, lead guitar; Bob Weir, rhythm guitar; Ron "Pigpen" McKernan, organ, harmonica; Phil Lesh, bass; and Bill Kruetzmann, drums. Mickey Hart (2nd drummer) and Tom Constanten (keyboards) added in 1968. Constanten left in 1970, Hart in 1971. Keith Godchaux (piano) and his wife Donna (vocals) joined in 1972. Pigpen died of a liver ailment on 3/8/73. Hart returned in 1975. Brent Mydland (keyboards) added in 1979, replacing Keith & Donna Godchaux.	
7/11/70	27	10	▲ 1. Workingman's Dead	Warner 1869
12/26/70	30	6	▲ 2. American Beauty	Warner 1893
10/16/71	25	6	3. Grateful Dead [L]	Warner 1935 [2]
1/06/73	24	8	● 4. Europe '72 [L]	Warner 2668 [3]
11/17/73	18	6	5. Wake Of The Flood	Grateful Dead 01
7/20/74	16	9	6. Grateful Dead From The Mars Hotel	Grateful Dead 102
9/20/75	12	9	7. Blues For Allah	Grateful Dead 494
9/10/77	28	4	8. Terrapin Station	Arista 7001
5/24/80	23	8	9. Go To Heaven	Arista 9508
10/03/81	29	3	10. Dead Set [L]	Arista 8606 [2]
			recorded live in New York City and San Francisco in 1980	
			GLEN GRAY & The Casa Loma Orchestra	
			Swing band organized in 1929. Glen died on 8/23/63 (57).	
2/23/57	18	9	1. Casa Loma In Hi-Fi! [I]	Capitol 747
6/29/59	28	2	2. Sounds Of The Great Bands! [I]	Capitol 1022
			THE CHARLES RANDOLPH GREAN SOUNDE	
			Charles is a former artist & repertoire director at RCA & Dot Records. Married to singer Betty Johnson.	
8/16/69	23	5	1. Quentin's Theme [I]	Ranwood 8055
			title cut is from TV's "Dark Shadows"	
			GEORGE GREELEY	
			Guest pianist with the Warner Bros. Orchestra.	
6/19/61	29	16	1. The Best Of The Popular Piano Concertos [I-K]	Warner 1410
			AL GREEN	
			Born in Forrest City, Arkansas on 4/13/46. Moved to Grand Rapids, Michigan at the age of 9. Signed to Hi Records by their A&R director, producer Willie Mitchell. Today, Al is a gospel singer & a minister at the Full Tabernacle Church in Memphis.	
2/26/72	8	20	● 1. **Let's Stay Together**	Hi 32070
			"Let's Stay Together"(1)	

DATE	POS	WKS	ARTIST—RECORD TITLE	LABEL & NO.
11/04/72	**4**	26	● 2. **I'm Still In Love With You**	Hi 32074
			"Look What You Done For Me"(4)	
			"I'm Still In Love With You"(3)	
2/03/73	**19**	11	3. Green Is Blues [E]	Hi 32055
			Al's first album on the HI label	
5/26/73	**10**	20	● 4. **Call Me**	Hi 32077
			"You Ought To Be With Me"(3)	
			"Call Me (Come Back Home)"(10)	
			"Here I Am (Come And Take Me)"(10)	
1/19/74	**24**	8	● 5. Livin' For You	Hi 32082
12/07/74	**15**	16	● 6. Al Green Explores Your Mind	Hi 32087
			"Sha-La-La (Make Me Happy)"(7)	
3/22/75	**17**	8	7. Al Green/Greatest Hits [G]	Hi 32089
10/11/75	**28**	6	8. Al Green Is Love	Hi 32092
			NORMAN GREENBAUM	
			Born on 11/20/42 in Malden, MA. Moved to the West Coast in 1965 and formed the psychedelic jug band, "Dr. West's Medicine Show & Junk Band".	
4/18/70	**23**	5	1. Spirit In The Sky	Reprise 6365
			"Spirit In The Sky"(3)	
			LORNE GREENE	
			Born on 2/12/15 in Ottawa, Canada. Chief news broadcaster for CBC radio, 1940-43. Moved to New York City in 1953. Best known as Ben Cartwright on TV's "Bonanza".	
1/16/65	**35**	4	1. Welcome To The Ponderosa	RCA 2843
			"Ringo"(1)	
			DICK GREGORY	
			Comedian. Civil rights activist.	
7/24/61	**23**	5	1. In Living Black & White [C]	Colpix 417
			HENRY GROSS	
			Rock singer, guitarist from Brooklyn. Original lead guitarist of Sha-Na-Na.	
4/12/75	**26**	3	1. Plug Me Into Something	A&M 4502
			GTR	
			British hard rock quintet featuring superstar guitarists Steve Hackett (Genesis) and Steve Howe (Yes & Asia), and Max Bacon (vocals).	
5/31/86	**11**	17	●● 1. GTR	Arista 8400
			VINCE GUARALDI TRIO	
			Vince was born on 7/17/32 in San Francisco. Jazz pianist formerly with Woody Herman and Cal Tjader. Died of a heart attack on 2/6/76 (43).	
4/13/63	**24**	7	1. Jazz Impressions of Black Orpheus [I]	Fantasy 3337
			"Cast Your Fate To The Wind"	
			featuring Vince's interpretations of 4 songs from the film "Black Orpheus"	

DATE	POS	WKS	ARTIST—RECORD TITLE	LABEL & NO.
			THE GUESS WHO	
			Rock group formed in Winnipeg, Canada, 1963. Consisted of Allan "Chad Allan" Kobel (guitar, vocals), Randy Bachman (lead guitar), Garry Peterson (drums), Bob Ashley (piano) and Jim Kale (bass). Recorded as The Reflections, and Chad Allan & The Expressions. Ashley replaced by new lead singer Burton Cummings in 1966. Allan left shortly thereafter. Bachman left in July, 1970, to form Bachman-Turner Overdrive. Replaced by Kurt Winter and Greg Leskiw. Leskiw and Kale left in 1972, replaced by Don McDougall and Bill Wallace. Domenic Troiano replaced both Winter and McDougall in 1974. Group disbanded in 1975; several reformations since then.	
3/07/70	9	23	● 1. **American Woman**	RCA 4266
			"No Time"(5)	
			"American Woman"(1)	
11/28/70	14	11	● 2. Share The Land	RCA 4359
			"Share The Land"(10)	
4/24/71	12	23	● 3. The Best of The Guess Who [G]	RCA 1004
10/14/72	39	1	4. Live At The Paramount (Seattle) [L]	RCA 4779
			ARLO GUTHRIE	
			Born on 7/10/47 in Coney Island, NY. Son of legendary folk singer Woody Guthrie.	
1/27/68	17	23	▲ 1. Alice's Restaurant	Reprise 6267
			side one is the 18 minute tale of "Alice's Restaurant Massacree"	
11/28/70	33	3	2. Washington County	Reprise 6411
			H	
			SAMMY HAGAR	
			Born on 10/13/47 in Monterey, CA. Rock singer, songwriter, guitarist. Lead singer of Montrose (1973-75). Replaced David Lee Roth as lead singer of Van Halen in 1985.	
2/20/82	28	14	● 1. Standing Hampton	Geffen 2006
1/29/83	17	14	● 2. Three Lock Box	Geffen 2021
11/03/84	32	9	▲ 3. VOA	Geffen 24043
			MERLE HAGGARD	
			Born in Bakersville, California on 4/6/37. Country singer, songwriter, guitarist. Served nearly 3 years in San Quentin prison on a burglary charge, 1957-60. Signed to Capitol Records in 1965 and then formed his backing band, The Strangers.	
8/20/83	37	1	▲ 1. Poncho & Lefty	Epic 37958
			MERLE HAGGARD/WILLIE NELSON	
			HAIRCUT ONE HUNDRED	
			British pop/rock sextet led by Nick Heyward.	
7/10/82	31	7	1. Pelican West	Arista 6600

DATE	POS	WKS	ARTIST—RECORD TITLE	LABEL & NO.
			BILL HALEY & His Comets	
			Born William John Clifton Haley Jr. on 7/6/25 in Highland Park, Michigan. Began career as a singer with a New England country band, the "Down Homers". Formed the "Four Aces of Western Swing" in 1948 and then in 1949 formed the Saddlemen, who recorded on various labels before signing with the Essex label (as Bill Haley & The Comets) in 1952, and then with Decca in 1954. The original Comets band who backed Haley on "Rock Around The Clock" were: Rudy Pompilli (sax), Al Pompilli (bass), Ralph Jones (drums) and Frannie Beecher (lead guitar). Bill died of a heart attack in Harlingen, Texas on 2/9/81.	
1/28/56	**12**	4	1. Rock Around The Clock [G]	Decca 8225
			"Shake, Rattle And Roll"(7-'54)	
			"Rock Around The Clock"(1)	
			"Burn That Candle"(9)	
10/13/56	**18**	5	2. Rock 'n Roll Stage Show	Decca 8345
			DARYL HALL	
			Born Daryl Franklin Hohl on 10/11/48 in Philadelphia. Half of Hall & Oates duo.	
9/20/86	**29**	6	1. Three Hearts in the Happy Ending Machine	RCA 7196
			"Dreamtime"(5)	
			DARYL HALL & JOHN OATES	
			Daryl Hall (see above) & John Oates (b: 4/7/49 in New York City) met while students at Temple University in 1967. Hall sang backup for many top soul groups, before teaming up with Oates in 1972. Duo's sophisticated "blue-eyed soul" style has earned them the #2 ranking (behind the Everly Brothers) as the all-time top duo of the rock era.	
5/22/76	**17**	11	● 1. Daryl Hall & John Oates	RCA 1144
			"Sara Smile"(4)	
9/18/76	**13**	35	● 2. Bigger Than Both Of Us	RCA 1467
			"Rich Girl"(1)	
10/30/76	**33**	4	● 3. Abandoned Luncheonette	Atlantic 7269
			"She's Gone"(7)	
9/24/77	**30**	5	● 4. Beauty On A Back Street	RCA 2300
10/07/78	**27**	6	● 5. Along The Red Ledge	RCA 2804
11/24/79	**33**	6	6. X-Static	RCA 3494
8/30/80	**17**	35	▲ 7. Voices	RCA 3646
			"Kiss On My List"(1)	
			"You Make My Dreams"(5)	
9/26/81	**5**	32	▲ 8. **Private Eyes**	RCA 4028
			"Private Eyes"(1)	
			"I Can't Go For That"(1)	
			"Did It In A Minute"(9)	
11/06/82	**3**	46	▲ 9. **H2O**	RCA 4383
			"Maneater"(1)	
			"One On One"(7)	
			"Family Man"(6)	
11/19/83	**7**	28	▲ 10. **Rock 'N Soul, Part 1** [G]	RCA 4858
			"Say It Isn't So"(2)	
			"Adult Education"(8)	

DATE	POS	WKS	ARTIST—RECORD TITLE	LABEL & NO.
10/27/84	5	31	▲ 11. **Big Bam Boom**	RCA 5309
			"Out Of Touch"(1)	
			"Method Of Modern Love"(5)	
10/05/85	21	8	● 12. Live At The Apollo with David Ruffin &	
			Eddie Kendrick　　　　　　　　　[L]	RCA 7035
			recorded at the re-opening of New York's Apollo Theatre - side 1 features guest vocalists Ruffin & Kendrick	
			JAN HAMMER - see JEFF BECK and TELEVISION SOUNDTRACKS	
			HERBIE HANCOCK	
			Born on 4/12/40 in Chicago. Jazz electronic keyboardist. Pianist with the Miles Davis band, 1963-68. Won an Oscar in 1987 for his "Round Midnight" film score.	
2/16/74	13	21	▲ 1. Head Hunters　　　　　　　　[I]	Columbia 32731
10/12/74	13	9	2. Thrust　　　　　　　　　　　[I]	Columbia 32965
11/08/75	21	4	3. 'Man-Child　　　　　　　　　[I]	Columbia 33812
4/21/79	38	3	4. Feets Don't Fail Me Now	Columbia 35764
			JERRY MURAD'S HARMONICATS	
			Harmonica trio formed in 1944: Jerry Murad, Al Fiore and Don Les.	
3/20/61	17	4	1. Cherry Pink And Apple Blossom White　[I]	Columbia 8356
			JOE HARNELL	
			Born on 8/2/24 in the Bronx. Conductor, arranger for Frank Sinatra, Peggy Lee and others. Musical director for many TV shows, including the Mike Douglas Show.	
1/26/63	3	27	1. **Fly Me To The Moon and the Bossa Nova Pops**　　　　　　　　　　　[I]	Kapp 3318
			EDDIE HARRIS	
			Born in 1936 in Chicago. Jazz tenor saxophonist.	
6/19/61	2(1)	22	1. **Exodus To Jazz**　　　　　　[I]	Vee-Jay 3016
9/07/68	36	1	2. The Electrifying Eddie Harris　[I]	Atlantic 1495
1/31/70	29	5	3. Swiss Movement　　　　　　[I-L]	Atlantic 1537
			LES McCANN & EDDIE HARRIS	
			recorded live at The Montreux Jazz Festival, Switzerland	
			EMMYLOU HARRIS	
			Born on 4/12/47 in Birmingham, Alabama. Contemporary country vocalist. Sang backup with Gram Parsons until his death in 1973.	
2/07/76	25	8	● 1. Elite Hotel	Reprise 2236
2/05/77	21	8	● 2. Luxury Liner	Warner 3115
2/25/78	29	5	3. Quarter Moon In A Ten Cent Town	Warner 3141
6/07/80	26	11	● 4. Roses In The Snow	Warner 3422
2/28/81	22	9	● 5. Evangeline	Warner 3508
			MAJOR HARRIS	
			Born on 2/9/47 in Richmond, VA. Sang with The Jarmels, early 60s. With The Delfonics, 1971-74.	
6/28/75	28	3	1. My Way	Atlantic 18119
			"Love Won't Let Me Wait"(5)	

DATE	POS	WKS	ARTIST—RECORD TITLE	LABEL & NO.
			RICHARD HARRIS	
			Born on 10/1/30 in Limerick, Ireland. Began prolific acting career in 1958. Portrayed King Arthur in the film version of "Camelot".	
6/01/68	4	16	1. **A Tramp Shining**	Dunhill 50032
			"MacArthur Park"(2)	
12/14/68	27	6	2. The Yard Went On Forever...	Dunhill 50042
11/10/73	25	9	3. Jonathan Livingston Seagull [T]	Dunhill 50160
			narration from the book - music composed by Terry James	
1/25/75	29	5	4. The Prophet by Kahlil Gibran [T]	Atlantic 18120
			Harris recites Gibran's classic work	
			ROLF HARRIS	
			Born in Perth, Australia on 3/30/30. Played piano from age nine. Moved to England in the mid-50s. Developed his unique "wobble board sound" out of a sheet of masonite. Had own BBC-TV series from 1970.	
8/17/63	29	4	1. Tie Me Kangaroo Down, Sport & Sun Arise [N]	Epic 26053
			"Tie Me Kangaroo Down, Sport"(3)	
			SAM HARRIS	
			Winner of TV's "Star Search" male vocalist category in 1984.	
11/17/84	35	3	● 1. Sam Harris	Motown 6103
			GEORGE HARRISON	
			Born on 2/25/43 in Liverpool, England. Formed his first group, the Rebels at age 13. Joined John Lennon and Paul McCartney in the Quarrymen in 1958; group later evolved into The Beatles, with Harrison as lead guitarist. Organized the Bangladesh benefit concerts at Madison Square Garden in 1971.	
12/19/70	1(7)	22	● 1. **All Things Must Pass**	Apple 639 [3]
			"My Sweet Lord"(1)	
			What Is Life"(10)	
1/08/72	2(6)	23	● 2. **The Concert For Bangla Desh** [L]	Apple 3385 [3]
			Madison Square Garden benefit concert on 8/1/71 - with guests Bob Dylan, Eric Clapton & Ringo Starr	
6/16/73	1(5)	15	● 3. **Living In The Material World**	Apple 3410
			"Give Me Love (Give Me Peace On Earth)"(1)	
1/04/75	4	9	● 4. **Dark Horse**	Apple 3418
10/11/75	8	7	● 5. **Extra Texture (Read All About It)**	Apple 3420
12/11/76	31	3	● 6. The Best of George Harrison [G]	Capitol 11578
			side 1: hits while with The Beatles; side 2: solo hits	
12/18/76	11	8	● 7. **Thirty-Three & 1/3**	Dark Horse 3005
			33 1/3: record playing speed and George's age	
3/17/79	14	9	● 8. George Harrison	Dark Horse 3255
6/20/81	11	7	9. Somewhere In England	Dark Horse 3492
			"All Those Years Ago"(2)	
			DEBBIE HARRY	
			Born on 7/1/45 in New York City. Lead singer of Blondie. In films "Unmade Beds", "Union City" and "Videodrome".	
9/05/81	25	4	● 1. KooKoo	Chrysalis 1347

DATE	POS	WKS	ARTIST—RECORD TITLE	LABEL & NO.
			COREY HART	
			Born in Montreal, Canada; raised in Spain and Mexico. Singer, songwriter, keyboardist.	
9/01/84	**31**	6	● 1. First Offense	EMI America 17117
			"Sunglasses At Night"(7)	
8/03/85	**20**	15	● 2. Boy In The Box	EMI America 17161
			"Never Surrender"(3)	
			FREDDIE HART	
			Born on 12/21/28 in Lochapoka, Alabama. Country singer, songwriter, guitarist.	
11/27/71	**37**	4	● 1. Easy Loving	Capitol 838
			DONNY HATHAWAY	
			Born on 10/1/45 in Chicago; raised in St. Louis; gospel singer beginning at age 3. R&B singer, songwriter, keyboardist, record producer and arranger. Committed suicide by jumping from the 15th floor of New York City's Essex House hotel on 1/13/79 (33). Also see Roberta Flack.	
3/25/72	**18**	23	● 1. Donny Hathaway Live [L]	Atco 386
5/20/72	**3**	21	● 2. **Roberta Flack & Donny Hathaway**	Atlantic 7216
			"Where Is The Love"(5)	
4/26/80	**25**	10	● 3. Roberta Flack Featuring Donny Hathaway	Atlantic 16013
			RICHIE HAVENS	
			Born on 1/21/41 in Brooklyn. Black folksinger/guitarist.	
5/15/71	**29**	7	1. Alarm Clock	Stormy F. 6005
			"Here Comes The Sun"	
			THE EDWIN HAWKINS' SINGERS	
			Formed by Edwin Hawkins and Betty Watson in Oakland in 1967 as the Northern California State Youth Choir. Member Dorothy Morrison went on to a solo career.	
5/17/69	**15**	8	1. Let Us Go Into The House Of The Lord	Pavilion 10001
			"Oh Happy Day"(4)	
			ISAAC HAYES	
			Born on 8/20/42 in Covington, TN. Soul singer, songwriter, keyboardist, record producer. Session musician for Otis Redding and other artists on the Stax label. Teamed with songwriter David Porter to compose "Soul Man", "Hold On! I'm A Comin'", and many others. Composed film score for "Shaft", "Tough Guys" and "Truck Turner".	
8/02/69	**8**	36	● 1. **Hot Buttered Soul**	Enterprise 1001
5/02/70	**8**	28	2. **The Isaac Hayes Movement**	Enterprise 1010
12/05/70	**11**	20	3. To Be Continued	Enterprise 1014
8/28/71	**1(1)**	29	4. **Shaft** [S-I]	Enterprise 5002 [2]
			3 of 15 tracks feature vocals	
			"Theme From Shaft"(1)	
12/18/71	**10**	15	5. **Black Moses**	Enterprise 5003 [2]
6/02/73	**14**	11	● 6. Live At The Sahara Tahoe [L]	Enterprise 5005 [2]
11/17/73	**16**	14	● 7. Joy	Enterprise 5007
7/05/75	**18**	9	● 8. Chocolate Chip	HBS 874
1/19/80	**39**	1	● 9. Don't Let Go	Polydor 6224

DATE	POS	WKS	ARTIST—RECORD TITLE	LABEL & NO.
			JUSTIN HAYWARD	
			Justin was born on 10/14/46 in Swindon, England. John Lodge was born on 7/20/45 in Birmingham, England. Justin (lead singer, lead guitar) and John (vocals, bass) joined The Moody Blues in the summer of 1966.	
4/19/75	16	8	1. Blue Jays	Threshold 14
			JUSTIN HAYWARD/JOHN LODGE	
			album title also refers to the name of their duo	
5/07/77	37	3	2. Songwriter	Deram 18073
			LEE HAZLEWOOD - see NANCY SINATRA	
			HEART	
			Rock band formed in Seattle in 1973. Originally known as The Army, then White Heart, shortened to Heart in 1974. Group features Ann Wilson (lead singer) and her sister Nancy (guitar, keyboards). Band moved to Vancouver, Canada in 1975 when their manager Mike Fisher was drafted, and signed with new Mushroom label. When amnesty was declared, group returned to Seattle and signed with the CBS Portrait label in 1976. In addition to the Wilson sisters, the lineup since 1982 includes guitarist Howard Leese, bassist Mark Andes and drummer Denny Carmassi.	
8/07/76	7	21	▲ 1. **Dreamboat Annie**	Mushroom 5005
			''Magic Man''(9)	
6/04/77	9	22	▲ 2. **Little Queen**	Portrait 34799
4/29/78	17	7	▲ 3. Magazine	Mushroom 5008
			recorded in 1976 but not released until 1978 because of a legal fight	
10/14/78	17	21	▲ 4. Dog & Butterfly	Portrait 35555
3/08/80	5	13	● 5. **Bebe Le Strange**	Epic 36371
12/06/80	13	12	● 6. Greatest Hits/Live [G-L]	Epic 36888 [2]
			6 of 18 tracks are live	
			''Tell It Like It Is''(8)	
6/19/82	25	4	7. Private Audition	Epic 38049
10/15/83	39	2	8. Passionworks	Epic 38800
7/27/85	1(1)	58	▲ 9. **Heart**	Capitol 12410
			''What About Love?''(10)	
			''Never''(4)	
			''These Dreams''(1)	
			''Nothin' At All''(10)	
			TED HEATH	
			Born Edward Heath on 3/30/00 in London, England. Died on 11/18/69. Trombonist, leader of own band since 1945.	
10/16/61	28	10	1. Big Band Percussion [I]	London P. 4 44002
9/15/62	36	2	2. Big Band Bash [I]	London P. 4 44017
			HEATWAVE	
			Multinational, interracial group formed in Germany by Johnnie and Keith Wilder of Dayton, OH. Johnnie injured in auto accident in 1979, paralyzed from neck down.	
9/17/77	11	12	▲ 1. Too Hot To Handle	Epic 34761
			''Boogie Nights''(2)	
5/06/78	10	13	▲ 2. **Central Heating**	Epic 35260
			''The Groove Line''(7)	
6/09/79	38	3	● 3. Hot Property	Epic 35970

DATE	POS	WKS	ARTIST—RECORD TITLE	LABEL & NO.
			NEAL HEFTI	
			Born on 10/29/22 in Hastings, Nebraska. Trumpeter most famous as arranger for Woody Herman (1944-46), Harry James, and Count Basie, then as composer of TV themes.	
2/05/55	8	2	1. **Music Of Rudolf Friml** [I]	"X" 3021
			10" album	
			RAY HEINDORF/MATTY MATLOCK	
			Ray Heindorf conducting the Warner Bros. Orchestra/ Matty Matlock & his Jazz Band. Also see Jack Webb.	
9/03/55	9	6	1. **Pete Kelly's Blues** [I]	Columbia 690
			MICHAEL HENDERSON	
			Soul singer from Yazoo City. MS. Toured with Stevie Wonder, Aretha Franklin, and Miles Davis. Also see Norman Connors.	
9/23/78	38	2	● 1. In The Night-Time	Buddah 5712
10/11/80	35	5	2. Wide Receiver	Buddah 6001
			JIMI HENDRIX	
			Born on 11/27/42 in Seattle. Died of a drug overdose in London on 9/18/70 (27). Legendary psychedelic-blues guitarist. Began career as a studio guitarist. In 1965, formed own band, Jimmy James & The Blue Flames. Created The Jimi Hendrix Experience in 1966, with Noel Redding on bass and Mitch Mitchell on drums. Formed new group in 1969, Band of Gypsys, with Buddy Miles on drums and Billy Cox on bass.	
9/16/67	5	77	▲ 1. **Are You Experienced?**	Reprise 6261
			"Purple Haze"/"Hey Joe"	
2/17/68	3	13	▲ 2. **Axis: Bold As Love**	Reprise 6281
11/02/68	1(2)	17	▲ 3. **Electric Ladyland**	Reprise 6307 [2]
8/09/69	6	17	▲ 4. **Smash Hits** [G]	Reprise 2025
5/02/70	5	23	● 5. **Band Of Gypsys** [L]	Capitol 472
			with Buddy Miles (drums) & Billy Cox (bass) - recorded New Year's Eve 1969 at New York's Fillmore East	
9/26/70	16	8	● 6. Monterey International Pop Festival [S-L]	Reprise 2029
			OTIS REDDING/THE JIMI HENDRIX EXPERIENCE	
			recorded June, 1967 & featured in film "Monterey Pop"	
3/06/71	3	17	● 7. **The Cry Of Love**	Reprise 2034
			Jimi's last self-authorized album	
10/16/71	15	9	● 8. Rainbow Bridge [S]	Reprise 2040
			recordings from 1968-1970	
3/11/72	12	9	● 9. Hendrix In The West [K-L]	Reprise 2049
3/29/75	5	9	● 10. **Crash Landing** [K]	Reprise 2204
			DON HENLEY	
			Born on 7/22/47 in Gilmer, Texas. Singer, songwriter, drummer. Worked with Glenn Frey backing Linda Ronstadt before forming the Eagles in 1971.	
9/25/82	24	20	● 1. I Can't Stand Still	Asylum 60048
			"Dirty Laundry"(3)	
12/22/84	13	30	▲ 2. Building The Perfect Beast	Geffen 24026
			"The Boys Of Summer"(5)	
			"All She Wants To Do Is Dance"(9)	

Jimi Hendrix died in 1970, but new albums of studio outtakes, concert performances, and greatest hits still appear regularly. *Crash Landing* (1975), eight unfinished cuts completed with posthumous accompaniment and produced by Alan Douglas and Tony Bongiovi, ironically proved to be one of Hendrix's biggest selling records ever.

Al Hirt, the son of a New Orleans police officer, turned away from classical music and started playing jazz trumpet in the 1940s, while keeping his job with an exterminating company. *Honey in the Horn* (1963), his first gold album, features compositions by Ray Charles, Hank Snow, and Ira Gershwin.

Buddy Holly died in a plane crash on Feb. 3, 1959 at age 22; *The Buddy Holly Story*, containing such classics as "Everyday," "Rave On," "Oh, Boy!," and "It's So Easy," was hastily compiled and released the following month. A second volume of the album was issued a year later. The 1978 film biography starring Gary Busey used the same title.

Engelbert Humperdinck, who was born Arnold Dorsey in 1936, hosted his own variety show on ABC-TV in 1970. The English singer reached gold status with his first eight albums, including *Engelbert* (1969), which features the 1968 hit, "Les Bicyclettes de Belsize."

The Isley Brothers won a Grammy in 1969, the year the group released *It's Our Thing* on its own label, T-Neck. Although the record company was named after the city of Teaneck, NJ, the Isley family actually hails from Cincinnati, OH.

Michael Jackson, aside from his many other record-breaking achievements, has the distinction of being the only singer to ever have a No. 1 hit with a song about a rat. "Ben," on the 1972 album of the same name, was the theme song for the sequel to *Willard*, a horror film about a boy and his collection of vicious rodents.

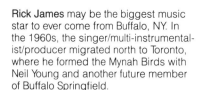

Rick James may be the biggest music star to ever come from Buffalo, NY. In the 1960s, the singer/multi-instrumentalist/producer migrated north to Toronto, where he formed the Mynah Birds with Neil Young and another future member of Buffalo Springfield.

Jan & Dean's professional career got off to a shaky start in 1958 when a recording the duo had made with a friend was released by a California label. Dean Torrence had just left on military service and couldn't be reached, so the other two—Jan & Arnie—put their names to the single, "Jennie Lee." Fortunately, Arnie soon lost interest in rock'n'roll and, upon his return, Torrence rejoined Jan Berry for a run of classic pop records.

Jefferson Airplane went through nine different lineups (1965–74) before becoming Jefferson Starship, of which there were eight versions. *Crown of Creation* (1968) is one of five albums by the longest-lasting incarnation.

Joan Jett and the Blackhearts has covered songs made popular by such artists as Gary Glitter, Tommy James and the Shondells, the Who, the Runaways (Jett's former band), Lesley Gore, the Dave Clark 5, and the Harry Simeone Chorale. *Album* (1983) contains Bobby Lewis' "Tossin' and Turnin'" and Sly Stone's "Everyday People."

Billy Joel was one of the featured artists at 1979's Havana Jam festival, the first joint Cuban-American music event held since 1959.

Elton John coaxed John Lennon to perform with him at a November 1974 Madison Square Garden concert by making the appearance the prize in a bet that Lennon's "Whatever Gets You Through the Night" (on which John sang backup) would make No. 1. At the show, Lennon sang that song with John, as well as "Lucy in the Sky with Diamonds" and "I Saw Her Standing There."

DATE	POS	WKS	ARTIST—RECORD TITLE	LABEL & NO.
			WOODY HERMAN	
			Born Woodrow Charles Herman on 5/16/13 in Milwaukee. Saxophonist, clarinetist in dance bands beginning in 1929. Formed own band in 1936. Band dubbed The Herman Herd in 1944. One of the most innovative and contemporary of all big-band leaders.	
2/19/55	**11**	2	1. The 3 Herds [K-I] recordings from 1945-1954	Columbia 592
			HERMAN'S HERMITS	
			Formed in Manchester, England in 1964. Named after a cartoon character in TV's "The Bullwinkle Show". Consisted of Peter "Herman" Noone (b: 11/5/47), vocals; Derek Leckenby and Keith Hopwood, guitars; Karl Green, bass; and Barry Whitman, drums. First called The Heartbeats. Noone left in 1972 for a solo career.	
3/27/65	**2**(4)	26	● 1. **Introducing Herman's Hermits** "Mrs. Brown You've Got A Lovely Daughter"(1)	MGM 4282
6/26/65	**2**(6)	24	● 2. **Herman's Hermits On Tour** "Can't You Hear My Heartbeat"(2) "Silhouettes"(5) "I'm Henry VIII, I Am"(1)	MGM 4295
11/27/65	**5**	27	● 3. **The Best Of Herman's Hermits** [G] "Wonderful World"(4) "Just A Little Bit Better"(7)	MGM 4315
4/30/66	**14**	7	4. Hold On! [S] "A Must To Avoid"(8) "Leaning On The Lamp Post"(9)	MGM 4342
1/07/67	**20**	7	● 5. The Best Of Herman's Hermits, Volume 2 [G] "Listen People"(3) "Dandy"(5)	MGM 4416
3/25/67	**13**	13	● 6. There's A Kind Of Hush All Over The World "There's A Kind Of Hush"(4)	MGM 4438
			EDDIE HEYWOOD	
			Born on 12/4/15 in Atlanta. Black jazz pianist, composer, arranger. Worked with Billie Holiday.	
5/25/59	**16**	4	1. Canadian Sunset [I] title song not the same version as with Hugo Winterhalter in 1956	RCA 1529
			HI-LO'S	
			Quartet formed in 1953, consisting of Gene Puerling, Clark Burroughs, Bob Morse and Bob Strasen. Numerous appearances on Rosemary Clooney's television show.	
4/13/57	**13**	3	1. Suddenly It's The Hi-Lo's	Columbia 952
7/22/57	**14**	7	2. Ring Around Rosie	Columbia 1006
			ROSEMARY CLOONEY & THE HI-LO'S	
10/14/57	**19**	4	3. Now Hear This	Columbia 1023
			AL HIBBLER	
			Born on 8/16/15 in Little Rock, Arkansas. Blind since birth, studied voice at Little Rock's Conservatory for the Blind. First recorded with Jay McShann for Decca in 1942. With Duke Ellington, 1943-51. Also recorded with Harry Carney, Tab Smith, Mercer Ellington and Billy Strayhorn.	
8/04/56	**20**	2	1. Starring Al Hibbler	Decca 8328

DATE	POS	WKS	ARTIST—RECORD TITLE	LABEL & NO.
			BERTIE HIGGINS	
			Singer, songwriter from Florida. Toured and recorded with the Roemans, 1964-66.	
6/12/82	38	3	1. Just Another Day In Paradise	Kat Family 37901
			"Key Largo"(8)	
			HIGH INERGY	
			Female soul group consisting of Barbara Mitchell, Linda Howard, Michelle Rumph and Vernessa Mitchell. Vernessa left in 1978, group continued as a trio.	
12/10/77	28	7	1. Turnin' On	Gordy 978
			DAN HILL	
			Born on 6/3/54 in Toronto, Canada.	
2/11/78	21	8	● 1. Longer Fuse	20th Century 547
			"Sometimes When We Touch"(3)	
			AL HIRT	
			Born Alois Maxwell Hirt on 11/7/22 in New Orleans. Trumpet virtuoso. Toured with Jimmy & Tommy Dorsey, Ray McKinley and Horace Heidt. Formed own dixieland combo (with clarinetist Pete Fountain) in the late 50s.	
8/14/61	21	32	1. The Greatest Horn In The World [I]	RCA 2366
3/10/62	24	5	2. Horn A-Plenty [I]	RCA 2446
6/06/64	8	38	● 3. **Cotton Candy** [I]	RCA 2917
9/19/64	9	20	● 4. **Sugar Lips**	RCA 2965
11/07/64	18	12	5. "Pops" Goes The Trumpet [I]	RCA 2729
			AL HIRT/BOSTON POPS/ARTHUR FIEDLER	
2/13/65	13	26	● 6. The Best Of Al Hirt [G-I]	RCA 3309
4/17/65	28	10	7. That Honey Horn Sound	RCA 3337
4/23/66	39	3	8. They're Playing Our Song [I]	RCA 3492
12/28/68	3	66	● 9. **Honey In The Horn**	RCA 2733
			Anita Kerr Singers do background vocals on some tracks	
			"Java"(4)	
			DON HO & The Aliis	
			Don was born on 8/13/30 in Oahu, Hawaii. Nightclub singer, actor.	
3/04/67	15	8	1. Tiny Bubbles	Reprise 6232
			JENNIFER HOLLIDAY	
			Born on 10/19/60 in Houston. Tony award winner for Best Actress in Broadway's "Dreamgirls".	
11/05/83	31	5	1. Feel My Soul	Geffen 4014
			THE HOLLIES	
			Formed in Manchester, England in 1962. Consisted of Allan Clarke, lead vocals; Graham Nash and Tony Hicks, guitar; Eric Haydock, bass; and Don Rathbone, drums. Clarke and Nash had worked as duo, the Guytones, added other members, became the Fourtones, Deltas, then The Hollies. First recorded for Parlophone in 1963. Rathbone left in 1963, replaced by Bobby Elliott. Haydock left in 1966, replaced by Bernie Calvert (first heard on "Bus Stop"). Nash left in December, 1968, replaced by Terry Sylvester, formerly in the Swingin' Blue Jeans. Regrouped in 1983 with Clarke, Nash, Hicks and Elliott.	
7/01/67	11	12	1. The Hollies' Greatest Hits [G]	Imperial 12350
4/11/70	32	4	2. He Ain't Heavy, He's My Brother	Epic 26538
			"He Ain't Heavy, He's My Brother"(7)	

DATE	POS	WKS	ARTIST—RECORD TITLE	LABEL & NO.
8/26/72	**21**	5	3. Distant Light *"Long Cool Woman (In A Black Dress)"*(2)	Epic 30958
8/10/74	**28**	2	4. Hollies *"The Air That I Breathe"*(6)	Epic 32574

BUDDY HOLLY

Born Charles Hardin Holley on 9/7/36 in Lubbock, Texas. Began recording (western & bop) demos with Bob Montgomery in 1954. Signed to Decca label in January, 1956, and recorded in Nashville as Buddy Holly & The Three Tunes (Sonny Curtis, lead guitar; Don Guess, bass; and Jerry Allison, drums). In February of 1957, Buddy assembled his backing group, The Crickets (Allison; Niki Sullivan, rhythm guitar; and Joel B. Mauldin, bass) for recordings at Norman Petty's studio in Clovis, New Mexico. Signed to Brunswick and Coral labels (subsidiaries of Decca Records). Because of contract arrangements, all Brunswick records released as The Crickets, and all Coral records released as Buddy Holly. Buddy moved to New York and split with The Crickets in the autumn of 1958. Buddy, Ritchie Valens and the Big Bopper were killed in a plane crash near Mason City, Iowa on 2/3/59 (22).

DATE	POS	WKS	ARTIST—RECORD TITLE	LABEL & NO.
4/27/59	**11**	20	● 1. The Buddy Holly Story [G] includes 4 songs with the Crickets *"That'll Be The Day"*(1) *"Peggy Sue"*(3) *"Oh, Boy!"*(10)	Coral 57279
4/20/63	**40**	1	2. Reminiscing [K] instrumental backing by the Fireballs dubbed in (1962)	Coral 57426

THE HOLLYRIDGE STRINGS

Stu Phillips - arranger/conductor.

DATE	POS	WKS	ARTIST—RECORD TITLE	LABEL & NO.
7/25/64	**15**	9	1. The Beatles Song Book [I]	Capitol 2116

HOLLYWOOD BOWL SYMPHONY ORCHESTRA - see LEONARD PENNARIO

HOLLYWOOD STUDIO ORCHESTRA

DATE	POS	WKS	ARTIST—RECORD TITLE	LABEL & NO.
3/27/61	**23**	1	1. Exodus [I] this is not the original soundtrack album	United Art. 6123

RUPERT HOLMES

Born on 2/24/47 in Cheshire, England. Moved to New York at age 6. Wrote and arranged for The Drifters, Platters, and Gene Pitney. Arranged/produced for Barbra Streisand.

DATE	POS	WKS	ARTIST—RECORD TITLE	LABEL & NO.
1/05/80	**33**	12	● 1. Partners In Crime *"Escape (The Pina Colada Song)"*(1) *"Him"*(6)	Infinity 9020

THE HONEYDRIPPERS

A rock superstar gathering: Robert Plant, Jimmy Page, Jeff Beck and Nile Rodgers.

DATE	POS	WKS	ARTIST—RECORD TITLE	LABEL & NO.
11/03/84	**4**	18	▲ 1. **Volume One** [M] *"Sea Of Love"*(3)	Es Paranza 90220

HOOTERS

Philadelphia rock quintet led by Rob Hyman & Eric Bazilian (arrangers, musicians and backing vocalists on Cyndi Lauper's "She's So Unusual" LP). Hooter: nickname of their keyboard-harmonica.

DATE	POS	WKS	ARTIST—RECORD TITLE	LABEL & NO.
9/28/85	**12**	30	● 1. Nervous Night *"All You Zombies"/"And We Danced"*	Columbia 39912

DATE	POS	WKS	ARTIST—RECORD TITLE	LABEL & NO.
4/12/69	28	7	**MARY HOPKIN** Born on 5/3/50 in Pontardame, Wales. Discovered by the model, Twiggy. 　　1. Post Card 　　　　produced by Paul McCartney 　　*"Those Were The Days"(2)*	Apple 3351
2/19/72	33	3	**NICKY HOPKINS** British session pianist for the Rolling Stones and others 　　1. Jamming With Edward!　　　　　　　　[I] 　　　　jam session with Ry Cooder, Mick Jagger, Bill Wyman & Charlie Watts	Rolling S. 39100
9/16/57 11/17/58 6/22/59	24 20 13	2 1 22	**LENA HORNE** Born on 6/30/17 in Brooklyn. Beautiful Broadway and movie musical star, long married to bandleader Lennie Hayton. Lena's remarkable career reached a new peak in the 1980s with her triumphant one-woman Broadway show. 　　1. Lena Horne at the Waldorf Astoria　　[L] 　　2. Give The Lady What She Wants 　　3. Porgy & Bess **LENA HORNE/HARRY BELAFONTE**	RCA 1028 RCA 1879 RCA 1507
10/25/86	3	35+	**BRUCE HORNSBY & THE RANGE** Piano-based, jazz influenced pop quintet led by singer, songwriter, pianist Hornsby, who was raised in Williamsburg, Virginia and moved to Los Angeles in 1980. ●　1. **The Way It Is** 　　　　originally released on RCA 8058 (with different cover) 　　*"The Way It Is"(1)* 　　*"Mandolin Rain"(4)*	RCA 5904
11/17/62 8/28/65	14 22	11 8	**VLADIMIR HOROWITZ** Classical pianist. Born in the U.S.S.R. 　　1. Vladimir Horowitz (Chopin, Schumann, Rachmaninoff, Liszt)　　　　　　　　[I] 　　2. Horowitz at Carnegie Hall - An Historic Return　　　　　　　　　　　　[I-L]	Columbia 6371 Columbia 728 [2]
2/27/61	8	18	**JOHNNY HORTON** Born on 4/3/29 in Tyler, Texas. Country singing star on the "Louisiana Hayride Radio Show" during the 50s. First recorded with Cormac Records in 1951. Married to Billie Jean Jones, widow of Hank Williams. Killed in an auto accident on 11/5/60. ▲　1. **Johnny Horton's Greatest Hits**　　　[G] 　　*"The Battle Of New Orleans"(1)* 　　*"Sink The Bismarck"(3)* 　　*"North To Alaska"(4)*	Columbia 8396
2/17/79	31	4	**HOT CHOCOLATE** Interracial rock-soul group formed in England by lead singer Errol Brown in 1970. 　　1. Every 1's A Winner 　　*"Every 1's A Winner"(6)*	Infinity 9002
8/15/70	30	5	**HOT TUNA** Formed by Jefferson Airplane members Jorma Kaukonen and Jack Casady. 　　1. Hot Tuna　　　　　　　　　　　　　[L]	RCA 4353

DATE	POS	WKS	ARTIST—RECORD TITLE	LABEL & NO.
			THELMA HOUSTON	
			Soul singer/actress from Leland, Mississippi. In films "Norman..Is That You?", "Death Scream" and "The Seventh Dwarf".	
2/26/77	**11**	16	1. Any Way You Like It	Tamla 345
			"Don't Leave Me This Way"(1)	
			WHITNEY HOUSTON	
			Born in 1963 in New Jersey. Billboard's "Artist of the Year" for 1986. Daughter of Cissy Houston and cousin of Dionne Warwick. Began career as a fashion model, then worked as a backing vocalist. Also see Teddy Pendergrass.	
6/15/85	**1**(14)	78	▲ 1. **Whitney Houston**	Arista 8212
			"You Give Good Love"(3)	
			"Saving All My Love For You"(1)	
			"How Will I Know"(1)	
			"Greatest Love Of All"(1)	
			HUDSON & LANDRY	
			Los Angeles disco jockeys (KGBS), Bob Hudson and Ron Landry.	
6/12/71	**30**	4	1. Hanging In There [C]	Dore 324
1/01/72	**33**	4	2. Losing Their Heads [C]	Dore 326
			THE HUES CORPORATION	
			Black vocal trio based in Los Angeles. Consisted of St. Clair Lee, Fleming Williams and H. Ann Kelley. Williams replaced by Tommy Brown after "Rock The Boat".	
7/20/74	**20**	7	1. Freedom For The Stallion	RCA 0323
			"Rock The Boat"(1)	
			HUGO & LUIGI	
			Producers, songwriters and label executives Hugo Peretti and Luigi Creator.	
5/11/63	**14**	8	1. The Cascading Voices of the Hugo & Luigi Chorus	RCA 2641
			THE HUMAN LEAGUE	
			British 6-member electronic pop band, featuring lead singer/synthesizer player Philip Oakey.	
4/03/82	**3**	20	• 1. **Dare**	A&M 4892
			"Don't You Want Me"(1)	
7/16/83	**22**	8	2. Fascination! [M]	A&M 12501
			"(Keep Feeling) Fascination"(8)	
11/01/86	**24**	12	3. Crash	A&M 5129
			"Human"(1)	
			HUMBLE PIE	
			Hard-rock band formed in late 1968 in Essex, England. Consisted of Peter Frampton (guitar, vocals), Steve Marriott (guitar, vocals), Greg Ridley (bass) and Jerry Shirley (drums). Frampton left, 1971, replaced by Clem Clempson. Disbanded in 1975.	
11/13/71	**21**	8	• 1. Performance-Rockin' The Fillmore [L]	A&M 3506 [2]
4/01/72	**6**	14	• 2. **Smokin'**	A&M 4342
11/18/72	**37**	4	3. Lost And Found [E-R]	A&M 3513 [2]
			reissue of their first two albums "Town And Country" & "As Safe As Yesterday Is"	
4/14/73	**13**	7	4. Eat It	A&M 3701 [2]
			side 4 recorded live in Glasgow, Scotland	

DATE	POS	WKS	ARTIST—RECORD TITLE	LABEL & NO.
			ENGELBERT HUMPERDINCK	
			Born Arnold George Dorsey on 5/2/36 in Madras, India. To Leicester, England in 1947. First recorded for Decca in 1958. Met Tom Jones' manager, Gordon Mills, in 1965, who suggested his name change to Engelbert Humperdinck (a famous German opera composer). Starred in his own musical variety TV series in 1970.	
7/01/67	7	31	● 1. **Release Me**	Parrot 71012
			"Release Me"(4)	
1/06/68	10	11	● 2. **The Last Waltz**	Parrot 71015
9/21/68	12	19	● 3. A Man Without Love	Parrot 71022
4/05/69	12	11	● 4. Engelbert	Parrot 71026
1/03/70	5	19	● 5. **Engelbert Humperdinck**	Parrot 71030
7/18/70	19	8	● 6. We Made It Happen	Parrot 71038
2/27/71	22	8	● 7. Sweetheart	Parrot 71043
9/18/71	25	5	● 8. Another Time, Another Place	Parrot 71048
12/25/76	17	8	▲ 9. After The Lovin'	Epic 34381
			"After The Lovin'"(8)	
			BOBBI HUMPHREY	
			Jazz flautist.	
2/22/75	30	4	1. Satin Doll	Blue Note 344
			IAN HUNTER	
			Born on 6/3/46 in Shrewsburg, England. Leader of "Mott The Hoople", 1969-74.	
6/02/79	35	6	1. You're Never Alone With A Schizophrenic	Chrysalis 1214
			DICK HYMAN	
			Born on 3/8/27 in New York City. Piano playing composer, conductor, arranger who toured Europe with Benny Goodman in 1950. Staff pianist at WMCA and WNBC-New York from 1951-57. Musical director of the Arthur Godfrey Show, 1958-62.	
11/25/57	21	2	1. 60 Great All Time Songs, Vol. 3 [I]	MGM 3537
			groups of medleys played by Dick on the piano	
6/21/69	30	8	2. Moog - The Electric Eclectics of Dick Hyman [I]	Command 938
			JANIS IAN	
			Born Janis Eddy Fink on 4/7/51, New York City. Singer/songwriter/pianist/guitarist.	
8/19/67	29	4	1. Janis Ian	Verve Folk. 3017
			"Society's Child"	
6/21/75	1(1)	24	▲ 2. **Between The Lines**	Columbia 33394
			"At Seventeen"(3)	
1/31/76	12	10	3. Aftertones	Columbia 33919
			ICICLE WORKS	
			Liverpool rock trio: Ian McNabb, Chris Layhe and Chris Sharrock.	
6/30/84	40	2	1. Icicle Works	Arista 8202

DATE	POS	WKS	ARTIST—RECORD TITLE	LABEL & NO.
			BILLY IDOL	
			Born William Broad on 11/30/55 in London, England. Leader of the London punk band, Generation X, 1977-81.	
2/25/84	6	38	▲ 1. **Rebel Yell**	Chrysalis 41450
			"Eyes Without A Face"(4)	
11/08/86	6	21	▲ 2. **Whiplash Smile**	Chrysalis 41514
			"To Be A Lover"(6)	
			JULIO IGLESIAS	
			Born on 9/23/43 in Madrid, Spain. Immensely popular Spanish singer, worldwide.	
4/30/83	32	9	▲ 1. Julio [F]	Columbia 38640
9/08/84	5	21	▲ 2. **1100 Bel Air Place**	Columbia 39157
			"To All The Girls I've Loved Before"(5-with Willie Nelson)	
			THE IMPRESSIONS	
			Soul group formed in Chicago in 1957. Group, originally known as The Roosters, consisted of Jerry Butler, Curtis Mayfield, Sam Gooden and brothers Arthur and Richard Brooks. Butler left for a solo career in 1958, replaced by Fred Cash. The Brooks brothers left in 1968, leaving Mayfield as the trio's leader. Mayfield left in 1970 for a solo career, replaced by Leroy Hutson. In 1972, Hutson was replaced by Reggie Torian and Ralph Johnson. Did film soundtrack for "Three The Hard Way". Butler, Mayfield, Gooden and Cash reunited for a tour in 1983.	
9/12/64	8	21	1. **Keep On Pushing**	ABC-Para. 493
			"Keep On Pushing"(10)	
			"Amen"(7)	
4/17/65	23	9	2. People Get Ready	ABC-Para. 505
5/04/68	35	5	3. We're A Winner	ABC 635
			LUTHER INGRAM	
			Born on 11/30/44 in Jackson, Tennessee. Soul singer, songwriter. First recorded for Smash in 1965. In the film "Wattstax".	
12/09/72	39	3	1. If Loving You Is Wrong I Don't Want To Be Right	Koko 2202
			"(If Loving You Is Wrong) I Don't Want To Be Right"(3)	
			INSTANT FUNK	
			9-man funk ensemble led by James Carmichael.	
3/10/79	12	13	● 1. Instant Funk	Salsoul 8513
			INXS	
			Rock sextet formed in Sydney, Australia: Michael Hutchence (lead singer), Kirk Pengilly, Garry Beers, and brothers Tim, Andy and Jon Farriss.	
2/22/86	11	16	1. Listen Like Thieves	Atlantic 81277
			"What You Need"(5)	
			THE IRISH ROVERS	
			Irish-born folk quintet. Group formed in Alberta, Canada in 1964.	
5/25/68	24	11	1. The Unicorn	Decca 74951
			"The Unicorn"(7)	

DATE	POS	WKS	ARTIST—RECORD TITLE	LABEL & NO.
			IRON BUTTERFLY	
			San Diego heavy-metal rock band. Consisted of Doug Ingle (lead vocals, keyboards), Erik Braunn (lead guitar), Lee Dorman (bass) and Ron Bushy (drums). Braunn left in late 1969, replaced by Mike Pinera and Larry Reinhardt.	
9/07/68	**4**	87	● 1. **In-A-Gadda-Da-Vida**	Atco 250
			side 2 is a 17 minute version of the album title	
2/22/69	**3**	19	● 2. **Ball**	Atco 280
5/23/70	**20**	6	3. Iron Butterfly Live [L]	Atco 318
			side 2 is a 19 minute version of "In-A-Gadda-Da-Vida"	
9/19/70	**16**	7	4. Metamorphosis	Atco 339
			with guitarists Mike Pinera & Larry Reinhardt	
			IRON MAIDEN	
			Heavy-metal quintet from London. Paul Di'anno, lead singer.	
5/22/82	**33**	5	▲ 1. The Number Of The Beast	Harvest 12202
			featuring new lead singer Bruce Dickinson	
6/18/83	**14**	14	▲ 2. Piece Of Mind	Capitol 12274
10/06/84	**21**	7	● 3. Powerslave	Capitol 12321
11/23/85	**19**	10	4. Live After Death [L]	Capitol 12441 [2]
			includes an 8 page color tour booklet	
10/18/86	**11**	18	● 5. Somewhere In Time	Capitol 12524
			THE ISLEY BROTHERS	
			R&B trio of brothers from Cincinnati. Formed in early 1950s as a gospel group. Consisted of O'Kelly, Ronald and Rudolph Isley. Moved to New York in 1957 and first recorded for Teenage Records. Trio added their younger brothers Ernie (guitar, drums) and Marvin Isley (bass, percussion) and brother-in-law Chris Jasper (keyboards), from 1973-84. Formed own label, T-Neck in 1969. O'Kelly died of a heart attack on 3/31/86 (48).	
5/17/69	**22**	7	1. It's Our Thing	T-Neck 3001
			"It's Your Thing"(20)	
9/09/72	**29**	8	2. Brother, Brother, Brother	T-Neck 3009
9/22/73	**8**	13	● 3. **3 + 3**	T-Neck 32453
			"That Lady"(6)	
10/05/74	**14**	9	● 4. Live It Up	T-Neck 33070
6/21/75	**1**(1)	18	◉ 5. **The Heat Is On**	T-Neck 33536
			"Fight The Power"(4)	
6/05/76	**9**	14	● 6. **Harvest For The World**	T-Neck 33809
4/23/77	**6**	14	▲ 7. **Go For Your Guns**	T-Neck 34432
4/22/78	**4**	14	▲ 8. **Showdown**	T-Neck 34930
6/23/79	**14**	7	● 9. Winner Takes All	T-Neck 36077 [2]
4/19/80	**8**	13	▲ 10. **Go All The Way**	T-Neck 36305
4/11/81	**28**	5	● 11. Grand Slam	T-Neck 37080
6/18/83	**19**	9	● 12. Between The Sheets	T-Neck 38674
			IT'S A BEAUTIFUL DAY	
			San Francisco group led by David LaFlamme.	
7/18/70	**28**	5	1. Marrying Maiden	Columbia 1058

DATE	POS	WKS	ARTIST—RECORD TITLE	LABEL & NO.
			BURL IVES	
			Born on 6/14/09 in Hunt Township, Illinois. One of America's best-known folk singers from the 1940s to 60s. Burl has won equal renown as a dramatic actor in movies, Broadway and TV.	
3/31/62	35	5	1. The Versatile Burl Ives!	Decca 4152
			"A Little Bitty Tear"(9)	
6/30/62	24	4	2. It's Just My Funny Way Of Laughin'	Decca 4279
			"Funny Way Of Laughin'"(10)	

J

DATE	POS	WKS	ARTIST—RECORD TITLE	LABEL & NO.
			FREDDIE JACKSON	
			Soul singer/songwriter; raised in Harlem. Backup singer for Melba Moore, Evelyn King, and others.	
7/13/85	10	36	▲ 1. **Rock Me Tonight**	Capitol 12404
			"You Are My Lady"	
11/22/86	23	26	▲ 2. Just Like The First Time	Capitol 12495
			JANET JACKSON	
			Born on 5/16/66 in Gary, Indiana. Sister of The Jacksons (youngest of 9 children). Debuted at age 7 at the MGM Grand in Las Vegas with her brothers. At age 10 she played Penny Gordon in the TV series "Good Times".	
3/29/86	1(2)	65+	▲ 1. **Control**	A&M 5106
			"What Have You Done For Me Lately"(4)	
			"Nasty"(3)	
			"When I Think Of You"(1)	
			"Control"(5)	
			"Let's Wait Awhile"(2)	
			JERMAINE JACKSON	
			Born on 12/11/54 in Gary, Indiana. Fourth oldest of the Jackson family. In Jackson 5 until group left Motown in 1976. Married Hazel Joy Gordy, daughter of Berry Gordy Jr., on 12/15/73.	
9/23/72	27	8	1. Jermaine	Motown 752
			"Daddy's Home"(9)	
5/03/80	6	17	● 2. **Let's Get Serious**	Motown 928
			"Let's Get Serious"(9)	
5/26/84	19	16	● 3. Jermaine Jackson	Arista 8203
			JOE JACKSON	
			Born on 8/11/55 in Burton-on-Trent, England. Singer, songwriter, pianist, featuring an ever-changing music style. Moved to New York City in 1982.	
6/02/79	20	11	● 1. Look Sharp!	A&M 4743
11/10/79	22	7	2. I'm The Man	A&M 4794
9/18/82	4	30	● 3. **Night And Day**	A&M 4906
			"Steppin' Out"(6)	
4/21/84	20	16	4. Body and Soul	A&M 5000
5/03/86	34	8	5. Big World [L]	A&M 6021 [2]
			3 sided album from a special live concert set - includes an 8 page booklet with lyrics in 6 different languages	

DATE	POS	WKS	ARTIST—RECORD TITLE	LABEL & NO.
			MICHAEL JACKSON	
			Born on 8/29/58 in Gary, Indiana. Lead singer of The Jackson 5/ Jacksons (7th of 9 children). His "Thriller" album, with sales of 40 million copies, is the best-selling album in history.	
2/26/72	**14**	12	1. Got To Be There	Motown 747
			"Got To Be There"(4)	
			"Rockin' Robin"(2)	
9/23/72	**5**	15	2. **Ben**	Motown 755
			"Ben"(1)	
9/08/79	**3**	52	▲ 3. **Off The Wall**	Epic 35745
			"Don't Stop 'Til You Get Enough"(1)	
			"Rock With You"(1)	
			"Off The Wall"(10)	
			"She's Out Of My Life"(10)	
12/25/82	**1(37)**	91	▲ 4. **Thriller**	Epic 38112
			the best selling album in history	
			"The Girl Is Mine"(2)	
			"Billie Jean"(1)	
			"Beat It"(1)	
			"Wanna Be Startin' Somethin'"(5)	
			"Human Nature"(7)	
			"P.Y.T. (Pretty Young Thing)"(10)	
			"Thriller"(4)	
			MILLIE JACKSON	
			Born on 7/15/44 in Thompson, GA. Soul singer, songwriter. To Newark, NJ in 1958. Professional singing debut at Club Zanibar in Hoboken, NJ in 1964. First recorded for MGM in 1969.	
12/07/74	**21**	12	● 1. Caught Up	Spring 6703
12/17/77	**34**	7	● 2. Feelin' Bitchy	Spring 6715
			THE JACKSONS	
			Quintet of brothers formed and managed by their father beginning in 1967 in Gary, Indiana. Consisted of Sigmund "Jackie" (b: 5/4/ 51), Toriano "Tito" (b: 10/15/53), Jermaine (b: 12/11/54), Marlon (b: 3/12/57) and lead singer Michael (b: 8/29/58). First recorded for Steeltown in 1968. Known as The Jackson 5 from 1968-75. Jermaine replaced by Randy (b: 10/29/61) in 1976. Jermaine rejoined the group for 1984's highly publicized "Victory" album and tour.	
			THE JACKSON 5:	
1/31/70	**5**	21	1. **Diana Ross Presents The Jackson 5**	Motown 700
			"I Want You Back"(1)	
6/06/70	**4**	21	2. **ABC**	Motown 709
			"ABC"(1)	
			"The Love You Save"(1)	
9/26/70	**4**	23	3. **Third Album**	Motown 718
			"I'll Be There"(1)	
			"Mama's Pearl"(2)	
5/08/71	**11**	14	4. Maybe Tomorrow	Motown 735
			"Never Can Say Goodbye"(2)	
10/16/71	**16**	11	5. Goin' Back To Indiana [TV]	Motown 742
			TV special with guests Bill Cosby & Tom Smothers	

DATE	POS	WKS	ARTIST—RECORD TITLE	LABEL & NO.
1/08/72	12	15	6. Jackson 5 Greatest Hits [G]	Motown 741
			"Sugar Daddy"(10)	
6/17/72	7	17	7. **Lookin' Through The Windows**	Motown 750
11/02/74	16	7	8. Dancing Machine	Motown 780
8/02/75	36	3	9. Moving Violation	Motown 829
			JACKSONS:	
1/29/77	36	3	● 10. The Jacksons	Epic 34229
			"Enjoy Yourself"(6)	
3/10/79	11	15	▲ 11. Destiny	Epic 35552
			"Shake Your Body (Down To The Ground)"(7)	
10/18/80	10	18	▲ 12. **Triumph**	Epic 36424
12/12/81	30	8	13. Jacksons Live [L]	Epic 37545 [2]
7/21/84	4	15	▲ 14. **Victory**	Epic 38946
			"State Of Shock"(3)	
			MICK JAGGER	
			Born Michael Phillip Jagger on 7/26/43 in Dartford, England. Lead singer of The Rolling Stones.	
3/16/85	13	12	▲ 1. She's The Boss	Columbia 39940
			"Just Another Night"	
			AHMAD JAMAL	
			Jazz pianist.	
9/22/58	3	01	1. **But Not For Me/Ahmad Jamal at the Pershing** [I-L]	Argo 628
11/17/58	11	16	2. Ahmad Jamal, Volume IV [I-L]	Argo 636
2/01/60	32	7	3. Jamal At The Penthouse [I]	Argo 646
			THE JAMES GANG	
			Cleveland hard-rock band. Lineup in 1969 consisted of Jim Fox (drums), Tom Kriss (bass) and Joe Walsh (guitar, keyboards, vocals). Kriss replaced by Dale Peters in 1970. Walsh left in late 1971, replaced by Dominic Troiano and Roy Kenner. Troiano left in 1973, replaced by Tommy Bolin. Group disbanded in 1976.	
8/29/70	20	12	● 1. James Gang Rides Again	ABC 711
5/08/71	27	16	● 2. Thirds	ABC 721
9/25/71	24	5	● 3. James Gang Live In Concert [L]	ABC 733
			BOB JAMES	
			Born on 12/25/39 in Marshall, Montana. Jazz fusion keyboardist. Did session work for many top stars beginning in late 60s. Producer/arranger for CTI/Kudo Records from 1973. Formed own label, Tappan Zee, in 1977.	
5/07/77	38	2	1. BJ4 [I]	CTI 7074
2/24/79	37	2	● 2. Touchdown [I]	Tappan Zee 35594
12/01/79	23	13	● 3. One On One [I]	Tappan Zee 36241
			BOB JAMES & EARL KLUGH	
			HARRY JAMES	
			Star trumpet player and bandleader. Died on 7/5/83 (67).	
11/12/55	10	2	1. **Harry James in Hi-Fi**	Capitol 654
			featuring vocals by Helen Forrest	

DATE	POS	WKS	ARTIST—RECORD TITLE	LABEL & NO.
			RICK JAMES	
			Born James Johnson on 2/1/52 in Buffalo. "Punk funk" singer, songwriter, guitarist. In Mynah Birds band with Neil Young, late 60s. To London, England, formed band Main Line. Returned to US and formed Stone City Band, did production work for Teena Marie, Mary Jane Girls, Eddie Murphy, and others.	
7/22/78	13	16	● 1. Come Get It!	Gordy 981
2/17/79	16	16	2. Bustin' Out Of L Seven	Gordy 984
12/01/79	34	3	3. Fire It Up	Gordy 990
5/30/81	3	27	▲ 4. **Street Songs**	Gordy 1002
6/12/82	13	10	● 5. Throwin' Down	Gordy 6005
9/10/83	16	12	● 6. Cold Blooded	Gordy 6043
			TOMMY JAMES & THE SHONDELLS	
			Group formed by James at age 12 in Niles, Michigan. Recorded "Hanky Panky" on the Snap label in 1963. Tommy re-located to Pittsburgh in 1965, after a disc jockey there popularized the tune. Original master was sold to Roulette, whereupon Tommy recruited a Pittsburgh group "The Raconteurs" to become the official Shondells. Consisted of Mike Vale (bass), Pete Lucia (drums), Eddie Gray (guitar) and Ronnie Rosman (organ).	
2/08/69	8	14	1. **Crimson & Clover**	Roulette 42023
			"Crimson & Clover"(1)	
			"Crystal Blue Persuasion"(2)	
12/27/69	21	10	2. The Best Of Tommy James & The Shondells [G]	Roulette 42040
			JAN & DEAN	
			Jan Berry (b: 4/3/41) and Dean Torrence (b: 3/10/40) formed group called the Barons while attending high school in Los Angeles. Jan & Dean and Barons member Arnie Ginsburg recorded "Jennie Lee" in Jan's garage. Dean left for a six month Army Reserve stint, whereupon Jan signed with Doris Day's label, Arwin, and the record was released as by Jan & Arnie. Upon Dean's return from the service, Arnie joined the Navy, and Jan & Dean signed with Herb Alpert's Dore label. Jan was critically injured in an auto accident on 4/19/66. Duo made a big comeback in 1978, after the showing of their biographical film "Dead Man's Curve".	
9/21/63	32	4	1. Surf City And Other Swingin' Cities	Liberty 7314
			"Surf City"(1)	
2/22/64	22	2	2. Drag City	Liberty 7339
			"Drag City"(10)	
1/16/65	40	1	3. The Little Old Lady From Pasadena	Liberty 7377
			"The Little Old Lady (From Pasadena)"(3)	
5/08/65	33	3	4. Command Performance/Live In Person [L]	Liberty 7403
			HORST JANKOWSKI	
			Born on 1/30/36 in Berlin, Germany. Jazz pianist.	
7/24/65	18	12	1. The Genius Of Jankowski! [I]	Mercury 60993
			"A Walk In The Black Forest"	
			AL JARREAU	
			Born on 3/12/40 in Milwaukee. Soul/jazz vocalist. Has won 4 Grammys.	
8/02/80	27	5	● 1. This Time	Warner 3434
8/29/81	9	20	▲ 2. **Breakin' Away**	Warner 3576
4/23/83	13	12	● 3. Jarreau	Warner 23801

DATE	POS	WKS	ARTIST—RECORD TITLE	LABEL & NO.

JAY & THE AMERICANS

Group formed in late 1959 by New York University students as the Harbor-Lites: John "Jay" Traynor (formerly with the Mystics), Sandy Yaguda, Kenny Vance (later a Hollywood musical director) and Howie Kane. Guitarist Marty Sanders joined during production of their first album in 1961. Traynor left after their first hit and was replaced by lead singer David "Jay" Black in 1962.

DATE	POS	WKS	ARTIST—RECORD TITLE	LABEL & NO.
1/15/66	21	5	1. Jay & The Americans Greatest Hits! [G]	United Art. 6453

JAZZ CRUSADERS - see CRUSADERS

JEFFERSON STARSHIP

Formed as Jefferson Airplane in San Francisco, 1965. Consisted of Marty Balin and Grace Slick (vocals), Paul Kantner (vocals, guitar), Jorma Kaukonen (guitar), Jack Casady (bass) and Spencer Dryden (drums). Slick and Dryden joined in 1966, replacing Signe Anderson and Skip Spence. Slick had been in the Great Society. Spence then formed Moby Grape. Dryden replaced by Joey Covington in 1970. Casady and Kaukonen left by 1974 to go full time with Hot Tuna. Balin left in 1971, rejoined in 1975, by which time group was renamed Jefferson Starship and consisted of Slick, Kantner, Papa John Creach (violin), David Freiberg (bass), Craig Chaquico (guitar), Pete Sears (bass) and John Barbata (drums). Slick left group from June, 1978 to January, 1981 due to personal problems. In 1979, singer Mickey Thomas joined, along with Aynsley Dunbar who replaced Barbata. Don Baldwin replaced Dunbar in 1982. Kantner left in 1984, and, due to legal difficulties, band's name was shortened to Starship, whose lineup includes Slick, Thomas, Sears, Chaquico and Baldwin.

JEFFERSON AIRPLANE:

DATE	POS	WKS	ARTIST—RECORD TITLE	LABEL & NO.
1/07/67	17	9	1. After Bathing At Baxter's	RCA 1511
5/06/67	3	29	● 2. **Surrealistic Pillow**	RCA 3766
			"Somebody To Love"(5)	
			"White Rabbit"(8)	
9/21/68	6	12	● 3. **Crown Of Creation**	RCA 4058
3/08/69	17	8	4. Bless It's Pointed Little Head [L]	RCA 4133
11/29/69	13	13	● 5. Volunteers	RCA 4238
12/12/70	12	14	● 6. The Worst Of Jefferson Airplane [G]	RCA 4459
9/18/71	11	11	● 7. Bark	Grunt 1001
9/09/72	20	9	● 8. Long John Silver	Grunt 1007

JEFFERSON STARSHIP:

DATE	POS	WKS	ARTIST—RECORD TITLE	LABEL & NO.
11/23/74	11	10	● 9. Dragon Fly	Grunt 0717
7/26/75	1(4)	32	● 10. **Red Octopus**	Grunt 0999
			"Miracles"(3)	
7/24/76	3	16	▲ 11. **Spitfire**	Grunt 1557
2/19/77	37	3	12. Flight Log (1966-1976) [K]	Grunt 1255 [2]
			anthology of Airplane, Starship, Hot Tuna, Slick and Kantner solo releases	
3/18/78	5	23	▲ 13. **Earth**	Grunt 2515
			"Count On Me"(8)	
2/24/79	20	5	● 14. Gold [G]	Grunt 3247
12/08/79	10	17	● 15. **Freedom At Point Zero**	Grunt 3452
5/09/81	26	16	● 16. Modern Times	Grunt 3848
11/13/82	26	11	17. Winds Of Change	Grunt 4372
7/07/84	28	8	● 18. Nuclear Furniture	Grunt 4921

DATE	POS	WKS	ARTIST—RECORD TITLE	LABEL & NO.
10/26/85	7	33	**STARSHIP:** ● 19. **Knee Deep In The Hoopla** *"We Built This City"(1)* *"Sara"(1)*	Grunt 5488
11/24/56	13	4	**GORDON JENKINS** Born on 5/12/10 in Webster Groves, MO. Pianist-arranger in early 30s with Isham Jones, Benny Goodman and others. Musical director and conductor for Decca Records beginning in 1945. Died on 5/1/84 (73). 1. Gordon Jenkins complete Manhattan Tower a musical narrative originally composed by Jenkins in 1945	Capitol 766
			WAYLON JENNINGS Born on 6/15/37 in Littlefield, Texas. While working as a DJ in Lubbock, Texas, Waylon befriended Buddy Holly. Holly produced Waylon's first record "Jole Blon" in 1958. Waylon then joined with Buddy's backing band as bass guitarist on the fateful "Winter Dance Party" tour in 1959. Established himself in the mid-70s as a leader of the "Outlaws" movement in Country music. Married to Jessi Colter since 1969.	
8/21/76	34	2	● 1. Are You Ready For The Country	RCA 1816
5/28/77	15	12	▲ 2. Ol' Waylon	RCA 2317
2/18/78	12	9	▲ 3. Waylon & Willie	RCA 2686
			WAYLON JENNINGS & WILLIE NELSON	
6/23/79	28	4	▲ 4. Greatest Hits [G]	RCA 3378
7/05/80	36	3	● 5. Music Man	RCA 3602
4/24/82	39	2	6. Black On Black	RCA 4247
5/17/86	21	25	**THE JETS** Wolfgramm family from Minneapolis consisting of eight siblings, ages 11-19. ● 1. The Jets *"Crush On You"(3)* *"You Got It All"(3)*	MCA 5667
			JETHRO TULL Progressive rock group formed in 1968 in Blackpool, England. Consisted of Ian Anderson (lead singer, flutist), Mick Abrahams (guitar), Glenn Cornick (bass) and Clive Bunker (drums). Named band after 18th century agriculturist Jethro Tull. Abrahams replaced by Martin Barre in 1968. Added keyboardist John Evans in 1970. Cornick replaced by Jeffrey Hammond-Hammond in 1971. Bunker left in late 1971 and was replaced by Barriemore Barlow, who in turn was replaced by John Glascock (died in 1979). Ian has revamped his lineup several times since then.	
10/25/69	20	9	● 1. Stand Up	Reprise 6360
5/16/70	11	17	● 2. Benefit	Reprise 6400
5/15/71	7	32	● 3. **Aqualung**	Reprise 2035
5/20/72	1(2)	20	● 4. **Thick As A Brick**	Reprise 2072
11/18/72	3	21	● 5. **Living In The Past** [K] primarily features unreleased material (1968-1971) - side 3 recorded live in Carnegie Hall	Chrysalis 2106 [2]
7/28/73	1(1)	14	● 6. **A Passion Play**	Chrysalis 1040
11/02/74	2(3)	23	● 7. **War Child**	Chrysalis 1067
10/04/75	7	8	● 8. **Minstrel In The Gallery**	Chrysalis 1082
1/31/76	13	9	▲ 9. M.U. - The Best Of Jethro Tull [G]	Chrysalis 1078

DATE	POS	WKS	ARTIST—RECORD TITLE	LABEL & NO.
6/05/76	**14**	7	10. Too Old To Rock 'N' Roll: Too Young To Die!	Chrysalis 1111
3/12/77	**8**	14	● 11. **Songs From The Wood**	Chrysalis 1132
5/06/78	**19**	8	● 12. Heavy Horses	Chrysalis 1175
10/28/78	**21**	8	● 13. Jethro Tull Live - Bursting Out [L]	Chrysalis 1201 [2]
10/13/79	**22**	5	● 14. Stormwatch	Chrysalis 1238
10/04/80	**30**	4	15. "A"	Chrysalis 1301
5/22/82	**19**	7	16. The Broadsword And The Beast	Chrysalis 1380
			JOAN JETT & THE BLACKHEARTS	
			Joan was born on 9/22/60 in Philadelphia. Played guitar with the Los Angeles female rock band The Runaways, 1975-78. Formed her backing band, The Blackhearts, in 1980. Starred in the 1987 film "Light Of Day" as the leader of a rock band called The Barbusters.	
2/06/82	**2(3)**	20	▲ 1. **I Love Rock-n-Roll**	Boardwalk 33243
			"I Love Rock 'N Roll"(1)	
			"Crimson And Clover"(7)	
7/23/83	**20**	10	● 2. Album	Blackheart 5437
			JOSE JIMENEZ - see BILL DANA	
			ANTONIO CARLOS JOBIM	
			Brazilian guitarist/pianist/vocalist.	
5/13/67	**19**	6	1. Francis Albert Sinatra & Antonio Carlos Jobim	Reprise 1021
			BILLY JOEL	
			Born William Martin Joel on 5/9/49 in Long Island, NY. Formed his first band in 1964, the Echoes, which later became the Lost Souls. Member of the Long Island group, The Hassles, late 60s, then formed a rock duo with The Hassles' drummer Jon Small, called Attila. Signed to Columbia Records in 1973. Involved in a serious motorcycle accident on Long Island in 1982. Married model Christie Brinkley in 1985.	
3/23/74	**27**	7	▲ 1. Piano Man	Columbia 32544
12/21/74	**35**	2	● 2. Streetlife Serenade	Columbia 33146
11/12/77	**2(6)**	70	▲ 3. **The Stranger**	Columbia 34987
			"Just The Way You Are"(3)	
11/04/78	**1(8)**	34	▲ 4. **52nd Street**	Columbia 35609
			"My Life"(3)	
3/22/80	**1(6)**	35	▲ 5. **Glass Houses**	Columbia 36384
			"You May Be Right"(7)	
			"It's Still Rock And Roll To Me"(1)	
10/03/81	**8**	10	▲ 6. **Songs In The Attic** [L]	Columbia 37461
			1980 concert tour recordings of pre-"Stranger" songs	
10/16/82	**7**	23	▲ 7. **The Nylon Curtain**	Columbia 38200
8/20/83	**4**	62	▲ 8. **An Innocent Man**	Columbia 38837
			"Tell Her About It"(1)	
			"Uptown Girl"(3)	
			"An Innocent Man"(10)	

DATE	POS	WKS	ARTIST—RECORD TITLE	LABEL & NO.
7/27/85	6	26	▲ 9. **Greatest Hits, Volume I & Volume II** [G]	Columbia 40121 [2]
			"You're Only Human (Second Wind)"(9)	
8/23/86	7	29	▲ 10. **The Bridge**	Columbia 40402
			"Modern Woman"(10)	
			"A Matter Of Trust"(10)	

ELTON JOHN

Born Reginald Kenneth Dwight on 3/25/47 in Pinner, Middlesex, England. Formed his first group, Bluesology, in 1966. Group backed visiting U.S. soul artists and later became Long John Baldry's backing band. Took the name of Elton John from the first names of Bluesology member Elton Dean and John Baldry. Teamed up with lyricist Bernie Taupin beginning in 1969. Formed own record label, Rocket Records, in 1973. Performed as the Pinball Wizard in the film version of "Tommy".

DATE	POS	WKS	ARTIST—RECORD TITLE	LABEL & NO.
10/31/70	4	28	● 1. **Elton John**	Uni 73090
			"Your Song"(8)	
1/23/71	5	20	● 2. **Tumbleweed Connection**	Uni 73096
4/17/71	36	4	● 3. **"Friends"** [S]	Paramount 6004
5/29/71	11	12	4. **11-17-70** [L]	Uni 93105
			title is date of a live New York radio concert broadcast	
12/04/71	8	25	● 5. **Madman Across The Water**	Uni 93120
6/24/72	1(5)	25	● 6. **Honky Chateau**	Uni 93135
			"Rocket Man"(6)	
			"Honky Cat"(8)	
2/17/73	1(2)	27	● 7. **Don't Shoot Me I'm Only The Piano Player**	MCA 2100
			"Crocodile Rock"(1)	
			"Daniel"(2)	
10/20/73	1(8)	53	● 8. **Goodbye Yellow Brick Road**	MCA 10003 [2]
			"Goodbye Yellow Brick Road"(2)	
			"Bennie And The Jets"(1)	
7/06/74	1(4)	20	● 9. **Caribou**	MCA 2116
			"Don't Let The Sun Go Down On Me"(2)	
			"The Bitch Is Back"(4)	
11/30/74	1(10)	20	● 10. **Elton John - Greatest Hits** [G]	MCA 2128
2/08/75	6	8	11. **Empty Sky** [E-R]	MCA 2130
			Elton's first album originally released in 1969	
6/07/75	1(7)	24	● 12. **Captain Fantastic And The Brown Dirt Cowboy**	MCA 2142
			"Someone Saved My Life Tonight"(4)	
11/08/75	1(3)	9	● 13. **Rock Of The Westies**	MCA 2163
			"Island Girl"(1)	
5/22/76	4	8	● 14. **Here And There** [L]	MCA 2197
			side 1: live in London; side 2: live in New York (both 1974)	
11/13/76	3	12	▲ 15. **Blue Moves**	MCA/Rocket 11004 [2]
			"Sorry Seems To Be The Hardest Word"(6)	
10/29/77	21	8	▲ 16. **Elton John's Greatest Hits, Volume II** [G]	MCA 3027
			"Lucy In The Sky With Diamonds"(1)	
			"Philadelphia Freedom"(1)	
			"Don't Go Breaking My Heart"(1)	

DATE	POS	WKS	ARTIST—RECORD TITLE	LABEL & NO.
11/18/78	15	7	▲ 17. A Single Man	MCA 3065
11/10/79	35	4	18. Victim Of Love	MCA 5104
6/07/80	13	9	● 19. 21 At 33	MCA 5121
			"Little Jeannie"(3)	
6/13/81	21	5	20. The Fox	Geffen 2002
5/15/82	17	8	● 21. Jump Up!	Geffen 2013
6/25/83	25	13	● 22. Too Low For Zero	Geffen 4006
			"I Guess That's Why They Call It The Blues"(4)	
7/28/84	20	14	● 23. Breaking Hearts	Geffen 24031
			"Sad Songs (Say So Much)"(5)	
			JOHNNY & THE HURRICANES Rock and roll instrumental band formed as the Orbits in Toledo, Ohio in 1958. Consisted of leader John Pocisk ("Paris"), saxophone; Paul Tesluk, organ; Dave Yorko, guitar; Lionel "Butch" Mattice, bass; and Tony Kaye, drums (replaced in late 1959 by Bill Savich). First recorded for Twirl in 1959. Paris had own label, Attila, from 1965-70.	
4/18/60	34	3	1. Stormsville [I]	Warwick 2010
			DON JOHNSON Actor born on 12/15/49, Flatt Creek, MO. Plays Sonny Crockett on TV's "Miami Vice".	
9/20/86	17	11	● 1. Heartbeat	Epic 40366
			"Heartbeat"(5)	
			FRANCE JOLI French-Canadian singer from Montreal, Canada. Age 16 in 1979.	
10/13/79	26	6	1. France Joli	Prelude 12170
			AL JOLSON One of America's all-time great entertainers. Born Asa Yoelson on 3/26/1886 in St. Petersburg, Russia; raised in Washington, DC. First appeared on Broadway in 1911 and for the next 20 years he was king of the American musical. Starred in 1927 film "The Jazz Singer", ushering in the age of sound motion picures. Died on 10/23/50.	
6/22/63	40	1	1. The Best Of Jolson [G] Al's recordings for the soundtracks "The Jolson Story" & "Jolson Sings Again"	Decca 169 [2]
			GRACE JONES Jamaican-born disco singer, fashion model, actress. Raised in Syracuse from age 12.	
7/11/81	32	4	1. Nightclubbing	Island 9624
			HOWARD JONES Born on 2/23/55 in Southampton, England. Pop singer, songwriter, synth wizard.	
5/04/85	10	21	● 1. **Dream Into Action**	Elektra 60390
			"Things Can Only Get Better"(5)	
6/14/86	34	6	2. Action Replay [M] 6 tracks; includes 3 remixes & 2 previously unreleased songs "No One Is To Blame"(4)	Elektra 60466

DATE	POS	WKS	ARTIST—RECORD TITLE	LABEL & NO.
			JACK JONES	
			Born on 1/14/38 in Los Angeles. Son of actor/singer Allan Jones, who had the hit "The Donkey Serenade" (POS 8) the year Jack was born.	
2/08/64	18	24	1. Wives And Lovers	Kapp 3352
2/06/65	11	11	2. Dear Heart	Kapp 3415
7/03/65	29	6	3. My Kind Of Town	Kapp 3433
9/03/66	9	15	4. **The Impossible Dream**	Kapp 3486
4/29/67	23	6	5. Lady	Kapp 3511
			JONAH JONES	
			Jazz trumpet player.	
3/10/58	7	17	1. **Muted Jazz** [I]	Capitol 839
4/28/58	7	19	2. **Swingin' On Broadway** [I]	Capitol 963
9/08/58	14	5	3. Jumpin' With Jonah [I]	Capitol 1039
			QUINCY JONES	
			Born Quincy Delight Jones, Jr. on 3/14/33 in Chicago. Composer, conductor, arranger, producer. Began as a jazz trumpeter, with Lionel Hampton, 1950-53. Music Director for Mercury Records in 1961, then Vice President in 1964. Wrote scores for many films, 1965-73. Scored TV series "Roots" in 1977. Produced Michael Jackson's "Thriller" album. Arranger and producer for hundreds of successful singers and orchestras. Winner of 19 Grammys.	
6/22/74	6	22	• 1. **Body Heat**	A&M 3617
9/06/75	16	11	2. Mellow Madness	A&M 4526
			this album introduces the Brothers Johnson	
3/05/77	21	6	• 3. Roots [TV]	A&M 4626
7/01/78	15	9	▲ 4. Sounds…And Stuff Like That!!	A&M 4685
4/18/81	10	26	▲ 5. **The Dude**	A&M 3721
			featuring James Ingram's vocals on "Just Once" & "One Hundred Ways"	
			RICKIE LEE JONES	
			Born on 11/8/54 in Chicago. Pop jazz-styled singer, songwriter. Moved to Los Angeles in 1977.	
4/28/79	3	24	▲ 1. **Rickie Lee Jones**	Warner 3296
			"Chuck E.'s In Love"(4)	
8/08/81	5	15	• 2. **Pirates**	Warner 3432
7/30/83	39	2	3. Girl At Her Volcano [M]	Warner 23805
			10" album - 2 of the 7 tracks are live performances	
			TOM JONES	
			Born Thomas Jones Woodward on 6/7/40 in Pontypridd, Wales. Worked local clubs as Tommy Scott, formed own trio, The Senators in 1963. Solo to London in 1964. Host of his own TV musical variety series from 1969-71.	
2/08/69	5	25	• 1. **Help Yourself**	Parrot 71025
4/19/69	14	13	• 2. The Tom Jones Fever Zone	Parrot 71019
4/26/69	13	21	• 3. Tom Jones Live! [L]	Parrot 71014
			originally recorded & released in 1967	
6/21/69	4	26	• 4. **This Is Tom Jones**	Parrot 71028
11/15/69	3	26	• 5. **Tom Jones Live In Las Vegas** [L]	Parrot 71031

DATE	POS	WKS	ARTIST—RECORD TITLE	LABEL & NO.
5/16/70	6	13	● 6. **Tom**	Parrot 71037
			"Without Love (There Is Nothing)"(5)	
12/05/70	23	3	● 7. I (Who Have Nothing)	Parrot 71039
5/29/71	17	9	● 8. She's A Lady	Parrot 71046
			"She's A Lady"(2)	

JANIS JOPLIN

Born on 1/19/43 in Port Arthur, Texas. White blues/rock singer. Nicknamed Pearl. To San Francisco in 1966, joined Big Brother & The Holding Company. Left band to go solo in 1968. Died of a heroin overdose in Hollywood on 10/4/70. The Bette Midler film "The Rose" was inspired by Joplin's life.

DATE	POS	WKS	ARTIST—RECORD TITLE	LABEL & NO.
10/18/69	5	16	● 1. **I Got Dem Ol' Kozmic Blues Again Mama!**	Columbia 9913
2/06/71	1(9)	23	▲ 2. **Pearl**	Columbia 30322
			"Me And Bobby McGee"(1)	
5/20/72	4	16	● 3. **Joplin In Concert** [L]	Columbia 31160 [2]
			<small>side 1: with Big Brother & The Holding Co.</small>	
			<small>side 2: with Full Tilt Boogie Band</small>	
8/18/73	37	2	▲ 4. Janis Joplin's Greatest Hits [G]	Columbia 32168

JOURNEY

Rock group formed in San Francisco in 1973. Consisted of Neal Schon, George Tickner (guitars), Gregg Rolie (keyboards, vocals), Ross Valory (bass) and Aynsley Dunbar (drums). Schon and Rolie had been in Santana. Tickner left in 1975. Steve Perry (lead vocals) added in 1978. Dunbar was replaced by Steve Smith in 1979. Jonathan Cain (keyboards) added in 1981, replacing Rolie. In 1986 group pared down to a 3-man core: Perry, Schon and Cain.

DATE	POS	WKS	ARTIST—RECORD TITLE	LABEL & NO.
3/25/78	21	13	▲ 1. Infinity	Columbia 34912
4/28/79	20	22	▲ 2. Evolution	Columbia 35797
3/22/80	8	17	▲ 3. **Departure**	Columbia 36339
2/21/81	9	12	▲ 4. **Captured** [L]	Columbia 37016 [2]
8/08/81	1(1)	58	▲ 5. **Escape**	Columbia 37408
			"Who's Crying Now"(4)	
			"Don't Stop Believin'"(9)	
			"Open Arms"(2)	
2/19/83	2(9)	42	▲ 6. **Frontiers**	Columbia 38504
			"Separate Ways (Worlds Apart)"(8)	
5/10/86	4	29	▲ 7. **Raised On Radio**	Columbia 39936
			"Be Good To Yourself"(9)	

JUDAS PRIEST

Heavy-metal rock band formed in Birmingham, England in 1973. Group consists of vocalist Rob Halford, guitarists K.K. Downing and Glenn Tipton, bassist Ian Hill and drummer Dave Holland.

DATE	POS	WKS	ARTIST—RECORD TITLE	LABEL & NO.
7/05/80	34	3	● 1. British Steel	Columbia 36443
5/23/81	39	2	2. Point Of Entry	Columbia 37052
8/07/82	17	21	▲ 3. Screaming For Vengeance	Columbia 38160
2/11/84	18	12	● 4. Defenders Of The Faith	Columbia 39219
4/19/86	17	11	● 5. Turbo	Columbia 40158

DATE	POS	WKS	ARTIST—RECORD TITLE	LABEL & NO.

K

BERT KAEMPFERT

Born on 10/16/23 in Hamburg, Germany. Multi-instrumentalist, bandleader, record producer, composer, arranger for Polydor Records in Germany. Produced the first Beatles' recording session. Died on 6/21/80 in Zug, Switzerland.

DATE	POS	WKS	ARTIST—RECORD TITLE	LABEL & NO.
12/31/60	1(5)	30	● 1. **Wonderland By Night** [I] "Wonderland By Night"(1)	Decca 74101
10/06/62	14	12	2. That Happy Feeling [I]	Decca 74305
2/27/65	5	27	● 3. **Blue Midnight** [I]	Decca 74569
10/09/65	27	10	4. The Magic Music Of Far Away Places [I]	Decca 74616
9/03/66	39	2	5. Strangers In The Night [I]	Decca 74795
12/17/66	30	6	● 6. Bert Kaempfert's Greatest Hits [G-I]	Decca 74810

KAJAGOOGOO

English pop/synth quintet led by Limahl.

DATE	POS	WKS	ARTIST—RECORD TITLE	LABEL & NO.
7/09/83	38	2	1. White Feathers "Too Shy"(5)	EMI America 17094

KANSAS

Progressive rock group formed in Topeka in 1970. Consisted of Steve Walsh (lead vocals, keyboards), Kerry Livgren (guitar & keyboards), Phil Ehart (drums), Robby Steinhardt (violin), Rich Williams (guitar) and Dave Hope (bass). Walsh left in 1981 and was replaced by John Elefante. Reformed lineup in 1986: Walsh, Ehart, Williams, Steve Morse and Billy Greer.

DATE	POS	WKS	ARTIST—RECORD TITLE	LABEL & NO.
12/11/76	5	26	▲ 1. **Leftoverture** "Carry On Wayward Son"	Kirshner 34224
10/29/77	4	33	▲ 2. **Point Of Know Return** "Dust In The Wind"(6)	Kirshner 34929
12/09/78	32	5	▲ 3. Two For The Show [L]	Kirshner 35660 [2]
6/16/79	10	9	● 4. **Monolith**	Kirshner 36008
10/11/80	26	8	● 5. Audio-Visions	Kirshner 36588
6/26/82	16	6	6. Vinyl Confessions	Kirshner 38002

PAUL KANTNER

Original member of Jefferson Airplane & Jefferson Starship.

DATE	POS	WKS	ARTIST—RECORD TITLE	LABEL & NO.
12/26/70	20	11	● 1. Blows Against The Empire	RCA 4448

PAUL KANTNER/JEFFERSON STARSHIP

with Grace Slick, Jerry Garcia, David Crosby & Graham Nash

KATRINA & THE WAVES

British-based pop/rock quartet fronted by Kansas-born Katrina Leskanich.

DATE	POS	WKS	ARTIST—RECORD TITLE	LABEL & NO.
5/25/85	25	9	1. Katrina And The Waves "Walking On Sunshine"(9)	Capitol 12400

DATE	POS	WKS	ARTIST—RECORD TITLE	LABEL & NO.
			SAMMY KAYE	
			Born on 3/13/10 in Rocky River, Ohio; died on 6/2/87 (cancer). Durable leader of popular "sweet" dance band with the slogan "Swing and Sway with Sammy Kaye". Also clarinet/alto saxman.	
8/04/56	20	1	1. My Fair Lady (For Dancing) [I]	Columbia 885
11/17/56	19	1	2. What Makes Sammy Swing and Sway [I]	Columbia 891
			KC & THE SUNSHINE BAND	
			Disco/R&B band formed in Florida in 1973 by lead singer, keyboardist Harry "KC" Casey and bassist Richard Finch. Integrated band contained from 7 to 11 members. Casey and Finch wrote, arranged and produced all of their hits.	
9/06/75	4	24	1. **KC And The Sunshine Band**	TK 603
			"Get Down Tonight"(1)	
			"That's The Way (I Like It)"(1)	
10/23/76	13	26	2. Part 3	TK 605
			"(Shake, Shake, Shake) Shake Your Booty"(1)	
			"I'm Your Boogie Man"(1)	
			"Keep It Comin' Love"(2)	
9/09/78	36	5	3. Who Do Ya (Love)	TK 607
			EDDIE KENDRICKS	
			Born on 12/17/39 in Union Springs, Alabama. Raised in Birmingham. Joined R&B group the Primes in Detroit in the late 50s. Group later evolved into The Temptations. Eddie was their lead singer from 1960-71. Eddie recently dropped the letter S from his last name.	
9/29/73	18	8	1. Eddie Kendricks	Tamla 327
			"Keep On Truckin'"(1)	
4/06/74	30	4	2. Boogie Down!	Tamla 330
			"Boogie Down"(2)	
4/17/76	38	2	3. He's A Friend	Tamla 343
			JOHN FITZGERALD KENNEDY	
			Tributes to President Kennedy who was assassinated on 11/22/63 (46).	
1/11/64	8	8	1. **The Presidential Years 1960-1963** [T]	20th Century 3127
			narrated by David Teig	
1/25/64	5	8	2. **That Was The Week That Was** [T]	Decca 9116
			the BBC telecast tribute to Kennedy on 11/23/63	
2/01/64	18	4	● 3. A Memorial Album [T]	Premier 2099
			narrated by Ed Brown - a broadcast by WMCA, New York on 11/22/63	
2/22/64	29	4	4. Four Days That Shocked The World [T]	Colpix 2500
			Nov. 22-25, 1963 (complete story narrated by Reid Collins)	
			STAN KENTON	
			Born on 2/19/12 in Wichita, Kansas. Died in Los Angeles on 8/25/79. Organized his first jazz band in 1941. Third person named to the Jazz Hall of Fame.	
9/08/56	13	2	1. Kenton in Hi-Fi [I]	Capitol 724
9/15/56	17	4	2. Cuban Fire! [I]	Capitol 731
11/20/61	16	28	3. Kenton's West Side Story [I]	Capitol 1609
			DICK KESNER & his Stradivarius Violin	
1/12/59	22	2	1. Lawrence Welk Presents Dick Kesner [I]	Brunswick 54044

DATE	POS	WKS	ARTIST—RECORD TITLE	LABEL & NO.
			CHAKA KHAN	
			Born Yvette Marie Stevens on 3/23/53 in Great Lakes, Illinois. Lead singer of Rufus from 1972-81.	
11/18/78	12	8	● 1. Chaka	Warner 3245
5/16/81	17	9	● 2. What Cha' Gonna Do For Me	Warner 3526
11/03/84	14	15	▲ 3. I Feel For You	Warner 25162
			"I Feel For You"(3)	
			GREG KIHN BAND	
			Greg is a rock singer, songwriter, guitarist from Baltimore. Formed band in Berkeley, California.	
8/01/81	32	5	1. Rockihnroll	Beserkley 10069
5/15/82	33	4	2. Kihntinued	Beserkley 60101
3/19/83	15	12	3. Kihnspiracy	Beserkley 60224
			"Jeopardy"(2)	
			ANDY KIM	
			Born Andrew Joachim on 12/5/46 in Montreal, Canada. His parents were from Lebanon. Pop singer, songwriter. Teamed with Jeff Barry to write "Sugar, Sugar".	
10/26/74	21	6	1. Andy Kim	Capitol 11318
			"Rock Me Gently"(1)	
			KING CRIMSON	
			English progressive rock group formed in 1969 by the eccentric Robert Fripp. Group featured an ever-changing lineup of top British artists.	
2/28/70	28	6	● 1. In The Court Of The Crimson King - An Observation By King Crimson	Atlantic 8245
9/19/70	31	5	2. In The Wake Of Poseidon	Atlantic 8266
			Greg Lake, lead singer on above 2 albums	
			KING FAMILY	
			Featuring songs by the entire cast of the TV show.	
7/31/65	34	4	1. The King Family Show!	Warner 1601
			B.B. KING	
			Born Riley B. King on 9/16/25 in Indianola, MS. To Memphis in 1946. Own radio show, 1949-50, where he was dubbed "The Beale Street Blues Boy", later shortened to "Blues Boy", then simply "B.B." First recorded for Bullet in 1949. The most famous blues singer/ guitarist in the world today.	
4/04/70	38	3	1. Completely Well	BluesWay 6037
			"The Thrill Is Gone"	
11/07/70	26	6	2. Indianola Mississippi Seeds	ABC 713
3/13/71	25	7	3. Live In Cook County Jail [L]	ABC 723
			BEN E. KING	
			Born Benjamin Earl Nelson on 9/23/38 in Henderson, NC. To New York in 1947. Worked with The Moonglows for six months while still in high school. Joined the Five Crowns in 1957, who became the new Drifters in 1959. Wrote lyrics to "There Goes My Baby", his first lead performance with The Drifters. Went solo in May of 1960.	
6/28/75	39	1	1. Supernatural	Atlantic 18132
			"Supernatural Thing"(5)	
8/20/77	33	5	2. Benny And Us	Atlantic 19105
			AVERAGE WHITE BAND & BEN E. KING	

Journey was formed in 1973 by ex-Santana guitarist Neal Schon, two ex-members of the little-known Frumious Bandersnatch, and Tubes drummer Prairie Prince. They called themselves the Golden Gate Rhythm Section and planned to be just a backing group, but after a Bay Area radio station held a name-the-band contest, the four became Journey and started to make their own music.

The King and I was originally produced in 1951 as a Broadway musical starring Yul Brynner and Gertrude Lawrence. The film, with Brynner and Deborah Kerr (her songs were sung by Marni Nixon), appeared in 1956 and yielded a No. 1 soundtrack. Although the songs were written by Rodgers and Hammerstein, conductor Alfred Newman won his eighth Academy Award for the film score.

The Kingston Trio, the leading folk group of the early 1960s, was formed by Hawaiians Bob Shane and Dave Guard and Californian Nick Reynolds, and reportedly served as the inspiration for Peter, Paul and Mary. *String Along with the Kingston Trio*, released in 1960, spent ten weeks at the top of the album charts.

The Kinks' *You Really Got Me* (1964) was the group's first American album. It includes the classic title track as well as "Bald Headed Woman," an odd tune recorded around the same time by the Who, and "Stop Your Sobbing," the song that launched the Pretenders' career the following decade.

Kiss has been incarnated and merchandised in many media, including comic books, dolls, and movies. The group's 1978 film was called *Kiss Meets the Phantom of the Park*; bassist/vocalist Gene Simmons has since done dramatic roles in other pictures. The group, which launched its career on the underground New York club scene in the early 1970s, was never photographed without full makeup until the release of *Lick It Up* in 1983. *Love Gun*, Kiss' third platinum album, was released in 1977.

Gladys Knight and the Pips had its first hit in 1961, but it wasn't until it cut "I Heard It Through the Grapevine" in 1967 that the quartet from Atlanta became a household name. Their biggest year for albums was 1973, when both *Neither One of Us* and *Imagination* reached No. 9.

Led Zeppelin was in the midst of a full-scale American tour in support of its 1973 album, *Houses of the Holy*, when $180,000 in Madison Square Garden box-office receipts was stolen from a safety deposit box in a New York hotel.

Brenda Lee (Tarpley) was born in Georgia in 1944 and reached singing stardom quickly. She won her first talent contest at 6, made her television debut and began her recording career at 11, and scored her first No. 1 single ("I'm Sorry") before turning 16. By age 21, Lee had released twenty-eight Top 40 singles.

John Lennon said in 1980, "After 10, 15, almost 20 years of being under contract, and having to produce two albums a year and a single every three months . . . I don't want to sell my soul again . . . to have a hit record. I've discovered I can live without it."

Gordon Lightfoot, who arranged and produced commercials in Toronto before launching a career with his own music, had his first American success in 1965, when a song he had written was recorded by Peter, Paul and Mary and became a hit single. Lightfoot began recording the following year, but didn't make the U.S. charts under his own name until 1969.

Little Richard spent the 1950s, 1960s, and 1970s alternating between careers as an outrageously anything-goes rock star and a God-fearing gospel singer. In the 1980s he added to his repertoire with a memorable piece of acting in the film *Down and Out in Beverly Hills* and a scandalous autobiography.

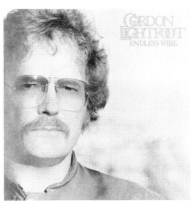

DATE	POS	WKS	ARTIST—RECORD TITLE	LABEL & NO.
			CAROLE KING	
			Born Carole Klein on 2/9/42 in Brooklyn. Singer, songwriter, pianist. Married lyricist Gerry Goffin in 1958, team wrote 4 #1 hits: "Will You Love Me Tomorrow", "Go Away Little Girl", "Take Good Care Of My Baby" and "The Loco-Motion". Divorced Goffin in 1968, first solo album in 1970. The most successful female songwriter of the rock era.	
4/24/71	1(15)	68	● 1. **Tapestry**	Ode 77009
			"It's Too Late"(1)	
12/18/71	1(3)	20	● 2. **Music**	Ode 77013
			"Sweet Seasons"(9)	
11/11/72	2(5)	20	● 3. **Rhymes & Reasons**	Ode 77016
6/30/73	6	15	● 4. **Fantasy**	Ode 77018
10/05/74	1(1)	13	● 5. **Wrap Around Joy**	Ode 77024
			"Jazzman"(2)	
			"Nightingale"(9)	
3/29/75	20	4	6. Really Rosie [TV]	Ode 77027
			from the original animated TV soundtrack	
2/07/76	3	14	● 7. **Thoroughbred**	Ode 77034
8/13/77	17	7	● 8. Simple Things	Capitol 11667
			EVELYN "CHAMPAGNE" KING	
			Born on 6/29/60 in the Bronx. To Philadelphia in 1970. Employed as cleaning woman at Sigma Studios when discovered.	
7/22/78	14	13	● 1. Smooth Talk	RCA 2466
			"Shame"(9)	
5/12/79	35	3	● 2. Music Box	RCA 3033
8/15/81	28	6	3. I'm In Love	RCA 3962
10/09/82	27	7	● 4. Get Loose	RCA 4337
			THE KINGSMEN	
			Rock band formed in Portland in 1957. Consisted of Jack Ely (lead singer, guitar), Lynn Easton (drums), Mike Mitchell (guitar), Bob Nordby (bass) and Don Gallucci (keyboards). After release of "Louie Louie" (featuring lead vocal by Ely), Easton took over leadership of band and replaced Ely as lead singer. America's premier Sixties garage band.	
2/22/64	20	28	1. The Kingsmen In Person [L]	Wand 657
			"Louie, Louie"(2)	
10/17/64	15	9	2. The Kingsmen, Volume II [L]	Wand 659
4/10/65	22	7	3. The Kingsmen, Volume 3 [L]	Wand 662
			"The Jolly Green Giant"(4)	
			THE KINGSTON TRIO	
			Folk trio formed in San Francisco in 1957. Consisted of Dave Guard (banjo), Bob Shane and Nick Reynolds (guitars). Big break came at San Francisco's Purple Onion, where they stayed for eight months. Guard left in 1961 to form the Whiskeyhill Singers. John Stewart replaced him. Disbanded in 1968, Shane formed New Kingston Trio. The originators of the folk music craze of the 60s.	
11/03/58	1(1)	45	● 1. **The Kingston Trio**	Capitol 996
			"Tom Dooley"(1)	
2/16/59	2(4)	12	● 2. **From The Hungry i** [L]	Capitol 1107
6/22/59	1(15)	32	● 3. **The Kingston Trio At Large**	Capitol 1199
11/09/59	1(8)	8	● 4. **Here We Go Again!**	Capitol 1258

DATE	POS	WKS	ARTIST—RECORD TITLE	LABEL & NO.
4/25/60	1(12)	54	● 5. **Sold Out**	Capitol 1352
8/15/60	1(10)	34	● 6. **String Along**	Capitol 1407
9/05/60	15	15	7. Stereo Concert [L]	Capitol 1183
			concert in Liberty Hall, El Paso, Texas	
12/05/60	11	4	8. The Last Month Of The Year [X]	Capitol 1446
2/27/61	2(1)	13	9. **Make Way!**	Capitol 1474
7/17/61	3	41	10. **Goin' Places**	Capitol 1564
10/16/61	3	46	11. **Close-Up**	Capitol 1642
			John Stewart replaces Dave Guard	
3/17/62	3	26	12. **College Concert** [L]	Capitol 1658
			concert on the campus of UCLA	
6/23/62	7	48	● 13. **The Best Of The Kingston Trio** [G]	Capitol 1705
8/25/62	7	18	14. **Something Special**	Capitol 1747
			with orchestral and chorus background	
1/05/63	16	23	15. New Frontier	Capitol 1809
4/06/63	4	23	16. **The Kingston Trio #16**	Capitol 1871
			"Reverend Mr. Black"(8)	
8/31/63	7	13	17. **Sunny Side!**	Capitol 1935
2/22/64	18	7	18. Time To Think	Capitol 2011
6/27/64	22	5	19. Back In Town [L]	Capitol 2081
			recorded at San Francisco's "Hungry i"	

THE KINKS

Rock group formed in London, England in 1963 by Ray Davies (lead singer, guitar) and his brother Dave Davies (lead guitar, vocals). Original lineup also included Peter Quaife (bass) and Mike Avory (drums). Numerous personnel changes during the 70s. Lineup in 1987 consisted of Ray & Dave Davies, Ian Gibbons (keyboards), Bob Henrit (drums) and Jim Rodford (bass).

DATE	POS	WKS	ARTIST—RECORD TITLE	LABEL & NO.
2/20/65	29	5	1. You Really Got Me	Reprise 6143
			"You Really Got Me"(7)	
5/01/65	13	11	2. Kinks-Size	Reprise 6158
			"All Day And All Of The Night"(7)	
			"Tired Of Waiting For You"(6)	
9/17/66	9	15	● 3. **The Kinks Greatest Hits!** [G]	Reprise 6217
1/09/71	35	3	4. Lola Versus Powerman and The Moneygoround, Part One	Reprise 6423
			"Lola"(9)	
3/19/77	21	8	5. Sleepwalker	Arista 4106
7/15/78	40	1	6. Misfits	Arista 4167
8/04/79	11	10	● 7. Low Budget	Arista 4240
7/05/80	14	14	● 8. One For The Road [L]	Arista 8401 [2]
9/26/81	15	9	● 9. Give The People What They Want	Arista 9567
6/25/83	12	12	10. State of Confusion	Arista 8018
			"Come Dancing"(6)	

DATE	POS	WKS	ARTIST—RECORD TITLE	LABEL & NO.
			KISS	
			Hard rock band formed in New York City in 1973. Consisted of Gene Simmons (bass), Paul Stanley (guitar), Ace Frehley (lead guitar) and Peter Criss (drums). Noted for elaborate makeup and highly theatrical stage shows. Criss replaced by Eric Carr in 1981. Frehley replaced by Vinnie Vincent in 1982. Group appeared without makeup for the first time in 1983 on album cover "Lick It Up". Mark St. John replaced Vincent in 1984. Bruce Kulick replaced St. John in 1985.	
6/07/75	32	3	● 1. Dressed To Kill	Casablanca 7016
11/01/75	9	17	● 2. **Alive!** [L]	Casablanca 7020 [2]
4/10/76	11	14	▲ 3. Destroyer	Casablanca 7025
			"Beth"(7)	
9/18/76	36	3	4. The Originals [R]	Casablanca 7032 [3]
			reissue of their first 3 albums	
11/20/76	11	26	▲ 5. Rock And Roll Over	Casablanca 7037
7/09/77	4	4	▲ 6. **Love Gun**	Casablanca 7057
11/26/77	7	14	▲ 7. **Alive II** [L]	Casablanca 7076 [2]
6/10/78	22	5	▲ 8. Double Platinum [G]	Casablanca 7100 [2]
			during October, 1978, each member of Kiss issued a solo album - all but Peter Criss' made the Top 40	
6/23/79	9	11	▲ 9. **Dynasty**	Casablanca 7152
7/12/80	35	4	● 10. Kiss Unmasked	Casablanca 7225
10/29/83	24	7	● 11. Lick It Up	Mercury 814297
			group shown unmasked for the first time	
10/20/84	19	17	▲ 12. Animalize	Mercury 822495
10/12/85	20	16	● 13. Asylum	Mercury 826099
			KLAATU	
			Canadian rock quartet. Anonymous first release had people speculating that they might be The Beatles reunited.	
4/30/77	32	3	1. Klaatu	Capitol 11542
			EARL KLUGH	
			Jazz acoustic guitarist.	
12/01/79	23	13	● 1. One On One [I]	Tappan Zee 36241
			BOB JAMES & EARL KLUGH	
6/11/83	38	3	2. Low Ride [I]	Capitol 12253
			KLYMAXX	
			Black female sextet formed in Los Angeles in 1979. Lead vocals and rap by Bernadette Cooper, Fenderella and Lorena Shelby.	
12/14/85	18	15	● 1. Meeting In The Ladies Room	Constell. 5529
			"I Miss You"(5)	
			THE KNACK	
			Rock group formed in Los Angeles in 1978. Consisted of Doug Fieger (lead singer, guitar), Berton Averre (guitar), Bruce Gary (drums) and Prescott Niles (bass). Disbanded in 1982.	
7/14/79	1(5)	22	▲ 1. **Get The Knack**	Capitol 11948
			"My Sharona"(1)	
3/08/80	15	9	● 2. But The Little Girls Understand	Capitol 12045

DATE	POS	WKS	ARTIST—RECORD TITLE	LABEL & NO.
			### GLADYS KNIGHT & THE PIPS	
			R&B family group from Atlanta. Formed in 1952 when Gladys was 8 years old. Consisted of Gladys (b: 5/28/44 in Atlanta), her brother Merald "Bubba" Knight and sister Brenda, and William and Elenor Guest. Named "Pips" for their manager, cousin James "Pip" Woods. First recorded for Brunswick in 1958. Brenda and Elenor replaced by cousins Edward Patten and Langston George in 1959. Langston left group in 1962 and group has remained a quartet with the same members ever since. Due to legal problems, Gladys could not record with the Pips from 1977-80.	
8/07/71	35	2	1. If I Were Your Woman	Soul 731
			"If I Were Your Woman"(9)	
3/31/73	9	10	2. **Neither One Of Us**	Soul 737
			"Neither One Of Us (Wants To Be The First To Say Goodbye)"(2)	
11/10/73	9	33	● 3. **Imagination**	Buddah 5141
			"Midnight Train To Georgia"(1)	
			"I've Got To Use My Imagination"(4)	
			"Best Thing That Ever Happened To Me"(3)	
7/13/74	35	3	● 4. Claudine [S]	Buddah 5602
			"On And On"(5)	
12/07/74	17	13	● 5. I Feel A Song	Buddah 5612
11/22/75	24	4	● 6. 2nd Anniversary	Buddah 5639
			title refers to their signing with Buddah Records	
3/20/76	36	4	7. The Best Of Gladys Knight & The Pips [G]	Buddah 5653
6/18/83	34	6	● 8. Visions	Columbia 38205
			### KOOL & THE GANG	
			R&B group formed in Jersey City, NJ in 1964 by bass player Robert "Kool" Bell as the Jazziacs. Session work in New York City, 1964-68. First recorded for De-Lite in 1969. Added lead singer James "J.T." Taylor in 1979. Current lineup consists of Robert Bell and his brother Ronald Bell (sax, keyboards), Taylor, George Brown (drums), Curtis "Fitz" Williams (keyboards) and Charles Smith (guitar). Jersey City group led by Robert "Kool" Bell (bass) & James Taylor (lead vocals on 13-18).	
2/23/74	33	4	● 1. Wild And Peaceful	De-Lite 2013
			"Jungle Boogie"(4)	
			"Hollywood Swinging"(6)	
10/20/79	13	28	▲ 2. Ladies' Night	De-Lite 9513
			"Ladies Night"(8)	
			"Too Hot"(5)	
11/22/80	10	24	▲ 3. **Celebrate!**	De-Lite 9518
			"Celebration"(1)	
10/24/81	12	30	▲ 4. Something Special	De-Lite 8502
			"Get Down On It"(10)	
10/23/82	29	12	● 5. As One	De-Lite 8505
1/21/84	29	10	● 6. In The Heart	De-Lite 8508
			"Joanna"(2)	
2/16/85	13	51	▲ 7. Emergency	De-Lite 822943
			"Misled"(10)	
			"Fresh"(9)	
			"Cherish"(2)	

DATE	POS	WKS	ARTIST—RECORD TITLE	LABEL & NO.
12/20/86	25	9	• 8. Forever "Victory"(10) "Stone Love"(10)	Mercury 830398
			AL KOOPER Top session keyboardist/guitarist. Founded Blood, Sweat & Tears.	
10/05/68	12	10	• 1. Super Session	Columbia 9701
			MIKE BLOOMFIELD/AL KOOPER/STEVE STILLS	
2/15/69	18	10	2. The Live Adventures Of Mike Bloomfield And Al Kooper [L]	Columbia 6 [2]
			ANDRE KOSTELANETZ & His Orchestra Russian immigrant. Conductor on radio and records. Died on 1/13/80 (78).	
10/01/55	4	11	1. **Meet Andre Kostelanetz** [K-I]	Columbia KZ 1
			KRAFTWERK German all-electronic duo: Ralf Hutter and Florian Schneider.	
3/08/75	5	11	1. **Autobahn** [I] side 1 is a 22 1/2 minute recording of "Autobahn"	Vertigo 2003
			KRIS KRISTOFFERSON Born on 6/22/36 in Brownsville, Texas. Singer, songwriter, actor. Married to Rita Coolidge, 1973-79. Wrote the #1 hit "Me And Bobby McGee".	
8/21/71	21	14	• 1. The Silver Tongued Devil And I	Monument 30679
9/22/73	31	4	• 2. Jesus Was A Capricorn "Why Me"	Monument 31909
10/13/73	26	6	• 3. Full Moon	A&M 4403
			KRIS KRISTOFFERSON & RITA COOLIDGE	
			KROKUS Heavy-metal band formed in Zurich, Switzerland featuring lead singer Marc Storace.	
6/11/83	25	8	• 1. Headhunter	Arista 9623
9/29/84	31	6	• 2. The Blitz	Arista 8243
			L	
			LaBELLE Vocal trio from Philadelphia consisting of Patti LaBelle, Sara Dash, and Nona Hendryx.	
2/15/75	7	11	• 1. **Nightbirds** "Lady Marmalade"(1)	Epic 33075
			PATTI LaBELLE Born Patricia Holt on 5/24/44 in Philadelphia. Lead singer of Patti LaBelle & The Bluebells, 1962-77.	
3/03/84	40	2	• 1. I'm In Love Again	Phil. Int. 38539
5/24/86	1(1)	19	▲ 2. **Winner In You** "On My Own"(1-with Michael McDonald)	MCA 5737

DATE	POS	WKS	ARTIST—RECORD TITLE	LABEL & NO.

FRANKIE LAINE

Born Frank Paul LoVecchio on 3/30/13 in Chicago. To Los Angeles, early 40s. First recorded for Exclusive in 1945, with Johnny Moore's Three Blazers. Signed to Mercury label in 1947. Dynamic style found favor with black and white audiences.

DATE	POS	WKS	ARTIST—RECORD TITLE	LABEL & NO.
4/20/57	13	12	1. Rockin'	Columbia 975
6/17/67	16	9	2. I'll Take Care Of Your Cares	ABC 604

LAKESIDE

9-man funk aggregation from Dayton, Ohio.

1/10/81	16	12	● 1. Fantastic Voyage	Solar 3720

LESTER LANIN & His Orchestra

Leader of society-styled dance bands. Albums 1-5 contain medleys of 25-50 songs with a party atmosphere background.

6/24/57	7	10	1. Dance To The Music Of Lester Lanin [I]	Epic 3340
11/11/57	18	2	2. Lester Lanin And His Orchestra [I]	Epic 3242
2/03/58	17	2	3. Lester Lanin At The Tiffany Ball [I]	Epic 3410
6/09/58	19	3	4. Lester Lanin Goes To College [I]	Epic 3474
11/17/58	12	4	5. Have Band, Will Travel [I]	Epic 3520
2/10/62	37	1	6. Twistin' in High Society! [I]	Epic 3825

MARIO LANZA

Born Alfredo Cocozza on 1/31/21 in Philadelphia. Mario Lanza became the most spectacularly popular operatic tenor since Caruso, his voice featured in seven movies (though no theatrical operas) before his death on 10/7/59 (38).

4/28/56	9	6	1. Serenade [S]	RCA 1996
3/17/58	7	8	2. Seven Hills Of Rome [S]	RCA 2211
			side 1: soundtrack; side 2: various Lanza recordings	
11/02/59	5	9	3. For The First Time [S]	RCA 2338
			Mario sings and stars in the above 3 films	
12/14/59	4	3	4. Lanza Sings Christmas Carols [X]	RCA 2333
5/16/60	4	41	5. Mario Lanza Sings Caruso Favorites [F]	RCA 2393
			recorded in Rome, June, 1959	

NICOLETTE LARSON

Born on 7/17/52 in Helena, Montana; raised in Kansas City. To San Francisco, 1974. Session vocalist with Neil Young, Linda Ronstadt, Van Halen, and many others.

1/20/79	15	12	● 1. Nicolette	Warner 3243
			"Lotta Love"(8)	

LAST POETS

Black protest poetry set to music.

8/29/70	29	7	1. The Last Poets	Douglas 3

CYNDI LAUPER

Born on 6/20/53 in Queens, New York. Recorded an album for Polydor Records in 1980 with the group, Blue Angel. Won a Grammy in 1984 as Best New Artist.

2/11/84	4	62	▲ 1. She's So Unusual	Portrait 38930
			"Girls Just Want To Have Fun"(2)	
			"Time After Time"(1)	
			"She Bop"(3)	
			"All Through The Night"(5)	
10/11/86	4	23	▲ 2. True Colors	Portrait 40313
			"True Colors"(1)	
			"Change Of Heart"(3)	

DATE	POS	WKS	ARTIST—RECORD TITLE	LABEL & NO.
			STEVE LAWRENCE	
			Born Sam Leibowitz on 7/8/35 in Brooklyn. Regular performer on the Steve Allen "Tonight Show" for 5 years. First recorded for King in 1953. Married to Eydie Gorme since 12/29/57.	
6/02/58	19	2	1. Here's Steve Lawrence	Coral 57204
			STEVE LAWRENCE & EYDIE GORME:	
3/02/63	27	7	2. Winners!	Columbia 8753
			"Go Away Little Girl"(1)	
			RONNIE LAWS	
			Born on 10/3/50 in Houston. R&B/jazz saxophonist. Brother of Hubert, Eloise and Debra Laws. With Earth, Wind And Fire, 1972-73.	
6/18/77	37	2	● 1. Friends And Strangers [I]	Blue Note 730
3/08/80	24	6	2. Every Generation	United Art. 1001
			LED ZEPPELIN	
			British heavy-metal rock supergroup formed in October, 1968. Consisted of Robert Plant (lead singer), Jimmy Page (lead guitar), John Paul Jones (bass, keyboards) and John Bonham (drums). First known as the New Yardbirds. Page had been in the Yardbirds, 1966-68. USA tour in 1973 broke many box-office records. Formed own label, Swan Song, in 1974. Plant seriously injured in an auto accident in Greece on 8/4/75. In concert film "The Song Remains The Same" in 1976. Bonham died on 9/25/80 at the age of 33 of asphyxiation. Group disbanded in December, 1980. Their most famous recording, "Stairway To Heaven" (on album "Led Zeppelin IV") was never released as a single.	
2/22/69	10	50	● 1. **Led Zeppelin**	Atlantic 8216
11/15/69	1(7)	29	● 2. **Led Zeppelin II**	Atlantic 8236
			"Whole Lotta Love"(4)	
10/24/70	1(4)	19	● 3. **Led Zeppelin III**	Atlantic 7201
			"Immigrant Song"	
11/27/71	2(4)	24	● 4. **Led Zeppelin IV (untitled)**	Atlantic 7208
			"Stairway To Heaven"	
4/21/73	1(2)	39	● 5. **Houses Of The Holy**	Atlantic 7255
3/15/75	1(6)	15	● 6. **Physical Graffiti**	Swan Song 200 [2]
4/24/76	1(2)	13	▲ 7. **Presence**	Swan Song 8416
11/06/76	2(3)	12	▲ 8. **The Soundtrack From The Film "The Song Remains The Same"** [S-L]	Swan Song 201 [2]
			soundtrack recorded live at Madison Square Garden	
9/08/79	1(7)	28	▲ 9. **In Through The Out Door**	Swan Song 16002
12/18/82	6	9	▲ 10. **Coda** [K]	Swan Song 90051
			previously unreleased recordings from 1969-1978	
			BRENDA LEE	
			Born Brenda Mae Tarpley on 12/11/44 in Lithonia, GA. Professional singer since age six. Signed to Decca Records in 1956. Became known as "Little Miss Dynamite". Successful Country singer since 1971.	
8/22/60	5	32	1. **Brenda Lee**	Decca 74039
			"Sweet Nothin's"(4)	
			"I'm Sorry"(1)	
			"That's All You Gotta Do"(6)	
11/21/60	4	9	2. **This Is.....Brenda**	Decca 74082
			"I Want To Be Wanted"(1)	
4/10/61	24	11	3. Emotions	Decca 74104
			"Emotions"(7)	

DATE	POS	WKS	ARTIST—RECORD TITLE	LABEL & NO.
9/11/61	**17**	10	4. All The Way *"Dum Dum"*(4)	Decca 74176
4/21/62	**29**	3	5. Sincerely	Decca 74216
11/17/62	**20**	4	6. Brenda, That's All *"You Can Depend On Me"*(6) *"Fool #1"*(3)	Decca 74326
3/23/63	**25**	8	7. All Alone Am I *"All Alone Am I"*(3)	Decca 74370
1/25/64	**39**	1	8. Let Me Sing *"Break It To Me Gently"*(4) *"Losing You"*(6)	Decca 74439
11/13/65	**36**	2	9. Too Many Rivers	Decca 74684
			PEGGY LEE Born Norma Jean Egstrom on 5/26/20 in Jamestown, ND. Jazz singer with Jack Wardlow band, 1936-40; Will Osborne, 1940-41; and Benny Goodman, 1941-43. Went solo in March, 1943. Films "Mister Music", 1950; "The Jazz Singer", 1953; and "Pete Kelly's Blues", 1955. Co-wrote many songs with husband Dave Barbour.	
9/17/55	**7**	10	1. **Songs from Pete Kelly's Blues** **PEGGY LEE & ELLA FITZGERALD**	Decca 8166
9/23/57	**20**	1	2. The Man I Love <small>orchestra conducted by Frank Sinatra</small>	Capitol 864
7/14/58	**15**	2	3. Jump For Joy	Capitol 979
12/08/58	**16**	1	4. Things Are Swingin'	Capitol 1049
4/11/60	**11**	44	5. Latin ala Lee!	Capitol 1290
2/09/63	**40**	1	6. Sugar 'N' Spice	Capitol 1772
5/04/63	**18**	9	7. I'm A Woman	Capitol 1857
			MICHEL LEGRAND Born on 2/24/32 in Paris, France. Pianist, composer, conductor and arranger. Scored over 50 motion pictures.	
5/28/55	**5**	16	1. **Holiday In Rome** [I]	Columbia 647
9/17/55	**13**	2	2. Vienna Holiday [I]	Columbia 706
6/30/56	**9**	4	3. **Castles In Spain** [I]	Columbia 888
			TOM LEHRER Satirist (in song) who performed on the TV show "That Was The Week That Was".	
12/11/65	**18**	19	1. That Was The Year That Was [C]	Reprise 6179
			ERICH LEINSDORF - see BOSTON SYMPHONY ORCHESTRA	
			JOHN LENNON Born on 10/9/40 in Liverpool, England. Founding member of The Beatles. Married Cynthia Powell on 8/23/62, had son Julian. Divorced Cynthia on 11/8/68. Met Yoko Ono (b: 2/18/34 in Japan) in 1966 and married her on 3/20/69. Formed Plastic Ono Band in 1969. To New York City in 1971. Fought deportation from USA, 1972-76, until he was granted a permanent visa. John was shot to death on 12/8/80 in New York City.	
1/24/70	**10**	13	● 1. **The Plastic Ono Band - Live Peace In Toronto 1969** [L] <small>9/13/69 concert featuring Eric Clapton on guitar</small>	Apple 3362

DATE	POS	WKS	ARTIST—RECORD TITLE	LABEL & NO.
12/26/70	6	12	● 2. **John Lennon/Plastic Ono Band** Plastic Ono Band: John's backing musicians - also see Yoko Ono/Plastic Ono Band	Apple 3372
10/02/71	1(1)	17	● 3. **Imagine** *"Imagine"(3)*	Apple 3379
11/24/73	9	11	● 4. **Mind Games**	Apple 3414
10/19/74	1(1)	11	● 5. **Walls And Bridges** *"Whatever Gets You Thru The Night"(1)* *"#9 Dream"(9)*	Apple 3416
3/15/75	6	9	6. **Rock 'N' Roll**	Apple 3419
11/15/75	12	6	7. Shaved Fish [G] *"Instant Karma"(3-'70)*	Apple 3421
12/06/80	1(8)	27	▲ 8. **Double Fantasy** 7 songs by John, and 7 by Yoko *"(Just Like) Starting Over"(1)* *"Woman"(2)* *"Watching The Wheels"(10)*	Geffen 2001
12/11/82	33	8	9. The John Lennon Collection [G]	Geffen 2023
2/11/84	11	10	● 10. Milk and Honey 6 songs by John and 6 by Yoko - recorded in 1980 *"Nobody Told Me"(5)*	Polydor 817160
			JULIAN LENNON Born John Charles Julian Lennon on 4/8/63. First child to be born to any of the Beatles.	
11/24/84	17	29	● 1. Valotte *"Valotte"(9)* *"Too Late For Goodbyes"(5)* title refers to the French studio where album was recorded	Atlantic 80184
4/19/86	32	5	● 2. The Secret Value of DayDreaming	Atlantic 81640
			THE LETTERMEN Harmonic vocal group formed in Los Angeles in 1960. Consisted of Tony Butala (b: 11/20/40), Jim Pike (b: 11/6/38) and Bob Engemann (b: 2/19/36). First recorded for Warner Brothers. Engemann replaced by Gary Pike (Jim's brother), 1968.	
3/10/62	6	25	1. **A Song For Young Love** *"The Way You Look Tonight"/"When I Fall In* *Love"(7)*	Capitol 1669
7/21/62	30	2	2. Once Upon A Time	Capitol 1711
3/14/64	31	3	3. A Lettermen Kind Of Love	Capitol 2013
4/17/65	27	5	4. Portrait Of My Love	Capitol 2270
9/18/65	13	10	5. The Hit Sounds Of The Lettermen	Capitol 2359
11/19/66	17	11	● 6. The Best Of The Lettermen [G]	Capitol 2554
8/05/67	31	4	7. Spring!	Capitol 2711
1/27/68	10	16	● 8. **The Lettermen!!!...and "Live!"** [L] *"Goin' Out Of My Head/Can't Take My Eyes Off* *You"(7)*	Capitol 2758
4/20/68	13	14	● 9. Goin' Out Of My Head	Capitol 2865
9/20/69	17	11	● 10. Hurt So Bad	Capitol 269
			LEVEL 42 Pop/soul/jazz foursome from Manchester, England, led by Mark King.	
5/10/86	18	13	1. World Machine *"Something About You"(7)*	Polydor 827487

DATE	POS	WKS	ARTIST—RECORD TITLE	LABEL & NO.
			GARY LEWIS & THE PLAYBOYS	
			Pop/rock group formed in Los Angeles in 1964. Consisted of Gary Lewis (vocals, drums), Al Ramsey, John West (guitars), David Walker (keyboards) and David Costell (bass). Lewis (b: 7/31/46) is the son of comedian Jerry Lewis. Group worked regularly at Disneyland in 1964. Lewis inducted into the Army on New Year's Day in 1967, resumed career after discharge in 1968.	
5/08/65	**26**	5	1. This Diamond Ring	Liberty 7408
			"This Diamond Ring"(1)	
10/30/65	**18**	5	2. A Session With Gary Lewis And The Playboys	Liberty 7419
			"Count Me In"(2)	
			"Save Your Heart For Me"(2)	
11/19/66	**10**	13	● 3. **Golden Greats** [G]	Liberty 7468
			HUEY LEWIS & THE NEWS	
			San Francisco 6-man rock band. Huey was born Hugh Cregg III on 7/5/50 in New York City. Joined the country-rock band Clover in the late 70s. Formed The News in 1980, consisting of Huey (lead singer), Chris Hayes (lead guitar), Mario Cipollina (bass), Bill Gibson (drums), Sean Hopper (keyboards) and Johnny Cola (sax, guitar).	
4/10/82	**13**	14	● 1. Picture This	Chrysalis 1340
			"Do You Believe In Love"(7)	
11/05/83	**1(1)**	71	▲ 2. **Sports**	Chrysalis 41412
			"Heart And Soul"(8)	
			"I Want A New Drug"(6)	
			"The Heart Of Rock & Roll"(6)	
			"If This Is It"(6)	
9/20/86	**1(1)**	40+	3. **Fore!**	Chrysalis 41534
			"Stuck With You"(1)	
			"Hip To Be Square"(3)	
			"Jacob's Ladder"(1)	
			"I Know What I Like"(9)	
			JERRY LEWIS	
			Born Joseph Levitch on 3/16/25 in Newark, NJ. Formed comedy team with Dean Martin in 1946 at Atlantic City. Film debut in 1949 in "My Friend Irma". National chairman in campaign against muscular dystrophy.	
12/22/56	**3**	19	1. **Jerry Lewis Just Sings**	Decca 8410
			"Rock-A-Bye Your Baby With A Dixie Melody"(10)	
			JERRY LEE LEWIS	
			Born on 9/29/35 in Ferriday, LA. Rock 'n roll singer, piano player. Played piano since age nine, professionally since age 15. First recorded for Sun in 1956. Appeared in the film "Disc Jockey Jamboree" in 1957. Career waned in 1958 after marriage to 13-year-old cousin, Myra Gale Brown, daughter of his bass player. Made comeback in country music beginning in 1968. "The Killer", surrounded by personal tragedies in the past 2 decades, survived several serious illnesses in the past 6 years. Cousin to country singer Mickey Gilley and TV evangelist Jimmy Swaggart.	
5/19/73	**37**	3	1. The Session	Mercury 803 [2]
			recorded in London with Peter Frampton, Rory Gallagher, Albert & Alvin Lee and others	

DATE	POS	WKS	ARTIST—RECORD TITLE	LABEL & NO.
			RAMSEY LEWIS	
			Ramsey formed the Gentlemen Of Swing, a jazz-oriented trio, in 1956 in Chicago. Consisted of Ramsey (b: 5/27/35, Chicago - piano); Eldee Young (bass) and Isaac "Red" Holt (drums). All had been in band called The Clefs, early 1950s. First recorded for Chess/Argo in 1956. Broke up in 1965, with Young and Holt forming the Young-Holt Trio. Lewis re-formed his trio with Cleveland Eaton, bass; and Maurice White (later with Earth, Wind & Fire), drums. Reunited with Young and Holt in 1983.	
9/11/65	**2**(1)	33	1. **The In Crowd** **[I-L]**	Argo 757
			"The 'In' Crowd"(5)	
3/12/66	**15**	15	2. Hang On Ramsey! **[I-L]**	Cadet 761
			above albums by The Ramsey Lewis Trio (Eldee Young & Red Holt)	
10/08/66	**16**	13	3. Wade In The Water **[I]**	Cadet 774
2/08/75	**12**	14	● 4. Sun Goddess	Columbia 33194
			with Earth, Wind & Fire on 2 of 6 cuts	
			ENOCH LIGHT & THE LIGHT BRIGADE	
			Enoch was born on 8/18/07 in Canton, Ohio. Died in New York City on 7/31/78. Conductor of own orchestra, The Light Brigade, since 1935. President of Grand Award label and managing director for Command Records, for whom he produced a long string of hit stereo percussion albums in the 60s. Enoch's studio musicians variously billed as Terry Snyder & The All-Stars, and The Command All-Stars. Also see Charleston City All-Stars/Los Admiradores/Tony Mottola.	
6/15/59	**38**	4	1. I Want To Be Happy Cha Cha's **[I]**	Grand Award 388
1/25/60	**1**(13)	14	● 2. **Persuasive Percussion** **[I]**	Command 800
1/25/60	**2**(5)	88	3. **Provocative Percussion** **[I]**	Command 806
8/22/60	**3**	41	4. **Persuasive Percussion, Volume 2** **[I]**	Command 808
9/19/60	**4**	43	5. **Provocative Percussion, Volume 2** **[I]**	Command 810
5/01/61	**3**	15	6. **Persuasive Percussion, Volume 3** **[I]**	Command 817
10/09/61	**1**(7)	57	7. **Stereo 35/MM** **[I]**	Command 826
			35/MM: magnetic film used in recording process	
2/17/62	**8**	22	8. **Stereo 35/MM, Volume Two** **[I]**	Command 831
3/03/62	**34**	5	9. Persuasive Percussion, Volume 4 **[I]**	Command 830
4/21/62	**27**	12	10. Great Themes From Hit Films **[I]**	Command 835
12/22/62	**8**	29	11. **Big Band Bossa Nova** **[I]**	Command 844
			GORDON LIGHTFOOT	
			Born on 11/17/38 in Orillia, Ontario, Canada. Folk/pop/country singer, songwriter, guitarist.	
1/30/71	**12**	12	● 1. Sit Down Young Stranger	Reprise 6392
			"If You Could Read My Mind"(5)	
7/03/71	**38**	3	2. Summer Side Of Life	Reprise 2037
3/16/74	**1**(2)	23	▲ 3. **Sundown**	Reprise 2177
			"Sundown"(1)	
			"Carefree Highway"(10)	
3/15/75	**10**	9	4. **Cold On The Shoulder**	Reprise 2206
1/03/76	**34**	4	▲ 5. Gord's Gold **[G]**	Reprise 2237 [2]
			record 1 features re-recordings of his Sixties songs	
7/17/76	**12**	26	▲ 6. Summertime Dream	Reprise 2246
			"Wreck Of The Edmund Fitzgerald"(2)	
2/11/78	**22**	7	● 7. Endless Wire	Warner 3149

DATE	POS	WKS	ARTIST—RECORD TITLE		LABEL & NO.
			THE LIMELITERS		
			Folk trio formed in Hollywood in 1959. Consisted of Glen Yarbrough (tenor), Lou Gottlieb (bass) and Alex Hassilev (baritone).		
2/27/61	5	42	1. **Tonight: In Person**	[L]	RCA 2272
			recorded at the Ash Grove, Hollywood, California		
10/02/61	40	2	2. The Limeliters		Elektra 7180
10/09/61	8	22	3. **The Slightly Fabulous Limeliters**	[L]	RCA 2393
2/17/62	14	21	4. Sing Out!		RCA 2445
6/16/62	25	11	5. Through Children's Eyes	[L]	RCA 2512
			featuring 70 children from Berkeley, California		
10/13/62	21	6	6. Folk Matinee		RCA 2547
3/09/63	37	2	7. Our Men In San Francisco	[L]	RCA 2609
			MARK LINDSAY		
			Born on 3/9/44 in Caldwell, Idaho. Lead singer of Paul Revere & The Raiders.		
3/28/70	36	4	1. Arizona		Columbia 9986
			"Arizona"(10)		
			LIPPS, INC.		
			Funk project from Minneapolis formed by producer, songwriter, multi-instrumentalist Steven Greenberg. Vocals by Miss Black Minnesota U.S.A. of 1976, Cynthia Johnson.		
5/03/80	5	13	● 1. **Mouth To Mouth**		Casablanca 7197
			"Funkytown"(1)		
			LITTLE FEAT		
			Los Angeles seminal rock sextet led by Lowell George (vocals) and Paul Barrere (lead guitar).		
11/16/74	36	2	● 1. Feats Don't Fail Me Now		Warner 2784
12/06/75	36	3	2. The Last Record Album		Warner 2884
6/04/77	34	4	3. Time Loves A Hero		Warner 3015
3/25/78	18	11	● 4. Waiting For Columbus	[L]	Warner 3140 [2]
12/15/79	29	7	5. Down On The Farm		Warner 3345
9/19/81	39	2	6. Hoy-Hoy!	[K]	Warner 3538 [2]
			LITTLE RICHARD		
			Born Richard Wayne Penniman on 12/25/35 in Macon, Georgia. R&B/rock and roll singer, piano player. Talent contest win led to first recordings for RCA-Victor in 1951. Worked with the Tempo Toppers, 1953-55. Earned degree in theology in 1961 and was ordained a minister. Left R&B for gospel music, 1959-62 and again in mid-70s. The key figure in the transition from R&B to rock 'n' roll. Appeared in 3 early rock 'n' roll films: "Don't Knock The Rock", "The Girl Can't Help It" and "Mister Rock 'n' Roll"; and in 1986 in comedy "Down & Out In Beverly Hills".		
8/05/57	13	5	1. Here's Little Richard	[G]	Specialty 2100
			"Long Tall Sally"(6)		
			"Jenny, Jenny"(10)		
			"Tutti-Frutti"		
			"Rip It Up"		
			"Ready Teddy"		

DATE	POS	WKS	ARTIST—RECORD TITLE	LABEL & NO.
			LITTLE RIVER BAND	
			Pop/rock group formed in Australia in 1975. Consisted of Glenn Shorrock (lead singer), Rick Formosa, Beeb Birtles and Graham Goble (guitars), Roger McLachlan (bass) and Derek Pellicci (drums). Formosa, McLachlan, replaced by David Briggs (guitar) and George McArdle (bass) after first album. Shorrock replaced by John Farnham in 1983. By 1985, after numerous changes, Goble was the only remaining original member. Shorrock returned in 1987, replacing Farnham.	
8/26/78	16	12	▲ 1. Sleeper Catcher	Harvest 11783
			"Reminiscing"(3)	
			"Lady"(10)	
8/18/79	10	15	▲ 2. **First Under The Wire**	Capitol 11954
			"Lonesome Loser"(6)	
			"Cool Change"(10)	
10/03/81	21	9	● 3. Time Exposure	Capitol 12163
			"The Night Owls"(6)	
			"Take It Easy On Me"(10)	
1/08/83	33	12	● 4. Little River Band/Greatest Hits [G]	Capitol 12247
			RICH LITTLE	
			Comedian/impressionist.	
2/27/82	29	6	1. The First Family Rides Again [C]	Boardwalk 33248
			with Melanie Chartoff, Michael Richards, Shelley Hack, Jenilee Harrison, Earle Doud (producer), & Vaughn Meader	
			LIVING STRINGS	
			European orchestra.	
2/27/61	26	6	1. Living Strings Play All The Music From Camelot [I]	RCA Camden 657
			LOBO	
			Born Kent Lavoie on 7/31/43 in Tallahassee, FL. Pop singer/songwriter/guitarist.	
12/16/72	37	7	1. Of A Simple Man	Big Tree 2013
			"I'd Love You To Want Me"(2)	
			"Don't Expect Me To Be Your Friend"(8)	
			NILS LOFGREN	
			Born in 1952 in Chicago. Pop-rock singer, guitarist. Leader of Grin, 1969-1974.	
5/22/76	32	3	1. Cry Tough	A&M 4573
4/23/77	36	2	2. I Came To Dance	A&M 4628
			LOGGINS & MESSINA	
			Kenny Loggins and ex-Buffalo Springfield/Poco member, Jim Messina (b: 12/5/47). Messina originally hired as producer for Loggins; however, they formed a partnership that lasted for 4 years.	
12/30/72	16	13	▲ 1. Loggins And Messina	Columbia 31748
			"Your Mama Don't Dance"(4)	
11/24/73	10	17	▲ 2. **Full Sail**	Columbia 32540
5/25/74	5	16	● 3. **On Stage** [L]	Columbia 32848 [2]
11/23/74	8	12	● 4. **Mother Lode**	Columbia 33175
9/20/75	21	8	5. So Fine	Columbia 33810
			featuring popular Fifties tunes	
2/07/76	16	9	● 6. Native Sons	Columbia 33578

DATE	POS	WKS	ARTIST—RECORD TITLE	LABEL & NO.
			KENNY LOGGINS	
			Born on 1/7/48 in Everett, WA. Pop/rock singer, songwriter, guitarist. With rock bands Second Helping and Gator Creek in the late 60s. Signed as a solo artist with Columbia in 1971 where he met and recorded with Jim Messina to 1976.	
6/11/77	27	7	▲ 1. Celebrate Me Home	Columbia 34655
8/05/78	7	17	▲ 2. **Nightwatch**	Columbia 35387
			"Whenever I Call You 'Friend'"(5)	
10/27/79	16	24	▲ 3. Keep The Fire	Columbia 36172
10/11/80	11	11	● 4. Kenny Loggins Alive [L]	Columbia 36738 [2]
			"I'm Alright"(live version)	
9/25/82	13	9	● 5. High Adventure	Columbia 38127
			GUY LOMBARDO & His Royal Canadians	
			Canadian - #1 dance band of the 30s & 40s. Died 11/5/77 (75).	
1/19/57	18	2	1. Your Guy Lombardo Medley [I]	Capitol 739
			medley of 40 tunes	
7/28/58	12	4	2. Berlin By Lombardo [I]	Capitol 1019
			medley of 40 Irving Berlin songs	
			JULIE LONDON	
			Born on 9/26/26 in Santa Rosa, California. Singer, actress. Played Dixie McCall on the TV series "Emergency".	
1/28/56	2(2)	14	1. **Julie Is Her Name**	Liberty 3006
			"Cry Me A River"(9)	
8/11/56	16	8	2. Lonely Girl	Liberty 3012
12/15/56	18	6	3. Calendar Girl	Liberty 9002
7/22/57	15	1	4. About The Blues	Liberty 3043
			LORETTA LONG - see CHILDREN'S section	
			CLAUDINE LONGET	
			Born on 1/29/42 in France. Singer, actress. Formerly married to Andy Williams.	
6/03/67	11	22	● 1. Claudine	A&M 4121
11/25/67	33	6	2. The Look Of Love	A&M 4129
6/01/68	29	5	3. Love Is Blue	A&M 4142
			TRINI LOPEZ	
			Born on 5/15/37 in Dallas. Pop/folk singer, guitarist. Discovered by Don Costa while performing at PJs nightclub in Los Angeles.	
8/03/63	2(6)	48	● 1. **Trini Lopez At PJ'S** [L]	Reprise 6093
			"If I Had A Hammer"(3)	
12/21/63	11	8	2. More Trini Lopez At PJ'S [L]	Reprise 6103
7/11/64	32	2	3. On The Move [L]	Reprise 6112
9/19/64	18	11	4. The Latin Album [F]	Reprise 6125
11/28/64	30	7	5. Live At Basin St. East [L]	Reprise 6134
2/27/65	18	9	6. The Folk Album	Reprise 6147
7/24/65	32	3	7. The Love Album	Reprise 6165
			LOS ADMIRADORES	
			Percussion group produced by Enoch Light.	
8/29/60	2(1)	46	1. **Bongos Bongos Bongos** [I]	Command 809
10/24/60	3	28	2. **Bongos/Flutes/Guitars** [I]	Command 812

DATE	POS	WKS	ARTIST—RECORD TITLE	LABEL & NO.
			LOS INDIOS TABAJARAS	
			Brazilian Indian brothers: Natalicio and Antenor Lima.	
11/30/63	7	11	1. **Maria Elena** [I]	RCA 2822
			"Maria Elena"(6)	
			LOVE UNLIMITED	
			Female soul trio from San Pedro, CA: sisters Glodean & Linda James, and Diane Taylor. Barry White, who later married Glodean, was their manager and producer.	
12/08/73	3	17	● 1. **Under The Influence Of...**	20th Century 414
			LOVE UNLIMITED ORCHESTRA	
			Studio orchestra conducted and arranged by Barry White.	
2/23/74	8	11	● 1. **Rhapsody In White** [I]	20th Century 433
			"Love's Theme"(1) - first appeared in Love Unlimited album	
			(#414 above)	
12/28/74	28	2	● 2. White Gold [I]	20th Century 458
			LOVERBOY	
			Rock quintet formed in Vancouver, Canada in 1978: Mike Reno (lead singer), Paul Dean (lead guitar), Scott Smith (bass), Matt Frenette (drums) and Doug Johnson (keyboards).	
3/28/81	13	17	▲ 1. Loverboy	Columbia 36762
			"Turn Me Loose"	
12/05/81	7	51	▲ 2. **Get Lucky**	Columbia 37638
			"Working For The Weekend"	
7/02/83	7	22	▲ 3. **Keep It Up**	Columbia 38703
			"Hot Girls In Love"	
9/21/85	13	21	▲ 4. Lovin' Every Minute Of It	Columbia 39953
			"Lovin' Every Minute Of It"(9)	
			"This Could Be The Night"(10)	
			THE LOVIN' SPOONFUL	
			Jug band rock group formed in New York City in 1965. Consisted of John Sebastian (lead vocals, songwriter, guitarist, harmonica), Zal Yanovsky (lead guitar), Steve Boone (bass) and Joe Butler (drums). Sebastian had been with the Even Dozen Jug Band; did session work at Elektra. Yanovsky and Sebastian were members of the Mugwumps with Cass Elliott and Denny Doherty (later with The Mamas & The Papas). Yanovsky replaced by Jerry Yester (keyboards) in 1967. Disbanded in 1968.	
5/07/66	10	11	1. **Daydream**	Kama Sutra 8051
			"You Didn't Have To Be So Nice"(10)	
			"Daydream"(2)	
7/16/66	32	7	2. Do You Believe In Magic	Kama Sutra 8050
			"Do You Believe In Magic"(9)	
			"Did You Ever Have To Make Up Your Mind"(2)	
1/21/67	14	8	3. Hums Of The Lovin' Spoonful	Kama Sutra 8054
			"Summer In The City"(1)	
			"Rain On The Roof"(10)	
			"Nashville Cats"(8)	
3/25/67	3	26	● 4. **The Best Of The Lovin' Spoonful** [G]	Kama Sutra 8056

DATE	POS	WKS	ARTIST—RECORD TITLE	LABEL & NO.
			NICK LOWE	
			Born on 3/25/49 in England. With Brinsley Schwarz (1970-75) and Rockpile. Married to Carlene Carter. Produced albums for Elvis Costello and Graham Parker & The Rumour.	
9/08/79	31	7	1. Labour Of Lust	Columbia 36087
			"Cruel To Be Kind"	
			L.T.D.	
			Jeffrey Osborne, lead singer of 10 man R&B/funk band from Greensboro, NC. L.T.D. means Love, Togetherness and Devotion.	
9/10/77	21	14	● 1. Something To Love	A&M 4646
			"(Every Time I Turn Around) Back In Love Again"(4)	
7/22/78	18	11	▲ 2. Togetherness	A&M 4705
8/04/79	29	6	● 3. Devotion	A&M 4771
9/20/80	28	8	4. Shine On	A&M 4819
			NORMAN LUBOFF Choir	
10/15/55	15	3	1. Songs Of The West	Columbia 657
7/14/56	19	2	2. Songs Of The South	Columbia 860
5/27/57	19	4	3. Calypso Holiday	Columbia 1000
1/13/58	22	1	4. Songs Of Christmas [X]	Columbia 926
			LULU	
			Born Marie Lawrie on 11/3/48 near Glasgow, Scotland. Formerly married to Maurice Gibb (Bee Gees), 1969-73.	
12/02/67	24	10	1. To Sir With Love	Epic 26339
			"To Sir With Love"(1) - also see Soundtrack of same title	
			ARTHUR LYMAN	
			Born on the island of Kauai, Hawaii in 1934. Plays vibraphone, guitar, piano and drums. Formerly with the Martin Denny Trio.	
5/12/58	6	62	1. **Taboo** [I]	HiFi 806
7/24/61	10	18	2. **Yellow Bird** [I]	HiFi 1004
			"Yellow Bird"(4)	
4/06/63	36	1	3. I Wish You Love [I]	HiFi 1009
			FRANKIE LYMON - see TEENAGERS	
			CHERYL LYNN	
			Born on 3/11/57 in Los Angeles. Soul singer. Discovered on TV's "Gong Show".	
1/27/79	23	6	● 1. Cheryl Lynn	Columbia 35486
			GLORIA LYNNE	
			Born on 11/23/31 in New York City. Jazz-styled vocalist.	
3/16/63	39	4	1. Gloria Lynne at the Las Vegas Thunderbird [L]	Everest 5208
4/18/64	27	10	2. Gloria, Marty & Strings	Everest 5220
			arranged and conducted by Marty Paich	

DATE	POS	WKS	ARTIST—RECORD TITLE		LABEL & NO.
			LYNYRD SKYNYRD		
			Southern rock band formed while in high school in Jacksonville, Florida in 1965. Named after their gym teacher Leonard Skinner. Nucleus of band consisted of Ronnie Van Zant (lead singer), Gary Rossington (guitar) and Allen Collins (guitar). Plane crash on 10/20/77 in Gillsburg, Mississippi killed Van Zant and members Steve and Cassie Gaines. Gary and Allen formed the Rossington Collins Band in 1980.		
5/25/74	12	19	● 1. Second Helping		MCA/Sounds 413
			"Sweet Home Alabama"(8)		
2/15/75	27	4	● 2. Lynyrd Skynyrd (pronounced leh-nerd skin-nerd)		MCA/Sounds 363
			"Free Bird"		
4/19/75	9	10	● 3. **Nuthin' Fancy**		MCA 2137
3/13/76	20	5	● 4. Gimme Back My Bullets		MCA 2170
10/16/76	9	15	▲ 5. **One More From The Road**	[L]	MCA 6001 [2]
11/19/77	5	15	▲ 6. **Street Survivors**		MCA 3029
			album released 3 days before the plane crash		
9/30/78	15	7	▲ 7. Skynyrd's First And…Last	[E]	MCA 3047
			recordings from 1970-1972		
1/05/80	12	11	▲ 8. Gold & Platinum	[G]	MCA 11008 [2]

M

DATE	POS	WKS	ARTIST—RECORD TITLE		LABEL & NO.
			MOMS MABLEY		
			Born Loretta Mary Aiken on 3/19/1897 in North Carolina. Died on 5/23/75. Bawdy comedienne. Charted 13 comedy albums on Billboard's pop albums charts.		
5/29/61	16	11	1. Moms Mabley At The "UN"	[C]	Chess 1452
12/11/61	39	1	2. Moms Mabley at The Playboy Club	[C]	Chess 1460
4/28/62	28	6	3. Moms Mabley At Geneva Conference	[C]	Chess 1463
9/29/62	27	4	4. Moms Mabley Breaks It Up	[C]	Chess 1472
3/02/63	19	5	5. Young Men, Si' - Old Men, No	[C]	Chess 1477
			JEANETTE MacDONALD & NELSON EDDY		
			Top movie duo of the '30s. Jeanette died on 1/14/65-63; Nelson died on 3/6/67-65.		
5/25/59	40	1	● 1. Favorites In Hi-Fi		RCA 1738
			MARY MacGREGOR		
			Pop singer from St. Paul.		
2/19/77	17	7	1. Torn Between Two Lovers		Ariola Am. 50015
			"Torn Between Two Lovers"(1)		
			MADONNA		
			Born Madonna Louise Ciccone on 8/16/58 in Bay City, MI. Starred in the film "Desperately Seeking Susan". Married to actor Sean Penn in 1985.		
2/18/84	8	36	▲ 1. **Madonna**		Sire 23867
			"Borderline"(10)		
			"Lucky Star"(4)		

DATE	POS	WKS	ARTIST—RECORD TITLE	LABEL & NO.
12/08/84	1(3)	51	▲ 2. **Like A Virgin** "Like A Virgin"(1) "Material Girl"(2) "Angel"(5) "Dress You Up"(5)	Sire 25157
7/19/86	1(5)	48	▲ 3. **True Blue** "Live To Tell"(1) "Papa Don't Preach"(1) "True Blue"(3) "Open Your Heart"(1) "La Isla Bonita"(4)	Sire 25442
			GEORGE MAHARIS Born on 9/1/33 in New York City. Played Buz Murdock on TV's "Route 66".	
7/14/62	10	8	1. **George Maharis Sings!**	Epic 26001
9/15/62	32	3	2. Portrait In Music	Epic 26021
			MAHAVISHNU ORCHESTRA - see JOHN McLAUGHLIN	
			MALO Latin-rock band formed by Jorge Santana (brother of Carlos).	
3/18/72	14	14	1. **Malo** "Suavecito"	Warner 2584
			THE MAMAS & THE PAPAS Quartet formed in New York City in 1963. Consisted of John Phillips (b: 8/30/35, Paris Island, SC); Holly Michelle Gilliam Phillips (b: 6/4/45, Long Beach, CA); Dennis Doherty (b: 11/29/41, Halifax, Nova Scotia) and Mama Cass Elliot. Phillips had been in the Journeymen, married Michelle Gilliam in 1962. Elliot had been in the Mugwumps with Doherty. Group moved to Los Angeles in 1964. Disbanded in 1968, reunited briefly in 1971. Michelle Phillips in films "Dillinger" and "Valentino". Formed new group in 1982: John and daughter MacKenzie Phillips, Dennis Doherty and Spanky McFarlane of Spanky & Our Gang.	
4/23/66	1(1)	1	● 1. **If You Can Believe Your Eyes And Ears** "California Dreamin'"(4) "Monday, Monday"(1)	Dunhill 50006
10/08/66	4	32	● 2. **The Mamas & The Papas** "I Saw Her Again"(5) "Words Of Love"(5)	Dunhill 50010
3/25/67	2(7)	25	● 3. **The Mamas & The Papas Deliver** "Dedicated To The One I Love"(2) "Creeque Alley"(5)	Dunhill 50014
11/25/67	5	18	● 4. **Farewell To The First Golden Era**　　　[G]	Dunhill 50025
6/22/68	15	11	5. The Papas & The Mamas	Dunhill 50031
			MANASSAS - see STEPHEN STILLS	

DATE	POS	WKS	ARTIST—RECORD TITLE	LABEL & NO.
			MELISSA MANCHESTER	
			Born on 2/15/51 in the Bronx, NY. Vocalist, pianist, composer. Studied with Paul Simon at University School of the Arts, early 70s. Former backup singer for Bette Midler.	
7/19/75	12	11	● 1. Melissa	Arista 4031
			"Midnight Blue"(6)	
2/28/76	24	8	2. Better Days & Happy Endings	Arista 4067
3/17/79	33	3	3. Don't Cry Out Loud	Arista 4186
			"Don't Cry Out Loud"(10)	
8/28/82	19	8	4. Hey Ricky	Arista 9574
			"You Should Hear How She Talks About You"(5)	
			HENRY MANCINI	
			Born on 4/16/24 in Cleveland. Leading film-TV composer/arranger/conductor. Staff composer for Universal Pictures, 1952-58. Won more Oscars (4) and Grammys (20) than any other pop artist.	
2/09/59	1(10)	97	● 1. **The Music From Peter Gunn** [TV-I]	RCA 1956
6/29/59	7	35	2. **More Music From Peter Gunn** [TV-I]	RCA 2040
3/28/60	2(1)	49	3. **Music From Mr. Lucky** [TV-I]	RCA 2198
5/08/61	28	26	4. Mr. Lucky Goes Latin [I]	RCA 2360
10/09/61	1(12)	96	● 5. **Breakfast At Tiffany's** [S-I]	RCA 2362
			"Moon River"	
3/10/62	28	7	6. Combo! [I]	RCA 2258
			recorded June, 1960	
6/30/62	37	1	7. Experiment In Terror [S-I]	RCA 2442
7/28/62	4	35	8. **Hatari!** [S-I]	RCA 2559
			"Baby Elephant Walk"	
2/23/63	12	23	9. Our Man In Hollywood	RCA 2604
			"Days Of Wine And Roses"	
7/06/63	5	11	10. **Uniquely Mancini** [I]	RCA 2692
2/01/64	6	18	11. **Charade** [S-I]	RCA 2755
4/25/64	8	41	● 12. **The Pink Panther** [S-I]	RCA 2795
8/15/64	15	7	13. The Concert Sound of Henry Mancini [I]	RCA 2897
			medleys of 30 tunes - with a 70-piece orchestra	
2/20/65	11	11	14. Dear Heart And Other Songs About Love	RCA 2990
6/07/69	5	19	● 15. **A Warm Shade Of Ivory** [I]	RCA 4140
			"Love Theme From Romeo & Juliet"(1)	
3/06/71	26	4	16. Mancini plays the Theme From Love Story	RCA 4466
			MANDRILL	
			Brooklyn Latin jazz/rock septet formed in 1968 by brothers Louis "Sweet Lou", Richard "Dr. Ric", and Carlos "Mad Dog" Wilson.	
5/12/73	28	8	1. Composite Truth	Polydor 5043
			MANFRED MANN	
			Rock group formed in England in 1964: Manfred Mann (real name: Michael Lubowitz), keyboards; Paul Jones, vocals; Mike Hugg, drums; Michael Vickers, guitar; and Tom McGuiness, bass. Manfred Mann formed his new 'Earth Band' in 1971, featuring Mick Rogers, vocals; Colin Pattenden, bass; and Chris Slade, drums. Mick replaced by Thompson (lead singer) in 1976.	
1/23/65	35	4	1. the Manfred Mann album	Ascot 16015
			"Do Wah Diddy Diddy"(1)	

DATE	POS	WKS	ARTIST—RECORD TITLE	LABEL & NO.
1/22/77	**10**	11	● 2. **The Roaring Silence**	Warner 2965
			"Blinded By The Light"(1)	
			<small>Chris Thompson replaces Mick Rogers as lead singer</small>	
3/24/84	**40**	2	3. Somewhere In Afrika	Arista 8194

CHUCK MANGIONE

Born on 11/29/40 in Rochester, NY. Flugelhorn, bandleader, composer. Recorded with older brother Gaspare ("Gap") as the Jazz Brothers for Riverside in 1960. To New York City in 1965, with Maynard Ferguson, Kai Winding, and Art Blakey's Jazz Messengers.

DATE	POS	WKS	ARTIST—RECORD TITLE	LABEL & NO.
2/18/78	**2(2)**	28	▲ 1. **Feels So Good** **[I]**	A&M 4658
			"Feels So Good"(4)	
9/30/78	**14**	10	● 2. Children Of Sanchez [S-I]	A&M 6700 [2]
7/28/79	**27**	6	3. An Evening Of Magic - Chuck Mangione	
			Live At The Hollywood Bowl [I-L]	A&M 6701 [2]
3/01/80	**8**	11	● 4. **Fun And Games** **[I]**	A&M 3715

THE MANHATTAN TRANSFER

Versatile vocal harmony quartet formed in New York City in 1972: Tim Hauser, Alan Paul, Janis Siegel and Cheryl Bentyne (replaced Laurel Masse in 1979).

DATE	POS	WKS	ARTIST—RECORD TITLE	LABEL & NO.
6/28/75	**33**	4	1. The Manhattan Transfer	Atlantic 18133
7/04/81	**22**	13	2. Mecca For Moderns	Atlantic 16036
			"Boy From New York City"(7)	

THE MANHATTANS

Soul group from Jersey City, NJ. Consisted of George "Smitty" Smith (d: 1970, spinal meningitis) lead; Winfred "Blue" Lovett, bass; Edward "Sonny" Bivins and Kenneth "Wally" Kelly, tenors; and Richard Taylor, baritone. Smith replaced by Gerald Alston in 1971. First recorded for Piney in 1962. Taylor left in 1977.

DATE	POS	WKS	ARTIST—RECORD TITLE	LABEL & NO.
6/19/76	**16**	12	● 1. The Manhattans	Columbia 33820
			"Kiss And Say Goodbye"(1)	
6/07/80	**24**	10	● 2. After Midnight	Columbia 36411
			"Shining Star"(5)	

BARRY MANILOW

Born on 6/17/46 in Brooklyn. Vocalist, pianist, composer. Studied at Juilliard, New York College of Music. Wrote jingles. On WCBS-TV series, "Callback". Worked at Continental Baths, New York in 1972, met Bette Midler, and became her director, arranger and accompanist. Produced her first two albums. Sang jingles for Dr. Pepper, Pepsi and McDonald's ("You Deserve A Break Today").

DATE	POS	WKS	ARTIST—RECORD TITLE	LABEL & NO.
1/11/75	**9**	11	● 1. **Barry Manilow II**	Arista 4016
			"Mandy"(1)	
10/04/75	**28**	6	● 2. Barry Manilow I	Arista 4007
			<small>above 2 albums previously released on the Bell label</small>	
			"Could It Be Magic"(6)	
11/29/75	**5**	9	● 3. **Tryin' To Get The Feeling**	Arista 4060
			"I Write The Songs"(1)	
			"Tryin' To Get The Feeling Again"(10)	
8/21/76	**6**	27	▲ 4. **This One's For You**	Arista 4090
			"Weekend In New England"(10)	
			"Looks Like We Made It"(1)	
5/28/77	**1(1)**	26	▲ 5. **Barry Manilow/Live** **[L]**	Arista 8500 [2]

DATE	POS	WKS	ARTIST—RECORD TITLE	LABEL & NO.
3/04/78	3	28	▲ 6. **Even Now**	Arista 4164
			"Can't Smile Without You"(3)	
			"Copacabana (At The Copa)"(8)	
			"Somewhere In The Night"(9)	
12/02/78	7	16	▲ 7. **Greatest Hits** [G]	Arista 8601 [2]
10/20/79	9	15	▲ 8. **One Voice**	Arista 9505
			"Ships"(9)	
12/20/80	15	9	▲ 9. Barry	Arista 9537
			"I Made It Through The Rain"(10)	
10/24/81	14	10	● 10. If I Should Love Again	Arista 9573
1/08/83	32	6	● 11. Here Comes The Night	Arista 9610
12/17/83	30	7	● 12. Barry Manilow/Greatest Hits, Vol. II [G [G]	Arista 8102
1/05/85	28	6	● 13. 2:00 AM Paradise Cafe	Arista 8254
			with jazz greats, Sarah Vaughan, Gerry Mulligan & Mel Torme	

HERBIE MANN

Born Herbert Jay Solomon on 4/16/30 in Brooklyn. Plays flute, saxophones and other reeds. First recorded with Mat Mathews Quintet for Brunswick in 1953. First recorded as a solo for Bethlehem in 1954.

DATE	POS	WKS	ARTIST—RECORD TITLE	LABEL & NO.
11/03/62	30	11	1. Herbie Mann at the Village Gate [I-L]	Atlantic 1380
6/21/69	22	17	2. Memphis Underground [I]	Atlantic 1522
			with Roy Ayers (vibes) & Larry Coryell (guitar)	
6/07/75	27	3	3. Discotheque [I]	Atlantic 1670

MANFRED MANN - see MANFRED

CHARLIE MANNA

Comedian from New York.

DATE	POS	WKS	ARTIST—RECORD TITLE	LABEL & NO.
9/11/61	27	14	1. Manna Overboard!! [C]	Decca 4159

MANTOVANI

Born Annunzio Paolo Mantovani on 11/15/05 in Venice, Italy. Died on 3/29/80. Played classical violin in England before forming his own orchestra in the early 30s. Achieved international fame twenty years later with his 40-piece orchestra and distinctive "cascading strings" sound.

DATE	POS	WKS	ARTIST—RECORD TITLE	LABEL & NO.
2/19/55	13	2	1. The Music Of Rudolf Friml [I]	London 1150
3/19/55	14	2	2. Waltz Time [I]	London 1094
			"Charmaine"(10-'51)	
7/09/55	8	8	● 3. **Song Hits From Theatreland** [I]	London 1219
5/26/56	12	7	4. Waltzes Of Irving Berlin [I]	London 1452
5/27/57	1(1)	73	● 5. **Film Encores** [I]	London 1700
12/09/57	4	6	● 6. **Christmas Carols** [X-I]	London 913
3/24/58	22	1	7. Mantovani Plays Tangos [I]	London 768
			above 2 albums released in 1953	
5/19/58	5	95	● 8. **Gems Forever...** [I]	London 3032
11/24/58	7	60	● 9. **Strauss Waltzes** [I]	London 685
			first released in 1953	
12/22/58	3	3	10. **Christmas Carols** [X-R]	London 913
2/16/59	13	46	11. Continental Encores [I]	London 3095
6/01/59	6	11	12. **Mantovani Stereo Showcase** [K-I]	London SS1
6/22/59	14	26	13. Film Encores, Vol. 2 [I]	London 3117

DATE	POS	WKS	ARTIST—RECORD TITLE	LABEL & NO.
12/21/59	16	3	14. Christmas Carols [X-R]	London 913
1/04/60	8	18	15. **All-American Showcase** [K-I]	London 3122 [2]
			1 side each: Sigmund Romberg/Victor Herbert/Irving Berlin/ Rudolf Friml	
3/28/60	11	30	16. The American Scene [I]	London 3136
			side 1 features the music of Stephen Foster	
7/25/60	21	30	17. Songs To Remember [I]	London 3149
12/05/60	2(5)	32	● 18. **Mantovani plays music from Exodus and other great themes** [I]	London 3231
12/19/60	8	3	19. **Christmas Carols** [X-R]	London 913
2/20/61	22	12	20. Operetta Memories [I]	London 3181
6/26/61	8	15	21. **Italia Mia** [I]	London 3239
8/21/61	29	5	22. Themes From Broadway [I]	London 3250
1/06/62	36	2	23. Christmas Carols [X-R]	London 913
6/16/62	8	19	24. **American Waltzes** [I]	London 248
11/03/62	24	8	25. Moon River and other great film themes [I]	London 249
6/01/63	10	13	26. **Latin Rendezvous** [I]	London 295
12/19/64	37	3	27. The Incomparable Mantovani [I]	London 392
5/01/65	26	8	28. The Mantovani Sound - Big Hits From Broadway And Hollywood [I]	London 419
4/16/66	23	8	29. Mantovani Magic [I]	London 448
11/26/66	27	7	30. Mr. Music...Mantovani [I]	London 474

TEENA MARIE
Born Mary Christine Brockert in Venice, CA in 1957. White soul singer, actress, guitarist, keyboardist, composer, producer.

DATE	POS	WKS	ARTIST—RECORD TITLE	LABEL & NO.
11/22/80	38	3	1. Irons In The Fire	Gordy 997
7/18/81	23	9	● 2. It Must Be Magic	Gordy 1004
3/02/85	31	12	● 3. Starchild	Epic 39528
			"Lovergirl"(4)	

THE MARKETTS
Hollywood, California instrumental surf quintet.

DATE	POS	WKS	ARTIST—RECORD TITLE	LABEL & NO.
3/14/64	37	2	1. Out Of Limits! [I]	Warner 1537
			"Out Of Limits"(3)	

BOB MARLEY & THE WAILERS
Bob & his Jamaican band are the masters of reggae. Bob died from brain cancer on 5/11/81 in Miami. Wrote Eric Clapton's hit "I Shot The Sheriff".

DATE	POS	WKS	ARTIST—RECORD TITLE	LABEL & NO.
5/15/76	8	14	1. **Rastaman Vibration**	Island 9383
			"Roots, Rock, Reggae"	
7/09/77	20	11	2. Exodus	Island 9498

THE MARSHALL TUCKER BAND
Southern rock band formed in South Carolina in 1971. Doug Gray, lead singer, Toy Caldwell, lead guitarist; George McCorkle, rhythm guitar; Paul Riddle, drums; Jerry Eubanks, sax; and Tommy Caldwell, bass (d: 4/30/80 - replaced by Franklin Wilkie).

DATE	POS	WKS	ARTIST—RECORD TITLE	LABEL & NO.
10/06/73	29	8	● 1. The Marshall Tucker Band	Capricorn 0112
3/30/74	37	3	● 2. A New Life	Capricorn 0124
10/11/75	15	8	● 3. Searchin' For A Rainbow	Capricorn 0161
7/24/76	32	5	4. Long Hard Ride	Capricorn 0170

The Mamas and the Papas rehearsed extensively on the island of St. Thomas before going to California and launching a career in the mid-1960s. In 1967, John Phillips wrote, produced, and played on the hippie pseudo-anthem "San Francisco (Be Sure to Wear Some Flowers in Your Hair)," which was recorded by onetime bandmate Scott McKenzie.

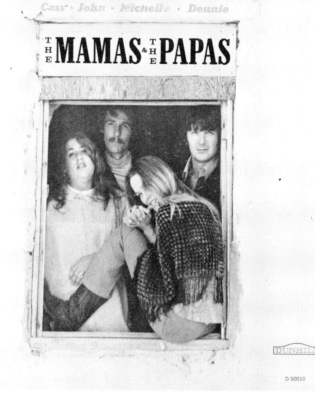

Henry Mancini was the first person to receive a gold album for a television series soundtrack: the memorable and distinctive theme music for "Peter Gunn" (NBC, 1958–61). Other shows and movies for which Mancini has provided music include "What's Happening!!," *Breakfast at Tiffany's*, and *Days of Wine and Roses*.

Manfred Mann was a group, but its namesake was a South African keyboard player who had studied classical music in New York and Vienna. In 1964, the London quintet became the third British Invasion group to have a No. 1 record in America: "Do Wah Diddy Diddy" was included on the group's first U.S. album, *The Manfred Mann Album*.

Johnny Mathis set records in basketball and track as a San Francisco high school student and won an athletic scholarship to college in the early 1950s. He was even invited to try out for the Olympics, but tried singing casually in a local club in which a talent scout happened to be. Mathis was signed to Columbia Records and began making records of an entirely different sort.

Bob & Doug McKenzie are actually Rick Moranis and Dave Thomas, two cast members of "SCTV." Canadian broadcasting regulations led the show to incorporate a routine in which a pair of backwoods brothers hosted an imaginary television show and drank lots of Canadian beer, muttering such Canadian colloquialisms as "hoser" and "Good day, eh?" That skit led to the comedy album *Great White North*, which also features Geddy Lee of Rush.

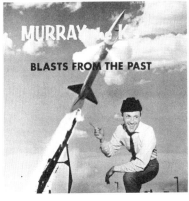

Moby Grape was one of the first 1960s rock groups to use what would become common 1970s promotional gimmicks on its records. Most of the tracks on the San Francisco band's debut album were simultaneously issued on 45s; *Wow* (1968), the group's second album, contained a bonus disc of jams and one cut that played at 78 RPM.

The Monkees' 1968 feature film, *Head*, has a screenplay written by Jack Nicholson and Bob Rafelson and includes appearances by such notables as Nicholson, Frank Zappa, Sonny Liston, Teri Garr, and stripper Carol Doda.

The Moody Blues' original guitarist and singer was Denny Laine ("Go Now"). Before Laine joined Paul McCartney's Wings in 1971, he was in a band called Balls, which was formed by four members of a group known as the Uglys. The Moody Blues, meanwhile, enjoyed success without him, scoring nine consecutive gold and platinum studio albums.

Van Morrison began his career as a Belfast teenager singing R&B with Them; he wrote "Gloria" (since covered most notably by the Shadows of Knight and Patti Smith) in 1965.

The Mothers of Invention parodied the Beatles' *Sgt. Pepper* cover on *We're Only in It for the Money* (1968), spelling "MOTHERS" with fruit and vegetables in front of a familiar-looking collage in which Frank Zappa wears a dress and pigtails.

Murray the K (Kaufman) was one of rock radio's legendary disc jockeys, helping keep New York airwaves exciting throughout the 1950s and 1960s. He billed himself as "the Fifth Beatle"; invented a language called "bop talk" that listeners adopted; and hosted incredible concerts at Brooklyn's Fox Theater, including one in 1967 at which the Who and Cream made their American debuts.

DATE	POS	WKS	ARTIST—RECORD TITLE	LABEL & NO.
4/02/77	23	15	▲ 5. Carolina Dreams	Capricorn 0180
6/03/78	22	5	● 6. Together Forever	Capricorn 0205
6/02/79	30	3	7. Running Like The Wind	Warner 3317
4/05/80	32	5	8. Tenth	Warner 3410

DEAN MARTIN

Born Dino Crocetti on 6/7/17 in Steubenville, OH. Vocalist, actor. To California in 1937, worked local clubs. Teamed with comedian Jerry Lewis in Atlantic City in 1946. First film, "My Friend Irma" in 1949. Team broke up after 16th film "Hollywood Or Bust" in 1956. Appeared in many films since then, own TV series from 1965-74.

DATE	POS	WKS	ARTIST—RECORD TITLE	LABEL & NO.
8/22/64	2(4)	32	● 1. **Everybody Loves Somebody**	Reprise 6130
			"Everybody Loves Somebody"(1)	
10/10/64	15	9	● 2. Dream With Dean	Reprise 6123
11/28/64	9	15	● 3. **The Door Is Still Open To My Heart**	Reprise 6140
			"The Door Is Still Open To My Heart"(6)	
3/13/65	13	9	● 4. Dean Martin Hits Again	Reprise 6146
10/02/65	13	16	● 5. (Remember Me) I'm The One Who Loves You	Reprise 6170
12/04/65	11	17	● 6. Houston	Reprise 6181
			"I Will"(10)	
5/14/66	40	2	● 7. Somewhere There's A Someone	Reprise 6201
1/21/67	34	3	8. The Dean Martin TV Show	Reprise 6233
9/16/67	20	16	● 9. Welcome To My World	Reprise 6250
7/13/68	26	12	● 10. Dean Martin's Greatest Hits! Vol. 1 [G]	Reprise 6301
2/08/69	14	9	● 11. Gentle On My Mind	Reprise 6330

STEVE MARTIN

Born in Waco, Texas in 1945. Raised in California. Popular television and film comedian. Comedy writer for the "Smothers Brothers Comedy Hour" TV show and others.

DATE	POS	WKS	ARTIST—RECORD TITLE	LABEL & NO.
10/15/77	10	11	▲ 1. **Let's Get Small** [C]	Warner 3090
11/11/78	2(6)	18	▲ 2. **A Wild And Crazy Guy** [C]	Warner 3238
10/20/79	25	5	● 3. Comedy Is Not Pretty! [C]	Warner 3392

AL MARTINO

Born Alfred Cini on 10/7/27 in Philadelphia. Encouraged by success of boyhood friend, Mario Lanza. Winner on Arthur Godfrey's "Talent Scouts" in 1952. Portrayed singer Johnny Fontane in the film "The Godfather", 1972.

DATE	POS	WKS	ARTIST—RECORD TITLE	LABEL & NO.
6/29/63	7	13	1. **I Love You Because**	Capitol 1914
			"I Love You Because"(3)	
10/26/63	9	21	2. **Painted, Tainted Rose**	Capitol 1975
2/29/64	13	10	3. Living A Lie	Capitol 2040
8/15/64	31	6	4. I Love You More And More Every Day/ Tears And Roses	Capitol 2107
			"I Love You More And More Every Day"(9)	
2/12/66	19	8	5. My Cherie	Capitol 2362
3/12/66	8	26	● 6. **Spanish Eyes**	Capitol 2435
8/12/67	23	4	7. Daddy's Little Girl	Capitol 2733

DATE	POS	WKS	ARTIST—RECORD TITLE	LABEL & NO.
			MARY JANE GIRLS	
			Female "funk & roll" quartet: Joanne McDuffie, Candice Ghant, Kim Wuletick and Yvette Marine. Formed and produced by Rick James.	
5/25/85	**18**	11	1. Only Four You	Gordy 6092
			"In My House"(7)	
			HUGH MASEKELA	
			Born Hugh Ramapolo Masekela on 4/4/39 in Wilbank, South Africa. Trumpeter, bandleader, arranger. Played trumpet since age 14. To England in 1959; New York City in 1960. Formerly married to Miriam Makeba. Formed own band in 1964.	
7/20/68	**17**	10	1. The Promise Of A Future	Uni 73028
			"Grazing In The Grass"(1)	
			DAVE MASON	
			Born on 5/10/46 in Worchester, England. Vocalist, composer, guitarist. Original member of Traffic.	
7/11/70	**22**	2	● 1. Alone Together	Blue Thumb 19
			with guests Leon Russell, Jim Capaldi, Rita Coolidge and Delaney & Bonnie	
11/30/74	**25**	4	● 2. Dave Mason	Columbia 33096
11/01/75	**27**	6	3. Split Coconut	Columbia 33698
			with guests The Manhattan Transfer, David Crosby and Graham Nash	
5/28/77	**37**	2	● 4. Let It Flow	Columbia 34680
			"We Just Disagree"	
			JOHNNY MATHIS	
			Born on 9/30/35 in San Francisco. Studied opera from age thirteen. Track scholarship, San Francisco State College. Invited to Olympic tryouts, chose singing career instead. To New York City in 1956. Ranks behind only Elvis Presley and Frank Sinatra as the top album artist of the rock era.	
9/09/57	**4**	26	1. **Wonderful Wonderful**	Columbia 1028
			the title song is not included on the album	
12/23/57	**2(4)**	84	● 2. **Warm**	Columbia 1078
4/07/58	**10**	12	3. **Good Night, Dear Lord**	Columbia 1119
4/14/58	**1(3)**	36	▲ 4. **Johnny's Greatest Hits** **[G]**	Columbia 1133
			"Wonderful! Wonderful!"/"It's Not For Me To Say"(5)	
			"Chances Are"(1)	
			"The Twelfth Of Never"(9)	
9/08/58	**6**	16	● 5. **Swing Softly**	Columbia 1165
12/15/58	**3**	4	▲ 6. **Merry Christmas** **[X]**	Columbia 1195
2/09/59	**4**	94	● 7. **Open Fire, Two Guitars**	Columbia 1270
7/27/59	**2(2)**	53	● 8. **More Johnny's Greatest Hits** **[G]**	Columbia 1344
			"A Certain Smile"/"Small World"	
9/21/59	**1(5)**	40	▲ 9. **Heavenly**	Columbia 1351
			"Misty"	
12/28/59	**10**	3	10. **Merry Christmas** **[X-R]**	Columbia 1195
1/18/60	**2(1)**	63	● 11. **Faithfully**	Columbia 8219
			"Maria"	
8/29/60	**4**	26	12. **Johnny's Mood**	Columbia 8326
10/03/60	**6**	25	13. **The Rhythms And Ballads Of Broadway**	Columbia 803 [2]
12/31/60	**10**	2	14. **Merry Christmas** **[X-R]**	Columbia 8021

DATE	POS	WKS	ARTIST—RECORD TITLE	LABEL & NO.
7/17/61	38	23	15. I'll Buy You A Star	Columbia 8423
9/04/61	2(7)	28	16. **Portrait Of Johnny** [G]	Columbia 8444
1/06/62	31	7	17. Merry Christmas [X-R]	Columbia 8021
3/24/62	14	12	18. Live It Up!	Columbia 8511
11/03/62	12	14	19. Rapture	Columbia 8715
12/22/62	12	2	20. Merry Christmas [X-R] made top 10 on Billboard's special Christmas charts (1963-68 & 1973)	Columbia 8021
4/27/63	6	17	21. **Johnny's Newest Hits** [G] ''Gina''(6) ''What Will Mary Say''(9)	Columbia 8816
9/21/63	20	9	22. Johnny	Columbia 8844
1/25/64	23	7	23. Romantically	Columbia 8898
2/29/64	13	16	24. Tender Is The Night	Mercury 60890
6/27/64	35	4	25. I'll Search My Heart and Other Great Hits [K]	Columbia 8943
12/26/64	40	1	26. This Is Love	Mercury 60942
5/14/66	9	16	27. **The Shadow Of Your Smile**	Mercury 61073
6/08/68	26	6	28. Love Is Blue	Columbia 9637
5/09/70	38	2	29. Raindrops Keep Fallin' On My Head	Columbia 1005
4/22/78	9	11	▲ 30. **You Light Up My Life** ''Too Much, Too Little, Too Late''(1-with Deniece Williams)	Columbia 35259
7/29/78	19	8	• 31. That's What Friends Are For **JOHNNY MATHIS & DENIECE WILLIAMS**	Columbia 35435
			MATTY MATLOCK - see RAY HEINDORF/ JACK WEBB	
			PAUL MAURIAT French conductor/arranger; born in 1925.	
2/10/68	1(5)	25	• 1. **Blooming Hits** [I] ''Love Is Blue''(1)	Philips 248
			ROBERT MAXWELL Born on 4/19/21 in New York City. Jazz harpist, composer. With NBC Symphony under Toscanini at age 17. Also see Mickey Mozart.	
5/23/64	17	12	1. Shangri-La [I]	Decca 74421
			BILLY MAY Born on 1/10/16 in Pittsburgh. Arranger/conductor/sideman for many of the big bands.	
3/05/55	7	6	1. **Sorta-May** [I]	Capitol 562
			JOHN MAYALL Born on 11/29/43 in Manchester, England. Bluesman John Mayall & his Bluesbreakers band spawned many of Britain's leading rock musicians.	
11/08/69	32	2	• 1. The Turning Point [L] featuring Jon Mark & Johnny Almond	Polydor 4004
4/11/70	33	4	2. Empty Rooms	Polydor 4010
10/31/70	22	5	3. USA Union featuring Harvey Mandel and other American artists	Polydor 4022

DATE	POS	WKS	ARTIST—RECORD TITLE	LABEL & NO.
			CURTIS MAYFIELD	
			Born on 6/3/42 in Chicago. Soul singer, songwriter, producer. With Jerry Butler in the gospel group Northern Jubilee Singers. Joined The Impressions in 1957. Wrote most of the hits for The Impressions and Jerry Butler. Own labels: Windy C, Mayfield, and Curtom. Went solo in 1970. Scored "Superfly", "Claudine", "A Piece Of The Action", "Short Eyes" film soundtracks. Appeared in "Short Eyes".	
10/24/70	**19**	18	● 1. Curtis	Curtom 8005
6/12/71	**21**	11	2. Curtis/Live! [L]	Curtom 8008 [2]
12/11/71	**40**	1	3. Roots	Curtom 8009
9/16/72	**1(4)**	30	● 4. **Superfly** [S]	Curtom 8014
			"Freddie's Dead"(4)	
			"Superfly"(8)	
6/23/73	**16**	10	● 5. Back To The World	Curtom 8015
7/06/74	**39**	1	6. Sweet Exorcist	Curtom 8601
			MAZE Featuring FRANKIE BEVERLY	
			Soul group formed in Philadelphia as the Butlers (later, Raw Soul); moved to San Francisco in 1972. Nucleus consisted of Frankie Beverly, vocalist; Wayne Thomas, Sam Porter, Robin Duhe, Roame Lowry and McKinley Williams.	
3/04/78	**27**	5	● 1. Golden Time Of Day	Capitol 11710
5/12/79	**33**	3	● 2. Inspiration	Capitol 11912
9/13/80	**31**	4	● 3. Joy And Pain	Capitol 12087
8/08/81	**34**	4	● 4. Live In New Orleans [L]	Capitol 12156 [2]
			side 4 contains new studio recordings	
6/04/83	**25**	5	5. We Are One	Capitol 12262
			MC5	
			Detroit hard rock quintet. Rob Tyner, lead singer.	
5/10/69	**30**	3	1. Kick Out The Jams [L]	Elektra 74042
			C.W. McCALL	
			Born Bill Fries on 11/15/28 in Audubon, Iowa. Advertising agent from Omaha.	
1/10/76	**12**	8	● 1. Black Bear Road	MGM 5008
			"Convoy"(1)	
			DAVID McCALLUM	
			Illya Kuryakin of TV's "The Man From U.N.C.L.E."	
4/16/66	**27**	8	1. Music - A Part Of Me [I]	Capitol 2432
			LES McCANN	
			Vocalist, piano. First recorded with Leroy Vinnegar, and Ron Jefferson, as Les McCann Ltd.	
1/31/70	**29**	5	1. Swiss Movement [I-L]	Atlantic 1537
			LES McCANN & EDDIE HARRIS	
			recorded live at the Montreux Jazz Festival, Switzerland	

DATE	POS	WKS	ARTIST—RECORD TITLE		LABEL & NO.

PAUL McCARTNEY

Born on 6/18/42 in Liverpool, England. Writer of over 50 Top 10 singles. Founding member/bass guitarist of The Beatles. Married Linda Eastman on 3/12/69. First solo album in 1970. Formed group Wings in 1971 with wife Linda (keyboards, backing vocals), Denny Laine (guitar) and Denny Seiwell (drums). Henry McCullough (guitar) joined in 1972. Seiwell and McCullough left in 1973. Joe English (drums) and James McCullough (guitar) joined in 1975. Also see Suzy & The Red Stripes.

DATE	POS	WKS	ARTIST—RECORD TITLE		LABEL & NO.
5/09/70	**1(3)**	20	● 1. **McCartney**		Apple 3363
			recorded at home by Paul as a one-man band		
			"Maybe I'm Amazed"		
			PAUL & LINDA McCARTNEY:		
6/05/71	**2(2)**	28	● 2. **RAM**		Apple 3375
			"Uncle Albert/Admiral Halsey"(1)		
			WINGS:		
12/25/71	**10**	10	● 3. **Wild Life**		Apple 3386
5/19/73	**1(3)**	16	● 4. **Red Rose Speedway**		Apple 3409
			"My Love"(1)		
12/22/73	**1(4)**	40	● 5. **Band On The Run**		Apple 3415
			"Helen Wheels"(10)		
			"Jet"(7)		
			"Band On The Run"(1)		
6/14/75	**1(1)**	17	● 6. **Venus And Mars**		Capitol 11419
			"Listen To What The Man Said"(1)		
4/10/76	**1(7)**	27	▲ 7. **Wings At The Speed Of Sound**		Capitol 11525
			"Silly Love Songs"(1)		
			"Let 'Em In"(3)		
12/25/76	**1(1)**	18	▲ 8. **Wings Over America**	[L]	Capitol 11593 [3]
			30 tracks from their 1976 U.S. tour		
			"Maybe I'm Amazed"(10)		
4/15/78	**2(6)**	16	▲ 9. **London Town**		Capitol 11777
			"With A Little Luck"(1)		
1/06/79	**29**	5	▲ 10. **Wings Greatest**	[G]	Capitol 11905
			"Another Day"(5-'71)		
			"Hi, Hi, Hi"(10-'73)		
			"Live And Let Die"(2-'73)		
			"Junior's Farm"(3-'75)		
7/07/79	**8**	11	▲ 11. **Back To The Egg**		Columbia 36057
			PAUL McCARTNEY:		
6/14/80	**3**	12	● 12. **McCartney II**		Columbia 36511
			recorded solely by Paul at his home		
			"Coming Up"(1)		
5/15/82	**1(3)**	18	▲ 13. **Tug Of War**		Columbia 37462
			"Ebony And Ivory"(1-with Stevie Wonder)		
			"Take It Away"(10)		
12/03/83	**15**	12	▲ 14. Pipes Of Peace		Columbia 39149
			"Say Say Say"(1-with Michael Jackson)		
11/10/84	**21**	10	● 15. Give my regards to Broad Street	[S]	Columbia 39613
			13 of 16 cuts are re-recordings of Beatles/McCartney hits		
			"No More Lonely Nights"(6)		
9/27/86	**30**	5	16. Press To Play		Capitol 12475

DATE	POS	WKS	ARTIST—RECORD TITLE	LABEL & NO.
2/21/81	34	4	**DELBERT McCLINTON** Born on 11/4/40 in Lubbock, TX. Played harmonica on Bruce Channel's hit "Hey Baby". Leader of the Ron-Dels. Also see Delbert & Glen. 1. The Jealous Kind *"Giving It Up For Your Love"(8)*	Capitol 12115
12/18/76	30	7	**MARILYN McCOO & BILLY DAVIS, JR.** Marilyn (b: 9/30/43) & husband Billy (b: 6/26/40) were members of the 5th Dimension. ● 1. I Hope We Get To Love In Time *"You Don't Have To Be A Star (To Be In My Show)"(1)*	ABC 952
6/14/75	12	9	**VAN McCOY** Born on 1/6/44 in Washington, DC; died on 7/6/79 in Englewood, NJ of a heart attack. Had own Rock'N label, 1960. Produced The Shirelles, Gladys Knight, and The Drifters Own MAXX label, mid-60s. 1. Disco Baby *"The Hustle"(1)*	Avco 69006
9/07/74	38	2	**GEORGE McCRAE** Born on 10/19/44 in West Palm Beach, Florida; died on 1/24/86 of cancer. Duets with wife Gwen McCrae, became her manager. 1. Rock Your Baby *"Rock Your Baby"(1)*	TK 501
			COUNTRY JOE McDONALD - **see COUNTRY JOE**	
9/11/82	6	11	**MICHAEL McDONALD** Vocalist, keyboardist. Member of Steely Dan in 1974. Lead singer of The Doobie Brothers from 1975-82. Also see Nicolette Larson. ● 1. **If That's What It Takes** *"I Keep Forgettin'"(4)*	Warner 23703
6/09/79	23	8	**McFADDEN & WHITEHEAD** R&B duo of Gene McFadden and John Whitehead from Philadelphia. Wrote songs for many Philadelphia soul acts. ● 1. McFadden & Whitehead *"Ain't No Stoppin' Us Now"*	Phil. Int. 35800
			BOB McGRATH - see CHILDREN'S section	
12/29/62	22	14	**JIMMY McGRIFF** Born on 4/3/36 in Philadelphia. Jazz/R&B organist and multi-instrumentalist. 1. I've Got A Woman [I]	Sue 1012
4/28/79	39	2	**McGUINN, CLARK & HILLMAN** Roger McGuinn (b: 7/13/42), vocals, guitar; Gene Clark (b: 11/17/44), guitar; & Chris Hillman (b: 6/4/42), bass. All are former members of the Byrds. 1. McGuinn, Clark & Hillman	Capitol 11910

DATE	POS	WKS	ARTIST—RECORD TITLE	LABEL & NO.

3/05/55	11	6	**THE McGUIRE SISTERS**
			Sisters Christine (b: 7/30/29), Dorothy (b: 2/13/30) and Phyllis (b: 2/14/31) from Middletown, Ohio. Replaced the Chordettes on the Arthur Godfrey Show in 1953. Phyllis went solo in 1964. Recently reunited.
			    1. By Request... [M]
			      10" album of 8 songs
			    "Sincerely"(1)
				Coral 56123

11/27/65	37	3	**BARRY McGUIRE**
			Born on 10/15/37 in Oklahoma City. Member of the New Christy Minstrels.
			    1. Eve Of Destruction
			    "Eve Of Destruction"(1)
				Dunhill 50003

2/06/82	8	13	**BOB & DOUG McKENZIE** Canadian comedians Rick Moranis and Dave Thomas of "SCTV". ● 1. Great White North [C] "Take Off"	Mercury 4034
			RAY McKINLEY - see GLENN MILLER	
3/10/73 7/21/73	15 14	11 7	**JOHN McLAUGHLIN** English-jazz fusion guitar virtuoso. 1. Birds Of Fire [I] **MAHAVISHNU ORCHESTRA** ● 2. Love Devotion Surrender [I] **CARLOS SANTANA/MAHAVISHNU JOHN McLAUGHLIN**	Columbia 31996 Columbia 32034

12/11/71
 	
2/03/73
3/21/81
	1(7)
	
	23
	28
		26
		
		7
		6
			DON McLEAN
			Born on 10/2/45 in New Rochelle, New York. Singer, songwriter, poet. The hit "Killing Me Softly With His Song" was written about Don.
			● 1. American Pie
			      "American Pie"(1)
			      "Vincent"
			    2. Don McLean
			    3. Chain Lightning
			      "Crying"(5)
				United Art. 5535
				
				United Art. 5651
				Millennium 7756

3/03/84	26	7	**CHRISTINE McVIE**
			Born in Birmingham, England on 7/12/43. Vocalist with Fleetwood Mac since 1970.
			    1. Christine McVie
			    "Got A Hold On Me"(10)
				Warner 25059

12/08/62
6/01/63
	1(12)
	4
		26
		11
			VAUGHN MEADER
			President John F. Kennedy imitator - produced by Bob Booker & Earle Doud.
			● 1. The First Family [C]
			    2. The First Family, volume two [C]
			      above albums feature Naomi Brossart as Jackie Kennedy
				Cadence 3060
				Cadence 3065

DATE	POS	WKS	ARTIST—RECORD TITLE	LABEL & NO.
			MEAT LOAF	
			Born Marvin Lee Aday on 9/27/47 in Dallas. Played Eddie in the film "The Rocky Horror Picture Show".	
5/13/78	14	28	▲ 1. Bat Out Of Hell	Cleve. I. 34974
			"Two Out Of Three Ain't Bad"	
			MECO	
			Discofied instrumentals by producer Meco Monardo (b: 11/29/39 in Johnsonburg, PA).	
9/10/77	13	9	▲ 1. Star Wars And Other Galactic Funk [I]	Millennium 8001
			"Star Wars Theme/Cantina Band"(1)	
			GEORGE MELACHRINO	
			Born on 5/1/09 in London of Greek parentage; died on 6/18/65. Multi-instrumentalist. First to use masses of strings to produce sentimental mood music.	
1/08/55	10	2	1. **Christmas in High Fidelity** [X-I]	RCA 1045
5/25/59	30	1	2. Under Western Skies [I]	RCA 1676
			MELANIE	
			Born Melanie Safka on 2/3/47 in Queens, NY. Neighborhood Records formed by Melanie and her husband/producer Peter Schekeryk.	
6/13/70	17	11	● 1. Candles In The Rain	Buddah 5060
			"Lay Down (Candles In The Rain)"(6)	
9/26/70	33	4	2. Leftover Wine [L]	Buddah 5066
12/11/71	15	14	● 3. Gather Me	Neighbor. 47001
			"Brand New Key"(1)	
			JOHN COUGAR MELLENCAMP	
			Born on 10/7/51 in Seymour, Indiana. Rock singer, songwriter, producer. Worked outside of music until 1975. First recorded for MCA in 1976.	
			JOHN COUGAR:	
5/16/81	37	3	1. Nothin' Matters And What If You Did	Riva 7403
5/29/82	1(9)	41	▲ 2. **American Fool**	Riva 7501
			"Hurts So Good"(2)	
			"Jack & Diane"(1)	
			JOHN COUGAR MELLENCAMP:	
11/12/83	9	36	▲ 3. **Uh-Huh**	Riva 7504
			"Crumblin' Down"(9)	
			"Pink Houses"(8)	
9/21/85	2(3)	41	▲ 4. **Scarecrow**	Riva 824865
			"Lonely Ol' Night"(6)	
			"Small Town"(6)	
			"R.O.C.K. In The U.S.A."(2)	
			HAROLD MELVIN & THE BLUE NOTES	
			Soul group from Philadelphia formed by Melvin in 1956. Teddy Pendergrass replaced lead singer John Atkins in 1970. Pendergrass left in 1976, replaced by David Ebo.	
5/03/75	26	12	● 1. To Be True	Phil. Int. 33148
12/27/75	9	12	● 2. **Wake Up Everybody**	Phil. Int. 33808

DATE	POS	WKS	ARTIST—RECORD TITLE	LABEL & NO.
			MEN AT WORK	
			Melbourne, Australia rock quintet formed in 1979. Colin Hay (lead singer, guitar), Ron Strykert (lead guitar), Greg Ham (sax, keyboards), Jerry Speiser (drums) and John Rees (bass). Speiser and Rees left in 1984.	
8/28/82	1(15)	48	▲ 1. **Business As Usual**	Columbia 37978
			"Who Can It Be Now?"(1)	
			"Down Under"(1)	
5/07/83	3	23	▲ 2. **Cargo**	Columbia 38660
			"Overkill"(3)	
			"It's A Mistake"(6)	
			MEN WITHOUT HATS	
			Techno-rock trio from Montreal, Canada. Ivan Doroschuk, singer, songwriter.	
8/20/83	13	14	• 1. Rhythm Of Youth	Backstreet 39002
			"The Safety Dance"(3)	
			SERGIO MENDES & BRASIL '66	
			Latin stylists originating from Brazil and led by pianist Mendes.	
10/15/66	7	30	• 1. **Sergio Mendes & Brasil '66**	A&M 4116
5/20/67	24	6	• 2. Equinox	A&M 4122
4/06/68	5	33	• 3. **Look Around**	A&M 4137
			"The Look Of Love"(4)	
12/21/68	3	16	• 4. **Fool On The Hill**	A&M 4160
			"The Fool On The Hill"(6)	
9/27/69	33	2	5. Crystal Illusions	A&M 4197
6/11/83	27	10	6. Sergio Mendes	A&M 4937
			"Never Gonna Let You Go"(4)	
			MERCY	
			Florida group led by Jack Sigler, Jr.	
7/12/69	38	3	1. The Mercy & Love (Can Make You Happy)	Sundi 803
			"Love (Can Make You Happy)"(2)	
			METALLICA	
			Heavy-metal San Francisco-based quartet - vocals: James Hetfield. Cliff Burton, bassist, killed in a bus crash in Sweden on 9/27/86 (24).	
4/12/86	29	7	• 1. Master Of Puppets	Elektra 60439
			MFSB	
			Large racially mixed studio band formed by producers Kenny Gamble and Leon Huff. Name means "Mothers, Fathers, Sisters, Brothers". Also see The Music Makers.	
3/09/74	4	14	• 1. **Love Is The Message** [I]	Phil. Int. 32707
			"TSOP (The Sound Of Philadelphia)"(1)	
1/10/76	39	2	2. Philadelphia Freedom [I]	Phil. Int. 33845
			MIAMI SOUND MACHINE	
			Miami group - Gloria M. Estefan, lead singer.	
3/01/86	21	21	▲ 1. **Primitive Love**	Epic 40131
			"Conga"(10)	
			"Bad Boy"(8)	
			"Words Get In The Way"(5)	

DATE	POS	WKS	ARTIST—RECORD TITLE	LABEL & NO.
			LEE MICHAELS	
			Born on 11/24/45 in Los Angeles. Rock organist/vocalist.	
9/11/71	16	12	1. "5th"	A&M 4302
			"Do You Know What I Mean"(6)	
			BETTE MIDLER	
			Born on 12/1/45 in Paterson, NJ. Vocalist, actress. Raised in Hawaii. In Broadway show "Fiddler On The Roof" for three years. Nominated for an Oscar in "The Rose". Recently starred in "Down & Out In Beverly Hills", "Ruthless People" and "Outrageous Fortune".	
1/13/73	9	23	● 1. **The Divine Miss M**	Atlantic 7238
			"Boogie Woogie Bugle Boy"(8)	
12/22/73	6	11	● 2. **Bette Midler**	Atlantic 7270
			accompanied by Barry Manilow (piano) on above 2 LPs	
2/07/76	27	6	3. Songs For The New Depression	Atlantic 18155
1/12/80	12	23	▲ 4. The Rose [S-L]	Atlantic 16010
			"The Rose"(3)	
12/13/80	34	3	5. Divine Madness [S-L]	Atlantic 16022
			film captures a live concert at Pasadena Civic Auditorium	
			MIDNIGHT STAR	
			8-man, 1-woman R&B/funk group formed at Kentucky State University.	
9/17/83	27	30	▲ 1. No Parking On The Dance Floor	Solar 60241
1/19/85	32	7	● 2. Planetary Invasion	Solar 60384
			MIDNIGHT STRING QUARTET	
			Snuff Garrett, producer.	
2/11/69	17	12	1. Rhapsodies For Young Lovers [I]	Viva 6001
			MIKE + THE MECHANICS	
			Rock quintet consisting of Mike Rutherford (Genesis), Paul Carrack (Ace), Paul Young, Peter Van Hooke and Adrian Lee.	
2/08/86	26	34	● 1. Mike + The Mechanics	Atlantic 81287
			"Silent Running"(6)	
			"All I Need Is A Miracle"(5)	
			BUDDY MILES	
			Born George Miles on 9/5/46 in Omaha. R&B vocalist, drummer. Prominent session musician. Worked as sideman in the Dick Clark Revue, 1963-64. With Wilson Pickett, 1965-66. In Michael Bloomfield's Electric Flag, 1967. In Jimi Hendrix's Band Of Gypsys, 1969-70.	
8/29/70	35	5	1. Them Changes	Mercury 61280
7/29/72	8	14	▲ 2. **Carlos Santana & Buddy Miles! Live!** [L]	Columbia 31308
			GLENN MILLER & His Orchestra	
			#1 dance band of all-time. Glenn disappeared on a plane flight from England to France on 12/15/44 (40).	
9/16/57	16	6	1. Marvelous Miller Moods [E]	RCA 1494
			Glenn Miller Army Air Force Band with Johnny Desmond (vocals) - from radio broadcasts during 1943-44	
12/09/57	17	4	2. The New Glenn Miller Orchestra In Hi Fi	RCA 1522
			directed by Ray McKinley (leader of the band after Glenn's death)	
2/24/58	19	3	3. The Glenn Miller Carnegie Hall Concert [E-L]	RCA 1506
			recorded on 10/06/39	

DATE	POS	WKS	ARTIST—RECORD TITLE	LABEL & NO.
			MITCH MILLER	
			Born on 7/4/11 in Rochester, NY. Producer/conductor/arranger. Oboe soloist with CBS Symphony, 1936-47. A&R executive for both Columbia and Mercury Records. Best known for his sing-along albums and TV show.	
7/14/58	**1(8)**	91	● 1. **Sing Along With Mitch**	Columbia 1160
11/10/58	**4**	22	● 2. **More Sing Along With Mitch**	Columbia 1243
12/29/58	**1(2)**	5	● 3. **Christmas Sing-Along With Mitch** [X]	Columbia 1205
3/23/59	**4**	96	● 4. **Still More! Sing Along With Mitch**	Columbia 1283
6/15/59	**11**	31	● 5. **Folk Songs Sing Along With Mitch**	Columbia 1316
8/31/59	**7**	00	● 6. **Party Sing Along With Mitch**	Columbia 1331
12/14/59	**8**	4	● 7. **Christmas Sing-Along With Mitch** [X-R]	Columbia 1205
1/04/60	**10**	91	8. **Fireside Sing Along With Mitch**	Columbia 1389
4/04/60	**8**	45	● 9. **Saturday Night Sing Along With Mitch**	Columbia 1414
6/27/60	**5**	54	● 10. **Sentimental Sing Along With Mitch**	Columbia 1457
10/10/60	**40**	16	11. March Along With Mitch [I]	Columbia 1475
10/31/60	**5**	42	● 12. **Memories Sing Along With Mitch**	Columbia 8342
12/19/60	**6**	3	● 13. **Christmas Sing-Along With Mitch** [X-R]	Columbia 8027
3/06/61	**9**	8	14. **Mitch's Greatest Hits** [G]	Columbia 8344
			"The Yellow Rose Of Texas"(1-'55)	
			"Song For A Summer Night"(8-'56)	
3/13/61	**5**	21	● 15. **Happy Times! Sing Along With Mitch**	Columbia 8368
6/12/61	**3**	20	● 16. **TV Sing Along With Mitch**	Columbia 8428
10/02/61	**6**	44	17. **Your Request Sing Along With Mitch**	Columbia 8471
12/04/61	**1(1)**	13	● 18. **Holiday Sing Along With Mitch** [X]	Columbia 8501
12/11/61	**9**	7	● 19. **Christmas Sing-Along With Mitch** [X-R]	Columbia 8027
3/10/62	**21**	7	20. Rhythm Sing Along With Mitch	Columbia 8527
7/21/62	**27**	5	21. Family Sing Along With Mitch	Columbia 8573
12/29/62	**33**	1	● 22. Holiday Sing Along With Mitch [X-R]	Columbia 8501
			made top 10 on Billboard's special Christmas charts (1963)	
12/29/62	**37**	1	● 23. Christmas Sing-Along With Mitch [X-R]	Columbia 8027
			MRS. MILLER	
			Mrs. Elva Miller. Tone-deaf singer from Claremont, California.	
6/04/66	**15**	10	1. Mrs. Miller's Greatest Hits	Capitol 2494
			featuring the novel operatic voice of housewife Mrs. Miller	
			ROGER MILLER	
			Born on 1/2/36 in Fort Worth, TX. Country vocalist, humorist, guitarist, composer. Raised in Erick, OK. To Nashville, mid-50s, began songwriting career. With Faron Young as writer and drummer in 1962. Won six Grammys in 1965. Own TV show in 1966. Songwriter of Broadway musical "Big River" (won Tony Award for Best Musical, 1985).	
12/12/64	**37**	2	● 1. Roger And Out [N]	Smash 67049
			"Dang Me"(7)	
			"Chug-A-Lug"(9)	
3/13/65	**4**	29	● 2. **The Return Of Roger Miller**	Smash 67061
			"King Of The Road"(4)	
8/07/65	**13**	9	3. The 3rd Time Around	Smash 67068
			"Engine Engine #9"(7)	
12/11/65	**6**	21	● 4. **Golden Hits** [G]	Smash 67073
			"England Swings"(8)	

DATE	POS	WKS	ARTIST—RECORD TITLE	LABEL & NO.
			STEVE MILLER BAND	
			Steve was born on 10/5/43 in Milwaukee. Raised in Dallas. Blues-rock singer, songwriter, guitarist. While at the University of Wisconsin-Madison, Steve led the blues-rock band, the Ardells, later known as the Fabulous Night Trains, featuring Boz Scaggs. To San Francisco in 1966, formed Steve Miller Band, which featured an ever-changing personnel.	
11/16/68	**24**	8	1. Sailor	Capitol 2984
			Boz Scaggs was a band member on above album	
7/05/69	**22**	8	2. Brave New World	Capitol 184
12/27/69	**38**	5	3. Your Saving Grace	Capitol 331
8/15/70	**23**	7	4. Number 5	Capitol 436
11/03/73	**2(1)**	20	● 5. **The Joker**	Capitol 11235
			"The Joker"(1)	
6/12/76	**3**	48	▲ 6. **Fly Like An Eagle**	Capitol 11497
			"Rock'n Me"(1)	
			"Fly Like An Eagle"(2)	
5/28/77	**2(2)**	27	▲ 7. **Book Of Dreams**	Capitol 11630
			"Jet Airliner"(8)	
12/23/78	**18**	9	▲ 8. Greatest Hits 1974-78 [G]	Capitol 11872
11/21/81	**26**	5	● 9. Circle Of Love	Capitol 12121
7/10/82	**3**	18	▲ 10. **Abracadabra**	Capitol 12216
			"Abracadabra"(1)	
			MILLS BROTHERS	
			Smooth vocal group from Piqua, Ohio. Consisted of John Jr. (b: 1911, d: 1936), Herbert (b: 1912), Harry (b: 1913, d: 6/28/82) and Donald (b: 1915). Originally featured unusual vocal style of imitating instruments. Achieved national fame via radio broadcasts and appearances in films. Father, John Sr., joined group in 1936, replacing John Jr., remained in group until 1956 (d: 12/8/67). Group continued as trio until 1982. Donald is currently singing with his son, John III.	
4/13/68	**21**	10	1. Fortuosity	Dot 25809
			"Cab Driver"	
			FRANK MILLS	
			Pianist, composer, producer, arranger.	
4/14/79	**21**	5	● 1. Music Box Dancer [I]	Polydor 6192
			"Music Box Dancer"(3)	
			STEPHANIE MILLS	
			Born in 1957 in Brooklyn. At age 15, she won starring role of Dorothy in the hit Broadway show "The Wiz". Played role for 5 years. Briefly married to Jeffrey Daniel of Shalamar in 1980.	
8/18/79	**22**	9	● 1. Whatcha Gonna Do...With My Lovin'?	20th Century 583
5/10/80	**16**	22	● 2. Sweet Sensation	20th Century 603
			"Never Knew Love Like This Before"(6)	
6/06/81	**30**	5	● 3. Stephanie	20th Century 700

DATE	POS	WKS	ARTIST—RECORD TITLE	LABEL & NO.
			RONNIE MILSAP	
			Born on 1/16/46 in Robbinsville, NC. Country singer, pianist, guitarist. Blind since birth, multi-instrumentalist by age 12. With J.J. Cale band, own band from 1965. Country Music Association Male Vocalist of the Year, 1974, 1976, 1977.	
2/14/81	36	4	▲ 1. Greatest Hits [G]	RCA 3772
10/03/81	31	3	● 2. There's No Gettin' Over Me	RCA 4060
			"(There's) No Gettin' Over Me"(5)	
6/11/83	36	3	3. Keyed Up	RCA 4670
			LIZA MINNELLI	
			Daughter of Judy Garland and director Vincente Minnelli.	
10/21/72	19	11	1. Liza With A "Z" [TV-L]	Columbia 31762
5/05/73	38	2	2. Liza Minnelli The Singer	Columbia 32149
			THE MIRACLES	
			R&B group formed at Northern High School in Detroit in 1955. Consisted of William "Smokey" Robinson (lead), Emerson and Bobby Rogers (tenors), Ronnie White (baritone) and Warren "Pete" Moore (bass). Emerson Rogers left in 1956 for US Army, replaced by Claudette Rogers Robinson, Smokey's wife. First recorded for End in 1958. Claudette retired in 1964. Smokey wrote many hit songs for his group and other Motown artists. Smokey went solo in 1972, replaced by William Griffin.	
5/29/65	21	14	1. Greatest Hits From The Beginning [G]	Tamla 254 [2]
			"Shop Around"(2-'61)	
			SMOKEY ROBINSON & THE MIRACLES:	
1/01/66	8	19	2. **Going To A Go-Go**	Tamla 267
11/11/67	28	7	3. Make It Happen	Tamla 276
			"The Tears Of A Clown"(1-'70)	
3/02/68	7	11	4. **Greatest Hits, Vol. 2** [G]	Tamla 280
			"I Second That Emotion"(4)	
8/16/69	25	8	5. Time Out for Smokey Robinson & The Miracles	Tamla 295
			"Baby, Baby Don't Cry"(8)	
1/03/76	33	10	6. City Of Angels	Tamla 339
			"Love Machine"(1)	
			MISSING PERSONS	
			Rock quintet. Dale Bozzio, lead singer (former Playboy bunny from Boston).	
11/13/82	17	26	● 1. Spring Session M	Capitol 12228
			title is an anagram of artist's name	
			MR. MISTER	
			Los Angeles-based pop/rock quartet: Richard Page, Steve George, Steve Farris and Pat Mastelotto.	
11/02/85	1(1)	34	▲ 1. **Welcome To The Real World**	RCA 8045
			"Broken Wings"(1)	
			"Kyrie"(1)	
			"Is It Love"(8)	
			THE CHAD MITCHELL TRIO	
			Chad Mitchell, Mike Kobluk and Joe Frazier; formed while sophomores at Gonzaga University in Spokane, Washington.	
6/02/62	39	1	1. Mighty Day On Campus [L]	Kapp 3262
			Jim McGuinn (Byrds) played guitar on above album	

DATE	POS	WKS	ARTIST—RECORD TITLE	LABEL & NO.
12/21/63	39	1	2. Singin' Our Mind	Mercury 60838
4/11/64	29	4	3. Reflecting	Mercury 60891

JONI MITCHELL

Born Roberta Joan Anderson on 11/7/43 in Alberta, Canada. Wrote the hit "Both Sides Now" and "Woodstock". Also see James Taylor.

DATE	POS	WKS	ARTIST—RECORD TITLE	LABEL & NO.
6/21/69	31	6	1. Clouds	Reprise 6341
4/25/70	27	9	▲ 2. Ladies Of The Canyon	Reprise 6376
			"Big Yellow Taxi"	
7/10/71	15	12	▲ 3. Blue	Reprise 2038
12/30/72	11	12	● 4. For The Roses	Asylum 5057
2/09/74	2(4)	31	● 5. **Court And Spark**	Asylum 1001
			"Help Me"(7)	
12/21/74	2(1)	14	● 6. **Miles Of Aisles** [L]	Asylum 202
			with Tom Scott & The L.A. Express	
12/13/75	4	10	● 7. **The Hissing Of Summer Lawns**	Asylum 1051
12/18/76	13	8	● 8. Hejira	Asylum 1087
1/14/78	25	4	● 9. Don Juan's Reckless Daughter	Asylum 701 [2]
7/14/79	17	9	10. Mingus	Asylum 505
			Joni performs music composed by Charles Mingus who died on 1/5/79 (56)	
10/18/80	38	3	11. Shadows And Light [L]	Asylum 704 [2]
			with guests Pat Metheny, Michael Brecker & Jaco Pastorius	
12/04/82	25	4	12. Wild Things Run Fast	Geffen 2019

MOBY GRAPE

Rock group from San Francisco.

DATE	POS	WKS	ARTIST—RECORD TITLE	LABEL & NO.
7/29/67	24	7	1. Moby Grape	Columbia 9498
			10 of 13 cuts released simultaneously on 45s	
5/18/68	20	6	2. Wow	Columbia 9613 [2]
			includes bonus LP titled "Grape Jam" (jam sessions with Al Kooper & Mike Bloomfield)	

DOMENICO MODUGNO

Born on 1/9/28 in Polignano a Mare, Italy. Singer/actor.

DATE	POS	WKS	ARTIST—RECORD TITLE	LABEL & NO.
9/15/58	8	6	1. **Nel Blu Dipinto Di Blu (Volare) and** **other Italian favorites** [F]	Decca 8808
			"Nel Blu Dipinto Di Blu"(1)	

MOLLY HATCHET

Southern hard rock sextet from Jacksonville, Florida. Danny Joe Brown, lead singer (replaced by John Farrar in 1980; Brown returned and replaced Farrar in 1983).

DATE	POS	WKS	ARTIST—RECORD TITLE	LABEL & NO.
10/06/79	19	18	▲ 1. Flirtin' With Disaster	Epic 36110
10/04/80	25	6	● 2. Beatin' The Odds	Epic 36572
12/26/81	36	3	3. Take No Prisoners	Epic 37480
			Jimmy Farrar, lead singer on above 2 albums	

EDDIE MONEY

Born Edward Mahoney on 3/2/49 in New York City. Rock singer discovered and subsequently managed by West Coast promoter Bill Graham.

DATE	POS	WKS	ARTIST—RECORD TITLE	LABEL & NO.
4/22/78	37	2	▲ 1. Eddie Money	Columbia 34909
			"Baby Hold On"	
2/03/79	17	10	● 2. Life For The Taking	Columbia 35598
9/06/80	35	4	3. Playing For Keeps	Columbia 36514

DATE	POS	WKS	ARTIST—RECORD TITLE	LABEL & NO.
8/21/82	20	13	● 4. No Control	Columbia 37960
10/18/86	20	21	5. Can't Hold Back	Columbia 40096
			"Take Me Home Tonight"(4)	

THE MONKEES

Formed in Los Angeles in 1965. Chosen from over 400 applicants for new Columbia TV series. Consisted of Davy Jones (b: 12/30/46, Manchester, England), vocals; Michael Nesmith (b: 12/30/42, Houston), guitar, vocals; Peter Tork (b: 2/13/44, Washington, DC), bass, vocals; and Micky Dolenz (b: 3/8/45, Tarzana, CA), drums, vocals. Dolenz had appeared in TV series "Circus Boy", using the name Mickey Braddock in 1956. Jones had been a race-horse jockey, and appeared in London musicals "Oliver" and "Pickwick". Tork had been in the Phoenix Singers; Nesmith had done session work for Stax/Volt. TV show dropped after 56 episodes, 1966-68. Tork left in 1968. Group disbanded in 1969; reformed (less Nesmith) in 1986.

DATE	POS	WKS	ARTIST—RECORD TITLE	LABEL & NO.
10/15/66	1(13)	49	● 1. **The Monkees**	Colgems 101
			"Last Train To Clarksville"(1)	
2/11/67	1(18)	45	● 2. **More Of The Monkees**	Colgems 102
			"I'm A Believer"(1)	
6/17/67	1(1)	41	● 3. **Headquarters**	Colgems 103
11/25/67	1(5)	19	● 4. **Pisces, Aquarius, Capricorn & Jones Ltd.**	Colgems 104
			"Pleasant Valley Sunday"(3)	
5/18/68	3	15	● 5. **The Birds, The Bees & The Monkees**	Colgems 109
			"Daydream Believer"(1)	
			"Valleri"(3)	
3/22/69	32	5	6. Instant Replay	Colgems 113
8/16/86	21	12	▲ 7. **Then & Now...The Best Of The Monkees** [G]	Arista 8432
			includes 3 new songs by Micky Dolenz & Peter Tork	

LOU MONTE

Born of Italian parentage on 4/2/17 in Lynhurst, NJ. Vocalist, guitarist.

DATE	POS	WKS	ARTIST—RECORD TITLE	LABEL & NO.
1/05/63	9	18	1. **Pepino The Italian Mouse & Other Italian Fun Songs** [N]	Reprise 6058
			"Pepino The Italian Mouse"(5)	

HUGO MONTENEGRO

Born in 1925; raised in New York City; died on 2/6/81. Conductor, composer.

DATE	POS	WKS	ARTIST—RECORD TITLE	LABEL & NO.
4/13/68	9	17	● 1. **Music From "A Fistful Of Dollars" & "For A Few Dollars More" & "The Good, The Bad And The Ugly"** [I]	RCA 3927
			"The Good, The Bad And The Ugly"(2)	

CHRIS MONTEZ

Born Christopher Montanez on 1/17/43 in Los Angeles. Protege of Ritchie Valens.

DATE	POS	WKS	ARTIST—RECORD TITLE	LABEL & NO.
9/03/66	33	4	1. The More I See You/Call Me	A&M 4115

WES MONTGOMERY

Jazz guitarist. First recorded for Pacific Jazz in 1957. Brother Monk plays bass, brother Buddy plays piano. Wes died on 6/15/68 (43).

DATE	POS	WKS	ARTIST—RECORD TITLE	LABEL & NO.
11/11/67	13	23	● 1. A Day In The Life [I]	A&M 3001
			"Windy"	
8/31/68	38	1	2. Down Here On The Ground [I]	A&M 3006

DATE	POS	WKS	ARTIST—RECORD TITLE	LABEL & NO.
			THE MOODY BLUES	
			Formed in Birmingham, England in 1964. Consisted of Denny Laine (guitar, vocals), Ray Thomas (flute, vocals), Mike Pinder (keyboards, vocals), Clint Warwick (bass) and Graeme Edge (drums). Laine and Warwick left in the summer of 1966, replaced by Justin Hayward (lead vocals, lead guitar) and John Lodge (vocals, bass). Patrick Moraz (formerly with Yes - keyboards), replaced Pinder in 1978.	
9/28/68	3	23	● 1. **Days Of Future Passed**	Deram 18012
			with The London Festival Orchestra	
			"Nights In White Satin" (2-'72)	
10/12/68	23	11	● 2. In Search Of The Lost Chord	Deram 18017
6/07/69	20	13	● 3. On The Threshold Of A Dream	Deram 18025
1/31/70	14	12	● 4. To Our Children's Children's Children	Threshold 1
9/19/70	3	17	● 5. **A Question Of Balance**	Threshold 3
8/21/71	2(3)	21	● 6. **Every Good Boy Deserves Favour**	Threshold 5
11/25/72	1(5)	23	● 7. **Seventh Sojourn**	Threshold 7
12/07/74	11	9	● 8. This Is The Moody Blues [G]	Threshold 12/13 [2]
7/02/77	26	5	9. Caught Live +5 [L]	London 690/1 [2]
			first 3 sides recorded live at the Royal Albert Hall in '69; side 4: previously unreleased studio recordings	
7/08/78	13	9	▲ 10. Octave	London 708
6/20/81	1(3)	23	▲ 11. **Long Distance Voyager**	Threshold 2901
			Patrick Moraz replaces Mike Pinder on keyboards	
9/24/83	26	6	12. The Present	Threshold 2902
5/17/86	9	22	● 13. **The Other Side Of Life**	Threshold 829179
			"Your Wildest Dreams"(9)	
			BOB MOORE	
			Born on 11/30/32 in Nashville. Top session bass player. Led the band on Roy Orbison's sessions for Monument Records. Also worked as sideman for Elvis Presley, Brenda Lee, Pat Boone and others.	
11/20/61	33	2	1. Mexico and Other Great Hits! [I]	Monument 4005
			"Mexico"(7)	
			DOROTHY MOORE	
			Born in Jackson, Mississippi in 1946. Lead singer of The Poppies.	
6/26/76	29	7	1. Misty Blue	Malaco 6351
			"Misty Blue"(3)	
			JANE MORGAN	
			Born Jane Currier in Boston, and raised in Florida. Popular singer in France before becoming successful in U.S. TV and night club entertaining.	
12/09/57	13	3	1. Fascination	Kapp 1066
			with the violins of The Troubadors	
			"Fascination"(7)	
			LEE MORGAN	
			Born on 7/10/38 in Philadelphia; fatally shot on 2/19/72. Jazz trumpeter.	
12/26/64	25	7	1. The Sidewinder [I]	Blue Note 84157

DATE	POS	WKS	ARTIST—RECORD TITLE	LABEL & NO.
			THE MORMON TABERNACLE CHOIR	
			375-voice choir directed by Richard P. Condie (died on 12/22/85).	
10/19/59	1(1)	27	● 1. **The Lord's Prayer**	Columbia 6068
			"Battle Hymn Of The Republic"	
12/28/59	5	2	2. **The Spirit Of Christmas** [X]	Columbia 6100
			VAN MORRISON	
			Born on 8/31/45 in Belfast, Ireland. Blue-eyed soul singer, songwriter. Leader of Them. Wrote the classic hit "Gloria".	
5/30/70	29	3	▲ 1. Moondance	Warner 1835
12/26/70	32	5	2. His Band And The Street Choir	Warner 1884
			"Domino"(9)	
11/13/71	27	6	● 3. Tupelo Honey	Warner 1950
9/02/72	15	12	4. Saint Dominic's Preview	Warner 2633
8/25/73	27	6	5. Hard Nose The Highway	Warner 2712
11/18/78	28	5	6. Wavelength	Warner 3212
			THE MOTELS	
			Martha Davis (b: 1/19/51), lead singer/songwriter of quintet from Los Angeles.	
5/29/82	16	15	● 1. All Four One	Capitol 12177
			"Only The Lonely"(9)	
10/22/83	22	8	● 2. Little Robbers	Capitol 12288
			"Suddenly Last Summer"(9)	
9/21/85	36	2	3. Shock	Capitol 12378
			MOTHERS OF INVENTION - **see FRANK ZAPPA**	
			MOTLEY CRUE	
			Los Angeles-based heavy metal band; Vince Neil (b: 2/8/61), lead singer.	
12/03/83	17	28	▲ 1. Shout At The Devil	Elektra 60289
7/20/85	6	18	▲ 2. **Theatre Of Pain**	Elektra 60418
			"Smokin' In The Boys Room"	
			MOTT THE HOOPLE	
			British glitter rock group led by vocalist Ian Hunter; included Bad Company's guitarist Mick Ralphs (left in 1973).	
10/13/73	35	4	1. Mott	Columbia 32425
5/18/74	28	7	2. The Hoople	Columbia 32871
1/04/75	23	4	3. Mott The Hoople Live [L]	Columbia 33282
			TONY MOTTOLA	
			Latin-style guitarist. Produced by Enoch Light.	
4/14/62	26	10	1. Roman Guitar [I]	Command 816
			MOUNTAIN	
			New York power-rock group led by Leslie West and Felix Pappalardi (fatally shot on 4/17/83 at the age of 44 in New York City). Also see West, Bruce & Laing.	
4/11/70	17	21	● 1. Mountain Climbing!	Windfall 4501
			"Mississippi Queen"	

DATE	POS	WKS	ARTIST—RECORD TITLE	LABEL & NO.
2/13/71	16	7	● 2. Nantucket Sleighride	Windfall 5500
1/22/72	35	3	3. Flowers Of Evil	Windfall 5501
			MTUME	
			Progressive funk band led by James Mtume. Mtume had been a percussionist with Miles Davis in early 70s.	
6/18/83	26	7	1. Juicy Fruit	Epic 38588
			MARIA MULDAUR	
			Maria (b: 9/12/43, New York City) and former husband Geoff Muldaur (divorced, 1972) were members of Jim Kweskin's Jug Band.	
3/16/74	3	21	● 1. **Maria Muldaur**	Reprise 2148
			"Midnight At The Oasis"(6)	
12/07/74	23	6	2. Waitress In The Donut Shop	Reprise 2194
			GERRY MULLIGAN'S Jazz Combo	
			Jazz baritone saxophonist.	
5/25/59	39	2	1. I Want To Live! [S-I]	United Art. 5006
			with Shelly Manne (drums) & Art Farmer (trumpet)	
			CHARLES MUNCH - see BOSTON SYMPHONY ORCHESTRA	
			MUPPETS - see CHILDREN'S section	
			MICHAEL MURPHEY	
			Progressive Country singer, songwriter from Austin, Texas.	
5/03/75	18	13	● 1. Blue Sky-Night Thunder	Epic 33290
			"Wildfire"(3)	
			EDDIE MURPHY	
			Born on 4/3/61 in Hempstead, NY. Comedian, actor. Regular on TV's "Saturday Night Live". Starred in films "Beverly Hills Cop", "Trading Places", "48 Hours" and "The Golden Child".	
1/14/84	35	3	▲ 1. Eddie Murphy: Comedian [C]	Columbia 39005
12/07/85	26	10	2. How Could It Be	Columbia 39952
			"Party All The Time"(2)	
			WALTER MURPHY	
			Born in New York City, 1952. Studied classical and jazz piano at Manhattan School of Music. Former arranger for Doc Severinson and "The Tonight Show" orchestra.	
10/02/76	15	6	● 1. A Fifth Of Beethoven	Private S. 2015
			"A Fifth Of Beethoven"(1)	
			MURRAY THE "K" - see RADIO/TV CELEBRITY COMPILATIONS	
			ANNE MURRAY	
			Born on 6/20/47 in Springhill, Nova Scotia. With CBC-TV show "Sing Along Jubilee". First recorded for Arc in 1969. On Glen Campbell's "Goodtime Hour" TV series from 1970.	
6/02/73	39	2	1. Danny's Song	Capitol 11172
			"Danny's Song"(7)	
7/13/74	24	6	2. Love Song	Capitol 11266
			"You Won't See Me"(8)	
10/19/74	32	2	● 3. Country [K]	Capitol 11324

DATE	POS	WKS	ARTIST—RECORD TITLE	LABEL & NO.
10/14/78	12	8	▲ 4. Let's Keep It That Way	Capitol 11743
			"You Needed Me"(1)	
3/10/79	23	6	● 5. New Kind Of Feeling	Capitol 11849
12/08/79	24	9	● 6. I'll Always Love You	Capitol 12012
11/01/80	16	17	▲ 7. Anne Murray's Greatest Hits [G]	Capitol 12110
			MUSICAL YOUTH	
			5 schoolboys (ages 11 to 16) from Birmingham, England. Dennis Seaton, lead singer.	
2/05/83	23	8	1. The Youth Of Today	MCA 5389
			"Pass The Dutchie"(10)	

N

DATE	POS	WKS	ARTIST—RECORD TITLE	LABEL & NO.
			JIM NABORS	
			Gomer Pyle on TV's "Andy Griffith Show" & "Gomer Pyle-U.S.M.C."	
12/03/66	24	7	● 1. Jim Nabors Sings Love Me With All Your Heart	Columbia 9358
7/04/70	34	3	2. The Jim Nabors Hour	Columbia 1020
			titled after his TV variety show (1969-1971)	
			NAKED EYES	
			English duo: Pete Byrne (vocals) and Rob Fisher (keyboards, synthesizer).	
6/04/83	32	4	1. Naked Eyes	EMI America 17089
			"Always Something There To Remind Me"(8)	
			GRAHAM NASH	
			Born on 2/2/42 in Blackpool, England. Co-founding member of The Hollies. Formed Crosby, Stills & Nash in 1970.	
6/19/71	15	11	● 1. Songs For Beginners	Atlantic 7204
2/23/74	34	3	2. Wild Tales	Atlantic 7288
			JOHNNY NASH	
			Born on 8/19/40 in Houston. Vocalist, guitarist, actor. Appeared on local TV from age 13. With Arthur Godfrey, TV and radio, from 1956-63. In film "Take A Giant Step" in 1959. Own label, JoDa, in 1965. Began recording in Jamaica, late 60s.	
11/18/72	23	8	1. I Can See Clearly Now	Epic 31607
			"I Can See Clearly Now"(1)	
			NAZARETH	
			Hard rock group formed in Scotland in 1969. Dan McCafferty, lead singer.	
2/14/76	17	9	● 1. Hair Of The Dog	A&M 4511
			"Love Hurts"(8)	
5/08/76	24	7	2. Close Enough For Rock 'N' Roll	A&M 4562
			NEKTAR	
			English art-rock quartet based in Germany.	
10/26/74	19	6	1. Remember The Future	Passport 98002
4/12/75	32	3	2. Down To Earth	Passport 98005

DATE	POS	WKS	ARTIST—RECORD TITLE	LABEL & NO.
			RICKY NELSON	
			Born Eric Hilliard Nelson on 5/8/40 in Teaneck, NJ. Died on 12/31/85 in a plane crash in DeKalb, Texas. Son of bandleader Ozzie Nelson and vocalist Harriet Hilliard. Rick and brother David appeared on Nelson's radio show from March, 1949, later on TV, 1952 to 1966. Formed own Stone Canyon Band in 1969. Films "Rio Bravo", "Wackiest Ship In The Army", and "Love And Kisses". One of the first teen idols of the rock era.	
11/11/57	**1**(2)	33	1. **Ricky**	Imperial 9048
			"Be-Bop Baby"(3)	
7/28/58	**7**	9	2. **Ricky Nelson**	Imperial 9050
			Poor Little Fool"(1)	
2/02/59	**14**	19	3. Ricky Sings Again	Imperial 9061
			"Believe What You Say"(4)	
			"Lonesome Town"(7)	
			"Never Be Anyone Else But You"(6)	
			"It's Late"(9)	
10/05/59	**22**	26	4. Songs By Ricky	Imperial 9082
			"Just A Little Too Much"(9)	
			"Sweeter Than You"(9)	
8/29/60	**18**	22	5. More Songs By Ricky	Imperial 9122
6/26/61	**8**	17	6. **Rick Is 21**	Imperial 9152
			"Travelin' Man"(1)	
			"Hello Mary Lou"(9)	
6/02/62	**27**	6	7. Album Seven By Rick	Imperial 9167
6/22/63	**20**	5	8. For Your Sweet Love	Decca 74419
1/18/64	**14**	12	9. Rick Nelson sings "For You"	Decca 74479
			"For You"(6)	
1/20/73	**32**	5	10. Garden Party	Decca 75391
			"Garden Party"(6)	
			SANDY NELSON	
			Born Sander Nelson on 12/1/38 in Santa Monica, CA. Rock 'n roll drummer. Became prominent studio musician. Heard on "Alley Oop", "To Know Him Is To Love Him", "A Thousand Stars", and many others. Lost portion of right leg in a motorcycle accident in 1963. Returned to performing in 1964.	
2/03/62	**6**	21	1. **Let There Be Drums** [I]	Imperial 9159
			"Let There Be Drums"(7)	
5/26/62	**29**	3	2. Drums Are My Beat! [I]	Imperial 9168
			WILLIE NELSON	
			Born on 4/30/33 in Abbott, Texas. Prolific country singer, songwriter. Pioneered "outlaw" country movement. Starred in several films including "The Electric Horseman" and "Honeysuckle Rose".	
11/15/75	**28**	5	▲ 1. Red Headed Stranger	Columbia 33482
			"Blue Eyes Crying In The Rain"	
2/18/78	**12**	9	▲ 2. Waylon & Willie	RCA 2686
			WAYLON JENNINGS & WILLIE NELSON	
6/17/78	**30**	3	▲ 3. Stardust	Columbia 35305
			an album of pop standards from 1926-1955 (produced by Booker T. Jones)	
1/13/79	**32**	4	▲ 4. Willie and Family Live [L]	Columbia 35642 [2]
			recorded at Harrah's, Lake Tahoe, Nevada	
7/07/79	**25**	5	● 5. One For The Road	Columbia 36064 [2]

DATE	POS	WKS	ARTIST—RECORD TITLE	LABEL & NO.
			WILLIE NELSON & LEON RUSSELL	
9/13/80	11	13	▲ 6. Honeysuckle Rose [S-L]	Columbia 36752 [2]
			"On The Road Again"	
3/21/81	31	6	▲ 7. Somewhere Over The Rainbow	Columbia 36883
10/03/81	27	6	▲ 8. Willie Nelson's Greatest Hits (& Some	
			That Will Be) [G]	Columbia 37542 [2]
3/27/82	2(4)	28	▲ 9. **Always On My Mind**	Columbia 37951
			"Always On My Mind"(5)	
5/21/83	39	1	10. Tougher Than Leather	Columbia 38248
8/20/83	37	1	▲ 11. Poncho & Lefty	Epic 37958
			MERLE HAGGARD/WILLIE NELSON	
			NENA	
			Gabriele "Nena" Kerner with 4-member backup group from West Germany.	
3/31/84	27	6	1. 99 Luftballons	Epic 39294
			"99 Luftballons"(2)	
			PETER NERO	
			Born on 5/22/34 in Brooklyn. Pop-jazz-classical pianist.	
8/07/61	34	22	1. Piano Forte [I]	RCA 2334
10/02/61	32	62	2. New Piano In Town [I]	RCA 2383
4/14/62	22	9	3. Young And Warm And Wonderful [I]	RCA 2484
8/11/62	16	12	4. For The Nero-Minded [I]	RCA 2536
3/30/63	40	1	5. The Colorful Peter Nero [I]	RCA 2618
4/13/63	5	18	6. **Hail The Conquering Nero**	RCA 2638
11/16/63	31	3	7. Peter Nero In Person [I-L]	RCA 2710
6/27/64	38	2	8. Reflections [I]	RCA 2853
12/25/71	23	10	● 9. Summer of '42 [I]	Columbia 31105
			THE NEW BIRTH	
			R&B vocal group portion of New Birth, Inc. (see Nite-Liters). Original group consisted of vocalists Londee Loren, Bobby Downs; Melvin Wilson, Leslie Wilson and Ann Bogan (aka: Love, Peace & Happiness); and soloist Alan Frye with instrumental backing by The Nite-Liters.	
5/26/73	31	4	1. Birth Day	RCA 4797
			THE NEW CHRISTY MINSTRELS	
			Folk/balladeer troupe named after the Christy Minstrels (formed in 1842 by Edwin "Pop" Christy). Group founded and led by Randy Sparks; Barry McGuire, member.	
10/27/62	19	8	1. The New Christy Minstrels	Columbia 8672
3/02/63	30	40	2. The New Christy Minstrels In Person [L]	Columbia 8741
6/29/63	20	7	3. Tall Tales! Legends & Nonsense	Columbia 8817
9/14/63	15	23	● 4. Ramblin' featuring Green, Green	Columbia 8855
5/16/64	9	20	5. **Today** [S]	Columbia 8959
			featuring songs from the film "Advance To The Rear"	
7/31/65	22	8	6. Chim Chim Cher-ee	Columbia 9169

DATE	POS	WKS	ARTIST—RECORD TITLE	LABEL & NO.
			NEW EDITION	
			R&B group formed in Boston, consisting of 5 boys (ages 13 to 15 in 1983): Ralph Tresvant, Ronald DeVoe, Michael Bivins, Ricky Bell and Bobby Brown (left for solo career in 1986).	
11/17/84	6	29	▲ 1. **New Edition**	MCA 5515
			"Cool It Now"(4)	
			"Mr. Telephone Man"	
1/11/86	32	15	▲ 2. All For Love	MCA 5679
			NEW RIDERS OF THE PURPLE SAGE	
			San Francisco country-rock band formed in 1969 by Jerry Garcia as an offshoot of the Grateful Dead. Garcia left after first album in 1971.	
10/30/71	39	2	1. New Riders Of The Purple Sage	Columbia 30888
6/17/72	33	6	2. Powerglide	Columbia 31284
			THE NEW SEEKERS	
			British-Australian group formed by former Seeker Keith Potger after disbandment of The Seekers in 1969. Consisted of Eve Graham, Lyn Paul, Peter Doyle, Marty Kristian and Paul Layton.	
1/29/72	37	2	1. We'd Like To Teach The World To Sing	Elektra 74115
			"I'd Like To Teach The World To Sing (In Perfect Harmony)"(7)	
			THE NEW VAUDEVILLE BAND	
			Creation of British composer/record producer Geoff Stephens.	
12/17/66	5	17	● 1. **Winchester Cathedral**	Fontana 27560
			"Winchester Cathedral"(1)	
			NEW WORLD THEATRE ORCHESTRA	
			Also shown as the Cinema Sound Stage Orchestra.	
10/21/57	8	4	1. **Around The World In 80 Days** [I]	Stereo-Fid. 2800
			NEW YORK PHILHARMONIC - see LEONARD BERNSTEIN	
			BOB NEWHART	
			Bob's situation comedy series debuted on 9/16/72. The "Bob Newhart Show" was a successful TV situation comedy from 1972-78. Bob's second TV sitcom, "Newhart", is a hit of the 80s.	
5/16/60	1(14)	08	● 1. **The Button-Down Mind Of Bob Newhart** [C]	Warner 1379
11/14/60	1(1)	70	● 2. **The Button-Down Mind Strikes Back!** [C]	Warner 1393
11/06/61	10	30	3. **Behind The Button-Down Mind Of Bob Newhart** [C]	Warner 1417
10/27/62	28	3	4. The Button-Down Mind On TV [C]	Warner 1467
			Bob hosted a comedy variety show from 1961-62	
			RANDY NEWMAN	
			Born on 11/28/43 in New Orleans. Singer, composer, pianist. Nephew of composers Alfred, Emil and Lionel Newman. Scored the films "Ragtime" and "The Natural".	
11/30/74	36	2	1. Good Old Boys	Reprise 2193
			background vocals by the Eagles' Glen Frey & Don Henley	
11/19/77	9	18	● 2. **Little Criminals**	Warner 3079
			guest appearances by members of the Eagles	
			"Short People"(2)	

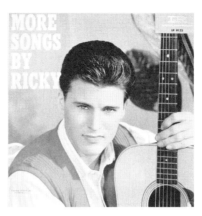

Nektar, a British progressive band of the 1970s, originally formed in Germany and included a nonmusical member, Mick Brockett on lights and visuals, in the five-man lineup. *Remember the Future* (1974) consists entirely of one piece in ten sections.

Ricky Nelson first appeared on his parents' television show, "The Adventures of Ozzie and Harriet," when he was 8. He began his professional singing career at 17 with a recording of Fats Domino's "I'm Walking" b/w "A Teenager's Romance" that reached No. 2 in the charts. By age 20, when *More Songs by Ricky* was released (1960), Nelson had twenty Top 40 singles to his credit.

Olivia Newton-John's first recognition as an entertainer came at age 12, when she won a Hayley Mills look-alike contest. Although born in London and raised in Australia, Newton-John hit it big in America as a country singer, only turning to rock and disco in the late 1970s.

Ted Nugent's early work with a psychedelic punk group, the Amboy Dukes, yielded one hit single, 1968's "Journey to the Center of the Mind." But Nugent's gonzo solo career brought the Detroit guitarist his greatest fame. The nickname "Motor City Madman" comes from a CB handle Nugent, a racing enthusiast, used in the early 1970s. *Cat Scratch Fever* (1977), his third solo album, reached the top twenty.

The Ohio Players backed Wilson Pickett on a 1962 single, but it wasn't until the arrival ten years later of keyboard player Walter "Junie" Morrison that the band began to have real national success.

Ozzy Osbourne's record company reportedly spent in the region of $75,000 to produce the horrific cover art for his 1983 *Bark at the Moon* album. The former Black Sabbath singer, who left that band in 1979 (after eight albums, five of them gold), reached No. 19 with his fourth solo studio album.

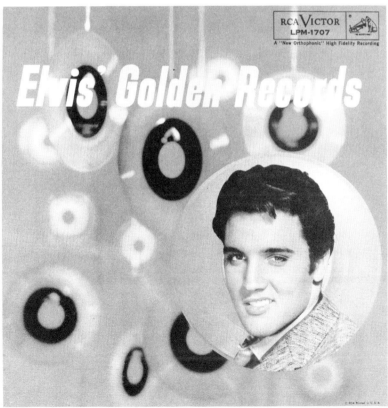

Robert Palmer interrupted his solo career in 1985 to front Power Station, a side project by members of Duran Duran. Although the resulting album and singles were top ten hits, Palmer decided not to join Power Station's tour, opting instead to finish his *Riptide* album. It was evidently a wise choice, as he wound up with a No. 1 single, "Addicted to Love."

Ray Parker Jr. learned to play guitar before his teens because he had broken his leg and was stuck at home. A band he formed at age 13 backed such stars as the Temptations and Stevie Wonder when they played Detroit, Parker's hometown. After becoming a top session guitarist, he launched Raydio, which scored four gold albums, and then went solo with *The Other Woman*.

Wilson Pickett started out in a Detroit R&B group called the Falcons, which also included Levi Stubbs' brother and the future author of "Mustang Sally." Pickett's biggest hit on his 1966 album *The Exciting Wilson Pickett* was "Land of 1000 Dances," which had been recorded by Fats Domino in 1962 and had reached the top thirty in a 1965 version by Cannibal and the Headhunters.

Pink Floyd's *Dark Side of the Moon*, which stayed on the *Billboard* charts well over a decade, only held the No. 1 spot for a week, in April 1973. Two subsequent albums spent more time in the top position, though neither approached *Dark Side*'s total sales. *The Wall*, a film made from the 1979 Floyd album, starred Bob Geldof.

Elvis Presley had only been a star for two years when RCA issued his first compilation album, containing an astonishing nine No. 1 hits. The album spent well over a year on the charts, peaking at No. 3. Although a 1957 release, *Elvis' Christmas Album*, reached No. 1, Presley didn't have another chart-topping album until 1960 with *G. I. Blues*.

DATE	POS	WKS	ARTIST—RECORD TITLE		LABEL & NO.
			JUICE NEWTON		
			Born Judy Cohen on 2/18/52 in Virginia Beach, VA. Pop/country-styled singer.		
4/25/81	**22**	34	▲ 1. Juice		Capitol 12136
			"Angel Of The Morning"(4)		
			"Queen Of Hearts"(2)		
			"The Sweetest Thing (I've Ever Known)"(7)		
6/05/82	**20**	8	● 2. Quiet Lies		Capitol 12210
			"Love's Been A Little Bit Hard On Me"(7)		
			WAYNE NEWTON		
			Born on 4/3/42 in Roanoke, Virginia. Singer, multi-instrumentalist. Las Vegas' #1 entertainer. First big break came in 1962 on the Jackie Gleason TV show. Bobby Darin saw Wayne, signed him up and produced his first charted single.		
6/05/65	**17**	8	1. Red Roses For A Blue Lady		Capitol 2335
8/19/72	**34**	5	2. Daddy Don't You Walk So Fast		Chelsea 1001
			"Daddy Don't You Walk So Fast"(4)		
			OLIVIA NEWTON-JOHN		
			Born on 9/26/48 in Cambridge, England. To Australia in 1953. At age 16 won talent contest trip to England, sang with Pat Carroll as Pat & Olivia. With group Toomorrow, in a British film of the same name. Consistent award winner in both pop and country. Films "Grease", 1978; "Xanadu", 1980; "Two Of A Kind", 1983.		
6/29/74	**1(1)**	20	● 1. **If You Love Me, Let Me Know**		MCA 411
			"If You Love Me (Let Me Know)"(5)		
			"I Honestly Love You"(1)		
3/08/75	**1(1)**	16	● 2. **Have You Never Been Mellow**		MCA 2133
			"Have You Never Been Mellow"(1)		
			"Please Mr. Please"(3)		
10/18/75	**12**	6	● 3. Clearly Love		MCA 2148
3/27/76	**13**	10	● 4. Come On Over		MCA 2186
11/27/76	**30**	4	● 5. Don't Stop Believin'		MCA 2223
8/27/77	**34**	4	6. Making A Good Thing Better		MCA 2280
11/12/77	**13**	13	▲ 7. Olivia Newton-John's Greatest Hits	[G]	MCA 3028
5/27/78	**1(12)**	39	▲ 8. Grease	[S]	RSO 4002 [2]
			5 songs by Olivia/others by various artists		
			"You're The One That I Want"(1)		
			"Hopelessly Devoted To You"(3)		
			"Summer Nights"(5)		
1/13/79	**7**	16	▲ 9. **Totally Hot**		MCA 3067
			"A Little More Love"(3)		
8/09/80	**4**	15	▲ 10. **Xanadu**	[S]	MCA 6100
			side 1: Olivia; side 2: ELO		
			"Magic"(1)		
			"Xanadu"(8)		
11/07/81	**6**	27	▲ 11. **Physical**		MCA 5229
			"Physical"(1)		
			"Make A Move On Me"(5)		
10/16/82	**16**	21	▲ 12. Olivia's Greatest Hits, Vol. 2	[G]	MCA 5347
			"Heart Attack"(3)		

DATE	POS	WKS	ARTIST—RECORD TITLE	LABEL & NO.
12/24/83	26	8	▲ 13. Two Of A Kind [S] 4 songs by Olivia/others by various artists "Twist Of Fate"(5)	MCA 6127
11/16/85	29	5	14. Soul Kiss	MCA 6151

MIKE NICHOLS & ELAINE MAY

Improvisational comedy team.

DATE	POS	WKS	ARTIST—RECORD TITLE	LABEL & NO.
7/13/59	39	1	1. Improvisations To Music [C] with Marty Rubenstein at the piano	Mercury 20376
1/23/61	10	8	2. An evening with Mike Nichols and Elaine May [OC-C] opened on Broadway on 10/8/60	Mercury 2200
3/24/62	17	9	3. Mike Nichols & Elaine May Examine Doctors [C]	Mercury 20680

STEVIE NICKS

Born Stephanie Nicks on 5/26/48 in Phoenix and raised in California. Became vocalist of Bay-area group Fritz and subsequently met guitarist Lindsey Buckingham. Teamed up and recorded album "Buckingham-Nicks" in 1973. Vocalist with Fleetwood Mac since January, 1975. Also see Robbie Patton.

DATE	POS	WKS	ARTIST—RECORD TITLE	LABEL & NO.
8/15/81	1(1)	45	▲ 1. Bella Donna "Stop Draggin' My Heart Around"(3) "Leather And Lace"(6)	Modern 139
7/09/83	5	22	▲ 2. The Wild Heart "Stand Back"(5)	Modern 90048
12/21/85	12	17	▲ 3. Rock A Little "Talk To Me"(4) "I Can't Wait"	Modern 90479

NIGHT RANGER

Rock quintet from California: Kelly Keagy (drums) and Jack Blades (bass), lead singers; Jeff Watson and Brad Gillis, guitars; Alan "Fitz" Gerald, keyboards.

DATE	POS	WKS	ARTIST—RECORD TITLE	LABEL & NO.
3/05/83	38	8	1. Dawn Patrol	Boardwalk 33259
5/05/84	15	29	▲ 2. Midnight Madness "Sister Christian"(5)	MCA 5456
6/15/85	10	25	▲ 3. 7 Wishes "Sentimental Street"(8) "Four In The Morning"/"Goodbye"	MCA/Camel 5593

NILSSON

Born Harry Edward Nelson, III on 6/15/41 in Brooklyn. Wrote Three Dog Night's hit "One"; scored the film "Skidoo" and TV's "The Courtship Of Eddie's Father". Close friend of John Lennon and Ringo Starr.

DATE	POS	WKS	ARTIST—RECORD TITLE	LABEL & NO.
4/10/71	25	8	1. The Point! [TV] songs & narration from his animated TV special	RCA 1003
2/05/72	3	19	● 2. Nilsson Schmilsson "Without You"(1) "Coconut"(8)	RCA 4515
8/05/72	12	13	● 3. Son Of Schmilsson	RCA 4717

DATE	POS	WKS	ARTIST—RECORD TITLE	LABEL & NO.
			THE NITTY GRITTY DIRT BAND	
			Country/rock/folk group from Long Beach, CA. Led by Jeff Hanna (vocals, guitar) and John McEuen (banjo, mandolin). Ex-Eagle Bernie Leadon replaced McEuen in 1987.	
9/14/74	28	6	1. Stars & Stripes Forever [L]	United Art. 184 [2]
			ALDO NOVA	
			Born Aldo Scarporuscio in Montreal. Rock singer, songwriter, guitarist, keyboards.	
4/03/82	8	16	● 1. **Aldo Nova**	Portrait 37498
			"Fantasy"	
			NU SHOOZ	
			Northwest Coast group centered around husband and wife team of guitarist, songwriter John Smith and lead singer Valerie Day.	
6/21/86	27	8	● 1. Poolside	Atlantic 81647
			"I Can't Wait"(3)	
			TED NUGENT	
			Born on 12/13/48 in Detroit. Heavy metal rock guitarist; leader of The Amboy Dukes.	
3/13/76	28	6	▲ 1. Ted Nugent	Epic 33692
10/16/76	24	8	▲ 2. Free-For-All	Epic 34121
			featuring vocals by Meat Loaf	
7/02/77	17	19	▲ 3. Cat Scratch Fever	Epic 34700
2/25/78	13	8	▲ 4. Double Live Gonzo! [L]	Epic 35069 [2]
11/18/78	24	10	▲ 5. Weekend Warriors	Epic 35551
6/09/79	18	6	● 6. State Of Shock	Epic 36000
6/07/80	13	9	● 7. Scream Dream	Epic 36404
			GARY NUMAN	
			Born Gary Webb on 3/8/58 in Hammersmith, England. Synthesized techno-rock artist.	
3/29/80	16	14	1. The Pleasure Principle	Atco 120
			"Cars"(9)	
			LAURA NYRO	
			Born Laura Nigro on 10/18/47 in Bronx, NY. White soul-gospel singer/songwriter. Wrote "Stone Soul Picnic", "Wedding Bell Blues", "And When I Die" and "Stoney End".	
11/22/69	32	3	1. New York Tendaberry	Columbia 9737

DATE	POS	WKS	ARTIST—RECORD TITLE	LABEL & NO.
			OAK RIDGE BOYS	
			Originally formed as a gospel quartet in Oak Ridge, TN during World War II. Many personnel changes. Switched to country/pop style in early 1970s with current lineup: Duane Allen, lead; Joe Bonsall, tenor; Bill Golden, baritone; and Richard Sterban, bass. Golden, a member since 1965, left in 1987 (replaced by the rhythm guitarist, Steve Sanders).	
7/04/81	14	10	▲ 1. Fancy Free	MCA 5209
			"Elvira"(5)	
3/06/82	20	9	● 2. Bobbie Sue	MCA 5294

DATE	POS	WKS	ARTIST—RECORD TITLE	LABEL & NO.
			RIC OCASEK	
			Born Richard Otcasek in Baltimore. Lead singer, guitarist of The Cars.	
2/05/83	**28**	9	1. Beatitude	Geffen 2022
11/01/86	**31**	5	2. This Side Of Paradise	Geffen 24098
			BILLY OCEAN	
			Born Leslie Sebastian Charles on 1/21/50 in Trinidad. Raised in England.	
9/22/84	**9**	57	▲ 1. **Suddenly**	Jive 8213
			"Caribbean Queen (No More Love On The Run)"(1)	
			"Loverboy"(2)	
			"Suddenly"(4)	
5/24/86	**6**	30	▲ 2. **Love Zone**	Jive 8409
			"There'll Be Sad Songs (To Make You Cry)"(1)	
			"Love Zone"(10)	
			ODYSSEY	
			New York soul/disco trio: Manila-born Tony Reynolds, and sisters Lillian and Louise Lopez, originally from the Virgin Islands.	
12/03/77	**36**	5	1. Odyssey	RCA 2204
			OHIO PLAYERS	
			Originally an R&B instrumental group called the Ohio Untouchables, formed in Dayton in 1959. Backup on The Falcons' records. Members during prime (1974-79): Marshall Jones, Clarence "Satch" Satchell, Jimmy "Diamond" Williams, Marvin "Merv" Pierce, Billy Beck, Ralph "Pee Wee" Middlebrook and Leroy "Sugarfoot" Bonner.	
6/08/74	**11**	22	● 1. Skin Tight	Mercury 705
11/30/74	**1(1)**	19	● 2. **Fire**	Mercury 1013
			"Fire"(1)	
8/23/75	**2(1)**	24	● 3. **Honey**	Mercury 1038
			"Love Rollercoaster"(1)	
6/19/76	**12**	9	● 4. Contradiction	Mercury 1088
11/27/76	**31**	4	● 5. Ohio Players Gold [G]	Mercury 1122
			THE O'JAYS	
			R&B group from Canton, Ohio formed in 1958 as the Triumphs. Consisted of Eddie Levert, Walter Williams, William Powell, Bobby Massey and Bill Isles. Recorded as the Mascots for King in 1961. Re-named by Cleveland dee-jay, Eddie O'Jay. Isles left in 1965. Massey left to become a record producer in 1971, Levert, Williams and Powell continued as a trio. Powell retired from touring due to illness, late 1975 (d: 5/26/77), replaced by Sammy Strain, formerly with Little Anthony & The Imperials.	
10/07/72	**10**	11	● 1. **Back Stabbers**	Phil. Int. 31712
			"Back Stabbers"(3)	
			"Love Train"(1)	
1/12/74	**11**	19	● 2. Ship Ahoy	Phil. Int. 32408
			"Put Your Hands Together"(10)	
			"For The Love Of Money"(9)	
8/10/74	**17**	7	● 3. The O'Jays Live In London [L]	Phil. Int. 32953
5/17/75	**11**	14	● 4. Survival	Phil. Int. 33150
12/06/75	**7**	17	▲ 5. **Family Reunion**	Phil. Int. 33807
			"I Love Music"(5)	

DATE	POS	WKS	ARTIST—RECORD TITLE	LABEL & NO.
10/16/76	20	6	● 6. Message In The Music	Phil. Int. 34245
6/11/77	27	5	● 7. Travelin' At The Speed Of Thought	Phil. Int. 34684
5/13/78	6	8	▲ 8. **So Full Of Love**	Phil. Int. 35355
			"Use Ta Be My Girl"(4)	
9/22/79	16	8	▲ 9. Identify Yourself	Phil. Int. 36027
9/27/80	36	3	10. The Year 2000	TSOP 36416
			MIKE OLDFIELD	
			Born on 5/15/53 in Reading, England. Classical rock multi-instrumentalist, composer.	
1/26/74	3	23	● 1. **Tubular Bells** [I]	Virgin 105
			"Tubular Bells"(7) - one 49 minute recording (excerpts used in film "The Exorcist")	
			OLIVER	
			Born William Oliver Swofford on 2/22/45 in North Wilkesboro, NC.	
9/06/69	19	10	1. Good Morning Starshine	Crewe 1333
			"Good Morning Starshine"(3)	
			"Jean"(2)	
			101 STRINGS	
			European orchestra under the direction of D.L. Miller.	
5/25/59	9	32	1. **The Soul of Spain** [I]	Somerset 6600
			this album was #1 for 46 of the 47 weeks that Billboard published a special "Best Selling Low Price LP's" chart (2/19/60-1/8/61)	
1/09/61	21	4	2. The Soul of Spain, Volume II [I]	Somerset 9900
			ROY ORBISON	
			Born on 4/23/36 in Vernon, Texas. Had own band, the Wink Westerners in 1952. Attended North Texas University with Pat Boone. First recorded for Jewel in early 1956. Toured with Sun Records shows to 1958. Toured with The Beatles in 1963.	
6/09/62	21	7	1. Crying	Monument 4007
			"Running Scared"(1)	
			"Crying"(2)	
9/15/62	14	48	● 2. Roy Orbison's Greatest Hits [G]	Monument 4009
			"Only The Lonely"(2)	
			"Blue Angel"(9)	
			"Dream Baby"(4)	
10/26/63	35	2	3. In Dreams	Monument 18003
			"In Dreams"(7)	
			"Blue Bayou"	
10/03/64	19	16	4. More Of Roy Orbison's Greatest Hits [G]	Monument 18024
			"It's Over"(9)	
			"Mean Woman Blues"(5)	
			ORCHESTRAL MANOEUVRES IN THE DARK	
			English electro-pop quartet: Paul Humphreys, Andrew McCluskey, Malcolm Holmes and Martin Cooper.	
11/02/85	38	5	1. Crush	A&M 5077
			"So In Love"	
			TONY ORLANDO - see DAWN	

DATE	POS	WKS	ARTIST—RECORD TITLE	LABEL & NO.
			ORLEANS Rock group founded in New York City by John Hall with brothers Lawrence and Lance Hoppen, Wells Kelly and Jerry Marotta. Hall and Marotta left in 1977, replaced by Bob Leinbach and R.A. Martin.	
10/11/75	33	5	1. Let There Be Music	Asylum 1029
			"Dance With Me"(6)	
10/02/76	30	5	2. Waking And Dreaming	Asylum 1070
			"Still The One"(5)	
			EUGENE ORMANDY - see PHILADELPHIA ORCHESTRA	
			JEFFREY OSBORNE Born on 3/9/48 in Providence, RI. Soul singer, songwriter, drummer. Ex-lead singer of L.T.D.	
9/03/83	25	23	● 1. Stay With Me Tonight	A&M 4940
11/24/84	39	4	● 2. Don't Stop	A&M 5017
7/12/86	26	11	● 3. Emotional	A&M 5103
			OZZY OSBOURNE Born John Osbourne on 12/3/48 in Birmingham, England. Heavy-metal artist; former lead singer of Black Sabbath.	
5/23/81	21	16	▲ 1. Blizzard Of Ozz	Jet 36812
11/28/81	16	23	▲ 2. Diary Of A Madman	Jet 37492
12/18/82	14	10	● 3. Speak Of The Devil [L]	Jet 38350 [2]
			recorded at The Ritz, New York	
12/17/83	19	11	▲ 4. Bark At The Moon	CBS Assoc. 38987
2/22/86	6	17	▲ 5. **The Ultimate Sin**	CBS Assoc. 40026
			LEE OSKAR Born on 3/24/48 in Copenhagen, Denmark. Harmonica player. Studio musician in Los Angeles. Original member of War.	
6/19/76	29	4	1. Lee Oskar	United Art. 594
			DONNY OSMOND Born on 12/9/57 in Ogden, Utah. Seventh son of George & Olive Osmond, Donny became a member of The Osmonds in 1963.	
7/24/71	13	18	● 1. The Donny Osmond Album	MGM 4782
			"Sweet And Innocent"(7)	
11/13/71	12	14	● 2. To You With Love, Donny	MGM 4797
			"Go Away Little Girl"(1)	
6/10/72	6	10	● 3. **Portrait Of Donny**	MGM 4820
			"Hey Girl"(9)	
			"Puppy Love"(3)	
8/05/72	11	14	● 4. Too Young	MGM 4854
1/06/73	29	6	● 5. My Best To You [G]	MGM 4872
4/14/73	26	7	6. Alone Together	MGM 4886
			"The Twelfth Of Never"(8)	
			DONNY & MARIE OSMOND Co-hosts of a musical/variety TV series, 1976-78.	
11/02/74	35	4	● 1. I'm Leaving It All Up To You	MGM 4968
			"I'm Leaving It (All) Up To You"(4)	
			"Morning Side Of The Mountain"(8)	

DATE	POS	WKS	ARTIST—RECORD TITLE		LABEL & NO.
			THE OSMONDS		
			Family group from Ogden, Utah. Alan (b: 6/22/49), Wayne (b: 8/28/51), Merrill (b: 4/30/53), Jay (b: 3/2/55) and Donny (b: 12/9/57). Began as a quartet in 1959, singing religious and barbershop-quartet songs. Regulars on Andy Williams' TV show from 1962-67. Alan, Wayne, Merrill and Jay are currently a hot Country act.		
2/06/71	**14**	10	● 1. Osmonds		MGM 4724
			"One Bad Apple"(1)		
7/03/71	**22**	10	● 2. Homemade		MGM 4770
2/05/72	**10**	13	● 3. **Phase-III**		MGM 4796
			"Yo-Yo"(3)		
			"Down By The Lazy River"(4)		
7/01/72	**13**	15	● 4. The Osmonds "Live"	[L]	MGM 4826 [2]
11/04/72	**14**	11	● 5. Crazy Horses		MGM 4851
			GILBERT O'SULLIVAN		
			Born Raymond O'Sullivan on 12/1/46 in Waterford, Ireland.		
8/19/72	**9**	14	1. **Gilbert O'Sullivan-Himself**		MAM 4
			"Alone Again (Naturally)"(1)		
			THE OUTFIELD		
			British pop/rock trio: Tony Lewis, lead singer; John Spinks, guitarist; and Alan Jackman, drums.		
3/29/86	**9**	29	▲ 1. **Play Deep**		Columbia 40027
			"Your Love"(6)		
			OUTLAWS		
			Southern rock band formed in Tampa in 1974. Consisted of guitarists Hughie Thomasson, Billy Jones and Henry Paul; Monte Yoho, drums; and Frank O'Keefe, bass (replaced by Harvey Arnold in 1977). Paul, Yoho, and Arnold left by 1980.		
9/20/75	**13**	6	● 1. Outlaws		Arista 4042
5/15/76	**36**	1	2. Lady In Waiting		Arista 4070
4/15/78	**29**	4	● 3. Bring It Back Alive	[L]	Arista 8300 [2]
2/07/81	**25**	7	● 4. Ghost Riders		Arista 9542
			THE OUTSIDERS		
			Cleveland rock quintet: Sonny Geraci, lead singer; Tom King, guitar; Bill Bruno, lead guitar; Mert Madsen, bass; and Rick Baker, drums.		
7/16/66	**37**	3	1. Time Won't Let Me		Capitol 2501
			"Time Won't Let Me"(5)		
			OZARK MOUNTAIN DAREDEVILS		
			Country-rock group from Springfield, MO. Nucleus consists of Larry Lee, keyboards, guitar; Steve Cash, harp; John Dillon, guitar; and Michael Granada, bass.		
6/22/74	**26**	5	● 1. The Ozark Mountain Daredevils		A&M 4411
2/08/75	**19**	8	2. It'll Shine When It Shines		A&M 3654
			"Jackie Blue"(3)		

DATE	POS	WKS	ARTIST—RECORD TITLE	LABEL & NO.

P

PABLO CRUISE

San Francisco pop/rock quartet formed in 1973. Consisted of Dave Jenkins, vocals, guitar; Bud Cockrell, vocals, bass (member of It's A Beautiful Day); Cory Lerios, keyboards; and Stephen Price, drums. Cockrell replaced by Bruce Day in 1977. John Pierce replaced Day, and guitarist Angelo Rossi joined group in 1980.

DATE	POS	WKS	ARTIST—RECORD TITLE	LABEL & NO.
7/02/77	19	17	▲ 1. A Place In The Sun	A&M 4625
			"Whatcha Gonna Do?"(6)	
7/15/78	6	14	▲ 2. **Worlds Away**	A&M 4697
			"Love Will Find A Way"(6)	
12/08/79	39	2	3. Part Of The Game	A&M 3712
8/22/81	34	5	4. Reflector	A&M 3726

PATTI PAGE

Born Clara Ann Fowler on 11/8/27 in Muskogee, Oklahoma. One of eleven children. Raised in Tulsa. On radio KTUL with Al Klauser & His Oklahomans, as "Ann Fowler", late 40s. Another singer was billed as "Patti Page" for the Page Milk Company show on KTUL. When she left, Fowler took her place and name. With the Jimmy Joy band in 1947. On Breakfast Club, Chicago radio, 1947; signed by Mercury Records. Used multi-voice effect on records from 1947. Own TV series "The Patti Page Show", 1955-58, and "The Big Record", 1957-58. In film "Elmer Gantry", 1960.

DATE	POS	WKS	ARTIST—RECORD TITLE	LABEL & NO.
11/24/56	18	2	1. Manhattan Tower	Mercury 20226
			a version of Gordon Jenkin's musical narrative	
6/26/65	27	7	2. Hush, Hush, Sweet Charlotte	Columbia 9153
			"Hush, Hush, Sweet Charlotte"(8)	

ROBERT PALMER

Born on 1/19/49 in Batley, England. Lead singer of supergroup The Power Station.

DATE	POS	WKS	ARTIST—RECORD TITLE	LABEL & NO.
8/25/79	19	8	1. Secrets	Island 9544
			"Bad Case Of Loving You"	
3/22/86	8	35	▲ 2. **Riptide**	Island 90471
			"Addicted To Love"(1)	
			"I Didn't Mean To Turn You On"(2)	

NORRIE PARAMOR

British conductor.

DATE	POS	WKS	ARTIST—RECORD TITLE	LABEL & NO.
9/08/56	18	3	1. In London, In Love... [I]	Capitol Int. 10025

GRAHAM PARKER & The Rumour

DATE	POS	WKS	ARTIST—RECORD TITLE	LABEL & NO.
5/26/79	40	2	1. Squeezing Out Sparks	Arista 4223
7/05/80	40	1	2. The Up Escalator	Arista 9517
			Bruce Springsteen sings on one track	

RAY PARKER JR.

Born in Detroit on 5/1/54. Prominent session guitarist in California, worked with Stevie Wonder, Barry White and others. Formed band Raydio in 1977.

RAYDIO:

DATE	POS	WKS	ARTIST—RECORD TITLE	LABEL & NO.
3/18/78	27	9	● 1. Raydio	Arista 4163
			"Jack And Jill"(8)	

DATE	POS	WKS	ARTIST—RECORD TITLE	LABEL & NO.
			RAY PARKER JR. & RAYDIO:	
5/10/80	33	5	● 2. Two Places At The Same Time	Arista 9515
5/02/81	13	16	● 3. A Woman Needs Love	Arista 9543
			"A Woman Needs Love (Just Like You Do)"(4)	
			RAY PARKER JR.:	
5/08/82	11	12	● 4. The Other Woman	Arista 9590
			"The Other Woman"(4)	
			MICHAEL PARKS	
			Portrayed Jim Bronson on TV's "Then Came Bronson".	
2/28/70	35	5	1. Closing The Gap	MGM 4646
5/30/70	24	6	2. Long Lonesome Highway	MGM 4662
			PARLIAMENT	
			"A Parliafunkadelicament Thang", a corporation of musicians led by producer, songwriter George Clinton. They recorded under various names for various groups including "Funkadelic", "Parliament", "Bootsy's Rubber Band", "Brides Of Funkenstein", "Parlet", and others. Also see George Clinton.	
4/10/76	13	17	▲ 1. Mothership Connection	Casablanca 7022
10/23/76	20	8	● 2. The Clones Of Dr. Funkenstein	Casablanca 7034
6/04/77	29	5	● 3. Parliament Live/P. Funk Earth Tour [L]	Casablanca 7053 [2]
1/21/78	13	19	▲ 4. Funkentelechy Vs. The Placebo Syndrome	Casablanca 7084
12/23/78	23	10	● 5. Motor-Booty Affair	Casablanca 7125
			THE ALAN PARSONS PROJECT	
			Duo formed in London, England in 1975. Consisted of Alan Parsons (guitar, keyboards, producer) and Eric Woolfson (vocals, keyboards, lyricist). Both had worked at the Abbey Road Studios; Parsons was an engineer, Woolfson a songwriter. Parsons engineered Pink Floyd's "Dark Side Of The Moon" and The Beatles' "Abbey Road" albums. Project features varying musicians and vocalists.	
7/04/76	38	4	1. Tales Of Mystery And Imagination - Edgar Allan Poe	20th Century 508
			musical interpretation of Poe's most notable works	
8/06/77	9	19	▲ 2. **I Robot**	Arista 7002
7/22/78	26	9	● 3. Pyramid	Arista 4180
9/22/79	13	12	● 4. Eve	Arista 9504
11/29/80	13	21	▲ 5. The Turn Of A Friendly Card	Arista 9518
7/10/82	7	21	▲ 6. **Eye In The Sky**	Arista 9599
			"Eye In The Sky"(3)	
3/24/84	15	13	● 7. Ammonia Avenue	Arista 8204
			DOLLY PARTON	
			Born on 1/19/46 in Sevier County, Tennessee. Worked on Knoxville radio show at age 11. First recorded for Gold Band in 1957. To Nashville in 1964. Replaced Norma Jean on the Porter Wagoner TV show, 1967-73. Went solo in 1974. Starred in films "Nine To Five", "The Best Little Whorehouse In Texas" and "Rhinestone".	
12/03/77	20	13	▲ 1. Here You Come Again	RCA 2544
			"Here You Come Again"(3)	
9/16/78	27	8	● 2. Heartbreaker	RCA 2797
7/21/79	40	1	● 3. Great Balls Of Fire	RCA 3361

DATE	POS	WKS	ARTIST—RECORD TITLE	LABEL & NO.
1/17/81	**11**	15	● 4. 9 to 5 and Odd Jobs	RCA 3852
			"9 to 5"(1)	
12/22/84	**31**	4	▲ 5. Once Upon A Christmas [X]	RCA 5307
			KENNY ROGERS & DOLLY PARTON	
			made top 10 on Billboard's special Christmas charts (1984)	
			THE PARTRIDGE FAMILY	
			Popularized through "The Partridge Family" TV series, with recordings by series stars David Cassidy (lead singer) and real-life stepmother Shirley Jones (backing vocals). David, son of actor Jack Cassidy, was born on 4/12/50 in New York City; raised in California. Shirley was born on 3/31/34 in Smithton, PA. Starred in film musicals "Oklahoma" and "The Music Man". Married David's father in 1956.	
11/07/70	**4**	36	● 1. **The Partridge Family Album**	Bell 6050
			"I Think I Love You"(1)	
4/03/71	**3**	23	● 2. **Up To Date**	Bell 6059
			"Doesn't Somebody Want To Be Wanted"(6)	
			"I'll Meet You Halfway"(9)	
9/04/71	**9**	22	● 3. **The Partridge Family Sound Magazine**	Bell 6064
4/01/72	**18**	7	● 4. The Partridge Family Shopping Bag	Bell 6072
10/07/72	**21**	10	● 5. The Partridge Family at home with their Greatest Hits [G]	Bell 1107
			PAUL & PAULA	
			Real names: Ray Hildebrand (b: 12/21/40, Joshua, TX) and Jill Jackson (b: 5/20/42, McCaney, TX). Formed duo at Howard Payne College, Brownwood, TX.	
3/16/63	**9**	8	1. **Paul & Paula Sing For Young Lovers**	Philips 078
			"Hey Paula"(1)	
			"Young Lovers"(6)	
			BILLY PAUL	
			Born Paul Williams on 12/1/34 in Philadelphia. Sang on Philadelphia radio broadcasts at age 11. First recorded for Jubilee in 1952.	
1/06/73	**17**	9	● 1. 360 Degrees Of Billy Paul	Phil. Int. 31793
			"Me And Mrs. Jones"(1)	
			LES PAUL & MARY FORD	
			Les was born Lester Polfus on 6/9/16 in Waukesha, WI. Mary was born Colleen Summer on 7/7/28 in Pasadena; died on 9/30/77. Paul is a self-taught guitarist. Worked local radio stations, then to Chicago, 1932-37. Own trio in 1936. With Fred Waring, 1938-41. Innovator in electric guitar and multitrack recordings. Married vocalist Mary Ford on 12/29/49; divorced in 1963.	
5/14/55	**15**	6	1. Les and Mary	Capitol 577
			10 songs feature Mary's vocals; 6 are instrumentals by Les	
			PEACHES & HERB	
			Soul duo from Washington, DC: Herb Fame (born Herbert Feemster, 1942) and Francine Barker (born Francine Hurd, 1947). Fame had been recording solo, Francine sang in vocal group, Sweet Things. Marlene Mack filled in for Francine, 1968-69. Reformed with Fame and Linda Green in 1977.	
6/24/67	**30**	6	1. Let's Fall In Love	Date 4004
			"Close Your Eyes"(8)	
2/17/79	**2(6)**	23	▲ 2. **2 Hot!**	Polydor 6172
			"Shake Your Groove Thing"(5)	
			"Reunited"(1)	
12/01/79	**31**	4	● 3. Twice The Fire	Polydor 6239

DATE	POS	WKS	ARTIST—RECORD TITLE	LABEL & NO.
			TEDDY PENDERGRASS	
			Born on 3/26/50 in Philadelphia. Worked local clubs, became drummer for Harold Melvin's Blue Notes in 1969; vocalist with same group in 1970. Went solo in 1976. Auto accident on 3/18/82 left him partially paralyzed.	
4/09/77	**17**	11	▲ 1. Teddy Pendergrass	Phil. Int. 34390
7/08/78	**11**	15	▲ 2. Life Is A Song Worth Singing	Phil. Int. 35095
6/30/79	**5**	14	▲ 3. **Teddy**	Phil. Int. 36003
1/26/80	**33**	4	● 4. Teddy Live! Coast To Coast [L]	Phil. Int. 36294 [2]
			side 4: interviews and new studio recordings	
8/23/80	**14**	16	▲ 5. TP	Phil. Int. 36745
10/10/81	**19**	7	● 6. It's Time For Love	Phil. Int. 37491
7/21/84	**38**	5	● 7. Love Language	Asylum 60317
			LEONARD PENNARIO	
			Classical pianist.	
6/08/59	**29**	1	1. Concertos under the Stars [I]	Capitol 8326
			with The Hollywood Bowl Symphony Orchestra, conducted by Carmen Dragon	
			STEVE PERRY	
			Born on 1/22/49 in Hanford, CA. Lead singer of Journey since 1978.	
5/05/84	**12**	18	▲ 1. Street Talk	Columbia 39334
			"Oh Sherrie"(3)	
			PET SHOP BOYS	
			British duo: Neil Tennant (vocals) and Chris Lowe.	
4/19/86	**7**	21	▲ 1. **Please**	EMI America 17193
			"West End Girls"(1)	
			"Opportunities"(10)	
			PETER & GORDON	
			Pop duo formed in London, England in 1963. Consisted of Peter Asher (b: 6/22/44) and Gordon Waller (b: 6/4/45). Toured USA in 1964, appeared on "Shindig", "Hullabaloo", Ed Sullivan TV shows. Disbanded in 1967. Asher went into production and management, including work with Linda Ronstadt and James Taylor.	
7/25/64	**21**	5	1. A World Without Love	Capitol 2115
			"A World Without Love"(1)	
			PETER, PAUL & MARY	
			Folk group formed in New York City in 1961. Consisted of Mary Travers (b: 11/7/37, Louisville); Peter Yarrow (b: 5/31/38, New York City); & Paul Stookey (b: 11/30/37, Baltimore). Yarrow had worked the Newport Folk Festival in 1960. Stookey had done TV work, and Travers had been in the Broadway musical "The Next President". Disbanded in 1971, reunited in 1978.	
6/02/62	**1(7)**	12	▲ 1. **Peter, Paul & Mary**	Warner 1449
			"If I Had A Hammer"(10)	
1/26/63	**2(9)**	71	● 2. **(Moving)**	Warner 1473
			"Puff The Magic Dragon"(2)	
10/26/63	**1(5)**	58	● 3. **In The Wind**	Warner 1507
			"Blowin' In The Wind"(2)	
			"Don't Think Twice, It's All Right"(9)	
8/29/64	**4**	25	● 4. Peter, Paul and Mary In Concert [L]	Warner 1555 [2]
5/01/65	**8**	26	● 5. **A Song Will Rise**	Warner 1589

DATE	POS	WKS	ARTIST—RECORD TITLE	LABEL & NO.
11/27/65	11	8	● 6. See What Tomorrow Brings	Warner 1615
9/17/66	22	9	7. Peter, Paul and Mary Album	Warner 1648
9/09/67	15	25	● 8. Album 1700	Warner 1700
			"I Dig Rock And Roll Music"(9)	
			"Leaving On A Jet Plane"(1)	
10/12/68	14	12	9. Late Again	Warner 1751
6/21/69	12	9	10. Peter, Paul and Mommy	Warner 1785
6/27/70	15	11	▲ 11. 10 Years Together/The Best Of Peter, Paul and Mary [G]	Warner 2552
			TOM PETTY & THE HEARTBREAKERS	
			Rock group formed in Los Angeles in 1975. Consisted of Tom Petty (b: 10/20/53, Gainesville, FL), guitar, vocals; Mike Campbell, guitar; Benmont Tench, keyboards; Ron Blair, bass; and Stan Lynch, drums. Petty, Campbell and Tench had been in Florida group Mudcrutch, early 70s. Backed Stevie Nicks on solo LP "Bella Donna". Blair left in 1982, replaced by Howard Epstein.	
7/01/78	23	8	● 1. You're Gonna Get It!	Shelter 52029
11/17/79	2(7)	29	▲ 2. **Damn The Torpedoes**	Backstreet 5105
			"Don't Do Me Like That"(10)	
5/23/81	5	17	▲ 3. **Hard Promises**	Backstreet 5160
11/27/82	9	22	● 4. **Long After Dark**	Backstreet 5360
4/13/85	7	18	▲ 5. **Southern Accents**	MCA 5486
			"Don't Come Around Here No More"	
1/18/86	22	9	6. Pack Up The Plantation - Live! [L]	MCA 8021 [2]
			PHILADELPHIA ORCHESTRA	
			Eugene Ormandy, conductor (d: 3/12/85 [85]). Also see Mormon Tabernacle Choir.	
5/26/62	17	11	1. The Magnificent Sound Of The Philadelphia Orchestra [K-I] *compiled from 16 of their albums*	Columbia 1 [2]
			ESTHER PHILLIPS	
			Real name: Esther Mae Jones. "Little Esther" had 5 Top 10 singles with Johnny Otis on the R&B charts in 1950. Died on 8/7/84 (48).	
9/20/75	32	6	1. What A Diff'rence A Day Makes *with jazz guitarist Joe Beck*	Kudu 23
			BOBBY "BORIS" PICKETT & The Crypt-Kickers	
			Born on 2/11/40 in Somerville, MA. Began recording career in Hollywood while aspiring to be an actor.	
12/15/62	19	3	1. The Original Monster Mash [N] *"Monster Mash"(1)*	Garpax 57001
			WILSON PICKETT	
			Born on 3/18/41 in Prattville, AL. Soul singer, songwriter. Sang in local gospel groups. To Detroit in 1955. With The Falcons, 1961-63. Career took off after recording in Memphis with guitarist, producer Steve Cropper.	
10/15/66	21	7	1. The Exciting Wilson Pickett *"Land Of 1000 Dances"(6)*	Atlantic 8129
1/27/68	35	8	2. The Best Of Wilson Pickett [G]	Atlantic 8151

DATE	POS	WKS	ARTIST—RECORD TITLE	LABEL & NO.
			PINK FLOYD	
			English progressive rock band formed in 1965: David Gilmour (replaced Syd Barrett in 1968), guitar; Roger Waters, bass; Nick Mason, drums; and Rick Wright, keyboards. Waters went solo in 1984. Band inactive, 1984-86. Gilmour, Mason and Wright regrouped in 1987.	
3/31/73	1(1)	63	● 1. **The Dark Side Of The Moon**	Harvest 11163
			although the LP has sold over 10 million copies, it is not certified platinum because RIAA rules an album cannot be considered for platinum if released prior to 1/1/76	
1/26/74	36	4	2. A Nice Pair [R]	Harvest 11257 [2]
			reissue of their first 2 British albums "The Piper At The Gates Of Dawn" & "A Saucerful Of Secrets"	
9/27/75	1(2)	15	▲ 3. **Wish You Were Here**	Columbia 33453
2/19/77	3	9	▲ 4. **Animals**	Columbia 34474
12/22/79	1(15)	35	▲ 5. **The Wall**	Columbia 36183 [2]
			"Another Brick In The Wall (Part II)"(1)	
12/19/81	31	7	● 6. A Collection Of Great Dance Songs [G]	Columbia 37680
			recordings from albums #5,7,10,11 & 12 above	
4/09/83	6	12	▲ 7. **The Final Cut**	Columbia 38243
			group now a trio (minus Rick Wright)	
			ROBERT PLANT	
			Born on 8/20/48 in Bromwich, England. Lead singer of Led Zeppelin and The Honeydrippers.	
7/24/82	5	14	● 1. **Pictures At Eleven**	Swan Song 8512
8/06/83	8	18	▲ 2. **The Principle Of Moments**	Es Paranza 90101
			"Big Log"/"In The Mood"	
6/22/85	20	8	● 3. Shaken 'N' Stirred	Es Paranza 90265
			PLASTIC ONO BAND - see JOHN LENNON	
			THE PLATTERS	
			R&B group formed in Los Angeles in 1953. Consisted of Tony Williams (b: 4/5/28, Elizabeth, NJ), lead; David Lynch, tenor; Paul Robi, baritone; Herb Reed, bass; and Zola Taylor. Taylor had formerly sung with Shirley Gunter's Queens. Group first recorded for Federal in 1954, with Alex Hodge instead of Robi, and without Zola Taylor. Hit "Only You" was written by manager Buck Ram and first recorded for Federal, who did not want to use it. To Mercury in 1955, recorded "Only You". Williams left to go solo, replaced by Sonny Turner in 1961. Taylor replaced by Sandra Dawn; Robi replaced by Nate Nelson (formerly in The Flamingos) in 1966. Several unrelated groups use this famous name today.	
7/14/56	7	26	1. **The Platters**	Mercury 20146
			"My Prayer"(1)	
1/19/57	12	8	2. The Platters, Volume Two	Mercury 20216
3/30/59	15	8	3. Remember When?	Mercury 20410
			"Smoke Gets In Your Eyes"(1)	
3/14/60	6	69	● 4. **Encore Of Golden Hits** [G]	Mercury 20472
			"Only You (And You Alone)"(5)	
			"The Great Pretender"(1)	
			"(You've Got) The Magic Touch"(4)	
			"Twilight Time"(1)	
11/14/60	20	16	● 5. More Encore Of Golden Hits [G]	Mercury 20591
			"Harbor Lights"(8)	

DATE	POS	WKS	ARTIST—RECORD TITLE	LABEL & NO.
			PLAYER	
			Pop/rock group formed in Los Angeles: Peter Beckett, vocals, guitar; John Crowley, vocals, guitar; Ronn Moss, bass; John Friesen, drums; Wayne Cooke, keyboards.	
1/28/78	26	6	● 1. Player	RSO 3026
			"Baby Come Back"(1)	
			"This Time I'm In It For Love"(10)	
11/04/78	37	2	● 2. Danger Zone	RSO 3036
			POCO	
			Los Angeles country-rock band formed by Rusty Young (pedal steel guitar) and Buffalo Springfield members Richie Furay (rhythm guitar) and Jim Messina (lead guitar). As of first single, group consisted of Furay, Messina, Young, George Grantham (drums) and Timothy B. Schmit (bass). Messina left in 1971, replaced by Paul Cotton, and Furay left in 1973. Grantham and Schmit (joins Eagles) left in 1977; replacements: Charlie Harrison, Kim Bullard and Steve Chapman.	
2/13/71	26	6	1. Deliverin' [L]	Epic 30209
10/20/73	38	2	2. Crazy Eyes	Epic 32354
			Richie Furay's last album as a member	
3/03/79	14	10	● 3. Legend	ABC 1099
			"Crazy Love"/"Heart Of The Night"	
			POINTER SISTERS	
			Soul group formed in Oakland in 1971, consisting of sisters Ruth, Anita, Bonnie and June Pointer. Parents were ministers. Group was originally a trio, joined by youngest sister June, in early 70s. First recorded for Atlantic in 1971. Backup work for Cold Blood, Elvin Bishop, Boz Scaggs, Grace Slick, and many others. Sang in nostalgic 1940s style, 1973-77. In film "Car Wash", 1976. Bonnie went solo in 1978; group continued as trio in new musical style.	
8/25/73	13	13	● 1. The Pointer Sisters	Blue Thumb 48
			"Yes We Can Can"	
8/09/75	22	7	2. Steppin	Blue Thumb 6021
2/03/79	13	10	● 3. Energy	Planet 1
			"Fire"(2)	
11/01/80	34	5	4. Special Things	Planet 9
			"He's So Shy"(3)	
7/18/81	12	14	● 5. Black & White	Planet 18
			"Slow Hand"(2)	
3/17/84	8	65	▲ 6. **Break Out**	Planet 4705
			"Automatic"(5)	
			"Jump (For My Love)"(3)	
			"I'm So Excited"(9-originally released on album #11 above)	
			"Neutron Dance"(6)	
4/20/85	24	25	▲ 7. Contact	RCA 5487
			"Dare Me"	
			POLICE	
			Rock trio formed in England in 1977: Gordon "Sting" Sumner (b: 10/2/51), vocals, bass; Andy Summers (b: 12/31/42), guitar; and Stewart Copeland (b: 7/16/52), drums. First guitarist was Henri Padovani, replaced by Summers in 1977. Copeland had been with Curved Air. Sting was in films "Dune", "The Bride" and "Plenty".	
3/31/79	23	11	▲ 1. Outlandos d'Amour	A&M 4753
			"Roxanne"	

DATE	POS	WKS	ARTIST—RECORD TITLE	LABEL & NO.
11/17/79	25	8	● 2. Reggatta de Blanc	A&M 4792
11/01/80	5	31	▲ 3. **Zenyatta Mondatta**	A&M 4831
			"De Do Do Do, De Da Da Da"(10)	
			"Don't Stand So Close To Me"(10)	
10/24/81	2(6)	30	▲ 4. **Ghost In The Machine**	A&M 3730
			"Every Little Thing She Does Is Magic"(3)	
			"Spirits In The Material World"	
7/02/83	1(17)	50	▲ 5. **Synchronicity**	A&M 3735
			"Every Breath You Take"(1)	
			"King Of Pain"(3)	
			"Wrapped Around Your Finger"(8)	
11/29/86	7	13	▲ 6. **Every Breath You Take - The Singles** [G]	A&M 3902

JEAN-LUC PONTY

French jazz-rock violinist - member of Mahavishnu Orchestra.

DATE	POS	WKS	ARTIST—RECORD TITLE	LABEL & NO.
10/29/77	35	3	1. Enigmatic Ocean [I]	Atlantic 19110
10/28/78	36	3	2. Cosmic Messenger [I]	Atlantic 19189

THE POWER STATION

Superstar quartet: Duran Duran's John Taylor (bass) & Andy Taylor (guitar); Chic's Tony Thompson (drums), and Robert Palmer (lead singer).

DATE	POS	WKS	ARTIST—RECORD TITLE	LABEL & NO.
4/20/85	6	25	▲ 1. **The Power Station**	Capitol 12380
			"Some Like It Hot"(6)	
			"Get It On"(9)	

PEREZ PRADO

Damaso Perez Prado - "King of the Mambo" bandleader, organist from Cuba and later Mexico City.

DATE	POS	WKS	ARTIST—RECORD TITLE	LABEL & NO.
5/25/59	22	3	1. "Prez" [I]	RCA 1556

ELVIS PRESLEY

The King of Rock & Roll. Born on 1/8/35 in Tupelo, Mississippi. Died on 8/16/77 in Memphis at the age of 42 due to heart failure caused by drug abuse. Won talent contest at age eight, singing "Old Shep". First played guitar at age eleven. Moved to Memphis in 1948. Sang in high school shows. Worked as an usher and truck driver after graduation. First recorded for Sun in 1954. Signed to RCA Records on 11/22/55. First film, "Love Me Tender" in 1956. In US Army from 3/24/58 to 3/5/60. In many films thereafter. NBC-TV special in 1968. Married Priscilla Beaulieu on 5/1/67; divorced on 10/11/73. Only child Lisa Marie, born on 2/1/68. Elvis' last live performance was in Indianapolis on 6/26/77.

DATE	POS	WKS	ARTIST—RECORD TITLE	LABEL & NO.
3/31/56	1(10)	48	● 1. **Elvis Presley**	RCA LPM-1254
			includes 5 Sun studio recordings	
11/10/56	1(5)	32	● 2. **Elvis**	RCA LPM-1382
			"Love Me"(2)	
5/13/57	3	9	3. **Peace In The Valley** [M]	RCA EPA-4054
			7" E.P. of sacred songs	
7/22/57	1(10)	29	● 4. **Loving You** [S]	RCA LPM-1515
			only side 1 has the soundtrack recordings	
			"(Let Me Be Your) Teddy Bear"(1)	
9/02/57	18	1	5. Loving You, Vol. II [M-S]	RCA EPA 2-1515
			7" E.P. - 4 songs from the soundtrack of previous album	
9/02/57	22	1	6. Love Me Tender [M-S]	RCA EPA-4006
			7" E.P. of songs from his first film	
			"Love Me Tender"(1)	

DATE	POS	WKS	ARTIST—RECORD TITLE		LABEL & NO.
9/30/57	**16**	1	7. Just For You	[M]	RCA EPA-4041
			7" E.P. - 3 of 4 songs from side 2 of "Loving You"		
12/02/57	**1(4)**	7	● 8. Elvis' Christmas Album	[X]	RCA LOC-1035
			with 10 pages of bound-in color photos of Elvis - includes all 4 songs from "Peace In The Valley" E.P.		
4/21/58	**3**	46	● 9. **Elvis' Golden Records**	[G]	RCA LPM-1707
			"Heartbreak Hotel"(1)		
			"I Want You, I Need You, I Love You"(1)		
			"Don't Be Cruel"(1)		
			"Hound Dog"(1)		
			"Too Much"(1)		
			"All Shook Up"(1)		
			"Jailhouse Rock"(1)		
9/15/58	**2(1)**	15	10. **King Creole**	[S]	RCA LPM-1884
			"Hard Headed Woman"(1)		
3/23/59	**19**	8	11. For LP Fans Only	[E]	RCA LPM-1990
			includes 4 Sun studio recordings - others from 1956		
9/21/59	**32**	8	12. A Date With Elvis	[E]	RCA LPM-2011
			includes 5 Sun studio recordings - others from 1956-57		
2/15/60	**31**	6	● 13. 50,000,000 Elvis Fans Can't Be Wrong - Elvis' Gold Records-Volume 2	[G]	RCA LPM-2075
			"Don't"(1)		
			"I Beg Of You"(8)		
			"Wear My Ring Around Your Neck"(2)		
			"One Night"(4)		
			"I Got Stung"(8)		
			"A Fool Such As I"(2)		
			"I Need Your Love Tonight"(4)		
			"A Big Hunk O' Love"(1)		
5/09/60	**2(3)**	44	14. **Elvis Is Back!**		RCA LSP-2231
			recorded shortly after his March 5th release from the Army		
10/31/60	**1(10)**	49	● 15. **G.I. Blues**	[S]	RCA LSP-2256
12/31/60	**33**	1	16. Elvis' Christmas Album	[X-R]	RCA LPM-1951
			repackage of LOC-1035 album (no photos)		
1/09/61	**13**	9	● 17. His Hand in Mine		RCA LSP-2328
			Elvis' first full album of sacred songs		
7/24/61	**1(3)**	17	18. **Something for Everybody**		RCA LSP-2370
10/30/61	**1(20)**	53	● 19. **Blue Hawaii**	[S]	RCA LSP-2426
			"Can't Help Falling In Love"(2)		
7/14/62	**4**	18	20. **Pot Luck**		RCA LSP-2523
12/08/62	**3**	21	● 21. **Girls! Girls! Girls!**	[S]	RCA LSP-2621
			"Return To Sender"(2)		
4/27/63	**4**	18	22. **It Happened At The World's Fair**	[S]	RCA LSP-2697
9/28/63	**3**	20	● 23. **Elvis' Golden Records, Volume 3**	[G]	RCA LSP-2765
			"Stuck On You"(1)		
			"It's Now Or Never"(1)		
			"Are You Lonesome To-night"(1)		
			"Surrender"(1)		
			"I Feel So Bad"(5)		
			"Little Sister"(5)		
			"(Marie's the Name) His Latest Flame"(4)		
			"Good Luck Charm"(1)		
			"She's Not You"(5)		

DATE	POS	WKS	ARTIST—RECORD TITLE		LABEL & NO.
4/04/64.	3	16	24. **Fun in Acapulco** includes 2 bonus songs not in the film *"Bossa Nova Baby"(8)*	[S]	RCA LSP-2756
4/18/64	6	15	25. **Kissin' Cousins** includes 2 bonus songs not in the film	[S]	RCA LSP-2894
11/28/64	1(1)	20	26. **Roustabout**	[S]	RCA LSP-2999
5/08/65	8	17	27. **Girl Happy** includes 1 bonus song not in the film	[S]	RCA LSP-3338
9/18/65	10	11	28. **Elvis For Everyone!** recordings from 2/57 to 1/64 (plus 1 Sun studio recording)	[K]	RCA LSP-3450
11/27/65	8	11	29. **Harum Scarum** includes 2 bonus songs not in the film	[S]	RCA LSP-3468
5/14/66	20	9	30. Frankie And Johnny	[S]	RCA LSP-3553
8/06/66	15	9	31. Paradise, Hawaiian Style includes 1 bonus song not in the film	[S]	RCA LSP-3643
12/03/66	18	10	32. Spinout includes 3 bonus songs not in the film	[S]	RCA LSP-3702
4/29/67	18	9	● 33. How Great Thou Art Elvis' 2nd full album of sacred songs *"Crying In The Chapel"(3)*		RCA LSP-3758
2/10/68	40	1	34. Clambake includes 5 bonus songs not in the film	[S]	RCA LSP-3893
5/11/68	33	4	35. Elvis' Gold Records, Volume 4 *"(You're the) Devil In Disguise"(3)*	[G]	RCA LSP-3921
1/25/69	8	14	● 36. **Elvis** NBC-TV special - Elvis' first live album	[TV-L]	RCA LPM-4088
6/14/69	13	15	● 37. From Elvis In Memphis first Memphis sessions since his 1955 Sun recordings *"In The Ghetto"(3)*		RCA LSP-4155
11/29/69	12	12	● 38. From Memphis To Vegas/From Vegas To Memphis record 1: Elvis in Person at the International Hotel, Las Vegas, Nevada; record 2: Elvis Back In Memphis (studio)	[L]	RCA LSP-6020 [2]
6/20/70	13	11	● 39. On Stage-February, 1970 recorded at the International Hotel, Las Vegas *"The Wonder Of You"(9)*	[L]	RCA LSP-4362
12/19/70	21	6	● 40. Elvis-That's The Way It Is 5 of 12 songs are live (Las Vegas)	[S-L]	RCA LSP-4445
1/30/71	12	10	● 41. Elvis Country ("I'm 10,000 Years Old")		RCA LSP-4460
6/26/71	33	5	42. Love Letters from Elvis all songs recorded in Nashville during June, 1970		RCA LSP-4530
7/15/72	11	18	● 43. Elvis As Recorded At Madison Square Garden the entire show of 6/10/72	[L]	RCA LSP-4776
11/25/72	22	11	44. Burning Love and hits from his movies, volume 2 featuring songs from 8 Elvis' films (1960-67) *"Burning Love"(2)*	[K]	RCA Camden 2595
3/10/73	1(1)	19	● 45. **Aloha from Hawaii via Satellite** RCA's first QuadraDisc - recorded on 1/14/73	[TV-L]	RCA VPSX-6089 [2]
8/10/74	33	4	46. Elvis Recorded Live On Stage In Memphis	[L]	RCA CPL-0606
7/30/77	3	17	▲ 47. **Moody Blue** recordings from 1974-77 (4 live; 6 recorded at Graceland)	[K-L]	RCA AFL-2428
10/29/77	5	7	▲ 48. **Elvis In Concert** record 1: from the CBS-TV Special record 2: from Elvis' final tour, June, 1977	[TV-L]	RCA APL-2587 [2]

DATE	POS	WKS	ARTIST—RECORD TITLE	LABEL & NO.
8/30/80	27	5	49. Elvis Aron Presley [K] 8 album boxed set: 1: An Early Live Performance/Monolog 2: An Early Benefit Performance 3: Collectors' Gold From The Movie Years 4: The TV Specials 5: The Las Vegas Years 6: Lost Singles 7: Elvis At The Piano/The Concert Years- Part 1 8: The Concert Years-Concluded	RCA CPL-3699 [8]
			BILLY PRESTON	
			Born on 9/9/46 in Houston. R&B vocalist, keyboardist. To Los Angeles at an early age. With Mahalia Jackson in 1956. Played piano in film "St. Louis Blues", 1958. Regular on "Shindig" TV show. Recorded with Beatles on "Get Back" and "Let It Be", worked Concert For Bangladesh, 1969. Prominent session man, played on Sly & The Family Stone hits. With Rolling Stones USA tour in 1975.	
7/01/72	32	8	1. I Wrote A Simple Song "Outa-Space"(2)	A&M 3507
6/30/73	32	6	2. Music Is My Life "Will It Go Round In Circles"(1)	A&M 3516
10/12/74	17	6	3. The Kids & Me "Nothing From Nothing"(1)	A&M 3645
			THE PRETENDERS	
			Rock quartet featuring American Chrissie Hynde (b: 9/7/51, Akron, Ohio), lead singer, songwriter, guitarist, and Englishmen James Honeyman-Scott, guitar (died on 6/16/82 - replaced by Robbie MacIntosh); Pete Farndon, bass (died on 4/14/83 - replaced in 1982 by Malcolm Foster); and Martin Chambers, drums. Numerous personnel changes since then. Chrissie married Jim Kerr of Simple Minds in 1984. Also see UB40.	
3/15/80	9	17	▲ 1. **Pretenders**	Sire 6083
5/02/81	27	4	2. Extended Play [M]	Sire 3563
8/29/81	10	9	3. **Pretenders II**	Sire 3572
2/04/84	5	22	▲ 4. **Learning To Crawl** "Back On The Chain Gang"(5)	Sire 23980
11/15/86	25	14	5. Get Close "Don't Get Me Wrong"(10)	Sire 25488
			ANDRE PREVIN	
			Pianist/conductor/arranger/composer born in Germany in 1929.	
6/29/59	16	21	1. Secret Songs For Young Lovers [I] with David Rose & His Orchestra "Like Young"	MGM 3716
7/04/60	25	15	2. Like Love [I]	Columbia 1437
			LEONTYNE PRICE	
			One of the great sopranos of opera.	
5/18/63	29	9	1. Giacomo Puccini: Madama Butterfly [F] with Richard Tucker (tenor), Rosalind Elias (mezzo-soprano), Philip Maero (baritone) & Erich Leinsdorf (conductor)	RCA 6160 [3]
			RAY PRICE	
			Country singer born on 1/12/26 in Perryville, Texas. Ray charted over 40 Top Ten hits on Billboard's Country charts.	
12/19/70	28	16	● 1. For The Good Times	Columbia 30106
			CHARLEY PRIDE	
			Born on 3/18/38 in Sledge, Mississippi. First black Country superstar. Charley's had 29 #1 hits on the Country charts.	
11/22/69	24	16	● 1. The Best Of Charley Pride [G]	RCA 4223
2/14/70	22	7	● 2. Just Plain Charley	RCA 4290

DATE	POS	WKS	ARTIST—RECORD TITLE	LABEL & NO.
9/12/70	30	2	● 3. Charley Pride's 10th Album	RCA 4367
1/15/72	38	2	● 4. Charley Pride Sings Heart Songs	RCA 4617
			"Kiss An Angel Good Mornin'"	

LOUIS PRIMA

Born on 12/7/11 in New Orleans; died on 8/24/78 in New Orleans. Durable jazz trumpeter-singer-composer-bandleader.

DATE	POS	WKS	ARTIST—RECORD TITLE	LABEL & NO.
1/16/61	9	11	1. **Wonderland By Night** [I]	Dot 25352

LOUIS PRIMA & KEELY SMITH

Husband and wife (divorced in 1962). Keely was born on 3/9/32 in Norfolk, VA; jazz-styled vocalist, first appeared with Prima in 1953. Back-up band: Sam Butera & The Witnesses.

DATE	POS	WKS	ARTIST—RECORD TITLE	LABEL & NO.
6/23/58	12	4	1. Las Vegas Prima Style [L]	Capitol 1010
5/25/59	37	2	2. Hey Boy! Hey Girl! [S]	Capitol 1160
			Louis & Keely portray Las Vegas entertainers in the film	

PRINCE

Born Prince Roger Nelson on 6/7/58 in Minneapolis. R&B vocalist, multi-instrumentalist, composer, producer, actor. Named for the Prince Roger Trio, led by his father. Self-taught musician - own band, Grand Central, in junior high school. Self-produced first album in 1978. Starred in films "Purple Rain", 1984, and "Under The Cherry Moon", 1986.

DATE	POS	WKS	ARTIST—RECORD TITLE	LABEL & NO.
12/15/79	22	10	▲ 1. Prince	Warner 3366
			"I Wanna Be Your Lover"	
11/14/81	21	5	▲ 2. Controversy	Warner 3601
11/27/82	9	56	▲ 3. **Prince **1999****	Warner 23720 [2]
			"Little Red Corvette"(6)	
			"Delirious"(8)	
7/14/84	1(24)	42	▲ 4. **Purple Rain** [S]	Warner 25110
			"When Doves Cry"(1)	
			"Let's Go Crazy"(1)	
			"Purple Rain"(2)	
			"I Would Die 4 U"(8)	
			"Take Me With U"	
			film is a semi-autobiographical story about Prince's career	
5/11/85	1(3)	27	▲ 5. **Around the World in a Day**	Paisley P. 25286
			"Raspberry Beret"(2)	
			"Pop Life"(7)	
4/19/86	3	17	▲ 6. **Parade** [S]	Paisley P. 25395
			music from the film "Under The Cherry Moon"	
			"Kiss"(1)	

PROCOL HARUM

British rock group led by Gary Brooker (vocals/piano) & Robin Trower (guitar, 1968-71).

DATE	POS	WKS	ARTIST—RECORD TITLE	LABEL & NO.
12/07/68	24	7	1. Shine On Brightly	A&M 4151
5/31/69	32	5	2. A Salty Dog	A&M 4179
8/01/70	34	6	3. Home	A&M 4261
5/22/71	32	5	4. Broken Barricades	A&M 4294
5/20/72	5	19	● 5. **Procol Harum Live In Concert with the Edmonton Symphony Orchestra** [L]	A&M 4335
			"Conquistador"	
4/21/73	21	7	6. Grand Hotel	Chrysalis 1037

DATE	POS	WKS	ARTIST—RECORD TITLE	LABEL & NO.
			DOROTHY PROVINE	
			Portrayed songstress Pinky Pinkham in the TV series "The Roaring Twenties".	
9/25/61	34	66	1. The Roaring 20's	Warner 1394
			medleys of 30 songs from the 20's	
			RICHARD PRYOR	
			Born in 1940 in Peoria, Illinois. Ribald comedian, actor. In films "Stir Crazy", "Silver Streak", "Superman III" and many others.	
10/19/74	29	8	● 1. That Nigger's Crazy [C]	Partee 2404
9/06/75	12	8	▲ 2. Is It Something I Said? [C]	Reprise 2227
10/23/76	22	7	● 3. Bicentennial Nigger [C]	Warner 2960
2/10/79	32	3	● 4. Wanted [C]	Warner 3364 [2]
5/01/82	21	7	5. Richard Pryor Live On The Sunset Strip [C-S]	Warner 3660
			filmed live at the Hollywood Palladium	
			GARY PUCKETT & THE UNION GAP	
			Formed in San Diego in 1967. Named after the town of Union Gap, WA. Consisted of Gary Puckett, vocals, guitar; Paul Whitebread, drums; Kerry Chater, bass; Dwight Bement, sax; and Gary Withem, keyboards.	
3/30/68	22	8	1. Woman, Woman	Columbia 9612
			"Woman, Woman"(4)	
6/29/68	21	11	● 2. Young Girl	Columbia 9664
			"Young Girl"(2)	
11/23/68	20	10	3. Incredible	Columbia 9715
			"Lady Willpower"(2)	
			"Over You"(7)	
			PURE PRAIRIE LEAGUE	
			Country-rock group formed in Cincinnati in 1971. Numerous personnel changes.	
6/21/75	24	6	1. Two Lane Highway	RCA 0933
6/21/75	34	6	● 2. Bustin' Out	RCA 4769
			"Amie"	
3/20/76	33	3	3. If The Shoe Fits	RCA 1247
7/12/80	37	3	4. Firin' Up	Casablanca 7212
			"Let Me Love You Tonight"(10)	
			BILL PURSELL	
			Pianist from Tulare, California. Appeared with the Nashville Symphony Orchestra. Taught musical composition at Vanderbilt University.	
4/13/63	28	6	1. Our Winter Love [I]	Columbia 1992
			arrangements by Bill Justis; orchestra directed by Grady Martin	
			"Our Winter Love"(9)	

DATE	POS	WKS	ARTIST—RECORD TITLE	LABEL & NO.

Q

QUARTERFLASH

Rock group from Portland, Oregon led by the husband-and-wife team of Marv and Rindy Ross. Originally known as Seafood Mama.

DATE	POS	WKS	ARTIST—RECORD TITLE	LABEL & NO.
12/12/81	8	21	▲ 1. **Quarterflash**	Geffen 2003
			"Harden My Heart"(3)	
8/06/83	34	4	2. Take Another Picture	Geffen 4011

SUZI QUATRO

Rock singer born on 6/3/50 in Detroit. Portrayed Leather Tuscadero on TV's "Happy Days" in 1977.

5/12/79	37	5	1. If You Knew Suzi...	RSO 3044
			"Stumblin' In"(4-with Chris Norman)	

QUEEN

Rock group formed in England in 1972. Consisted of Freddie Mercury, vocals; Brian May, guitar; John Deacon, bass; and Roger Taylor, drums. May and Taylor had been in the group Smile. Mercury had recorded as Larry Lurex. Wrote soundtrack for the film "Flash Gordon", 1980.

4/05/75	12	10	● 1. Sheer Heart Attack	Elektra 1026
			"Killer Queen"	
1/24/76	4	28	● 2. **A Night At The Opera**	Elektra 1053
			"Bohemian Rhapsody"(9)	
1/15/77	5	8	● 3. **A Day At The Races**	Elektra 101
			"Somebody To Love"	
12/03/77	3	21	▲ 4. **News Of The World**	Elektra 112
			"We Are The Champions"(4)	
			"We Will Rock You"	
12/09/78	6	11	▲ 5. **Jazz**	Elektra 166
7/14/79	16	7	● 6. Queen Live Killers [L]	Elektra 702 [2]
7/19/80	1(5)	31	▲ 7. **The Game**	Elektra 513
			"Crazy Little Thing Called Love"(1)	
			"Another One Bites The Dust"(1)	
1/10/81	23	7	8. Flash Gordon [S]	Elektra 518
11/14/81	14	13	▲ 9. Greatest Hits [G]	Elektra 564
6/05/82	22	5	● 10. Hot Space	Elektra 60128
3/24/84	23	9	● 11. The Works	Capitol 12322

QUICKSILVER MESSENGER SERVICE

San Francisco acid-rock group featuring John Cipollina (guitar) and David Freiberg (bass - joined Jefferson Starship in 1973). Many personnel changes.

4/26/69	27	6	1. Happy Trails [L]	Capitol 120
			includes several studio tracks	
2/07/70	25	5	2. Shady Grove	Capitol 391
9/05/70	27	8	3. Just For Love	Capitol 498
1/30/71	26	4	4. What About Me	Capitol 630
			Nicky Hopkins (piano) featured on above 3 albums	

DATE	POS	WKS	ARTIST—RECORD TITLE	LABEL & NO.
			QUIET RIOT	
			Heavy-metal rock quartet from Los Angeles: Kevin DuBrow, lead singer; Carlos Cavazo, guitar; Frankie Banoli, drums; Rudy Sarzo, bass (replaced by Chuck Wright, 1985). Dubrow left group, early 1987.	
7/16/83	**1(1)**	36	▲ 1. **Metal Health**	Pasha 38443
			"Cum On Feel The Noize"(5)	
8/11/84	**15**	10	▲ 2. Condition Critical	Pasha 39516
9/06/86	**31**	9	3. QR III	Pasha 40321
			CARMEL QUINN	
			Quinn sings favorites from her native country, Ireland.	
4/02/55	**4**	10	1. **Arthur Godfrey presents Carmel Quinn**	Columbia 629

R

DATE	POS	WKS	ARTIST—RECORD TITLE	LABEL & NO.
			EDDIE RABBITT	
			Born Edward Thomas on 11/27/44 in Brooklyn. Country singer, songwriter, guitarist. Raised in East Orange, NJ. First recorded for 20th Century, 1964. Moved to Nashville in 1968. Became established after Elvis Presley recorded his song "Kentucky Rain".	
9/27/80	**19**	15	▲ 1. Horizon	Elektra 276
			"Drivin' My Life Away"(5)	
			"I Love A Rainy Night"(1)	
9/12/81	**23**	8	● 2. Step By Step	Elektra 532
			"Step By Step"(5)	
1/22/83	**31**	7	3. Radio Romance	Elektra 60160
			"You And I"(7-with Crystal Gayle)	
			GERRY RAFFERTY	
			Born on 4/16/47 in Paisley, Scotland. Singer, songwriter, guitarist. Co-leader of Stealers Wheel.	
6/03/78	**1(1)**	23	▲ 1. **City to City**	United Art. 840
			"Baker Street"(2)	
6/23/79	**29**	6	● 2. Night Owl	United Art. 958
			RAIDERS - see PAUL REVERE	
			RAINBOW	
			Hard-rock band led by British guitarist Ritchie Blackmore and bassist Roger Glover, both members of Deep Purple. Group disbanded upon reformation of Deep Purple, 1984.	
10/04/75	**30**	4	1. Ritchie Blackmore's R-A-I-N-B-O-W	Oyster 6049
5/29/82	**30**	5	2. Straight Between The Eyes	Mercury 4041
10/29/83	**34**	4	3. Bent Out Of Shape	Mercury 815305
			BONNIE RAITT	
			Born on 11/8/49 in Burbank, CA. Blues-rock singer, guitarist. Daughter of Broadway's John Raitt.	
5/14/77	**25**	4	● 1. Sweet Forgiveness	Warner 2990
11/10/79	**30**	5	2. The Glow	Warner 3369
4/03/82	**38**	3	3. Green Light	Warner 3630

PRETENDERS

The Pretenders was the first (but not the last, thanks to Pet Shop Boys) band led by a onetime rock critic to record a platinum album. Ohio's Chrissie Hynde wrote for Britain's *New Musical Express* before forming the Pretenders with three nonjournalists in 1978.

Prince's own awesome musical achievements are evidently not enough as far as he's concerned. In addition to his own prodigious output of the past few years, Prince—using that name as well as Jamie Starr and Christopher—has written and produced material for the Time, the Bangles, Sheila E, Vanity 6, Apollonia, Jill Jones, Deborah Allen, Mazarati, and others.

Gary Puckett and the Union Gap, formed in California and garbed in Civil War uniforms, had an impressive string of four consecutive gold singles in 1967 and 1968, despite criticism that they were all essentially the same song.

Johnnie Ray was discovered by a local disc jockey in 1951 while performing in a Detroit nightclub. Ray had his first hit, 1951's "Cry," with a song written by an amateur composer who worked at a dry cleaner.

The Righteous Brothers, Bill Medley and Bobby Hatfield, first performed together at a 1962 high school prom in Anaheim, CA and cut its first album the following year. Notwithstanding its title, *This Is New!* (1965), this album of early material was released by the duo's first record company after it had switched to Phil Spector's Philles label, on which it made its classic hits.

Marty Robbins was discovered and signed to Columbia Records in 1951 while performing on a radio program in Phoenix, AZ. He dabbled in rockabilly, blues, and rock'n'roll (recording Arthur Crudup's "That's All Right" the same year Elvis Presley did) before settling into country music; he became a top-selling artist and a member of the Country Music Hall of Fame.

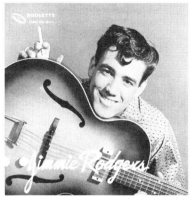

Jimmie Rodgers, not to be confused with the legendary country star of the same name who died in 1933, was a folk singer who had a number of hits in the late 1950s. Rodgers' career was almost aborted when he neglected to leave his address after auditioning for Roulette Records, who found and signed him six months later.

The Rolling Stones paid tribute of some sort to the Beatles on the three-dimensional cover of *Their Satanic Majesties Request* (1967) by burying tiny photos of the Fab Four amidst the flower arrangement.

The Rolling Stones' *Sticky Fingers* (1971) was the band's second No. 1 album, and the first album released on Rolling Stones Records. Although Andy Warhol, who was also responsible for creating the familiar lips and tongue logo, designed the controversial cover to include a working zipper, later editions of the record substituted an embossed imitation.

Sam the Sham and the Pharaohs came from Texas, where singer/organist Domingo Samudio was born and raised. The group wore pseudo-Arab garb and traveled in a hearse; its two biggest hits were "Wooly Bully" (1965), which more or less singlehandedly invented cheesy 1960s Tex-Mex organ rock, and "Li'l Red Riding Hood" (1966).

Boz Scaggs and Steve Miller played together as Dallas grade-school classmates, and later as college pals in Wisconsin. When Miller eventually headed to San Francisco, Scaggs went to Europe, subsequently rejoining his old friend's band for two 1968 albums.

Bob Seger made eight albums before striking it big with a live album that he recorded in Detroit in 1976 with backing by the Silver Bullet Band. *Stranger in Town* (1978) contains four hit singles: "Still the Same," "Hollywood Nights," "We've Got Tonite," and "Old Time Rock & Roll."

DATE	POS	WKS	ARTIST—RECORD TITLE	LABEL & NO.
			RAM JAM	
			East Coast rock quartet led by Bill Bartlett (lead guitarist of The Lemon Pipers). Member Howie Blauvelt played bass in Billy Joel's group The Hassles.	
10/15/77	34	4	1. Ram Jam	Epic 34885
			"Black Betty"	
			SID RAMIN	
			Conductor, arranger from Boston.	
5/25/63	34	4	1. New Thresholds in Sound [I]	RCA 2658
			BOOTS RANDOLPH	
			Born in Paducah, Kentucky. Premier Nashville session saxophonist.	
4/22/67	36	4	● 1. Boots with Strings [I]	Monument 18066
			RARE EARTH	
			Rock group from Detroit. Nucleus consisted of Gil Bridges, saxophone, flute; John Persh, trombone, bass; and Pete Rivera, drums. Worked as Sunliners, 1960's. Added Ed Guzman, percussion, 1970, and Ray Monette (replaced Rob Richards), guitar; Mark Olson replaced Kenneth James, keyboards, 1971. Many changes ensued.	
3/14/70	12	3	1. Get Ready	Rare Earth 507
			"Get Ready"(4)	
			side 2 is a 21-1/2 minute version of the title song	
7/18/70	15	18	2. Ecology	Rare Earth 514
			"(I Know) I'm Losing You"(7)	
8/14/71	28	11	3. One World	Rare Earth 520
			"I Just Want To Celebrate"(7)	
1/29/72	29	4	4. Rare Earth In Concert [L]	Rare Earth 534 [2]
			THE RASCALS	
			Blue-eyed soul/pop quartet formed in New York City in 1964. Consisted of Felix Cavaliere, Dino Danelli, Eddie Brigati and Gene Cornish. All except Danelli had been in Joey Dee's Starliters. Brigati and Cornish left in 1971, replaced by Robert Popwell, Buzzy Feiten and Ann Sutton. Group disbanded in 1972.	
			THE YOUNG RASCALS:	
6/11/66	15	14	● 1. The Young Rascals	Atlantic 8123
			"Good Lovin'"(1)	
3/18/67	14	24	● 2. Collections	Atlantic 8134
8/19/67	5	21	● 3. **Groovin'**	Atlantic 8148
			"Groovin'"(1)	
			"A Girl Like You"(10)	
			"How Can I Be Sure"(4)	
			RASCALS:	
3/09/68	9	12	4. **Once Upon A Dream**	Atlantic 8169
7/27/68	1(1)	32	● 5. **Time Peace/The Rascals' Greatest Hits** [G]	Atlantic 8190
			"A Beautiful Morning"(3)	
4/05/69	17	6	● 6. Freedom Suite	Atlantic 901 [2]
			record 2 entitled "Music Music" is all instrumental	
			"People Got To Be Free"(1)	

DATE	POS	WKS	ARTIST—RECORD TITLE	LABEL & NO.
			RASPBERRIES	
			Cleveland pop/rock quartet: Eric Carmen, lead singer, guitar; Wally Bryson, lead guitar; David Smalley, bass; Jim Bonfanti, drums. Smalley and Bonfanti replaced by Scott McCarl and Michael McBride, 1974. Carmen went solo, 1975.	
1/20/73	36	4	1. Fresh	Capitol 11123
			RATT	
			Hard-rock quintet from Los Angeles - Stephen Pearcy, lead singer.	
6/16/84	7	26	▲ 1. **Out Of The Cellar**	Atlantic 80143
6/29/85	7	18	▲ 2. **Invasion Of Your Privacy**	Atlantic 81257
11/01/86	26	7	▲ 3. Dancin' Undercover	Atlantic 81683
			LOU RAWLS	
			Born on 12/1/35 in Chicago. With the Pilgrim Travelers gospel group, 1957-59. Summer replacement TV show "Lou Rawls & The Golddiggers" in 1969. In films "Angel Angel, Down We Go" and "Believe In Me". Voice of many Budweiser beer ads.	
5/27/57	18	14	1. Too Much!	Capitol 2713
6/18/66	4	38	● 2. **Lou Rawls Live!** [L]	Capitol 2459
10/08/66	7	22	● 3. **Lou Rawls Soulin'**	Capitol 2566
3/04/67	20	10	4. Lou Rawls Carryin' On!	Capitol 2632
9/09/67	29	2	5. That's Lou	Capitol 2756
7/31/76	7	12	▲ 6. **All Things In Time**	Phil. Int. 33957
			"You'll Never Find Another Love Like Mine"(2)	
			RAY, GOODMAN & BROWN	
			Soul group consisting of Harry Ray, tenor; Al Goodman, bass; and Billy Brown, falsetto. Formerly known as The Moments.	
3/01/80	17	11	● 1. Ray, Goodman & Brown	Polydor 6240
			"Special Lady"(5)	
			JOHNNIE RAY	
			Born on 1/10/27 in Dallas, Oregon. Has worn hearing aid since age 14. First recorded for Okeh in 1951. Famous for emotion-packed delivery, with R&B influences. Appeared in three films. Active into the 1980s. Now lives in Hollywood.	
3/02/57	19	2	1. The Big Beat	Columbia 961
			RAYDIO - see RAY PARKER JR.	
			READY FOR THE WORLD	
			Black sextet - Melvin Riley, Jr., lead singer.	
8/31/85	17	30	▲ 1. Ready For The World	MCA 5594
			"Oh Sheila"(1)	
			LEON REDBONE	
			Mysterious performer of 1920s and 1930s blues and ragtime.	
2/26/77	38	4	1. Double Time	Warner 2971
			OTIS REDDING	
			Born on 9/9/41 in Dawson, GA. Killed in a plane crash in Lake Monona in Madison, WI on 12/10/67. Soul singer, songwriter, producer, pianist. First recorded with Johnny Jenkins & The Pinetoppers on Confederate in 1960. Own label, Jotis. Plane crash also killed four members of the Bar-Kays.	
7/22/67	36	3	1. King & Queen	Stax 716

DATE	POS	WKS	ARTIST—RECORD TITLE	LABEL & NO.
			OTIS REDDING/CARLA THOMAS	
9/09/67	32	4	2. Otis Redding Live In Europe　　　　[L]	Volt 416
1/27/68	9	19	3. **History Of Otis Redding**　　　　[G]	Volt 418
3/30/68	4	20	4. **The Dock Of The Bay**	Volt 419
			"(Sittin' On) The Dock Of The Bay"(1)	
9/26/70	16	8	● 5. Monterey International Pop Festival　　　　[S-L]	Reprise 2029
			OTIS REDDING/THE JIMI HENDRIX EXPERIENCE	
			recorded June, 1967 & featured in film "Monterey Pop"	
			HELEN REDDY	
			Born on 10/25/42 in Melbourne, Australia. Family was in show business. Helen made stage debut at age four. Own TV series, early 1960's. Migrated to New York in 1966. Married Jeff Wald, agent with William Morris talent agency. To Los Angeles in 1968.	
1/06/73	14	17	● 1. I Am Woman	Capitol 11068
			"I Am Woman"(1)	
8/25/73	8	15	● 2. **Long Hard Climb**	Capitol 11213
			"Delta Dawn"(1)	
			"Leave Me Alone (Ruby Red Dress)"(3)	
5/04/74	11	14	● 3. Love Song For Jeffrey	Capitol 11284
			"You And Me Against The World"(9)	
11/23/74	8	16	● 4. **Free And Easy**	Capitol 11348
			"Angie Baby"(1)	
8/09/75	11	10	● 5. No Way To Treat A Lady	Capitol 11418
			"Ain't No Way To Treat A Lady"(8)	
12/20/75	5	11	● 6. **Helen Reddy's Greatest Hits**　　　[G]	Capitol 11467
8/14/76	16	8	● 7. Music, Music	Capitol 11547
			LOU REED	
			Born Louis Firbank on 3/2/44 in the New York City area. Lead singer, composer of New York seminal rock band, the Velvet Underground.	
3/24/73	29	9	1. Transformer	RCA 4807
			produced by David Bowie	
			"Walk On The Wild Side"	
10/19/74	10	7	2. **Sally Can't Dance**	RCA 0611
			DELLA REESE	
			Born Delloreese Patricia Early on 7/6/31 in Detroit. With Mahalia Jackson troupe, 1945-49, Erskine Hawkins, early 1950s. Solo since 1957. Great actress/singer on many TV shows. Own series "Della", 1970. Della Rogers of TV series "Chico & The Man", 1976-78. Film "Let's Rock", 1958.	
3/07/60	35	2	1. Della	RCA 2157
			JIM REEVES	
			Born on 8/20/24 in Panola County, Texas. Killed in a plane crash on 7/31/64 in Nashville. Aspirations of professional baseball career cut short by ankle injury. Deejay at KWKH, Shreveport, LA, home of the "Louisiana Hayride", early 1950s. First recorded for Macy's in 1950. Joined "Hayride" cast following first country hit "Mexican Joe" in 1953. Joined Grand Ole Opry in 1955. Own ABC-TV series in 1957. Film "Kimberley Jim", 1963. Posthumously, he continued to have many Top 10 Country hits through 1980.	
5/23/60	18	26	1. He'll Have To Go	RCA 2223
			"He'll Have To Go"(2)	
9/05/64	30	2	2. Moonlight and Roses	RCA 2854

DATE	POS	WKS	ARTIST—RECORD TITLE		LABEL & NO.
9/19/64	9	18	● 3. **The Best Of Jim Reeves**	[G]	RCA 2890
7/16/66	21	10	● 4. Distant Drums	[K]	RCA 3542
			R.E.M.		
			Athens, Georgia rock quartet: Michael Stipe, Pete Buck, Mike Mills and Bill Berry.		
7/30/83	36	3	1. Murmur		I.R.S. 70604
5/26/84	27	6	2. Reckoning		I.R.S. 70044
7/06/85	28	14	3. Fables Of The Reconstruction		I.R.S. 5592
9/06/86	21	12	● 4. Lifes Rich Pageant		I.R.S. 5783
			REO SPEEDWAGON		
			Rock quintet from Champaign, IL: Kevin Cronin (lead vocals, rhythm guitar), Gary Richrath (lead guitar), Neal Doughty (keyboards), Bruce Hall (bass) and Alan Gratzer (drums). Name taken from a 1911 fire truck.		
6/03/78	29	5	▲ 1. You can Tune a piano, but you can't Tuna fish		Epic 35082
9/08/79	33	5	● 2. Nine Lives		Epic 35988
12/27/80	1(15)	50	▲ 3. **Hi Infidelity**		Epic 36844
			"Keep On Loving You"(1)		
			"Take It On The Run"(5)		
7/10/82	7	16	▲ 4. **Good Trouble**		Epic 38100
			"Keep The Fire Burnin'"(7)		
2/02/85	7	21	5. **Wheels are turnin'**		Epic 39593
			"Can't Fight This Feeling"(1)		
			RETURN TO FOREVER		
			Jazz/rock band: Chick Corea (keyboards), Stanley Clarke (bass), Lenny White (drums), Al Di Meola (guitar).		
11/23/74	32	4	1. Where Have I Known You Before	[I]	Polydor 6509
4/05/75	39	2	2. No Mystery	[I]	Polydor 6512
5/22/76	35	3	3. Romantic Warrior	[I]	Columbia 34076
5/14/77	38	2	4. Musicmagic		Columbia 34682
			PAUL REVERE & THE RAIDERS		
			Pop/rock group formed in Portland in 1960. Band formed around Paul Revere (keyboards) and Mark Lindsay (lead singer). To Los Angeles in 1965. On daily ABC-TV show "Where The Action Is" in 1965. Group had many personnel changes throughout their career.		
3/12/66	5	19	● 1. **Just Like Us!**		Columbia 9251
7/02/66	9	15	● 2. **Midnight Ride**		Columbia 9308
			"Kicks"(4)		
1/14/67	9	17	● 3. **The Spirit Of '67**		Columbia 9395
			"Hungry"(6)		
			"Good Thing"(4)		
5/27/67	15	19	● 4. Greatest Hits	[G]	Columbia 9462
9/23/67	25	7	5. Revolution!		Columbia 9521
			"Him or Me-What's It Gonna Be?"(5)		
			Freddy Weller joins group as lead guitarist		
			RAIDERS:		
7/03/71	19	11	6. Indian Reservation		Columbia 30768
			"Indian Reservation"(1)		

DATE	POS	WKS	ARTIST—RECORD TITLE	LABEL & NO.
			DEBBIE REYNOLDS	
			Born Mary Reynolds on 4/1/32 in El Paso, TX. Leading lady of 50s musicals, and later in comedies. Married Eddie Fisher on 9/26/55; divorced by 1959. Mother of actress Carrie Fisher.	
6/11/66	23	4	1. The Singing Nun　　　　　　　　　　　　　[S]	MGM 7
			film is a fictionalized story about Soeur Sourire	
			ROBERT RHEIMS	
1/05/59	25	1	1. Merry Christmas in Carols　　　　　　　[X-I]	Rheims 6006
1/04/60	39	1	2. We Wish You A Merry Christmas　　　　　[X]	Rheims 6008
			EMITT RHODES	
			Lead singer of Merry-Go-Round.	
1/09/71	29	7	1. Emitt Rhodes	Dunhill 50089
			"Fresh As A Daisy"	
			RHYTHM HERITAGE	
			Los Angeles studio group assembled by producers Steve Barri and Michael Omartian.	
4/24/76	40	2	1. Disco-Fied　　　　　　　　　　　　　　[I]	ABC 934
			"Theme From S.W.A.T."(1)	
			CHARLIE RICH	
			Born on 12/14/32 in Colt, Arkansas. Rockabilly/country singer, pianist, songwriter. First played jazz and blues. Own jazz group, the Velvetones, mid-1950s, while in US Air Force. Session work with Sun Records in 1958.	
12/08/73	8	32	▲　1. **Behind Closed Doors**	Epic 32247
			"The Most Beautiful Girl"(1)	
3/30/74	36	2	●　2. There Won't Be Anymore　　　　　　[E]	RCA 0433
4/06/74	24	11	●　3. Very Special Love Songs	Epic 32531
12/28/74	25	9	4. The Silver Fox	Epic 33250
			LIONEL RICHIE	
			Born on 6/20/49 in Tuskegee, Alabama. Grew up on the campus of Tuskegee Institute where his grandfather worked. Former lead singer of the Commodores. Appeared in the film "Thank God It's Friday".	
10/30/82	3	38	▲　1. **Lionel Richie**	Motown 6007
			"Truly"(1)"You Are"(4)	
			"My Love"(5)	
11/12/83	1(3)	78	▲　2. **Can't Slow Down**	Motown 6059
			"All Night Long (All Night)"(1)	
			"Running With The Night"(7)	
			"Hello"(1)	
			"Stuck On You"(3)	
			"Penny Lover"(8)	
8/30/86	1(2)	38	▲　3. **Dancing On The Ceiling**	Motown 6158
			"Dancing On The Ceiling"(2)	
			"Love Will Conquer All"(9)	
			"Ballerina Girl"(7)	

DATE	POS	WKS	ARTIST—RECORD TITLE	LABEL & NO.
			SVIATOSLAV RICHTER	
			Classical pianist from Russia.	
12/12/60	5	20	1. **Brahms: Piano Concerto No. 2** [I]	RCA 2466
			with the Chicago Symphony Orchestra; Erich Leinsdorf, conducting	
			NELSON RIDDLE	
			Born on 6/1/21 in Oradell, NJ; died on 10/6/85. Trombonist-arranger with Charlie Spivak and Tommy Dorsey in the 40s. One of the most in-demand of all arranger-conductors for many top artists, including Frank Sinatra (several classic 50s albums), Nat King Cole, Ella Mae Morse, and, more recently, Linda Ronstadt; also arranger and musical director for many films.	
5/27/57	20	1	1. Hey…Let Yourself Go! [I]	Capitol 814
2/17/58	20	1	2. C'mon…Get Happy! [I]	Capitol 893
			THE RIGHTEOUS BROTHERS	
			Blue-eyed soul duo: Bill Medley (b: 9/19/40, Santa Ana, CA), baritone; and Bobby Hatfield (b: 8/10/40, Beaver Dam, WI), tenor. Both sang in local Los Angeles groups, formed duo in 1962. First recorded as the Paramours for Smash in 1962. On "Hullaballoo" and "Shindig" TV shows. Split up, 1968-74, Medley went solo, replaced by Billy Walker, then rejoined Hatfield in 1974.	
2/06/65	4	19	1. **You've Lost That Lovin' Feelin'**	Philles 4007
			"You've Lost That Lovin' Feelin'"(1)	
2/06/65	11	9	2. Right Now! [E]	Moonglow 1001
2/06/65	14	10	3. Some Blue-Eyed Soul [E]	Moonglow 1002
7/17/65	9	18	4. **Just Once In My Life…**	Philles 4008
			"Just Once In My Life"(9)	
			"Unchained Melody"(4)	
8/07/65	39	1	5. This Is New! [E]	Moonglow 1003
2/05/66	16	11	6. Back To Back	Philles 4009
			"Ebb Tide"(5)	
5/07/66	7	19	● 7. **Soul & Inspiration**	Verve 5001
			"(You're My) Soul And Inspiration"(1)	
10/15/66	32	6	8. Go Ahead And Cry	Verve 5004
11/11/67	21	5	● 9. Greatest Hits [G]	Verve 5020
			Philles and Moonglow label hits	
9/28/74	27	8	10. Give It To The People	Haven 9201
			"Rock And Roll Heaven"(3)	
			JEANNIE C. RILEY	
			Born Jeannie Carolyn Stephenson on 10/19/45 in Anson, Texas. Country singer.	
11/02/68	12	12	● 1. Harper Valley P.T.A.	Plantation 1
			all songs about characters mentioned in the title song	
			"Harper Valley P.T.A."(1)	
			MINNIE RIPERTON	
			Born on 11/8/47 in Chicago; died of cancer on 7/12/79 in Los Angeles. Recorded as "Andrea Davis" on Chess in 1966. In Rotary Connection, 1967-70. In Stevie Wonder's backup group, Wonderlove, in 1973.	
10/26/74	4	18	● 1. **Perfect Angel**	Epic 32561
			"Lovin' You"(1)	
6/14/75	18	8	2. Adventures In Paradise	Epic 33454

DATE	POS	WKS	ARTIST—RECORD TITLE	LABEL & NO.
8/25/79	29	4	3. Minnie	Capitol 11936
9/27/80	35	4	4. Love Lives Forever	Capitol 12097
			recordings from 1978 with new accompaniment	
			CYRIL RITCHARD	
			British actor.	
1/09/61	19	8	1. Alice In Wonderland: The Mad Tea Party/The Lobster Quandrille　　　　[T]	Riverside 1406
			Cyril reads (and sings) selections from the classic story	
			THE RITCHIE FAMILY	
			Philadelphia disco group named for arranger/producer Ritchie Rome. Group featured various session singers and musicians.	
10/02/76	30	7	1. Arabian Nights	Marlin 2201
			LEE RITENOUR	
			Born on 1/11/52 in Los Angeles. Guitarist, composer, arranger. Top session guitarist, has appeared on more than 200 albums. Nicknamed "Captain Fingers".	
6/13/81	26	7	1. "Rit"	Elektra 331
			"Is It You"	
			JOAN RIVERS	
			Popular comedienne. Former host of "The Late Show", 1986-87.	
5/14/83	22	6	1. What Becomes A Semi-Legend Most?　　[C]	Geffen 4007
			JOHNNY RIVERS	
			Born John Ramistella on 11/7/42 in New York City; raised in Baton Rouge. Rock and roll singer, guitarist, composer, producer. Recorded with the Spades for Suede in 1956. Named Johnny Rivers by deejay Alan Freed in 1958. To Los Angeles in 1961. Own Soul City label, 1966.	
7/11/64	12	20	1. Johnny Rivers At The Whisky a Go Go　　[L]	Imperial 12264
			"Memphis"(2)	
12/12/64	38	1	2. Here We a Go Go Again!　　[L]	Imperial 12274
7/31/65	21	6	3. Meanwhile Back At The Whisky a Go Go [L　[L]	Imperial 12284
			"Seventh Son"(7)	
2/05/66	33	5	4. Changes	Imperial 12334
			"Poor Side Of Town"(1)	
11/05/66	29	9	● 5. Johnny Rivers' Golden Hits　　[G]	Imperial 12324
7/08/67	14	8	6. Rewind	Imperial 12341
			"Baby I Need Your Lovin'"(3)	
			"The Tracks Of My Tears"(10)	
7/27/68	5	16	● 7. **Realization**	Imperial 12372
			"Summer Rain"	
7/12/69	26	10	● 8. A Touch Of Gold　　[G]	Imperial 12427
			MARTY ROBBINS	
			Born Martin Robinson on 9/26/25 in Glendale, Arizona; died of a heart attack on 12/8/82. Country singer, guitarist, composer. Own radio show with K-Bar Cowboys, late 1940s. Own TV show, "Western Caravan", KPHO-Phoenix, 1951. First recorded for Columbia in 1952. Regular on Grand Ole Opry since 1953. Had own label, Robbins, 1958. Stock car racer. Films "Road To Nashville" and "Guns Of A Stranger".	
12/28/59	6	1	▲　1. **Gunfighter Ballads and Trail Songs**	Columbia 1349
			"El Paso"(1)	

DATE	POS	WKS	ARTIST—RECORD TITLE	LABEL & NO.
1/09/61	21	12	2. More Gunfighter Ballads and Trail Songs	Columbia 1481
1/12/63	35	1	3. Devil Woman	Columbia 1918

SMOKEY ROBINSON

Born William Robinson on 2/19/40 in Detroit. Formed The Miracles (then called the Matadors) at Northern High School in 1955. First recorded for End in 1958. Married Miracles' member Claudette Rogers in 1963. Left Miracles on 1/29/72. Wrote dozens of hit songs for Motown artists. Vice President of Motown Records.

DATE	POS	WKS	ARTIST—RECORD TITLE	LABEL & NO.
6/14/75	36	3	1. A Quiet Storm	Tamla 337
1/05/80	17	11	2. Where There's Smoke..	Tamla 366
			"Cruisin'"(4)	
4/05/80	14	12	3. Warm Thoughts	Tamla 367
4/04/81	10	17	● 4. **Being With You**	Tamla 375
			"Being With You"(2)	
3/13/82	33	4	5. Yes It's You Lady	Tamla 6001

ROCKPILE

British pop/rock quartet: Dave Edmunds, Nick Lowe, Billy Bremner, Terry Williams.

DATE	POS	WKS	ARTIST—RECORD TITLE	LABEL & NO.
11/29/80	27	10	1. Seconds Of Pleasure	Columbia 36886
			includes a 7" EP of Edmunds & Lowe singing 4 Everly Brothers' tunes	

ROCKWELL

Born Kennedy Gordy on 3/15/64 in Detroit. Son of Motown chairman, Berry Gordy, Jr.

DATE	POS	WKS	ARTIST—RECORD TITLE	LABEL & NO.
3/03/84	15	12	● 1. Somebody's Watching Me	Motown 6052
			"Somebody's Watching Me"(2)	

JIMMIE RODGERS

Born on 9/18/33 in Camas, Washington. Vocalist, guitarist, pianist. Formed first group while in the Air Force. Own NBC-TV variety series in 1959. Career hampered following mysterious assault in Los Angeles on 12/1/67, which left him with a fractured skull. Returned to performing on 1/28/69.

DATE	POS	WKS	ARTIST—RECORD TITLE	LABEL & NO.
12/16/57	15	3	1. Jimmie Rodgers	Roulette 25020
			"Honeycomb"(1)	
			"Kisses Sweeter Than Wine"(3)	

TOMMY ROE

Born on 5/9/42 in Atlanta. Pop/rock singer, guitarist, composer. Formed band, The Satins, at Brown High School, worked local dances, late 1950s. Group recorded for Judd in 1960. Moved to Britain, mid-1960s, returned in 1969.

DATE	POS	WKS	ARTIST—RECORD TITLE	LABEL & NO.
4/26/69	25	8	1. Dizzy	ABC 683
			"Dizzy"(1)	
1/17/70	21	13	2. 12 In A Roe/A Collection of Tommy Roe's Greatest Hits [G]	ABC 700
			"Jam Up Jelly Tight"(8)	

ROGER

Roger Troutman from Hamilton, Ohio. Leader of family group Zapp.

DATE	POS	WKS	ARTIST—RECORD TITLE	LABEL & NO.
10/24/81	26	6	● 1. The Many Facets Of Roger	Warner 3594

ERIC ROGERS

DATE	POS	WKS	ARTIST—RECORD TITLE	LABEL & NO.
12/04/61	37	3	1. The Percussive Twenties [I]	London P. 4 44006

DATE	POS	WKS	ARTIST—RECORD TITLE	LABEL & NO.
			KENNY ROGERS	
			Born on 8/21/38 in Houston. With high school band, the Scholars in 1958. Bass player of jazz group, the Bobby Doyle Trio, recorded for Columbia. In Kirby Stone Four and The New Christy Minstrels, mid-1960s. Formed The First Edition in 1967. Went solo in 1973. Starred in films "The Gambler", "Coward Of The County" and "Six Pack". Also see Dottie West.	
6/11/77	30	4	● 1. Kenny Rogers	United Art. 689
			"Lucille"(5)	
9/24/77	39	2	● 2. Daytime Friends	United Art. 754
3/18/78	33	4	▲ 3. Ten Years Of Gold [G]	United Art. 835
			side 1: new versions of his First Edition hits	
2/24/79	12	21	▲ 4. The Gambler	United Art. 934
			"She Believes In Me"(5)	
10/06/79	5	26	▲ 5. **Kenny**	United Art. 979
			"You Decorated My Life"(7)	
			"Coward Of The County"(3)	
4/26/80	12	11	▲ 6. Gideon	United Art. 1035
			"Don't Fall In Love With A Dreamer"(4-with Kim Carnes)	
10/18/80	1(2)	36	▲ 7. **Kenny Rogers' Greatest Hits** [G]	Liberty 1072
			"Lady"(1)	
7/11/81	6	13	▲ 8. **Share Your Love**	Liberty 1108
			album produced by Lionel Richie	
			"I Don't Need You"(3)	
12/26/81	34	3	▲ 9. Christmas [X]	Liberty 51115
8/14/82	34	7	● 10. Love Will Turn You Around	Liberty 51124
3/12/83	18	12	● 11. We've Got Tonight	Liberty 51143
			"We've Got Tonight"(6-with Sheena Easton)	
10/01/83	6	24	▲ 12. **Eyes That See In The Dark**	RCA 4697
			album produced by Barry Gibb	
			"Islands In The Stream"(1-with Dolly Parton)	
11/26/83	22	11	▲ 13. Twenty Greatest Hits [G]	Liberty 51152
10/13/84	31	8	▲ 14. What About Me?	RCA 5043
12/22/84	31	4	▲ 15. Once Upon A Christmas [X]	RCA 5307
			KENNY ROGERS & DOLLY PARTON	
			KENNY ROGERS & THE FIRST EDITION	
			Original lineup: Kenny Rogers, Thelma Camacho, Mike Settle, Terry Williams and Mickey Jones. All but Jones were members of The New Christy Minstrels. Hosted own syndicated TV variety show, "Rollin", in 1972. Officially disbanded in 1975.	
			THE FIRST EDITION:	
5/02/70	26	6	1. Something's Burning	Reprise 6385
			THE ROLLING STONES	
			British R&B influenced rock group formed in London in January, 1963. Consisted of Mick Jagger (b: 7/26/43), vocals; Keith Richards (b: 12/18/43), lead guitar; Brian Jones (b: 2/28/42), guitar; Bill Wyman (b: 10/24/36), bass; and Charlie Watts (b: 6/2/41), drums. Jagger was the lead singer of Blues, Inc. Took name from a Muddy Waters' song. Promoted as the 'bad boys' in contrast to The Beatles. First UK tour, with Ronettes in 1964. Jones left group shortly before	

DATE	POS	WKS	ARTIST—RECORD TITLE	LABEL & NO.
			drowning on 7/3/69. Replaced by Mick Taylor (b: 1/17/48). Taylor replaced by Ron Wood, 1975. Film "Gimme Shelter", a documentary of their controversial Altamont concert on 12/6/69. Considered by many as the world's greatest rock band of all-time.	
7/25/64	**11**	12	1. England's Newest Hit Makers/The Rolling Stones	London 375
			"Not Fade Away"/"Tell Me"	
11/28/64	3	20	2. **12 x 5**	London 402
			"Time Is On My Side"(6)	
			"It's All Over Now"	
4/10/65	5	29	3. **The Rolling Stones, Now!**	London 420
			"Heart Of Stone"	
8/14/65	**1**(3)	35	● 4. **Out Of Our Heads**	London 429
			"The Last Time"(9)	
			"(I Can't Get No) Satisfaction"(1)	
12/18/65	4	22	● 5. **December's Children (and everybody's)**	London 451
			"Get Off Of My Cloud"(1)	
			"As Tears Go By"(6)	
4/23/66	3	35	● 6. **Big Hits (High Tide And Green Grass)** [G]	London 1
			"19th Nervous Breakdown"(2)	
7/16/66	**2**(2)	26	● 7. **Aftermath**	London 476
			"Paint It, Black"(1)	
12/31/66	6	11	● 8. **got Live if you want it!** [L]	London 493
			recorded at the Royal Albert Hall, London	
2/25/67	**2**(4)	19	● 9. **Between The Buttons**	London 499
			"Ruby Tuesday"(1)	
			"Let's Spend The Night Together"	
7/29/67	3	18	● 10. **Flowers** [G]	London 509
			"Mothers Little Helper"(8)	
			"Have You Seen Your Mother, Baby, Standing In The Shadow?"(9)	
12/23/67	**2**(6)	13	● 11. **Their Satanic Majesties Request**	London 2
12/21/68	5	13	● 12. **Beggars Banquet**	London 539
9/20/69	**2**(2)	16	● 13. **Through The Past, Darkly (Big Hits Vol. 2)** [G]	London 3
			"Jumpin' Jack Flash"(3)	
			"Honky Tonk Women"(1)	
12/13/69	3	19	● 14. **Let It Bleed**	London 4
			Brian Jones' last appearance/Mick Taylor's first with band	
10/17/70	6	10	● 15. **'Get Yer Ya-Ya's Out!'** [L]	London 5
			recorded at New York's Madison Square Garden, November, 1969	
5/15/71	**1**(4)	26	● 16. **Sticky Fingers**	Rolling S. 59100
			"Brown Sugar"(1)	
1/08/72	4	30	● 17. **Hot Rocks 1964-1971** [G]	London 606/7 [2]
6/10/72	**1**(4)	17	● 18. **Exile On Main St.**	Rolling S. 2900 [2]
			"Tumbling Dice"(7)	
1/20/73	9	12	● 19. **More Hot Rocks (big hits & fazed cookies)** [G]	London 626/7 [2]
9/29/73	**1**(4)	19	● 20. **Goats Head Soup**	Rolling S. 59101
			"Angie"(1)	
11/09/74	**1**(1)	11	● 21. **It's Only Rock 'N Roll**	Rolling S. 79101
6/21/75	8	8	22. **Metamorphosis** [K]	Abkco 1

DATE	POS	WKS	ARTIST—RECORD TITLE	LABEL & NO.
6/28/75	6	9	● 23. **Made In The Shade** [G]	Rolling S. 79102
5/08/76	1(4)	14	▲ 24. **Black And Blue**	Rolling S. 79104
			Ron Wood's first appearance with band	
			"Fool To Cry"(10)	
10/15/77	5	7	● 25. **Love You Live** [L]	Rolling S. 9001 [2]
6/24/78	1(2)	32	▲ 26. **Some Girls**	Rolling S. 39108
			"Miss You"(1)	
			"Beast Of Burden"(8)	
7/19/80	1(7)	20	▲ 27. **Emotional Rescue**	Rolling S. 16015
			"Emotional Rescue"(3)	
4/04/81	15	5	● 28. **Sucking In The Seventies** [G]	Rolling S. 16028
9/12/81	1(9)	30	▲ 29. **Tattoo You**	Rolling S. 16052
			"Start Me Up"(2)	
7/03/82	5	10	● 30. **"Still Life" (American Concert 1981)** [L]	Rolling S. 39113
11/26/83	4	12	▲ 31. **Undercover**	Rolling S. 90120
			"Undercover Of The Night"(9)	
4/12/86	4	15	▲ 32. **Dirty Work**	Rolling S. 40250
			"Harlem Shuffle"(5)	

THE ROMANTICS

Rock quartet from Detroit. Wally Palmar, lead singer.

DATE	POS	WKS	ARTIST—RECORD TITLE	LABEL & NO.
12/17/83	14	15	● 1. In Heat	Nemperor 38880
			"Talking In Your Sleep"(3)	

LINDA RONSTADT

Born on 7/15/46 in Tucson, Arizona. While in high school formed folk trio, The Three Ronstadts (with sister and brother). To Los Angeles in 1964. Formed the Stone Poneys with Bobby Kimmel (guitar) and Ken Edwards (keyboards); recorded for Sidewalk in 1965. Went solo in 1968. In 1971 formed backing band with Glenn Frey, Don Henley, Randy Meisner and Bernie Leadon (later became the Eagles). In "Pirates Of Penzance" operetta in New York City, 1980, also in film of same name in 1983.

DATE	POS	WKS	ARTIST—RECORD TITLE	LABEL & NO.
12/14/74	1(1)	19	● 1. **Heart Like A Wheel**	Capitol 11358
			"You're No Good"(1)	
			"When Will I Be Loved"(2)	
10/11/75	4	10	● 2. **Prisoner In Disguise**	Asylum 1045
			"Heat Wave"(5)	
9/04/76	3	15	▲ 3. **Hasten Down The Wind**	Asylum 1072
			"That'll Be The Day"	
12/18/76	6	15	▲ 4. **Greatest Hits** [G]	Asylum 1092
			includes her hits on Capitol	
10/01/77	1(5)	23	▲ 5. **Simple Dreams**	Asylum 104
			"Blue Bayou"(3)	
			"It's So Easy"(5)	
10/07/78	1(1)	16	▲ 6. **Living In The USA**	Asylum 155
			"Ooh Baby Baby"(7)	
3/15/80	3	17	▲ 7. **Mad Love**	Asylum 510
			"How Do I Make You"(10)	
			"Hurt So Bad"(8)	
11/15/80	26	10	● 8. Greatest Hits, Volume Two [G]	Asylum 516
10/30/82	31	6	● 9. Get Closer	Asylum 60185

DATE	POS	WKS	ARTIST—RECORD TITLE	LABEL & NO.
10/08/83	3	25	▲ 10. **What's New**	Asylum 60260
12/15/84	13	11	▲ 11. Lush Life	Asylum 60387
			above 2 arranged and conducted by Nelson Riddle	
			THE ROOFTOP SINGERS	
			Folk trio: Erik Darling, Willard Svanoe and Lynne Taylor (d: 1982). Disbanded in 1967. Darling was a member of The Tarriers in 1956, and The Weavers, 1958-62. Taylor was a vocalist with Benny Goodman.	
3/02/63	15	7	1. Walk Right In!	Vanguard 9123
			"Walk Right In"(1)	
			EDMUNDO ROS	
			London-based bandleader. Native of Caracas, Venezuela.	
5/25/59	28	2	1. Hollywood Cha Cha Cha [I]	London 152
9/22/62	31	5	2. Dance Again [I]	London P. 4 44015
			ROSE ROYCE	
			Eight-member backing band formed in Los Angeles, early 70s. Backed Edwin Starr as Total Concept Unlimited in 1973. Backed The Temptations, became regular band for Undisputed Truth. Lead vocalist Gwen Dickey added, name changed to Rose Royce in 1976. Did soundtrack for the film "Car Wash".	
12/18/76	14	13	● 1. Car Wash [S]	MCA 6000 [2]
			"Car Wash"(1)	
			"I Wanna Get Next To You"(10)	
9/17/77	9	14	▲ 2. **Rose Royce II/In Full Bloom**	Whitfield 3074
9/23/78	28	6	● 3. Rose Royce III/Strikes Again!	Whitfield 3227
			DAVID ROSE	
			Born on 6/15/10 in London, England; moved to Chicago at an early age. Conductor, composer, arranger for numerous films and TV series. TV series included "The Red Skelton Show", "Bonanza" and "Little House On The Prairie". Married briefly to Martha Raye and Judy Garland.	
7/07/62	3	28	● 1. **The Stripper and other fun Songs for the family** [I]	MGM 4062
			"The Stripper"(1)	
			DIANA ROSS	
			Born Diane Earle on 3/26/44 in Detroit. In vocal group, the Primettes, first recorded for LuPine in 1960. Lead singer of The Supremes, 1961-69. Went solo in late 1969. Oscar nominee for the film "Lady Sings The Blues", 1971. In films "Mahogany" and "The Wiz". Also see The Supremes.	
7/18/70	19	18	1. Diana Ross	Motown 711
			"Ain't No Mountain High Enough"(1)	
12/23/72	1(2)	24	2. **Lady Sings The Blues** [S]	Motown 758 [2]
			Diana portrayed Billie Holiday in the film	
7/28/73	5	15	3. **Touch Me In The Morning**	Motown 772
			"Touch Me In The Morning"(1)	
12/08/73	26	5	4. Diana & Marvin	Motown 803
			DIANA ROSS & MARVIN GAYE	
12/13/75	19	10	5. Mahogany [S-I]	Motown 858
			Diana sings only the title song - instrumentals conducted by Lee Holdridge	
			"Theme From Mahogany (Do You Know Where You're Going To)"(1)	

DATE	POS	WKS	ARTIST—RECORD TITLE	LABEL & NO.
3/27/76	5	18	6. **Diana Ross**	Motown 861
			"Love Hangover"(1) - also includes "Theme From Mahogany"	
8/14/76	13	14	7. Diana Ross' Greatest Hits [G]	Motown 869
10/22/77	18	12	8. Baby It's Me	Motown 890
10/22/77	29	12	9. An Evening With Diana Ross [L]	Motown 877 [2]
			recorded at the Ahmanson Theatre, Los Angeles	
7/07/79	14	17	● 10. The Boss	Motown 923
6/21/80	2(2)	34	▲ 11. **Diana**	Motown 936
			"Upside Down"(1)	
			"I'm Coming Out"(5)	
3/28/81	32	4	12. To Love Again [K]	Motown 951
			"It's My Turn"(9)	
11/14/81	15	20	▲ 13. Why Do Fools Fall In Love	RCA 4153
			"Why Do Fools Fall In Love"(7)	
			"Mirror, Mirror"(8)	
11/21/81	37	3	● 14. All The Great Hits [G]	Motown 960 [2]
			includes medleys with the Supremes	
			"Endless Love"(1-with Lionel Richie)	
10/30/82	27	7	● 15. Silk Electric	RCA 4384
			"Muscles"(10)	
8/06/83	32	4	16. Ross	RCA 4677
10/06/84	26	16	● 17. Swept Away	RCA 5009
			"Missing You"(10)	
			ROSSINGTON COLLINS BAND	
			Band formed by 4 surviving members of Lynyrd Skynyrd, including Gary Rossington and Allen Collins. Dale Krantz, female lead singer.	
7/19/80	13	13	● 1. Anytime, Anyplace, Anywhere	MCA 5130
10/17/81	24	5	2. This Is The Way	MCA 5207
			ROTARY CONNECTION	
			Canadian rock/R&B sextet. Minnie Riperton, lead singer.	
5/04/68	37	4	1. Rotary Connection	Cadet Concept 312
			DAVID LEE ROTH	
			Born on 10/10/55 in Bloomington, Indiana. Former lead singer of Van Halen.	
2/23/85	15	20	▲ 1. Crazy From The Heat [M]	Warner 25222
			"California Girls"(3)	
			"Just A Gigolo/I Ain't Got Nobody"	
7/26/86	4	21	▲ 2. **Eat 'Em And Smile**	Warner 25470
			ROXY MUSIC	
			English art-rock band. Nucleus consisted of Bryan Ferry (vocals, keyboards), Phil Manzanera (guitar) and Andy Mackey (horns).	
3/08/75	37	3	1. Country Life	Atco 106
4/14/79	23	8	2. Manifesto	Atco 114
8/09/80	35	3	3. Flesh + Blood	Atco 102

DATE	POS	WKS	ARTIST—RECORD TITLE	LABEL & NO.
			THE ROYAL PHILHARMONIC ORCHESTRA	
			British - Louis Clark, conductor (born in Birmingham, England - arranger for ELO).	
12/12/81	4	22	▲ 1. **Hooked On Classics** [I]	RCA 4194
			"Hooked On Classics"(10)	
9/18/82	33	7	● 2. Hooked On Classics II (Can't Stop the Classics) [I]	RCA 4373
			THE ROYAL SCOTS DRAGOON GUARDS	
			The Pipes and Drums and The Military Band of Scotland's armoured regiment.	
7/22/72	34	5	1. Amazing Grace [I]	RCA 4744
			ARTHUR RUBINSTEIN	
			Classical pianist. Born in Lodz, Poland; died on 12/20/82 (95).	
2/13/61	30	1	1. Heart of the Piano Concerto [I]	RCA 2495
			favorite movements from 6 piano concertos	
			ED RUDY - see BEATLES	
			DAVID RUFFIN	
			Born on 1/18/41 in Meridian, MS. Brother of Jimmy Ruffin. With Dixie Nightingales gospel group. Recorded for Anna in 1960. Co-lead singer of The Temptations, 1963-68.	
6/28/69	31	7	1. My Whole World Ended	Motown 685
			"My Whole World Ended (The Moment You Left Me)"(9)	
1/17/76	31	6	2. Who I Am	Motown 849
			"Walk Away From Love"(9)	
			RUFUS Featuring CHAKA KHAN	
			Soul group from Chicago. Band was first known as Smoke, then Ask Rufus. Varying membership. Included Tony Maiden (guitar), Nate Morgan, Kevin Murphy (keyboards), Bobby Watson (bass), Andre Fischer (drums) and Chaka Khan (lead singer). After Khan went solo in 1978, vocals were by Maiden and David Wolinski.	
8/03/74	4	11	● 1. **Rags To Rufus**	ABC 809
			"Tell Me Something Good"(3)	
1/25/75	7	12	● 2. **Rufusized**	ABC 837
			"Once You Get Started"(10)	
12/06/75	7	24	● 3. **Rufus featuring Chaka Khan**	ABC 909
			"Sweet Thing"(5)	
2/12/77	12	10	▲ 4. Ask Rufus	ABC 975
2/25/78	14	14	● 5. Street Player	ABC 1049
11/24/79	14	16	● 6. Masterjam	MCA 5103
			RUN-D.M.C.	
			Pop trio from Queens, New York: Joseph Simmons (Run), Daryll McDaniels (D.M.C.) and Jason Mizell (Jam Master Jay).	
6/21/86	3	49	▲ 1. **Raising Hell**	Profile 1217
			"Walk This Way"(4)	

DATE	POS	WKS	ARTIST—RECORD TITLE	LABEL & NO.
			TODD RUNDGREN	
			Born on 6/22/48 in Upper Darby, PA. Virtuoso musician, songwriter, producer, engineer. Leader of groups Nazz and Utopia. Produced Meat Loaf's "Bat Out Of Hell" album and produced albums for Badfinger, Grand Funk Railroad, The Tubes, Patti Smith and many others.	
12/15/73	29	18	● 1. Something/Anything?	Bearsville 2066 [2]
			"Hello It's Me"(5)	
			"I Saw The Light"	
6/17/78	36	2	2. Hermit Of Mink Hollow	Bearsville 6981
			"Can We Still Be Friends"	
			RUSH	
			Canadian power-rock trio: Geddy Lee (b: 7/29/53), vocals, bass; Alex Lifeson (b: 8/27/53), guitar; Neil Peart (b: 9/12/52), drums. Also see Bob & Doug McKenzie.	
11/20/76	40	2	▲ 1. All The World's A Stage [L]	Mercury 7508 [2]
10/08/77	33	5	● 2. A Farewell To Kings	Mercury 1184
2/09/80	4	15	▲ 3. **Permanent Waves**	Mercury 4001
3/07/81	3	29	▲ 4. **Moving Pictures**	Mercury 4013
			"Limelight"/"Tom Sawyer"	
11/14/81	10	14	● 5. **Exit...Stage Left** [L]	Mercury 7001 [2]
10/02/82	10	11	▲ 6. **Signals**	Mercury 4063
			"New World Man"	
5/05/84	10	12	▲ 7. **Grace Under Pressure**	Mercury 818476
11/02/85	10	14	▲ 8. **Power Windows**	Mercury 826098
			PATRICE RUSHEN	
			Born on 9/30/54 in Los Angeles. Jazz/soul vocalist, pianist, songwriter. Much session work with Jean Luc-Ponty, Lee Ritenour and Stanley Turrentine.	
3/01/80	39	2	1. Pizzazz	Elektra 243
5/15/82	14	8	2. Straight From The Heart	Elektra 60015
			"Forget Me Nots"	
7/28/84	40	3	3. Now	Elektra 60360
			LEON RUSSELL	
			Born on 4/2/41 in Lawton, Oklahoma. Vocalist, songwriter, top multi-instrumentalist sessionman. Formed Shelter Records with British producer Denny Cordell in 1970. Recorded as Hank Wilson in 1973. Married Mary McCreary (vocalist with Little Sister, part of Sly Stone's "family") in 1976. Own label, Paradise, 1976. Wrote "Superstar" and "This Masquerade". Also see Joe Cocker.	
6/12/71	17	10	● 1. Leon Russell & The Shelter People	Shelter 8903
7/29/72	2(4)	20	● 2. **Carney**	Shelter 8911
			"Tight Rope"	
7/14/73	9	12	● 3. **Leon Live** [L]	Shelter 8917 [3]
			recorded at the Long Beach Arena, Long Beach, California	
9/29/73	28	5	4. Hank Wilson's Back, Vol. I	Shelter 8923
			an album of Country & Western songs	
7/13/74	34	3	5. Stop All That Jazz	Shelter 2108
5/31/75	30	7	● 6. Will O' The Wisp	Shelter 2138
			"Lady Blue"	
6/12/76	34	4	7. Wedding Album	Paradise 2943

DATE	POS	WKS	ARTIST—RECORD TITLE	LABEL & NO.
			LEON & MARY RUSSELL (wife Mary McCreary)	
12/04/76	**40**	1	● 8. Best Of Leon [G]	Shelter 52004
7/07/79	**25**	5	● 9. One For The Road	Columbia 36064 [2]
			WILLIE NELSON & LEON RUSSELL	
			## BOBBY RYDELL	
			Born Robert Ridarelli on 4/26/42 in Philadelphia. Regular on Paul Whiteman's amateur TV show, 1951-54. Drummer with Rocco & The Saints, which included Frankie Avalon on trumpet in 1956. First recorded for Veko in 1957. Films "Bye Bye Birdie" and "That Lady From Peking". Currently performing an oldies revue with fellow Philadelphians Frankie Avalon and Fabian.	
2/27/61	**12**	8	1. Bobby's Biggest Hits [G]	Cameo 1009
			"We Got Love"(6)	
			"Wild One"(2)	
			"Swingin' School"(5)	
			"Volare"(4)	
12/25/61	**7**	11	2. **Bobby Rydell/Chubby Checker**	Cameo 1013
			"Jingle Bell Rock"	
			## MITCH RYDER & THE DETROIT WHEELS	
			Rock quintet from Detroit. Originally known as Billy Lee & The Rivieras. Renamed by their producer Bob Crewe.	
2/25/67	**23**	7	1. Breakout...!!!	New Voice 2002
			"Devil With A Blue Dress On & Good Golly Miss Molly"(4)	
5/06/67	**34**	3	2. Sock It To Me!	New Voice 2003
			"Sock It To Me-Baby!"(6)	
1/20/68	**37**	4	3. All Mitch Ryder Hits! [G]	New Voice 2004
			# S	
			## SADE	
			Born Helen Folasade Adu on 1/16/59 in Nigeria; moved to London at age 4.	
3/09/85	**5**	27	▲ 1. **Diamond Life**	Portrait 39581
			"Smooth Operator"(5)	
12/21/85	**1(2)**	27	▲ 2. **Promise**	Portrait 40263
			"The Sweetest Taboo"(5)	
			## SSGT BARRY SADLER	
			Born in New Mexico in 1941. Staff Sergeant of the U.S. Army Special Forces (aka Green Berets). Served in Vietnam until injuring leg in booby trap.	
3/12/66	**1(5)**	20	● 1. **Ballads of the Green Berets**	RCA 3547
			"The Ballad Of The Green Berets"(1)	
			## SAGA	
			Canadian rock quintet: Michael Sadler, lead singer; brothers Jim and Ian Crichton, Jim Gilmour and Steve Negus.	
1/08/83	**29**	13	● 1. Worlds Apart	Portrait 38246

DATE	POS	WKS	ARTIST—RECORD TITLE	LABEL & NO.
10/24/60	22	13	**MORT SAHL** Topical satirist. 1. Mort Sahl At The Hungry i [C]	Verve 15012
10/07/72	38	2	**SAILCAT** Country-rock duo: Court Pickett and John Wyker. 1. Motorcycle Mama	Elektra 75029
7/06/63	14	8	**KYU SAKAMOTO** Native of Kawasaki, Japan. One of 520 people killed in the crash of the Japan Airlines 747 near Tokyo on 8/12/85 (43). 1. Sukiyaki and other Japanese hits [F] "Sukiyaki"(1)	Capitol 10349
2/07/76	14	14	**SALSOUL ORCHESTRA** Disco orchestra conducted by Philadelphia producer-arranger Vincent Montana, Jr. 1. The Salsoul Orchestra [I]	Salsoul 5501
8/14/65	26	5	**SAM THE SHAM & THE PHAROAHS** Rock & roll group formed in the early 60s featuring lead singer Domingo "Sam" Samudio (b: 1940, Dallas). First recorded for Dingo in 1965. Samudio went solo in 1970. Formed new band in 1974. On soundtrack "The Border" in 1982. 1. Wooly Bully "Wooly Bully"(2)	MGM 4297
2/01/69	20	4	**SAN SEBASTIAN STRINGS** Music composed by Anita Kerr (with sound effects), featuring narration of the poetry of Rod McKuen. 1. Home To The Sea [I-T]	Warner 1764
11/26/66	13	10	**THE SANDPIPERS** Los Angeles-based trio - met in the Mitchell Boys Choir. Jim Brady (b: 8/24/44), Michael Piano (b: 10/26/44) and Richard Shoff (b: 4/30/44). • 1. Guantanamera "Guantanamera"(9)	A&M 4117
5/06/57 2/24/58	4 17	18 4	**TOMMY SANDS** Born on 8/27/37 in Chicago. Pop singer and actor. Mother was a vocalist with Art Kassel's band. Married Nancy Sinatra in 1960; divorced in 1965. Film's "Sing Boy Sing", "Mardi Gras", "Babes In Toyland", and "The Longest Day". 1. **Steady Date with Tommy Sands** 2. Sing Boy Sing [S] Tommy portrays fictional singer Virgil Walker in the film	Capitol 848 Capitol 929
4/08/78	29	3	**SAMANTHA SANG** Born on 8/5/53 in Melbourne, Australia. Began career on Melbourne radio as Cheryl Gray at age 8. • 1. Emotion "Emotion"(3)	Private S. 7009
1/14/78	25	8	**SANTA ESMERALDA** Spanish-flavored disco studio project produced by Nicolas Skorsky and Jean-Manuel De Scarano. • 1. Don't Let Me Be Misunderstood	Casablanca 7080

DATE	POS	WKS	ARTIST—RECORD TITLE	LABEL & NO.
			SANTANA	
			Latin-rock group formed in San Francisco in 1966. Consisted of Carlos Santana (b: 7/20/47, Autlan de Navarro, Mexico), vocals, guitar; Gregg Rolie, keyboards; and David Brown, bass. Added percussionists Michael Carabello, Jose Chepitos Areas and Michael Shrieve in 1969. Worked Fillmore West and Woodstock in 1969. Neal Schon, guitar, added in 1971. Santana began solo work in 1972. Schon and Rolie formed Journey.	
9/27/69	4	42	▲ 1. **Santana**	Columbia 9781
			"Evil Ways"(9)	
10/10/70	1(6)	40	▲ 2. **Abraxas**	Columbia 30130
			"Black Magic Woman"(4)	
			"Oye Como Va"	
10/16/71	1(5)	23	● 3. **Santana III**	Columbia 30595
			"Everybody's Everything"	
11/11/72	8	17	▲ 4. **Caravanserai**	Columbia 31610
12/15/73	25	9	● 5. Welcome	Columbia 32445
8/24/74	17	11	▲ 6. Santana's Greatest Hits [G]	Columbia 33050
11/23/74	20	5	7. Borboletta	Columbia 33135
4/17/76	10	11	● 8. **Amigos**	Columbia 33576
1/29/77	27	4	● 9. Festival	Columbia 34423
11/12/77	10	8	● 10. **Moonflower** [L]	Columbia 34914 [2]
			set also features some new studio recordings	
11/11/78	27	5	● 11. Inner Secrets	Columbia 35600
11/03/79	25	6	12. Marathon	Columbia 36154
5/02/81	9	21	● 13. **Zebop!**	Columbia 37158
			"Winning"	
9/11/82	22	10	14. Shango	Columbia 38122
			"Hold On"	
			CARLOS SANTANA	
			Mexican-born rock and jazz-fusion guitarist (Santana leader).	
7/29/72	8	14	▲ 1. **Carlos Santana & Buddy Miles! Live!** [L]	Columbia 31308
			recorded in Hawaii's Diamond Head volcano crater	
7/21/73	14	7	● 2. Love Devotion Surrender [I]	Columbia 32034
			CARLOS SANTANA/MAHAVISHNU JOHN McLAUGHLIN	
5/14/83	31	4	3. Havana Moon	Columbia 38642
			with guests: Willie Nelson, Booker T. Jones and The Fabulous Thunderbirds	
			SANTO & JOHNNY	
			Brooklyn-born guitar duo: Santo Farina (b: 10/24/37) on steel guitar, and his brother Johnny (b: 4/30/41) on rhythm guitar.	
1/18/60	20	29	1. Santo & Johnny [I]	Canadian-Am. 1001
			"Sleep Walk"(1)	
9/26/60	11	21	2. Encore [I]	Canadian-Am. 1002
			SAVOY BROWN	
			British blues-rock band led by guitarist Kim Simmonds. Many personnel changes.	
11/21/70	39	1	1. Looking In	Parrot 71042
4/15/72	34	7	2. Hellbound Train	Parrot 71052

DATE	POS	WKS	ARTIST—RECORD TITLE	LABEL & NO.
			LEO SAYER	
			Born Gerard Sayer on 5/21/48 in Shoreham, England. With Patches in early 70s. Songwriting team with David Courtney, 1972-75. Own TV show in England, early 80s.	
4/19/75	**16**	7	1. Just A Boy	Warner 2836
			"Long Tall Glasses (I Can Dance)"(9)	
1/22/77	**10**	14	▲ 2. **Endless Flight**	Warner 2962
			"You Make Me Feel Like Dancing"(1)	
			"When I Need You"(1)	
11/05/77	**37**	2	3. Thunder In My Heart	Warner 3089
12/27/80	**36**	6	4. Living In A Fantasy	Warner 3483
			"More Than I Can Say"(2)	
			BOZ SCAGGS	
			Born: William Royce Scaggs on 6/8/44 in Ohio. Raised in Texas. Joined Steve Miller's band, The Marksmen, in 1959. Joined R&B band, The Wigs, in 1963. To Europe in 1964, toured as a folksinger. Rejoined Miller in 1967, solo since 1969.	
5/01/76	**2(5)**	53	▲ 1. **Silk Degrees**	Columbia 33920
			"Lowdown"(3)	
			"Lido Shuffle"	
12/10/77	**11**	14	▲ 2. Down Two Then Left	Columbia 34729
4/19/80	**8**	21	▲ 3. **Middle Man**	Columbia 36106
12/06/80	**24**	14	● 4. Hits! [G]	Columbia 36841
			SCANDAL	
			New York-based rock band led by Patty Smyth and Zack Smith.	
5/28/83	**39**	3	1. Scandal [M]	Columbia 38194
8/18/84	**17**	14	▲ 2. Warrior	Columbia 39173
			"The Warrior"(7)	
			KERMIT SCHAFER	
			Collection of 'bloopers' by radio & TV producer Schafer. Died on 3/8/79.	
1/27/58	**17**	1	1. Pardon My Blooper! Volume 6 [C]	Jubilee 6
			narrator: George de Holczer	
			LALO SCHIFRIN	
			Argentinian pianist/conductor/composer.	
12/29/62	**35**	2	1. Bossa Nova - New Brazilian Jazz [I]	Audio Fidel. 1981
			JOHN SCHNEIDER	
			Born in Mt. Kisco, New York in 1955. Country singer, actor. Bo Duke of TV's "The Dukes Of Hazzard".	
8/08/81	**37**	3	1. Now Or Never	Scotti Br. 37400
			DICK SCHORY'S Percussion Pops Orchestra	
6/29/59	**11**	26	1. Music For Bang, Baa room and Harp [I]	RCA 1866
5/11/63	**13**	9	2. Supercussion [I]	RCA 2613

DATE	POS	WKS	ARTIST—RECORD TITLE	LABEL & NO.
			SCORPIONS	
			German heavy-metal rock quintet: Rudolf Schenker (Michael's brother), lead guitar; Klaus Meine, lead singer; Matthias Jabs, guitar; Francis Buchholz, bass; and Herman Rarebell, drums.	
4/10/82	10	18	▲ 1. **Blackout**	Mercury 4039
3/24/84	6	27	▲ 2. **Love At First Sting**	Mercury 814981
			"Rock You Like A Hurricane"	
7/20/85	14	16	▲ 3. World Wide Live [L]	Mercury 824344 [2]
			TOM SCOTT	
			Born on 5/19/48 in Los Angeles. Pop-jazz-fusion saxophonist. Session work for Joni Mitchell, Steely Dan, Carole King and others. Composer of films and TV scores.	
5/03/75	18	8	1. Tom Cat [I]	Ode 77029
			GIL SCOTT-HERON & BRIAN JACKSON	
			Keyboard duo: Gil is the lyricist; Brian composes the music.	
3/22/75	30	3	1. The First Minute Of A New Day	Arista 4030
			featuring backup group: The Midnight Band	
			SEA LEVEL	
			Jazzy blues-rock 7-man band formed by 3 members of The Allman Brothers Band.	
3/04/78	31	3	1. Cats On The Coast	Capricorn 0198
			SEALS & CROFTS	
			Pop duo: Jim Seals (b: 10/17/41, Sidney, TX), guitar, fiddle, saxophone; and Dash Crofts (b: 8/14/40, Cisco, TX), drums, mandolin, keyboards, guitar. With Dean Beard, recorded for Edmoral and Atlantic in 1957. To Los Angeles in 1958. With the Champs from 1958-65. Own group, the Dawnbreakers, late 60s. Entire band converted to Baha'i faith in 1969.	
10/14/72	7	33	● 1. **Summer Breeze**	Warner 2629
			"Summer Breeze"(6)	
5/05/73	4	31	● 2. **Diamond Girl**	Warner 2699
			"Diamond Girl"(6)	
3/23/74	14	16	● 3. Unborn Child	Warner 2761
5/03/75	30	5	● 4. I'll Play For You	Warner 2848
11/22/75	11	11	▲ 5. Greatest Hits [G]	Warner 2886
5/29/76	37	10	● 6. Get Closer	Warner 2907
			"Get Closer"(6)	
			THE SEARCHERS	
			Liverpool, England rock quartet formed in 1960: Mike Pender and John McNally (vocals, guitars), Tony Jackson (vocals, bass) and Chris Curtis (drums). Worked as backup band for Johnny Sandon, toured England, worked Star Club in Hamburg, Germany. Left Sandon in 1962. Jackson replaced by Frank Allen in 1965. Curtis replaced by Billy Adamson in 1969. Active into the 80s.	
6/13/64	22	8	1. Meet The Searchers/Needles & Pins	Kapp 3363
			JOHN SEBASTIAN	
			Born on 3/17/44 in New York City. Lead singer of The Lovin' Spoonful.	
4/18/70	20	7	1. John B. Sebastian	MGM 4654
			album also released on Reprise 6379	

DATE	POS	WKS	ARTIST—RECORD TITLE	LABEL & NO.
			NEIL SEDAKA	
			Born on 3/13/39 in Brooklyn. Pop singer, songwriter, pianist. Studied piano since elementary school. Formed songwriting team with lyricist Howard Greenfield while attending Lincoln High School (partnership lasted over 20 years). Recorded with The Tokens on Melba in 1956. Attended Juilliard School for classical piano. Prolific hit songwriter. Career revived in 1974 after signing with Elton John's new Rocket label.	
2/08/75	23	8	● 1. Sedaka's Back	Rocket 463
			compilation of cuts from 3 albums made in Britain	
			"Laughter In The Rain"(1)	
11/08/75	16	10	● 2. The Hungry Years	Rocket 2157
			"Bad Blood"(1)	
			"Breaking Up Is Hard To Do"(8)	
5/15/76	26	5	3. Steppin' Out	Rocket 2195
			THE SEEKERS	
			Pop/folk Australian-born quartet: Judith Durham (b: 7/3/43), lead singer; Keith Potger, guitar; Bruce Woodley, Spanish guitar; and Athol Guy, standup bass. Potger formed the New Seekers in 1970.	
3/25/67	10	12	1. **Georgy Girl**	Capitol 2431
			"Georgy Girl"(2)	
			BOB SEGER	
			Born on 5/6/45 in Ann Arbor, Michigan; raised in Detroit. Rock singer, songwriter, guitarist. First recorded in 1966, formed the System in 1968. Left music to attend college in 1969, returned in 1971. Formed own backing group, The Silver Bullet Band in 1976: Alto Reed (horns), Robyn Robbins (keyboards), Drew Abbott (guitar), Chris Campbell (bass) and Charlie Allen Martin (drums). Campbell is the only remaining original member.	
			BOB SEGER & THE SILVER BULLET BAND:	
6/12/76	34	2	▲ 1. 'Live' Bullet [L]	Capitol 11523 [2]
			recorded at Cobo Hall, Detroit, Michigan	
1/08/77	8	23	▲ 2. **Night Moves**	Capitol 11557
			"Night Moves"(4)	
6/03/78	4	33	▲ 3. **Stranger in Town**	Capitol 11698
			"Still The Same"(4)	
			"Old Time Rock & Roll"	
3/15/80	1(6)	43	▲ 4. **Against The Wind**	Capitol 12041
			"Fire Lake"(6)	
			"Against The Wind"(5)	
9/26/81	3	21	▲ 5. **Nine Tonight** [L]	Capitol 12182 [2]
			"Tryin' To Live My Life Without You"(5)	
1/15/83	5	23	▲ 6. **The Distance**	Capitol 12254
			"Shame On The Moon"(2)	
4/26/86	3	28	▲ 7. **Like A Rock**	Capitol 12398
			THE SERENDIPITY SINGERS	
			Pop/folk group organized at the University of Colorado.	
4/11/64	11	18	1. The Serendipity Singers	Philips 115
			"Don't Let The Rain Come Down (Crooked Little Man)"(6)	
			SESAME STREET - see CHILDREN'S section	

DATE	POS	WKS	ARTIST—RECORD TITLE	LABEL & NO.
			CHARLIE SEXTON	
			Austin, Texas rock singer/guitarist.	
2/15/86	**15**	13	1. Pictures For Pleasure	MCA 5629
			SHA NA NA	
			Fifties rock & roll specialists led by John "Bowzer" Baumann. Formed at Columbia University in 1969. Own syndicated TV show beginning in 1977. Henry Gross was a member, left in 1970. Many personnel changes.	
6/09/73	**38**	2	● 1. The Golden Age Of Rock 'N' Roll [L]	Kama Sutra 2073 [2]
			SHALAMAR	
			Black vocal trio formed in Los Angeles in 1978: Jody Watley and Jeffrey Daniels (both dancers from TV's "Soul Train") and Howard Hewett. Watley and Daniels replaced by Delisa Davis and Micki Free in 1984.	
2/09/80	**23**	11	● 1. Big Fun	Solar 3479
			"The Second Time Around"(8)	
3/28/81	**40**	2	● 2. Three For Love	Solar 3577
5/08/82	**35**	3	● 3. Friends	Solar 28
9/17/83	**38**	2	4. The Look	Solar 60239
			"Dead Giveaway"	
			SHANNON	
			Brenda Shannon Greene from Washington, DC. Began singing career at York University.	
3/10/84	**32**	4	● 1. Let The Music Play	Mirage 90134
			"Let The Music Play"(8)	
			DEL SHANNON	
			Born Charles Westover on 12/30/39 in Coopersville, Michigan. With US Army "Get Up And Go" radio show in Germany. Discovered by Ann Arbor deejay/producer Ollie McLaughlin. Formed own label, Berlee, in 1963. Wrote "I Go To Pieces" for Peter & Gordon. To Los Angeles in 1966, production work.	
7/06/63	**12**	9	1. Little Town Flirt	Big Top 1308
			"Runaway"(1)	
			"Hats Off To Larry"(5)	
			BOB SHARPLES	
			Bandleader from Bury, Lancashire, England.	
10/16/61	**11**	25	1. Pass In Review [I]	London P. 4 44001
			featuring patriotic songs	
			ROBERT SHAW Chorale	
			Shaw organized his singing group in 1948.	
12/23/57	**5**	4	● 1. **Christmas Hymns And Carols** [X]	RCA 1711
12/22/58	**13**	3	2. Christmas Hymns And Carols [X-R]	RCA 1711
			made top 10 on Billboard's special Christmas charts (1963)	
5/25/59	**21**	1	3. Deep River and Other Spirituals	RCA 2247
6/08/63	**27**	7	4. This Is My Country	RCA 2662
			with the RCA Victor Symphony Orchestra	
			ROLAND SHAW Orchestra	
			English.	
6/19/65	**38**	1	1. Themes From The James Bond Thrillers [I]	London 412

"**77 Sunset Strip**," one of the coolest television detective shows of all time, starred Efrem Zimbalist Jr., Roger Smith, and Edd Byrnes as Kookie, who began as a punky parking lot attendant. During the show's first season, Byrnes had a hit single, featuring a duet with Connie Stevens,"Kookie, Kookie (Lend Me Your Comb)."

David Seville and the Chipmunks employed a very simple technique—voices sped up with a tape recorder—to sell millions of adorable records, win several Grammy awards, and get a weekly animated series on television. Alvin, Simon, Theodore, and David Seville were all the creation of songwriter Ross Bagdasarian; since his death in 1972 his son has kept the Chipmunks alive on record.

Del Shannon, born Charles Westover, took his surname from a would-be wrestler and, "inspired by a Cadillac Coupe DeVille," came up with "Del." On a 1963 tour in support of "Little Town Flirt," he played London's Royal Albert Hall on a bill with the Beatles. Shannon liked the group's then current single, "From Me to You," enough to record it , thus becoming the first American artist to cover a Lennon-McCartney song.

Allan Sherman, born in Chicago in 1924, was the creator-producer of "I've Got a Secret" in the 1950s. He became a recording artist in 1962 with *My Son, the Folk Singer*, an album of satiric, Jewish folk/comedy. *My Son, the Celebrity* was his second chart-topper in a string of three.

Carly Simon first recorded in 1964 in a duo with her sister, Lucy, and didn't make her solo debut until 1971. She found immediate success when a single from the album, "That's the Way I've Always Heard It Should Be," reached the top ten. Simon's third album, *No Secrets*, released the following year, went No. 1, earning her a gold album and the Grammy award for "Best New Artist."

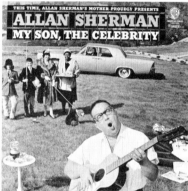

Frank Sinatra won "Album of the Year" and "Best Vocal Performance, Male" Grammys for his 1959 *Come Dance with Me!* album, which remained on the charts nearly three years. In 1961, the singer/actor founded Reprise Records and signed such cronies as Sammy Davis Jr. and Dean Martin. After Sinatra sold the label to Warner Bros. in 1963, it became home to such un-Sinatralike artists as T. Rex and Captain Beefheart.

Nancy Sinatra made her commercial breakthrough in 1966 with the million-selling single "These Boots Are Made for Walkin'." *Boots*, featuring such contemporary fare as the Rolling Stones' "As Tears Go By" and the Statler Brothers' "Flowers on the Wall," likewise went gold. The following year, Sinatra recorded "Somethin' Stupid" with her father and had her second No. 1 single.

The Smothers Brothers parlayed a popular folk music/comedy act into a successful television career in the 1960s, beginning as a regular feature on "The Steve Allen Show" (1961). Tom (guitar) and Dick (bass) starred in a bizarre 1965 sitcom, but made their real mark with the influential and controversial "Smothers Brothers Comedy Hour" (1967–70).

South Pacific was filmed in 1958, with Rossanno Brazzi, Mitzi Gaynor, and Frances Nuyen singing Rodgers and Hammerstein's delightful songs. The soundtrack album was an unprecedented smash, spending five years on the charts, including thirty-one weeks at No. 1. It was also England's first million-selling album ever. Twenty-five years later, Captain Sensible of the Damned had a No. 1 British hit with his recording of "Happy Talk."

Rick Springfield, the first person ever to rhyme the word "moot" in a hit single ("Jessie's Girl"), had American hits as early as 1972. But it wasn't until he began playing a doctor on the soap opera "General Hospital" in the 1980s that his music career gathered momentum. *Living in Oz* (1983) was the Australian native's third in a string of four consecutive platinum albums.

DATE	POS	WKS	ARTIST—RECORD TITLE	LABEL & NO.
			GEORGE SHEARING Quintet	
			English piano stylist. Born blind. Moved to U.S. in 1947.	
10/06/56	20	1	1. Velvet Carpet [I]	Capitol 720
10/07/57	13	3	2. Black Satin [I]	Capitol 858
8/25/58	17	2	3. Burnished Brass [I]	Capitol 1038
7/25/60	11	35	4. White Satin	Capitol 1334
5/12/62	27	9	5. Nat King Cole Sings/George Shearing Plays	Capitol 1675
			SHEILA E.	
			Born Sheila Escovedo on 12/12/59 in San Francisco. R&B vocalist, percussionist. Daughter of percussionist Pete Escovedo.	
9/01/84	28	9	● 1. Sheila E. in The Glamorous Life *"The Glamorous Life"(7)*	Warner 25107
			ALLAN SHERMAN	
			Born on 11/30/24 in Chicago; died on 11/21/73. Began as a professional comedy writer for Jackie Gleason, Joe E. Lewis and others. Creator-producer of TV's "I've Got A Secret".	
11/10/62	1(2)	29	● 1. **My Son, The Folk Singer** [C]	Warner 1475
1/26/63	1(1)	19	2. **My Son, The Celebrity** [C]	Warner 1487
1/26/63	1(1)	19	3. **My Son, The Celebrity**	Warner 1487
8/24/63	1(8)	24	4. **My Son, The Nut** [C] *"Hello Mudduh, Hello Fadduh!"(2)*	Warner 1501
5/16/64	25	6	5. Allan In Wonderland [C]	Warner 1539
1/02/65	32	5	6. For Swingin' Livers Only!	Warner 1569
			BOBBY SHERMAN	
			Born on 7/22/44 in Santa Monica, CA. Regular on TV's "Shindig" and played Jeremy Bolt on TV's "Here Come The Brides". Currently involved in TV production.	
11/22/69	11	15	● 1. Bobby Sherman *"Little Woman"(3)*	Metromedia 1014
4/18/70	10	12	● 2. **Here Comes Bobby** *"La La La (If I Had You)"(9)* *"Easy Come, Easy Go"(9)*	Metromedia 1028
10/24/70	20	8	● 3. With Love, Bobby *"Julie, Do Ya Love Me"(5)*	Metromedia 1032
			THE SHIRELLES	
			R&B "girl group" from Passaic, NJ. Consisted of Shirley Owens Alston (b: 6/10/41), Beverly Lee (b: 8/3/41), Doris Kenner (b: 8/2/41) and Addie "Micki" Harris (b: 1/22/40, d: 6/10/82). Formed in junior high school as the Poquellos. First recorded for Tiara in 1958. Kenner left group in 1968, returned in 1975. Alston left for solo career in 1975.	
2/09/63	19	18	1. The Shirelles Greatest Hits [G] *"Will You Love Me Tomorrow"(1)* *"Dedicated To The One I Love"(3)* *"Mama Said"(4)*	Scepter 507
			DON SHIRLEY	
			Pianist, organist. Born in Kingston, Jamaica on 1/27/27.	
4/02/55	14	4	1. Tonal Expressions [I]	Cadence 1001

DATE	POS	WKS	ARTIST—RECORD TITLE	LABEL & NO.
			THE SHOCKING BLUE	
			Dutch rock quartet: Mariska Veres (lead singer), Robbie van Leeuwen (guitar), Cor van Beek (drums) and Klaasje van der Wal (bass). Disbanded in 1974.	
3/07/70	31	3	1. The Shocking Blue	Colossus 1000
			"Venus"(1)	
			SILVER CONVENTION	
			German studio disco act assembled by producer Michael Kunze and writer/arranger Silvester Levay. Female vocal trio formed in 1976 consisting of Penny McLean, Ramona Wolf and Linda Thompson.	
10/25/75	10	10	● 1. **Save Me**	Midland Int. 1129
			"Fly, Robin, Fly"(1)	
5/01/76	13	10	2. Silver Convention	Midland Int. 1369
			"Get Up And Boogie (That's Right)"(2)	
			GENE SIMMONS	
			Born Gene Klein on 8/25/49 in Queens, NY. Bass guitarist of Kiss.	
11/11/78	22	12	▲ 1. Gene Simmons	Casablanca 7120
			SIMON & GARFUNKEL	
			Folk/rock duo from New York City: Paul Simon and Art Garfunkel. Recorded as Tom & Jerry in 1957. Duo had split before first hit in 1965; Simon was working solo in England, and Garfunkel was in graduate school. They reformed and stayed together until 1971. Reunited in 1981 for national tour.	
2/12/66	30	3	● 1. Wednesday Morning, 3 AM	Columbia 9049
			contains original unmixed version of "The Sounds Of Silence"	
4/09/66	21	33	● 2. Sounds of Silence	Columbia 9269
			"The Sounds Of Silence"(1)	
			"I Am A Rock"(3)	
11/19/66	4	60	▲ 3. **Parsley, Sage, Rosemary and Thyme**	Columbia 9363
			"Homeward Bound"(5)	
			"Scarborough Fair/Canticle"	
3/23/68	1(9)	47	● 4. **The Graduate** [S]	Columbia 3180
			includes 4 previously released Simon & Garfunkel songs - the two "Mrs. Robinson" cuts are not the hit versions	
5/25/68	1(7)	40	▲ 5. **Bookends**	Columbia 9529
			"Mrs. Robinson"(1)	
			side 2: singles hits previously unavailable on an album	
2/28/70	1(10)	24	▲ 6. **Bridge Over Troubled Water**	Columbia 9914
			"The Boxer"(7)	
			"Bridge Over Troubled Water"(1)	
			"Cecilia"(4)	
7/08/72	5	22	▲ 7. **Simon And Garfunkel's Greatest Hits** [G]	Columbia 31350
3/13/82	6	11	▲ 8. **The Concert In Central Park** [L]	Warner 3654 [2]
			recorded in New York City's Central Park on 9/19/81	
			CARLY SIMON	
			Born on 6/25/45 in New York City. Pop vocalist/songwriter. Father is co-founder of Simon & Schuster publishing company. Married James Taylor on 11/3/72, separated in 1982.	
7/03/71	30	7	1. Carly Simon	Elektra 74082
			"That's The Way I've Always Heard It Should Be"(10)	
2/12/72	30	6	● 2. Anticipation	Elektra 75016

DATE	POS	WKS	ARTIST—RECORD TITLE	LABEL & NO.
12/23/72	**1**(5)	23	● 3. **No Secrets**	Elektra 75049
			"You're So Vain"(1)	
2/09/74	3	16	● 4. **Hotcakes**	Elektra 1002
			"Mockingbird"(5-with James Taylor)	
5/10/75	10	9	5. **Playing Possum**	Elektra 1033
12/20/75	17	9	● 6. The Best Of Carly Simon [G]	Elektra 1048
7/04/76	29	4	7. Another Passenger	Elektra 1064
5/13/78	10	17	▲ 8. **Boys In The Trees**	Elektra 128
			"You Belong To Me"(6)	
11/01/80	36	4	9. Come Upstairs	Warner 3443
			"Jesse"	

PAUL SIMON

Born on 11/5/41 in Newark, NJ; raised in Queens, NY. Vocalist, composer, guitarist. Met Art Garfunkel in high school, recorded together as Tom & Jerry in 1957. Worked as Jerry Landis, Paul Kane, Harrison Gregory and True Taylor in early 60s. To England from 1963-64. Returned to USA and recorded first album with Garfunkel in 1965. Went solo in 1971. In films "Annie Hall" and "One-Trick Pony".

DATE	POS	WKS	ARTIST—RECORD TITLE	LABEL & NO.
2/19/72	4	18	▲ 1. **Paul Simon**	Columbia 30750
			"Mother And Child Reunion"(4)	
6/09/73	2(2)	24	▲ 2. **There Goes Rhymin' Simon**	Columbia 32280
			"Kodachrome"(2)	
			"Loves Me Like A Rock"(2)	
4/13/74	33	3	● 3. Paul Simon In Concert/Live Rhymin' [L]	Columbia 32855
11/01/75	**1**(1)	29	● 4. **Still Crazy After All These Years**	Columbia 33540
			"My Little Town"(9 - Simon & Garfunkel)	
			"50 Ways To Leave Your Lover"(1)	
12/17/77	18	9	▲ 5. Greatest Hits, Etc. [G]	Columbia 35032
			"Slip Slidin' Away"(5)	
9/06/80	12	13	● 6. One-Trick Pony [S]	Warner 3472
			Paul starred in the film	
			"Late In The Evening"(6)	
12/03/83	35	8	7. Hearts And Bones	Warner 23942
9/27/86	3	39+	▲ 8. **Graceland**	Warner 25447

NINA SIMONE

Born Eunice Waymon on 2/21/33 in Tryon, SC. Jazz-influenced vocalist, pianist, composer. Attended Juilliard School of Music in New York City. Devoted more time to political activism in 70s, infrequent recording.

DATE	POS	WKS	ARTIST—RECORD TITLE	LABEL & NO.
3/06/61	23	5	1. Nina At Newport [L]	Colpix 412

SIMPLE MINDS

Scottish rock group; current lineup: Jim Kerr, lead singer (married to Chrissie Hynde of the Pretenders); Michael MacNeil, keyboards; Charles Burchill, guitar; Mel Gaynor, drums; and John Gibbin, bass.

DATE	POS	WKS	ARTIST—RECORD TITLE	LABEL & NO.
11/16/85	10	29	● 1. **Once Upon A Time**	A&M 5092
			"Alive & Kicking"(3)	
			"Sanctify Yourself"	

DATE	POS	WKS	ARTIST—RECORD TITLE	LABEL & NO.
			SIMPLY RED British pop sextet led by vocalist Mick "Red" Hucknall.	
5/31/86	**16**	28	● 1. Picture Book	Elektra 60452
			"Holding Back The Years"(1)	
			FRANK SINATRA Born Francis Albert Sinatra on 12/12/15 in Hoboken, NJ. With Harry James, 1939-40, first recorded for Brunswick in 1939; with Tommy Dorsey, 1940-42. Went solo in late 1942 and charted 40 Top 10 hits through 1954. Appeared in many films from 1941 on. Won an Oscar for the film "From Here To Eternity" in 1953. Own TV show in 1957. Own record company, Reprise, 1961, sold to Warner Bros. in 1963. Announced his retirement in 1970, but made comeback in 1973. Regarded by many as the greatest popular singer of the 20th century.	
5/28/55	**2**(18)	33	1. in the Wee Small Hours	Capitol 581
3/31/56	**2**(1)	50	● 2. songs for Swingin' Lovers!	Capitol 653
			"I've Got You Under My Skin"	
12/22/56	**8**	17	● 3. This is Sinatra! [G]	Capitol 768
			"Young At Heart"(2-'54)	
			"Three Coins In The Fountain"(7-'54)	
			"Learnin' The Blues"(1)	
			"Love And Marriage"(5)	
			"(Love Is) The Tender Trap"(7)	
3/02/57	**5**	14	4. Close To You	Capitol 789
			featuring The Hollywood String Quartet	
5/27/57	**2**(1)	36	5. a Swingin' Affair!	Capitol 803
9/23/57	**3**	21	6. Where are you?	Capitol 855
11/11/57	**2**(1)	27	7. Pal Joey [S]	Capitol 912
			Frank plays Joey Evans and sings on 6 of the tracks	
			"The Lady Is A Tramp"	
12/30/57	**18**	2	● 8. a Jolly Christmas from Frank Sinatra [X]	Capitol 894
2/03/58	**1**(5)	56	9. Come fly with me	Capitol 920
6/02/58	**12**	1	10. The Frank Sinatra Story [K]	Columbia 6 [2]
			"All Or Nothing At All"/"You'll Never Know"/ "Nancy"	
4/28/58	**8**	7	11. This Is Sinatra, Volume Two [G]	Capitol 982
			"Hey! Jealous Lover"(3)	
9/29/58	**1**(5)	81	● 12. Frank Sinatra sings for Only The Lonely	Capitol 1053
2/09/59	**2**(5)	03	● 13. Come Dance With Me!	Capitol 1069
6/01/59	**8**	11	14. Look to Your Heart [K]	Capitol 1164
8/31/59	**2**(2)	42	15. No One Cares	Capitol 1221
8/22/60	**1**(9)	38	● 16. Nice 'n' Easy	Capitol 1417
2/13/61	**3**	22	17. Sinatra's Swingin' Session!!!	Capitol 1491
2/13/61	**18**	36	18. Sinatra and Swingin' Brass	Reprise 1005
			"I Get A Kick Out Of You"	
4/10/61	**4**	60	19. All The Way [G]	Capitol 1538
			"All The Way"(2)	
			"Witchcraft"(6)	
			"High Hopes"	
5/08/61	**4**	20	20. Ring-A-Ding Ding!	Reprise 1001
			the first album for Sinatra's own record company	

DATE	POS	WKS	ARTIST—RECORD TITLE	LABEL & NO.
8/21/61	8	12	21. **Come Swing With Me!**	Capitol 1594
8/28/61	6	18	22. **Sinatra Swings**	Reprise 1002
			"That Old Black Magic"	
11/19/61	3	23	23. **I Remember Tommy...**	Reprise 1003
			songs popularized by Tommy Dorsey	
3/17/62	8	20	24. **Sinatra & Strings**	Reprise 1004
			"Night And Day"/"Misty"/"Stardust"	
5/05/62	19	23	25. Point Of No Return	Capitol 1676
8/25/62	15	9	26. Sinatra Sings...of love and things [K]	Capitol 1729
11/24/62	25	8	27. All Alone	Reprise 1007
2/09/63	5	22	28. **Sinatra-Basie**	Reprise 1008
			FRANK SINATRA/COUNT BASIE	
7/06/63	6	11	29. **The Concert Sinatra**	Reprise 1009
10/19/63	8	17	● 30. **Sinatra's Sinatra**	Reprise 1010
			newly recorded Sinatra favorites	
4/25/64	10	16	31. **Days Of Wine And Roses, Moon River, and other academy award winners**	Reprise 1011
9/12/64	13	15	32. **It Might As Well Be Swing**	Reprise 1012
			FRANK SINATRA/COUNT BASIE	
2/06/65	19	12	33. Softly, As I Leave You	Reprise 1013
7/17/65	9	32	34. **Sinatra '65**	Reprise 6167
9/25/65	5	46	● 35. **September Of My Years**	Reprise 1014
			"It Was A Very Good Year"	
1/15/66	9	20	● 36. **A Man And His Music** [K]	Reprise 1016 [2]
			an anthology of Sinatra's career, narrated and sung by him	
2/19/66	30	3	37. My Kind Of Broadway	Reprise 1015
6/18/66	34	2	38. Moonlight Sinatra	Reprise 1018
7/02/66	1(1)	43	● 39. **Strangers In The Night**	Reprise 1017
			"Strangers In The Night"(1)	
9/10/66	9	15	● 40. **Sinatra At The Sands** [L]	Reprise 1019 [2]
			with Count Basie & The Orchestra	
1/21/67	6	22	● 41. **That's Life**	Reprise 1020
			"That's Life"(4)	
5/13/67	19	6	42. Francis Albert Sinatra & Antonio Carlos Jobim	Reprise 1021
			Jobim: Brazilian songwriter/guitarist/vocalist	
9/30/67	24	9	43. Frank Sinatra	Reprise 1022
			"Somethin' Stupid"(1-with Nancy Sinatra)	
1/18/69	18	7	● 44. Cycles	Reprise 1027
5/17/69	11	8	● 45. My Way	Reprise 1029
9/27/69	30	5	46. A Man Alone & Other Songs of Rod McKuen	Reprise 1030
11/17/73	13	10	● 47. Ol' Blue Eyes Is Back	Reprise 2155
1/04/75	37	2	48. Sinatra - The Main Event Live [L]	Reprise 2207
			recorded at New York's Madison Square Garden - with Woody Herman & The Young Thundering Herd	
5/03/80	17	12	● 49. Trilogy: Past, Present, Future	Reprise 2300 [3]
			"Theme From New York, New York"	

DATE	POS	WKS	ARTIST—RECORD TITLE	LABEL & NO.
			NANCY SINATRA	
			Born on 6/8/40 in Jersey City, NJ. First child of Frank and Nancy Sinatra. Moved to Los Angeles while a child. Made national TV debut with father and Elvis Presley in 1959. Married to Tommy Sands, 1960-65. Appeared on "Hullabaloo", "American Bandstand", and own specials, mid-60s. In films "For Those Who Think Young", "Get Yourself A College Girl", "The Oscar" and "Speedway".	
3/26/66	5	24	● 1. **Boots**	Reprise 6202
			"These Boots Are Made For Walkin'"(1)	
3/18/67	18	6	2. Sugar	Reprise 6239
			"Sugar Town"(5)	
3/16/68	37	4	3. Movin' With Nancy [TV]	Reprise 6277
			guests: Frank Sinatra, Dean Martin & Lee Hazlewood	
5/25/68	13	18	● 4. Nancy & Lee	Reprise 6273
			NANCY SINATRA & LEE HAZLEWOOD	
			THE SINGING NUN	
			Sister Luc-Gabrielle (real name: Jeanine Deckers) from the Fichermont, Belgium convent. Recorded under the name Soeur Sourire ("Sister Smile"). Committed suicide on 3/31/85 (52).	
11/23/63	1(10)	18	● 1. **The Singing Nun** [F]	Philips 203
			"Dominique"(1)	
			SISTER SLEDGE	
			Sisters Debbie, Joni, Kim and Kathie Sledge from North Philadelphia. First recorded as Sisters Sledge for Money Back in 1971. .	
3/24/79	3	19	▲ 1. **We Are Family**	Cotillion 5209
			"He's The Greatest Dancer"(9)	
			"We Are Family"(2)	
3/29/80	31	5	2. Love Somebody Today	Cotillion 16012
			SKYY	
			Brooklyn R&B/pop-funk octet. Vocals by sisters Denise, Delores and Bonnie Dunning.	
2/06/82	18	11	● 1. Skyy Line	Salsoul 8548
			SLADE	
			English hard-rock quartet: Noddy Holder (b: 6/15/50), lead singer; David Hill, guitar; Jim Lea, bass, keyboards; and Don Powell, drums.	
6/16/84	33	4	1. Keep Your Hands Off My Power Supply	CBS Assoc. 39336
			"Run Runaway"	
			FELIX SLATKIN	
			St. Louis native. Virtuoso violinist, conductor, composer, arranger. Worked with many film and record companies. Died on 2/9/63 (47).	
5/11/63	20	7	1. Our Winter Love [I]	Liberty 7287
			SLAVE	
			Funk band from Dayton, Ohio. Steve Arrington, studio vocalist and later a member, 1978-82. Numerous personnel changes.	
6/18/77	22	12	● 1. Slave	Cotillion 9914
			PERCY SLEDGE	
			Born in 1941 in Leighton, Alabama. Worked local clubs with Esquires Combo until going solo.	
8/06/66	37	2	1. When A Man Loves A Woman	Atlantic 8125
			"When A Man Loves A Woman"(1)	

DATE	POS	WKS	ARTIST—RECORD TITLE	LABEL & NO.
			GRACE SLICK	
			Born Grace Wing on 10/30/39 in Chicago. Female lead singer of Jefferson Airplane, Jefferson Starship, and Starship.	
4/26/80	32	4	1. Dreams	RCA 3544
			SLY & THE FAMILY STONE	
			San Francisco funk/rock band featuring Sly Stone (Sylvester Stewart), brother Freddie Stone, sister Rose Stone and Larry Graham (1-5).	
5/03/69	13	24	▲ 1. Stand!	Epic 26456
			"Everyday People"(1)	
11/14/70	2(1)	27	▲ 2. **Greatest Hits** [G]	Epic 30325
			"Hot Fun In The Summertime"(2)	
			"Thank You (Falettinme Be Mice Elf Agin)"(1)	
11/13/71	1(2)	19	● 3. **There's A Riot Goin' On**	Epic 30986
			"Family Affair"(1)	
7/07/73	7	16	● 4. **Fresh**	Epic 32134
8/17/74	15	7	● 5. Small Talk	Epic 32930
			SLY FOX	
			Black-and-white duo: Gary "Mudbone" Cooper (P-Funk) and Michael Camacho.	
4/26/86	31	4	1. Let's Go All The Way	Capitol 12367
			"Let's Go All The Way"(7)	
			SMITH	
			Los Angeles-based rock quintet fronted by St. Louis blues rocker Gayle McCormick.	
11/01/69	17	11	1. a group called Smith	Dunhill 50056
			"Baby It's You"(5)	
			JIMMY SMITH	
			Born on 12/8/25 in Norristown, Pennsylvania. Jazz organist. Both parents were piano players. Won Major Bowes Amateur Show in 1934. With father (James, Sr.) in song and dance team, 1942. With Don Gardner & The Sonotones, recorded for Bruce in 1953. A pioneer of the jazz organ, Smith first recorded with own trio for Blue Note in 1956. Began doing vocals in 1966.	
4/21/62	28	5	1. Midnight Special [I]	Blue Note 84078
			with Stanley Turrentine (sax) & Kenny Burrell (guitar)	
7/21/62	10	20	2. **Bashin'** [I]	Verve 8474
			"Walk On The Wild Side"	
3/23/63	14	8	3. Back At The Chicken Shack [I]	Blue Note 84117
			with Stanley Turrentine & Kenny Burrell	
5/25/63	11	15	4. Hobo Flats [I]	Verve 8544
11/30/63	25	7	5. Any Number Can Win [I]	Verve 8552
5/23/64	16	15	6. Who's Afraid Of Virginia Woolf? [I]	Verve 8583
10/31/64	12	13	7. The Cat [I]	Verve 8587
7/10/65	35	4	8. Monster [I]	Verve 8618
10/30/65	15	10	9. Organ Grinder Swing [I]	Verve 8628
			featuring Kenny Burrell (guitar) & Grady Tate (drums)	
5/28/66	28	10	10. Get My Mojo Workin' [I]	Verve 8641

DATE	POS	WKS	ARTIST—RECORD TITLE	LABEL & NO.
			KATE SMITH	
			Tremendously popular soprano who was for years one of the most-listened-to of all radio singers, and later hosted a TV series. Kate introduced the classic hit "God Bless America". Died on 6/17/86 (79).	
4/16/66	36	5	1. How Great Thou Art	RCA 3445
			KEELY SMITH	
			Born on 3/9/32 in Norfolk, Virginia. Also see Louis Prima.	
10/20/58	14	8	1. Politely!	Capitol 1073
5/25/59	23	4	2. Swingin' Pretty	Capitol 1145
1/04/60	40	1	3. Be My Love	Dot 3241
			O.C. SMITH	
			Born Ocie Lee Smith on 6/21/32 in Mansfield, LA. Raised in Los Angeles. Sang while in US Air Force, 1951-55. First recorded for Cadence in 1956. With Count Basie from 1961-63.	
11/23/68	19	10	1. Hickory Holler Revisited	Columbia 9680
			"Little Green Apples"(2)	
			PATTI SMITH GROUP	
			Born on 12/31/46 in Chicago; raised in New Jersey. Poet-turned-punk rocker.	
5/27/78	20	8	1. Easter	Arista 4171
			"Because The Night"	
5/26/79	18	7	2. Wave	Arista 4221
			produced by Todd Rundgren	
			REX SMITH	
			Born in Jacksonville, FL. Vocalist, actor. Starred in several Broadway musicals.	
5/12/79	19	8	● 1. Sooner Or Later	Columbia 35813
			"You Take My Breath Away"(10)	
			SAMMI SMITH	
			Born on 8/5/43 in Orange, California; raised in Oklahoma. Country singer.	
3/27/71	33	4	1. Help Me Make It Through The Night	Mega 1000
			"Help Me Make It Through The Night"(8)	
			THE SMOTHERS BROTHERS	
			Comedians Tom (b: 2/2/37), guitar; and Dick Smothers (b: 11/20/39), standup bass. Hosts of their own TV comedy variety series from 1967-70.	
11/24/62	26	11	● 1. The Two Sides Of The Smothers Brothers [C]	Mercury 20675
			side 1: comedy; side 2: serious singing	
5/04/63	27	22	● 2. (Think Ethnic!) [C]	Mercury 20777
1/04/64	13	10	3. Curb Your Tongue, Knave! [C]	Mercury 20862
6/20/64	23	7	4. It Must Have Been Something I Said! [C]	Mercury 20904
1/29/66	39	2	5. Mom Always Liked You Best! [C]	Mercury 21051
			SNIFF 'n' the TEARS	
			British rock group led by Paul Roberts (vocals) and Loz Netto (guitar).	
10/06/79	35	3	1. Fickle Heart	Atlantic 19242
			"Driver's Seat"	

DATE	POS	WKS	ARTIST—RECORD TITLE	LABEL & NO.
			PHOEBE SNOW Born Phoebe Laub on 7/17/52 in New York City; raised in New Jersey. Vocalist, guitarist, songwriter. Began performing in Greenwich Village in the early 70s.	
11/16/74	4	22	● 1. **Phoebe Snow**	Shelter 2109
			"Poetry Man"(5)	
2/21/76	13	10	● 2. Second Childhood	Columbia 33952
11/27/76	29	7	3. It Looks Like Snow	Columbia 34387
			TERRY SNYDER & THE ALL-STARS - see **ENOCH LIGHT** (Terry died on 3/15/63-47)	
			SOFT CELL British electro-rock duo: Marc Almond (vocals) & David Ball (synthesizer).	
3/20/82	22	18	1. Non-Stop Erotic Cabaret	Sire 3647
			"Tainted Love"(8)	
			SONNY & CHER Husband and wife duo: Sonny and Cher Bono. Session singers for Phil Spector. First recorded as Caesar & Cleo for Vault in 1963. Married in 1963; divorced in 1974. Films "Good Times", 1966 and "Chastity", 1968. Own CBS-TV variety series from 1971-74. Brief TV reunion in 1975.	
9/04/65	2(8)	25	● 1. **Look At Us**	Atco 177
			"I Got You Babe"(1)	
6/04/66	34	6	2. The Wondrous World Of Sonny & Cher	Atco 183
9/02/67	23	10	3. The Best of Sonny & Cher [G]	Atco 219
12/04/71	35	2	● 5. Sonny & Cher Live [L]	Kapp 3654
3/11/72	14	15	● 6. All I Ever Need Is You	Kapp 3660
			"All I Ever Need Is You"(7)	
			"A Cowboy's Work Is Never Done"(8)	
			THE S.O.S. BAND Atlantic funk/R&B band. Mary Davis, lead singer. Name means "Sounds Of Success".	
7/12/80	12	11	● 1. S.O.S.	Tabu 36332
			"Take Your Time (Do It Right)"(3)	
			DAVID SOUL Born David Solberg on 8/28/43 in Chicago. Ken Hutchinson of TV's "Starsky & Hutch." Began career as a folksinger and appeared several times on "The Merv Griffin Show" as "The Covered Man" (wore a ski mask).	
4/23/77	40	1	1. David Soul	Private S. 2019
			"Don't Give Up On Us"(1)	
			SOUNDS ORCHESTRAL English - Johnny Pearson on piano.	
6/19/65	11	9	1. Cast Your Fate To The Wind [I]	Parkway 7046
			"Cast Your Fate To The Wind"(10)	

DATE	POS	WKS	ARTIST—RECORD TITLE	LABEL & NO.
			THE SOUTHER, HILLMAN, FURAY BAND	
			Country-rock sextet formed as a supergroup featuring veterans J.D. Souther, Chris Hillman, and Richie Furay.	
8/03/74	11	11	● 1. The Souther, Hillman, Furay Band	Asylum 1006
7/26/75	39	1	2. Trouble In Paradise	Asylum 1036
			SPANDAU BALLET	
			English quintet: Tony Hadley (lead singer), Gary Kemp (guitar), Steve Norman (sax), Martin Kemp (bass) and John Keeble (drums).	
10/08/83	19	8	1. True	Chrysalis 41403
			"True"(4)	
			SPINNERS	
			In 1961, an R&B vocal group from Ferndale High School near Detroit, originally named the Domingoes, became the Spinners. Many personnel changes ensued until their hit lineup in 1972 included: Bobbie Smith, Phillipe Wynne, Billy Henderson, Henry Fambrough and Pervis Jackson. Wynne (d: 7/14/84) left group in 1977, replaced by John Edwards.	
5/12/73	14	11	● 1. Spinners	Atlantic 7256
			"I'll Be Around"(3)	
			"Could It Be I'm Falling In Love"(4)	
4/06/74	16	14	● 2. Mighty Love	Atlantic 7296
12/28/74	9	14	● 3. **New And Improved**	Atlantic 18118
			"Then Came You"(1-with Dionne Warwick)	
8/16/75	8	16	● 4. **Pick Of The Litter**	Atlantic 18141
			"They Just Can't Stop It the (Games People Play)"(5)	
1/17/76	20	9	5. Spinners Live! [L]	Atlantic 910 [2]
8/14/76	25	9	● 6. Happiness Is Being With The Detroit Spinners	Atlantic 18181
			"The Rubberband Man"(2)	
4/09/77	26	4	7. Yesterday, Today & Tomorrow	Atlantic 19100
3/22/80	32	4	8. Dancin' And Lovin'	Atlantic 19256
			"Working My Way Back To You/Forgive Me, Girl"(2)	
			SPIRIT	
			Los Angeles eclectic rock group: Jay Ferguson (lead singer), Mark Andes (bass), Ed Cassidy (drums), Randy California (guitar) and John Locke (keyboards). Ferguson and Andes left to form Jo Jo Gunne, mid-1971. Andes became an original member of Firefall in 1975 and later joined Heart in 1983. Los Angeles rock fusion group - Jay Ferguson, lead singer.	
8/31/68	31	16	1. Spirit	Ode 44004
2/08/69	22	12	2. The Family That Plays Together	Ode 44014
			SPLIT ENZ	
			Sextet from New Zealand, led by brothers Tim and Neil Finn.	
11/15/80	40	2	1. True Colours	A&M 4822
			record pressed in laser-etched vinyl	

DATE	POS	WKS	ARTIST—RECORD TITLE	LABEL & NO.
			RICK SPRINGFIELD	
			Born on 8/23/49 in Sydney, Australia. Singer, actor, composer. With top Australian teen idol band, Zoot, before going solo in 1972. Turned to acting in late 70s, played Noah Drake on the TV soap opera "General Hospital", early 80s. Starred in the film "Hard To Hold" in 1984.	
9/30/72	**35**	4	1. Beginnings	Capitol 11047
			"Speak To The Sky"	
6/27/81	**7**	38	▲ 2. **Working Class Dog**	RCA 3697
			"Jessie's Girl"(1)	
			"I've Done Everything For You"(8)	
4/03/82	**2**(3)	15	▲ 3. **Success Hasn't Spoiled Me Yet**	RCA 4125
			"Don't Talk To Strangers"(2)	
5/07/83	**12**	24	▲ 4. Living in Oz	RCA 4660
			"Affair Of The Heart"(9)	
4/21/84	**16**	9	▲ 5. Hard To Hold [S]	RCA 4935
			Rick starred in the film	
			"Love Somebody"(5)	
5/11/85	**21**	11	● 6. Tao	RCA 5370
			BRUCE SPRINGSTEEN	
			Born on 9/23/49 in Freehold, NJ. Rock singer, songwriter, guitarist. Worked local clubs in New Jersey and Greenwich Village, mid-60s. Own E-Street Band in 1973, consisted of Clarence Clemons (saxophone), David Sancious and Danny Federici (keyboards), Gary Tallent (bass) and Vini Lopez (drums). Sancious and Lopez replaced by Roy Bittan and Max Weinberg. Miami Steve Van Zandt (guitar) joined group in 1975. Wrote Earth Band's "Blinded By The Light" and the Pointer Sisters' "Fire". After "Born To Run", a court injunction prevented the release of any new albums until 1978. "The Boss" is America's #1 rock star of the past decade.	
9/20/75	**3**	12	▲ 1. **Born To Run**	Columbia 33795
6/17/78	**5**	17	▲ 2. **Darkness on the Edge of Town**	Columbia 35318
11/01/80	**1**(4)	22	▲ 3. **The River**	Columbia 36854 [2]
			"Hungry Heart"(5)	
10/09/82	**3**	11	● 4. Nebraska	Columbia 38358
			recorded on a 4-track cassette recorder at home	
6/23/84	**1**(7)	96	▲ 5. **Born In The U.S.A.**	Columbia 38653
			"Dancing In The Dark"(2)	
			"Cover Me"(7)	
			"Born In The U.S.A."(9)	
			"I'm On Fire"(6)	
			"Glory Days"(5)	
			"I'm Goin' Down"(9)	
			"My Hometown"(6)	
11/29/86	**1**(7)	15	▲ 6. **Bruce Springsteen & The E Street Band**	Columbia 40558 [5]
			Live l975-1985 [L]	
			contains 40 songs & includes 36 page color booklet with lyrics	
			"War"(8)	
			SPYRO GYRA	
			Buffalo-based jazz/pop band led by sax man Jay Beckenstein.	
6/09/79	**27**	17	● 1. Morning Dance [I]	Infinity 9004
4/05/80	**19**	8	● 2. Catching The Sun [I]	MCA 5108

DATE	POS	WKS	ARTIST—RECORD TITLE	LABEL & NO.
			SQUEEZE	
			English pop/rock quintet led by Chris Difford & Glenn Tilbrook.	
6/26/82	32	4	1. Sweets From A Stranger	A&M 4899
			BILLY SQUIER	
			Born on 5/12/50 in Wellesley, MA. Hard rock singer, songwriter, guitarist.	
6/20/81	5	38	▲ 1. **Don't Say No**	Capitol 12146
			"The Stroke"	
8/21/82	5	29	▲ 2. **Emotions in Motion**	Capitol 12217
8/11/84	11	14	▲ 3. Signs of Life	Capitol 12361
			JO STAFFORD	
			Born on 11/12/20 in Coalinga, California. Member of Tommy Dorsey's vocal group, the Pied Pipers, 1940-42. Married to orchestra leader, Paul Weston.	
12/29/56	13	8	1. Ski Trails	Columbia 910
			with husband Paul Weston, conductor; and the Norman Luboff Choir	
			PAUL STANLEY	
			Born Paul Eisen on 1/20/52 in Queens, New York. Rhythm guitarist of Kiss.	
12/16/78	40	2	▲ 1. Paul Stanley	Casablanca 7123
			THE STAPLE SINGERS	
			Family soul group consisting of Roebuck "Pop" Staples (b: 12/28/15, Winoma, MS), with his son Pervis (who left in 1971) and daughters Cleotha, Yvonne, and lead singer Mavis Staples. Roebuck was a blues guitarist in his teens, later with the Golden Trumpets gospel group. Moved to Chicago in 1935. Formed own gospel group in the early 50s. First recorded for United in 1953. Mavis recorded solo, early 70s.	
4/15/72	19	12	1. Bealtitude: Respect Yourself	Stax 3002
			"I'll Take You There"(1)	
11/29/75	20	8	2. Let's Do It Again [S]	Curtom 5005
			"Let's Do It Again"(1)	
			STARGARD	
			Disco trio: Rochelle Runnells, Debra Anderson and Janice Williams. Appeared as "The Diamonds" in film "Sgt. Pepper's Lonely Hearts Club Band".	
3/18/78	26	6	1. Stargard	MCA 2321
			STARLAND VOCAL BAND	
			Pop quartet: Bill and wife Taffy Danoff, John Carroll and Margot Chapman. Bill and Taffy had fronted Fat City folk quintet. Danoff co-wrote "Take Me Home, Country Roads" with friend, John Denver. Denver owned Windsong record label.	
7/10/76	20	10	1. Starland Vocal Band	Windsong 1351
			"Afternoon Delight"(1)	
			RINGO STARR	
			Born Richard Starkey on 7/7/40 in Liverpool, England. Ringo joined The Beatles following ousting of drummer Pete Best in 1962. First solo album in 1970. Films "Candy" (made in 1967, released in 1969), "The Magic Christian", "200 Motels", "Born To Boogie", "Blindman", "That'll Be The Day" and "Cave Man". Married actress Barbara Bach in 1982.	

DATE	POS	WKS	ARTIST—RECORD TITLE	LABEL & NO.
5/23/70	22	6	1. Sentimental Journey	Apple 3365
11/17/73	2(2)	19	● 2. **Ringo**	Apple 3413
			featuring backing by the other 3 Beatles	
			"Photograph"(1)	
			"You're Sixteen"(1)	
			"Oh My My"(5)	
12/07/74	8	12	● 3. **Goodnight Vienna**	Apple 3417
			guests: John Lennon and Elton John	
			"Only You"(6)	
			"No No Song"(3)	
12/27/75	30	5	4. Blast From Your Past [G]	Apple 3422
			"It Don't Come Easy"(4)	
			"Back Off Boogaloo"(9)	
10/23/76	28	6	5. Ringo's Rotogravure	Atlantic 18193
			guests: McCartney & Lennon, Eric Clapton, Peter Frampton	
			STARS ON	
			Session musicians from Holland, performing hit song medleys.	
6/20/81	9	8	● 1. **Stars On Long Play**	Radio 16044
			side 1: Beatles' medley	
			DAKOTA STATON	
			Jazz stylist born in Pittsburgh on 6/3/31.	
2/24/58	4	45	1. **The Late, Late Show**	Capitol 876
10/27/58	22	1	2. Dynamic!	Capitol 1054
6/08/59	23	9	3. Crazy He Calls Me	Capitol 1170
			STEELY DAN	
			Los Angeles-based pop/jazz-styled group formed by Donald Fagen (keyboards, vocals) and Walter Becker (bass, vocals). Group, primarily known as a studio unit, featured Fagen and Becker with various studio musicians. Duo went their separate ways, 1981.	
2/10/73	17	17	● 1. Can't Buy A Thrill	ABC 758
			"Do It Again"(6)	
			"Reeling In The Years"	
9/15/73	35	3	● 2. Countdown To Ecstasy	ABC 779
5/04/74	8	19	● 3. **Pretzel Logic**	ABC 808
			"Rikki Don't Lose That Number"(4)	
4/19/75	13	9	● 4. Katy Lied	ABC 846
5/29/76	15	9	● 5. The Royal Scam	ABC 931
10/15/77	3	51	▲ 6. **Aja**	ABC 1006
			"Peg"/"Deacon Blues"	
12/09/78	30	9	▲ 7. Greatest Hits [G]	ABC 1107 [2]
12/13/80	9	19	▲ 8. **Gaucho**	MCA 6102
			"Hey Nineteen"(10)	
			STEPPENWOLF	
			Hard rock quintet formed in Los Angeles in 1967. Original lineup: John Kay (born Joachim Krauledat on 4/12/44 in Tilsit, East Germany), vocals, guitar; Michael Monarch, guitar; Goldy McJohn, keyboards; Nick St. Nicholas, bass; Mars Bonfire (Dennis Edmonton), guitar, and brother Jerry Edmonton, drums. All but Monarch were members of the Canadian group, Sparrow. Many personnel changes except for Kay, McJohn and Jerry Edmonton.	
7/27/68	6	25	● 1. **Steppenwolf**	Dunhill 50029
			"Born To Be Wild"(2)	

DATE	POS	WKS	ARTIST—RECORD TITLE		LABEL & NO.
10/19/68	3	24	● 2. **The Second**		Dunhill 50037
			"Magic Carpet Ride"(3)		
3/29/69	7	11	3. **At Your Birthday Party**		Dunhill 50053
			"Rock Me"(10)		
8/02/69	29	6	4. Early Steppenwolf	[E-L]	Dunhill 50060
			recorded in 1967 when band was known as Sparrow - side 2 is a 21-1/2 minute version of "The Pusher"		
12/06/69	17	16	● 5. **Monster**		Dunhill 50066
4/25/70	7	15	● 6. **Steppenwolf 'Live'**	[L]	Dunhill 50075 [2]
11/21/70	19	7	● 7. Steppenwolf 7		Dunhill 50090
3/13/71	24	9	● 8. Steppenwolf Gold/Their Great Hits	[G]	Dunhill 50099

CAT STEVENS

Born Steven Georgiou on 7/21/47 in London, England. Began career playing folk music at Hammersmith College in 1966. Contracted tuberculosis in 1968, and spent over a year recuperating. Adopted new style when he reemerged. Lived in Brazil, mid-70s. Converted to Muslim religion, late 1979, took name Yusef Islam.

DATE	POS	WKS	ARTIST—RECORD TITLE		LABEL & NO.
2/13/71	8	44	● 1. **Tea for the Tillerman**		A&M 4280
			"Wild World"		
10/16/71	2(1)	37	● 2. **Teaser And The Firecat**		A&M 4313
			"Peace Train"(7)		
			"Morning Has Broken"(6)		
10/28/72	1(3)	26	● 3. **Catch Bull At Four**		A&M 4365
8/04/73	3	15	● 4. **Foreigner**		A&M 4391
4/20/74	2(3)	25	● 5. **Buddha And The Chocolate Box**		A&M 3623
			"Oh Very Young"(10)		
7/26/75	6	11	● 6. **Greatest Hits**	[G]	A&M 4519
			"Another Saturday Night"(6)		
12/13/75	13	13	● 7. Numbers		A&M 4555
5/28/77	7	12	● 8. **Izitso**		A&M 4702
1/20/79	33	4	9. Back To Earth		A&M 4735

RAY STEVENS

Born Ray Ragsdale on 1/24/41 in Clarkdale, Georgia. Attended Georgia State University, studied music theory and composition. Production work, mid-60s. Numerous appearances on Andy Williams TV show, late 60s. Own TV show in summer of 1970. Featured on "Music Country" TV show, 1973-74. The #1 novelty recording artist of the rock era.

DATE	POS	WKS	ARTIST—RECORD TITLE		LABEL & NO.
7/04/70	35	3	1. Everything Is Beautiful		Barnaby 35005
			"Everything Is Beautiful"(1)		

AL STEWART

Born on 9/5/45 in Glasgow, Scotland. Pop-rock singer, composer, guitarist.

DATE	POS	WKS	ARTIST—RECORD TITLE		LABEL & NO.
4/12/75	30	3	1. Modern Times		Janus 7012
11/20/76	5	21	▲ 2. **Year Of The Cat**		Janus 7022
			"Year Of The Cat"(8)		
10/14/78	10	14	▲ 3. **Time Passages**		Arista 4190
			"Time Passages"(7)		
10/04/80	37	4	4. 24 Carrots		Arista 9520

DATE	POS	WKS	ARTIST—RECORD TITLE	LABEL & NO.
			AMII STEWART	
			Born in Washington, DC in 1956. Disco singer, dancer, actress. In the Broadway musical "Bubbling Brown Sugar".	
3/31/79	**19**	9	● 1. Knock On Wood	Ariola 50054
			"Knock On Wood"(1)	
			JERMAINE STEWART	
8/16/86	**32**	5	1. Frantic Romantic	Arista 8395
			"We Don't Have To Take Our Clothes Off"(5)	
			JOHN STEWART	
			Born on 9/5/39 in San Diego. Member of the Kingston Trio from 1961-67. Wrote "Daydream Believer".	
6/16/79	**10**	14	1. **Bombs Away Dream Babies**	RSO 3051
			"Gold"(5-with Stevie Nicks)	
			ROD STEWART	
			Born on 1/10/45 in London, England. Worked as a folksinger in Europe, early 60s. Recorded for English Decca in 1964. With the Hoochie Coochie Men, Steampacket, and Shotgun Express. Joined Jeff Beck Group, 1967-69. With Faces from 1969-75, also recorded solo during this time. Left Faces in December, 1975. Also see Jeff Beck and Faces.	
7/11/70	**27**	7	1. Gasoline Alley	Mercury 61264
6/26/71	**1(4)**	35	● 2. **Every Picture Tells A Story**	Mercury 609
			"Maggie May"(1)	
8/12/72	**2(3)**	21	● 3. **Never A Dull Moment**	Mercury 646
8/11/73	**31**	3	● 4. Sing It Again Rod [G]	Mercury 680
11/09/74	**13**	5	5. Smiler	Mercury 1017
9/20/75	**9**	10	● 6. **Atlantic Crossing**	Warner 2875
7/31/76	**2(5)**	30	▲ 7. **A Night On The Town**	Warner 2938
			"Tonight's The Night (Gonna Be Alright)"(1)	
11/26/77	**2(6)**	27	▲ 8. **Foot Loose & Fancy Free**	Warner 3092
			"You're In My Heart (The Final Acclaim)"(4)	
1/06/79	**1(3)**	24	▲ 9. **Blondes Have More Fun**	Warner 3261
			"Da Ya Think I'm Sexy?"(1)	
12/01/79	**22**	7	▲ 10. Rod Stewart Greatest Hits [G]	Warner 3373
12/06/80	**12**	15	▲ 11. Foolish Behaviour	Warner 3485
			"Passion"(5)	
11/28/81	**11**	20	▲ 12. Tonight I'm Yours	Warner 3602
			"Young Turks"(5)	
7/09/83	**30**	4	13. Body Wishes	Warner 23877
7/07/84	**18**	19	● 14. Camouflage	Warner 25095
			"Infatuation"(6)	
			"Some Guys Have All The Luck"(10)	
7/26/86	**28**	7	15. Rod Stewart	Warner 25446
			"Love Touch"(6)	

DATE	POS	WKS	ARTIST—RECORD TITLE	LABEL & NO.
			STEPHEN STILLS	
			Born on 1/3/45 in Dallas. Member of Buffalo Springfield and Crosby, Stills & Nash.	
10/05/68	12	10	● 1. Super Session	Columbia 9701
			MIKE BLOOMFIELD/AL KOOPER/STEVE STILLS	
12/05/70	3	16	● 2. Stephen Stills	Atlantic 7202
			guests: Jimi Hendrix, Eric Clapton, David Crosby, Graham Nash	
			"Love The One You're With"	
7/24/71	8	9	● 3. **Stephen Stills 2**	Atlantic 7206
5/06/72	4	15	● 4. **Manassas**	Atlantic 903 [2]
6/02/73	26	6	5. Down The Road	Atlantic 7250
			above 2 albums feature Stills' band, Manassas	
7/12/75	19	6	6. Stills	Columbia 33575
6/19/76	31	3	7. Illegal Stills	Columbia 34148
10/30/76	26	6	● 8. Long May You Run	Reprise 2253
			STILLS-YOUNG BAND (Neil Young)	
			STING	
			Born Gordon Sumner on 10/2/51 in Wallsend, England. Lead singer, bass guitarist of the Police. Nicknamed Sting because of a yellow & black jersey he liked to wear.	
7/20/85	2(6)	37	▲ 1. **The Dream Of The Blue Turtles**	A&M 3750
			"If You Love Somebody Set Them Free"(3)	
			"Fortress Around Your Heart"(8)	
			THE KIRBY STONE FOUR	
			Kirby Stone (b: 4/27/18 in New York City), Eddie Hall, Larry Foster and Mike Gardner. Kirby was musical director for various TV shows.	
8/25/58	13	9	1. Baubles, Bangles And Beads	Columbia 1211
			STORIES	
			New York rock quartet: Ian Lloyd, lead singer, bass; Michael Brown (founding member of Left Banke), keyboards; Steve Love, guitar; and Bryan Madey, drums. Brown left group in 1973, replaced by Ken Aaronson, bass; and Ken Bichel, keyboards.	
9/01/73	29	6	1. About Us	Kama Sutra 2068
			"Brother Louie"(1)	
			STRAWBERRY ALARM CLOCK	
			West Coast psychedelic rock sextet: Ed King (lead guitar), Mark Weitz (keyboards), Lee Freeman (guitar), Gary Lovetro (bass), George Bunnel (bass) and Randy Seol (drums). King joined Lynyrd Skynyrd, 1973-75.	
12/02/67	11	13	1. Incense And Peppermints	Uni 73014
			"Incense And Peppermints"(1)	
			STRAY CATS	
			Long Island, New York rockabilly trio: Brian Setzer (b: 4/10/60), lead singer, guitar; Lee Rocker (Leon Drucher), string bass; and Slim Jim Phantom (Jim McDonell), drums. Group disbanded in 1984.	
9/04/82	2(15)	37	▲ 1. **Built For Speed**	EMI America 17070
			"Rock This Town"(9)	
			"Stray Cat Strut"(3)	
9/17/83	14	10	● 2. Rant n' Rave with the Stray Cats	EMI America 17102
			"(She's) Sexy + 17"(5)	

DATE	POS	WKS	ARTIST—RECORD TITLE	LABEL & NO.
			BARBRA STREISAND	
			Born Barbara Joan Streisand on 4/24/42 in Brooklyn. Made Broadway debut in "I Can Get It For You Wholesale", 1962. Lead role in Broadway's "Funny Girl", 1964. Film debut in "Funny Girl", 1968 (tied with Katharine Hepburn for Best Actress Oscar), also starred in "A Star Is Born", "Hello Dolly", "Funny Lady", "The Way We Were" and many others. Produced, directed and starred in the film "Yentl", 1983.	
5/04/63	8	78	● 1. **The Barbra Streisand Album**	Columbia 8807
			"Happy Days Are Here Again"	
9/28/63	2(3)	47	● 2. **The Second Barbara Streisand Album**	Columbia 8854
3/14/64	5	8	● 3. **The Third Album**	Columbia 8954
5/02/64	2(3)	40	● 4. **Funny Girl** [OC]	Capitol 2059
			based on the early life of Fanny Brice	
10/10/64	1(5)	48	● 5. **People**	Columbia 9015
			"People"(5)	
5/29/65	2(3)	46	● 6. **My Name Is Barbra**	Columbia 9136
11/13/65	2(3)	31	▲ 7. **My Name Is Barbra, Two...**	Columbia 9209
4/23/66	3	22	● 8. **Color Me Barbra**	Columbia 9278
12/03/66	5	13	9. **Je m'appelle Barbra**	Columbia 9347
12/02/67	12	12	10. Simply Streisand	Columbia 9482
11/09/68	12	31	▲ 11. Funny Girl [S]	Columbia 3220
			screen version of the above Broadway musical	
11/09/68	30	13	12. A Happening In Central Park [L]	Columbia 9710
9/20/69	31	4	13. What About Today?	Columbia 9816
3/21/70	32	2	▲ 14. Barbra Streisand's Greatest Hits [G]	Columbia 9968
2/27/71	10	11	▲ 15. **Stoney End**	Columbia 30378
			"Stoney End"(6)	
9/25/71	11	15	● 16. Barbra Joan Streisand	Columbia 30792
12/16/72	19	8	▲ 17. Live Concert At The Forum [L]	Columbia 31760
2/23/74	1(2)	12	▲ 18. **The Way We Were**	Columbia 32801
			not the soundtrack album (see Soundtracks)	
			"The Way We Were"(1)	
11/30/74	13	11	● 19. ButterFly	Columbia 33095
4/12/75	6	9	● 20. **Funny Lady** [S]	Arista 9004
			film is the sequel to "Funny Girl"	
11/15/75	12	10	● 21. Lazy Afternoon	Columbia 33815
12/25/76	1(6)	28	▲ 22. **A Star Is Born** [S-L]	Columbia 34403
			Kris Kristofferson sings on 5 of the 12 tracks (all but 4 tracks are live) - third version of the 1937 film classic	
			"Evergreen"(1)	
7/02/77	3	14	▲ 23. **Streisand Superman**	Columbia 34830
			"My Heart Belongs To Me"(4)	
6/24/78	12	13	▲ 24. Songbird	Columbia 35375
12/02/78	1(3)	17	▲ 25. **Barbra Streisand's Greatest Hits, Volume 2** [G]	Columbia 35679
			"You Don't Bring Me Flowers"(1-with Neil Diamond)	
7/21/79	20	9	● 26. The Main Event [S]	Columbia 36115
			3 versions of title song - others by various artists	
			"The Main Event/Fight"(3)	

DATE	POS	WKS	ARTIST—RECORD TITLE	LABEL & NO.
11/10/79	7	14	▲ 27. **Wet**	Columbia 36258
			"No More Tears (Enough Is Enough)"(1-with Donna Summer)	
10/11/80	**1**(3)	33	▲ 28. **Guilty**	Columbia 36750
			"Woman In Love"(1)	
			"Guilty"(3-with Barry Gibb)	
			"What Kind Of Fool"(10-with Barry Gibb)	
12/12/81	10	15	▲ 29. **Memories** [K]	Columbia 37678
12/03/83	9	13	▲ 30. **Yentl** [S]	Columbia 39152
			Barbra is the first woman to produce, direct, and write a film and perform its title role	
11/03/84	19	11	▲ 31. Emotion	Columbia 39480
11/30/85	**1**(3)	24	▲ 32. **The Broadway Album**	Columbia 40092
			Barbra sings 14 of her favorite Broadway tunes	

STRYPER

Christian heavy-metal band: Michael Sweet (vocals), Robert Sweet, Oz Fox, and Tim Gaines.

DATE	POS	WKS	ARTIST—RECORD TITLE	LABEL & NO.
11/29/86	32	12	● 1. To Hell With The Devil	Enigma 73237

THE STYLISTICS

Soul group from Philadelphia, formed in 1968. Consisted of Russell Thompkins, Jr. (b: 3/21/51), lead; Airrion Love, James Smith, James Dunn and Herbie Murrell. Thompkins, Love, and Smith had sang with the Percussions; Murrell and Dunn with the Monarchs from 1965-68. First recorded for Sebring in 1969.

DATE	POS	WKS	ARTIST—RECORD TITLE	LABEL & NO.
1/15/72	23	18	● 1. The Stylistics	Avco 33023
			"You Are Everything"(9)	
			"Betcha By Golly, Wow"(3)	
1/27/73	32	9	● 2. Round 2: The Stylistics	Avco 11006
			"I'm Stone In Love With You"(10)	
			"Break Up To Make Up"(5)	
6/22/74	14	7	● 3. Let's Put It All Together	Avco 69001

STYX

Chicago-based rock quintet: Dennis DeYoung (vocals, keyboards), Tommy Shaw (lead guitar), James Young (guitar), and twin brothers John (drums) and Chuck Panozzo (bass). Shaw replaced John Curulewski in 1976. Most songs written by Dennis DeYoung and/or Tommy Shaw.

DATE	POS	WKS	ARTIST—RECORD TITLE	LABEL & NO.
2/22/75	20	6	● 1. Styx II	Wooden N. 1012
			originally released in 1973 (Styx I did not chart)	
			"Lady"(6)	
9/03/77	6	37	▲ 2. **The Grand Illusion**	A&M 4637
			"Come Sail Away"(8)	
10/07/78	6	28	▲ 3. **Pieces of Eight**	A&M 4724
10/13/79	**2**(1)	26	▲ 4. **Cornerstone**	A&M 3711
			"Babe"(1)	
1/31/81	**1**(3)	35	▲ 5. **Paradise Theater**	A&M 3719
			"The Best Of Times"(3)	
			"Too Much Time On My Hands"(9)	
3/19/83	3	22	▲ 6. **Kilroy Was Here**	A&M 3734
			"Mr. Roboto"(3)	
			"Don't Let It End"(6)	
5/05/84	31	6	7. Caught In The Act - Live [L]	A&M 6514 [2]

DATE	POS	WKS	ARTIST—RECORD TITLE	LABEL & NO.
			SUGARLOAF	
			Denver rock quartet: Jerry Corbetta (lead singer, keyboards), Bob Webber (guitar), Bob Raymond (bass) and Bob MacVittie (drums). Robert Yeazel (guitar, vocals) joined in 1971. By 1974, Myron Pollock replaced MacVittie, and Yeazel had left.	
10/03/70	**24**	10	1. Sugarloaf	Liberty 7640
			"Green-Eyed Lady"(3)	
			DONNA SUMMER	
			Born LaDonna Adrian Gaines on 12/31/48 in Boston. With group Crow, played local clubs. In German production of "Hair", European productions of "Godspell", "The Me Nobody Knows" and "Porgy And Bess". Settled in Germany, where she recorded "Love To Love You Baby". In the film "Thank God It's Friday" in 1979. Married Bruce Sudano of Brooklyn Dreams in 1980. The Queen of Disco.	
12/13/75	**11**	13	● 1. Love To Love You Baby	Oasis 5003
			"Love To Love You Baby"(2)	
5/01/76	**21**	9	● 2. A Love Trilogy	Oasis 5004
11/20/76	**29**	5	● 3. Four Seasons Of Love	Casablanca 7038
6/18/77	**18**	18	● 4. I Remember Yesterday	Casablanca 7056
			"I Feel Love"(6)	
12/03/77	**26**	10	● 5. Once Upon A Time…	Casablanca 7078 [2]
9/16/78	**1(1)**	32	▲ 6. **Live And More** [L]	Casablanca 7119 [2]
			one of four sides is a studio recording	
			"MacArthur Park"(1)	
			"Heaven Knows"(4)	
5/12/79	**1(6)**	26	▲ 7. **Bad Girls**	Casablanca 7150 [2]
			"Hot Stuff"(1)	
			"Bad Girls"(1)	
			"Dim All The Lights"(2)	
11/10/79	**1(1)**	23	▲ 8. **On The Radio-Greatest Hits-Volumes I & II** [G]	Casablanca 7191 [2]
			"Last Dance"(3)	
			"No More Tears (Enough Is Enough)"(1-with Barbra Streisand)	
			"On The Radio"(5)	
11/08/80	**13**	8	● 9. The Wanderer	Geffen 2000
			"The Wanderer"(3)	
8/21/82	**20**	9	● 10. Donna Summer	Geffen 2005
			"Love Is In Control (Finger On The Trigger)"(10)	
7/23/83	**9**	15	● 11. **She Works Hard For The Money**	Mercury 812265
			"She Works Hard For The Money"(3)	
10/13/84	**40**	2	12. Cats Without Claws	Geffen 24040
			SUPERTRAMP	
			British rock quintet: Roger Hodgson (vocals, guitar), Rick Davies (vocals, keyboards), John Helliwell (sax), Dougie Thomson (bass) and Bob Benberg (drums). Hodgson went solo in 1983.	
5/17/75	**38**	3	● 1. Crime Of The Century	A&M 3647
			"Bloody Well Right"/"Dreamer"	
5/14/77	**16**	17	● 2. Even In The Quietest Moments…	A&M 4634
			"Give A Little Bit"	

DATE	POS	WKS	ARTIST—RECORD TITLE		LABEL & NO.
4/07/79	1(6)	48	▲ 3. **Breakfast In America**		A&M 3708
			"The Logical Song"(6)		
			"Take The Long Way Home"(10)		
10/11/80	8	11	● 4. **Paris**	[L]	A&M 6702 [2]
			recorded at the Paris Pavillon on 11/29/79		
11/13/82	5	17	● 5. **…famous last words…**		A&M 3732
			"It's Raining Again"		
6/15/85	21	10	6. Brother Where You Bound		A&M 5014
			first album without Roger Hodgson		

THE SUPREMES

R&B vocal group from Detroit, formed as the Primettes in 1959. Consisted of lead singer Diana Ross (b: 3/26/44), Mary Wilson (b: 3/6/44) and Florence Ballard (b: 6/30/43; d: 2/22/76 of cardiac arrest). Recorded for LuPine in 1960. Signed to Motown's Tamla label in 1960. Changed name to The Supremes in 1961. Ballard discharged from group in 1967, replaced by Cindy Birdsong, formerly with The Blue Belles. Ross left in 1969 for solo career, replaced by Jean Terrell. Birdsong left in 1972, replaced by Lynda Laurence. Terrell and Laurence left in 1973; Mary Wilson reformed group with Scherrie Payne (sister of Freda Payne) and Cindy Birdsong. Birdsong left again in 1976, replaced by Susaye Greene. In 1978, Wilson toured England with Karen Ragland and Karen Jackson, but lost rights to the name "Supremes" thereafter.

DATE	POS	WKS	ARTIST—RECORD TITLE		LABEL & NO.
10/31/64	2(4)	48	1. **Where Did Our Love Go**		Motown 621
			"Where Did Our Love Go"(1)		
			"Baby Love"(1)		
			"Come See About Me"(1)		
1/23/65	21	8	2. A Bit Of Liverpool		Motown 623
9/11/65	6	17	3. **More Hits By The Supremes**		Motown 627
			"Stop! In The Name Of Love"(1)		
			"Back In My Arms Again"(1)		
12/04/65	11	24	4. The Supremes at the Copa	[L]	Motown 636
4/02/66	8	14	5. **I Hear A Symphony**		Motown 643
			"I Hear A Symphony"(1)		
			"My World Is Empty Without You"(5)		
10/08/66	1(2)	31	6. **The Supremes A' Go-Go**		Motown 649
			"Love Is Like An Itching In My Heart"(9)		
			"You Can't Hurry Love"(1)		
2/25/67	6	17	7. **The Supremes sing** **Holland-Dozier-Holland**		Motown 650
			Brian Holland, Lamont Dozier, Eddie Holland		
			"You Keep Me Hangin' On"(1)		
			"Love Is Here And Now You're Gone"(1)		
7/01/67	20	7	8. The Supremes Sing Rodgers & Hart		Motown 659
			songwriting team: Richard Rodgers & Lorenz Hart		
			DIANA ROSS & THE SUPREMES:		
10/07/67	31	49	9. Diana Ross & the Supremes Greatest Hits, Volume 3	[G]	Motown 702
5/11/68	18	9	10. Reflections		Motown 665
			"Reflections"(2)		
			"In And Out Of Love"(9)		
12/21/68	2(1)	14	11. **Diana Ross & the Supremes Join the** **Temptations**		Motown 679
			"I'm Gonna Make You Love Me"(2)		

DATE	POS	WKS	ARTIST—RECORD TITLE	LABEL & NO.
12/28/68	**14**	7	12. Love Child	Motown 670
			"Love Child"(1)	
1/11/69	**1(1)**	19	13. **TCB** [TV]	Motown 682
			DIANA ROSS & THE SUPREMES with THE TEMPTATIONS	
7/05/69	**24**	6	14. Let The Sunshine In	Motown 689
			"I'm Livin' In Shame"(10)	
11/15/69	**28**	3	15. Together	Motown 692
			DIANA ROSS & THE SUPREMES with THE TEMPTATIONS	
12/20/69	**33**	7	16. Cream Of The Crop	Motown 694
			"Someday We'll Be Together"(1)	
12/20/69	**38**	2	17. On Broadway [TV]	Motown 699
			DIANA ROSS & THE SUPREMES with THE TEMPTATIONS	
1/31/70	**1(5)**	6	18. **Diana Ross and the Supremes Greatest Hits** [G]	Motown 663 [2]
			"The Happening"(1)	
			THE SUPREMES:	
6/06/70	**25**	6	19. Right On	Motown 705
			"Up The Ladder To The Roof"(10)	
			THE SURFARIS	
			Teenage surf band from Glendora, California. Consisted of Ron Wilson (drummer), Jim Fuller (lead guitar), Bob Berryhill (rhythm guitar), Pat Connolly (bass) and Jim Pash (sax, clarinet).	
9/07/63	**15**	16	1. Wipe Out [I]	Dot 25535
			"Wipe Out"(2)	
			SURVIVOR	
			Midwest rock quintet: Dave Bickler (lead singer), Jim Peterik (keyboards), Frankie Sullivan (guitar), Gary Smith (drums) and Dennis Johnson (bass). Smith and Johnson replaced by Marc Droubay and Stephan Ellis in 1981. Bickler replaced by Jimi Jamison in 1984.	
7/03/82	**2(4)**	19	▲ 1. **Eye Of The Tiger**	Scotti Br. 38062
			"Eye Of The Tiger"(1)	
3/09/85	**16**	44	2. Vital Signs	Scotti Br. 39578
			"High On You"(8)	
			"The Search Is Over"(4)	
			BILLY SWAN	
			Born on 5/12/43 in Cape Girardeau, Missouri. Singer, songwriter, keyboardist, guitarist. Produced Tony Joe White's first three albums.	
1/04/75	**21**	7	1. I Can Help	Monument 33279
			"I Can Help"(1)	
			SWEET	
			English rock band: Brian Connolly (lead singer), Steve Priest (bass, vocals), Andy Scott (guitar, keyboards) and Mick Tucker (drums).	
9/27/75	**25**	6	● 1. Desolation Boulevard	Capitol 11395
			"Ballroom Blitz"(5)	
			"Fox On The Run"(5)	
3/20/76	**27**	7	2. Give Us A Wink	Capitol 11496
			SWINGLE SINGERS	
			Ward Swingle (American) & his wordless French singers.	
11/23/63	**15**	24	1. Bach's Greatest Hits [I]	Philips 097

DATE	POS	WKS	ARTIST—RECORD TITLE	LABEL & NO.
			SWITCH	
			Soul/funk sextet from Detroit. Discovered by Jermaine Jackson.	
11/18/78	37	4	1. Switch	Gordy 980
8/11/79	37	4	2. Switch II	Gordy 988
			SYLVESTER	
			Born Sylvester James in Los Angeles. Moved to San Francisco in 1967. With vocal group, the Cockettes. In film "The Rose".	
9/30/78	28	6	● 1. Step II	Fantasy 9556
			T	
			TACO	
			Born Taco Ockerse in 1955 to Dutch parents in Jaharta, IN. German-based singer.	
8/06/83	23	11	1. After Eight	RCA 4818
			"Puttin' On The Ritz"(4)	
			TALKING HEADS	
			New York City-based 'new wave' quartet: David Byrne (lead singer, guitar), Jerry Harrison (keyboards, guitar), Tina Weymouth (bass) and husband Chris Frantz (drums). Also see Tom Tom Club.	
10/28/78	29	5	● 1. More Songs About Buildings And Food	Sire 6058
			"Take Me To The River"	
9/15/79	21	10	● 2. Fear Of Music	Sire 6076
11/15/80	19	9	● 3. Remain In Light	Sire 6095
			above 3 albums produced by Brian Eno	
5/08/82	31	4	4. The Name Of This Band Is Talking Heads [L]	Sire 3590 [2]
7/02/83	15	25	● 5. Speaking In Tongues	Sire 23883
			"Burning Down The House"(9)	
7/06/85	20	24	▲ 6. Little Creatures	Sire 25305
10/18/86	17	16	● 7. True Stories	Sire 25512
			contains new versions of songs featured in film "True Stories"	
			A TASTE OF HONEY	
			Soul/disco quartet: Janice Marie Johnson (vocals, guitar), Hazel Payne (vocals, bass), Perry Kimble (keyboards) and Donald Johnson (drums). Reformed as a duo in 1980 with Janice Johnson and Hazel Payne.	
7/29/78	6	14	▲ 1. A Taste of Honey	Capitol 11754
			"Boogie Oogie Oogie"(1)	
5/23/81	36	4	2. Twice As Sweet	Capitol 12089
			"Sukiyaki"(3)	
			TAVARES	
			Family R&B group from New Bedford, MA. Consisted of brothers Ralph, Antone "Chubby", Feliciano "Butch", Arthur "Pooch", and Perry Lee "Tiny" Tavares. Worked as Chubby & The Turnpikes from 1964-69.	
9/27/75	26	5	1. In The City	Capitol 11396
			"It Only Takes A Minute"(10)	

Squeeze's first record, a 1977 maxi-single called *Packet of Three,* was produced by John Cale and released on London's Deptford Fun City Records. After issuing its fifth A&M album, *Sweets from a Stranger,* in 1982, Squeeze disbanded and leaders Chris Difford and Glenn Tilbrook made an album on their own. In 1984, the pair reformed Squeeze with original piano player Jools Holland.

Steely Dan ultimately became a highly regarded jazz-art-rock ensemble, but its founders, Walter Becker and Donald Fagen, had to pay some bizarre dues first. They sold a song to Barbra Streisand, played in Jay and the Americans, and wrote mainstream pop for the Grass Roots. *Aja,* issued in 1977, reached the top five and was Steely Dan's first platinum record.

Rod Stewart began making solo albums in 1969 while still a member of the Jeff Beck Group and continued releasing albums under his own name throughout his years with Faces. *Atlantic Crossing* was Stewart's first album after he disbanded that group in 1975 and yielded a British No. 1 hit with "Sailing."

The Stray Cats emigrated from Long Island to London in 1980 and quickly found an audience for leader Brian Setzer's retro-rockabilly stylings. America was slow to catch the buzz: although the trio had its first U.K. hit album in early 1981, no records were even released in the U.S. until more than a year later.

Styx began in Chicago as a mid-1960s band called the Tradewinds, not becoming Styx until 1970. Once the hits began in 1974, Styx became (literally) golden, with a string of eight huge albums including five that were certified platinum. *Kilroy Was Here* (1983) featured the hit "Mr. Roboto"; the band mounted a major theatrical production for the subsequent tour.

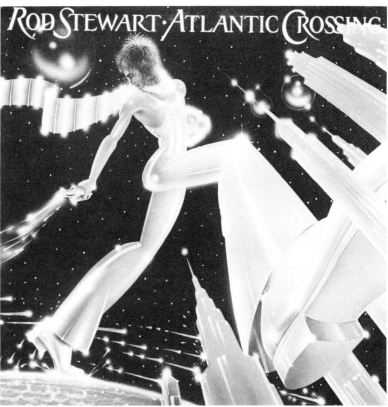

Supertramp, which originally formed as a quartet in 1969, took its name from the 1910 novel *The Autobiography of a Supertramp*. The group did not play its first American concert until its 1974 album, *Crime of the Century,* had been on the charts for over half a year. *Even in the Quietest Moments* was the group's second gold album, and its first to reach the top twenty.

Talking Heads has been far more productive during the past decade than seven studio and two live albums might indicate. The group starred in the film *Stop Making Sense;* singer/guitarist David Byrne later directed *True Stories* and recorded several albums outside the group. Tina Weymouth and Chris Frantz have made two Tom Tom Club albums; Jerry Harrison issued two solo albums and produced a Violent Femmes record.

James Taylor released *One Man Dog,* his fourth album, the same month he married Carly Simon and then took a year-and-a-half off from recording. Carole King, Linda Ronstadt, and Taylor's brothers Alex and Hugh and sister Kate helped out on the album, which reached the top five and went gold.

The Temptations' second album (1965) consisted entirely of songs written by Motown labelmate Smokey Robinson, who gave the group such classics as "My Girl" and "The Way You Do the Things You Do." In 1985, members David Ruffin and Eddie Kendricks rerecorded both songs live at the Apollo Theatre with Hall & Oates.

George Thorogood and the Destroyers covered songs by Hank Williams, Bo Diddley, Chuck Berry, Willie Dixon, and Brownie McGee on its second album, *Move It On Over* (1978), which went Top 40 and collected a gold record. Three years later, the R&B band from Delaware played on several Rolling Stones' concert dates.

DATE	POS	WKS	ARTIST—RECORD TITLE	LABEL & NO.
7/24/76	**24**	11	2. Sky High!	Capitol 11533
			"Heaven Must Be Missing An Angel"	

JAMES TAYLOR

Born on 3/12/48 in Boston. Singer, songwriter, guitarist. With older brother Alex in the Fabulous Corsairs, 1964. In New York group the Flying Machine, 1967, with friend Danny Kortchmar. Moved to England in 1968, recorded for Peter Asher. Married Carly Simon on 11/3/72; filed for divorce in 1982. In film "Two Lane Blacktop" with Dennis Wilson in 1973. Sister Kate and brothers Alex and Livingston also recorded.

DATE	POS	WKS	ARTIST—RECORD TITLE	LABEL & NO.
4/18/70	**3**	54	▲ 1. **Sweet Baby James**	Warner 1843
			"Fire And Rain"(3)	
5/08/71	**2(4)**	31	▲ 2. **Mud Slide Slim And The Blue Horizon**	Warner 2561
			"You've Got A Friend"(1)	
12/16/72	**4**	12	● 3. **One Man Dog**	Warner 2660
7/27/74	**13**	10	4. Walking Man	Warner 2794
6/14/75	**6**	15	● 5. **Gorilla**	Warner 2866
			"How Sweet It Is (To Be Loved By You)"(5)	
7/10/76	**16**	14	● 6. In The Pocket	Warner 2912
12/18/76	**23**	7	▲ 7. Greatest Hits　　　　　　　　[G]	Warner 2979
7/16/77	**4**	24	▲ 8. JT	Columbia 34811
			"Handy Man"(4)	
5/19/79	**10**	10	● 9. **Flag**	Columbia 36058
3/21/81	**10**	12	● 10. **Dad Loves His Work**	Columbia 37009
			"Her Town Too"(with J.D. Souther)	
12/07/85	**34**	8	11. That's Why I'm Here	Columbia 40052

JOHNNIE TAYLOR

Born on 5/5/37 in West Memphis, Arkansas. With gospel group, the Highway QC's in Chicago, early 50s. In vocal group the Five Echoes, recorded for Sabre in 1954. In The Soul Stirrers gospel group before going solo.

DATE	POS	WKS	ARTIST—RECORD TITLE	LABEL & NO.
3/27/76	**5**	11	● 1. **Eargasm**	Columbia 33951
			"Disco Lady"(1)	

TEARS FOR FEARS

British duo: Roland Orzabal (vocals, guitar, keyboards) & Curt Smith (vocals, bass). Adopted name from Arthur Yanoff's book "Prisoners Of Pain". Assisted by Manny Elias (drums) and Ian Stanley (keyboards).

DATE	POS	WKS	ARTIST—RECORD TITLE	LABEL & NO.
4/20/85	**1(5)**	55	▲ 1. **Songs From The Big Chair**	Mercury 824300
			"Everybody Wants To Rule The World"(1)	
			"Shout"(1)	
			"Head Over Heels"(3)	

TEENAGERS featuring Frankie Lymon

R&B group formed as the Premiers in the Bronx, New York in 1955. Lead singer, Lymon (b: 9/30/42, New York City), died of a drug overdose on 2/28/68. Other members included Herman Santiago, Jimmy Merchant (tenors); Joe Negroni (baritone - d: 9/5/78); and Sherman Garnes (bass, d: 2/26/77). Group in films "Rock, Rock, Rock" and "Mister Rock 'n' Roll".

DATE	POS	WKS	ARTIST—RECORD TITLE	LABEL & NO.
1/19/57	**19**	1	1. The Teenagers featuring Frankie Lymon	Gee 701
			"Why Do Fools Fall In Love"(6)	

DATE	POS	WKS	ARTIST—RECORD TITLE	LABEL & NO.
			THE TEMPTATIONS	
			Soul group formed in Detroit in 1960. Consisted of Eddie Kendricks, Paul Williams (d: 8/17/73), Melvin Franklin, Otis Williams and David Ruffin (joined in 1963). Originally called the Primes and Elgins, first recorded for Miracle in 1961. Ruffin replaced by Dennis Edwards in 1968. Kendricks and Paul Williams left in 1971, replaced by Damon Harris and Richard Street. Harris left in 1975, replaced by Glenn Leonard. Edwards left group, 1977-79, replaced by Louis Price. Edwards left again in 1984, rejoined in 1987. America's all-time favorite soul group.	
5/29/65	**35**	3	1. The Temptations Sing Smokey	Gordy 912
			tribute to songwriter/producer Smokey Robinson	
			"My Girl"(1)	
1/01/66	**11**	19	2. Temptin' Temptations	Gordy 914
8/13/66	**12**	18	3. Gettin' Ready	Gordy 918
1/14/67	**5**	65	4. **The Temptations Greatest Hits** **[G]**	Gordy 919
			"Beauty Is Only Skin Deep"(3)	
4/15/67	**10**	18	5. **Temptations Live!** **[L]**	Gordy 921
8/19/67	**7**	18	6. **With A Lot O' Soul**	Gordy 922
			"(I Know) I'm Losing You"(8)	
			"All I Need"(8)	
			"You're My Everything"(6)	
1/27/68	**13**	14	7. The Temptations in a Mellow Mood	Gordy 924
6/22/68	**13**	14	8. Wish It Would Rain	Gordy 927
			"I Wish It Would Rain"(4)	
12/21/68	**2(1)**	13	9. **Diana Ross & the Supremes Join the Temptations**	Motown 679
			"I'm Gonna Make You Love Me"(2)	
1/11/69	**1(1)**	19	10. **TCB** **[TV]**	Motown 682
			DIANA ROSS & THE SUPREMES with THE TEMPTATIONS	
2/01/69	**15**	9	11. Live At The Copa **[L]**	Gordy 938
			Dennis Edwards replaces David Ruffin	
3/22/69	**4**	26	12. **Cloud Nine**	Gordy 939
			"Cloud Nine"(6)	
			"Run Away Child, Running Wild"(6)	
8/16/69	**24**	10	13. The Temptations Show **[TV]**	Gordy 933
			with guests Kaye Stevens & George Kirby	
10/25/69	**5**	19	14. **Puzzle People**	Gordy 949
			"I Can't Get Next To You"(1)	
11/15/69	**28**	3	15. Together	Motown 692
			DIANA ROSS & THE SUPREMES with THE TEMPTATIONS	
12/27/69	**38**	1	16. On Broadway **[TV]**	Motown 699
			DIANA ROSS & THE SUPREMES with THE TEMPTATIONS	
4/11/70	**9**	18	17. **Psychedelic Shack**	Gordy 947
			"Psychedelic Shack"(7)	
9/05/70	**21**	6	18. Live at London's Talk of The Town **[L]**	Gordy 953
10/10/70	**15**	12	19. Temptations Greatest Hits II **[G]**	Gordy 954
			"Ball Of Confusion (That's What The World Is Today)"(3)	
5/22/71	**16**	15	20. Sky's The Limit	Gordy 957
			"Just My Imagination (Running Away With Me)"(1)	

DATE	POS	WKS	ARTIST—RECORD TITLE	LABEL & NO.
2/19/72	**24**	8	21. Solid Rock	Gordy 961
			Damon Harris replaces Eddie Kendricks	
9/16/72	**2(2)**	25	22. **All Directions**	Gordy 962
			"Papa Was A Rollin' Stone"(1)	
3/24/73	**7**	14	23. **Masterpiece**	Gordy 965
			"Masterpiece"(7)	
1/26/74	**19**	8	24. 1990	Gordy 966
3/22/75	**13**	16	25. A Song For You	Gordy 969
12/20/75	**40**	2	26. House Party	Gordy 973
5/15/76	**29**	6	27. Wings Of Love	Gordy 971
6/05/82	**37**	2	28. Reunion	Gordy 6008
			Ruffin & Kendricks return for this album	

10cc

English art-rock group which evolved from Hotlegs. Consisted of Eric Stewart (formerly of The Mindbenders), guitar; Graham Gouldman, bass; Lol Creme, guitar, keyboards; and Kevin Godley, drums. Godley and Creme left in 1976, replaced by drummer Paul Burgess. Added members Rick Fenn, Stuart Tosh and Duncan MacKay in 1978. Gouldman later in duo, Wax. Also see Godley & Creme.

DATE	POS	WKS	ARTIST—RECORD TITLE	LABEL & NO.
6/28/75	**15**	10	1. The Original Soundtrack	Mercury 1029
			"I'm Not In Love"(2)	
5/28/77	**31**	5	2. Deceptive Bends	Mercury 3702
			"The Things We Do For Love"(5)	

TEN YEARS AFTER

British blues-rock quartet: Alvin Lee (vocals, guitar), Leo Lyons (bass) Chick Churchill (keyboards) and Ric Lee (drums).

DATE	POS	WKS	ARTIST—RECORD TITLE	LABEL & NO.
9/13/69	**20**	7	1. SSSH	Deram 18029
4/25/70	**14**	8	2. Cricklewood Green	Deram 18038
12/19/70	**21**	8	3. Watt	Deram 18050
9/11/71	**17**	10	▲ 4. A Space In Time	Columbia 30801
			"I'd Love To Change The World"	
7/28/73	**39**	2	5. Recorded Live [L]	Columbia 32290 [2]

JOE TEX

Born Joseph Arrington, Jr. on 8/8/33 in Rogers, Texas; died of a heart attack on 8/13/82. Sang with local gospel groups. Won recording contract at Apollo Theater talent contest in 1954. First recorded for King in 1955. Became a convert to Muslim faith, changed name to Joseph Hazziez in July, 1972.

DATE	POS	WKS	ARTIST—RECORD TITLE	LABEL & NO.
5/06/72	**17**	11	1. I Gotcha	Dial 6002
			"I Gotcha"(2)	

THIN LIZZY

Dublin, Ireland rock quartet led by Phil Lynott. Phil died on 1/4/86 (35).

DATE	POS	WKS	ARTIST—RECORD TITLE	LABEL & NO.
6/05/76	**18**	10	● 1. Jailbreak	Mercury 1081
			"The Boys Are Back In Town"	
10/29/77	**39**	2	2. Bad Reputation	Mercury 1186

DATE	POS	WKS	ARTIST—RECORD TITLE	LABEL & NO.
			38 SPECIAL	
			Florida Southern-rock sextet: Donnie Van Zant (younger brother of Lynyrd Skynyrd's Ronnie Van Zant), lead singer; Don Barnes, Jeff Carlisi, Steve Brookins, Jack Grondin and Larry Jungstrom (replaced Ken Lyons in 1979).	
3/14/81	18	18	▲ 1. Wild-Eyed Southern Boys	A&M 4835
6/05/82	10	11	▲ 2. **Special Forces**	A&M 4888
			"Caught Up In You"(10)	
12/10/83	22	20	▲ 3. Tour De Force	A&M 4971
5/24/86	17	20	● 4. Strength In Numbers	A&M 5115
			B.J. THOMAS	
			Born Billy Joe Thomas on 8/27/42 in Hugo, Oklahoma; raised in Roseburg, Texas (near Houston). With the Triumphs, worked local clubs, recorded for Hickory in 1964. Went solo in 1966. Became a born-again Christian in 1976 and began a successful Gospel recording career.	
1/31/70	12	23	● 1. Raindrops Keep Fallin' On My Head	Scepter 580
			"Raindrops Keep Fallin' On My Head"(1)	
			CARLA THOMAS	
			Born on 12/21/42 in Memphis. Daughter of Rufus Thomas. First recorded with Rufus for Satellite in 1960. Had several duets with Otis Redding.	
7/22/67	36	3	1. King & Queen	Stax 716
			OTIS REDDING & CARLA THOMAS	
			THOMPSON TWINS	
			British-based trio: Tom Bailey (b: 1/18/56, England), lead singer, synthesizer; Alannah Currie (b: 9/28/57, New Zealand), xylophone, percussion; Joe Leeway (b: South Africa), conga, snythesizer. Leeway left in 1986.	
3/26/83	34	4	1. Side Kicks	Arista 6607
			"Lies"	
3/31/84	10	24	▲ 2. **Into The Gap**	Arista 8200
			"Hold Me Now"(3)	
10/26/85	20	24	● 3. Here's To Future Days	Arista 8276
			"Lay Your Hands On Me"(6)	
			"King For A Day"(8)	
			GEORGE THOROGOOD & THE DESTROYERS	
			Delaware rock & blues quartet. Lineup since 1980: Thorogood (vocals, guitar), Billy Blough (bass), Jeff Simon (drums) and Hank Carter (sax).	
3/31/79	33	7	● 1. Move It On Over	Rounder 3024
4/06/85	32	15	● 2. Maverick	EMI America 17145
9/20/86	33	4	3. Live [L]	EMI America 17214
			BILLY THORPE	
			English-born singer, guitarist; raised in Australia. Superstar artist in Australia.	
9/29/79	39	1	1. Children Of The Sun	Polydor 6228
			originally released on Capricorn 0221	

DATE	POS	WKS	ARTIST—RECORD TITLE		LABEL & NO.
			THE THREE DEGREES		
			Philadelphia R&B trio discovered by Richard Barrett. Originally consisted of Fayette Pinkney, Linda Turner and Shirley Porter. Turner and Porter replaced by Sheila Ferguson and Valerie Holiday in 1966.		
1/18/75	**28**	5	1. The Three Degrees		Phil. Int. 32406
			"When Will I See You Again"(2)		
			THREE DOG NIGHT		
			Los Angeles pop/rock group formed in 1968 featuring lead singers Danny Hutton (b: 9/10/42), Cory Wells (b: 2/5/42) and Chuck Negron (b: 6/8/42). Disbanded in the mid-70s.		
4/05/69	**11**	26	● 1. Three Dog Night		Dunhill 50048
			"One"(5)		
7/26/69	**16**	27	● 2. Suitable for Framing		Dunhill 50058
			"Easy To Be Hard"(4)		
			"Eli's Coming"(10)		
12/06/69	**6**	24	● 3. **Captured Live At The Forum**	[L]	Dunhill 50068
5/09/70	**8**	20	● 4. **It Ain't Easy**		Dunhill 50078
			"Mama Told Me (Not To Come)"(1)		
12/19/70	**14**	22	● 5. Naturally		Dunhill 50088
			"Joy To The World"(1)		
			"Liar"(7)		
3/06/71	**5**	30	● 6. **Golden Bisquits**	[G]	Dunhill 50098
10/23/71	**8**	21	● 7. **Harmony**		Dunhill 50108
			"An Old Fashioned Love Song"(4)		
			"Never Been To Spain"(5)		
8/12/72	**6**	19	● 8. **Seven Separate Fools**		Dunhill 50118
			"Black & White"(1)		
3/31/73	**18**	9	● 9. Around The World With Three Dog Night	[L]	Dunhill 50138 [2]
11/10/73	**26**	6	● 10. Cyan		Dunhill 50158
4/27/74	**20**	8	● 11. Hard Labor		Dunhill 50168
			"The Show Must Go On"(4)		
1/11/75	**15**	8	● 12. Joy To The World-Their Greatest Hits	[G]	Dunhill 50178
			THREE SUNS		
			Instrumental (organ/accordion/guitar) trio.		
5/28/55	**13**	9	1. Soft and Sweet	[I]	RCA 1041
8/18/56	**19**	1	2. High Fi and Wide	[I]	RCA 1249
1/26/57	**16**	6	3. Midnight For Two	[I]	RCA 1333
			TIERRA		
			East Los Angeles group led by brothers Steve and Rudy Salas. Both formerly with El Chicano.		
3/07/81	**38**	4	1. City Nights		Boardwalk 36995
			'TIL TUESDAY		
			Boston pop quartet: Aimee Mann (lead singer, bass), Michael Hausmann (drums), Robert Holmes (guitar) and Joey Pesce (keyboards).		
6/01/85	**19**	12	● 1. Voices Carry		Epic 39458
			"Voices Carry"(8)		

DATE	POS	WKS	ARTIST—RECORD TITLE	LABEL & NO.
			JOHNNY TILLOTSON	
			Born on 4/20/39 in Jacksonville, Florida; raised in Palatka, Florida. On local radio "Young Folks Revue" from age nine, had own band in high school. Deejay on WWPF. Appeared on the "Toby Dowdy" TV show in Jacksonville, then own show. Signed by Cadence Records in 1958. In the film "Just For Fun".	
8/25/62	8	10	1. **It Keeps Right On A-Hurtin'**	Cadence 3058
			"It Keeps Right On A-Hurtin'"(3)	
			THE TIME	
			Funk group formed in Minneapolis by Prince in 1981. Original lineup: Morris Day (lead singer), Terry Lewis, Jimmy "Jam" Harris, Monte Moir, Jesse Johnson and Jellybean Johnson. Disbanded in 1984. Day and Jesse Johnson went solo; Lewis and Harris have become a highly successful songwriting-producing team.	
10/02/82	26	8	● 1. What Time Is It?	Warner 23701
8/25/84	24	34	▲ 2. Ice Cream Castle	Warner 25109
			TINY TIM	
			Born Herbert Khaury on 4/12/30 in New York City. Novelty singer, ukulele player. National phenomenon when he married "Miss Vicki" on "The Tonight Show" on 12/18/69.	
6/08/68	7	10	1. **God Bless Tiny Tim** [N]	Reprise 6292
			"Tip-Toe Thru' The Tulips With Me"	
			TOBY BEAU	
			Texas pop quintet: Danny McKenna, Rob Young, Balde Silva, Steve Zipper and Ron Rose.	
9/02/78	40	1	1. Toby Beau	RCA 2771
			"My Angel Baby"	
			TOM TOM CLUB	
			Studio project headed by Chris Frantz and wife Tina Weymouth of the Talking Heads.	
2/20/82	23	10	● 1. Tom Tom Club	Sire 3628
			LILY TOMLIN	
			Member of TV's "Laugh-In" series (1970-73). TV/film actress. In films "9 To 5", "All of Me", and Broadway's "The Search For Signs of Intelligent Life In The Universe".	
4/10/71	15	11	1. This is a Recording [C]	Polydor 4055
			TOMMY TUTONE	
			San Francisco rock band led by Tommy Heath (lead singer) & Jim Keller (lead guitar).	
4/17/82	20	8	1. Tommy Tutone-2	Columbia 37401
			"867-5309/Jenny"(4)	
			TOTO	
			Pop/rock group formed in Los Angeles in 1978. Consisted of Bobby Kimball (vocals), Steve Lukather (guitar), David Paich and Steve Porcaro (keyboards), David Hungate (bass) and Jeff Porcaro (drums). Prominent session musicians, most notably behind Boz Scaggs in the late 70s. Hungate was replaced by Mike Porcaro in 1983. Kimball replaced by Fergie Frederiksen in 1984; Frederiksen replaced by Joseph Williams (conductor John's son) in 1986.	
12/09/78	9	20	▲ 1. **Toto**	Columbia 35317
			"Hold The Line"(5)	

DATE	POS	WKS	ARTIST—RECORD TITLE	LABEL & NO.
12/15/79	37	3	● 2. Hydra	Columbia 36229
5/08/82	4	42	▲ 3. **Toto IV**	Columbia 37728
			"Rosanna"(2)	
			"Africa"(1)	
			"I Won't Hold You Back"(10)	
11/29/86	40	2	4. Fahrenheit	Columbia 40273

TOWER OF POWER

Integrated Oakland-based R&B/funk band formed by sax player Emilio "Mimi" Castillo in the late 60s. Lenny Williams sang lead from 1972-75.

DATE	POS	WKS	ARTIST—RECORD TITLE	LABEL & NO.
7/28/73	15	8	1. Tower Of Power	Warner 2681
4/06/74	26	5	2. Back to Oakland	Warner 2749
2/22/75	22	5	3. Urban Renewal	Warner 2834
			Lenny Williams, lead singer on above 3 albums	

PETE TOWNSHEND

Born on 5/19/45 in London. Lead guitarist/songwriter of The Who.

DATE	POS	WKS	ARTIST—RECORD TITLE	LABEL & NO.
5/24/80	5	19	● 1. **Empty Glass**	Atco 100
			"Let My Love Open The Door"(9)	
7/24/82	26	9	2. All The Best Cowboys Have Chinese Eyes	Atco 149
4/09/83	35	4	3. Scoop [K]	Atco 90063 [2]
			primarily a collection of Townshend's demo recordings	
12/28/85	26	11	● 4. White City - A Novel	Atco 90473

TRAFFIC

British rock band - original lineup: Steve Winwood (keyboards, guitar), Dave Mason (guitar), Jim Capaldi (drums) and Chris Wood (flute, sax; d: 7/12/83). Many personnel changes during the group's 7 year existence.

DATE	POS	WKS	ARTIST—RECORD TITLE	LABEL & NO.
12/21/68	17	8	1. Traffic	United Art. 6676
5/24/69	19	7	2. Last Exit	United Art. 6702
7/25/70	5	16	● 3. **John Barleycorn Must Die**	United Art. 5504
10/16/71	26	7	4. Welcome To The Canteen [L]	United Art. 5550
12/18/71	7	20	● 5. **The Low Spark Of High Heeled Boys**	Island 9306
2/17/73	6	12	● 6. **Shoot Out At The Fantasy Factory**	Island 9323
11/24/73	29	5	7. Traffic-On The Road [L]	Island 9336 [2]
10/05/74	9	10	● 8. **When The Eagle Flies**	Asylum 1020

PAT TRAVERS

Canadian blues-rock guitarist/vocalist.

DATE	POS	WKS	ARTIST—RECORD TITLE	LABEL & NO.
9/01/79	29	4	1. Pat Travers Band Live! Go For What You Know [L]	Polydor 6202
			"Boom Boom (Out Go The Lights)"	
4/12/80	20	12	2. Crash And Burn	Polydor 6262
4/25/81	37	2	3. Radio Active	Polydor 6313

JOHN TRAVOLTA

Born on 2/18/54 in Englewood, New Jersey. Vinnie Barbarino on the TV series "Welcome Back Kotter". Starred in the films "Saturday Night Fever", "Grease", "Urban Cowboy", "Blow Out" and others.

DATE	POS	WKS	ARTIST—RECORD TITLE	LABEL & NO.
7/17/76	39	4	1. John Travolta	Midland Int. 1563
			"Let Her In"(10)	

DATE	POS	WKS	ARTIST—RECORD TITLE	LABEL & NO.
			T. REX	
			British rock group led by Marc Bolan (born Marc Feld on 9/30/48 in London; killed in an auto accident on 9/16/77).	
3/18/72	32	5	1. Electric Warrior	Reprise 6466
			"Bang A Gong (Get It On)"(10)	
10/07/72	17	11	2. The Slider	Reprise 2095
			TRIUMPH	
			Canadian hard-rock trio formed in Toronto in 1975. Consisted of Gil Moore (drums, vocals), Rik Emmett (guitar, vocals) and Mike Levine (keyboards, bass).	
4/19/80	32	6	1. Progessions Of Power	RCA 3524
10/17/81	23	9	● 2. Allied Forces	RCA 3902
2/12/83	26	12	● 3. Never Surrender	RCA 4382
2/02/85	35	7	4. Thunder Seven	MCA 5537
10/25/86	33	5	5. The Sport Of Kings	MCA 5786
			TRIUMVIRAT	
			German synthesized rock trio.	
7/26/75	27	5	1. Spartacus	Capitol 11392
			ROBIN TROWER	
			Born on 3/9/45 in London, England. Rock guitarist - member of Procol Harum. James Dewar, vocalist (except on "B.L.T." album).	
5/11/74	7	21	● 1. **Bridge Of Sighs**	Chrysalis 1057
3/08/75	5	9	● 2. **For Earth Below**	Chrysalis 1073
4/03/76	10	7	3. **Robin Trower Live!** [L]	Chrysalis 1089
10/16/76	24	6	● 4. Long Misty Days	Chrysalis 1107
10/22/77	25	6	● 5. In City Dreams	Chrysalis 1148
10/07/78	37	4	6. Caravan To Midnight	Chrysalis 1189
4/05/80	34	3	7. Victims Of The Fury	Chrysalis 1215
4/25/81	37	3	8. B.L.T.	Chrysalis 1324
			B.L.T.: Jack Bruce, Bill Lordan, Robin Trower	
			THE TUBES	
			San Francisco theatre rock troupe led by Fee Waybill.	
7/18/81	36	4	1. The Completion Backward Principle	Capitol 12151
4/30/83	18	14	2. Outside Inside	Capitol 12260
			"She's A Beauty"(10)	
			IKE & TINA TURNER	
			Husband and wife R&B duo: Ike Turner (b: 11/5/31, Clarksdale, MS), guitar, and Annie Mae Bullock (b: 11/26/38, Nutbush, TN), vocals. Married in 1958. Turner was a deejay at Clarksdale's WROX. Formed own band and recorded for RPM in 1951. First recorded with Tina for Federal in 1957. Ike developed dynamic stage show "The Ike & Tina Turner Revue" around Tina and her female backing group, The Ikettes. Tina went solo in 1974, and they were divorced in 1976.	
3/13/71	25	8	1. Workin' Together	Liberty 7650
			"Proud Mary"(4)	
7/31/71	25	11	● 2. Live At Carnegie Hall/What You Hear Is What You Get [L]	United Art. 9953 [2]

DATE	POS	WKS	ARTIST—RECORD TITLE	LABEL & NO.
			TINA TURNER	
			Born Annie Mae Bullock on 11/26/38 in Nutbush, Tennessee. R&B/ rock vocalist, actress. Half of Ike & Tina Turner duo. In films "Tommy" and "Mad Max Beyond Thunderdome".	
6/30/84	3	71	▲ 1. **Private Dancer**	Capitol 12330
			"What's Love Got To Do With It"(1)	
			"Better Be Good To Me"(5)	
			"Private Dancer"(7)	
10/04/86	4	17	▲ 2. **Break Every Rule**	Capitol 12530
			"Typical Male"(2)	
			THE TURTLES	
			Pop, folk rock group formed at Westchester High School in Los Angeles in 1961, and led by Mark Volman (b: 4/19/47, Los Angeles) and Howard Kaylan (b: Howard Kaplan on 6/22/47, New York City). First called the Nightriders; then the Crossfires. Recorded for Capco in 1963. Name changed to The Turtles in 1965. Many personnel changes except for Volman and Kaylan. Group disbanded in 1970. Volman and Kaylan joined the Mothers Of Invention. Went out as a duo in 1972 and recorded as Phlorescent Leech & Eddie and later as Flo & Eddie. Did soundtrack for the film "Strawberry Shortcake". Toured again as The Turtles in 1985.	
5/20/67	25	7	1. Happy Together	White Whale 7114
			"Happy Together"(1)	
			"She'd Rather Be With Me"(3)	
12/16/67	7	16	● 2. **The Turtles! Golden Hits** [G]	White Whale 7115
			DWIGHT TWILLEY	
			Born on 6/6/51 in Tulsa, Oklahoma. Rock singer, songwriter, pianist. Formed the Dwight Twilley Band with Phil Seymour (bassist, drummer) in 1974.	
4/14/84	39	3	1. Jungle	EMI America 17107
			"Girls"	
			TWISTED SISTER	
			Long Island, New York heavy-metal quintet led by Dee Snider.	
8/04/84	15	26	▲ 1. **Stay Hungry**	Atlantic 80156
			"We're Not Gonna Take It"	
			BONNIE TYLER	
			Born on 6/8/53 in Skewen, South Wales. Distinctive raspy vocals caused by operation to remove throat modules in 1976.	
6/10/78	16	8	● 1. It's A Heartache	RCA 2821
			"It's A Heartache"(3)	
9/10/83	4	17	▲ 2. **Faster Than The Speed Of Night**	Columbia 38710
			"Total Eclipse Of The Heart"(1)	
			THE TYMES	
			Smooth soul group formed in Philadelphia in 1956. Consisted of George Williams (lead singer), George Hilliard, Donald Banks, Albert Berry and Norman Burnett. First called the Latineers.	
8/24/63	15	9	1. So Much In Love	Parkway 7032
			"So Much In Love"(1)	
			"Wonderful! Wonderful!"(7)	

DATE	POS	WKS	ARTIST—RECORD TITLE	LABEL & NO.

U

DATE	POS	WKS	ARTIST—RECORD TITLE	LABEL & NO.
			UB40	
			British integrated reggae octet. Ali Campbell, lead singer. Took name from a British unemployment benefit form.	
4/14/84	39	3	● 1. Labour of Love	A&M 4980
10/05/85	40	3	2. Little Baggariddim [M]	A&M 5090
			"I Got You Babe"(with Chrissie Hynde)	
			UFO	
			British hard-rock group led by Phil Mogg (vocals) & Michael Schenker (guitar).	
7/23/77	23	12	1. Lights Out	Chrysalis 1127
			TRACEY ULLMAN	
			Born on 12/30/59 in England. Actress, singer, comedienne. Own variety-style TV show on new Fox Broadcasting Co. network in 1987.	
4/28/84	34	5	1. You Broke My Heart In 17 Places	MCA 5471
			"They Don't Know"(8)	
			ULTIMATE SPINACH	
			Psychedelic rock quintet from Boston.	
4/20/68	34	4	1. Ultimate Spinach	MGM 4518
			UNION GAP - see GARY PUCKETT	
			UNITED STATES MARINE BAND	
6/22/63	22	6	1. The United States Marine Band [I]	RCA 2687
			UNITED STATES NAVY BAND	
6/22/63	38	1	1. The United States Navy Band	RCA 2688
			with The Sea Chanters on 2 tracks	
			URIAH HEEP	
			British hard rock band. Key members: David Byron (lead singer), Mick Box (lead guitar) and Ken Hensley (keyboards).	
8/26/72	23	13	● 1. Demons And Wizards	Mercury 630
			"Easy Livin"	
1/06/73	31	8	● 2. The Magician's Birthday	Mercury 652
6/09/73	37	5	● 3. Uriah Heep Live [L]	Mercury 7503 [2]
11/03/73	33	3	● 4. Sweet Freedom	Warner 2724
8/24/74	38	2	● 5. Wonderworld	Warner 2800
			USA for AFRICA	
			USA: United Support of Artists - a collection of 46 major artists formed to help the suffering people of Africa and the U.S.A.	
4/20/85	1(3)	11	▲ 1. **We Are The World**	Columbia 40043
			tracks contributed by Northern Lights (Canada's superstar artists), Bruce Springsteen, Prince, Huey Lewis, Chicago, Tina Turner, Pointer Sisters, Kenny Rogers, Steve Perry	
			"We Are The World"(1-featuring 46 major recording artists)	

DATE	POS	WKS	ARTIST—RECORD TITLE	LABEL & NO.
			UTOPIA	
			Veteran pop/rock group with own recording studio near Woodstock, New York. Consists of Todd Rundgren (guitar), Kasim Sulton (bass), Roger Powell (keyboards) and Willie Wilcox (drums).	
12/14/74	34	2	1. Todd Rundgren's Utopia	Bearsville 6954
2/16/80	32	5	2. Adventures In Utopia	Bearsville 6991
			"Set Me Free"	
			U2	
			Rock band formed in Dublin, Ireland in 1976. Consisted of Paul "Bono" Hewson (vocals), Dave "The Edge" Evans (guitar), Adam Clayton (bass) and Larry Mullen Jr. (drums). Emerged as 1987's leading rock act.	
4/02/83	12	16	▲ 1. War	Island 90067
			"New Year's Day"/"Sunday Bloody Sunday"	
1/07/84	28	13	▲ 2. Under A Blood Red Sky [M-L]	Island 90127
10/27/84	12	22	▲ 3. The Unforgettable Fire	Island 90231
6/29/85	37	1	4. Wide Awake In America [L]	Island 90279
			side A: live; side B: outtakes from "The Unforgettable Fire" LP album dropped by Billboard after charting for 1 week because it was only a four-cut album that listed for less than $5.98	
			V	
			JERRY VALE	
			Born Genero Vitaliano on 7/8/32 in Bronx, New York. Pop ballad singer.	
4/13/63	34	4	1. Arrivederci, Roma	Columbia 8755
10/26/63	22	6	2. The Language Of Love	Columbia 8843
3/21/64	28	6	3. Till The End Of Time	Columbia 8916
10/17/64	26	6	4. Be My Love	Columbia 8981
4/24/65	30	5	5. Have You Looked Into Your Heart	Columbia 9113
4/30/66	38	1	6. It's Magic	Columbia 9244
			RITCHIE VALENS	
			Born Richard Valenzuela on 5/13/41 in Pacoima, California. Latin rock and roll singer, songwriter, guitarist. Killed in the plane crash that also took the lives of Buddy Holly and the Big Bopper on 2/3/59. In the film "Go Johnny Go".	
4/06/59	23	5	1. Ritchie Valens	Del-Fi 1201
			"Donna"(2)	
			"La Bamba"	
			FRANKIE VALLI	
			Born Francis Castellucio on 5/3/37 in Newark, New Jersey. Recorded his first solo single in 1953 as Frank Valley on the Corona label. Formed own group, the Variatones in 1955, and changed their name to the Four Lovers in 1956, which evolved into The 4 Seasons by 1961. Began solo work in 1965.	
8/26/67	34	2	1. Frankie Valli-Solo	Philips 247
			"Can't Take My Eyes Off You"(2)	

DATE	POS	WKS	ARTIST—RECORD TITLE	LABEL & NO.
			VAN HALEN	
			Hard-rock band formed in Pasadena, California in 1974. Consisted of David Lee Roth (b: 10/10/55), vocals; Eddie Van Halen (b: 1/26/57), guitar; Michael Anthony (b: 6/20/55), bass; and Alex Van Halen (b: 5/8/55), drums. The Van Halen brothers were born in Nijmegen, The Netherlands, and moved to Pasadena in 1968. Sammy Hagar replaced Roth as lead singer in 1985.	
4/15/78	19	12	▲ 1. Van Halen	Warner 3075
			"You Really Got Me"	
4/21/79	6	18	▲ 2. **Van Halen II**	Warner 3312
			"Dance The Night Away"	
4/19/80	6	13	▲ 3. **Women and Children First**	Warner 3415
5/30/81	5	12	▲ 4. **Fair Warning**	Warner 3540
5/08/82	3	16	▲ 5. **Diver Down**	Warner 3677
			"(Oh) Pretty Woman"	
1/28/84	2(5)	53	▲ 6. **1984 (MCMLXXXIV)**	Warner 23985
			"Jump(1)"	
			"I'll Wait"/"Panama"	
4/12/86	1(3)	32	▲ 7. **5150**	Warner 25394
			Sammy Hagar replaces David Lee Roth as lead singer - 5150: New York Police code for the criminally insane; also the name of Eddie Van Halen's recording studio	
			"Why Can't This Be Love"(3)	
			LUTHER VANDROSS	
			Born on 4/20/51 in New York City. Soul singer, producer, songwriter. Began career singing commercial jingles, then became a top session vocalist, arranger.	
10/10/81	19	10	● 1. Never Too Much	Epic 37451
10/30/82	20	12	▲ 2. Forever, For Always, For Love	Epic 38235
1/28/84	32	9	▲ 3. Busy Body	Epic 39196
4/20/85	19	17	▲ 4. The Night I Fell In Love	Epic 39882
11/08/86	14	32	5. Give Me The Reason	Epic 40415
			VANGELIS	
			Born Evangelos Papathanassiou in Greece. Keyboardist, composer. Formed rock band, Aphrodites Child, in France with Demis Roussos, 1968-early 70s. Also see Jon & Vangelis.	
2/20/82	1(4)	20	▲ 1. **Chariots Of Fire** [S-I]	Polydor 6335
			film is based on the true story of 2 members of Britain's 1924 Olympic team	
			"Chariots Of Fire-Titles"(1)	
			VANILLA FUDGE	
			Psychedelic rock quartet formed in New York in 1966. Consisted of Mark Stein (lead singer, keyboards), Vinnie Martell (guitar), Tim Bogert (bass) and Carmine Appice (drums).	
9/23/67	6	39	● 1. **Vanilla Fudge**	Atco 224
			"You Keep Me Hangin' On"(6)	
3/09/68	17	9	2. The Beat Goes On	Atco 237
8/10/68	20	9	3. Renaissance	Atco 244
3/15/69	16	9	4. Near the Beginning [L]	Atco 278
			side 2 recorded live	
11/01/69	34	4	5. Rock & Roll	Atco 303

DATE	POS	WKS	ARTIST—RECORD TITLE	LABEL & NO.
			GINO VANNELLI	
			Born on 6/16/52 in Montreal, Canada. Pop/soul-styled singer, songwriter.	
9/11/76	32	5	1. The Gist of The Gemini	A&M 4596
1/07/78	33	4	2. A Pauper In Paradise	A&M 4664
			side 2 with the Royal Philharmonic Orchestra	
11/04/78	13	11	▲ 3. Brother To Brother	A&M 4722
			"I Just Wanna Stop"(4)	
4/25/81	15	14	4. Nightwalker	Arista 9539
			"Living Inside Myself"(6)	
			SARAH VAUGHAN	
			Born on 3/27/24 in Newark, New Jersey. Jazz singer. Studied piano, 1931-39. Won amateur contest at the Apollo Theater in 1942, which led to her joining Earl Hine's band as vocalist and second pianist. Later joined Billy Eckstine's band and recorded for Continental in 1944. Went solo in 1945. Married manager George Treadwell in 1947. Dubbed "The Divine One". Still active in the 80s.	
11/24/56	20	2	1. Linger Awhile	Columbia 914
12/01/56	21	5	2. Sassy	EmArcy 36089
4/13/57	14	10	3. Great Songs From Hit Shows	Mercury 100 [2]
8/19/57	14	9	4. Sarah Vaughan sings George Gershwin	Mercury 101 [2]
			STEVIE RAY VAUGHAN & Double Trouble	
			Lead guitarist on David Bowie's "Let's Dance" album.	
9/03/83	38	3	1. Texas Flood	Epic 38734
7/07/84	31	8	2. Couldn't Stand The Weather	Epic 39304
			recorded at Montreux Jazz Festival 1985; Austin Opera House and Dallas Starfest, 1986	
10/26/85	34	6	3. Soul To Soul	Epic 40036
			BILLY VAUGHN	
			Born Richard Vaughn on 4/12/19 in Glasgow, Kentucky. Organized the Hilltoppers vocal group in 1952. Music director for Dot Records - arranger/conductor for Pat Boone, Gale Storm, The Fontane Sisters and many other Dot artists. Billy had more pop hits than any other orchestra leader during the rock era.	
4/21/58	5	56	● 1. **Sail Along Silv'ry Moon** [I]	Dot 3100
			"Sail Along Silvery Moon"(5)	
			"Raunchy"(10)	
10/13/58	15	45	2. Billy Vaughn Plays The Million Sellers [I]	Dot 3119
5/04/59	20	3	3. Billy Vaughn Plays [I]	Dot 3156
5/25/59	7	47	● 4. **Blue Hawaii** [I]	Dot 3165
1/18/60	36	1	5. Golden Saxophones [I]	Dot 3205
3/21/60	1(2)	48	● 6. **Theme from A Summer Place** [I]	Dot 3276
8/15/60	5	33	7. **Look For A Star** [I]	Dot 3322
12/19/60	5	15	8. **Theme from The Sundowners** [I]	Dot 3349
5/08/61	11	20	9. Orange Blossom Special and Wheels [I]	Dot 3366
10/09/61	17	9	10. Golden Waltzes [I]	Dot 3280
12/04/61	20	15	11. Berlin Melody [I]	Dot 3396
3/24/62	18	11	12. Greatest String Band Hits	Dot 3409
6/09/62	14	13	13. Chapel By The Sea [I]	Dot 3424

DATE	POS	WKS	ARTIST—RECORD TITLE	LABEL & NO.
10/06/62	10	10	14. **A Swingin' Safari** [I]	Dot 3458
2/16/63	17	12	15. 1962's Greatest Hits [I]	Dot 25497
7/06/63	15	6	16. Sukiyaki and 11 Hawaiian Hits [I]	Dot 25523
3/06/65	18	9	17. Pearly Shells [I]	Dot 25605
11/13/65	31	6	18. Moon Over Naples [I]	Dot 25654

BOBBY VEE

Born Robert Velline on 4/30/43 in Fargo, North Dakota. Formed band, The Shadows, with his brother and a friend in 1959. After Buddy Holly's death in a plane crash, The Shadows filled in on Buddy's next scheduled show in Fargo. First recorded for Soma in 1959. In films "Swingin' Along", "It's Trad, Dad", "Play It Cool", "C'mon Let's Live A Little" and "Just For Fun".

DATE	POS	WKS	ARTIST—RECORD TITLE	LABEL & NO.
3/20/61	18	2	1. Bobby Vee	Liberty 7181
			"Devil Or Angel"(6)	
			"Rubber Ball"(6)	
12/01/62	24	9	2. Bobby Vee's Golden Greats [G]	Liberty 7245

THE VENTURES

Guitar-based instrumental rock and roll band formed in the Seattle/Tacoma, Washington area. Consisted of lead guitarist Nokie Edwards (b: 5/9/39), bass and lead guitarist Bob Bogle (b: 1/16/37), rhythm guitarist Don Wilson (b: 2/10/37), and drummer Howie Johnson. First recorded for own label, Blue Horizon, in 1959. Johnson was injured in an auto accident, and was replaced by Mel Taylor in 1963. Taylor went solo in 1967, returned in 1978. Edwards left in 1968, replaced by Jerry McGee, returned in 1972. Added keyboardist John Durrill in 1969. Latest recordings featured Edwards, Bogle, Wilson and Taylor.

DATE	POS	WKS	ARTIST—RECORD TITLE	LABEL & NO.
12/05/60	11	13	1. Walk Don't Run [I]	Dolton 8003
			"Walk-Don't Run"(2)	
7/31/61	39	14	2. Another Smash!!! [I]	Dolton 8006
2/03/62	24	12	3. Twist With The Ventures [I]	Dolton 8010
1/19/63	8	11	● 4. **The Ventures play Telstar, The Lonely Bull** [I]	Dolton 8019
6/01/63	30	5	5. "Surfing" [I]	Dolton 8022
10/12/63	30	2	6. Let's Go! [I]	Dolton 8024
2/15/64	27	7	7. (The) Ventures In Space [I]	Dolton 8027
8/22/64	32	4	8. The Fabulous Ventures [I]	Dolton 8029
11/07/64	17	10	9. Walk, Don't Run, Vol. 2 [I]	Dolton 8031
			"Walk-Don't Run '64"(8)	
4/10/65	31	5	10. The Ventures Knock Me Out! [I]	Dolton 8033
8/28/65	27	9	11. The Ventures On Stage [I-L]	Dolton 8035
10/23/65	16	20	12. The Ventures a go-go [I]	Dolton 8037
4/23/66	33	3	13. Where The Action Is [I]	Dolton 8040
8/20/66	39	2	14. Go With The Ventures! [I]	Dolton 8045
11/05/66	33	6	15. Wild Things! [I]	Dolton 8047
5/17/69	11	14	● 16. Hawaii Five-O [I]	Liberty 8061
			"Hawaii Five-O"(4)	

DATE	POS	WKS	ARTIST—RECORD TITLE	LABEL & NO.
			VILLAGE PEOPLE	
			New York campy disco group: Victor Willis, Randy Jones, David Hodo, Felipe Rose, Glenn Hughes and Alexander Briley. In film "Can't Stop The Music", 1980.	
7/29/78	**24**	8	▲ 1. Macho Man	Casablanca 7096
11/11/78	**3**	26	▲ 2. **Cruisin'**	Casablanca 7118
			"Y.M.C.A."(2)	
4/14/79	**8**	13	▲ 3. **Go West**	Casablanca 7144
			"In The Navy"(3)	
11/17/79	**32**	5	● 4. Live and Sleazy [L]	Casablanca 7183 [2]
			record 1: live; record 2: studio	
			THE VILLAGE STOMPERS	
			Greenwich Village, New York dixieland-styled band.	
11/23/63	**5**	14	1. **Washington Square** [I]	Epic 26078
			"Washington Square"(2)	
			GENE VINCENT	
			Born Vincent Eugene Craddock on 2/11/35 in Norfolk, Virginia; died from an ulcer hemorrhage on 10/12/71. Innovative rock and roll singer, songwriter, guitarist. Injured left leg in motorcycle accident in 1953, had to wear steel brace thereafter. Formed own band, The Bluecaps, in Norfolk in 1956. Appeared in films "The Girl Can't Help It" and "Hot Rod Gang". To England from 1960-67. Injured in car crash that killed Eddie Cochran in England in 1960.	
			GENE VINCENT & His Blue Caps:	
9/29/56	**16**	2	1. Bluejean Bop!	Capitol 764
			BOBBY VINTON	
			Born Stanley Robert Vinton on 4/16/35 in Canonsburg, Pennsylvania. Father was a bandleader. Formed own band while in high school. Toured as backing band for Dick Clark's "Caravan of Stars" in 1960. Left band for a singing career in 1962. Own TV series from 1975-78.	
8/18/62	**5**	14	1. **Roses Are Red**	Epic 26020
			"Roses Are Red (My Love)"(1)	
			"Mr. Lonely"(1-'64)	
9/07/63	**10**	18	2. **Blue Velvet**	Epic 26068
			"Blue On Blue"(3)	
			"Blue Velvet"(1)	
2/22/64	**8**	12	3. **There! I've Said It Again**	Epic 26081
			"There! I've Said It Again"(1)	
			"My Heart Belongs To Only You"(9)	
8/22/64	**31**	4	4. Tell Me Why	Epic 26113
12/05/64	**12**	14	● 5. Bobby Vinton's Greatest Hits [G]	Epic 26098
1/30/65	**18**	7	6. Mr. Lonely	Epic 26136
			album 1 above also contains the hit version of the title song	
2/01/69	**21**	6	7. I Love How You Love Me	Epic 26437
			"I Love How You Love Me"(9)	
12/21/74	**16**	7	● 8. Melodies Of Love	ABC 851
			"My Melody Of Love"(3)	

DATE	POS	WKS	ARTIST—RECORD TITLE	LABEL & NO.
			THE VOGUES Vocal group formed in Turtle Creek, PA in 1960. Consisted of Bill Burkette (lead), Hugh Geyer & Chuck Blasko (tenors) and Don Miller (baritone). Met in high school.	
12/07/68	29	4	1. Turn Around, Look At Me	Reprise 6314
			"Turn Around, Look At Me"(7)	
			"My Special Angel"(7)	
4/05/69	30	6	2. Till	Reprise 6326
			VOYAGE European disco group. Sylvia Mason, lead singer.	
7/01/78	40	2	1. Voyage	Marlin 2213

W

DATE	POS	WKS	ARTIST—RECORD TITLE	LABEL & NO.
			JOHN WAITE Born on 7/4/55 in England. Lead singer of The Babys.	
8/04/84	10	17	● 1. **No Brakes**	EMI America 17124
			"Missing You"(1)	
10/05/85	36	3	2. Mask Of Smiles	EMI America 17164
			RICK WAKEMAN English - former keyboardist of the Strawbs and Yes.	
5/19/73	30	13	● 1. The Six Wives of Henry VIII [I]	A&M 4361
6/22/74	3	16	● 2. **Journey To The Centre Of The Earth** [L]	A&M 3621
			with the London Symphony Orchestra	
5/03/75	21	6	3. The Myths and Legends of King Arthur and the Knights of the Round Table	A&M 4515
			with the English Chamber Choir and orchestra	
			JOE WALSH Born on 11/20/47 in Wichita, Kansas. Rock singer/songwriter/guitarist. Member of The James Gang (1969-71) and the Eagles (1975-82).	
8/18/73	6	20	● 1. **The Smoker You Drink, The Player You Get**	Dunhill 50140
			"Rocky Mountain Way"	
2/01/75	11	10	● 2. So What	Dunhill 50171
4/17/76	20	9	3. You Can't Argue With A Sick Mind [L]	ABC 932
6/17/78	8	14	▲ 4. **But Seriously, Folks...**	Asylum 141
			"Life's Been Good"	
6/13/81	20	9	5. There Goes The Neighborhood	Asylum 523
			WALTER WANDERLEY Brazilian organist/pianist/composer. Died of cancer on 9/4/86 (55).	
11/19/66	22	9	1. Rain Forest [I]	Verve 8658
			"Summer Samba"	

DATE	POS	WKS	ARTIST—RECORD TITLE	LABEL & NO.
			WANG CHUNG	
			British pop/rock group: Jack Hues (lead singer, guitar, keyboards), Nick Feldman (bass, keyboards) and Darren Costin (drums). Costin left in 1985.	
6/23/84	**30**	6	1. Points On The Curve	Geffen 4004
			"Dance Hall Days"	
			WAR	
			Latin jazz/funk band formed in Long Beach, California in 1969. Consisted of Lonnie Jordan (keyboards), Howard Scott (guitar), Charles Miller (saxophone), B.B. Dickerson (bass), Harold Brown and "Papa" Dee Allen (percussion) and Lee Oskar (harmonica). Eric Burdon's backup band until 1971. Dickerson replaced by Luther Rabb. Alice Tweed Smyth (vocals) added in 1978. Pat Rizzo (horns) and Ron Hammond (percussion) added in 1979. Tweed left in 1982.	
			ERIC BURDON & WAR:	
7/11/70	**18**	13	1. Eric Burdon Declares "War"	MGM 4663
			"Spill The Wine"(3)	
			WAR:	
3/04/72	**16**	22	● 2. All Day Music	United Art. 5546
12/16/72	**1(2)**	25	● 3. **The World Is A Ghetto**	United Art. 5652
			"The World Is A Ghetto"(7)	
			"The Cisco Kid"(2)	
9/08/73	**6**	14	● 4. **Deliver The Word**	United Art. 128
			"Gypsy Man"(8)	
4/06/74	**13**	11	● 5. War Live! [L]	United Art. 193 [2]
7/12/75	**8**	19	● 6. **Why Can't We Be Friends?**	United Art. 441
			"Why Can't We Be Friends?"(6)	
			"Low Rider"(7)	
9/04/76	**6**	13	▲ 7. **Greatest Hits** [G]	United Art. 648
			"Summer"(7)	
8/06/77	**23**	7	● 8. Platinum Jazz [K]	Blue Note 690 [2]
12/17/77	**15**	12	● 9. Galaxy	MCA 3030
			ANITA WARD	
			Born on 12/20/57 in Memphis. R&B/disco vocalist.	
6/09/79	**8**	10	1. **Songs Of Love**	Juana 200,004
			"Ring My Bell"(1)	
			FRED WARING & The PENNSYLVANIANS	
			Glee club/bandleader since early 20s. Died on 7/29/84 (84).	
9/09/57	**25**	1	1. Fred Waring And The Pennsylvanians In Hi-Fi	Capitol 845
12/23/57	**6**	3	2. **Now Is The Caroling Season** [X]	Capitol 896
12/22/58	**19**	1	3. Now Is The Caroling Season [X-R]	Capitol 896
			RUSTY WARREN	
			Singer/storyteller of adult comedy.	
11/07/60	**8**	10	1. **Knockers Up!** [C]	Jubilee 2029
5/29/61	**21**	12	2. Sin-Sational [C]	Jubilee 2034
2/10/62	**31**	5	3. Rusty Warren Bounces Back [C]	Jubilee 2039
12/01/62	**22**	11	4. Rusty Warren In Orbit [C]	Jubilee 2044

DATE	POS	WKS	ARTIST—RECORD TITLE		LABEL & NO.
			DIONNE WARWICK		
			Born on 12/12/40 in East Orange, New Jersey. In church choir from age 6. With the Drinkard Singers gospel group. Formed trio, the Gospelaires, with sister Dee Dee and their aunt Cissy Houston. Much backup studio work in New York, late 50s. Added an "e" to her last name for a time in the early 70s. Burt Bacharach and Hal David's main "voice" for the songs they composed.		
7/01/67	18	15	● 1. Here Where There is Love		Scepter 555
			"Alfie"		
11/11/67	22	6	2. The Windows of The World		Scepter 563
			"I Say A Little Prayer"(4)		
12/02/67	10	23	3. **Dionne Warwick's Golden Hits, Part One**	[G]	Scepter 565
			"Anyone Who Had A Heart"(8-'64)		
3/16/68	6	18	● 4. **Valley of the Dolls**		Scepter 568
			"(Theme From) Valley Of The Dolls"(2)		
			"Do You Know The Way To San Jose"(10)		
1/18/69	18	11	5. Promises, Promises		Scepter 571
			"This Girl's In Love With You"(7)		
4/19/69	11	9	6. Soulful		Scepter 573
9/20/69	31	5	● 7. Dionne Warwick's Greatest Motion Picture Hits	[K]	Scepter 575
11/22/69	28	4	8. Dionne Warwick's Golden Hits, Part 2	[G]	Scepter 577
			"Message To Michael"(8-'66)		
5/09/70	23	14	9. I'll Never Fall In Love Again		Scepter 581
			"I'll Never Fall In Love Again"(6)		
1/09/71	37	4	10. Very Dionne		Scepter 587
8/18/79	12	13	▲ 11. Dionne		Arista 4230
			album produced by Barry Manilow		
			"I'll Never Love This Way Again"(5)		
8/30/80	23	6	12. No Night So Long		Arista 9526
11/27/82	25	10	13. Heartbreaker		Arista 9609
			album produced by Barry Gibb		
			"Heartbreaker"(10)		
1/11/86	12	13	● 14. Friends		Arista 8398
			"That's What Friends Are For"(1-with Elton John, Stevie Wonder & Gladys Knight)		
			DINAH WASHINGTON		
			Born Ruth Lee Jones on 8/29/24 in Tuscaloosa, Alabama; died on 12/14/63 (overdose of alcohol and pills). R&B/blues vocalist, pianist. Moved to Chicago in 1927. With Sallie Martin Gospel Singers, 1940-41, and local club work in Chicago, 1941-43. With Lionel Hampton, 1943-46. First recorded for Keynote in 1943. Solo touring from 1946. Married seven times.		
2/01/60	34	22	1. What a diff'rence a day makes!		Mercury 20479
			"What A Diff'rence A Day Makes"(8)		
1/23/61	10	7	2. **Unforgettable**		Mercury 20572
7/28/62	33	4	3. Dinah '62		Roulette 25170
			GROVER WASHINGTON, JR.		
			Born on 12/12/43 in Buffalo. Jazz/R&B saxophonist. Own band, the Four Clefs, at age 16. Session work in Philadelphia, where he now resides.		
4/05/75	10	17	1. **Mister Magic**	[I]	Kudu 20
11/22/75	10	7	2. **Feels So Good**	[I]	Kudu 24

DATE	POS	WKS	ARTIST—RECORD TITLE	LABEL & NO.
2/12/77	31	6	3. A Secret Place [I]	Kudu 32
2/04/78	11	9	4. Live At The Bijou [I-L]	Kudu 3637 [2]
11/18/78	35	5	5. Reed Seed [I]	Motown 910
			backed by the jazz ensemble, Locksmith	
5/19/79	24	6	6. Paradise [I]	Elektra 182
3/29/80	24	6	7. Skylarkin' [I]	Motown 933
1/24/81	5	27	▲ 8. **Winelight** [I]	Elektra 305
			"Just The Two Of Us"(2-with Bill Withers)	
1/23/82	28	5	9. Come Morning [I]	Elektra 562
			ROGER WATERS	
			Pink Floyd's bassist.	
6/02/84	31	7	1. The Pros and Cons of Hitch Hiking	Columbia 39290
			JOHNNY "GUITAR" WATSON	
			Born on 2/3/35 in Houston. Funk/R&B vocalist, guitarist, pianist. First recorded (as Young John Watson) for Federal in 1952.	
5/21/77	20	13	● 1. A Real Mother For Ya	DJM 7
			WAYLON & WILLIE - **see WAYLON JENNINGS/WILLIE NELSON**	
			WE FIVE	
			California pop quintet: Beverly Bivens (lead singer), Mike Stewart (brother of John Stewart), Pete Fullerton, Bob Jones and Jerry Burgan.	
12/11/65	32	6	1. You Were On My Mind	A&M 4111
			"You Were On My Mind"(3)	
			WEATHER REPORT	
			Jazz/fusion quintet led by Josef Zawinul (keyboards) and Wayne Shorter (sax).	
6/28/75	31	4	1. Tale Spinnin' [I]	Columbia 33417
4/30/77	30	5	● 2. Heavy Weather [I]	Columbia 34418
			WEAVERS	
			Folk quartet: Pete Seeger, Lee Hays (d: 8/26/81), Fred Hellerman and Ronnie Gilbert.	
3/13/61	24	1	1. The Weavers at Carnegie Hall [E-L]	Vanguard 9010
			recorded on Christmas Eve, 1955	
			JACK WEBB	
			Jack narrates the introduction to songs played by a 7-man jazz combo led by Matty Matlock (clarinet) - also see Ray Heindorf.	
9/03/55	2(2)	2	1. **Pete Kelly's Blues** [T-I]	RCA 1126
			played by the same band which did the scoring for the film	
			ANDREW LLOYD WEBBER - **see SOUNDTRACKS**	
			TIM WEISBERG	
			Born in 1943 in Hollywood. Studied classical flute as an adolescent. Performs pop-oriented music with a jazz appeal.	
9/23/78	8	13	1. **Twin Sons Of Different Mothers**	Full Moon 35339
			DAN FOGELBERG & TIM WEISBERG	

DATE	POS	WKS	ARTIST—RECORD TITLE	LABEL & NO.
			ERIC WEISSBERG	
			Bluegrass musician.	
2/17/73	1(3)	14	● 1. **Dueling Banjos** [I] except for the title song, all tunes performed by Weissberg & Marshall Brickman "New Dimensions in Banjo & Bluegrass" "Dueling Banjos"(2-by Weissberg & Steve Mandell)	Warner 2683
			BOB WELCH	
			Born on 7/31/46 in Los Angeles, California. Guitarist, vocalist with Fleetwood Mac (1971-74). Formed British rock group, Paris, 1976.	
11/12/77	12	29	▲ 1. **French Kiss** "Sentimental Lady"(8)	Capitol 11663
3/17/79	20	5	● 2. Three Hearts	Capitol 11907
			LAWRENCE WELK	
			Born on 3/11/03 in Strasburg, North Dakota. Accordionist and polka/ sweet bandleader since the mid-20s. Band's style labeled "champagne music". Own national TV musical variety show began on 7/2/55 and ran into the 70s.	
1/28/56	5	11	1. **Lawrence Welk and His Sparkling** **Strings** [I]	Coral 57011
3/31/56	13	2	2. TV Favorites	Coral 57025
3/31/56	18	2	3. Shamrocks and Champagne	Coral 57036
5/12/56	6	17	4. **Bubbles In The Wine** title song is Lawrence's theme song	Coral 57038
8/18/56	10	30	5. **Say It With Music** [I] medleys of 36 dance favorites	Coral 57041
8/25/56	17	4	6. Champagne Pops Parade	Coral 57078
10/20/56	18	1	7. Moments To Remember [I]	Coral 57068
12/22/56	8	3	8. **Merry Christmas** [X]	Coral 57093
3/16/57	20	1	9. Pick-a-Polka! [I]	Coral 57067
5/20/57	17	5	10. Waltz with Lawrence Welk [I] medleys of 24 favorite waltzes	Coral 57119
10/21/57	19	2	11. Lawrence Welk plays Dixieland [I] featuring Pete Fountain on clarinet	Coral 57146
12/23/57	18	3	12. Jingle Bells [X]	Coral 57186
12/19/60	4	26	13. **Last Date** [I]	Dot 3350
1/30/61	1(11)	50	● 14. **Calcutta!** [I] "Calcutta"(1)	Dot 3359
8/07/61	2(1)	41	15. **Yellow Bird** [I] above 2 albums feature Frank Scott on harpsichord	Dot 3389
1/13/62	4	43	16. **Moon River** [I]	Dot 3412
6/09/62	6	12	17. **Young World** [I]	Dot 3428
9/29/62	9	10	18. **Baby Elephant Walk and Theme From The** **Brothers Grimm** [I]	Dot 3457
4/13/63	20	12	19. 1963's Early Hits [I]	Dot 25510
4/20/63	34	5	20. Waltz Time [I]	Dot 25499
9/07/63	33	6	21. Scarlett O'Hara [I]	Dot 25528
2/15/64	29	3	22. Wonderful! Wonderful! [I]	Dot 25552
5/16/64	37	3	23. Early Hits Of 1964 [I]	Dot 25572
12/31/66	12	18	● 24. Winchester Cathedral [I]	Dot 25774

DATE	POS	WKS	ARTIST—RECORD TITLE	LABEL & NO.
			MARY WELLS	
			Born on 5/13/43 in Detroit. R&B vocalist. First artist to record on the Motown label. Married for a time to Cecil Womack, brother of Bobby Womack.	
7/18/64	**18**	12	1. Greatest Hits [G]	Motown 616
			"The One Who Really Loves You"(8)	
			"You Beat Me To The Punch"(9)	
			"My Guy"(1)	
			WEST, BRUCE & LAING	
			Power-rock trio: Leslie West (guitar/vocals-Mountain), Jack Bruce (bass-Cream) and Corky Laing (drums-Mountain).	
12/09/72	**26**	6	1. Why Dontcha	Windfall 31929
			PAUL WESTON	
			Top arranger and conductor of mood music since 1934. Married to Jo Stafford.	
10/29/55	**15**	2	1. Mood For 12 [I]	Columbia 693
9/01/56	**12**	5	2. Solo Mood [I]	Columbia 879
			both albums feature same group of 12 big band soloists	
			WHAM!	
			Pop duo from Bushey, England: George Michael (b: George Michael Panos on 6/26/63), lead singer, and Andrew Ridgely (b: 1/26/63), guitarist. Disbanded in 1986.	
11/17/84	**1(3)**	56	▲ 1. **Make It Big**	Columbia 39595
			"Wake Me Up Before You Go-Go"(1)	
			"Careless Whisper"(1)	
			"Everything She Wants"(1)	
			"Freedom"(3)	
7/26/86	**10**	11	▲ 2. **Music From The Edge Of Heaven**	Columbia 40285
			"I'm Your Man"(3)	
			"A Different Corner"(7-George Michael)	
			"The Edge Of Heaven"(10)	
			THE WHISPERS	
			Los Angeles soul group formed in 1964. Consisted of Gordy Harmon, twin brothers Walter and Wallace "Scotty" Scott, Marcus Hutson and Nicholas Caldwell. First recorded for Dore in 1964. Harmon replaced by Leaveil Degree in 1973.	
2/09/80	**6**	17	▲ 1. **The Whispers**	Solar 3521
			"And The Beat Goes On"	
2/14/81	**23**	11	● 2. Imagination	Solar 3578
4/03/82	**35**	4	● 3. Love Is Where You Find It	Solar 27
5/07/83	**37**	3	4. Love For Love	Solar 60216
			WHITESNAKE	
			British heavy-metal band. Current lineup: David Coverdale (vocals), John Sykes (guitar), Neil Murray (bass) and Aynsley Dunbar (drums). Coverdale and early members Jon Lord and Ian Paice were members of Deep Purple.	
8/25/85	**40**	2	● 1. Slide it in	Geffen 4018

DATE	POS	WKS	ARTIST—RECORD TITLE	LABEL & NO.
			BARRY WHITE	
			Born on 9/12/44 in Galveston, Texas; raised in Los Angeles. Soul singer, songwriter, keyboardist, producer, arranger. With Upfronts vocal group, recorded for Lummtone in 1960. A&R man for Mustang/Bronco, 1966-67. Formed Love Unlimited in 1969, which included future wife Glodean James. Leader of 40-piece Love Unlimited Orchestra.	
6/02/73	**16**	10	● 1. I've Got So Much To Give	20th Century 407
			"I'm Gonna Love You Just A Little More Baby"(3)	
12/08/73	**20**	16	● 2. Stone Gon'	20th Century 423
			"Never, Never Gonna Give Ya Up"(7)	
9/14/74	**1(1)**	13	● 3. **Can't Get Enough**	20th Century 444
			"Can't Get Enough Of Your Love, Babe"(1)	
			"You're The First, The Last, My Everything"(2)	
4/26/75	**17**	8	● 4. Just Another Way To Say I Love You	20th Century 466
			"What Am I Gonna Do With You"(8)	
11/29/75	**23**	5	● 5. Barry White's Greatest Hits [G]	20th Century 493
9/24/77	**8**	13	▲ 6. **Barry White Sings For Someone You Love**	20th Century 543
			"It's Ecstasy When You Lay Down Next To Me"(4)	
12/16/78	**36**	2	▲ 7. Barry White The Man	20th Century 571
			PAUL WHITEMAN	
			The #1 orchestra leader of the 1920s. Died on 12/29/67 (77).	
1/19/57	**20**	1	1. Paul Whiteman/50th Anniversary	Grand Award 901 [2]
			reunion with many of the great alumni of the Whiteman Orchestra: Tommy & Jimmy Dorsey, Bing Crosby, Hoagy Carmichael, Jack Teagarden & others	
			ROGER WHITTAKER	
			Born on 3/22/36 in Nairobi, Kenya. British MOR singer.	
6/07/75	**31**	5	● 1. "The Last Farewell" and other hits	RCA 0855
			THE WHO	
			Rock group formed in London, England in 1964. Consisted of Roger Daltrey (b: 3/1/44), lead singer; Pete Townshend (b: 5/19/45), guitar, vocals; John Entwistle (b: 10/9/44), bass; and Keith Moon (b: 8/23/47), drums. Originally known as the High Numbers in 1964. All but Moon had been in The Detours. Developed stage antics of destroying their instruments. Made rock opera "Tommy" in 1969, became a film in 1975. Solo work by members began in 1972. Moon died on 9/7/78 of a drug overdose, replaced by Kenney Jones. In films "The Kids Are Alright" and "Quadrophenia", 1979. Eleven fans trampled and died at their concert in Cincinnati, 12/3/79. Group's status is currently in limbo. Regrouped at "Live Aid" in 1986.	
11/30/68	**39**	2	1. Magic Bus-The Who On Tour [K]	Decca 75064
6/14/69	**4**	47	● 2. **Tommy**	Decca 7205 [2]
			also see Rock Operas and Soundtrack versions	
			"Pinball Wizard"	
6/06/70	**4**	24	● 3. **Live At Leeds** [L]	Decca 79175
8/21/71	**4**	20	● 4. **Who's next**	Decca 79182
			"Won't Get Fooled Again"	
11/20/71	**11**	8	● 5. Meaty Beaty Big And Bouncy [G]	Decca 79184
11/10/73	**2(1)**	18	● 6. **Quadrophenia**	MCA 10004
			Townshend's second rock opera	
11/02/74	**15**	8	● 7. Odds & Sods [K]	Track 2126
			previously unreleased recordings from 1964-72	

Johnny Tillotson first sang on radio at the age of 9; as a teenager, he was a regular on a local Florida television show. *It Keeps Right On A-Hurtin'* (1962) is named for a top ten song he wrote and recorded; it has since been recorded by nearly 100 other artists. Besides his singing career, Tillotson has done some acting and even hosted a Junior Miss pageant.

Tommy, Pete Townshend's ground-breaking rock opera, exists as three entirely different albums: the Who's 1969 original; the 1975 film soundtrack; and this sumptuously packaged 1972 version, played by the London Symphony Orchestra and sung by the Who and such guest stars as Rod Stewart, Steve Winwood, Ringo Starr, and Richard Harris. Interestingly, while all three records placed in the top five, none reached No. 1.

Robin Trower began his career in a 1962 London R&B band called the Paramounts and spent five years as Procol Harum's guitarist before launching his solo career in 1973. In 1981, he made two albums with bassist Jack Bruce. *B.L.T.,* the first, with drummer Bill Lordan, comes from the musicians' initials and was Trower's last Top 40 album to date.

Ike & Tina Turner's 1970 album contains the massive crossover hit version of John Fogerty's "Proud Mary," which earned a Grammy and a gold record. The album proved to be the pair's biggest seller in a decade of working together. Despite the cooperative title, Tina found far greater stardom after divorcing Ike in 1976.

Urban Cowboy, the 1980 film that starred John Travolta and Debra Winger, launched a nationwide fad of Western clothes and mechanical bulls. The country/rock soundtrack album didn't equal the success of a previous Travolta movie album (*Saturday Night Fever,* the biggest selling soundtrack of all time), but it did reach No. 3 and achieve platinum status.

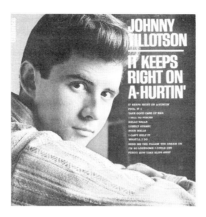

U2's first public notoriety came in 1978, when the newly formed Dublin quartet won a £500 prize in a local talent contest co-sponsored by Harp lager. Five years later, the group had its first platinum album with *War*, which contains "New Year's Day" and "Sunday Bloody Sunday."

Ritchie Valens died in the 1959 plane crash that also killed Buddy Holly and the Big Bopper. He was only 17 and had been a recording artist for merely eight months, yet he had two chart singles to his credit. Valens' life story was made into a 1987 movie, *La Bamba*.

Bobby Vee was born and raised in Fargo, ND. In 1959, the Velline brothers' band, the Shadows, was hired to fill in at a concert Buddy Holly was scheduled to play days after his sudden death; Vee was 15 at the time. His 1962 compilation album contains seven top twenty singles, all originally issued in the first two years of his recording career.

The Ventures made a demo tape of "Walk, Don't Run," but no record company the group approached would release it. When the mother of one of the quartet's members put out the single herself in 1960, it became a regional—then national—hit, launching a long career of successful and influential guitar instrumentals. Although the Ventures named its first album after that song, *Vol. 2* was its sixteenth album, released four years later.

Gene Vincent's characteristic limp came from a 1955 car crash in Franklin, VA, near where 20-year-old Eugene Craddock was stationed in the Navy. A year later, Gene Vincent and the Blue Caps had its first top ten single with "Be-Bop-A-Lula," originally issued as a B-side.

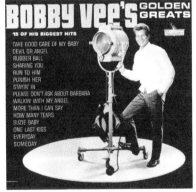

DATE	POS	WKS	ARTIST—RECORD TITLE	LABEL & NO.
11/01/75	8	14	● 8. **The Who By Numbers**	MCA 2161
			"Squeeze Box"	
9/09/78	2(2)	13	▲ 9. **Who Are You**	MCA 3050
7/07/79	8	11	▲ 10. **The Kids Are Alright** [S-L]	MCA 11005 [2]
			film features interviews & performances from the group's past 15 years	
4/04/81	4	14	▲ 11. **Face Dances**	Warner 3516
			"You Better You Bet"	
9/25/82	8	10	● 12. **It's Hard**	Warner 23731

WHODINI

New York rap duo: Jalil "Whodini" Hutchins and John Fletcher.

DATE	POS	WKS	ARTIST—RECORD TITLE	LABEL & NO.
1/26/85	35	5	▲ 1. Escape	Jive 8251
6/28/86	35	4	● 2. Back In Black	Jive 8407
			Grandmaster Dee joins group	

WILD CHERRY

White funk band formed in Steubenville, Ohio in 1976. Consisted of Bob Parissi (lead vocals, guitar), Bryan Bassett (guitar), Mark Avsec (keyboards), Allen Wentz (bass) and Ron Beitle (drums).

DATE	POS	WKS	ARTIST—RECORD TITLE	LABEL & NO.
8/07/76	5	15	▲ 1. **Wild Cherry**	Sweet City 34195
			"Play That Funky Music"(1)	

ANDY WILLIAMS

Born Howard Andrew Williams on 12/3/28 in Wall Lake, Iowa. Formed quartet with his brothers and eventually moved to Los Angeles. With Bing Crosby on hit "Swingin' On A Star", 1944. With comedienne Kay Thompson in mid-40s. Went solo in 1952. On Steve Allen's "Tonight Show" from 1952-55. Own NBC-TV variety series, 1962-67 and 1969-71. In film "I'd Rather Be Rich", 1964. One of America's greatest Pop/MOR singers. Formerly married to Claudine Longet.

DATE	POS	WKS	ARTIST—RECORD TITLE	LABEL & NO.
1/25/60	38	1	1. Lonely Street	Cadence 3030
			"Lonely Street"(5)	
3/24/62	19	8	2. "Danny Boy" and other songs I love to sing	Columbia 8551
6/02/62	3	06	● 3. **Moon River & Other Great Movie Themes**	Columbia 8609
11/10/62	16	22	4. Warm And Willing	Columbia 8679
4/20/63	1(16)	61	● 5. **Days of Wine and Roses**	Columbia 8815
			"Can't Get Used To Losing You"(2)	
2/01/64	9	16	● 6. **The Wonderful World Of Andy Williams**	Columbia 8937
			with members of Andy's family	
5/23/64	5	27	● 7. **The Academy Award Winning "Call Me Irresponsible"**	Columbia 8971
10/10/64	5	20	● 8. **The Great Songs From "My Fair Lady" and other Broadway hits**	Columbia 9005
4/24/65	4	45	● 9. **Dear Heart**	Columbia 9138
3/12/66	23	8	10. Andy Williams' Newest Hits [K]	Columbia 9183
6/11/66	6	18	● 11. **The Shadow of Your Smile**	Columbia 9299
3/04/67	21	11	12. In The Arms Of Love	Columbia 9333
5/27/67	5	35	● 13. **Born Free**	Columbia 9480
12/09/67	8	11	● 14. **Love, Andy**	Columbia 9566
6/29/68	9	24	● 15. **Honey**	Columbia 9662
5/31/69	9	10	● 16. **Happy Heart**	Columbia 9844
11/22/69	27	6	● 17. **Get Together With Andy Williams**	Columbia 9922
			with The Osmonds on 3 tracks	

DATE	POS	WKS	ARTIST—RECORD TITLE	LABEL & NO.
2/27/71	**3**	16	▲ 18. **Love Story**	Columbia 30497
			"(Where Do I Begin) Love Story"(9)	
5/20/72	**29**	8	● 19. Love Theme From "The Godfather"	Columbia 31303

DENIECE WILLIAMS

Born Deniece Chandler on 6/3/51 in Gary, Indiana. Soul vocalist, songwriter. Recorded for Toddlin' Town, early 60s. Member of Wonderlove, Stevie Wonder's backup group, 1972-75.

DATE	POS	WKS	ARTIST—RECORD TITLE	LABEL & NO.
3/05/77	**33**	6	● 1. This is Niecy	Columbia 34242
7/29/78	**19**	8	● 2. That's What Friends Are For	Columbia 35435
5/15/82	**20**	7	3. Niecy	ARC 37952
			"It's Gonna Take A Miracle"(10)	
6/16/84	**26**	6	4. Let's Hear It For The Boy	Columbia 39366
			"Let's Hear It For The Boy"(1)	

HANK WILLIAMS, JR.

Born Randall Hank Williams, Jr. on 5/26/49 in Shreveport, LA; raised in Nashville. Country singer, songwriter, guitarist. Son of country music's first superstar, Hank Williams.

DATE	POS	WKS	ARTIST—RECORD TITLE	LABEL & NO.
3/13/65	**16**	13	● 1. Your Cheatin' Heart [S]	MGM 4260
			film is Hank Williams' life story (Hank is played by George Hamilton - songs sung by Hank, Jr.)	

MASON WILLIAMS

Born on 8/24/38 in Abilene, Texas. Folk guitarist, songwriter, author. Wrote for the Smothers Brothers TV show.

DATE	POS	WKS	ARTIST—RECORD TITLE	LABEL & NO.
8/17/68	**14**	8	1. The Mason Williams Phonograph Record	Warner 1729
			"Classical Gas"(2)	

ROBIN WILLIAMS

Mork of TV series "Mork & Mindy". In films "Moscow On The Hudson", "Club Paradise".

DATE	POS	WKS	ARTIST—RECORD TITLE	LABEL & NO.
7/28/79	**10**	12	● 1. **Reality...What A Concept** [C]	Casablanca 7162

ROGER WILLIAMS

Born Louis Weertz in 1925 in Omaha. Learned to play the piano by age 3. Educated at Drake University, Idaho State University, and Juilliard School of Music. Took lessons from Lenny Tristano and Teddy Wilson. Win on Arthur Godfrey's "Talent Scouts" led to recording contract.

DATE	POS	WKS	ARTIST—RECORD TITLE	LABEL & NO.
3/31/56	**19**	2	1. Roger Williams [I]	Kapp 1012
			"Autumn Leaves"(1)	
8/25/56	**19**	3	2. Daydreams [I]	Kapp 1031
10/27/56	**16**	2	3. Roger Williams plays the wonderful Music of the Masters [I]	Kapp 1040
			classical melodies	
3/23/57	**6**	57	● 4. **Songs Of The Fabulous Fifties** [I]	Kapp 5000 [2]
10/07/57	**20**	5	5. Almost Paradise [I]	Kapp 1063
11/04/57	**19**	4	6. Songs Of The Fabulous Forties [I]	Kapp 5003 [2]
3/31/58	**4**	73	● 7. **Till** [I]	Kapp 1081
2/23/59	**10**	65	8. **Near You** [I]	Kapp 1112
			"Near You"(10)	
6/15/59	**11**	14	● 9. More Songs Of The Fabulous Fifties [I]	Kapp 1130
10/26/59	**8**	29	10. **With These Hands** [I]	Kapp 1147
12/28/59	**12**	2	11. Christmas Time [X-I]	Kapp 1164
4/04/60	**25**	22	12. Always [I]	Kapp 1172

DATE	POS	WKS	ARTIST—RECORD TITLE	LABEL & NO.
12/19/60	5	14	13. **Temptation** [I]	Kapp 1217
10/23/61	35	?	14. Songs Of The Soaring '60s [I]	Kapp 1251
3/31/62	9	19	15. **Maria** [I]	Kapp 3266
11/17/62	27	4	16. Mr. Piano [I]	Kapp 3290
3/07/64	27	4	17. The Solid Gold Steinway [I]	Kapp 3354
7/30/66	24	11	18. I'll Remember You [I]	Kapp 3470
12/17/66	7	23	● 19. **Born Free** [I]	Kapp 3501
			"Born Free"(7)	
			FLIP WILSON	
			Host of his own TV variety show (1970-74).	
2/17/68	34	5	1. Cowboys & Colored People [C]	Atlantic 8149
5/23/70	17	9	● 2. "The Devil made me buy this dress" [C]	Little David 1000
			HANK WILSON - see LEON RUSSELL	
			JACKIE WILSON	
			Born on 6/9/34 in Detroit; died on 1/21/84. Worked solo until 1953, then joined Billy Ward's Dominoes as Clyde McPhatter's replacement. Solo since 1957. Career waned by 1964. Collapsed from a stroke on stage at the Latin Casino in Camden, New Jersey on 9/25/75 and spent the rest of his life in hospitals.	
7/20/63	36	2	1. Baby Workout	Brunswick 754110
			"Baby Workout"(5)	
			NANCY WILSON	
			Born on 2/20/37 in Chillicothe, Ohio. Jazz stylist with Rusty Bryant's Carolyn Club Band in Columbus. First recorded for Dot in 1956.	
7/07/62	30	5	1. Nancy Wilson/Cannonball Adderley	Capitol 1657
4/20/63	18	21	2. Broadway-My Way	Capitol 1828
8/31/63	11	20	3. Hollywood-My Way	Capitol 1934
2/01/64	4	26	4. **Yesterday's Love Songs/Today's Blues**	Capitol 2012
6/13/64	10	24	5. **Today, Tomorrow, Forever**	Capitol 2082
9/19/64	4	19	6. **How Glad I Am**	Capitol 2155
2/27/65	24	18	7. The Nancy Wilson Show! [L]	Capitol 2136
			recorded at the Cocoanut Grove in Los Angeles	
7/31/65	7	11	8. **Today-My Way**	Capitol 2321
10/16/65	17	8	9. Gentle Is My Love	Capitol 2351
6/25/66	15	12	10. A Touch Of Today	Capitol 2495
10/29/66	35	3	11. Tender Loving Care	Capitol 2555
4/01/67	35	3	12. Nancy-Naturally	Capitol 2634
8/05/67	40	1	13. Just For Now	Capitol 2712
			WINGS - see PAUL McCARTNEY	
			EDGAR WINTER	
			Born on 12/28/46 in Beaumont, Texas. Rock singer, keyboardist, saxophonist. Younger brother of Johnny Winter. Group included Rick Derringer and Dan Hartman, 1972-75.	
			EDGAR WINTER'S WHITE TRASH:	
4/15/72	23	9	● 1. Roadwork [L]	Epic 31249 [2]
			EDGAR WINTER GROUP:	
3/03/73	3	25	▲ 2. **They Only Come Out At Night**	Epic 31584
			album introduces Ronnie Montrose & Dan Hartman in group	
			"Frankenstein"(1)	
			"Free Ride"	

DATE	POS	WKS	ARTIST—RECORD TITLE	LABEL & NO.
6/15/74	**13**	13	● 3. Shock Treatment	Epic 32461
			Rick Derringer replaces Montrose as lead guitarist (Rick also appears on previous 3 albums)	
			JOHNNY WINTER	
			Born on 2/23/44 in Leland, Mississippi. Blues-rock guitarist, vocalist. Both Johnny and brother Edgar are albinos.	
5/17/69	**24**	8	1. Johnny Winter	Columbia 9826
5/29/71	**40**	2	● 2. Live/Johnny Winter And [L]	Columbia 30475
5/05/73	**22**	11	3. Still Alive And Well	Columbia 32188
			JONATHAN WINTERS	
			Comedian; master of improvisation.	
2/01/60	**18**	40	1. The Wonderful World Of Jonathan Winters [C]	Verve 15009
9/19/60	**25**	23	2. Down To Earth [C]	Verve 15011
7/03/61	**19**	6	3. Here's Jonathan [C]	Verve 15025
			STEVE WINWOOD	
			Born on 5/12/48 in Birmingham, England. Rock singer, keyboardist, synthesizer player, guitarist. Lead singer of The Spencer Davis Group, Blind Faith and Traffic.	
7/30/77	**22**	10	1. Steve Winwood	Island 9494
2/14/81	**3**	26	● 2. **Arc Of A Diver**	Island 9576
			"While You See A Chance"(7)	
9/04/82	**28**	6	3. Talking Back To The Night	Island 9777
7/26/86	**3**	48+	▲ 4. **Back in the High Life**	Island 25448
			"Higher Love"(1)	
			"The Finer Things"(8)	
			BILL WITHERS	
			Born on 7/4/38 in Slab Fork, WV. Black vocalist, guitarist, composer. Moved to California in 1967 and made demo records of his songs. First recorded for Sussex in 1970, produced by Booker T. Jones. Made professional singing debut on 6/26/71. Married to actress Denise Nicholas.	
9/25/71	**39**	1	1. Just As I Am	Sussex 7006
			"Ain't No Sunshine"(3)	
6/17/72	**4**	25	● 2. **Still Bill**	Sussex 7014
			"Lean On Me"(1)	
			"Use Me"(2)	
2/04/78	**39**	3	● 3. Menagerie	Columbia 34903
			PETER WOLF	
			Born Peter Blankfield on 3/7/46 in the Bronx. Lead singer of The J. Geils Band until 1983.	
8/25/84	**24**	8	1. Lights Out	EMI America 17121
			BOBBY WOMACK	
			Born on 3/4/44 in Cleveland. Soul vocalist, guitarist, songwriter. Sang in family gospel group, the Womack Brothers. Group recorded for Sar as The Valentinos and The Lovers, 1962-64. Toured as guitarist with Sam Cooke. Solo recording for Him label in 1965. Back-up guitarist on many sessions, including Wilson Pickett Box Tops, Joe Tex, Aretha Franklin and Janis Joplin. Married for a time to Sam Cooke's widow.	
8/25/73	**37**	1	1. Facts Of Life	United Art. 043
2/20/82	**29**	6	2. The Poet	Beverly G. 10000

DATE	POS	WKS	ARTIST—RECORD TITLE		LABEL & NO.
			STEVIE WONDER		
			Born Steveland Morris on 5/13/50 in Saginaw, Michigan. Singer, songwriter, multi-instrumentalist, producer. Blind since birth. Signed to Motown in 1960, did backup work. First recorded in 1962, as "Little Stevie Wonder". Married to Syreeta Wright from 1970-72. Near-fatal auto accident on 8/6/73. Winner of 16 Grammy Awards. In films "Bikini Beach" and "Muscle Beach Party".		
7/27/63	1(1)	13	1. **Little Stevie Wonder/The 12 Year Old Genius**	[L]	Tamla 240
			"Fingertips"(1)		
9/24/66	33	3	2. Up-Tight Everything's Alright		Tamla 268
			"Uptight (Everything's Alright)"(3)		
			"Blowin' In The Wind"(9)		
7/06/68	37	4	3. Greatest Hits	[G]	Tamla 282
11/01/69	34	4	4. My Cherie Amour		Tamla 296
			"My Cherie Amour"(4)		
			"Yester-Me, Yester-You, Yesterday"(7)		
9/12/70	25	5	5. Signed Sealed & Delivered		Tamla 304
			"Signed, Sealed, Delivered I'm Yours"(3)		
			"Heaven Help Us All"(9)		
6/10/72	21	11	6. Music Of My Mind		Tamla 314
12/30/72	3	30	7. **Talking Book**		Tamla 319
			"Superstition"(1)		
			"You Are The Sunshine Of My Life"(1)		
8/25/73	4	58	8. **Innervisions**		Tamla 326
			"Higher Ground"(4)		
			"Living For The City"(8)		
8/17/74	1(2)	11	9. **Fulfillingness' First Finale**		Tamla 332
			"You Haven't Done Nothin"(1)		
			"Boogie On Reggae Woman"(3)		
10/16/76	1(14)	44	10. **Songs In The Key Of Life**		Tamla 340 [2]
			double LP also includes a bonus 4 song 7" E.P.		
			"I Wish"(1)		
			"Sir Duke"(1)		
2/04/78	34	3	11. Looking Back	[K]	Motown 804 [3]
			compilation of recordings from 1962-1971		
11/24/79	4	15	12. **Journey Through The Secret Life of Plants**		Tamla 371 [2]
			"Send One Your Love"(4)		
11/15/80	3	25	▲ 13. **Hotter Than July**		Tamla 373
			"Master Blaster (Jammin')"(5)		
5/29/82	4	8	● 14. **Stevie Wonder's Original Musiquarium I**	[G]	Tamla 6002 [2]
			compilation of hits from 1972-1982		
			"That Girl"(4)		
9/29/84	4	21	▲ 15. **The Woman in Red**	[S]	Motown 6108
			"I Just Called To Say I Love You"(1)		
			featuring Dionne Warwick on 3 songs		
10/19/85	5	29	▲ 16. **In Square Circle**		Tamla 6134
			"Part-Time Lover"(1)		
			"Go Home"(10)		

DATE	POS	WKS	ARTIST—RECORD TITLE	LABEL & NO.
			WOODY WOODBURY	
			Adult comedy storyteller.	
3/07/60	10	55	1. **Woody Woodbury Looks at love and life** [C]	Stereoddities 1
6/13/60	16	38	2. Woody Woodbury's Laughing Room [C]	Stereoddities 2
			BETTY WRIGHT	
			Born on 12/21/53 in Miami. Soul singer. In family gospel group Echoes Of Joy, from 1956. First recorded for Deep City in 1966. Hostess of TV talk shows in Miami.	
9/09/78	26	7	1. Betty Wright Live [L]	Alston 4408
			GARY WRIGHT	
			Born on 4/26/43 in Creskill, New Jersey. Pop/rock singer, songwriter, keyboardist. Appeared in "Captain Video" TV series at age seven. In Broadway play "Fanny". Co-leader of Spooky Tooth.	
2/14/76	7	35	▲ 1. **The Dream Weaver**	Warner 2868
			"Dream Weaver"(2)	
			"Love Is Alive"(2)	
1/29/77	23	9	2. The Light of Smiles	Warner 2951
			TAMMY WYNETTE	
			Born Virginia Wynette Pugh on 5/5/42 near Tupelo, Mississippi. Top female country singer, with over 15 #1 country hits. Discovered by producer Billy Sherrill. Married to country star George Jones from 1968-75.	
11/08/69	37	2	● 1. Tammy's Greatest Hits [G]	Epic 26486

Y

DATE	POS	WKS	ARTIST—RECORD TITLE	LABEL & NO.
			"WEIRD AL" YANKOVIC	
			Los Angeles novelty singer, accordion player. Specializes in song parodies.	
3/31/84	17	11	● 1. "Weird Al" Yankovic In 3-D [N]	Rock 'n' R. 39221
			"Eat It"	
			YARBROUGH & PEOPLES	
			Dallas soul duo: Cavin Yarbrough and Alisa Peoples. Discovered by The Gap Band.	
2/14/81	16	11	● 1. The Two Of Us	Mercury 3834
			GLENN YARBROUGH	
			Born on 1/12/30 in Milwaukee. Lead singer of the Limeliters (1959-63).	
7/10/65	35	3	1. Baby The Rain Must Fall	RCA 3422
			THE YARDBIRDS	
			Legendary rock group formed in Surrey, England in 1963. Consisted of Keith Relf (d: 5/14/76), vocals, harmonica; Anthony "Top" Topham and Chris Dreja, guitars; Paul "Sam" Samwell-Smith, bass, keyboards; and Jim McCarty, drums. Formed as the Metropolitan Blues Quartet at Kingston Art School. Topham replaced by Eric Clapton in 1963. Clapton replaced by Jeff Beck in 1965. Samwell-Smith replaced by Chris Dreja on bass and Jimmy Page added on guitar	

DATE	POS	WKS	ARTIST—RECORD TITLE	LABEL & NO.
			in 1966. Beck left in December of 1966. Group disbanded in July, 1968. Page formed the New Yardbirds in October of 1968, which evolved into Led Zeppelin. Relf and McCarty formed Renaissance in 1969. Keith Relf later in Armageddon, 1975. McCarty later in Illusion, 1977.	
5/27/67	28	8	1. The Yardbirds' Greatest Hits [G] *"Shapes Of Things"*	Epic 26246
			YES	
			Progressive rock group formed in London, England in 1968. Consisted of Jon Anderson (vocals), Peter Banks (guitar), Tony Kaye (keyboards), Chris Squire (bass) and Bill Bruford (drums). Banks replaced by Steve Howe in 1971. Kaye replaced by Rick Wakeman in 1971. Bruford left to join King Crimson, replaced by Alan White, late 1972. Wakeman replaced by Patrick Moraz in 1974, rejoined in 1976 when Moraz left. Wakeman and Anderson left in 1980, replaced by The Buggles' Trevor Horne (guitar) and Geoff Downes (keyboards). Group disbanded in 1980. Howe and Downes went with Asia. Reformed in 1983 with Anderson, Kaye, Squire, White, and Trevor Rabin (guitar).	
1/22/72	40	1	● 1. The Yes Album	Atlantic 8243
2/05/72	4	21	● 2. **Fragile** Rick Wakeman replaces Tony Kaye on keyboards *"Roundabout"*	Atlantic 7211
10/21/72	3	15	● 3. **Close To The Edge**	Atlantic 7244
6/02/73	12	10	● 4. **Yessongs** [L] Alan White replaces Bill Bruford on drums	Atlantic 100 [3]
2/09/74	6	11	● 5. **Tales From Topographic Oceans**	Atlantic 908
1/04/75	5	9	● 6. **Relayer** Patrick Moraz replaces Rick Wakeman on keyboards	Atlantic 18122
3/29/75	17	5	7. Yesterdays [K] featuring cuts from their first 2 albums (uncharted) "Yes" and "Time and a Word"	Atlantic 19134
8/06/77	8	12	● 8. **Going For The One** Rick Wakeman returns as a replacement for Patrick Moraz	Atlantic 19106
10/21/78	10	7	▲ 9. **Tormato**	Atlantic 19202
9/13/80	18	7	10. Drama Geoff Downes & Trevor Horn replace Wakeman & Anderson	Atlantic 16019
12/03/83	5	28	▲ 11. **90125** reformed group: Jon Anderson, Trevor Rabin (guitars), Chris Squire, Alan White and Tony Kaye *"Owner Of A Lonely Heart"*(1)	Atco 90125
			YOUNG-HOLT UNLIMITED	
			Chicago instrumental soul group: Eldee Young, bass; Isaac "Red" Holt, drums (both of the Ramsey Lewis Trio) and Don Walker, piano. Walker left by 1968.	
2/01/69	9	14	1. **Soulful Strut** [I] *"Soulful Strut"*(3)	Brunswick 754144
			JESSE COLIN YOUNG	
			Born Perry Miller. Leader of the Youngbloods.	
7/20/74	37	3	1. Light Shine	Warner 2790
4/19/75	26	4	2. Songbird	Warner 2845
5/08/76	34	3	3. On The Road [L]	Warner 2913

DATE	POS	WKS	ARTIST—RECORD TITLE	LABEL & NO.
			NEIL YOUNG	
			Born on 11/12/45 in Toronto, Canada. Rock singer, songwriter, guitarist. Formed rock band, the Mynah Birds, featuring lead singer Rick James, early 60s. Moved to Los Angeles in 1966 and formed Buffalo Springfield. Went solo in 1969 with backing band, Crazy Horse. Joined with Crosby, Stills & Nash in 1970.	
8/08/70	34	5	▲ 1. Everybody Knows This Is Nowhere	Reprise 6349
			"Cinnamon Girl"/"Down By The River"	
9/19/70	8	21	▲ 2. **After The Gold Rush**	Reprise 6383
3/04/72	1(2)	25	▲ 3. **Harvest**	Reprise 2032
			"Heart Of Gold"(1)	
11/03/73	22	6	● 4. Time Fades Away [L]	Reprise 2151
			guests: David Crosby & Graham Nash	
8/10/74	16	9	● 5. On The Beach	Reprise 2180
7/26/75	25	5	6. Tonight's The Night	Reprise 2221
12/20/75	25	7	7. Zùma	Reprise 2242
10/30/76	26	6	● 8. Long May You Run	Reprise 2253
			STILLS-YOUNG BAND (Stephen Stills)	
7/16/77	21	9	● 9. American Stars 'N Bars	Reprise 2261
			guests: Linda Ronstadt & Emmylou Harris	
10/28/78	7	11	● 10. **Comes A Time**	Reprise 2266
7/28/79	8	17	▲ 11. **Rust Never Sleeps**	Reprise 2295
12/15/79	15	13	● 12. Live Rust [L]	Reprise 2296 [2]
12/06/80	30	6	13. Hawks & Doves	Reprise 2297
11/28/81	27	9	14. Re-ac-tor	Reprise 2304
1/29/83	19	7	15. Trans	Geffen 2018
			PAUL YOUNG	
			Born on 1/17/56 in Bedfordshire, England. Pop/rock vocalist, guitarist.	
6/29/85	19	24	● 1. The Secret Of Association	Columbia 39957
			"Everytime You Go Away"(1)	

DATE	POS	WKS	ARTIST—RECORD TITLE	LABEL & NO.
			ZAGER & EVANS	
			Lincoln, Nebraska duo: Denny Zager and Rick Evans. Disbanded in 1969.	
8/16/69	30	5	1. 2525 (Exordium & Terminus)	RCA 4214
			"In The Year 2525"(1)	
			ZAPP	
			Dayton, Ohio funk band formed by the Troutman brothers: Roger "Zapp", Lester and Larry. Bootsy Collins produced and played on first session. Also see Roger.	
10/04/80	19	7	● 1. Zapp	Warner 3463
			with Bootsy Collins (guitars)	
8/28/82	25	6	● 2. Zapp II	Warner 23583
9/24/83	39	2	3. Zapp III	Warner 23875

DATE	POS	WKS	ARTIST—RECORD TITLE	LABEL & NO.
			FRANK ZAPPA	
			Born on 12/21/40 in Baltimore, Maryland. Singer, songwriter, guitarist. Rock music's leading satirist. Formed The Mothers Of Invention in 1965. In films "200 Motels" and "Baby Snakes". Father of Dweezil and Moon Unit.	
			MOTHERS OF INVENTION:	
4/13/68	30	4	1. We're Only In It For The Money	Verve 5045
			album art work is a parody of the Beatles' "Sgt. Pepper" LP	
9/04/71	38	3	2. The Mothers/Fillmore East-June 1971 [L]	Bizarre 2042
11/17/73	32	4	● 3. Over-nite Sensation	DiscReet 2149
5/11/74	10	15	● 4. **Apostrophe (')**	DiscReet 2175
			FRANK ZAPPA	
			"Don't Eat The Yellow Snow"	
11/09/74	27	3	5. Roxy & Elsewhere [L]	DiscReet 2202 [2]
8/02/75	26	5	6. One Size Fits All	DiscReet 2216
			FRANK ZAPPA:	
4/28/79	21	8	7. Sheik Yerbouti	Zappa 1501 [2]
			"Dancin' Fool"	
9/29/79	27	5	8. Joe's Garage, Act I	Zappa 1603
7/17/82	23	6	9. Ship arriving too late to save a drowning witch	Barking P. 38066
			"Valley Girl"	
			ZEBRA	
			Rock trio founded in New Orleans. Consisted of Randy Jackson (lead singer), Felix Hanemann (bass) and Guy Gelso (drums).	
7/23/83	29	7	1. Zebra	Atlantic 80054
			WARREN ZEVON	
			Born on 1/24/47 in Canada. Parents were Russian immigrants. Singer, songwriter, pianist. Wrote Linda Ronstadt's "Poor Poor Pitiful Me".	
3/25/78	8	13	● 1. **Excitable Boy**	Asylum 118
			above album produced by Jackson Browne	
			"Werewolves Of London"	
3/15/80	20	8	2. Bad Luck Streak In Dancing School	Asylum 509
			THE ZOMBIES	
			British rock quintet: Rod Argent (keyboards), Colin Blunstone (vocals), Paul Atkinson (guitar), Chris White (bass) and Hugh Grundy (drums). Group disbanded in late 1967. Rod later formed Argent, in 1969.	
5/01/65	39	1	1. The Zombies	Parrot 71001
			"She's Not There"(2)	
			"Tell Her No"(6)	
			ZZ TOP	
			Boogie-rock trio formed in Houston, Texas in 1969. Consisted of Billy Gibbons (vocals, guitar), Dusty Hill (vocals, bass) and Frank Beard (drums). All were born in 1949 in Texas. Gibbons had been lead guitarist in Moving Sidewalks, a Houston psychedelic rock band. Hill and Beard had played in American Blues, based in Dallas. Inactive from 1977-79.	
9/29/73	8	25	● 1. **Tres Hombres**	London 631
5/31/75	10	21	● 2. **Fandango!** [L]	London 656
			side 1: live; side 2: studio	

DATE	POS	WKS	ARTIST—RECORD TITLE	LABEL & NO.
1/29/77	**17**	8	● 3. Tejas	London 680
12/22/79	**24**	14	▲ 4. Deguello	Warner 3361
8/15/81	**17**	12	● 5. El Loco	Warner 3593
4/23/83	**9**	82	▲ 6. **Eliminator**	Warner 23774
			"Legs"(8)	
11/16/85	**4**	36	▲ 7. **Afterburner**	Warner 25342
			"Sleeping Bag"(8)	

DATE	POS	WKS	ALBUM TITLE	LABEL & NO.
			SOUNDTRACKS	

The film stars are listed directly below the title. Also shown are the Composer (cp)/Conductor (cd)/Lyricist (ly)/Music Writer (mu)/Performer (pf)/ Songwriter [music & lyrics] (sw). The following symbols are also used in this section: [I] Instrumental/[M] Musical/[O] Oldies/[R] Reissue/[V] Various Artists.

DATE	POS	WKS	ALBUM TITLE	LABEL & NO.
			Advance to the Rear - see New Christy Minstrels Glenn Ford/Stella Stevens/Melvyn Douglas	
4/07/84	12	12	● 1. Against All Odds [V] Rachel Ward/Jeff Bridges/James Woods side 2: instrumentals - cp/pf: Larry Carlton/Michel Colombier *"Against All Odds (Take A Look At Me Now)"* *(1-Phil Collins)*	Atlantic 80152
12/05/60	7	22	2. **Alamo, The** [I+V] John Wayne/Richard Widmark/Laurence Harvey cp/cd: Dimitri Tiomkin	Columbia 8358
4/12/80	36	3	3. All That Jazz [M] Roy Scheider/Jessica Lange - cd: Ralph Burns	Casablanca 7198
3/15/80	7	15	● 4. **American Gigolo** [I+V] Richard Gere/Lauren Hutton side 2: instrumentals - cp/pf: Giorgio Moroder *"Call Me"(1-Blondie)*	Polydor 6259
10/06/73	10	41	● 5. **American Graffiti** [V-O] director George Lucas' 1st major film - stars Ronny Howard & newcomers Richard Dreyfuss, Cindy Williams & Harrison Ford - also see "More American Graffiti"	MCA 8001 [2]
5/06/78	31	4	6. American Hot Wax [V-O] based on the life of disc jockey Alan Freed - record 1: live; record 2: original '50s recordings	A&M 6500 [2]
7/10/82	35	6	▲ 7. Annie [M] Aileen Quinn (Annie)/Carol Burnett/Albert Finney mu: Charles Strouse/ly: Martin Charnin; cd: Ralph Burns - also see Original Cast ('77)	Columbia 38000
1/09/61	18	5	8. Apartment, The [I] Jack Lemmon/Shirley MacLaine/Fred MacMurray cp: Adolph Deutsch; cd: Mitchell Powell	United Art. 3105
			April Love - see Pat Boone Pat Boone/Shirley Jones	
4/13/57	1(10)	88	9. **Around The World In 80 Days** [I] David Niven/Cantinflas/Robert Newton/Shirley MacLaine cp/cd: Victor Young - also see New World Theatre Orchestra	Decca 79046
10/10/81	32	7	10. Arthur (The Album) [I+V] Dudley Moore/Liza Minnelli/John Gielgud side 2: instrumentals - cp: Burt Bacharach *"Arthur's Theme"* (1-Christopher Cross)	Warner 3582
8/10/85	12	14	● 11. Back To The Future [V] Michael J. Fox/Christopher Lloyd/Lea Thompson/Crispin Glover *"The Power Of Love"(1-Huey Lewis & The News)*	MCA 6144
			Beach Party - see Annette Annette/Frankie Avalon/Robert Cummings	
6/23/84	14	9	● 12. Beat Street, Volume 1 [V] Rae Dawn Chong/Guy Davis	Atlantic 80154
4/25/60	6	55	13. **Ben-Hur** [I] Charlton Heston - cp: Miklos Rozsa; cd: Carlo Savina includes a full-color book about the movie	MGM 1
1/26/85	1(2)	36	▲ 14. **Beverly Hills Cop** [V] Eddie Murphy/Judge Reingold/Lisa Eilbacher/John Ashton *"Neutron Dance"(6-Pointer Sisters)* *"The Heat Is On" (2-Glenn Frey)* *"Axel F"(3-Harold Faltermeyer)*	MCA 5547

DATE	POS	WKS	ALBUM TITLE	LABEL & NO.
11/12/83	**17**	19	▲ 15. Big Chill [V-O] William Hurt/Glenn Close/Jobeth Williams/Jeff Goldblum	Motown 6062
2/02/63	**33**	6	16. Billy Rose's Jumbo [M] Doris Day/Stephen Boyd/Jimmy Durante/Martha Raye mu: Richard Rodgers; ly: Lorenz Hart; cd: George Stoll	Columbia 2260
			Black Caesar - see James Brown Fred Williamson/Art Lund/Julius Harris	
			Blue Hawaii - see Elvis Presley Elvis (Chad Gates)/Joan Blackman/Angela Lansbury	
			Blues Brothers - see Blues Brothers John Belushi/Dan Aykroyd	
4/13/68	**12**	13	17. Bonnie And Clyde [I] Warren Beatty/Faye Dunaway - cp: Charles Strouse includes excerpts of the original dialogue - also see Flatt & Scruggs	Warner 1742
			Breakfast at Tiffany's - see Henry Mancini Audrey Hepburn/George Peppard	
3/30/85	**17**	13	● 18. Breakfast Club, The [V] Molly Ringwald/Anthony Michael Hall/Emilio Estevez/ Paul Gleason/Judd Nelson/Ally Sheedy *"Don't You (Forget About Me)"(1-Simple Minds)*	A&M 5045
6/16/84	**8**	14	▲ 19. **Breakin'** [V] Lucinda Dickey/Adolfo Quinones/Michael Chambers *"Breakin'...There's No Stopping Us"(9-Ollie & Jerry)*	Polydor 821919
1/10/70	**16**	26	● 20. Butch Cassidy And The Sundance Kid [I+V] Paul Newman/Robert Redford - cp/cd: Burt Bacharach *"Raindrops Keep Fallin' On My Head"(1-B.J. Thomas)*	A&M 4227
5/11/63	**2(2)**	41	21. **Bye Bye Birdie** [M] Ann-Margret/Jesse Pearson/Janet Leigh/Dick Van Dyke mu: Charles Strouse; ly: Lee Adams; cd: Johnny Green - also see Original Cast ('60)	RCA 1081
5/12/73	**25**	9	● 22. Cabaret [M] Liza Minnelli/Michael York/Joel Grey mu: John Kander; ly: Fred Ebb - also see Original Cast ('67)	ABC 752
12/23/67	**11**	23	▲ 23. Camelot [M] Richard Harris/Vanessa Redgrave - mu: Frederick Loewe; ly: Alan Jay Lerner; cd: Alfred Newman - also see Original Cast ('61) *Living Strings/Percy Faith*	Warner 1712
5/02/60	**3**	20	24. **Can-Can** [M] Frank Sinatra/Shirley MacLaine/Maurice Chevalier/Louis Jourdan sw: Cole Porter; cd: Nelson Riddle	Capitol 1301
			Car Wash - see Rose Royce George Carlin/Richard Pryor/Ivan Dixon	
2/25/56	**2(1)**	56	● 25. **Carousel** [M] Gordon MacRae/Shirley Jones - mu: Richard Rodgers; ly: Oscar Hammerstein II; cd: Alfred Newman - also see Original Cast (special version '62)	Capitol 694
6/10/67	**22**	9	26. Casino Royale [I] Peter Sellers/David Niven - cp/cd: Burt Bacharach	Colgems 5005
			Chariots of Fire - see Vangelis Ian Charleson/Ben Cross	
			Children of Sanchez - see Chuck Mangione Anthony Quinn/Dolores Del Rio/Katy Jurado	
			Clambake - see Elvis Presley Elvis (Scott Heywood)/Shelley Fabares/Will Hutchins	
			Claudine - see Gladys Knight & the Pips James Earl Jones/Diahann Carroll	

DATE	POS	WKS	ALBUM TITLE		LABEL & NO.
6/29/63	2(3)	14	27. **Cleopatra** Elizabeth Taylor/Richard Burton/Rex Harrison cp/cd: Alex North	[I]	20th Century 5008
4/08/72	34	5	28. Clockwork Orange Malcolm McDowell/Patrick Magee - features classical pieces & the electronic synthesizer compositions of Walter Carlos	[I]	Warner 2573
1/21/78	17	8	● 29. Close Encounters Of The Third Kind Richard Dreyfuss/Teri Garr - cp/cd: John Williams	[I]	Arista 9500
5/17/80	40	1	● 30. Coal Miner's Daughter based on Loretta Lynn's life - Sissy Spacek plays Loretta & performs the vocals		MCA 5107
12/01/58	21	1	31. Damn Yankees Tab Hunter/Gwen Verdon - sw: Richard Adler/Jerry Ross - also see Original Cast ('55)	[M]	RCA 1047
1/22/55	4	16	32. **Deep In My Heart** features many stars - based on the life and the melodies of Sigmund Romberg - cd: Adolph Deutsch	[M]	MGM 3153
			Divine Madness - see Bette Midler		
5/28/66	1(1)	15	● 33. **Doctor Zhivago** Omar Sharif/Julie Christie - cp/cd: Maurice Jarre	[I]	MGM 6
			Don't Knock the Twist - see Chubby Checker		
10/18/69	6	41	● 34. **Easy Rider** Peter Fonda/Dennis Hopper/Jack Nicholson featuring songs by Jimi Hendrix, Steppenwolf & The Byrds	[V]	Dunhill 50063
			Eddie & the Cruisers - see John Cafferty Michael Pare/Tom Berenger		
			Eddie Duchin Story - see Carmen Cavallaro Tyrone Power/Kim Novak		
9/08/62	35	3	35. El Cid Charlton Heston/Sophia Loren - cp/cd: Miklos Rozsa	[I]	MGM 3977
			Elvis - That's the Way It Is - see Elvis Presley		
5/17/80	4	17	● 36. **Empire Strikes Back** Mark Hamill/Harrison Ford/Carrie Fisher cp/cd: John Williams; pf: London Symphony Orchestra also see Various-Jazz section "Empire Jazz"/Meco	[I]	RSO 4201 [2]
8/15/81	9	14	● 37. **Endless Love** Brooke Shields/Martin Hewitt *"Endless Love"(1-Diana Ross & Lionel Richie)*	[I+V]	Mercury 2001
8/07/82	37	5	● 38. **E.T. The Extra-Terrestrial** Henry Thomas/Peter Coyote/Dee Wallace - cp/cd: John Williams	[I]	MCA 6109
1/16/61	1(14)	55	● 39. **Exodus** Paul Newman/Eva Marie Saint - cp/cd: Ernest Gold - also see Hollywood Studio Orchestra	[I]	RCA 1058
			Experiment in Terror - see Henry Mancini Glenn Ford/Lee Remick/Stefanie Powers		
7/26/80	7	16	▲ 40. **Fame** inspired by the students of New York's High School of The Performing Arts *"Fame"(4-Irene Cara)*	[M]	RSO 3080
1/01/72	30	4	● 41. **Fiddler on the Roof** Topol - mu: Jerry Bock; ly: Sheldon Harnick; cd: John Williams - also see Original Cast ('64)	[M]	United Art. 10900 [2]
10/12/59	22	9	42. Five Pennies Danny Kaye/Louis Armstrong based on the life of bandleader Loring "Red" Nichols	[M]	Dot 29500
			Flash Gordon - see Queen Sam Jones/Melody Anderson/Max Von Sydow		
5/07/83	1(2)	54	▲ 43. **Flashdance** Jennifer Beals/Michael Nouri *"Flashdance...What A Feeling"(1-Irene Cara)* *"Maniac"(1-Michael Sembello)*	[V]	Casablanca 811492

DATE	POS	WKS	ALBUM TITLE	LABEL & NO.
2/03/62	**15**	24	44. Flower Drum Song [M] Nancy Kwan/James Shigeta/Miyoshi Umeki mu: Richard Rodgers; ly: Oscar Hammerstein II; cd: Alfred Newman - also see Original Cast ('59)	Decca 79098
5/13/78	**5**	12	▲ 45. FM [V] Michael Brandon/Eileen Brennan/Alex Karras/Martin Mull featuring songs by 17 top rock artists	MCA 12000 [2]
3/10/84	**1(10)**	27	▲ 46. Footloose [V] Kevin Bacon/Lori Singer - "Footloose"(1-Kenny Loggins) *"Let's Here It For The Boy"(1-Deniece Williams)* *"Almost Paradise"(7-Mike Reno & Ann Wilson)* Frankie & Johnny - see Elvis Presley Elvis (Johnny)/Donna Douglas (Frankie)/Nancy Kovack Friends - see Elton John Sean Bury/Anicee Alvina	Columbia 39242
7/25/64	**27**	6	47. From Russia with Love [I] Sean Connery/Daniela Bianchi - cp/cd: John Barry Fun in Acapulco - see Elvis Presley Elvis (Mike Windgren)/Ursula Andress/Elsa Cardenas Funny Girl - see Barbra Streisand (both Soundtrack & Original Cast) Barbra Streisand/Omar Sharif	United Art. 5114
7/14/84	**6**	17	▲ 48. **Ghostbusters** [V] Bill Murray/Dan Aykroyd/Sigourney Weaver *"Ghostbusters"(1-Ray Parker Jr.)* G.I. Blues - see Elvis Presley Elvis (Tulsa McCauley) *Juliet Prowse/James Douglas*	Arista 8246
12/29/56	**16**	7	49. Giant [I] Elizabeth Taylor/Rock Hudson/James Dean cp/cd: Dimitri Tiomkin	Capitol 773
6/23/58	**1(10)**	43	● 50. **Gigi** [M] Leslie Caron/Maurice Chevalier/Louis Jordan ly: Alan Jay Lerner/mu: Frederick Loewe; cd: Andre Previn **Girls! Girls! Girls! - see Elvis Presley** Elvis (Ross Carpenter)/Stella Stevens/Laurel Goodwin **Give My Regards to Broad Street - see Paul McCartney** Paul McCartney/Bryan Brown/Ringo Starr	MGM 3641
4/29/72	**21**	14	51. Godfather, The [I] Marlon Brando/Al Pacino/James Caan/Robert Duvall cp: Nino Rota; cd: Carlo Savina	Paramount 1003
2/06/65	**1(3)**	36	52. **Goldfinger** [I] Sean Connery/Gert Frobe (Goldfinger) - cp/cd: John Barry *"Goldfinger"(8-Shirley Bassey)*	United Art. 5117
12/23/67	**24**	9	53. Gone With The Wind [I] first album taken directly from the film sound track (premiered in 1939) - cp/cd: Max Steiner	MGM 10
3/16/68	**4**	21	● 54. **Good, The Bad and The Ugly** [I] Clint Eastwood/Lee Van Cleef - cp/cd: Ennio Morricone - also see Hugo Montenegro	United Art. 5172
5/27/78	**1(12)**	39	▲ 55. **Grease** [M] Olivia Newton-John/John Travolta *"You're The One That I Want"(1)* *"Summer Nights"(5)* *"Hopelessly Devoted To You"(3-Olivia solo)* *"Grease"(1-Frankie Valli)*	RSO 4002 [2]

DATE	POS	WKS	ALBUM TITLE	LABEL & NO.
1/26/63	**10**	13	56. **Gypsy** [M] Rosalind Russell/Natalie Wood/Karl Malden - mu: Jule Styne; ly: Stephen Sondheim - also see Original Cast ('59)	Warner 1480
			Hard Day's Night - see Beatles	
			Hard to Hold - see Rick Springfield	
			Harum Scarum - see Elvis Presley Elvis (Johnny Tyronne)/Mary Ann Mobley/Fran Jeffries	
			Hatari! - see Henry Mancini John Wayne/Red Buttons/Hardy Kruger	
			Having a Wild Weekend - see Dave Clark Five	
8/29/81	**12**	13	● 57. Heavy Metal [V] animated film - featuring songs by 13 rock artists	Asylum 90004 [2]
2/03/58	**25**	1	58. Helen Morgan Story Ann Blyth (portrays Helen)/Paul Newman vocals performed by Gogi Grant; cd: Ray Heindorf	RCA 1030
			Help! - see Beatles	
			Hey Boy! Hey Girl! - see Louis Prima & Keely Smith	
			Hey, Let's Twist! - see Joey Dee	
8/25/56	**5**	28	59. **High Society** [M] adapted from the play "Philadelphia Story" Bing Crosby/Grace Kelly/Frank Sinatra - sw: Cole Porter *"True Love"(3-Bing Crosby & Grace Kelly)*	Capitol 750
			Hold On! - see Herman's Hermits Peter Noone/Shelley Fabares/Sue Ane Langdon	
			Honeysuckle Rose - See Willie Nelson Willie Nelson/Dyan Cannon/Amy Irving/Slim Pickens	
4/20/63	**4**	34	● 60. **How The West Was Won** features many top stars - cd: Alfred Newman	MGM 5
			I Want to Live - see Gerry Mulligan Susan Hayward	
			It Happened at the World's Fair - see Elvis Presley Elvis (Mike Edwards)/Joan O'Brien/Gary Lockwood	
			James Bond - see: Casino Royale/Spy Who Loved Me/ From Russia With Love/Thunderball/ Goldfinger/You Only Live Twice/ Live And Let Die/also: Roland Shaw	
8/30/75	**30**	4	61. Jaws [I] Roy Scheider/Richard Dreyfuss/Robert Shaw cp/cd: John Williams	MCA 2087
			Jazz Singer - see Neil Diamond Neil Diamond/Laurence Oliver/Lucie Arnaz	
8/11/73	**21**	8	● 62. Jesus Christ Superstar [M] Ted Neely/Yvonne Elliman/Carl Anderson/Barry Dennen mu: Andrew Lloyd Webber; ly: Tim Rice also see Various ('70) *Original Cast ('72)*	MCA 11000 [2]
			Jonathan Livingston Seagull - see Neil Diamond James Franciscus/Juliet Mills - also see Richard Harris	
3/09/68	**19**	11	63. Jungle Book Disney cartoon based on Rudyard Kipling's "Mowgli" stories sw: Richard M. Sherman/Robert B. Sherman	Disneyland 3948
8/02/86	**30**	9	64. Karate Kid Part II [V] Ralph Macchio/Noriyuki "Pat" Morita *"Glory Of Love"(1-Peter Cetera)*	United Art. 40414
			Kids Are Alright - see Who	

DATE	POS	WKS	ALBUM TITLE		LABEL & NO.
7/21/56	**1**(1)	30	● 65. **King And I** [M]		Capitol 740
			Yul Brynner/Deborah Kerr - mu: Richard Rodgers; ly: Oscar Hammerstein II; cd: Alfred Newman		
			King Creole - see Elvis Presley		
			Elvis (Danny Fisher)/Carolyn Jones/Walter Matthau		
11/06/61	**10**	24	66. **King of Kings** [I]		MGM 2
			Jeffrey Hunter (Jesus Christ) - cp/cd: Miklos Rozsa includes a full-color book about the movie		
			Kissin' Cousins - see Elvis Presley		
			Elvis (Josh Morgan/Jodie Tatum)/Arthur O'Connell		
			Lady Sings the Blues - see Diana Ross		
			Diana Ross/Billy Dee Williams/Richard Pryor		
			Last Waltz - see Band		
3/23/63	**2**(2)	40	67. **Lawrence Of Arabia** [I]		Colpix 514
			Peter O'Toole/Alec Guinness/Anthony Quinn cp/cd: Maurice Jarre; pf: London Philharmonic Orchestra		
			Let It Be - see Beatles		
			Let's Do It Again - see Staple Singers		
			Sidney Poitier/Bill Cosby/Jimmie Walker/John Amos		
8/11/73	**17**	7	68. Live And Let Die [I]		United Art. 100
			Roger Moore/Jane Seymour - cp/cd: George Martin		
			"Live And Let Die"(2-Paul McCartney & Wings)		
2/03/79	**39**	2	69. Lord Of The Rings [I]		Fantasy 1 [2]
			animated film based on the novels of J.R.R. Tolkien cp/cd: Leonard Rosenman - also see Bo Hansson		
			Love Me or Leave Me - see Doris Day		
			Doris Day/James Cagney/Cameron Mitchell		
			Love Me Tender - see Elvis Presley		
			Elvis (Clint)/Richard Egan/Debra Paget		
1/23/71	**2**(6)	22	● 70. **Love Story** [I]		Paramount 6002
			Ali MacGraw/Ryan O'Neal - cp/cd: Francis Lai		
			Loving You - see Elvis Presley		
			Elvis (Deke Rivers)/Lizabeth Scott/Dolores Hart		
			Mad Dogs & Englishmen - see Joe Cocker		
9/21/85	**39**	2	71. Mad Max Beyond Thunderdome		Capitol 12429
			Mel Gibson/Tina Turner - cp/cd: Maurice Jarre		
			"We Don't Need Another Hero (Thunderdome)"(2-Tina Turner)		
			Magical Mystery Tour - see Beatles		
			Mahogany - see Diana Ross		
			Diana Ross/Billy Dee Williams/Anthony Perkins		
			Main Event - see Barbra Streisand		
			Barbra Streisand/Ryan O'Neal		
1/28/67	**10**	44	● 72. **Man And A Woman** [F]		United Art. 5147
			Jean-Louis Trintignant/Anouk Aimee - cp: Francis Lai grand prize winner of the 1966 Cannes Film Festival		
3/24/56	**2**(4)	17	73. **Man With The Golden Arm** [I]		Decca 78257
			Frank Sinatra/Eleanor Parker/Kim Novak cp/cd: Elmer Bernstein jazz sequences played by Shorty Rogers & His Giants		
12/05/64	**1**(14)	78	● 74. **Mary Poppins** [M]		Buena Vista 4026
			Julie Andrews/Dick Van Dyke/David Tomlinson/Glynis Johns sw: Richard M. Sherman/Robert B. Sherman; cd: Irwin Kostal		
			McVicar - see Roger Daltrey		

DATE	POS	WKS	ALBUM TITLE	LABEL & NO.
9/20/69	**19**	19	● 75. Midnight Cowboy [I+V] Dustin Hoffman/Jon Voight *"Everybody's Talkin'"*(6-Nilsson)	United Art. 5198
7/27/63	**15**	13	76. Mondo Cane [I] documentary depicting various cultures around the world - cp: Riz Ortolani & Nino Oliviero	United Art. 5105
			Monterey Pop - see Otis Redding/Jimi Hendrix	
			Muppet Movie - see Muppets (Children's section)	
8/11/62	**2(6)**	35	● 77. **Music Man** **[M]** Robert Preston/Shirley Jones - cp: Meredith Willson; cd: Ray Heindorf - also see Original Cast ('58)	Warner 1459
1/05/63	**14**	11	78. Mutiny On The Bounty [I] Marlon Brando/Trevor Howard cp: Bronislau Kaper; cd: Robert Armbruster includes a full-color souvenir book	MGM 4
10/31/64	**4**	77	● 79. **My Fair Lady** **[M]** Audrey Hepburn/Rex Harrison/Stanley Holloway mu: Frederick Loewe; ly: Alan Jay Lerner; cd: Andre Previn also see Percy Faith/Sammy Kaye/Andy Williams/Original Cast ('56)	Columbia 2600
1/30/61	**2(5)**	53	80. **Never On Sunday** **[I]** Melina Mercouri/Jules Dassin - cp/cd: Manos Hadjidakis	United Art. 5070
12/04/82	**38**	3	81. Officer And A Gentleman [V] Richard Gere/Debra Winger/David Keith/Louis Gossett, Jr. *"Up Where We Belong"*(1-Joe Cocker & Jennifer Warnes) includes songs by ZZ Top, Pat Benatar and Dire Straits	Island 90017
9/17/55	**1(4)**	62	● 82. **Oklahoma!** **[M]** Gordon MacRae/Shirley Jones - mu: Richard Rodgers; ly: Oscar Hammerstein II; cd: Jay Blackton	Capitol 595
5/10/69	**20**	8	● 83. **Oliver!** **[M]** Mark Lester (Oliver)/Ron Moody/Jack Wild/Oliver Reed sw: Lionel Bart; cd: John Green also see Original Cast ('62)/Mantovani	Colgems 5501
			One-Trick Pony - see Paul Simon	
4/26/86	**38**	2	84. Out Of Africa [I] Meryl Streep/Robert Redford - cp/cd: John Barry	MCA 6158
12/06/69	**28**	4	● 85. Paint Your Wagon [M] Lee Marvin/Clint Eastwood/Jean Seberg mu: Frederick Loewe; ly: Alan Jay Lerner	Paramount 1001
9/23/57	**9**	14	86. **Pajama Game** **[M]** Doris Day/John Raitt - sw: Richard Adler/Jerry Ross; cd: Ray Heindorf	Columbia 5210
			Pal Joey - see Frank Sinatra Frank Sinatra/Rita Hayworth/Kim Novak	
			Paradise, Hawaiian Style - see Elvis Presley Elvis (Rick Richards)/Suzanne Leigh/James Shigeta	
			Pat Garrett & Billy the Kid - see Bob Dylan James Coburn/Kris Kristofferson/Jason Robards	
			Pete Kelly's Blues - see Peggy Lee & Ella **Fitzgerald/Ray Heindorf &** **Matty Matlock/Jack Webb** Jack Webb/Janet Leigh/Peggy Lee/Lee Marvin	
5/05/56	**6**	18	87. **Picnic** **[I]** William Holden/Kim Novak/Rosalind Russell cp: George Duning; cd: Morris Stoloff *"Moonglow and Theme From Picnic"*(1-Morris Stoloff)	Decca 78320

DATE	POS	WKS	ALBUM TITLE		LABEL & NO.
			Pink Panther - see Henry Mancini		
			Peter Sellers/David Niven/Robert Wagner/Capucine		
8/03/59	8	58	● 88. **Porgy and Bess** [M]		Columbia 2016
			Sidney Poitier/Dorothy Dandridge - mu: George Gershwin;		
			ly: DuBose Heyward/Ira Gershwin; cd: Andre Previn		
			also see Harry Belafonte/Ray Charles/Percy Faith/		
			Leontyne Price		
3/22/86	5	17	● 89. **Pretty In Pink** [V]		A&M 5113
			Molly Ringwald/Harry Dean Stanton/Jon Cryer/Andrew McCarthy		
			"If You Leave"(4-Orchestral Manoeuvres In The Dark)		
			Purple Rain - see Prince		
			Prince/Apollonia Kotero/Morris Day		
			Quadrophenia - see Who		
			Phil Daniels/Leslie Ash/Sting		
			Rainbow Ridge - see, Jimi Hendrix		
6/18/83	20	6	90. Return Of The Jedi [I]		RSO 811767
			Mark Hamill/Harrison Ford/Carrie Fisher/Billy Dee Williams		
			cp/cd: John Williams; pf: London Symphony Orchestra		
			Richard Pryor Live on the Sunset Strip - see Richard Pryor		
3/09/57	16	9	91. Rock, Pretty Baby		Decca 8429
			Sal Mineo/John Saxon/Luana Patten		
			cp: Henry Mancini; pf: Jimmy Daley & The Ding-A-Lings		
4/23/77	4	14	▲ 92. **Rocky**		United Art. 693
			Sylvester Stallone/Talia Shire - cp/cd: Bill Conti		
			"Gonna Fly Now"(1-Bill Conti)		
7/24/82	15	10	● 93. **Rocky III**		Liberty 51130
			Sylvester Stallone/Talia Shire/Mr. T - cp/cd: Bill Conti		
			"Eye Of The Tiger"(1-Survivor)		
12/28/85	10	16	▲ 94. **Rocky IV** [V]		Scotti Br. 40203
			Sylvester Stallone/Talia Shire/Burt Young/Carl Weathers		
			"Burning Heart"(2-Survivor)		
			"Living In America" (4-James Brown)		
			"No Easy Way Out"(Robert Tepper)		
6/30/62	5	20	95. **Rome Adventure** [I]		Warner 1458
			Troy Donahue/Suzanne Pleshette/Angie Dickinson		
			cp: Max Steiner - side 2: "Neapolitan Favorites" by The		
			Cafe Milano Orch.		
			"Al Di La"(6-Emilio Pericoli)		
5/03/69	2(2)	31	● 96. **Romeo & Juliet**		Capitol 2993
			Leonard Whiting/Olivia Hussey - cp/cd: Nino Rota		
			includes dialogue highlights		
			Rose, The - see Bette Midler		
			Bette Midler/Alan Bates/Frederic Forrest		
			Roustabout - see Elvis Presley		
			Elvis (Charlie Rogers)/Barbara Stanwyck/Joan Freeman		
7/19/86	20	9	● 97. **Ruthless People** [V]		Epic 40398
			Danny DeVito/Bette Midler/Judge Reinhold/Helen Slater		
			"Modern Woman"(10-Billy Joel)		
			St. Louis Blues - see Nat King Cole		
12/10/77	1(24)	54	▲ 98. **Saturday Night Fever** [V]		RSO 4001 [2]
			John Travolta - biggest selling soundtrack album of all-time		
			"If I Can't Have You"(1-Yvonne Elliman) - also see Bee Gees		

DATE	POS	WKS	ALBUM TITLE		LABEL & NO.
			Serenade - see Mario Lanza		
			Mario Lanza/Joan Fontaine		
			Seven Hills of Rome - see Mario Lanza		
			Mario Lanza/Renato Roscel/Marisa Allasio		
8/12/78	5	12	▲ 99. **Sgt. Pepper's Lonely Hearts Club Band**	[M]	RSO 4100 [2]
			Peter Frampton/Bee Gees - sw: John Lennon/Paul McCartney film inspired by the Beatles "Sgt. Pepper's" album		
			"Got To Get You Into My Life"(9-Earth, Wind & Fire)		
			Shaft - see Isaac Hayes		
			Richard Roundtree/Moses Gunn/Gwenn Mitchell		
			Sing Boy Sing - See Tommy Sands		
			Tommy Sands/Lili Gentle/Edmond O'Brien		
			Singing Nun - see Debbie Reynolds		
			Debbie Reynolds/Ricardo-Montalban/Greer Garson		
			Song Remains the Same - see Led Zeppelin		
4/10/65	1(2)	61	● 100. **Sound Of Music, The**	[M]	RCA 2005
			Julie Andrews/Christopher Plummer - story of Maria Trapp's family - mu: Richard Rodgers; ly: Oscar Hammerstein II; cd: Irwin Kostal - also see Original Cast ('59)		
3/31/58	1(31)	65	● 101. **South Pacific**	[M]	RCA 1032
			Rossano Brazzi/Mitzi Gaynor/John Kerr - mu: Richard Rodgers; ly: Oscar Hammerstein II; cd: Alfred Newman		
			Sparkle - see Aretha Franklin		
			Irene Cara/Philip Thomas/Lonette McKee		
			Spinout - see Elvis Presley		
			Elvis (Mike McCoy)/Shelley Fabares/Diana McBain		
11/05/77	40	2	102. **Spy Who Loved Me**	[I]	United Art. 774
			Roger Moore/Barbara Bach - cp/cd: Marvin Hamlisch		
			"Nobody Does It Better"(2-Carly Simon)		
8/10/85	21	11	● 103. **St. Elmo's Fire**	[V]	Atlantic 81261
			Emilio Estevez/Rob Lowe/Andrew McCarthy/Demi Moore/Judd Nelson/Ally Sheedy/Mare Winningham		
			"St. Elmo's Fire (Man In Motion)"(1-John Parr)		
11/22/86	31	11	104. **Stand By Me**	[V-O]	Atlantic 81677
			Wil Wheaton/River Phoenix/Corey Feldman/Jerry O'Connell		
			"Stand By Me"(9-Ben E. King)		
			Star Is Born - see Barbra Streisand		
			Barbra Streisand/Kris Kristofferson		
7/02/77	2(3)	22	▲ 105. **Star Wars**	[I]	20th Century 541 [2]
			Mark Hamill/Harrison Ford/Carrie Fisher/Alec Guinness cp/cd: John Williams; pf: London Symphony Orchestra		
			"Star Wars (Main Title)"(1) - also see Meco/Zubin Mehta		
1/21/78	36	2	● 106. **Star Wars, The Story Of**		20th Century 550
			storyline excerpts from the film - narrator: Roscoe Browne		
5/19/62	12	15	107. **State Fair**	[M]	Dot 29011
			Pat Boone/Ann-Margret/Bobby Darin - mu: Richard Rodgers; ly: Oscar Hammerstein II; cd: Alfred Newman		
7/30/83	6	14	▲ 108. **Staying Alive**	[V]	RSO 813269
			John Travolta - side 1: Bee Gees; side 2: Various Artists		
			"Far From Over"(10-Frank Stallone)		
3/02/74	1(5)	23	● 109. **Sting, The**	[I]	MCA 390
			Paul Newman/Robert Redford/Robert Shaw - cp: Scott Joplin; cd/pianist: Marvin Hamlisch		
			"The Entertainer"(3-Marvin Hamlisch)		

DATE	POS	WKS	ALBUM TITLE		LABEL & NO.
7/14/84	32	6	110. Streets Of Fire Michael Pare/Diane Lane/Rick Moranis/Amy Madigan *"I Can Dream About You"(6-Dan Hartman)* Superfly - see Curtis Mayfield Ron O'Neal/Carl Lee/Julius Harris	[V]	MCA 5492
12/07/85	29	4	111. Sweet Dreams - The Life And Times Of Patsy Cline Jessica Lange/Ed Harris - featuring Patsy's original vocals		MCA 6149
11/24/84	34	4	● 112. Teachers Nick Nolte/Jobeth Williams/Judd Hirsch/Ralph Macchio features songs by 38 Special, Joe Cocker and 8 others	[V]	Capitol 12371
5/20/78	10	15	▲ 113. **Thank God It's Friday** Jeff Goldblum/Valerie Landsburg - includes bonus 12" single *"Last Dance"(3-Donna Summer)* **That's the Way of the World - see Earth, Wind & Fire**	[V]	Casablanca 7099 [2]
1/22/55	6	8	114. **There's No Business Like Show Business** Ethel Merman/Donald O'Connor/Dan Dailey - sw: Irving Berlin	[M]	Decca 8091
5/13/67	16	12	● 115. **Thoroughly Modern Millie** Julie Andrews/Mary Tyler Moore/Carol Channing cd: Andre Previn	[M]	Decca 71500
1/22/66	10	13	116. **Thunderball** Sean Connery/Claudine Auger - cp/cd: John Barry	[I]	United Art. 5132
11/15/80	37	4	117. Times Square Tim Curry/Trini Alvarado/Robin Johnson featuring recordings by 20 rock artists	[V]	RSO 4203 [2]
11/11/67	16	11	118. To Sir, With Love Sidney Poitier/Judy Geeson *"To Sir With Love"(1-Lulu)*	[I+V]	Fontana 67569
5/30/64	38	31	119. Tom Jones Albert Finney/Susannah York - cp/cd: John Addison	[I]	United Art. 5113
4/12/75	2(1)	19	● 120. **Tommy** rock opera featuring Roger Daltrey, Ann-Margret, Oliver Reed, Elton John - all but 4 songs written by Pete Townshend also see The Who/Various "Rock Operas"	[M]	Polydor 9502 [2]
6/14/86	1(5)	33	▲ 121. **Top Gun** Tom Cruise/Kelly McGillis/Val Kilmer/Anthony Edwards *"Danger Zone"(2-Kenny Loggins)* *"Take My Breath Away"(1-Berlin)* **Trouble Man - see Marvin Gaye** Robert Hooks/Paul Winfield/Ralph Waite/Paul Kelly	[V]	Columbia 40323
12/24/83	26	8	▲ 122. Two Of A Kind John Travolta/Olivia Newton-John *"Twist Of Fate"(5-Olivia Newton-John)*	[V]	MCA 6127
10/05/68	24	11	● 123. 2001: A Space Odyssey Gary Lockwood/Keir Dullea features classical music by various orchestras	[I]	MGM 13
8/15/64	11	16	124. Unsinkable Molly Brown Debbie Reynolds/Harve Presnell - sw: Meredith Willson; cd: Robert Armbruster - also see Original Cast ('60)	[M]	MGM 4232
6/07/80	3	23	▲ 125. **Urban Cowboy** John Travolta/Debra Winger *"Lookin' For Love"(5-Johnny Lee)*	[V]	Asylum 90002 [2]
2/24/68	11	9	126. Valley Of The Dolls Barbara Parkins/Patty Duke/Sharon Tate/Susan Hayward sw: Dory & Andre Previn; cd: Johnny Williams		20th Century 4196
7/13/85	38	4	127. View To A Kill, A Roger Moore/Tanya Roberts/Christopher Walken/Grace Jones - cp/cd: John Barry - "A View To A Kill"(1-Duran Duran)	[I]	Capitol 12413

DATE	POS	WKS	ALBUM TITLE	LABEL & NO.
3/23/85	11	12	▲ 128. Vision Quest [V] Matthew Modine/Linda Fiorentino/Michael Schoeffling *"Only The Young"*(9-Journey) *"Crazy For You"*(1-Madonna)	Geffen 24063
9/08/62	33	2	129. Walk On The Wild Side [I] Laurence Harvey/Jane Fonda - cp/cd: Elmer Bernstein Wattstax - see Concerts	Ava 4
3/02/74	20	5	● 130. Way We Were [I] Barbra Streisand/Robert Redford - cp: Marvin Hamlisch	Columbia 32830
11/20/61	1(54)	44	▲ 131. **West Side Story** **[M]** Natalie Wood/Richard Beymer/Rita Moreno/George Chakiris mu: Leonard Bernstein; ly: Stephen Sondheim; cd: Johnny Green also see Ferrante & Teicher/Stan Kenton/Original Cast ('58)	Columbia 2070
8/21/65	14	10	132. What's New Pussycat? [I+V] Peter Sellers/Peter O'Toole - mu: Burt Bacharach; ly: Hal David - "What's New Pussycat?"(3-Tom Jones)	United Art. 5117
12/07/85	17	12	● 133. White Nights [V] Mikhail Baryshnikov/Gregory Hines/Geraldine Page/Helen Mirren *"Separate Lives"*(1-Phil Collins & Marilyn Martin) Wild Angels - see Davie Allan Peter Fonda/Nancy Sinatra - cp/cd: Mike Curb	Atlantic 81273
9/21/68	12	12	134. Wild In The Streets Christopher Jones/Diana Varsi/Shelley Winters sw: Barry Mann/Cynthia Weil; cd: Mike Curb	Tower 5099
11/25/78	40	1	● 135. Wiz, The [M] a soul musical version of "The Wizard Of Oz" Diana Ross/Michael Jackson; sw: Charlie Smalls; cd: Quincy Jones - also see Original Cast ('75) Woman In Red - see Stevie Wonder Gene Wilder/Charles Grodin/Judith Ivey/Gilda Radner Woodstock - see Concerts Xanadu - see Olivia Newton-John/ELO Olivia Newton-John/Gene Kelly Yellow Submarine - see Beatles Yentl - see Barbra Streisand Barbra Streisand/Mandy Patinkin/Amy Irving	MCA 14000 [2]
11/05/77	17	5	● 136. You Light Up My Life Didi Conn/Joe Silver - cp/cd: Joseph Brooks	Arista 4159
8/19/67	27	6	137. You Only Live Twice [I] Sean Connery - cp/cd: John Barry Young at Heart - see Doris Day Your Cheatin' Heart - see Hank Williams, Jr. George Hamilton/Susan Oliver/Red Buttons/Arthur O'Connell	United Art. 5155
7/17/65	26	23	138. Zorba The Greek [I] Anthony Quinn/Irene Papas - cp/cd: Mikis Theodorakis also see Original Cast "Zorba"('69-an adaptation)	20th Century 4167

SOUNDTRACK COMPILATIONS

DATE	POS	WKS	ALBUM TITLE	LABEL & NO.
1/23/61	2(3)	63	1. **Great Motion Picture Themes** **[I]** *"Exodus"* Ferrante & Teicher/*"Never On Sunday"* Don Costa	United Art. 3122
6/23/62	31	3	2. Original Motion Picture Hit Themes *"Town Without Pity"* Gene Pitney/*"Tonight"* Ferrante & Teicher	United Art. 3197

DATE	POS	WKS	ALBUM TITLE	LABEL & NO.
			ORIGINAL CASTS The original cast stars are listed directly below the title. Also shown are the Lyricist (ly)/Music Writer (mu)/Songwriter (sw).	
4/21/62	21	6	1. All American Ray Bolger/Eileen Herlie/Ron Husmann mu: Charles Strouse; ly: Lee Adams	Columbia 2160
12/30/57	12	5	2. Annie Get Your Gun Mary Martin/John Raitt - sw: Irving Berlin - San Francisco/ Los Angeles production selected by NBC for a TV spectacular (introduced on Broadway in 1946 - starring Ethel Merman)	Capitol 913
2/09/57	20	1	3. Bells are Ringing Judy Holliday/Sydney Chaplin - mu: Jule Styne; ly: Betty Comden/Adolph Green	Columbia 5170
7/18/60	12	25	4. Bye Bye Birdie Chita Rivera/Dick Van Dyke/Kay Medford/Dick Gautier (Conrad Birdie) - mu: Charles Strouse; ly: Lee Adams - also see Soundtrack ('63)	Columbia 5510
3/25/67	37	3	5. Cabaret Jill Haworth/Jack Gilford/Bert Convy/Lotte Lenya mu: John Kander; ly: Fred Ebb - also see Soundtrack ('72)	Columbia 3040
1/23/61	1(6)	52	● 6. Camelot Richard Burton/Julie Andrews/Robert Goulet mu: Frederick Loewe; ly: Alan Jay Lerner also see Percy Faith/Soundtrack ('67)	Columbia 2031
6/12/61	1(1)	29	7. **Carnival** Anna Maria Alberghetti/James Mitchell - sw: Bob Merrill	MGM 3946
11/17/62	12	12	8. Carousel version of the Rodgers & Hammerstein musical - produced by Enoch Light and featuring vocalists Alfred Drake & Roberta Peters - also see Soundtrack ('56)	Command 843
4/29/57	15	1	9. Cinderella Julie Andrews - mu: Richard Rodgers; ly: Oscar Hammerstein a special CBS-TV production (3/31/57)	Columbia 5190
6/11/55	6	12	10. **Damn Yankees** Gwen Verdon/Stephen Douglass/Ray Walston sw: Richard Adler/Jerry Ross - also see Soundtrack ('58)	RCA 1021
3/06/61	12	11	11. Do Re Mi Phil Silvers/Nancy Walker - mu: Jule Styne; ly: Betty Comden/Adolph Green	RCA 2002
6/12/82	11	15	12. Dreamgirls Jennifer Holliday/Loretta Devine/Cleavant Derricks mu: Henry Krieger; ly: Tom Eyen	Geffen 2007
			Evening with Mike Nichols and Elaine May - see Mike Nichols & Elaine May	
1/22/55	7	2	13. Fanny Ezio Pinza/Walter Slezak/Florence Henderson - sw: Harold Rome	RCA 1015
12/26/64	7	60	● 14. **Fiddler On The Roof** Zero Mostel/Maria Karnilova/Beatrice Arthur mu: Jerry Bock; ly: Sheldon Harnick also see Soundtrack ('71)	RCA 1093
1/11/60	7	44	15. **Fiorello!** Tom Bosley/Patricia Wilson/Ellen Hanley/Howard Da Silva mu: Jerry Bock; ly: Sheldon Harnick	Capitol 1321
1/12/59	1(3)	02	● 16. **Flower Drum Song** Miyoshi Umeki/Larry Blyden/Pat Suzuki - mu: Richard Rodgers; ly: Oscar Hammerstein II - also see Sountrack ('61)	Columbia 2009
			Funny Girl - see Barbra Streisand (both Original Cast and Soundtrack) Barbra Streisand/Sydney Chaplin - mu: Jule Styne; ly: Bob Merrill	
2/15/64	33	3	17. Girl Who Came To Supper Jose Ferrer/Florence Henderson - sw: Noel Coward	Columbia 2420

Dionne Warwick, who added an "e" to her surname in the early 1970s, was discovered by songwriters Burt Bachrach and Hal David in 1961; she went on to have numerous hits singing their material. Among the classic collaborations: "Walk on By," "Do You Know the Way to San Jose?," and "I Say a Little Prayer," which was her first gold single and appeared on her 1967 album, *The Windows of the World*.

The Who's final album with drummer Keith Moon, who died a month after its release, was 1978's *Who Are You*, which proved to be the group's biggest chart success, hitting the No. 2 position for two weeks. Pete Townshend wrote the title track about a drunken confrontation he had with two of the Sex Pistols in a London nightclub.

Andy Williams has not only had an enormously successful singing career of his own, with hit records beginning in 1956, but he must claim responsibility for launching the Osmonds into national stardom. Williams discovered them performing at Disneyland and featured them on his long-running television show. *Lonely Street* (1960) was Williams' first hit album.

Jackie Wilson won a Golden Gloves boxing championship at age 16, but fortunately became a professional singer in 1952 when he replaced Clyde McPhatter in the Dominoes. Wilson's career took off in the late 1950s with "Lonely Teardrops." The single for which his 1963 album, *Baby Workout*, was titled reached No. 5 in the charts.

The Edgar Winter Group featured two future stars besides Johnny Winter's multifarious younger brother. Dan Hartman had great success as a singer ("I Can Dream About You" from the *Streets of Fire* soundtrack) and producer (James Brown's "Living in America" from *Rocky IV*); guitarist Ronnie Montrose's first solo record went gold and introduced future Van Halen member Sammy Hagar.

STEREO PAS 71001

SHE'S NOT THERE • TELL HER NO • WHAT MORE CAN I DO • IT'S ALRIGHT WITH ME
YOU'VE REALLY GOT A HOLD ON ME • WOMAN • SUMMERTIME • I DON'T WANT TO KNOW
WORK 'N' PLAY • CAN'T NOBODY LOVE YOU • SOMETIMES • I'VE GOT MY MOJO WORKING

Johnny Winter's big break came when a 1968 *Rolling Stone* article raved about the Texan's stunning guitar playing. From local beginnings in a group called Johnny Winter and the Black Plague, the albino blues player became a national phenomenon.

Stevie Wonder was discovered at age 12 by a neighbor whose brother was in the Miracles; his first album, aptly if immodestly titled *The 12 Year Old Genius*, was a chart-topper. For the next decade, however, despite enormous popularity and numerous hit singles, Wonder's albums didn't crack the top twenty. *Music of My Mind* (1972) only reached No. 21, but was followed by *Talking Book* (No. 3) and six more smash studio albums.

Woodstock Two, a double album, was issued ten months after the three-record *Woodstock* set and further chronicled the music played at the greatest live concert event of all time (Aug. 16–18, 1969). Among the performers featured on this volume are Jimi Hendrix, Joan Baez, Melanie, Mountain, Canned Heat, and Jefferson Airplane.

Yes' original late-1960s lineup made two albums that were later compiled on a 1975 retrospective, *Yesterdays.* The group's third album introduced guitarist Steve Howe, who stayed with Yes until 1980, when he helped form Asia. Other Yes alumni include keyboard stars Rick Wakeman and Patrick Moraz (later of the Moody Blues) and drummer Bill Bruford (later of King Crimson).

The Zombies, signed to its first recording contract on the strength of a tape of George Gershwin's "Summertime," appeared in the 1965 film, *Bunny Lake Is Missing.* Although *The Zombies* (1965) features two classic early hits, the group's best-selling American single, "Time of the Season," wasn't released until more than a year after it had broken up.

DATE	POS	WKS	ALBUM TITLE	LABEL & NO.
7/08/72	**34**	12	● 18. Godspell Stephen Nathan/David Haskell - sw: Stephen Schwartz based upon the gospel according to St. Matthew	Bell 1102
2/13/65	**36**	3	19. Golden Boy Sammy Davis, Jr./Billy Daniels - mu: Charles Strouse; ly: Lee Adams	Capitol 2124
7/20/59	**13**	41	20. Gypsy Ethel Merman/Jack Klugman/Sandra Church - mu: Jule Styne; ly: Stephen Sondheim - based on memoirs of Gypsy Rose Lee also see Soundtrack ('62)	Columbia 2017
11/23/68	**1(13)**	59	● 21. **Hair** Gerome Ragni/James Rado/Lynn Kellogg - mu: Galt MacDermot; ly: Gerome Ragni/James Rado	RCA 1150
2/29/64	**1(1)**	58	● 22. **Hello, Dolly!** Carol Channing/David Burns/Eileen Brennan - sw: Jerry Herman	RCA 1087
1/18/64	**38**	1	23. Here's Love Janis Paige/Craig Stevens - sw: Meredith Willson based on "Miracle On 34th Street"	Columbia 2400
12/18/61	**19**	19	24. How To Succeed In Business Without Really Trying Robert Morse/Rudy Vallee - sw: Frank Loesser	RCA 1066
12/05/60	**9**	17	25. **Irma La Douce** Elizabeth Seal/Keith Michell/Clive Revill mu: Marguerite Monnot; original lyrics: Alexandre Breffort	Columbia 2029
1/08/72	**31**	12	26. Jesus Christ Superstar Ben Vereen/Jeff Fenbolt/Yvonne Elliman/Bob Bingham mu: Andrew Lloyd Webber; ly: Tim Rice also see Various ('70)/Soundtrack ('73)	Decca 1503
12/29/56	**19**	3	27. Li'l Abner Edith Adams/Peter Palmer/Howard St. John/Stubby Kaye mu: Gene de Paul; ly: Johnny Mercer	Columbia 5150
8/20/66	**23**	14	● 28. Mame Angela Lansbury/Beatrice Arthur - sw: Jerry Herman based on the movie "Auntie Mame"	Columbia 3000
2/18/67	**31**	13	● 29. Man of La Mancha Richard Kiley/Irving Jacobson/Joan Diener - mu: Mitch Leigh; ly: Joe Darion - an adaptation of "Don Quixote" - featuring the song "The Impossible Dream"	Kapp 4505
11/20/61	**10**	27	30. **Milk and Honey** Robert Weede/Mimi Benzell/Molly Picon - sw: Jerry Herman	RCA 1065
12/01/62	**14**	13	31. Mr. President Robert Ryan/Nanette Fabray - sw: Irving Berlin	Columbia 2270
8/04/56	**11**	4	32. Most Happy Fella, The Robert Weede/Jo Sullivan - sw: Frank Loesser	Columbia 2330
2/24/58	**1(12)**	55	● 33. **Music Man, The** Robert Preston/Barbara Cook - sw: Meredith Willson also see Soundtrack ('62)	Capitol 990
4/28/56	**1(15)**	11	▲ 34. **My Fair Lady** Rex Harrison/Julie Andrews - mu: Frederick Loewe; ly: Alan Jay Lerner - adapted from Bernard Shaw's "Pygmalion" - also see Soundtrack ('64)	Columbia 5090
8/05/57	**17**	3	35. New Girl in Town Gwen Verdon/Thelma Ritter/George Wallace - sw: Bob Merrill	RCA 1027
4/28/62	**5**	27	36. **No Strings** Richard Kiley/Diahann Carroll - sw: Richard Rodgers	Capitol 1695
11/03/62	**4**	53	● 37. **Oliver!** Clive Revill/Georgia Brown/Bruce Prochnik (Oliver) sw: Lionel Bart - also see Soundtrack ('68)/Mantovani	RCA 2004
2/15/64	**37**	2	38. 101 In The Shade Robert Horton/Inga Swenson/Stephen Douglass mu: Harvey Schmidt; ly: Tom Jones	RCA 1085

DATE	POS	WKS	ALBUM TITLE	LABEL & NO.
4/02/55	4	8	**39. Peter Pan** Mary Martin/Cyril Ritchard - mu: Mark Charlap/Jule Styne; ly: Carolyn Leigh/Betty Comden/Adolph Green	RCA 1019
1/06/62	36	2	40. Sail Away Elaine Stritch/James Hurst - sw: Noel Coward	Capitol 1643
6/22/63	15	8	41. She Loves Me Barbara Cook/Daniel Massey/Barbara Baxley/Jack Cassidy mu: Jerry Bock; ly: Sheldon Harnick	MGM 4118 [2]
4/16/55	9	6	42. **Silk Stockings** Hildegarde Neff/Don Ameche/Gretchen Wyler - sw: Cole Porter	RCA 1016
12/21/59	1(16)	27	● 43. **Sound Of Music, The** Mary Martin/Theodore Bikel - mu: Richard Rodgers; ly: Oscar Hammerstein II - also see Soundtrack ('65)	Columbia 2020
11/24/62	3	22	44. **Stop The World-I Want To Get Off** Anthony Newley/Anna Quayle - sw: Leslie Bricusse/ Anthony Newley	London 88001
1/09/61	15	12	45. Tenderloin Maurice Evans/Ron Husmann/Wayne Miller/Eileen Rodgers mu: Jerry Bock; ly: Sheldon Harnick	Capitol 1492
12/26/60	6	13	46. **Unsinkable Molly Brown** Tammy Grimes/Harve Presnell - sw: Meredith Willson also see Soundtrack ('64)	Capitol 1509
3/17/58	5	13	● 47. **West Side Story** Carol Lawrence/Larry Kert/Chita Rivera/Art Smith mu: Leonard Bernstein; ly: Stephen Sondheim also see Soundtrack ('61)	Columbia 5230
5/09/64	28	3	48. What Makes Sammy Run? Steve Lawrence/Sally Ann Howes/Robert Alda - sw: Ervin Drake	Columbia 2440
1/23/61	6	26	49. **Wildcat** Lucille Ball/Keith Andes - mu: Cy Coleman; ly: Carolyn Leigh	RCA 1060

DATE	POS	WKS	ALBUM TITLE		LABEL & NO.

TELEVISION SHOWS

The stars of the show are listed directly below the title.

DATE	POS	WKS	ALBUM TITLE		LABEL & NO.
11/27/71	8	12	● 1. **All In The Family**	[C]	Atlantic 7210
			Carroll O'Connor/Jean Stapleton/Rob Reiner/Sally Struthers comedy excerpts from the show		
8/23/69	18	8	2. Dark Shadows	[I]	Philips 314
			Jonathan Frid/David Selby - cp/cd: Robert Cobert		
10/12/85	1(11)	22	▲ 3. **Miami Vice**	[V]	MCA 6150
			Don Johnson/Philip Michael Thomas - includes 5 instrumentals composed & performed by Jan Hammer - "Miami Vice"(1-Jan Hammer)		
			"You Belong To The City"(2-Glenn Frey)		
			Mr. Lucky - see Henry Mancini		
5/09/60	30	2	4. One Step Beyond (Music From)	[I]	Decca 8970
			from the "Alcoa Presents" TV series - Harry Lubin conducts the Berliner Symphoniker orchestra		
			Peter Gunn - see Henry Mancini		
			Roaring Twenties - see Dorothy Provine		
			Roots - see Quincy Jones		
2/05/77	38	3	5. Saturday Night Live!	[C]	Arista 4107
			John Belushi/Dan Aykroyd/Chevy Chase/Jane Curtin & cast		
			Sesame Street - see Children's section		
4/20/59	3	21	6. **77 Sunset Strip**	[I]	Warner 1289
			Efrem Zimbalist, Jr./Roger Smith/Ed "Kookie" Byrnes musical director: Warren Barker		
1/12/74	34	7	7. Sunshine		MCA 387
			TV film starring Christina Raines and Cliff DeYoung music composed by John Denver; vocals by Cliff DeYoung		
1/18/75	30	3	● 8. Tonight Show/Here's Johnny	[C]	Casablanca 1296 [2]
			actual musical and comedy excerpts from the TV show hosted by Johnny Carson since 10/1/62		
11/10/58	2(4)	85	9. **Victory At Sea, Vol 2**	[I]	RCA 2226
9/25/61	7	19	10. **Victory At Sea, Vol. 3**	[I]	RCA 2523
			above 2 albums are orchestral suites from the NBC-TV series which featured actual film of World War II naval battles cp: Richard Rodgers; cd: Robert Russell Bennett		

DATE	POS	WKS	ALBUM TITLE	LABEL & NO.
			# LABEL COMPILATIONS A sampling of artists and songs are listed below each title.	
			ATLANTIC	
11/24/56	**20**	2	1. Rock & Roll Forever 14 selections by Atlantic's top R&B artists	Atlantic 1239
9/02/67	**12**	14	2. The Super Hits "Respect" Aretha Franklin/"Good Lovin'" Young Rascals	Atlantic 501
			CAPITOL	
6/01/59	**5**	3	3. **What's New? on Capitol Stereo, vol. 1** preview of 12 new Capitol stereo albums	Capitol SN-1
			COLUMBIA	
6/12/61	**1(9)**	39	4. **Stars For A Summer Night** 25 performances by 22 pop and classical artists	Columbia 1 [2]
			END	
2/27/61	**19**	5	5. 12 + 3 = 15 Hits Flamingos/Chantels/Little Anthony & The Imperials/Dubs	End 310
			ORIGINAL SOUND	
9/28/59	**12**	88	6. Oldies But Goodies "Earth Angel" Penguins/"In The Still Of The Night" 5 Satins	Original Snd. 5001
9/11/61	**12**	20	7. Oldies But Goodies, Vol. 3 "Come Go With Me" Dell-Vikings/"Sea Cruise" Frankie Ford	Original Snd. 5004
9/11/61	**15**	20	8. Oldies But Goodies, Vol. 4 "Silhouettes" Rays/"Blue Suede Shoes" Carl Perkins	Original Snd. 5005
8/04/62	**16**	11	9. Oldies But Goodies, Vol. 5 "Alley-Oop" Hollywood Argyles/"Little Star" Elegants	Original Snd. 5007
7/06/63	**31**	14	10. Oldies But Goodies, Vol. 6 "Raindrops" Dee Clark/"Quarter To Three" Gary U.S. Bonds	Original Snd. 5011
			RCA	
10/15/55	**9**	9	11. **Pop Shopper** 12 selections from RCA Victor's album releases	RCA 12-13
11/30/59	**2(7)**	39	● 12. **60 Years Of Music America Loves Best** performances by RCA Victor artists, from Caruso to Belafonte	RCA 6072 [2]
10/31/60	**6**	24	13. **60 Years Of Music America Loves Best, Volume II** 30 performances by RCA artists, from Sousa to Eddie Fisher	RCA 6088 [2]
9/25/61	**5**	12	14. **Sixty Years Of Music America Loves Best, Volume III (Popular)** "Frenesi" Artie Shaw/"Night And Day" Frank Sinatra	RCA 1509

DATE	POS	WKS	ALBUM TITLE	LABEL & NO.
			## RADIO/TV CELEBRITY COMPILATIONS Collections of hits gathered together by famous radio and TV names.	
8/11/73	**27**	7	● 1. Dick Clark/20 Years Of Rock N' Roll original hits from 1953-1972	Buddah 5133 [2]
1/27/62	**26**	7	2. Murray the K's Blasts From The Past *"Sweet Little 16" Chuck Berry/"Bo Diddley" Bo Diddley*	Chess 1461
			## CONCERTS/FESTIVALS	
5/02/81	**36**	3	1. Concerts For The People Of Kampuchea December, 1979 four day benefit concert in London, England The Who/Paul McCartney/Pretenders/Rockestra and 6 others	Atlantic 7005 [2]
8/26/72	**40**	2	2. Fillmore: The Last Days Bill Graham's Fillmore-San Francisco rock shows ran from 11/6/65-7/4/71 - album includes a booklet & 7" interview record	Fillmore 31390 [3]
1/05/80	**19**	9	● 3. No Nukes/The MUSE Concerts For A Non-Nuclear Future benefit concerts at New York's Madison Square Garden Jackson Browne/Bruce Springsteen/Tom Petty/Doobie Bros.	Asylum 801 [3]
4/17/82	**29**	5	4. Secret Policeman's Other Ball/ The Music Sting/Jeff Beck & Eric Clapton/Phil Collins/Donovan above 2 albums are benefit concerts recorded in London for Amnesty International	Island 9698
3/24/73	**28**	6	● 5. Wattstax: The Living Word [S] Isaac Hayes/Staple Singers/Rufus & Carla Thomas/Eddie Floyd	Stax 3010 [2]
6/06/70	**1(4)**	36	● **6. Woodstock** [S] film of historic rock festival near Woodstock, New York on August 15-17, 1969 - Jimi Hendrix/Crosby, Stills, Nash & Young/Santana/The Who/Ten Years After/Joe Cocker/Sha-Na-Na	Cotillion 500 [3]
4/10/71	**7**	9	● **7. Woodstock Two** [S] more songs from the festival - Jefferson Airplane/Joan Baez/ Melanie/Mountain/Canned Heat/Butterfield Blues Band	Cotillion 400 [2]
			## ROCK OPERAS/ CONCEPT ALBUMS	
11/21/70	**1(3)**	65	● **1. Jesus Christ Superstar** a rock opera featuring Ian Gillan (Jesus), Murray Head and Yvonne Elliman - mu: Andrew Lloyd Webber; ly: Tim Rice also see Soundtrack and Original Cast versions	Decca 7206 [2]
2/14/76	**10**	14	▲ **2. The Outlaws** Waylon Jennings, Willie Nelson, Jessi Colter, Tompall Glaser	RCA 1321
12/23/72	**5**	13	● **3. Tommy** featuring the London Symphony Orchestra and English Chamber Choir with guests Pete Townshend, Roger Daltrey, Rod Stewart, Ringo Starr and others - also see The Who/Soundtrack versions	Ode 99001 [2]

DATE	POS	WKS	ALBUM TITLE	LABEL & NO.
7/09/55	5	10	**JAZZ** 1. **I Like Jazz!** **[K]** a sampling of the development of jazz (ragtime, swing, etc.)	Columbia 1
8/18/79	21	6	**DANCE/DISCO/RAP** ● 1. Night At Studio 54 specially sequenced disco favorites at the New York club	Casablanca 7161 [2]
7/17/82	15	27	**AEROBICS** Albums for aerobic exercising - with music, narration, instructions and illustrations. ▲ 1. Jane Fonda's Workout Record music: Jacksons/REO Speedwagon/Brothers Johnson/Boz Scaggs	Columbia 38054 [2]
5/24/80 8/29/70 10/27/79 12/22/79	35 23 32 26	4 9 5 4	**CHILDREN'S** Children oriented albums. ▲ 1. Mickey Mouse Disco disco songs performed by session musicians ● 2. Sesame Street Book & Record **[TV]** Loretta Long/Bob McGrath/Jim Henson's Muppets & cast ● 3. The Muppet Movie **[S]** *"Rainbow Connection" - Kermit* ▲ 4. A Christmas Together **[X]** **JOHN DENVER & THE MUPPETS**	Disneyland 2504 Columbia 1069 Atlantic 16001 RCA 3451

DATE	POS	WKS	ARTIST—RECORD TITLE	LABEL & NO.

12/30/57	**19**	3	**CHRISTMAS** .
			The following various artist/specialty Christmas album made Billboard's regular Top LPs charts.
			    1. Merry Christmas [EP]
			       7" E.P. (originally released as a 10" LP in 1952)
			       Ames Brothers/Don Cornell/Johnny Desmond/Eileen Barton
			       For the years 1963 through 1973, Billboard did not chart Christmas albums on their regular Top LPs charts. Instead, they issued special Christmas charts for 3-4 weeks during each Christmas season. These special charts were discontinued from 1974 through 1982 when Billboard again charted Christmas albums on their regular album charts. For the years 1983 and 1984, Billboard again issued special Christmas charts; however, they also listed the best selling Christmas albums on their regular Top LPs charts. The following list includes only those albums which made the TOP 10 of Billboard's special CHRISTMAS ALBUMS chart and never made Billboard's regular Top LPs charts.
				Coral 82003

12/07/68	**1(2)**	8	**HERB ALPERT & THE TIJUANA BRASS** ● 1. Alpert, Herb, & The Tijuana Brass Christmas Album [2 yrs.] [I]	A&M 4166

12/02/67	**9**	1	**JULIE ANDREWS**
			2. A Christmas Treasure
			    with the orchestra. Harpsichord & arrangements of
			    Andre Previn
				RCA 3829

12/03/66	**6**	5	**JOAN BAEZ** 3. Noel [2 yrs.]	Vanguard 79230
12/05/64	**6**	3	**BEACH BOYS** ● 4. The Beach Boys' Christmas Album [2 yrs.] *"Little Saint Nick"/"The Man With All The Toys"*	Capitol 2164
12/14/68	**10**	1	**TONY BENNETT** 5. Snowfall/The Tony Bennett Christmas Album	Columbia 9739
12/19/70	**9**	1	**BOSTON POPS ORCHESTRA/ARTHUR FIEDLER** 6. A Christmas Festival [I]	Polydor 5004
12/25/71	**6**	1	**BRADY BRUNCH** 7. Merry Christmas from the Brady Bunch	Paramount 5026
12/13/69	**10**	1	**JAMES BROWN** 8. A Soulful Christmas	King 1040
12/07/68	**1(2)**	6	**GLEN CAMPBELL** ● 9. That Christmas Feeling [2 yrs.]	Capitol 2978
12/13/69	**7**	1	**JOHNNY CASH** 10. The Christmas Spirit	Columbia 8917
12/21/63	**9**	1	**CHIPMUNKS** 11. Christmas with the Chipmunks, Vol. 2 [N]	Liberty 7334
12/21/63	**1(2)**	39	**NAT KING COLE** ● 12. The Christmas Song [12 yrs.]	Capitol 1967

DATE	POS	WKS	ARTIST—RECORD TITLE	LABEL & NO.
12/05/70	5	2	**PERRY COMO** ● 13. The Perry Como Christmas Album	RCA 4016
12/12/70	10	1	**RAY CONNIFF** 14. Here We Come A-Caroling	Columbia GP 3
12/19/64	9	2	**BING CROSBY/FRANK SINATRA/FRED WARING** 15. 12 Songs Of Christmas	Reprise 2022
12/15/84	9	1	**PLACIDO DOMINGO** 16. Christmas with Placido Domingo with the Vienna Symphony Orchestra	CBS 37245
12/01/73	3	3	**JOSE FELICIANO** 17. Jose Feliciano "Feliz Navidad"	RCA 4421
12/05/64	3	4	**JOHN GARY** 18. The John Gary Christmas Album	RCA 2940
12/17/66	9	2	**EYDIE GORME & The TRIO LOS PANCHOS** 19. Navidad means Christmas [F]	Columbia 9357
12/07/63	4	6	**ROBERT GOULET** 20. This Christmas I Spend With You [2 yrs.]	Columbia 8876
12/08/73	4	2	**MERLE HAGGARD** 21. Merle Haggard's Christmas Present (Something Old, Something New) "If We Make It Through December"	Capitol 11230
12/05/70	1(6)	16	**JACKSON 5** 22. Christmas Album [4 yrs.]	Motown 713
12/13/69	2(1)	2	**MAHALIA JACKSON** 23. Christmas with Mahalia	Columbia 9727
12/07/63	10	2	**BERT KAEMPFERT** 24. Christmas Wonderland [I]	Decca 74441
12/18/65	8	2	**KING FAMILY** 25. Christmas With The King Family	Warner 1627
12/16/72	7	1	**BRENDA LEE** 26. Merry Christmas from Brenda Lee "Rockin' Around The Christmas Tree"	Decca 74583
12/19/64	8	2	**RAMSEY LEWIS TRIO** 27. More Sounds Of Christmas [I]	Argo 745
12/15/84	8	2	**BARBARA MANDRELL** 28. Christmas At Our House	MCA 5519

DATE	POS	WKS	ARTIST—RECORD TITLE	LABEL & NO.
12/14/63	7	3	**MANTOVANI** 29. Christmas Greetings From Mantovani [2 yrs.] [I]	London 338
12/03/66	1(1)	14	**DEAN MARTIN** ● 30. The Dean Martin Christmas Album [4 yrs.]	Reprise 6222
12/12/64	8	2	**AL MARTINO** 31. A Merry Christmas	Capitol 2165
11/30/63 12/06/69	2(2) 1(1)	7 15	**JOHNNY MATHIS** 32. Sounds Of Christmas [2 yrs.] ● 33. Give Me Your Love For Christmas [4 yrs.]	Mercury 60837 Columbia 9923
12/11/65 12/20/69	8 3	1 4	**MORMON TABERNACLE CHOIR** ● 34. The Joy of Christmas _{with Leonard Bernstein conducting the New York Philharmonic} 35. Handel: Messiah [3 yrs.] _{with Eugene Ormandy conducting The Philadelphia Orchestra featured vocalists: Eileen Farrell (soprano) & William Warfield (baritone)}	Columbia 6499 Columbia 607 [2]
12/09/67	1(1)	17	**JIM NABORS** ● 36. Jim Nabors' Christmas Album [6 yrs.]	Columbia 9531
12/28/63	5	1	**NEW CHRISTY MINSTRELS** 37. Merry Christmas!	Columbia 8896
12/03/66	10	3	**WAYNE NEWTON** 38. Songs For A Merry Christmas	Capitol 2588
12/04/71	1(4)	6	**PARTRIDGE FAMILY** ● 39. A Partridge Family Christmas Card [2 yrs.]	Bell 6066
12/17/83	6	4	**LUCIANO PAVAROTTI** ● 40. O Holy Night [2 yrs.] _{with Kurt Adler conducting the National Philharmonic (recorded 1976)}	London 26473
12/05/70 12/04/71	2(3) 1(3)	5 12	**ELVIS PRESLEY** 41. Elvis' Christmas Album [2 yrs.] _{8 of 10 songs are from his 1957 Christmas album} *"If Every Day Was Like Christmas"/"Mama Liked The Roses"* ▲ 42. Elvis sings The Wonderful World of Christmas [3 yrs.] _{an all new Christmas LP (recorded May, 1971)}	RCA Camden 2428 RCA LSP-4579
12/12/70	5	6	**CHARLEY PRIDE** 43. Christmas in My Home Town [3 yrs.]	RCA 4406
12/02/67	2(1)	5	**LOU RAWLS** 44. Merry Christmas Ho! Ho! Ho!	Capitol 2790
12/09/67	10	1	**PAUL REVERE & THE RAIDERS** 45. A Christmas Present...And Past	Columbia 9555

DATE	POS	WKS	ARTIST—RECORD TITLE	LABEL & NO.
12/07/68	8	2	**ROBERT SHAW CHORALE & ORCHESTRA** 46. Handel: Messiah *"Messiah" was composed by George Frideric Handel from 8/22 to 9/14, 1741*	RCA 6175 [3]
12/12/70	2(1)	3	**BOBBY SHERMAN** 47. Bobby Sherman Christmas Album	Metromedia 1038
12/03/66	5	4	**HARRY SIMEONE CHORALE** 48. O Bambino/The Little Drummer Boy [3 yrs.] includes Simeone's new recording of "The Little Drummer Boy"	Kapp 3450
12/13/69	3	2	**SINATRA FAMILY** 49. The Sinatra Family Wish You A Merry Christmas Frank and daughters Nancy & Tina, and son Frank Jr.	Reprise 1026
12/05/64	8	1	**JIMMY SMITH** 50. Christmas '64 [I]	Verve 8604
12/11/65	6	3	**SUPREMES** 51. Merry Christmas	Motown 638
12/19/70 12/17/83	4 6	5 2	**TEMPTATIONS** 52. The Temptations' Christmas Card [3 yrs.] 53. Give Love At Christmas	Gordy 951 Gordy 998
12/18/65	9	2	**VENTURES** 54. The Ventures' Christmas Album [I]	Dolton 8038
11/30/63 12/18/65	1(9) 1(3)	26 12	**ANDY WILLIAMS** ● 55. The Andy Williams Christmas Album [8 yrs.] ● 56. Merry Christmas [4 yrs.]	Columbia 8887 Columbia 9220
12/09/72 12/01/73 12/08/73 12/05/70 12/23/72 12/06/69	7 7 1(1) 7 6 8	3 1 3 1 3 2	**VARIOUS ARTISTS** 57. Christmas Album, The features songs by Barbra Streisand, Mahalia Jackson, Johnny Mathis, Frank Sinatra, Tony Bennett, Johnny Cash & 14 others 58. Christmas Greetings from Nashville features Eddy Arnold, Chet Atkins, Jim Reeves & 7 others 59. Motown Christmas, A Temptations/Stevie Wonder/Jackson Five/Miracles/Supremes 60. Peace On Earth Beach Boys/Glen Campbell/Nat King Cole/Lettermen + 13 others 61. Phil Spector's Christmas Album Crystals/Ronettes/Darlene Love/Bob B. Soxx & Blue Jeans - reissue of "A Christmas Gift For You" (Philles/1963) 62. Soul Christmas Otis Redding/Clarence Carter/Joe Tex plus 5 others	Columbia 30763 [2] RCA 0262 Motown 795 [2] Capitol 585 [2] Apple 3400 Atco 269

DATE	POS	WKS	ALBUM TITLE	LABEL & NO.
			## CLASSICAL	
			Various artist compilations.	
9/25/61	6	9	1. **Sixty Years Of Music America Loves Best, Volume III (Red Seal)**	RCA 2574
			Caruso/Fiedler/Toscanini plus 9 more classical greats	
5/25/63	39	3	2. Sound of Genius	Columbia SGS 1 [2]
			19 favorites by 18 of Columbia's greatest classical artists	
6/16/62	24	9	3. Summer Festival	RCA 6097 [2]
			19 favorites by 20 of RCA's greatest classical artists	
			## COMEDY	
			Comedy concept productions.	
1/26/63	27	4	1. Other Family, The	Laurie 5000
			starring Larry Foster, Marty Brill and Toby Deane	
11/12/66	40	2	2. Our Wedding Album or The Great Society Affair	Jamie 3028
			spoof of President Johnson's family - with Kenny Solms, Gail Parent, Fannie Flagg, Robert Klein & Jo Ann Worley	
1/26/63	35	4	3. President Strikes Back!	Kapp 1322
			an answer album to Vaughn Meader's "The First Family" starring Marc London and Sylvia Miles	
12/04/65	3	14	• 4. **Welcome to the LBJ Ranch!**	Capitol 2423
			featuring the actual recorded voices of political leaders	
5/07/66	22	5	5. When You're In Love The Whole World Is Jewish	Kapp 4506
			starring Betty Walker, Lou Jacobi, Frank Gallop and 4 others	
10/23/65	9	14	6. **You Don't Have To Be Jewish**	Kapp 4503
			starring Betty Walker, Lou Jacobi, Frank Gallop and 5 others	
			## MISCELLANEOUS	
			The following albums, because of their unusual content, are listed in this section and are categorized with special headings.	
			### CARS	
2/29/64	27	2	1. Big Sounds Of The Drags!	Capitol 2001
			actual sounds of drag racing at a quarter-mile track	
7/27/63	7	31	2. **Shut Down**	Capitol 1918
			"Shut Down" Beach Boys/"Black Denim Trousers" Cheers, plus 10 other car songs	
			### MINSTREL SHOW	
5/26/56	9	9	3. **Gentlemen, Be Seated**	Epic 3238
			recreation of a complete minstrel show (conducted by Allen Roth) - also see Eric Rogers "Vaudeville"	
			### RADIO	
3/29/69	31	7	4. Themes Like Old Times	Viva 36018 [2]
			180 of the most famous original radio themes	

THE
RECORD
HOLDERS

TOP ARTIST AND ALBUM ACHIEVEMENTS

THE TOP 100 ARTISTS (A–Z)

ARTIST	RANK	ARTIST	RANK
HERB ALPERT & THE TIJUANA BRASS	15	KISS	77
JOAN BAEZ	57	LED ZEPPELIN	36
BEACH BOYS	17	JOHN LENNON	71
BEATLES	5	ENOCH LIGHT	30
BEE GEES	31	HENRY MANCINI	19
HARRY BELAFONTE	18	BARRY MANILOW	52
PAT BOONE	62	MANTOVANI	8
DAVID BOWIE	46	DEAN MARTIN	96
DAVE BRUBECK QUARTET	70	JOHNNY MATHIS	6
GLEN CAMPBELL	55	PAUL McCARTNEY/WINGS	22
CARPENTERS	100	MITCH MILLER	7
RAY CHARLES	28	STEVE MILLER BAND	87
CHUBBY CHECKER	76	JONI MITCHELL	83
CHICAGO	20	MONKEES	82
ERIC CLAPTON	48	MOODY BLUES	42
NAT KING COLE	33	RICKY NELSON	95
COMMODORES	56	OLIVIA NEWTON-JOHN	39
PERRY COMO	80	PETER, PAUL & MARY	34
RAY CONNIFF	10	ELVIS PRESLEY	2
BILL COSBY	81	QUEEN	65
CREEDENCE CLEARWATER REVIVAL	92	KENNY ROGERS	64
JOHN DENVER	38	ROLLING STONES	3
NEIL DIAMOND	21	LINDA RONSTADT	50
DOOBIE BROTHERS	63	DIANA ROSS	37
DOORS	59	SANTANA	40
BOB DYLAN	11	BOB SEGER	91
EAGLES	74	SIMON & GARFUNKEL	61
EARTH, WIND & FIRE	44	FRANK SINATRA	1
ELECTRIC LIGHT ORCHESTRA	84	BRUCE SPRINGSTEEN	85
TENNESSEE ERNIE FORD	53	CAT STEVENS	68
FOREIGNER	88	ROD STEWART	35
ARETHA FRANKLIN	24	BARBRA STREISAND	4
MARVIN GAYE	78	DONNA SUMMER	66
JACKIE GLEASON	79	SUPREMES	27
GRAND FUNK RAILROAD	47	JAMES TAYLOR	54
DARYL HALL & JOHN OATES	58	TEMPTATIONS	12
GEORGE HARRISON	86	THREE DOG NIGHT	49
ISAAC HAYES	90	VAN HALEN	89
HEART	98	BILLY VAUGHN	23
JIMI HENDRIX	51	VENTURES	99
AL HIRT	97	WAR	93
ISLEY BROTHERS	67	DIONNE WARWICK	75
JACKSON 5/JACKSONS	45	LAWRENCE WELK	16
JEFFERSON AIRPLANE/STARSHIP	26	WHO	43
JETHRO TULL	32	ANDY WILLIAMS	14
BILLY JOEL	41	ROGER WILLIAMS	24
ELTON JOHN	13	NANCY WILSON	72
JOURNEY	93	STEVIE WONDER	29
CAROLE KING	73	YES	69
KINGSTON TRIO	9	NEIL YOUNG	60

THE TOP 100 ARTISTS OF THE ROCK ERA

ARTIST	POINTS	ARTIST	POINTS
1. FRANK SINATRA	3571	26. JEFFERSON AIRPLANE/STARSHIP	1104
2. ELVIS PRESLEY	3081	27. SUPREMES	1091
3. ROLLING STONES	2554	28. RAY CHARLES	1090
4. BARBRA STREISAND	2318	29. STEVIE WONDER	1033
5. BEATLES	2316	30. ENOCH LIGHT	982
6. JOHNNY MATHIS	2279	31. BEE GEES	955
7. MITCH MILLER	2055	32. JETHRO TULL	947
8. MANTOVANI	1929	33. NAT KING COLE	940
9. KINGSTON TRIO	1772	34. PETER, PAUL & MARY	929
10. RAY CONNIFF	1678	35. ROD STEWART	897
11. BOB DYLAN	1611	36. LED ZEPPELIN	890
12. TEMPTATIONS	1530	37. DIANA ROSS	857
13. ELTON JOHN	1524	38. JOHN DENVER	839
14. ANDY WILLIAMS	1358	39. OLIVIA NEWTON-JOHN	834
15. HERB ALPERT & THE TIJUANA BRASS	1350	40. SANTANA	826
16. LAWRENCE WELK	1345	41. BILLY JOEL	819
17. BEACH BOYS	1283	42. MOODY BLUES	818
18. HARRY BELAFONTE	1254	43. WHO	817
19. HENRY MANCINI	1252	44. EARTH, WIND & FIRE	804
20. CHICAGO	1252	45. JACKSON 5	798
21. NEIL DIAMOND	1220	46. DAVID BOWIE	787
22. PAUL McCARTNEY	1151	47. GRAND FUNK RAILROAD	783
23. BILLY VAUGHN	1134	48. ERIC CLAPTON	770
24. ARETHA FRANKLIN	1131	49. THREE DOG NIGHT	764
25. ROGER WILLIAMS	1131	50. LINDA RONSTADT	758

THE TOP 100 ARTISTS OF THE ROCK ERA

ARTIST	POINTS	ARTIST	POINTS
51. JIMI HENDRIX	755	76. CHUBBY CHECKER	620
52. BARRY MANILOW	743	77. KISS	615
53. TENNESSEE ERNIE FORD	734	78. MARVIN GAYE	606
54. JAMES TAYLOR	728	79. JACKIE GLEASON	606
55. GLEN CAMPBELL	725	80. PERRY COMO	601
56. COMMODORES	716	81. BILL COSBY	594
57. JOAN BAEZ	709	82. MONKEES	590
58. DARYL HALL & JOHN OATES	708	83. JONI MITCHELL	579
59. DOORS	700	84. ELECTRIC LIGHT ORCHESTRA	578
60. NEIL YOUNG	694	85. BRUCE SPRINGSTEEN	573
61. SIMON & GARFUNKEL	690	86. GEORGE HARRISON	571
62. PAT BOONE	683	87. STEVE MILLER BAND	564
63. DOOBIE BROTHERS	681	88. FOREIGNER	564
64. KENNY ROGERS	674	89. VAN HALEN	559
65. QUEEN	672	90. ISAAC HAYES	558
66. DONNA SUMMER	670	91. BOB SEGER	558
67. ISLEY BROTHERS	667	92. CREEDENCE CLEARWATER REVIVAL	557
68. CAT STEVENS	664	93. WAR	556
69. YES	659	94. JOURNEY	556
70. DAVE BRUBECK QUARTET	653	95. RICKY NELSON	553
71. JOHN LENNON	644	96. DEAN MARTIN	549
72. NANCY WILSON	639	97. AL HIRT	548
73. CAROLE KING	632	98. HEART	547
74. EAGLES	625	99. VENTURES	545
75. DIONNE WARWICK	624	100. CARPENTERS	539

Artist's points are calculated using the following formula:

1. Each artist's Top 40 albums are awarded points based on their highest charted position (No. 1 = 40 points; No. 2 = 39 points; etc.) and added.
2. Bonus points are awarded to each album based on its highest charted position (Nos. 1-5 = 25 points; Nos. 6-10 = 20 points; Nos. 11-20 = 15 points; Nos. 21-30 = 10 points; Nos. 31-40 = 5 points).
3. Total weeks charted are added in.
4. Total weeks an album held the No. 1 position are also added in.

When two artists combine for a hit album (Examples: Supremes/Temptations; Kenny Rogers/Dolly Parton), the full point value is given to each artist.

Artists such as "Simon and Garfunkel," "Sonny & Cher," and "Loggins & Messina" are considered regular recording teams and their points are not split or shared by either of the artists individually.

THE TOP 25 ARTISTS BY DECADE

ARTIST	POINTS	ARTIST	POINTS

THE FIFTIES 1955—59

1. FRANK SINATRA		1390
2. JOHNNY MATHIS		1178
3. MANTOVANI		1140
4. MITCH MILLER		965
5. HARRY BELAFONTE		880
6. ELVIS PRESLEY		842
7. ROGER WILLIAMS		753
8. TENNESSEE ERNIE FORD		656
9. PAT BOONE		619
10. LAWRENCE WELK		609
11. JACKIE GLEASON		606
12. KINGSTON TRIO		580
13. RAY CONNIFF		458
14. PERRY COMO		458
15. NAT KING COLE		442
16. BILLY VAUGHN		343
17. FOUR FRESHMEN		318
18. VAN CLIBURN		285
19. RICKY NELSON		279
20. DAVE BRUBECK QUARTET		266
21. HENRY MANCINI		261
22. BING CROSBY		258
23. MARIO LANZA		255
24. SHELLEY BERMAN		254
25. LESTER LANIN		233

THE SIXTIES

1. FRANK SINATRA		2066
2. BEATLES		1712
3. ELVIS PRESLEY		1695
4. ANDY WILLIAMS		1249
5. HERB ALPERT & THE TIJUANA BRASS		1249
6. RAY CONNIFF		1220
7. KINGSTON TRIO		1192
8. ROLLING STONES		1148
9. MITCH MILLER		1090
10. RAY CHARLES		1090
11. BARBRA STREISAND		1081
12. JOHNNY MATHIS		983
13. SUPREMES		983
14. TEMPTATIONS		973
15. ENOCH LIGHT		970
16. BEACH BOYS		963
17. HENRY MANCINI		962
18. PETER, PAUL & MARY		877
19. BILLY VAUGHN		791
20. MANTOVANI		789
21. LAWRENCE WELK		736
22. NANCY WILSON		639
23. CHUBBY CHECKER		620
24. JOAN BAEZ		577
25. BOB DYLAN		576

THE SEVENTIES

1. ELTON JOHN		1301
2. CHICAGO		996
3. ROLLING STONES		942
4. BOB DYLAN		907
5. NEIL DIAMOND		880
6. PAUL McCARTNEY/WINGS		871
7. BARBRA STREISAND		865
8. JETHRO TULL		833
9. JOHN DENVER		803
10. GRAND FUNK RAILROAD		751
11. CAT STEVENS		664
12. ROD STEWART		661
13. JAMES TAYLOR		645
14. CAROLE KING		632
15. LED ZEPPELIN		624
16. JACKSON 5		623
17. SANTANA		610
18. BEE GEES		603
19. JEFFERSON AIRPLANE/STARSHIP		599
20. EARTH, WIND & FIRE		598
21. NEIL YOUNG		590
22. DOOBIE BROTHERS		590
23. DAVID BOWIE		580
24. STEVIE WONDER		578
25. DIANA ROSS		578

THE EIGHTIES 1980—86

1. BILLY JOEL		534
2. PAT BENATAR		496
3. DARYL HALL & JOHN OATES		488
4. KENNY ROGERS		471
5. ROLLING STONES		464
6. JOURNEY		455
7. PRINCE		449
8. VAN HALEN		437
9. RUSH		424
10. BRUCE SPRINGSTEEN		420
11. GENESIS		405
12. POLICE		385
13. BOB SEGER		373
14. BARBRA STREISAND		372
15. DURAN DURAN		372
16. AC/DC		363
17. LIONEL RICHIE		352
18. KOOL & THE GANG		344
19. NEIL DIAMOND		340
20. STEVIE WONDER		331
21. RICK SPRINGFIELD		329
22. MADONNA		326
23. ALABAMA		326
24. JOHN COUGAR MELLENCAMP		320
25. CARS		319

TOP ARTIST ACHIEVEMENTS*

ARTIST	POINTS	ARTIST	POINTS

THE MOST TOP 40 ALBUMS

ARTIST	POINTS
1. FRANK SINATRA	49
2. ELVIS PRESLEY	49
3. ROLLING STONES	32
4. BARBRA STREISAND	32
5. JOHNNY MATHIS	31
6. MANTOVANI	30
7. RAY CONNIFF	28
8. TEMPTATIONS	28
9. BEATLES	27
10. BOB DYLAN	27
11. LAWRENCE WELK	24
12. MITCH MILLER	23
13. ELTON JOHN	23
14. NEIL DIAMOND	21
15. ARETHA FRANKLIN	21
16. BEACH BOYS	20
17. KINGSTON TRIO	19
18. ANDY WILLIAMS	19
19. ROGER WILLIAMS	19
20. JEFFERSON AIRPLANE/STARSHIP	19
21. SUPREMES	19
22. BILLY VAUGHN	18
23. NAT KING COLE	17
24. DIANA ROSS	17
25. HARRY BELAFONTE	16

THE MOST WEEKS AT NO. 1

ARTIST	POINTS
1. BEATLES	119
2. ELVIS PRESLEY	64
3. KINGSTON TRIO	46
4. ELTON JOHN	39
5. ROLLING STONES	38
6. HARRY BELAFONTE	37
7. MONKEES	37
8. FLEETWOOD MAC	37
9. MICHAEL JACKSON	37
10. BEE GEES	31
11. LED ZEPPELIN	28
12. EAGLES	27
13. PRINCE	27
14. HERB ALPERT & THE TIJUANA BRASS	26
15. SIMON & GARFUNKEL	26
16. BARBRA STREISAND	22
17. HENRY MANCINI	22
18. CHICAGO	22
19. PAUL McCARTNEY	22
20. FRANK SINATRA	20
21. ENOCH LIGHT	20
22. CAROLE KING	19
23. BRUCE SPRINGSTEEN	18
24. PINK FLOYD	18
25. STEVIE WONDER	17

THE MOST NO. 1 ALBUMS

ARTIST	POINTS
1. BEATLES	15
2. ELVIS PRESLEY	9
3. ROLLING STONES	9
4. ELTON JOHN	7
5. PAUL McCARTNEY/WINGS	7
6. BARBRA STREISAND	6
7. LED ZEPPELIN	6
8. KINGSTON TRIO	5
9. HERB ALPERT & THE TIJUANA BRASS	5
10. CHICAGO	5
11. FRANK SINATRA	4
12. EAGLES	4
13. MONKEES	4
14. ALLAN SHERMAN	4
15. MITCH MILLER	3
16. BOB DYLAN	3
17. SUPREMES	3
18. STEVIE WONDER	3
19. BEE GEES	3
20. JOHN DENVER	3
21. OLIVIA NEWTON-JOHN	3
22. LINDA RONSTADT	3
23. SIMON & GARFUNKEL	3
24. DONNA SUMMER	3
25. JOHN LENNON	3

THE MOST TOP TEN ALBUMS

ARTIST	POINTS
1. FRANK SINATRA	31
2. ROLLING STONES	30
3. ELVIS PRESLEY	25
4. BEATLES	23
5. BARBRA STREISAND	20
6. JOHNNY MATHIS	18
7. MITCH MILLER	17
8. KINGSTON TRIO	14
9. BOB DYLAN	14
10. MANTOVANI	13
11. ELTON JOHN	13
12. BEACH BOYS	13
13. RAY CONNIFF	12
14. ANDY WILLIAMS	12
15. CHICAGO	12
16. NEIL DIAMOND	12
17. PAUL McCARTNEY/WINGS	12
18. TEMPTATIONS	10
19. LAWRENCE WELK	10
20. STEVIE WONDER	10
21. LED ZEPPELIN	10
22. HERB ALPERT & THE TIJUANA BRASS	9
23. HARRY BELAFONTE	9
24. HENRY MANCINI	9
25. WHO	9

*Ties are broken according to artist rank in the "The Top 100 Artists of the Rock Era" section.

THE TOP 100 ALBUMS (A–Z)

ALBUM TITLE	RANK	ALBUM TITLE	RANK
Abbey Road	38	In Through The Out Door	89
All Things Must Pass	94	Judy At Carnegie Hall	29
American Fool	57	Kingston Trio At Large	20
American Pie	92	Led Zeppelin II	88
Around The World In 80 Days	43	Licensed To Ill	91
Asia	62	Long Run	61
Beatles '65	60	Love Is The Thing	71
Beatles, The [White Album]	66	Love Me Or Leave Me	11
Belafonte	98	Loving You	49
Blood, Sweat & Tears	85	Magical Mystery Tour	75
Blue Hawaii	8	Mary Poppins	22
Bookends	87	Meet The Beatles!	39
Born In The U.S.A.	83	Miami Vice	40
Breakfast At Tiffany's	33	Modern Sounds In Country And Western	
Breakfast In America	100	Music	24
Bridge Over Troubled Water	51	Monkees, The	31
Brothers In Arms	55	More Of The Monkees	9
Bruce Springsteen & The E Street Band Live		Music From Peter Gunn	42
1975–1985	96	Music Man	32
Business As Usual	18	My Fair Lady	14
Button-Down Mind Of Bob Newhart	21	My Son, The Nut	78
Calcutta!	37	Nice 'n' Easy	59
Calypso	4	No Jacket Required	84
Camelot	99	Pearl	67
Captain Fantastic And The Brown Dirt		Persuasive Percussion	28
Cowboy	93	Peter, Paul & Mary	82
Cheap Thrills	76	Purple Rain	7
Chicago V	68	Rumours	5
Cosmo's Factory	65	Saturday Night Fever	6
Days of Wine and Roses	13	Sgt. Pepper's Lonely Hearts Club Band	16
Double Fantasy	77	Sing Along With Mitch	69
Elton John—Greatest Hits	52	Singing Nun	53
Elvis Presley	47	Slippery When Wet	80
Emotional Rescue	95	Sold Out	34
Exodus	25	Songs In The Key Of Life	26
52nd Street	73	Sound Of Music	12
First Family	36	South Pacific	3
Footloose	50	Stars For A Summer Night	58
4	45	Stereo 35/MM	86
Frampton Comes Alive!	44	String Along	48
G.I. Blues	46	Synchronicity	10
Gigi	41	Tapestry	15
Going Places	97	Tattoo You	64
Goodbye Yellow Brick Road	72	Tchaikovsky: Piano Concerto No. 1	81
Graduate, The	56	Thriller	2
Grease	35	Wall, The	19
Hair	30	West Side Story	1
Hard Day's Night	27	What Now My Love	54
Help!	63	Whipped Cream & Other Delights	70
Here We Go Again!	79	Whitney Houston	23
Hi Infidelity	17	Wings At The Speed Of Sound	90
Hotel California	74		

THE TOP 100 ALBUMS OF THE ROCK ERA

Following is a listing, in rank order, of the Top No. 1 Albums from 1955 through 1986. The ranking is based on the total weeks at No. 1. Ties are broken by the total weeks in the Top 40.

Columnar headings show the following data:

PK YR : Year album reached its peak position
WKS T40 : Total weeks in the Top 40
WKS No. 1: Total weeks album held the No. 1 position
† : Album still in Top 40 as of the June 20, 1987 issue

PK YR	WKS T40	WKS NO. 1	ALBUM TITLE/ARTIST
62	144	54	1. WEST SIDE STORY Soundtrack
83	91	37	2. THRILLER Michael Jackson
58	165	31	3. SOUTH PACIFIC Soundtrack
56	84	31	4. CALYPSO Harry Belafonte
77	59	31	5. RUMOURS Fleetwood Mac
78	54	24	6. SATURDAY NIGHT FEVER Bee Gees/Soundtrack
84	42	24	7. PURPLE RAIN Prince/Soundtrack
61	53	20	8. BLUE HAWAII Elvis Presley/Soundtrack
67	45	18	9. MORE OF THE MONKEES Monkees
83	50	17	10. SYNCHRONICITY Police
55	28	17	11. LOVE ME OR LEAVE ME Doris Day/Soundtrack
60	127	16	12. THE SOUND OF MUSIC Original Cast
63	61	16	13. DAYS OF WINE AND ROSES Andy Williams
56	311	15	14. MY FAIR LADY Original Cast
71	68	15	15. TAPESTRY Carole King
67	63	15	16. SGT. PEPPER'S LONELY HEARTS CLUB BAND Beatles
81	50	15	17. HI INFIDELITY REO Speedwagon
82	48	15	18. BUSINESS AS USUAL Men At Work
80	35	15	19. THE WALL Pink Floyd
59	32	15	20. THE KINGSTON TRIO AT LARGE Kingston Trio
60	108	14	21. THE BUTTON-DOWN MIND OF BOB NEWHART Bob Newhart
65	78	14	22. MARY POPPINS Soundtrack
86	78	14	23. WHITNEY HOUSTON Whitney Houston
62	59	14	24. MODERN SOUNDS IN COUNTRY AND WESTERN MUSIC Ray Charles
61	55	14	25. EXODUS Soundtrack
76	44	14	26. SONGS IN THE KEY OF LIFE Stevie Wonder
64	14	14	27. A HARD DAY'S NIGHT Beatles/Soundtrack
60	114	13	28. PERSUASIVE PERCUSSION Enoch Light/Terry Snyder
61	73	13	29. JUDY AT CARNEGIE HALL Judy Garland
69	59	13	30. HAIR Original Cast

TOP 100 ALBUMS OF THE ROCK ERA

PK YR	WKS T40	WKS NO. 1	ALBUM TITLE/ARTIST
66	49	13	31. THE MONKEES Monkees
58	155	12	32. THE MUSIC MAN Original Cast
62	96	12	33. BREAKFAST AT TIFFANY'S Henry Mancini/Soundtrack
60	54	12	34. SOLD OUT Kingston Trio
78	39	12	35. GREASE Soundtrack/Olivia Newton-John
62	26	12	36. THE FIRST FAMILY Vaughn Meader
61	50	11	37. CALCUTTA! Lawrence Welk
69	32	11	38. ABBEY ROAD Beatles
64	27	11	39. MEET THE BEATLES! Beatles
85	22	11	40. MIAMI VICE TV Soundtrack
58	143	10	41. GIGI Soundtrack
59	97	10	42. THE MUSIC FROM PETER GUNN Henry Mancini/TV Soundtrack
57	88	10	43. AROUND THE WORLD IN 80 DAYS Soundtrack
76	56	10	44. FRAMPTON COMES ALIVE! Peter Frampton
81	52	10	45. 4 Foreigner
60	49	10	46. G.I. BLUES Elvis Presley/Soundtrack
56	48	10	47. ELVIS PRESLEY Elvis Presley
60	34	10	48. STRING ALONG Kingston Trio
57	29	10	49. LOVING YOU Elvis Presley/Soundtrack
84	27	10	50. FOOTLOOSE Soundtrack
70	24	10	51. BRIDGE OVER TROUBLED WATER Simon & Garfunkel
74	20	10	52. ELTON JOHN—GREATEST HITS Elton John
63	18	10	53. THE SINGING NUN Singing Nun
66	59	9	54. WHAT NOW MY LOVE Herb Alpert & The Tijuana Brass
85	55	9	55. BROTHERS IN ARMS Dire Straits
68	47	9	56. THE GRADUATE Simon & Garfunkel/Soundtrack
82	41	9	57. AMERICAN FOOL John Cougar
61	39	9	58. STARS FOR A SUMMER NIGHT Various Artists
60	38	9	59. NICE 'N' EASY Frank Sinatra
65	38	9	60. BEATLES '65 Beatles
79	36	9	61. THE LONG RUN Eagles
82	35	9	62. ASIA Asia
65	33	9	63. HELP! Beatles/Soundtrack
81	30	9	64. TATTOO YOU Rolling Stones
70	27	9	65. COSMO'S FACTORY Creedence Clearwater Revival
68	25	9	66. THE BEATLES [WHITE ALBUM] Beatles
71	23	9	67. PEARL Janis Joplin
72	20	9	68. CHICAGO V Chicago
58	191	8	69. SING ALONG WITH MITCH Mitch Miller & The Gang
65	141	8	70. WHIPPED CREAM & OTHER DELIGHTS Herb Alpert & The Tijuana Brass

TOP 100 ALBUMS OF THE ROCK ERA

PK YR	WKS T40	WKS NO. 1	ALBUM TITLE/ARTIST
57	66	8	71. LOVE IS THE THING Nat King Cole
73	53	8	72. GOODBYE YELLOW BRICK ROAD Elton John
78	34	8	73. 52ND STREET Billy Joel
77	32	8	74. HOTEL CALIFORNIA Eagles
68	30	8	75. MAGICAL MYSTERY TOUR Beatles/Soundtrack
68	29	8	76. CHEAP THRILLS Big Brother & The Holding Company
80	27	8	77. DOUBLE FANTASY John Lennon
63	24	8	78. MY SON, THE NUT Allan Sherman
59	8	8	79. HERE WE GO AGAIN! Kingston Trio
86	40†	8	80. SLIPPERY WHEN WET Bon Jovi
58	125	7	81. TCHAIKOVSKY: PIANO CONCERTO NO. 1 Van Cliburn
62	112	7	82. PETER, PAUL & MARY Peter, Paul & Mary
84	96	7	83. BORN IN THE U.S.A. Bruce Springsteen
85	70	7	84. NO JACKET REQUIRED Phil Collins
69	66	7	85. BLOOD, SWEAT & TEARS Blood, Sweat & Tears
61	57	7	86. STEREO 35/MM Enoch Light
68	40	7	87. BOOKENDS Simon & Garfunkel
69	29	7	88. LED ZEPPELIN II Led Zeppelin
79	28	7	89. IN THROUGH THE OUT DOOR Led Zeppelin
76	27	7	90. WINGS AT THE SPEED OF SOUND Paul McCartney/Wings
87	27†	7	91. LICENSED TO ILL Beastie Boys
72	26	7	92. AMERICAN PIE Don McLean
75	24	7	93. CAPTAIN FANTASTIC AND THE BROWN DIRT COWBOY Elton John
71	22	7	94. ALL THINGS MUST PASS George Harrison
80	20	7	95. EMOTIONAL RESCUE Rolling Stones
86	15	7	96. BRUCE SPRINGSTEEN & THE E STREET BAND LIVE 1975–1985 Bruce Springsteen
66	107	6	97. GOING PLACES Herb Alpert & The Tijuana Brass
56	62	6	98. BELAFONTE Harry Belafonte
61	52	6	99. CAMELOT Original Cast
79	48	6	100. BREAKFAST IN AMERICA Supertramp

TOP 35 ALBUMS

PK YR	WKS T40	WKS NO. 1	TITLE/ARTIST
			## THE FIFTIES 1955—59
58	165	31	1. SOUTH PACIFIC Soundtrack
56	84	31	2. CALYPSO Harry Belafonte
55	28	17	3. LOVE ME OR LEAVE ME Doris Day/Soundtrack
56	311	15	4. MY FAIR LADY Original Cast
59	32	15	5. THE KINGSTON TRIO AT LARGE Kingston Trio
58	155	12	6. THE MUSIC MAN Original Cast
58	143	10	7. GIGI Soundtrack
59	97	10	8. THE MUSIC FROM PETER GUNN Henry Mancini/TV Soundtrack
57	88	10	9. AROUND THE WORLD IN 80 DAYS Soundtrack
56	48	10	10. ELVIS PRESLEY Elvis Presley
57	29	10	11. LOVING YOU Elvis Presley/Soundtrack
58	191	8	12. SING ALONG WITH MITCH Mitch Miller & The Gang
57	66	8	13. LOVE IS THE THING Nat King Cole
59	8	8	14. HERE WE GO AGAIN! Kingston Trio
58	125	7	15. TCHAIKOVSKY: PIANO CONCERTO NO. 1 Van Cliburn
56	62	6	16. BELAFONTE Harry Belafonte
55	27	6	17. STARRING SAMMY DAVIS, JR. Sammy Davis, Jr.
58	81	5	18. FRANK SINATRA SINGS FOR ONLY THE LONELY Frank Sinatra
59	61	5	19. EXOTICA Martin Denny
58	56	5	20. COME FLY WITH ME Frank Sinatra
59	40	5	21. HEAVENLY Johnny Mathis
56	32	5	22. ELVIS Elvis Presley
56	262	4	23. OKLAHOMA! Soundtrack
57	7	4	24. ELVIS' CHRISTMAS ALBUM Elvis Presley
58	236	3	25. JOHNNY'S GREATEST HITS Johnny Mathis
59	102	3	26. FLOWER DRUM SONG Original Cast
58	33	2	27. RICKY Ricky Nelson
55	23	2	28. LONESOME ECHO Jackie Gleason
55	20	2	29. CRAZY OTTO Crazy Otto
58	5	2	30. CHRISTMAS SING-ALONG WITH MITCH Mitch Miller & The Gang
56	230	1	31. THE KING AND I Soundtrack
59	173	1	32. FILM ENCORES Mantovani
58	145	1	33. THE KINGSTON TRIO Kingston Trio
56	99	1	34. THE EDDY DUCHIN STORY Carmen Cavallaro/Soundtrack
58	7	1	35. MERRY CHRISTMAS Bing Crosby

TOP 40 ALBUMS

PK YR	WKS T40	WKS NO. 1	TITLE/ARTIST
			## THE SIXTIES
62	144	54	1. WEST SIDE STORY Soundtrack
61	53	20	2. BLUE HAWAII Elvis Presley/Soundtrack
67	45	18	3. MORE OF THE MONKEES Monkees
60	127	16	4. THE SOUND OF MUSIC Original Cast
63	61	16	5. DAYS OF WINE AND ROSES Andy Williams
67	63	15	6. SGT. PEPPER'S LONELY HEARTS CLUB BAND Beatles
60	108	14	7. THE BUTTON-DOWN MIND OF BOB NEWHART Bob Newhart
65	78	14	8. MARY POPPINS Soundtrack
62	59	14	9. MODERN SOUNDS IN COUNTRY AND WESTERN MUSIC Ray Charles
61	55	14	10. EXODUS Soundtrack
64	14	14	11. A HARD DAY'S NIGHT Beatles/Soundtrack
60	114	13	12. PERSUASIVE PERCUSSION Enoch Light/Terry Snyder
61	73	13	13. JUDY AT CARNEGIE HALL Judy Garland
69	59	13	14. HAIR Original Cast
66	49	13	15. THE MONKEES Monkees
62	96	12	16. BREAKFAST AT TIFFANY'S Henry Mancini/Soundtrack
60	54	12	17. SOLD OUT Kingston Trio
62	26	12	18. THE FIRST FAMILY Vaughn Meader
61	50	11	19. CALCUTTA! Lawrence Welk
69	32	11	20. ABBEY ROAD Beatles
64	27	11	21. MEET THE BEATLES! Beatles
60	49	10	22. G.I. BLUES Elvis Presley/Soundtrack
60	34	10	23. STRING ALONG Kingston Trio
63	18	10	24. THE SINGING NUN Singing Nun
66	59	9	25. WHAT NOW MY LOVE Herb Alpert & The Tijuana Brass
68	47	9	26. THE GRADUATE Simon & Garfunkel/Soundtrack
61	39	9	27. STARS FOR A SUMMER NIGHT Various Artists
60	38	9	28. NICE 'N' EASY Frank Sinatra
65	38	9	29. BEATLES '65 Beatles
65	33	9	30. HELP! Beatles/Soundtrack
68	25	9	31. THE BEATLES (WHITE ALBUM) Beatles
65	141	8	32. WHIPPED CREAM & OTHER DELIGHTS Herb Alpert & The Tijuana Brass
68	30	8	33. MAGICAL MYSTERY TOUR Beatles/Soundtrack
68	29	8	34. CHEAP THRILLS Big Brother & The Holding Company
63	24	8	35. MY SON, THE NUT Allan Sherman
62	112	7	36. PETER, PAUL & MARY Peter, Paul & Mary
69	66	7	37. BLOOD, SWEAT & TEARS Blood, Sweat & Tears
61	57	7	38. STEREO 35/MM Enoch Light
68	40	7	39. BOOKENDS Simon & Garfunkel
69	29	7	40. LED ZEPPELIN II Led Zeppelin

TOP 40 ALBUMS

PK YR	WKS T40	WKS NO. 1	TITLE/ARTIST
			## THE SEVENTIES
77	59	31	1. RUMOURS Fleetwood Mac
78	54	24	2. SATURDAY NIGHT FEVER Bee Gees/Soundtrack
71	68	15	3. TAPESTRY Carole King
76	44	14	4. SONGS IN THE KEY OF LIFE Stevie Wonder
78	39	12	5. GREASE Soundtrack/Olivia Newton-John
76	56	10	6. FRAMPTON COMES ALIVE! Peter Frampton
70	24	10	7. BRIDGE OVER TROUBLED WATER Simon & Garfunkel
74	20	10	8. ELTON JOHN—GREATEST HITS Elton John
79	36	9	9. THE LONG RUN Eagles
70	27	9	10. COSMO'S FACTORY Creedence Clearwater Revival
71	23	9	11. PEARL Janis Joplin
72	20	9	12. CHICAGO V Chicago
73	53	8	13. GOODBYE YELLOW BRICK ROAD Elton John
78	34	8	14. 52ND STREET Billy Joel
77	32	8	15. HOTEL CALIFORNIA Eagles
79	28	7	16. IN THROUGH THE OUT DOOR Led Zeppelin
76	27	7	17. WINGS AT THE SPEED OF SOUND Paul McCartney/Wings
72	26	7	18. AMERICAN PIE Don McLean
75	24	7	19. CAPTAIN FANTASTIC AND THE BROWN DIRT COWBOY Elton John
71	22	7	20. ALL THINGS MUST PASS George Harrison
79	48	6	21. BREAKFAST IN AMERICA Supertramp
70	40	6	22. ABRAXAS Santana
77	28	6	23. A STAR IS BORN Barbra Streisand
79	26	6	24. SPIRITS HAVING FLOWN Bee Gees
79	26	6	25. BAD GIRLS Donna Summer
75	15	6	26. PHYSICAL GRAFFITI Led Zeppelin
76	57	5	27. EAGLES/THEIR GREATEST HITS 1971–1975 Eagles
75	43	5	28. ONE OF THESE NIGHTS Eagles
74	42	5	29. YOU DON'T MESS AROUND WITH JIM Jim Croce
79	30	5	30. MINUTE BY MINUTE Doobie Brothers
73	27	5	31. CHICAGO VI Chicago
72	26	5	32. FIRST TAKE Roberta Flack
72	25	5	33. HONKY CHATEAU Elton John
73	24	5	34. BROTHERS AND SISTERS Allman Brothers Band
73	23	5	35. NO SECRETS Carly Simon
77	23	5	36. SIMPLE DREAMS Linda Ronstadt
72	23	5	37. SEVENTH SOJOURN Moody Blues
74	23	5	38. THE STING Soundtrack
71	23	5	39. SANTANA III Santana
75	22	5	40. CHICAGO IX—CHICAGO'S GREATEST HITS Chicago

TOP 40 ALBUMS

PK YR	WKS T40	WKS NO. 1	TITLE/ARTIST
			## THE EIGHTIES 1980—86
83	91	37	1. THRILLER Michael Jackson
84	42	24	2. PURPLE RAIN Prince/Soundtrack
83	50	17	3. SYNCHRONICITY Police
81	50	15	4. HI INFIDELITY REO Speedwagon
82	48	15	5. BUSINESS AS USUAL Men At Work
80	35	15	6. THE WALL Pink Floyd
86	78	14	7. WHITNEY HOUSTON Whitney Houston
85	22	11	8. MIAMI VICE TV Soundtrack
81	52	10	9. 4 Foreigner
84	27	10	10. FOOTLOOSE Soundtrack
85	55	9	11. BROTHERS IN ARMS Dire Straits
82	41	9	12. AMERICAN FOOL John Cougar
82	35	9	13. ASIA Asia
81	30	9	14. TATTOO YOU Rolling Stones
86	40†	8	15. SLIPPERY WHEN WET Bon Jovi
80	27	8	16. DOUBLE FANTASY John Lennon
84	96	7	17. BORN IN THE U.S.A. Bruce Springsteen
85	70	7	18. NO JACKET REQUIRED Phil Collins
87	27†	7	19. LICENSED TO ILL Beastie Boys
80	20	7	20. EMOTIONAL RESCUE Rolling Stones
86	15	7	21. BRUCE SPRINGSTEEN & THE E STREET BAND LIVE 1975–1985 Bruce Springsteen
80	43	6	22. AGAINST THE WIND Bob Seger & The Silver Bullet Band
82	38	6	23. BEAUTY AND THE BEAT Go-Go's
80	35	6	24. GLASS HOUSES Billy Joel
85	55	5	25. SONGS FROM THE BIG CHAIR Tears For Fears
86	48	5	26. TRUE BLUE Madonna
86	33	5	27. TOP GUN Soundtrack
80	31	5	28. THE GAME Queen
82	21	5	29. MIRAGE Fleetwood Mac
82	29	4	30. FREEZE-FRAME J. Geils Band
86	29	4	31. THIRD STAGE Boston
81	23	4	32. MISTAKEN IDENTITY Kim Carnes
80	22	4	33. THE RIVER Bruce Springsteen
82	20	4	34. CHARIOTS OF FIRE Vangelis/Soundtrack
83	78	3	35. CAN'T SLOW DOWN Lionel Richie
85	56	3	36. MAKE IT BIG Wham!
85	51	3	37. LIKE A VIRGIN Madonna
81	35	3	38. PARADISE THEATER Styx
80	33	3	39. GUILTY Barbra Streisand
86	32	3	40. 5150 Van Halen

†: Album still in Top 40 as of the June 20, 1987 issue.

NO. 1 ALBUMS LISTED CHRONOLOGICALLY

For the years 1958 through 1963, when separate stereo and mono charts were published each week, there are special columns on the right side of the page to show the weeks each album held the No. 1 spot on each of these pop charts. If an album peaked at No. 1 on both the mono and stereo charts in the same week, it is counted as only one week at No. 1. Therefore, the grand total of an album's weeks at No. 1 on all charts may equal more than the total shown on the left side of the page.

The date shown is the earliest date that an album hit No. 1 on any of the three pop charts. Some dates are duplicated because different albums peaked at No. 1 on the same date on different charts.

DATE: Date album first hit the No. 1 position.
WKS: Total weeks album held the No. 1 position.
*: Album appeared non-consecutively at the No. 1 position.

CHARTS COLUMN:
1 CH: One chart published
ST: Stereo chart
MO: Mono chart

The No. 1 album of each year is shown in bold type and is based on total weeks at the No. 1 spot. Ties are broken by total weeks charted. The album qualifies for the award only in the year that it first peaked at No. 1.

313 albums have hit the No. 1 position on *Billboard*'s pop charts from 1955 through 1986.

DATE	WKS	ALBUM TITLE	ARTIST
		1955	
5/28	2	1. CRAZY OTTO	Crazy Otto
6/11	6	2. STARRING SAMMY DAVIS JR.	Sammy Davis, Jr.
7/23	2	3. LONESOME ECHO	Jackie Gleason
8/6	17	4. **LOVE ME OR LEAVE ME**	Doris Day/Soundtrack

Two albums from 1954 continued into 1955 at the No. 1 spot: "The Student Prince," Mario Lanza (eighteen wks.), and "Music, Martinis And Memories," Jackie Gleason (two wks.). For all of 1955 and up to 3/24/56, the album chart was published mainly on a bi-weekly basis. The chart was considered "frozen" for a nonpublished week and, therefore, each position on the published chart was counted twice. In addition to these bi-weekly "frozen" charts, there were five other weeks of unpublished charts that did not count toward weeks at the No. 1 spot.

DATE	WKS	ALBUM TITLE	ARTIST
		1956	
1/28	4	1. OKLAHOMA!	Soundtrack
3/24	6	2. BELAFONTE	Harry Belafonte
5/5	10	3. ELVIS PRESLEY	Elvis Presley
7/14	15*	4. MY FAIR LADY	Original Cast
		Peaked at No. 1 in four consecutive years: '56 (8 wks.), '57 (1 wk.), '58 (3 wks.), & '59 (3 wks.–Stereo chart)	
9/8	31*	5. **CALYPSO**	Harry Belafonte
10/6	1	6. THE KING AND I	Soundtrack
10/13	1	7. THE EDDY DUCHIN STORY	Carmen Cavallaro/Soundtrack
12/8	5	8. ELVIS	Elvis Presley

Beginning with 3/24/56, *Billboard* published the album chart on a weekly basis. From the first of the year to that date, there were two published charts, two frozen charts, and seven weeks of unpublished charts.

DATE	WKS	ALBUM TITLE	ARTIST
		1957	
5/27	8	1. LOVE IS THE THING	Nat King Cole
7/22	10*	2. **AROUND THE WORLD IN 80 DAYS**	Soundtrack
7/29	10	3. LOVING YOU	Elvis Presley/Soundtrack
12/16	4*	4. ELVIS' CHRISTMAS ALBUM	Elvis Presley
12/30	1	5. MERRY CHRISTMAS	Bing Crosby

DATE	WKS	ALBUM TITLE	ARTIST	Multiple Charts 1 CH	ST	MO

1958

DATE	WKS	ALBUM TITLE	ARTIST	1 CH	ST	MO
1/20	2	1. RICKY	Ricky Nelson	2	—	—
2/10	5	2. COME FLY WITH ME	Frank Sinatra	5	—	—
3/17	12*	3. THE MUSIC MAN	Original Cast	12	—	—
5/19	31*	4. **SOUTH PACIFIC** *3 wks. No. 1 in '58; 28 wks., No. 1 on Stereo charts beginning 5/25/59*	Soundtrack	3	28	—
6/9	3*	5. JOHNNY'S GREATEST HITS	Johnny Mathis	3	—	—
7/21	10*	6. GIGI *3 wks. No. 1 in '58; 3 wks. No. 1 on Stereo chart in '59; and 4 wks. No. 1 on Mono charts beginning 5/29/59*	Soundtrack	6	—	4
8/11	7*	7. TCHAIKOVSKY: PIANO CONCERTO NO. 1	Van Cliburn	7	—	—
10/6	8*	8. SING ALONG WITH MITCH	Mitch Miller	8	—	—
10/13	5	9. FRANK SINATRA SINGS FOR ONLY THE LONELY	Frank Sinatra	5	—	—
11/24	1	10. THE KINGSTON TRIO	Kingston Trio	1	—	—
12/29	2	11. CHRISTMAS SING-ALONG WITH MITCH	Mitch Miller	2	—	—

1959

DATE	WKS	ALBUM TITLE	ARTIST	1 CH	ST	MO
2/2	3	1. FLOWER DRUM SONG	Original Cast	3	—	—
2/23	10	2. THE MUSIC FROM PETER GUNN	Henry Mancini	10	—	—
		5/25/59: Separate Stereo and Mono charts begin				
6/22	5	3. EXOTICA	Martin Denny	—	—	5
7/13	1	4. FILM ENCORES	Mantovani	—	1	—
7/27	15	5. **THE KINGSTON TRIO AT LARGE**	Kingston Trio	—	—	15
11/9	5	6. HEAVENLY	Johnny Mathis	—	—	5
12/14	8	7. HERE WE GO AGAIN!	Kingston Trio	—	2	8

1960

DATE	WKS	ALBUM TITLE	ARTIST	1 CH	ST	MO
1/11	1	1. THE LORD'S PRAYER	Mormon Tabernacle Choir	—	1	—
1/25	16	2. **THE SOUND OF MUSIC**	Original Cast	—	15	12
4/25	13*	3. PERSUASIVE PERCUSSION	Enoch Light/ Terry Snyder	—	13	—
5/2	2*	4. THEME FROM A SUMMER PLACE	Billy Vaughn	—	—	2
5/9	12*	5. SOLD OUT	Kingston Trio	—	3	10
7/25	14*	6. THE BUTTON-DOWN MIND OF BOB NEWHART	Bob Newhart	—	—	14
8/29	10*	7. STRING ALONG	Kingston Trio	—	10	5
10/24	9*	8. NICE 'N' EASY	Frank Sinatra	—	9	1
12/5	10*	9. G.I. BLUES	Elvis Presley/ Soundtrack	—	2	8

DATE	WKS	ALBUM TITLE	ARTIST	Multiple Charts		
				1 CH	ST	MO
		1961				
1/9	1	1. THE BUTTON-DOWN MIND STRIKES BACK!	Bob Newhart	—	—	1
1/16	5*	2. WONDERLAND BY NIGHT	Bert Kaempfert	—	—	5
1/23	14*	3. EXODUS	Soundtrack	—	14	3
3/13	11*	4. CALCUTTA!	Lawrence Welk	—	11	8
6/5	6	5. CAMELOT	Original Cast	—	—	6
7/17	9	6. STARS FOR A SUMMER NIGHT	Various Artists	—	9	4
7/17	1	7. CARNIVAL	Original Cast	—	—	1
8/21	3	8. SOMETHING FOR EVERYBODY	Elvis Presley	—	—	3
9/11	13	9. JUDY AT CARNEGIE HALL	Judy Garland	—	9	13
11/18	7	10. STEREO 35/MM	Enoch Light	—	7	—
12/11	20	11. **BLUE HAWAII**	Elvis Presley/ Soundtrack	—	4	20
		1962				
1/13	1	1. HOLIDAY SING ALONG WITH MITCH	Mitch Miller	—	1	—
2/10	12*	2. BREAKFAST AT TIFFANY'S	Henry Mancini/ Soundtrack	—	12	—
5/5	54*	3. **WEST SIDE STORY** *Most weeks at No. 1 for the 1955–85 era*	Soundtrack	—	53	12
6/23	14	4. MODERN SOUNDS IN COUNTRY AND WESTERN MUSIC	Ray Charles	—	1	14
10/20	7*	5. PETER, PAUL & MARY *Returned to the No. 1 spot for one week on 10/26/63*	Peter, Paul & Mary	1	—	6
12/1	2	6. MY SON, THE FOLK SINGER	Allan Sherman	—	—	2
12/15	12	7. THE FIRST FAMILY	Vaughn Meader	—	—	12
		1963				
3/9	1	1. MY SON, THE CELEBRITY	Allan Sherman	—	—	1
3/9	1	2. JAZZ SAMBA	Stan Getz/Charlie Byrd	—	1	—
3/16	5	3. SONGS I SING ON THE JACKIE GLEASON SHOW	Frank Fontaine	—	—	5
5/4	16	4. **DAYS OF WINE AND ROSES**	Andy Williams	1	11	15
		8/17/63: Stereo & Mono charts combined into one single chart				
8/24	1	5. LITTLE STEVIE WONDER/THE 12 YEAR OLD GENIUS	Stevie Wonder	1	—	—
8/31	8	6. MY SON, THE NUT	Allan Sherman	8	—	—
11/2	5	7. IN THE WIND	Peter, Paul & Mary	5	—	—
12/7	10	8. THE SINGING NUN	Singing Nun	10	—	—

DATE	WKS	ALBUM TITLE	ARTIST

1964

DATE	WKS	ALBUM TITLE	ARTIST
2/15	11	1. MEET THE BEATLES!	Beatles
5/2	5	2. THE BEATLES' SECOND ALBUM	Beatles
6/6	1	3. HELLO, DOLLY!	Original Cast
6/13	6	4. HELLO, DOLLY!	Louis Armstrong
7/25	14	5. **A HARD DAY'S NIGHT**	Beatles/Soundtrack
10/31	5	6. PEOPLE	Barbra Streisand
12/5	4	7. BEACH BOYS CONCERT	Beach Boys

1965

DATE	WKS	ALBUM TITLE	ARTIST
1/2	1	1. ROUSTABOUT	Elvis Presley/Soundtrack
1/9	9	2. BEATLES '65	Beatles
3/13	14*	3. **MARY POPPINS**	Soundtrack
3/20	3	4. GOLDFINGER	Soundtrack
7/10	6	5. BEATLES VI	Beatles
8/21	3	6. OUT OF OUR HEADS	Rolling Stones
9/11	9	7. HELP!	Beatles/Soundtrack
11/13	2	8. THE SOUND OF MUSIC	Soundtrack
11/27	8*	9. WHIPPED CREAM & OTHER DELIGHTS	Herb Alpert & The Tijuana Brass

1966

DATE	WKS	ALBUM TITLE	ARTIST
1/8	6	1. RUBBER SOUL	Beatles
3/5	6*	2. GOING PLACES	Herb Alpert & The Tijuana Brass
3/12	5	3. BALLADS OF THE GREEN BERETS	SSgt Barry Sadler
5/21	1	4. IF YOU CAN BELIEVE YOUR EYES AND EARS	Mamas & The Papas
5/28	9*	5. WHAT NOW MY LOVE	Herb Alpert & The Tijuana Brass
7/23	1	6. STRANGERS IN THE NIGHT	Frank Sinatra
7/30	5	7. "YESTERDAY" . . . AND TODAY	Beatles
9/10	6	8. REVOLVER	Beatles
10/22	2	9. THE SUPREMES A' GO-GO	Supremes
11/5	1	10. DOCTOR ZHIVAGO	Soundtrack
11/12	13	11. **THE MONKEES**	Monkees

1967

DATE	WKS	ALBUM TITLE	ARTIST
2/11	18	1. **MORE OF THE MONKEES**	Monkees
6/17	1	2. SOUNDS LIKE	Herb Alpert & The Tijuana Brass
6/24	1	3. HEADQUARTERS	Monkees
7/1	15	4. SGT. PEPPER'S LONELY HEARTS CLUB BAND	Beatles
10/14	2	5. ODE TO BILLIE JOE	Bobbie Gentry
10/28	5	6. DIANA ROSS AND THE SUPREMES GREATEST HITS	Supremes
12/2	5	7. PISCES, AQUARIUS, CAPRICORN & JONES LTD.	Monkees

DATE	WKS	ALBUM TITLE	ARTIST
		## 1968	
1/6	8	1. MAGICAL MYSTERY TOUR	Beatles
3/2	5	2. BLOOMING HITS	Paul Mauriat
4/6	9*	3. THE GRADUATE	Simon & Garfunkel/Soundtrack
5/25	7*	4. BOOKENDS	Simon & Garfunkel
7/27	2	5. THE BEAT OF THE BRASS	Herb Alpert & The Tijuana Brass
8/10	4	6. WHEELS OF FIRE	Cream
9/7	4*	7. WAITING FOR THE SUN	Doors
9/28	1	8. TIME PEACE/THE RASCALS' GREATEST HITS	Rascals
10/12	8*	9. CHEAP THRILLS	Big Brother & The Holding Company
11/16	2	10. ELECTRIC LADYLAND	Jimi Hendrix Experience
12/21	5*	11. WICHITA LINEMAN	Glen Campbell
12/28	9*	12. **THE BEATLES [WHITE ALBUM]**	Beatles
		## 1969	
2/8	1	1. TCB	Supremes & Temptations
3/29	7*	2. BLOOD, SWEAT & TEARS	Blood, Sweat & Tears
4/26	13	3. **HAIR**	Original Cast
8/23	4	4. JOHNNY CASH AT SAN QUENTIN	Johnny Cash
9/20	2	5. BLIND FAITH	Blind Faith
10/4	4	6. GREEN RIVER	Creedence Clearwater Revival
11/1	11*	7. ABBEY ROAD	Beatles
12/27	7*	8. LED ZEPPELIN II	Led Zeppelin
		## 1970	
3/7	10	1. **BRIDGE OVER TROUBLED WATER**	Simon & Garfunkel
5/16	1	2. DEJA VU	Crosby, Stills, Nash & Young
5/23	3	3. McCARTNEY	Paul McCartney
6/13	4	4. LET IT BE	Beatles/Soundtrack
7/11	4	5. WOODSTOCK	Various Artists/Soundtrack
8/8	2	6. BLOOD, SWEAT & TEARS 3	Blood, Sweat & Tears
8/22	9	7. COSMO'S FACTORY	Creedence Clearwater Revival
10/24	6*	8. ABRAXAS	Santana
10/31	4	9. LED ZEPPELIN III	Led Zeppelin

DATE	WKS	ALBUM TITLE	ARTIST
		## 1971	
1/2	7	1. ALL THINGS MUST PASS	George Harrison
2/20	3*	2. JESUS CHRIST SUPERSTAR	Various Artists
2/27	9	3. PEARL	Janis Joplin
5/15	1	4. 4 WAY STREET	Crosby, Stills, Nash & Young
5/22	4	5. STICKY FINGERS	Rolling Stones
6/19	15	6. **TAPESTRY**	Carole King
10/2	4	7. EVERY PICTURE TELLS A STORY	Rod Stewart
10/30	1	8. IMAGINE	John Lennon
11/6	1	9. SHAFT	Isaac Hayes/Soundtrack
11/13	5	10. SANTANA III	Santana
12/18	2	11. THERE'S A RIOT GOIN' ON	Sly & The Family Stone
		## 1972	
1/1	3	1. MUSIC	Carole King
1/22	7	2. AMERICAN PIE	Don McLean
3/11	2	3. HARVEST	Neil Young
3/25	5	4. AMERICA	America
4/29	5	5. FIRST TAKE	Roberta Flack
6/3	2	6. THICK AS A BRICK	Jethro Tull
6/17	4	7. EXILE ON MAIN ST.	Rolling Stones
7/15	5	8. HONKY CHATEAU	Elton John
8/19	9	9. **CHICAGO V**	Chicago
10/21	4	10. SUPERFLY	Curtis Mayfield/Soundtrack
11/18	3	11. CATCH BULL AT FOUR	Cat Stevens
12/9	5	12. SEVENTH SOJOURN	Moody Blues
		## 1973	
1/13	5	1. NO SECRETS	Carly Simon
2/17	2	2. THE WORLD IS A GHETTO	War
3/3	2	3. DON'T SHOOT ME I'M ONLY THE PIANO PLAYER	Elton John
3/17	3	4. DUELING BANJOS	Eric Weissberg
4/7	2	5. LADY SINGS THE BLUES	Diana Ross/Soundtrack
4/21	1	6. BILLION DOLLAR BABIES	Alice Cooper
4/28	1	7. THE DARK SIDE OF THE MOON	Pink Floyd
5/5	1	8. ALOHA FROM HAWAII VIA SATELLITE	Elvis Presley
5/12	2	9. HOUSES OF THE HOLY	Led Zeppelin
5/26	1	10. THE BEATLES/1967–1970	Beatles
6/2	3	11. RED ROSE SPEEDWAY	Paul McCartney & Wings
6/23	5	12. LIVING IN THE MATERIAL WORLD	George Harrison
7/28	5*	13. CHICAGO VI	Chicago
8/18	1	14. A PASSION PLAY	Jethro Tull
9/8	5	15. BROTHERS AND SISTERS	Allman Brothers Band
10/13	4	16. GOATS HEAD SOUP	Rolling Stones
11/10	8	17. **GOODBYE YELLOW BRICK ROAD**	Elton John

DATE	WKS	ALBUM TITLE	ARTIST
		## 1974	
1/5	1	1. THE SINGLES 1969–1973	Carpenters
1/12	5	2. YOU DON'T MESS AROUND WITH JIM	Jim Croce
2/16	4	3. PLANET WAVES	Bob Dylan
3/16	2	4. THE WAY WE WERE	Barbra Streisand
3/30	3*	5. JOHN DENVER'S GREATEST HITS	John Denver
4/13	4*	6. BAND ON THE RUN	Paul McCartney & Wings
4/27	1	7. CHICAGO VII	Chicago
5/4	5	8. THE STING	Soundtrack (Marvin Hamlisch)
6/22	2	9. SUNDOWN	Gordon Lightfoot
7/13	4	10. CARIBOU	Elton John
8/10	1	11. BACK HOME AGAIN	John Denver
8/17	4	12. 461 OCEAN BOULEVARD	Eric Clapton
9/14	2	13. FULFILLINGNESS' FIRST FINALE	Stevie Wonder
9/28	1	14. BAD COMPANY	Bad Company
10/5	1	15. ENDLESS SUMMER	Beach Boys
10/12	1	16. IF YOU LOVE, LET ME KNOW	Olivia Newton-John
10/19	1	17. NOT FRAGILE	Bachman-Turner Overdrive
10/26	1	18. CAN'T GET ENOUGH	Barry White
11/2	1	19. SO FAR	Crosby, Stills, Nash & Young
11/9	1	20. WRAP AROUND JOY	Carole King
11/16	1	21. WALLS AND BRIDGES	John Lennon
11/23	1	22. IT'S ONLY ROCK 'N ROLL	Rolling Stones
11/30	10	23. **ELTON JOHN—GREATEST HITS**	Elton John
		## 1975	
2/8	1	1. FIRE	Ohio Players
2/15	1	2. HEART LIKE A WHEEL	Linda Ronstadt
2/22	1	3. AWB	Average White Band
3/1	2	4. BLOOD ON THE TRACKS	Bob Dylan
3/15	1	5. HAVE YOU NEVER BEEN MELLOW	Olivia Newton-John
3/22	6	6. PHYSICAL GRAFFITI	Led Zeppelin
5/3	2	7. CHICAGO VIII	Chicago
5/17	3	8. THAT'S THE WAY OF THE WORLD	Earth, Wind & Fire/Soundtrack
6/7	7*	9. **CAPTAIN FANTASTIC AND THE BROWN DIRT COWBOY** *Album debuted at No. 1*	Elton John
7/19	1	10. VENUS AND MARS	Paul McCartney/Wings
7/26	5	11. ONE OF THESE NIGHTS	Eagles
9/6	4*	12. RED OCTOPUS	Jefferson Starship
9/13	1	13. THE HEAT IS ON	Isley Brothers
9/20	1	14. BETWEEN THE LINES	Janis Ian
10/4	2	15. WISH YOU WERE HERE	Pink Floyd
10/18	2	16. WINDSONG	John Denver
11/8	3	17. ROCK OF THE WESTIES *Album debuted at No. 1*	Elton John
12/6	1	18. STILL CRAZY AFTER ALL THESE YEARS	Paul Simon
12/13	5	19. CHICAGO IX—CHICAGO'S GREATEST HITS	Chicago

DATE	WKS	ALBUM TITLE	ARTIST
		## 1976	
1/17	3	1. GRATITUDE	Earth, Wind & Fire
2/7	5	2. DESIRE	Bob Dylan
3/13	5*	3. EAGLES/THEIR GREATEST HITS 1971–1975	Eagles
4/10	10*	4. FRAMPTON COMES ALIVE!	Peter Frampton
4/24	7*	5. WINGS AT THE SPEED OF SOUND	Paul McCartney/Wings
5/1	2	6. PRESENCE	Led Zeppelin
5/15	4*	7. BLACK AND BLUE	Rolling Stones
7/31	2	8. BREEZIN'	George Benson
9/4	1	9. FLEETWOOD MAC	Fleetwood Mac
10/16	14*	10. **SONGS IN THE KEY OF LIFE** *Album debuted at No. 1*	Stevie Wonder
		## 1977	
1/15	8*	1. HOTEL CALIFORNIA	Eagles
1/22	1	2. WINGS OVER AMERICA	Paul McCartney/Wings
2/12	6	3. A STAR IS BORN	Barbra Streisand/Soundtrack
4/2	31*	4. **RUMOURS**	Fleetwood Mac
7/16	1	5. BARRY MANILOW/LIVE	Barry Manilow
12/3	5	6. SIMPLE DREAMS	Linda Ronstadt
		## 1978	
1/21	24	1. **SATURDAY NIGHT FEVER**	Bee Gees/Soundtrack
7/8	1	2. CITY TO CITY	Gerry Rafferty
7/15	2	3. SOME GIRLS	Rolling Stones
7/29	12*	4. GREASE	Soundtrack
9/16	2*	5. DON'T LOOK BACK	Boston
11/4	1	6. LIVING IN THE USA	Linda Ronstadt
11/11	1	7. LIVE AND MORE	Donna Summer
11/18	8*	8. 52ND STREET	Billy Joel
		## 1979	
1/6	3	1. BARBRA STREISAND'S GREATEST HITS, VOLUME 2	Barbra Streisand
2/3	1	2. BRIEFCASE FULL OF BLUES	Blues Brothers
2/10	3	3. BLONDES HAVE MORE FUN	Rod Stewart
3/3	6*	4. SPIRITS HAVING FLOWN	Bee Gees
4/7	5*	5. MINUTE BY MINUTE	Doobie Brothers
5/19	6*	6. BREAKFAST IN AMERICA	Supertramp
6/16	6*	7. BAD GIRLS	Donna Summer
8/11	5	8. GET THE KNACK	Knack
9/15	7	9. IN THROUGH THE OUT DOOR	Led Zeppelin
11/3	9	10. **THE LONG RUN**	Eagles

DATE	WKS	ALBUM TITLE	ARTIST

1980

DATE	WKS	ALBUM TITLE	ARTIST
1/5	1	1. ON THE RADIO—GREATEST HITS—VOLUMES I & II	Donna Summer
1/12	1	2. BEE GEES GREATEST	Bee Gees
1/19	15	3. **THE WALL**	Pink Floyd
5/3	6	4. AGAINST THE WIND	Bob Seger & The Silver Bullet Band
6/14	6	5. GLASS HOUSES	Billy Joel
7/26	7	6. EMOTIONAL RESCUE	Rolling Stones
9/13	1	7. HOLD OUT	Jackson Browne
9/20	5	8. THE GAME	Queen
10/25	3*	9. GUILTY	Barbra Streisand
11/8	4	10. THE RIVER	Bruce Springsteen
12/13	2	11. KENNY ROGERS' GREATEST HITS	Kenny Rogers
12/27	8	12. DOUBLE FANTASY	John Lennon/Yoko Ono

1981

DATE	WKS	ALBUM TITLE	ARTIST
2/21	15*	1. **HI INFIDELITY**	REO Speedwagon
4/4	3*	2. PARADISE THEATER	Styx
6/27	4	3. MISTAKEN IDENTITY	Kim Carnes
7/25	3	4. LONG DISTANCE VOYAGER	Moody Blues
8/15	1	5. PRECIOUS TIME	Pat Benatar
8/22	10*	6. 4	Foreigner
9/5	1	7. BELLA DONNA	Stevie Nicks
9/12	1	8. ESCAPE	Journey
9/19	9	9. TATTOO YOU	Rolling Stones
12/26	3	10. FOR THOSE ABOUT TO ROCK WE SALUTE YOU	AC/DC

1982

DATE	WKS	ALBUM TITLE	ARTIST
2/6	4	1. FREEZE-FRAME	J. Geils Band
3/6	6	2. BEAUTY AND THE BEAT	Go-Go's
4/17	4	3. CHARIOTS OF FIRE	Vangelis/Soundtrack
5/15	9*	4. ASIA	Asia
5/29	3	5. TUG OF WAR	Paul McCartney
8/7	5	6. MIRAGE	Fleetwood Mac
9/11	9	7. AMERICAN FOOL	John Cougar
11/13	15	8. **BUSINESS AS USUAL**	Men At Work

1983

DATE	WKS	ALBUM TITLE	ARTIST
2/26	37*	1. **THRILLER**	Michael Jackson
6/25	2	2. FLASHDANCE	Soundtrack
7/23	17*	3. SYNCHRONICITY	Police
1/26	1	4. METAL HEALTH	Quiet Riot
12/3	3	5. CAN'T SLOW DOWN	Lionel Richie

DATE	WKS	ALBUM TITLE	ARTIST

1984

DATE	WKS	ALBUM TITLE	ARTIST
4/21	10	1. FOOTLOOSE	Soundtrack
6/30	1	2. SPORTS	Huey Lewis & The News
7/7	7*	3. BORN IN THE U.S.A.	Bruce Springsteen
8/4	24	4. **PURPLE RAIN**	Prince & The Revolution/Soundtrack

1985

DATE	WKS	ALBUM TITLE	ARTIST
2/9	3	1. LIKE A VIRGIN	Madonna
3/2	3	2. MAKE IT BIG	Wham!
3/23	1	3. CENTERFIELD	John Fogerty
3/30	7*	4. NO JACKET REQUIRED	Phil Collins
4/27	3	5. WE ARE THE WORLD	USA for Africa
6/1	3	6. AROUND THE WORLD IN A DAY	Prince
6/22	2	7. BEVERLY HILLS COP	Soundtrack
7/13	5*	8. SONGS FROM THE BIG CHAIR	Tears For Fears
8/10	2	9. RECKLESS	Bryan Adams
8/31	9	10. BROTHERS IN ARMS	Dire Straits
11/2	11*	11. **MIAMI VICE**	TV Soundtrack
12/21	1	12. HEART	Heart

1986

DATE	WKS	ALBUM TITLE	ARTIST
1/25	3	1. THE BROADWAY ALBUM	Barbra Streisand
2/15	2	2. PROMISE	Sade
3/1	1	3. WELCOME TO THE REAL WORLD	Mr. Mister
3/8	14*	4. **WHITNEY HOUSTON**	Whitney Houston
4/26	3	5. 5150	Van Halen
7/5	2	6. CONTROL	Janet Jackson
7/19	1	7. WINNER IN YOU	Patti LaBelle
7/26	5*	8. TOP GUN	Soundtrack
8/16	5	9. TRUE BLUE	Madonna
9/27	2	10. DANCING ON THE CEILING	Lionel Richie
10/18	1	11. FORE!	Huey Lewis & The News
10/25	8*	12. SLIPPERY WHEN WET	Bon Jovi
11/1	4	13. THIRD STAGE	Boston
11/29	7	14. BRUCE SPRINGSTEEN & THE E STREET BAND LIVE 1975–1985	Bruce Springsteen

ALBUMS OF LONGEVITY
Albums Charted Sixty Weeks Or More In The Top 40

PK YR	PK POS	WKS T40	TITLE/ARTIST
56	1	311	1. MY FAIR LADY Original Cast
56	1	262	2. OKLAHOMA! Soundtrack
58	1	236	3. JOHNNY'S GREATEST HITS Johnny Mathis
56	1	230	4. THE KING AND I Soundtrack
58	1	191	5. SING ALONG WITH MITCH Mitch Miller & The Gang
57	2	185	6. HYMNS Tennessee Ernie Ford
59	1	173	7. FILM ENCORES Mantovani
58	1	165	8. SOUTH PACIFIC Soundtrack
65	1	161	9. THE SOUND OF MUSIC Soundtrack
58	1	155	10. THE MUSIC MAN Original Cast
58	1	145	11. THE KINGSTON TRIO Kingston Trio
62	1	144	12. WEST SIDE STORY Soundtrack
58	1	143	13. GIGI Soundtrack
65	1	141	14. WHIPPED CREAM & OTHER DELIGHTS Herb Alpert & The Tijuana Brass
60	1	127	15. THE SOUND OF MUSIC Original Cast
58	1	125	16. TCHAIKOVSKY: PIANO CONCERTO NO. 1 Van Cliburn
59	4	122	17. MORE SING ALONG WITH MITCH Mitch Miller & The Gang
66	1	115	18. DOCTOR ZHIVAGO Soundtrack
60	1	114	19. PERSUASIVE PERCUSSION Enoch Light/Terry Snyder
62	5	113	20. WEST SIDE STORY Original Cast
62	1	112	21. PETER, PAUL & MARY Peter, Paul & Mary
59	2	112	22. FROM THE HUNGRY I Kingston Trio
61	8	110	23. KNOCKERS UP! Rusty Warren
60	1	108	24. THE BUTTON-DOWN MIND OF BOB NEWHART Bob Newhart
66	1	107	25. GOING PLACES Herb Alpert & The Tijuana Brass
60	3	107	26. BELAFONTE AT CARNEGIE HALL Harry Belafonte
63	3	106	27. MOON RIVER & OTHER GREAT MOVIE THEMES Andy Williams
59	2	103	28. COME DANCE WITH ME! Frank Sinatra
59	1	102	29. FLOWER DRUM SONG Original Cast
58	3	101	30. BUT NOT FOR ME/AHMAD JAMAL AT THE PERSHING Ahmad Jamal
60	7	100	31. PARTY SING ALONG WITH MITCH Mitch Miller & The Gang
60	17	100	32. CONNIE'S GREATEST HITS Connie Francis
56	1	99	33. THE EDDY DUCHIN STORY Carmen Cavallaro/Soundtrack
59	1	97	34. THE MUSIC FROM PETER GUNN Henry Mancini/TV Soundtrack
62	1	96	35. BREAKFAST AT TIFFANY'S Henry Mancini/Soundtrack
84	1	96	36. BORN IN THE U.S.A. Bruce Springsteen
59	2	96	37. INSIDE SHELLEY BERMAN Shelley Berman
59	4	96	38. STILL MORE! SING ALONG WITH MITCH Mitch Miller & The Gang
58	5	95	39. GEMS FOREVER Mantovani
59	4	94	40. OPEN FIRE, TWO GUITARS Johnny Mathis

ALBUMS OF LONGEVITY
Albums Charted Sixty Weeks Or More In The Top 40

PK YR	PK POS	WKS T40	TITLE/ARTIST
83	1	91	41. THRILLER Michael Jackson
60	10	91	42. FIRESIDE SING ALONG WITH MITCH Mitch Miller & The Gang
57	1	88	43. AROUND THE WORLD IN 80 DAYS Soundtrack
60	2	88	44. PROVOCATIVE PERCUSSION Enoch Light/Command All-Stars
59	12	88	45. OLDIES BUT GOODIES Various Artists
69	4	87	46. IN-A-GADDA-DA-VIDA Iron Butterfly
61	2	86	47. TIME OUT FEATURING "TAKE FIVE" Dave Brubeck Quartet
59	2	85	48. VICTORY AT SEA, VOL. 2 TV Soundtrack
56	1	84	49. CALYPSO Harry Belafonte
58	2	84	50. WARM Johnny Mathis
62	5	83	51. I LEFT MY HEART IN SAN FRANCISCO Tony Bennett
83	9	82	52. ELIMINATOR ZZ Top
58	1	81	53. FRANK SINATRA SINGS FOR ONLY THE LONELY Frank Sinatra
60	4	81	54. ITALIAN FAVORITES Connie Francis
80	6	81	55. CHRISTOPHER CROSS Christopher Cross
65	1	78	56. MARY POPPINS Soundtrack
86	1	78	57. WHITNEY HOUSTON Whitney Houston
83	1	78	58. CAN'T SLOW DOWN Lionel Richie
63	8	78	59. THE BARBRA STREISAND ALBUM Barbra Streisand
65	4	77	60. MY FAIR LADY Soundtrack
68	5	77	61. ARE YOU EXPERIENCED? Jimi Hendrix Experience
61	1	73	62. JUDY AT CARNEGIE HALL Judy Garland
58	4	73	63. TILL Roger Williams
59	5	72	64. HAVE 'TWANGY' GUITAR—WILL TRAVEL Duane Eddy
84	1	71	65. SPORTS Huey Lewis & The News
63	2	71	66. (MOVING) Peter, Paul & Mary
84	3	71	67. PRIVATE DANCER Tina Turner
85	1	70	68. NO JACKET REQUIRED Phil Collins
61	1	70	69. THE BUTTON-DOWN MIND STRIKES BACK! Bob Newhart
78	2	70	70. THE STRANGER Billy Joel
62	10	70	71. JOAN BAEZ IN CONCERT Joan Baez
62	13	70	72. JOAN BAEZ, VOL. 2 Joan Baez
60	6	69	73. ENCORE OF GOLDEN HITS Platters
71	1	68	74. TAPESTRY Carole King
76	1	68	75. FLEETWOOD MAC Fleetwood Mac
57	1	66	76. LOVE IS THE THING Nat King Cole
69	1	66	77. BLOOD, SWEAT & TEARS Blood, Sweat & Tears
85	1	66	78. RECKLESS Bryan Adams
64	3	66	79. HONEY IN THE HORN Al Hirt
61	34	66	80. THE ROARING 20'S Dorothy Provine

ALBUMS OF LONGEVITY
Albums Charted Sixty Weeks Or More In The Top 40

PK YR	PK POS	WKS T40	TITLE/ARTIST
71	1	65	81. JESUS CHRIST SUPERSTAR Various Artists
86	1	65†	82. CONTROL Janet Jackson
67	5	65	83. THE TEMPTATIONS GREATEST HITS Temptations
84	8	65	84. BREAK OUT Pointer Sisters
60	10	65	85. NEAR YOU Roger Williams
67	1	63	86. SGT. PEPPER'S LONELY HEARTS CLUB BAND Beatles
73	1	63	87. THE DARK SIDE OF THE MOON Pink Floyd
61	2	63	88. GREAT MOTION PICTURE THEMES Soundtrack Compilation
60	2	63	89. FAITHFULLY Johnny Mathis
56	1	62	90. BELAFONTE Harry Belafonte
83	4	62	91. AN INNOCENT MAN Billy Joel
84	4	62	92. SHE'S SO UNUSUAL Cyndi Lauper
59	6	62	93. TABOO Arthur Lyman
61	32	62	94. NEW PIANO IN TOWN Peter Nero
63	1	61	95. DAYS OF WINE AND ROSES Andy Williams
59	1	61	96. EXOTICA Martin Denny
58	5	61	97. NEARER THE CROSS Tennessee Ernie Ford
66	4	60	98. PARSLEY, SAGE, ROSEMARY AND THYME Simon & Garfunkel
61	4	60	99. ALL THE WAY Frank Sinatra
65	7	60	100. FIDDLER ON THE ROOF Original Cast
60	7	60	101. STRAUSS WALTZES Mantovani

PK YR: Year album reached its peak position
PK POS: Highest charted position album attained
WKS T40: Total weeks charted in Top 40
    †: Album still in Top 40 as of the June 20, 1987 issue

INDEX TO ALBUMS OF LONGEVITY (A-Z BY ARTIST)

CHECK OUT THE CHARTS
If you're serious about pop music, the Top

Joel Whitburn's TOP POP ALBUMS 1955–1985

The only book to list complete chart data for *every* album that made *Billboard*'s weekly "Top Pop Albums" charts. Arranged by artist, it lists over 14,000 titles and 3,000 artists. So, whether an album charted at position 200 for one week or hit No. 1 for fifty weeks, it's listed here in this complete chart history of the rock era.
516 pages. Softcover $50.

Joel Whitburn's TOP POP SINGLES 1955–1986

The complete history of *Billboard*'s "Hot 100" and other pop charts, plus thousands of new artist biographies. A complete up-to-date listing, by artist and by title, of each of the nearly 18,000 singles to appear on *Billboard*'s pop charts.
Over 730 pages. Hardcover $60. Softcover $50.

Joel Whitburn's POP ANNUAL 1955–1986

Every pop programmer's dream: a book that lists all of *Billboard*'s Pop and "Hot 100" charted singles in rank order, year by year. And now, for the first time, the book lists the playing time of each record and features "Time Capsules" highlighting each year's major events! Also includes a complete A–Z song-title section.
Over 670 pages. Hardcover $60. Softcover $50.

Joel Whitburn's POP MEMORIES 1890–1954

From Edison to Elvis—the first book to document the history of America's recorded popular music from its very beginnings. Find out who had the hit versions of those popular standards you've heard for generations. Arranged by artist and by title, the book lists over 12,000 songs and 1,500 artists.
660 pages. Hardcover $60. Softcover $50.

Billboard's MUSIC YEARBOOK 1986

Get your Record Research books up-to-date! Lists every 1986 hit to make *Billboard*'s nine major charts, in one easy-to-use tome. Introduces a section on the highly requested "Album Rock Tracks" chart.
Over 200 pages. Softcover $30.

Billboard's MUSIC YEARBOOK 1985

The complete story of 1985's charted music in one concise volume. Covers eleven major *Billboard* charts. Updates all previous Record Research books and includes data on the exciting new "Top Pop Compact Disks" chart.
240 pages. Softcover $30.

FROM TOP TO BOTTOM
40 Albums list is just the tip of the charts.

Billboard's **MUSIC YEARBOOK 1983—MUSIC YEARBOOK 1984**

Two comprehensive books listing complete chart data on each of the records to appear on the fourteen major *Billboard* charts in 1983 and 1984. Updates all previous Record Research books, plus complete data on 6 additional charts.
Softcover $30 each (1983 edition: 276 pages/1984 edition: 264 pages).

Joel Whitburn's **BUBBLING UNDER THE HOT 100** 1959–1981

Lists over 4,000 of the "hits that might have been." Includes many regional hits that never made it nationally, and the near-hits by the superstars! The only reference book of its kind.
240 pages. Softcover $30.

Joel Whitburn's **TOP 2000 1955–1985** Compiled by Joel Whitburn

The 2,000 hottest singles of the rock era, compared side-by-side, hit-by-hit. Rank Section lists records in order of all-time popularity from No. 1 to No. 2000, along with complete chart data for each title. Also includes a Title Section and Artist Section.
144 pages. Softcover $30.

UP AND COMING!
TOP R&B SINGLES 1942–1986
TOP COUNTRY SINGLES 1984–1986
BILLBOARD'S TOP VIDEOCASSETTES 1979–1987

For more information on the complete line of Record Research books, write for a free catalog. When ordering the above books, please include a check or money order for full amount plus $4.00 for postage and handling. Overseas orders add $4.00 per book. All Canadian orders must be paid in U.S. dollars.

P.O. BOX 200
MENOMONEE FALLS, WISCONSIN 53051